THE CENTENNIAL EDITION

OF THE WORKS OF

SIDNEY LANIER

GENERAL EDITOR

CHARLES R. ANDERSON

LANIER, AGE THIRTY-TWO, 1874

Charles D. Lanier Collection, Johns Hopkins University

CENTENNIAL EDITION

VOLUME IX

SIDNEY LANIER

LETTERS

1874—1877

EDITED BY

CHARLES R. ANDERSON AND AUBREY H. STARKE

BALTIMORE

THE JOHNS HOPKINS PRESS

1945

PRINTED IN THE UNITED STATES OF AMERICA

CONTENTS

ILLUSTRATIONS

LETTERS
1 8 7 4 — 1 8 7 7

CHRONOLOGY

1874	Jan.	Moved to 64 Center St. Began friendship with R. M. Johnston and Innes Randolph.
	Winter–Spring	Ill. Composed music. Began career as professional musician, in Peabody Orchestra (until Mar. 28) and other concerts, including tour to the Middle West with Jenny Busk (Apr.).
	Apr. 28	Left for Georgia. Spent May–June in Brunswick and Macon.
	July–Aug.	At " Sunnyside," Griffin, Ga. Wrote " Corn," composed music.
	Sept.–Nov.	In New York seeking new career in the arts and trying to get music and poems published.
	Dec.	In Macon, concert (Dec. 23). Returned to Baltimore (Dec. 28).
1875	Jan. 2	Peabody Orchestra season began, lasting until Mar. 20.
	Winter	" Corn " published in *Lippincott's* (Feb.), beginning of national reputation. Met Gibson Peacock, Charlotte Cushman, and Baltimore and Philadelphia *literati*.
	Spring	Ill. Wrote " The Symphony " (Mar.). Trip to Philadelphia, New York, and Boston (Apr. 4–12) re: commission to write *Florida*.
	Apr. 13	Left for the South. Spent the next three months in Georgia and Florida collecting material for his travel book.
	June	" The Symphony " and " The Power of Prayer " published.
	July–Nov.	In Philadelphia and New York writing *Florida* (published *c.* Nov. 15), short poems, and prose. Met Bayard Taylor (Aug. 28) and New York *literati*. Trip to Boston to see Charlotte Cushman (Nov. 2-10), met Longfellow and Lowell.
	Nov. 13–28	In Macon. Returned to Baltimore, 66 Center St.
	Dec. 4	Peabody Orchestra season began, lasting until Mar. 18, 1876.
1876	Winter–Spring	Wrote " Cantata " for Centennial (Jan.) and " Psalm of the West " (Mar.). Published " Sketches of India " (Jan.–Apr.).
	Apr. 11	Left for the South. Spent a month in Montgomery and Macon.
	May 10	Attended performance of " Centennial Meditation of Columbia."
	May–June	In Philadelphia and New York. Joined by wife and children.
	July–Oct.	At a farm near West Chester, Pa. " The Psalm of the West " published (July). Wrote " Clover " and " The Waving of the Corn." Seriously ill.
	Nov.–Dec.	In Philadelphia with the Peacocks. *Poems* published by Lippincott's (Nov. 12). Desperately ill. Left for winter in Florida, arriving in Tampa Dec. 21.
1877	Winter	In Tampa, regaining health. Wrote numerous short poems.
	Apr.–May	Spent a month each in Brunswick and Macon.
	June–July	In Baltimore, Washington, New York, and Philadelphia seeking employment.
	Aug.–Sept.	At a farm near Chadd's Ford, Pa., ill. Wrote short poems. Trips to Washington and Baltimore seeking employment.
	Oct. 5	Returned to Baltimore after an absence of 18 months. Joined by family at 55 Lexington St. (Oct. 28). Moved to 33 Denmead St. (Dec. 22).
	Dec. 15	Peabody Orchestra season began, lasting until Mar. 16, 1878.

1874

To Mary Day Lanier [1]

Baltimore, January 3rd 1874.

Dear Heartsease, Canst thou imagine a man who is at the same time nothing but a sigh ? Or a heart that is only a longing-for-a-heart? Or a me, that is wholly a dream-of-thee ?

—— I am just come from our Concert. We opened with a Symphony of Mozart, in G minor. An *allegro* movement, full of delicious interchanges betwixt the wind and the strings, comes presently to an abrupt end; then a long *Andante,* in 6/8 time, which seems to be a record of sweetest confidences whispered between the first flute and the first violins, – as if they were two young girls just commencing a friendship ! – and of occasional intrusions of the Oboe (as of a girl *de trop*), as well as of sage advice volunteered here and there by the elderly Bassoons. Finally this conversation ends: and thereto succeeds a minuett, stately yet coquettish, courteous yet piquant, grave with the measured steps of dignitaries and of queenly women, yet illumined by the gleam of bright eyes and the flash of silver shoe-buckles. Then the Finale closes all, with a great outburst of joy, which breaks out in a thousand lovely phases of self-repetition, and at last completely and satisfactorily expresses itself.

— But thou, My Soul of-sweet-talk and of-girlhood, and of courtesy and piquancy, and of joyful satisfaction and completeness, – thou wert not by me, and therefore my heart was in pain although in heaven.

—— Then a lady named Thompson howled dismally a beautiful air from the Barber of Seville.

Then should have come a Concerto for Oboe, with Orchestra; but Oboe's lips were chapped, he vowed, – until he almost

[1] Previously published, *Scribner's,* XXV, 631 (May, 1899) ; reprinted, *Letters* (New York, 1899), pp. 89-91.

shook his spectacles off – that he *könnte nicht es spielen*; whereupon *Maestro Hamerik* announced the fact, and added that Mr.
Sidney Lanier and Mr. Henry Wysham had kindly consented
to play a simple melody in place of the Oboe Concerto. Then
those two gentlemen appeared, and, amid great applause,
advanced to the front. They played "Adieu, Dear Land,"
S. L. taking first, and H. C. W. skirmishing about as second,
Mr. Hamerik palpitating a lovely accompaniment on the piano.
Ah, My Friend, need I tell thee how the heart of this same S. L.
did beat along through every note of this lovely song, – am I
not too an exile from my dear Land, – which is always the land
where thou art ? We brought down the house, and responded
to a thundering *encore* with Annie Laurie, (wh. I hate with all
my heart, but Harry liketh it, and insisted, and we had not time
to discuss).

Then came our *pièce de résistance,* The "Dream of Xmas"
Overture by Ferdinand Hiller. Sweet Heaven,– how shall I tell
thee the gentle melodies, the gracious surprises, the frosty glitter
of starlights, and flashing of icy *spiculae* and of frozen surfaces,
the hearty chanting of peace and good will to men, the thrilling
pathos of virginal thoughts and trembling anticipations and
lofty prophecies, the solemn and tender breathings-about of the
coming reign of forgiveness and of love, and the final confusion
of innumerable angels flying through the heavens and jubilantly
choiring together ?

—— But thou, alas, – thou more beautiful than any in that
throng !– wert not by me, and my heart was still at once in
heaven and in pain.

—— We closed with a grand March of Mendellsohn's, found
after his death, and played by us tonight for the first time in
this country: – the strangest combination of Mendellsohn's most
beautiful effects, – particularly of reeds – with a singularly-
interpolated old highland-pibroch sort of air in the middle, as
if the ghost of "The March of the Cameron Men" were flitting
about through the loveliest modern Orchestral harmonies.

—— But alas, and alas, and forever alas, – thou wert not by,
and therefore, although in heaven, yet nevertheless in pain,
was the heart of thy

                    lover.——

TO MARY DAY LANIER

Baltimore, Jany 4th 1874

And now one little word to thee, dear Heliotrope,—after several letters to various people wh. have quite disabled my sword-arm—by way of benediction and final blessing upon the labors of this day.

I have not told thee that I found some twenty houses at which I had to call, on New Year's day: and that I made my calls very successfully. I might have called at a hundred: but I refused to go anywhere where I had not already been,—not liking to be introduced for the first time, on a day when one is expected to call on one's *friends*.

New Year's night, I went by invitation to the house of J. Stricker Jenkins. This gentleman spends an enormous yearly income upon paintings, and engravings; and his house is a fairy palace. O, Sweet Heart-of-my-heart, if thou mightst have gazed with me upon a certain Miranda, standing by a high rock over-looking the sea, hair and scarf blown backward by the wind, looking, with all her soul in her eyes, toward the god-like form of her future lover! How thy gray eyes would have glowed and widened, and how full would have been my soul! I wd. not let them take me round, catalogue in hand, on the absurd business of looking at a house-full of pictures in a couple of hours: but took my chair before my lovely Miranda,[2] and gave myself to that, and to a wonderful Romeo and Juliet. Then we were taken up stairs to other rooms and shown all manner of magnificent things: then I played the Swamp-Robin, and Wysham and I a duo: then we had a charming supper. My particular cicerone was Miss *Vandervoort,* sister of Mrs. Jenkins. Miss V. is a slim lady, with gray hair, very fashionably dressed, and Cousin, or sister, (I did not distinctly make out

[2] See Lanier's letter of Jan. 31, 1874, and note 16, below, for his poem " On Huntingdon's ' Miranda ' " (I, 32) inspired by this picture. There also survives a fragmentary MS of a musical composition by Lanier entitled " Mem. for ' Miranda ' " (Charles D. Lanier Collection, Johns Hopkins University), which may have been inspired by the same painting or may have been a setting for his poem. The painting itself, by Daniel Huntington (1816-1906), was sold at auction for $430.00, May 2-3, 1876, and cannot now be located. (Letter from Frick Art Reference Library, New York, to Dr. J. C. French, Oct. 29, 1942.)

which,) to thy Vandervorts in New York. My heart leaped
when I heard her name: I thought she must know *thee!*

— This morning to church with Mrs. Bird: being pressed to
dinner, thereafter, I said no,—desiring to think over many
things,—and took some oysters in solitary style at a restaurant.
Mrs. B. sent thee a-many messages, all loving and thoughtful.
I have told her thou art the finest letter-writer in the world.

— Did Harry receive the mortgage and note wh. I drew up
and sent him some weeks ago? Tell this dear old Cubbie I
wasn't "worrited" about the check, and didn't mean to make
that impression on him.

Kiss thy father for me.   ×   ×   ×   ×   ×.[3] But say thou
naught to him, that I think so: for that wd. distress his good
heart.

— I wd. all the stars that shine on thee this night did burn
with the same tender fire that liveth ever in the heart of thy

lover.

To Robert S. Lanier

4

Baltimore, Md. January 4th 1873

My dear Father:

I was very glad to get your letter, and to learn
that you keep in perfect health in spite of the severe work you
appear to have been doing. You lead, however, the most
enviable life any man could desire: towit, one full of work,
and of uninterrupted capacity for work. This no one can
appreciate more than I do: since my own labor is so often
stopped by ill-health, and so much of my time must necessarily
be devoted to mere bodily precautions.

How much, – you do not know; else you would abandon all
idea (as I have) of the possibility of my practising law, either
in Macon or elsewhere. To write, for any length of time
beyond a few minutes, results in very distressing consequences

---

[3] A passage is deleted in the MS at this point, probably Lanier's comment on
the account of Charles Day contained in Mary Day Lanier's letter of Dec. 28,
1873: "Dear Father is quiet and sad, suffering from this unaccustomed aimless life wh. allows him too much time for sorrowful retrospects and anticipations. I wish I had more time to devote to him for I could cheer him somewhat
if there were ample opportunity."

to me: and this effectually debars me from Office practice. To speak long, or often, would be equally injurious to me. What sort of lawyer, then, can one be, who can neither write a Bill in Equity, nor make a jury speech, – without a hemorrhage? — I speak of this because I observe from your letter that you still find difficulty in reconciling yourself to my course. There is really no other way now known to me, by which I can secure any immediate income.

Can you, within a week, send me a hundred and fifty dollars? I have a matter outstanding which will be due within that time. Address me, "care of H. C. Wysham Esq. 41 Lexington St, Baltimore."

Our Symphony Orchestra has been very successful. The concerts are fully attended, and are said to be better than ever before. It is quite impossible for me to describe the delight I take in interpreting the great works which we bring out every Saturday night: particularly now that I am beginning to acquire some ease in playing with so many other instruments, – a novelty that at first put me up to the severest strain of attention.

I have quite a circle of influential friends, here, and have received the pleasantest evidences of kindly feeling, from many quarters.

I hope Mama is better than when you wrote. Give her and Pringle a great deal of love, from

Your Son

S. L.

To Clifford A. Lanier

Baltimore, Md Jany, 4th 1874

My dear Brother:

Your Xmas gift (and Wilsie's) came to me safely. The spirit of it is lodged *in* my heart; the body of it is mostly *about* my heart. I laid it out in a vest, a pair of cloth over-gaiters, india-rubbers, a cravat, and a pair of gloves, for myself: – thus wearing your love, as it were, all warm and protective, upon neck, hands, feet and body. T'other half of it, tho', gave me most pleasure; for it goes to buy a pair of kid shoes for my Heartsease yonder in the South.

– Indeed, dear, dear Clifford, your thoughtful kindness touched me too deeply for any words: – and I would rather not say anything more about it.

———"———
"

We gave a very successful Concert last night. Wysham and I played a flute duo which brought down the house, with a hearty *encore*. How can I tell you how keenly I wish for you, as I sit in my place in the Orchestra and help to render the immortal harmonies of the great tone-poets? – It has been a tremendous trial of patience, of nerve, of skill, to me, – this Orchestral business. Having had no musical education whatever, knowing nothing save what I had "picked up" in the most desultory way, unacquainted even with the meaning of a Conductor's motions, – and at the same time suddenly saddled with the duty of interpreting a responsible part in works which I had never even heard before, in company, too, with old musicians most of whom have been playing ever since they were children and doing nothing else–, all this nearly made my spirit give way many times: and when, in addition, came fearful illness, so that for two weeks I cd. scarcely sit in my chair on the stage, and even when able to sit up, could scarcely breathe, – I many times wondered whether the heavens were really going to deny me, after all, this last desperate little hope of making a pitiful living. But I worried it through, and was never absent, save from one rehearsal.

– I'm not very well; can only write for a few minutes at a time; and consequently my work progresses very slowly. But I'm improving all the time, and hope to be in full activity ere long.

If I could but hear something financially cheerful from you! Can I not?

Kiss my slender Wilsie, with a special and most tender fervor, for me. Where is Aunt Jane, and why answers she not my letter? I send a great deal of love to Grandmother & Aunt Lucy, and all the kinsfolk. I'm going to move soon, so write me "Care of H. C. Wysham, 41 Lexington St."

Yr. bro.

S. L.

To George W. F. Price [4]

Baltimore, Md,   Jany 8th 1874.

My dear Mr. Price:

I was glad to get your letter, not only because it brought me news of you (of whom I used to hear many things from my Tuskeegee cousins), but because it also gave me the opportunity to cicerone you in among the labyrinthine beauties of the Silver Böhm flutes.

To reply to your inquiries categorically: – one who plays the old flute *can* learn the Böhm, with a little practice and perseverance. Of course the difficuty experienced will vary with the fixedness of the players's fingering—depending as that does on the length of time he has used the old flute—, and also with his natural knack of " catching " things: but I should say that an average player would in the course of a couple of weeks,— practicing (say) a half hour a day, have quite conquered all the purely *dry* drudgery of learning the new instrument, so as to render all the subsequent practicing a matter of *pleasure* as well as work.

To your second question, I answer that the Böhm is on the whole not more difficult to manipulate than the old flute. The highest six notes of the Böhm—that is, from [high *f*] to [high *c* above the staff]—are, I think, more difficult than the corresponding notes on the old flute, for they involve the simultaneous action of two fingers, often, which being almost impossible in rapid passages, other *special* fingerings have to be used that require some time to become familiar. On the other hand, however, all the notes below those mentioned are

[4] George W. F. Price was a native of Alabama and a graduate of the state university in 1848. In Apr., 1870, as president of the East Alabama Female College, at Tuskegee, Ala., he had invited Lanier to deliver " an Address upon the occasion of the Art Levee " of his college; but Lanier had apparently not accepted the invitation. In 1874, when he wrote Lanier for information concerning the Silver Böhm Flute, he was president of the Huntsville Female College, at Huntsville, Ala. In 1880 he founded at Nashville, Tenn., the Nashville College for Young Ladies, of which he remained president until his death. This is the only letter by Lanier to Price that has been found, but six surviving letters by Price to Lanier indicate a correspondence extending into Sept., 1874.

In the third paragraph, the words in brackets have been substituted for the music symbols in the MS.

easier than on the old flute: and as these latter are used far oftener than the others, I am sure it is a very safe assertion that the Böhm is on the whole quite as easily fingered as the old flute.

Third, as to the tone of the silver flute: I reply that you can, in my judgment, get any sort of tone you like from a silver flute, and that it is purely a matter of lip and *embouchure*. By spreading the lips and blowing steadily you can get the cornet tone (of course nothing like so loud, but the same in quality): a little change of lip will give you the wooden flute tone: another change will give you a lovely *pianissimo* flowing like melted amber, in *adagio* passages, and gurgling like a swift brook, in more rapid ones. This last tone I believe is peculiar to the Silver flute: and is not often heard, since the *power* of the silver flute has tempted almost all the great players to cultivate the strong tones of the instrument, to the exclusion of the rest. To my own ear, this last tone is best of all: it goes straight into people's hearts and stirs them, like the faint odors of violets and heliotropes, suggesting things infinitely sweet and high and lovely.

Finally, in reply to the P. S. question; a part of the splendid endowment given by Mr. Peabody was for musical encouragement, and, amongst other things, has been devoted to maintaining a first-class Orchestra of thirty-five musicians, who are to render the greatest works of the greatest Masters in a series of Symphony Concerts during this winter. I am *Flauto Primo* in this Orchestra: and to that extent only am officially connected with the Peabody Institute. I came to Baltimore particularly to consult some books in the Peabody Library which bear upon the subject of a long poem I'm writing.[5] I ought to mention, perhaps, that my physicians have declared it to be a matter of life and death with me to abandon my profession,—the law; and that I have done so. I hope to get some permanent occupation,—such as a professorship, or the like,—in this part of the land before long: but have yet made no efforts in that direction.

——————— So!—you see what a fearsome screed you have brought upon yourself, by a few questions about the Böhm flute. The keen desire I have to get Art at its best, as well as

[5] "The Jacquerie" (see note 145, 1873).

a more personal hope of seeing you enjoy the greatly-increased powers and capabilities of the silver flute,—must be my apology for answering so voluminously.

I should add, in conclusion, that I have had one of Badger's $240 Silver Böhm flutes for five months, and that I am greatly pleased with it. I believe him to be a faithful craftsman, and know that he takes great pride in his " children,"—as he calls his flutes. If you should ever conclude to order one from him, it will give me pleasure to superintend its construction, to advance any hints in relation to size of holes and shape of embouchure, and to examine it thoroughly when finally made.

Should you write me again, address me " 64 Centre St, Baltimore, Md."

Very truly Yours

Sidney Lanier

To Mary Day Lanier [6]

[Baltimore, Jan. 10, 1874?]

O Twin, O Twin, how my heart is throbbing ! If I might only look into thine eyes, and get the comfort of those eloquent and unfathomable sympathies that live in the gray thereof !   I am just from our Third Symphony Concert.   We played, first, a Symphony of Hayden's: then a violin Concerto, (for violin and Orchestra), of Mendellsohn: then Wolfram's song, from Tannhäuser: then Beethoven's great *concerto* for Piano and Orchestra.   Then Miss Busk sang some lovely things of Schubert's, " Restless Love ", and " Impatience ": then we all dashed at Mozart's scrambling " *Entführung* ", – The " Abduction from the Seraglio " Overture.

——   The Beethoven concerto, the Mendellsohn Concerto, the Wolfram's Song, — these will kill me if I do not hear them some day with thee. I dare not talk about them, more.

[6] Excerpt previously published, *Scribner's*, XXV, 732 (June 1899) ; reprinted, *Letters* (New York, 1899), pp. 114-115—where it is marked " not dated " and placed after a letter dated March 18, 1876. Conjectural dating from the evidence of the third sentence, since the third concert of the Peabody Orchestra was held on Saturday, Jan. 10, 1874.

We had the largest audience ever assembled in the Peabody Hall. Even the aisles were crowded with ladies, standing.

—— Now, – in thine ear, of all the ears in the world, be it whispered, — I could conduct a concert far, far better than this one. How well I now understand the foundation which music has, in the culture of the soul ! A broad and liberal Spirit, wielding the *bâton* tonight, could have set the hearts of fifteen hundred people a-fire. As it was, they were (merely) greatly pleased.

—— There is a certain heaven in store for me: it is to play, with thine accompaniment, some day, certain songs out of a " Schubert's Album " wh. I have. O if thou cdst. hear the passion, the melodious eloquence, the pleading pathos, wherewith my dear Silvertongue rendereth these ! And thou art the only woman in the world that cd. get into the hearts of them. – I play them with a Lady, here, sometimes: and they are so beautiful, that all her blood cometh into her cheeks, and her eyes gleam and flash.[7] But as for Silvertongue, it will have no kiss but mine: and as for me, I thirst for none in all the world but thine; none but thine.

— Now the sweet garden where thy kisses grow, God keep it lit bright, and sunshiny, and dewy, — prayeth thy faithful

lover.

To Mary Day Lanier

[Baltimore, Jan. 20, 1874?] [8]

It is far in the night but I can not resist the temptation to tell thee ——— have I told it thee before? — that thou art simply the Sweetest Lady that God hath yet made, and that I am very madly in love with thee.

— Thou art particularly and specifically sweet – for this night – in respect of thy trustfulness. Here I have put thee

[7] Referred to in Lanier's letter of Jan. 20, 1874 (below), as " Miss M."

[8] Conjectural dating from the evidence of the following letter, Jan. 22, where Lanier says he has 'just come from the second of Theodore Thomas's concerts, referred to in the present letter as scheduled for " tomorrow night and the night after."

off week after week, with no knowledge of my plans; and thou
hast said no word until thy little timid inquiry of today re-
mindeth me how good and how beautiful a soul thou art in
this matter.

—   Definite knowledge, indeed, I can not give thee: nor
say further than that I am fixed in my determination to live
here.   I have several plans in view, to that end: but thou wilt
not desire me to pain myself by telling thee the details of what
may be all frustrated, – as so many of my plans are.   I decided
to take no pupils: principally because I do not think it well to
" pick up " a living in that way.   My aim is to get some settled
occupation here wh. will allow me to pursue my musical and
poetic endeavors, until such time as I shall be able to devote
myself entirely to them.   This I am trying to do, with all
my strength.

There are a thousand advantages in living here.   How I
long to see thee in midst of these people, – that is only known
to the God who hath heard the prayers and seen the tears of
my lonesome longing.   But I think it will be compassed ere
long.

Also will I send thee funds in a few days.

—   That thou shdst. ask me if thou mayst know the name
of the lady with whom I play the   Schubert's songs!   I send
thee her last note.   It accompanied a nice little Pocket Inhaler,
— for introducing the Carbolate of Iodine to the lungs —
and is a fair and good note, meseemeth.

—   Aye, Thomas' Orchestra playeth for me, tomorrow night
and night after.   My heart is all alive.   I will send thee the
programme.   Thou shalt be with me, and sit by me: and shall
take the worship wh. this music will crush out of my soul as it
were a lady's fingers crushing a flower's odor out.

—   My little Harry!   Did he indeed say my name?   How
thou makest mine arms ache for him.

Thou art to separately kiss all the numerous men, old and
young, great and small, short and tall, baby and all, for thy

lover.

Perhaps I ought to tell thee that the " cough " mentioned in
Miss M.'s note is simply a very feeble little clearing of the
throat wh. she hath sometimes beheld at rehearsal, and is no

cough at all.   I have no more than thou hast seen me have
all summer.

To Mary Day Lanier [9]

[Baltimore,] Jany 22nd 1874

Aye: Thomas hath played for me: two nights.   I am just
from the second Concert: having walked home with my fair
friend, whose note I sent thee yesterday.

────── The mere memory and unsubstantial heart's-ideal of
thee, is better than the actual presence and eye-embodiment of
any other woman in the world.

── I am beginning, in midst of the stormy glories of the
Orchestra, to feel my heart sure, and my soul discriminating.
Not less do I thrill, to ride upon the great surges: but I am
growing calm enough to see the star that should light the
musician, and presently my hand will be firm enough to hold
the helm and guide the ship that way. *Now,* I am very
quiet: I am waiting. – The music of the modern Orchestra
is greatly defective in the *f, ff,* and *fff* passages.   When the
frenzy of the *finale* comes upon these players of Thomas', for
instance: it is too much a frenzy.   The Orchestral voices are
in each other's way, it is rather a noise, than music.   And the
invention of the Orchestral Composers, since Beethoven, is so
poor !   We hear so much that we privately forgive, in consideration of some special little strain that we liked, E. G :   the
Rubinstein piece, " Ivan IV ", tonight.   It was, of course, all
in the Russian tone: but at least one half of it was noise.   In
the midst of the uproar, suddenly a dead silence; then the four
'cellos glided into a r[e]ligious quartette, simple as the open
heavens, beautiful beyond description.   The proportion between this quartette, and the noise, was too greatly in favor
of the latter.

To see Thomas lead, ───is music, itself !   His baton
is alive, full of grace, of symmetry; he maketh no gestures, he
readeth his score almost without looking at it, he seeth everybody, heareth everything, warneth every man, encourageth every

[9] Previously published, *Scribner's,* XXV, 631-632 (May, 1899) ; reprinted,
Letters (New York, 1899), pp. 91-92.

instrument, quietly, firmly, marvellously. Not the slightest shade of nonsense, not the faintest spark of affectaction, not the minutest grain of *effect*, is in him.

He taketh the Orchestra in his hand, as if it were a pen, – and writeth with it.

— Ah, Heartsease, Heartsease, thou wert with me, there: thy sweet, comforting Spirit stayed by me. God in Heaven, – how I love thee, my Fine-Soul.

—— I grieve that thou and thy good father read the [Baltimore] Sun: – so much that I have purveyed me a package of stamped newspaper wrappers, wherein I purpose to send thee daily the Baltimore " Gazette ", wh. I read every morning. I sent thee a copy this day. The Sun is a mere *news*paper: it is much like the Herald, of N. Y. The Gazette is a very civilized Journal, indeed. The musical and dramatic critic of the Gazette is an old friend of mine whom I used to meet at my poor Emmet Robinson's house, in Petersburg.[10]

— Well: the still small voice of thy blessed little watch crieth, kiss her, and come away. So, purse thy sweet lips: there: and there, again, a thousand times : and now, dear Heartsease, God wrap thee in the night as it were the velvety petal of some great, dark, ravishing-perfumed flower, – until morning come to thee and to thy

lover.——

To Mary Day Lanier [11]

Baltimore,   Jany 23rd 1874

The truth is, dear Friend, thou hast quite spoiled me for all the other people in the world, and I do believe there is naught but disappointment in store for me, as to the rest of mankind, male and female, friendly and otherwise.

[10] Innes Randolph (1837-1887) had moved to Baltimore from Richmond, Va., in 1868. A man of varied interests he combined the practice of law with newspaper work, usually as critic of the arts; tried his hand at music, painting, sculpture, and the drama; and wrote poems and short stories. (See the Baltimore *Sun*, Apr. 29, 1887.)

[11] Excerpt previously published, *Scribner's*, XXV, 749 (June, 1899); reprinted, *Letters* (New York, 1899), p. 107—where it is merely dated " 1874 " and is placed out of order, after a letter of Nov. 8, 1874.

—   This remark is made apropos of thine inquiry as to
my " Jonathan ".[12] Alas, alas, – what shall I say? I fear
that there is a little reactionary period always, in these matters:
and I try very hard to allow for that.   But he is not *large*
enough. For instance, in Music; he doth not love music
much, he loveth *playing* it infinitely.   The great deeps, the
wild heights, the passionate cities, the happy vales, the dear,
secret springs, the broad and generous-bosomed rivers, the
manifold exquisite flowers, the changeful seasons, the starry
skies, the present, the past, the future – – – of the world of
music; – into these he hath not been, into these will he never
enter. A twittering solo of Briccialdi, a languishing waltz-
flirtation of Terschak, an old-time Rondo of Kuhlau: if he
could have these every day, he wd. not ask further boon of
Music.   Yet, he is prodigiously vain of his musical acquirement: and there is no musical virtue wh. he doth not stoutly
claim.   Moreover, there is a certain finicalness, a lack of innate
dignity, an absence of anything like a great aim or high ideal,
a tendency to be content with cheap triumphs and showings-
off, – wh. fit not to my liking.   Moreover, I think he putteth
off too many matters on the lady that is his wife.   'Tis a
fearsome creature, truly, – this wife: but fearsome through her
weakness, rather than through any bad intent.   I fear this
latter consideration hath not weight enough with him.
—   Dream thou not, though, that we are less friends than at
first. I dine there every day, he coming always to my room
for me: and I try to make some diversion from the numerous
troubles whereof the wife hath always a store to regale him
with.   After dinner he cometh back to my room with me:
and we have Kuhlau, *en duo*, some of wh. I greatly enjoy.   I
always remember too, that he hath not a mate, infinitely sweet,
as I have, to present ever before him the glorious ideal of one's
youth, to keep him ever trustful in the brightness and reality
and sufficiency of love, to hold him ever self-watchful and
solicitious to be all that is high and manly and noble, in order
to maintain himself in some way worthy of his unapproachable
Beloved.   Having not this, how much ought I, – I who have
thee, thou Inspiration, thou Creator of genius by love, thou

[12] H. C. Wysham.

Reward of labor by dainty sweetness, thou dear Star that art at once a far-off beautiful world and a Brightness intimately mixed with all the tissues of my soul, shining simultaneously in heaven and in the water therebeneath, – how much I say ought *I* to forgive, in *him*!

— We are the best of friends, and " run " together, always. This confidence is quite for thine ear, – into which I pour my most secret heart so joyfully.

— I think of thee with wonder, that groweth and groweth. Thou art so large in thy soul, so keen and quick and sure in thine intuitions, so beautiful in thy judgments and sweet conclusions. Dear Heartsease, thou wilt break my heart with sheer loveliness.

—— I continually fight away the thought that thou art there where the malarial devils may wound thee. The agony of my yearning to take thee away to this brighter climate where there is frost and snow and vigorous life, – O my wife, my Wife, how will I tell thee the tears I have shed in this behalf?

— But I am clear that thou must *stimulate*, in whatever best way thou findest. Purvey thee, therefore, the cask full of beer, again: and imbibe the same *hourly* : beginning with small doses, and increasing gradually. I command thee, do it. Drinkest much milk? I have known some who were made bilious, always, thereby: and *I* have never been bilious since the milk-drinking days of last summer.

— I was to have seen thy Letty [Yonge] Wrenshall some nights ago: but just as I was starting, Mr. W. came and informed me that Jack had had the croup, and Mrs. Letty was weary with nursing the same; so I went not. Am to go tomorrow morn, to make another appointment.

— I will be compelled to retire from social life. I will have three engagements for every night in the week, if matters go on; and work will be impossible.

— My father writeth that what with a carbuncle on his leg, and an overwhelming rush of business, he hath been unable to write thee: and beggeth that I will inform thee of this pressure, and of his continual thought of thee and of the boys. I will make inquiry as to the miniature. Willie's portrait is a monstrous caricature, and I think it shd. be incontinently cast into the fire, and burned.[18]

—   And now Time crieth, Have done: wherefore, praying that thou mayst inhale and breathe the very love of God through this night, – lingering, leaveth thee

thy

lover.

To Mary Day Lanier

[Baltimore,] Jany 28th 1874

At three I dined with Mrs. Bird, on canvass-backs and Champagne: meeting Minnie [Gresham] Machen and Mrs. Tom Gresham, (who is here staying with Minnie), and also Miss Walton Johnson, daughter of Col. R. M., " Philemon Perch," [14] of the Dukesborough Tales: wh. over, I dashed over to Wysham's, to call on Isobel and her friend Miss Emily Andrews, whom she hath brought home with her from New York. Then back to my room, in the twilight, where I have just picked up my flute and made a wailing *Sehnsucht* for thee that shall some day make thine ears tingle with knowledge of how I longed for thee.

——" — Yesterday at five, Mrs. Bird took me, by appointment, to see Miss [Elise?] Gelstin. 'Tis a rich girl, a most unfathomably silly woman, a rare transparent crystal of affectations,—and withal the most wonderful singer in America. I had to use much eloquence, and to say all sorts of pretty things to her, before she wd. sing, her father being recently dead. Finally, she went to her piano,—the best one, by the way, I ever heard—and after a little prelude, evidently impromptu but simply wonderful for artistic propriety and finish, she sang one of Franz' beautiful German songs. Just such singing have

---

[18] " Willie's portrait " was a photograph of Mrs. Clifford Lanier, sent as a Christmas gift; the "miniature" was to be painted from a photograph of the late Janie Lamar Day (see Mary Day Lanier's letters of Jan. 4 and Feb. 22, 1874).

[14] Pseudonym under which Richard Malcolm Johnston published *The Dukesborough Tales* in 1871.

I never heard before. She wept and sobbed and shrieked, with
melody so beautiful that it was painful and with agony so
melodious that it was fascinating. Then she sang " Bereft," in
the same manner.

—— Thou, thou, thou, Large Soul, Sweet Understanding
Soul, thou wert not there, and it was far, far too beautiful to
listen to alone, my heart was like ice for lack of thee, I suffered, and hurried my good Mrs. Bird away.

—— I enclose thee a pleasant letter from Mr. [George] Price,
President of Huntsville Female College. Thou wilt enjoy the
good-hearted tone thereof, and there are some fine touches
in it.

I am pretty well. The two hours' playing at each rehearsal,
wh. used to fatigue me greatly, does not so now. I improve
much in the technique of the flute, and am studying composition. How delightfully thou and I cd. pass life, in this place!
'Tis full of warm-hearted people, who without knowing it,
are languishing for some one such as thou art.[15] God grant it.
God send thee quickly, quickly, to thy famishing

lover.

To Mary Day Lanier

Balto. Jany 31st 1874.

I wrote thee of Huntingdon's lovely picture of Miranda, wh.
I saw at Col. Jenkins'. She standeth, with one arm stretched
along the top of a rock, upon an eminence overlooking the
sea, gazing at her future lover as he cometh along the strand.
Her hair is blown backward by the wind, and in all her posture
and expression is the sweet intangible ideal of perfect womanhood, serene and healthy, contrasted with the new disturbing
element wh. now, with her first sight of a young man, enters
into her heart.

—— Well, then, placing thee where she standeth, I remark,
as follows, towit:

---

[15] The last eight words in this sentence have been heavily marked over in the
MS; the reading here given is therefore tentative.

Miranda.[16]

I

The Storm hath blown thee a lover, Sweet,
And set him at thy very feet.
— But the wind's twice paid for grace so rare,
In that he hath thy holy hair
To kiss and to sing through and to flare
Like a torch-flame in the passionate air,
    Thou rose-and-white Miranda.

II

Eyes in a blaze, eyes in a daze,
Bold with love, cold with amaze,
Warm thrilling eyes, fast-filling eyes
'Twixt the flame and the shame of love's surpise,
— Ye draw yon prince-soul into your blue
As hot skies drink up a drop of dew,
    Divine eyes of Miranda.

III

And if I were yon stolid stone
Thy marvellous white arm leaneth on,
Thy touch would turn me to a heart
And I would palpitate, and start,
—— Content, when thou wert gone, to be
A dumb rock by a lonesome sea
    Forever, O Miranda!

Attend to these following imperious commands, from me
thy tyrant. First, do thou straightway copy off for me, fairly,
and send the same to me, the poem, the one sweet burst of
music out of thy heart!—that *thou* didst write.[17] I wish it,
particularly: obey me thereupon: an thou send it not presently,
I will invent some dire torture for thee that shall by contrast
make Nero to shine in history as an Angel of Mercy.

Secondly, send me the name, and precise designation, of that
most superlative thing of Chopin, wh. thou playest as none else

---

[16] Published in the New York *Evening Post*, Mar. 6, 1874, as " On Huntingdon's ' Miranda ' " (I, 32).

[17] " The Bequest," June 16, 1867 (see letter from Mary Day, printed in VII,
293-294, of the present edition).

can, and wh. I love as it were a part of thee,[18]—I mean that wh. commenceth,

I wish to arrange it for Orchestra, and will not rest till this old dream of mine shall be realized.

I return thee the parlous poems thou sendest. The " Lines " are perfect:—I regard the fact that there are people existing along in the world, who write these things, unharmed—when there is so much nitro-glycerine and giant-powder and acrolites and things of that nature about in easy reach—as the very strongest proof which could possibly be adduced of God's infinite forbearance. Surely it is only Divine love, wh. cd. at once possess the power, and resist the temptation,—to exterminate " M. A. Glaze." What a fascinating thing it is, this " Lines." One verse sticketh in my craw, ineradicably:

> The oldest he was years not six,
> And the youngest only eleven months old,
> But often she had left them there alone
> As by the neighbors I have been told.

—The careful statement of ages contained in the first two lines compelleth the mind to enter into a pleasing contemplation of the admirable regularity and system with which these domestic treasures must have made their appearance in the world: and the equally careful reference in the last line to the poet's authorities for the statement contained in the third,— (the *neighbors* told him)—speaketh marvellous well for his painstaking endeavor at historical accuracy.

—" As for " The Bather," it hath some rare sweet strokes. Thou hadst marked the ones I like best: save one wh. I have circled with a ⟨⟩. I cd. wish he had said naught of blushes, and the like. These allusions take the picture forever off the footing of a pure sweet statue, and set the imagination off on the sensuous road.

---

[18] Identified by Mary Day Lanier in her letter of Feb. 5, 1874, as " The Chopin Nocturne . . . No. 2—in ' Deux Nocturnes—pour Piano '—Opus 37. In G. Moll. W. G." Lanier's transcription is slightly inaccurate.

Address thy letters to me, hereafter, at " 64 Centre St, Baltimore, Md." instead of to Wysham's care. The little mouse [?] is in a great tiff with me, for disagreeing with him in opinion about the pitch of his flute wh. I think is sharp in the high notes. Alas, I daily see 'tis a finical soul, and I fear there are some melancholy explanations of what I took to be craziness [?] – But further thereanent some other time.[19]

I am tolerably well, vigorous, and bright. Write me, bravely, if thou likest my Miranda. Thine honest opinion will guide me, whether or not to publish the same.

—— As for thee, how dear thou art! Hast thou seen, on some quiet summer day, a large white cloud, resting tranquilly upon the bouyant air afar off in the horizon, and shining in the sunlight?

So, upon the up-bearing strength of thy love, so, in the never-failing light of thy love, resteth and dreameth happily, thy

lover.

To Mary Day Lanier [20]

Bo.   Feby. 3rd 1874

O, if thou cdst. hear a symphony of Gade's, wh. we rehearsed this morning! It is lovely, not with the passionate loveliness that bringeth pain, but with the dainty and childlike, yet strong, loveliness of a mountain (say) all covered with flowers and many-colored rocks and green leaves and sparkling springs –

—— Now may God bless thy wise heart and thy beautiful eyes:– I had just written so far when in cometh thy birth-

---

[19] A slip of paper has been pasted over this paragraph, partially obscuring its legibility; the reading here given is therefore tentative. In her letter of Feb. 5, 1874, Mary Day Lanier wrote: " I am too sorry for these clouds thou perceivest upon thy friendship and thy friend. Sweetheart, how could he have written that soulful, noble letter to thee in N. Y. were he hopelessly ' finical '? Think how hard his life has been. Why, his soul must feel like the foot of a Chinese lady of quality, from trying to fit itself to its surroundings. I have read from him some generous, passionate outbursts, some reverent confessions of faith, which tend to stay my hope in all these discouragements."

[20] Excerpt previously published, *Scribner's*, XXV, 632 (May 1899) ; reprinted, *Letters* (New York, 1899), p. 92.

MARY DAY LANIER IN 1874

Charles D. Lanier Collection, Johns Hopkins University

day gift.[21]　I am yet in the first ecstasy of it.　I cannot speak coherently thereanent, who is this good man that hath at last put upon paper thy divine eyes and brows, thy forehead's glorious expanse, and the perfect oval of thy lovelit face, I cd. kiss him, he is an artist, he is one of the old Masters.　God bless his Camera, and send him a wife faintly like to thee, – faintly, I say, for is none other greatly like thee – it was an inspiration to pose thee so that the exquisite long curve of thy cheek and chin cd. show itself, sloping like a mile-long ripple, made by a swallow's-wing, that slowly advanceth over a still lake, dost thou grow ever and ever more beautiful? as I study this face, I find it the loveliest human countenance I ever saw, it hath in it both that which I saw when I left it and something more, born since that moment, — I know not what – of intangible bravery and hope and trust –, it is like Heaven and the Spirits are visible wh. do inhabit it, namely, Kisses, and Bright Wits, and Keen Intelligences, and Loving Previsions, and Sweet Honesties, and Dainty Girl-Fancies, and Passionate Purities, and Celestial Longings, and Womanly Ideals, and Wifely Self-Abandonments, and Lovely Mother-Raptures, and Open-Armed Faiths, and Strong-handed Hopes, and Meek-faced Humilities, and Charitable Religions, and Clinging Friendships, and manifold Man-Loves and Nature-Loves and Art-Loves, and where gottest thou these dimples in the corners of thy mouth? was it from kissing young Prince Hal? and O, how unclouded and wrinkleless is thy broad brow, and how Eve-young thy cheeks are! and how can I to tell thee, dear Heliotrope-and-Tube-rose-and-Violet-all-in-One, how my spirit is drunk with *thee* as Spinoza was called the God-drunken man because all his thoughts and sayings were interfused with the idea of God? and is it possible that this fine-stranded hair, – whose touch is like thine own, and whose coils I have covered with kisses and wound about my neck, – was but lately on thy sweet round very head, and lay mayhap but lately along thy cheek and even across thy perfect mouth? — and now I will tell thee that I have two other birth-day gifts, one an exquisite white-silk neck-kerchief for protecting the throat in cold weather, from my

[21] The photograph of Mary Day Lanier described in this paragraph is apparently the one reproduced on the opposite page (first reproduced in Mims, p. 98, and ascribed to the year 1873).

friend Mrs. Martin, and t'other a visit from Wysham who
hath come over and brought his flute and played some Kuhlau
duos with me in marvellous token of amity.

— I hope soon to get a place, as teacher, wh. will make me
feel safe to bring thee here.   — My God, how beautiful is
this hope!, and am going to Col. [R. M.] Johnson's tomorrow-
night, to talk with him over the prospect, – and to read him
also some of the " Jacquerie." [22]

If thou gettest the Baltimore " Sun " of today, in the upper
right-hand corner of the 1st page thou wilt find some account
of a Masque Ball.   I played, there, as one of the Orchestra,
in a sort of Concert lasting until twelve O'clock, when the
dancing commenced and I yielded my desk to Flauto Secondo.
Some of the Tableaux were comical beyond description, and I
will tell thee about them on some happy day when I have thine
ear to kiss and to whisper into.   Now must I cease this fearsome screed, and betake me to copying some of my Jacquerie
wherewith to regale my friend tomorrow.

I was paid seven extra dollars today, being *honorarium* for
playing in St. Paul's Church O' Christmas, and therewith I am
going immediately to purvey me a dainty pocket-case of velvet
for thy most dear *eidolon*.   So that I may have the same without harm next my heart, always.   How humbly, how wholly,
how devoutly, do I thank thee for this thoughtful sweet act !

—— May this night be as fair and as full of stars to thee, as
thy picture face is to me, – wisheth thy

lover.——

To Mary Day Lanier [23]

[Baltimore,] Fb. 7th 1874.

Meseemeth 'tis a fearsome long time since I have kneeled
and worshipped before thee with tangible prayer, – for with
*in*tangible and wordless invocations I am always at my devo-

---

[22] This is the first clear evidence of the beginning of the friendship between
Lanier and Richard Malcolm Johnston. Apparently Lanier did not begin teaching
at Johnston's Pen Lucy School until four years later (see his letter of Feb. 24,
1878, and note 27, 1878).

[23] Previously published, *Scribner's*, XXV, 632 (May, 1899) ; reprinted, *Letters*
(New York, 1899), pp. 92-93.

tions and my life is nothing but a church-service in thy praise
—, 'tis three days since I have written thee.
Thy picture sanctifieth my room and my days with an infinite
comfort. Thy letter is now here, of 2nd . I freely forgive
the " artist " his laziness as to young Hal,[24] and I can even find
in my heart to condone his " general aggravating-ness " toward
thee, – because he hath been the first to catch any faintest
semblance of thee in the photographic way. Perhaps some day
Heaven will weary of flouting my plans, – so that I may have
thee painted upon ivory. There will come forth a face shall
go down to posterity for a miracle of loveliness and a model
for all women to look like who desire to be to their lovers, as
thou art to me, at once Wife, Comrade, Teacher, Inspiration,
Sweetheart, Religion, Friend, Country, Music, Ambition, Love,
Hope, Longing, Heaven. Aye, this is just *thou*, to me : take
the sweet essences of all these, and fuse them by some exquisite
alchemy of fragrances into one perfect Lady : – thou resultest.
————— Randolph's criticism in the " Gazette " on the
English and American Music [25] was in the main just, – though
of course a little exaggerated, to eke out the spiciness thereof.
He and I had a good laugh over it, next morning. I was disappointed in Sterndale Bennetts' Music. If I had not heard so
much better, perhaps I wd. have enjoyed it : – and he does occasionally get off a beautiful idea –: but his music is too unsubstantial, you bring nothing away with you from it, it is much
like Mendellsohn-and-water. The other pieces of the programme were equally unsubstantial. The Overture to " De-
borah " was pretty, – nothing more: the " Fugue ", by Deems,
was a very good fugue doubtless, but was abominably dismal music; and the march by Rosewald (who is leader of
our first violins) was decidedly the best piece on the programme, but was somewhat marred by a palpable imitation of

[24] In her letter of Jan. 30, 1874, Mary Day Lanier had written that the Brunswick photographer was too impatient to take a picture of the baby, Henry
Wysham Lanier.
[25] Randolph's criticism (Baltimore *Gazette,* Jan. 26, 1874) accords with
Lanier's: he was very severe on the Fantasie Overture of Sir William Sterndale
Bennett, slightly less so on the Symphony Concerto of Mr. Boise of Cleveland,
and mildly complimentary to J. H. Rosewald's Wedding March in C. He added,
however, that it was particularly fitting that the Peabody Institute should sponsor
the works of contemporary American and English composers.

wind effects in a march of Mendellsohn's we played some weeks ago. Our concert tonight is to be a very beautiful one in the Orchestral features. We are to play the "Fernand Cortez" Overture, by Spontini, The "Water-Carrier" Overture, by Cherubini, The "Fantastic Symphony," by Mercadante, and the "William Tell" Overture, by Rossini. This last has a celebrated Flute solo, in a beautiful Pastoral Scene, and I have had many compliments on my rendition of it, at the rehearsals. I do not think much of it, though: 'tis not the sort of playing I like most for the flute, and is more admired for its difficulty, I think, than for its beauty.

I have not time now to answer thine interrogatories but will endeavor to examine myself soon, and execute same.

—— My Jonathan is full of love again, and hath but now brought over a duo for me to practice, for next Sunday night. Start not ! 'Tis a Charity Concert, and are we not allowed to lift the poor out of the ditch o' Sundays ?

—— As all these snow flakes fly to the earth and have rest in a vast and white content, so fly to thee and rest in thee all the thoughts, wishes, and acts of thy

lover.

To Mary Day Lanier [26]

Bo. Feb. 7th 1874

Yes, yes, God bless thee forever, and infinitely, and in some new and marvellous exquisite fashion, – there *is*, as thou sayest, more of "my wife" in this picture than any other that hath been taken. How cloudless the face is, how noble and high and majestical with all great loves and ideals!   Dream not that I can say anything too full of praise for thee : – but, honor bright, do I din too much love into thine ear?   I do not think thou *canst* tire of it, it is so fervent and true-worshipful : but – one hundred and thirty days of it, or thereabout – – – – .?

———— I am just from the Concert. It was splendidly successful. The Orchestra was in fine trim, the audience in a good humor, the singing delightful, the piano playing simply

[26] Previously published, *Scribner's*, XXV, 745 (June, 1899) ; reprinted, *Letters* (New York, 1899), pp. 94-95.

exquisite. The Tell overture went off well, save that the 'cellos, which have a beautiful introduction, were not as well harmonized as might be. I had another triumph in the Pastoral Scene: When Oboe and I had finished our long interchange of confidences, the audience broke into applause wh. was only stilled by the continuance of the overture: and the Conductor came down and said it was beautifully played.[27] My greatest trouble in playing has been to keep in tune with the Oboe: the tone of that instrument is so strange, so strident, and so indecisive when one is close to the player, (he sitteth immediately behind me) that I have infinite difficulty in accommodating my pitch to his. Some of the notes on his instrument, too, are incorrect: and, inasmuch as he *cannot* change his tones, and as my music is often written in octaves above his, I have to use the utmost caution and skill in turning the embouchure in and out, so as to be in perfect accord with him. For some weeks I did not succeed in this, and suffered untold agonies thereanent: but I believe I have now discovered all his quips and his quirks, and tonight we were in lovely harmony with each other. I read far better than at first: and am greatly improved in the matter of keeping time in the Orchestra. How much I have learned in the last two months ! I am not yet an artist, though, on the flute. The technique of the instrument has many depths wh. I had not thought of, before: and I wd. not call myself a virtuoso within a year. I feel sure that in that time I cd. do anything possible to the instrument. But thou wdst. not know my tone, now ! How I wish I might play for thee ! I have just composed a thing I call " Longing." [28] It is all full of thee, and I have not

[27] Innes Randolph, describing the William Tell Overture in the Baltimore *Gazette,* Feb. 9, 1874, said: " Then, the Shepherd's pipe, and the Alpine horn call to each other from hill to hill—so finely done by Messrs. Lannier [*sic*] and Stowasser that the overture was interrupted by applause."

Lanier's comments, in the following sentences, on the oboe are also reflected by the *Gazette* critic: " To the first hautbois we have listened carefully during several concerts, hesitating to speak, but we are compelled to say that he has a very bad instrument. His tone is superb, but the instrument is not in tune with itself, besides not being exactly in the pitch of the rest."

[28] The original musical composition here described is obviously the same as that referred to in Lanier's letter of Jan. 28, 1874, above. A fragmentary MS of eight bars entitled " Mem. Sehnsucht " has survived (Charles D. Lanier Collection, Johns Hopkins University).

played it for anyone, save for myself, when my heart is quite too full. I suspect the people in the house think I am stark-mad, in the twilights, when I send this strenuous sigh out on the air. Suppose a tuberose shd. just breathe itself out in perfume, and disappear utterly in a sweet breath: – thus my heart in this melody.

Well, here is a picture of Badger, he hath just sent me, and one of his house and grapery.[29] Thou wdst. marvel to hear how this battered soul talketh about thy lover. I believe he is one of the truest lovers I ever had. He thinketh there was never a flutist like me. This is all simply because I touched his heart. I doubt not he has heard many flutists with far more technique than I have.

— Now God send thee some joy as perfect-sweet as thou art to thy

lover.

To Mary Day Lanier [30]

Bo. Feby. 8th 1874.

If the constituents and guardians of my childhood, – those good Presbyterians who believed me a model for the Sunday-school children of all time, – cd. have witnessed my acts and doings this day, I know not what groans of sorrowful regret wd. arise in my behalf. For, – the same being Sunday – I went at two O'clock to rehearse with an Orchestra in which I was engaged, under Herr Lenschow, for the Concert of the Germania Männerchor, of Baltimore, wh. is to be next Wednesday night. I carried *thee* with me, and so I felt safe and happy. Having arrived at the beautiful new hall wh. this Männerchor have just built, – and the opening of which is the occasion of the concert – I found they were waiting for me, and so quickly took my seat and fell-to. First, a Concerto for Violin and

---

[29] Both pictures have survived (Charles D. Lanier Collection, Johns Hopkins University).

[30] Previously published, *Scribner's*, XXV, 632-633 (May, 1899); reprinted, *Letters* (New York, 1899), pp. 95-97.

In the middle of the first paragraph the words in brackets have been substituted for the music symbols in the MS.

Orchestra, by DeBeriot, light, lovely, airy, and wondrous delicate: then the " Jübel " (Jubilee) Overture, of Weber, full of
glory and triumph, ending with " God Save the Queen," wh. is
set in four sharps and carrieth the poor straining Flauto Primo
clear up to [high c above the staff] and thereabouts, without
pity: then in filed a great Chorus of male and female voices,
and we all plunged into the great " Athalia " of Mendellsohn,
for Orchestra and Chorus. Borne on the noble surges of the
upswelling tones, I floated hither and thither in that sea of
glory-turned-into-music. Presently I found myself playing
almost alone, in Octaves with a lovely Soprano voice; I turned
my eyes involuntarily, as we sailed along together, and my gaze
fell full upon a pair of beautiful liquid gazelle-eyes wh. by a
similar impulse, I suppose, had sought mine; She — I mean
the Eyes – looked me full in the face a moment, then with a
half-smile, full of dignity and sweetness, turned to her notes
again: wh. also I had to do, never having seen or heard the
piece before; and so, mutually cheered by this dumb exchange
of sympathy, we sang and played together to the end of the
piece, wh. occupied, I shd. think, near three-quarters of an
hour. When we had finished, I rushed to Herr Lenschow and
procured a presentation to the fair Soprano. I found her a
charming young woman, bright-faced and witty, – Miss Pagels,
by name – and had a little really refreshing Champagny talk
with her.

She recognized me, – she said – immediately on looking at
me, having seen me at the Peabody Concerts : then she paid
some pretty compliments to " Blackbirds," and altogether made
herself exceedingly agreeable. I thought all the time how thy
great eyes wd. have sparkled and deepened and widened, cdst.
thou have been, with thy very lips, and self, a third in this
little meeting. Something in her eyes, her gestures, – a certain
trick of the hair – I know not what, – was so like thee that I
half-loved her on the spot.

– – – Then we played a cavatina from Ernani, sung by a stout
German lady: then the " Sonnenuntergang " (Sunset) by
Flomma, for Chorus of mens' voices and Orchestra. Then I
took a great draught of beer, and found it was six O'clock. I
had had nothing to eat since eight this morning; so hied me to
a restaurant, and dined on oysters and a chop. Then home,

laid me down for twenty minutes, rose, dressed in full concert-suit. Then came Wysham, and we fared forth to the great Hall of The Masonic Temple. Here we found a large audience assembled to hear a concert for the benefit of the Carmelite Nuns; and, being quickly called, forth stepped the little man and I on the stage, and dashed into the elaborate tootle-ty-tootle-ty of Robboni's duo on themes from Rigoletto. I did laugh inwardly as I looked about the hall, to see the big Irishmen, servant-maids and all, good Catholics every one, gazing and listening rapt. They encored us, and we responded with " Adieu, Dear Land." Then, home: and here sit I, with thy wondrous face breathing all manner of loves and dear womanly sweetnesses into my heart out of the mute portrait, – wondering whether thou art, at this moment, undressing the elf,[31] or feeling Charley's pulse, or taking young Hal to thy breast, or feeding little Daughter, or kissing thy father, or stroking dear Harry's head, or coddling Mammy or holding one of thy long and mysterious conferences with Rena anent the towels or that missing sheet. Whichsoever of these thou art doing, I wd. to God I might see thee and hear thee at it: for I am famished for the tone of thy voice, for the lovely sight of thy motherly ministrations and housewifely movings-about, Bohemianism and compliments fill not my heart, thou, thou, dear Wife, my beautiful Lady, my worshipful Mistress, my Tuberose, My sweet wise Sweetheart, thou alone bringest me the highest-of-life, thou art my Only-One, and when I am far from thee I have no comfort save in thinking how utterly and simply and devoutly I am thy

Lover.

To Mary Day Lanier [32]

Bo.   Feb. 12th 1874

I have not a particle of business news to tell thee, and I wonder that thou art not utterly out of patience with me, that I send thee no money and no plans. To give thee both, in a few

---

[31] " The Elf " and " Prince Elfin " were nicknames for Sidney Lanier, Jr.
[32] Previously published, *Scribner's*, XXV, 745-746 (June, 1899); reprinted, *Letters* (New York, 1899), pp. 97-98.

days; that is my hope and expectation. ——— Sometimes I think God has not a particle of pity for me. I do not blame Him, for I do not deserve any . —— But being hard on *me*, He is therefore necessarily hard on *thee*, — and this ——— O my Friend, I am glad I *cannot* tell thee how bitter and how mournful this maketh my heart, when with excess of love and excess of vain waiting I am overborne.

That I write thus to thee, – Thou Sweet Courageous Soul that sendest me such brave and heartsome and beautiful letters ! – is only proof how hurt my heart is, and how wholly I reverence *thee*, for thou knowest that to thee alone in the world do I reveal my sorrows.

— To offset this Jeremiad, I may tell thee that from a hundred indications I gather that I have conquered myself a place, here, as an orchestral player. The prejudices, the cliques, the claques, the difficulties, I had to encounter were innumerable and appalling: but by straightforward behavior and hard work and steady improvement, I have finally managed to beat down and trample on every one of them. I believe my Tell solo, on Saturday night, quite gave the *coup de grâce* to them, and the managers of the smaller Orchestras about town have freely proffered engagements for odd occasions, although I do not belong to the " Musical Union " which embraceth nearly all the musicians in town and wh. obligeth all its members to employ each other in preference to outsiders.[33] I played last night with the Germania Maennerchor Orchestra: next week I am to play with the Liederkranz; and have four other engagements, of similar character. I was also engaged to play solos in two concerts at Wheeling, Va: but this has been postponed until after Lent. Miss Busk asked me some nights ago if I wd. take a tour with her, in the Spring; and the leader of the Harmonie Maennerchor has engaged me for a solo at their next concert, the date of wh. is not yet determined.

I am copying off, – in order to try the publishers therewith – a *Danse des Moucherons*,[34] (Midge – dance) wh. I have written

[33] Lanier did join the union. His certificate of permission to play (Charles D. Lanier Collection) is dated Mar. 21, 1874; date of expiration, May 1, 1874.

[34] " Danse des Moucherons " survives in MS, in the possession of Henry W. Lanier. The first sheet (reproduced in S. T. Williams, *The American Spirit in Letters*, New Haven, 1926, p. 256) contains the inscription: " To Henry C. Wy-

for flute and piano, and wh. I think enough of to let it go forward as Op. 1. Dost thou remember one morning last summer, Charley and I were walking in the upper part of the yard, before breakfast, and saw a swarm of gnats, of whose strange evolutions we did relate to thee a marvellous tale ? I have put the grave oaks, the quiet shade, the sudden sunlight, the fantastic, contrariwise and ever-shifting midge-movements, the sweet hills afar off, and *thee* with thy earnest wide eyes, — all, in the piece, and thus *I* like it: but I know not if others will, I have not played it for anybody.

— Good Night, thou, for whom into each moment I compress an eternity of love.

To Mary Day Lanier

Bo. Feb. 16th 1874.

I am so sleepy and so tired that I scarcely can hold my pen. I rehearsed two hours with the Peabody Orchestra today, and then two hours with the Liederkranz, who give a concert tomorrow night. Coming home, I found Wysham and Cockey [35] waiting in my room, and played flute trios with them for an

---

sham. Dec. 25, 1873." The second sheet (reproduced in Starke, opposite p. 174) contains an account of its origin similar to the one in the present letter—which, with its reference to the " hills afar off," indicates Marietta, Ga., as the locale. Five years later, in relating the incident as an illustration in his lectures on Shakespeare at the Johns Hopkins University, Lanier described a different and somewhat more romantic setting—a lonely horseback ride on the coast of Georgia (III, 407-410). The phenomenon, of course, could have been witnessed on two separate occasions. The composition has never been published, but there is available a wax recording of its performance by the orchestra of the Peabody Institute at the centenary exercises held on Feb. 3, 1942. (There also survive in the Charles D. Lanier Collection, Johns Hopkins University, the following: (1.) two MS copies, by H. W. Lanier, of " Danse des Moucherons "—one for flute and piano, one for flute only; (2.) a fragmentary orchestration in Lanier's autograph entitled " Gnats "; and (3.) three fragments in one of Lanier's staff books entitled: " Mem. Symphony. / The Woods," " Theme. Gnats," " Tema. Gnats.")

[35] Dr. Charles Henry Cockey (1844-1904), practising physician, Professor of Microscopy and one of the founders of the Baltimore University Hospital, and an amateur flute player. For many years he also served as principal of the Baltimore Grammar School, No. 18; it is possible that the " charity class of street-boys," which Lanier mentions teaching, came through his connection with Dr. Cockey. (See Eugene F. Cordell, *The Medical Annals of Maryland, 1799-1899*, Baltimore, 1903; and the Baltimore *Sun*, Nov. 21, 1904.)

hour: then fared forth to a charity class of street-boys, wh. I teach every Monday and Thursday night: and thence home again. I wd. not write thee such a wretched scrawl: but I am oppressed with an intolerable sense of irreligion, such as I have heard miners describe, who had been in the "diggings" for years without seeing a woman, or a baby, or going to church: sooth to say, it is four days since I wrote thee, and this long cessation of worship maketh me to feel barbaric and utterly horrible. Therefore I scratch thee this little illegible prayer, tonight, half-careless whether or not thou canst read it, half-content in that I can write myself once more thy faithful, thy ever longing

lover.

TO MARY DAY LANIER

[Baltimore,] Feby. 21st 1874

Thou art the prettiest Critic in the world, and what thou say'st of my poem is perfectly just, from the stand-point of thine understanding of it.[36] By the "*shame* of love's surprise," I really did not intend to convey the idea of the blush of the conscious and impure boarding-school girl, but rather the *humility* of a soul, hitherto free as air, now suddenly feeling itself in bondage and as it were a thrall. But I will change the line, and will adopt entire thine emendation; for the "fear" which thou suggestst is a better sentiment than mine. I will also perfect the metre of the two last lines of the 2nd verse, wh. is not to my liking, requiring too much tripping of tongue.

My Child, thou art a fair and great poet. Didst thou indeed inquire of God, long ago, if it were possible He cd. need, so sorely as *thou* didst, the love of that poor "Heart," – wh. after all did never die, no, By Heaven ! but only slept till the wound wh. Monsieur Brain dealt him was healed, and then woke fresh, strong and even more and more thy loving knight ?[37] Didst thou indeed inquire if heaven shone brighter

---

[36] Mary Day Lanier's letter of Feb. 5, 1874, contained an extended criticism of her husband's poem, " On Huntingdon's ' Miranda.' "

[37] The allusion is to Mary Day Lanier's poem, " The Bequest," which was an answer to " The Tournament. Joust First," by Lanier (see note 53, 1867).

for this love wh. thou thoughtest was ascended thither ?
Didst thou indeed finally comfort thy soul with remembering that the last words of this wounded Heart were a love-
message to thee, thou Only-Beloved ? – My heart trembleth all
through, to read thy poem, now. It is too beautiful. I thank
thee for it, inexpressibly.

— Read in the programme wh. I enclose, (of our concert last
night,)[38] how King Valdemar said: "Let God have Heaven,
if he will give me my woods and my lady !" – I, who love
the woods as passionately as King Valdemar, love my lady
better than he : for I wd. leave out the woods, in *my* cry, and
I freely resign all, so God will give me thee, thee alone, thou
divine Heartsease and Sweetest Sweet, to whom arise unceasingly the faithful aspirations and true-love longings of thy

lover.

To Mary Day Lanier

Bo.   Mch. 5th 1874

Last night, according to appointment, I fared forth to thy Letty
Yonge Wrenshall, and found the same all beaming and rosy-
radiant, and took the same on my arm, and marched away
(having previously given Jack a rare tumble in his crib and
well-nigh broken my heart therein by reason of big sighs for
my own young men) to the Latrobe's, towit, W. H. B. Latrobe,[39] bridge-builder, of the Baltimore Bridge Company.
There came also Conductor Hamerik, and, after some talk,

---

[38] A concert of the "Grand Duchess" Orchestra at the Concordia Theatre.
In his letter of Feb. 20, 1874 (here omitted), Lanier complained that this
playing about in local orchestras took up too much of his time ("two long
rehearsals today: . . . *three,* yesterday, taking seven hours") and did not pay.
On Feb. 22 Mary Day Lanier wrote: "I tremble lest thou overstrain thy lungs
some day, in so long flute-playing. . . . One little step too far thou mayst be
unable to retrace for months or forever." But in his reply of Feb. 28, 1874
(here omitted), Lanier reassured her: "Fear not that I will play too much. In
the matter of lungs I am, for *me,* in fine condition, and my general state of health
is fully as good as at any time in five years past."

[39] This is probably a slip for either Benjamin Henry Latrobe (1806-1878) or
his son Charles Hazlehurst Latrobe (1834-1902), both of whom were civil
engineers and bridge-builders in Baltimore. The name of a second son, J. H. B.
Latrobe, a lawyer, may have been responsible for Lanier's error.

my flute was haled forth.   I vowed I wd. not put finger to key for anybody but Schubert, and so forthwith, into my beloved Schubert's Album we plunged, Hamerik playing the accompaniments with such intense and loving fervor and such artistic perfection as wd. have delighted the inmost craving of thy heart. Song after song, we played: sweet, brief, passionate outgleamings of melody, writ as (thou mayst remember) I have so often contended all lyric poetry must be, *i.e.*, each poem expressing but a single idea, and expressing *that* in the shortest manner possible, and in the simplest, noblest, most beautiful, and most musical words. As for thy Letty, she was a picture, and I am sure these lovely songs found lodgment in her heart. Hamerik was so enthused that he invited me to play a couple of them at the next concert, – just to show the singers, he said, how to render Schubert's music.

— When I play these songs with thee, – then, dear Wife, life will be full.

— Thy Letty discourseth most sweetly upon thee, and for this I love her.   That any one shd. love thee, – that is grace enough.

— May thy soul float upon the glory of the Spring, into Paradise, – aspireth thy

lover.

To Mary Day Lanier

Bo. Mch. 8th 1874.

Ah, do I not remember that fair day,[40] when the haze was in the sky, and the sun was dreaming, and the boat floated idly, and thy gray lustrous eyes shone from under the heap of the Jessamine bells ? It is but a few days since I was at Col. Johnson's, spending the evening, when the talk fell upon Jessamines, and I did straightway burst into a description of that same day wh. fairly made them stare, with the fervor thereof.

It is worth living a lifetime for, thou dainty Soul, to get but one such letter from thee, as that with the Jessamines. These

---

[40] The reference is apparently to the time of Lanier's first meeting with Mary Day in the spring of 1863.

are exquisite twins, – thy words and Jessamine blooms – : and
it is well that thou sendest them together, to float hand in hand
into my heart and abide there as Spirits of beauty forever.
—— Here is a programme of last night's Concert. I wd. thou
mightst have heard the Concerto of Henselt, and the " Fair
Ellen " Cantata, and the Schubert March.   I have not now
time to enlarge thereupon.

May the strong and tender cloud of my worship support thy
soul up in among the stars this night, midst of a heaven of
serene dreams, – fervently prayeth thy

lover.

To Robert S. Lanier

Bo. Mch. 11th 1874.

My dear Father:
Your kind letter of 7th inst., enclosing check
for $40.00 is here, and gives me great pleasure.   I had written
you only a few days before.

I believe (–in answer to yr. inquiry about my health) I wrote
you that I was quite strong, for *me*, in the matter of lungs: and
in general condition I am fully as well off as when I last saw
you.

If I could only obtain some sort of foothold, here, which would
leave me at all easy in mind, I am sure I could soon place
myself on a secure foundation in my favorite pursuits, – I mean,
in literature and music, as an author. I am all the time working
to this end: and am now trying to secure a place in one of the
large female schools of this city, where I can teach for three
or four hours a day, without responsibility.   There are such
positions, here, and if I can get one, it will suit me admirably,
and will enable me to bring my family here.

I could never tell you how hampered are all my efforts, by the
physical disabilities which I have been so long enduring. I can
not write for more than fifteen minutes at a time without severe
pain:– and this prevents me from taking many places which I
could secure through several friends that I have here. –   This
is but one of a dozen ways in which the wretched disease
thwarts me at every step.   It also makes me very slow in
advancing my literary work.

I have a couple of pieces for Flute, – one for Flute & Piano, and one for Flute alone – nearly ready for publication.[41]   A poem of mine, written on Huntington's painting of " Miranda " (wh. I saw at Col. J. Stricker Jenkin's house in Baltimore) appears in the New York " Evening Post " (William Cullen Bryant's paper) of March 6th :   I have ordered some extra copies and will send you one.

I have not done much with the " Jacquerie," save to think over the plot, and recast some of it.

I have made a great many pleasant acquaintances, and some very delightful friendships, here: and, if I had time to attend to social duties, could soon know the whole town.   But I have been obliged to decline going out much: for my time was greatly occupied with the necessary practice to enable me to discharge the duties of my new position, and with my work.

I expect to run home early in April.   I long to see all of you.   Kiss Mama for me, and condole with Master Pringle in my behalf, anent the chills.   Yr. Son

S. L.

To Mary Day Lanier

Bo.   Mch. 11th 1874

It is three days since I have sent a prayer to the sweet South-country that holdeth thee.   O why can I not bring thee into these more bracing airs?   Some day the burning of this desire will surely scorch Heaven into letting me have its fulfillment.

A letter cometh from Harry, and saith thou wert, or had been, ill with chills, and weary with spring-lassitudes.   This doubleth the flame in my heart, and, thou wdst. stare if thou cdst. know the wild expedients wh., in the mere extravagance of pain of longing, I devise to get thee here.

This is a noble place to board, where I am; and the ladies are now " thinking over " what they'll charge for thee and the babies and Rena and me, to have two bedrooms and a parlor of our own.   The house is in a hundred yards of the Academy (Peabody), only a short three-minutes' walk from thy Letty

[41] Presumably " Danse des Moucherons " and " Blackbirds " (or " Swamp Robin ").

Wrenschall, less than that from Mrs. Bird's and from another dear friend of mine whom I long for thee to know, – hight Mary Jones – and in five minutes walk of a lovely church of thy persuasion. The people (as I mean of the house) are Miss Mary Ann Young, her sister Miss Tina (abridgment of I know not what) – both ladies being somewhere about thirty –, another sister, Mrs. Richardson, and her husband (in the hardware trade) – childless –, and the Uncle of these ladies, Mr. Charles B. Young, a gentleman seventy two years of age, yet who started off on a business trip to *Mexico* a month ago, and will be gone a month still! – and who is altogether the youngest, liveliest, wittiest, most " travelled " old gentleman that you shall find in a summer's day. They are gentle-people, all; have been rich, but say nothing of it, and are always at once quiet, merry, and simple. There is but one boarder, besides myself. That is Miss Seaton, formerly of Washington (thy Father will remember, if thou dost not, the ancient firm of Gales and Seaton, proprietors of the old National Intelligencer, in Washington, for many years: and the lady I speak of is daughter of that Seaton), who hath written a very successful life of her father, and is now engaged in some work for Harper's Magazine. She is a charming person, making me think always of thy Mrs. Whittle: is quite deaf, and cometh not to table, but liveth in a mystic Olympian recess far upstairs. I have seen little of her, until recently. We met on the street today, and walked merrily home together through the roaring March wind. As we came upstairs together, I handed her the New York " Evening Post ", which containeth my " Miranda." She has just sent it back, with the enclosed note, wh. with all other of my praises I lay at thy feet, for it is thou that writest in me.[42]

— The ladies declare they are longing for some children to pet. And O, if thou cdst. live but a little while on the glorious bread and butter, and noble beef, and delicate fish,

---

[42] Eight surviving notes from Josephine Seaton to Lanier, 1874-1880, reveal that he frequently sent his poems to her for criticism. She also offered to help him in that part of his work that was an irksome interruption to his inspiration, by doing research for him in the Mercantile and Peabody Libraries. She had recently published a biography of her father, *William Winston Seaton of the National Intelligencer* (1871).

and snowy potatoes, and such hominy as wd. cause Warren [43]
to murder his wife and then hang himself for very shame and
remorse (they cook the hominy in a bottle, as thou makest thy
famous beef-tea), and eggs and milk wh. wd. heap coals of
fire on all the cows' and hens' heads in Cobb County, and
splendid water, and delicious wine at a dollar and a half a
gallon (I've got to look back and see how this sentence commenced: – ah, "live on," these things.), – I sh. have thee a
portly matron ere long, with an arm like a myrtle bough. And
no more freezing o' nights with getting up to the children, nor
having *them* frozen with being uncovered. On the coldest
winter day, I dress in any part of my room with perfect comfort, and never think of temperature while indoors. We wd.
have no trouble with fires, water, or that ilk: not to speak of
many other conveniences wh. I will not here dilate upon.

And we will have our own parlor and a noble piano, whereupon a teacher will make thee exercise thy soulfull fingers
daily: – and then my soul will dry some of her tears, thou dear,
unearthly-sweet, long-suffering Beloved! Wdst. not like this?
'Tis a ravishing dream to thy

lover.

I forgot to say that a nice place for thy father, and for Harry
whenever he is ready to come, can be secured within a few
yards: also that I will send thee a copy of the Post in a day
or two.

To Mary Day Lanier [44]

Bo. Mch. 15th 1874

So, then: here is a poem wh. hath lain in my heart like an opal
in the earth, ever since that blessèd day when thy two gray
eyes dawned on me. Of course, since I have written it to print,
I cannot make it such as *I* desire, in artistic design: for the
forms of today require a certain trim smugness and clean-

---

[43] A negro servant in the boarding-house in Marietta where the Laniers had
stayed the previous summer.

[44] Excerpt previously published, W. H. Ward, "Memorial," *Poems* (New
York, 1884), p. 244, as a note to "My Two Springs" (I, 32), the poem inclosed
in this letter. (A fragmentary musical composition survives in one of Lanier's staff

shaven propriety in the face and dress of a poem, and I must win a hearing by conforming in some degree to these tyrannies, – with a view to overturning them in the future. Written so, it is not nearly so beautiful as I wd. have it: and I therefore have another, still in my heart, which I will some day write, for *myself*. Yet, this one gives me some peace : thou dear one, it is so sweet to print thee, at all, and to show people how noble and how rare thou art, and the devotion wh. breatheth through this little poem will make people [know?] 'tis a marvellous wife that hath all these things in her two eyes.

And so, now, no more, for lack of time. Within three weeks I shall see thee.   My God !

To Mary Day Lanier

Bo. Mch. 21st 1874

Nay, Sweet Soul, my plans are too embryonic, yet, for thee to do more than dream on ; and I do *not* think to move thee *here* before June, – tho' of course thou canst not stay in B'k later than the early May, else I wd. have no Wife.   I have not thought where to place thee for the summer. I *did* think, when I wrote thee of the house, here, that I might bring thee on here in the summer; but two or three days of warm weather wh. we have recently had, convince me that neither thou nor I cd. stand it. Of thy summer destination, we will talk when I see thee.

Also will we talk of another matter whereof thou speakest.

books, Charles D. Lanier Collection, Johns Hopkins University, entitled " The Spring that feeds the Lake of Dreams," echoing a line in this poem.)

Mary Day Lanier received the MS at Brunswick, Mar. 22, 1874, and wrote to her husband the same day:

" And here is my Poem. I *ought* to be ' calmly unafraid to die' after reading this: for it is satisfaction enough for one life to have read these words from *thee*. It has been my intense desire for lo! these many years to have one of thy sweet songs all mine own.

" Thou hast right royally granted my petition, my King.

" I feel too much to say more of this crown which thy love hath set upon my head."

I thought, when I wrote thee, that I wd. get a position to teach, for some three hours a day, an advanced class of young ladies, – wh. wd. pay well and leave me time for my beloved pursuits whereof my heart and my brain become more and more full, day by day. But the prospect of getting the same recedeth somewhat, – and I rather think God (heavy odds !) is against me.

I am invited by Miss Busk [45] to go on a short Concert tour with her, – to Wheeling, Va, Columbus, Ohio, and intermediate places, – early in April: wh. will keep me ten days later from thee, likely. – It is of course my plain duty, to go (–for they offer me, to pay all my expenses and give me twenty per cent of the net receipts) – my plain duty to *thee*, – otherwise nothing under heaven cd. keep me away from thee ten days – or ten minutes, longer than my present engagement lasts. – – – – For I do so need thee, Wise Sweetheart ! – thy counsel, thy talk, thy suggestions based on thy firm woman's-intuition. I am indeed come to a place where two roads lead off: I do not quite know wh. to take :– thou canst tell me : – hereof thou and I will talk: God speed the time !
Thou art so wondrous generous, in declaring thou canst wait. I have many plans, upon *one* of wh. I am perfectly sure I can fall back for a little time.

Think not, from aught I have said herein, that I see any reason to retreat from my chosen life. Not at all. To be poet and musician, – that will I be, or naught. A sacred fire burneth in every vein, wh. is hotter and steadier and stronger than ever before.
So thou seest I have now no plan for the summer (save of course to take thee away from B'k, where thou wdst. expire), until I discuss and make one, with thee.

I pray thee embrace thy father and thy brother for thy

lover.——

---

[45] Miss Jenny Busk (see Lanier's letter of Apr. 19, 1874, below). She had been soloist with the Peabody Orchestra during the present season.

To Robert S. Lanier

64 Centre St.

Bo. Mch. 21st 1874

My dear Father:

Yr. last letter mentions that you need some one in the office. I write a hasty line to say that if this shd. be so, I will be glad to know, after consultation between you and Uncle Clifford, what you can afford to pay an assistant. It might suit me, – in the execution of some plans I have – to engage with you for at least a year. I only write this to prevent you from engaging any one else, before letting me know. I shall see you in April, – with how much pleasure, only a soul capable of as much lonesomeness as mine is, can tell!

Am greatly pushed for time.

Kiss Mama for me, and give Pringle a quinine pill with my compliments. Love to Uncle C.   from

Your Son

S. L.

To Mary Day Lanier

Bo. Mch. 25th 1874

I know not exactly why, – but somehow I can scarce bring myself, now, to put pen to paper in thy behalf. Perhaps the ecstasy of the Hope of seeing thee ere long rendereth the mere delight of writing thee a positive pain, by contrast. Why is it? —— Last night I was at a *musicale* at the Jenkins', and had a gorgeous evening. They are the people of whom I wrote thee some time ago, as having a magnificent collection of paintings. 'Twas there I saw the " Miranda." Col. Jenkins found my little poem in the Evening Post, and gave me a lovely photograph of the picture, wh. I shall delight to hear thee rave over, when I show it thee. – I played but one piece, – a duo with Wysham, – and refused to play a solo: not liking to put out my fancies in such a crowd. Thy lover hath had so many triumphs, dear Love, in all save business! He cd. never tell

thee the good things wh. have been done and said anent him. –
Why is it, then, that God bringeth all my business purposes to
such naught?

——   I am to leave B⁰ on the 14ᵗʰ April next; on a concert
tour, with Miss Busk, and others. We go to Columbus, Ohio,
taking some half dozen places *en route.* They are to pay all
my expenses and give me twenty per cent of the net profits.
From Columbus I shall proceed directly onward to thee, and
shd. reach thee, I fancy, in about a couple of days: wh. wd.
bring me into the fair vision of thine eyes about the 25ᵗʰ April.
——   I am eager to know that thou likest my poem anent
thine eyes.
——   Thou art so dear, Little Maydie, to thy

lover!

To Mary Day Lanier

[Baltimore, Mar. 31, 1874?] [46]

Dear Eloise, thine Abelard crieth, My God, My God, of what
avail in the world is a man so utterly half and incomplete, as
am I without daily sight and hearing of My Love ?
——   In truth there is nothing in my heart but thee. Whatever of the beautiful shall arise out of my soul, – is but a rose-
breath whereof thou art the breathing Rose.   Stand, all ye
rose-tenders of Heaven, in wingéd circle about my Rose, and
wave off the winter forever !

″
————————
″

———— I have been again to Mr. Winans, spent a pleasant
evening, played for him, captured him, and have cordial invitations to return. ——″—— T'other night I met Miss Estelle
Nathan, – daughter of the Nathan Murder, thou rememberest ?
— and finding her a rare piquant soul, made essay at the same;
whereupon a charming little flirtation; continued on Sunday
night, when I called (at her invitation) at the Cohens', her
cousins, where she hath been sojourning: the whole ending in

---

[46] Conjectural dating from pencil memorandum by Mary Day Lanier at top of
first page.

a very pleasant friendship and warm invitations to her home
in New York whither she returned yesterday . ——″—— Met a
Miss Holt, sister of Holt & Williams, Publishers: a charming
person, full of life, talk and art, much travelled, tall as a pine-
tree, dressed in startling adornments, good and sweet, – who
finally talked to me of Miss Haynes, her friend, and thus made
me love her, because *thou* also knewest Miss Haynes, n'est ce
pas, have I not heard thee discourse of Miss Haynes ? 'Twas
apropos of Nillson: Miss H. was laughing at the Nillson worship, and instanced pious Miss Haynes, rigid Miss Haynes, who
is actually a devotee of Nilsson, bringeth her to house among
the tender young shootlet-girls, and giveth operatic parties in
her behalf. ——″————

These being my last weeks in town, and wishing to prepare the
way to have many pleasant callers upon thee when we shall
come here to live (as we will, some day) I have accepted many
invitations, and usually have engagements from two deep to
four deep every evening.   I am always in such a passion of
longing for thee, at these places, that I can scarcely enjoy
aught: yet to stay in my room wd. not help aught.
——″—— Thou art so patient. – It was cutting, after thy gracious
letter when thou declaredst thyself happy in thinking of seeing
me on the 4th April, – to write thee that it wd. be the 24th
instead.   Twenty extra days from thee : – naught less strong
than love-of-thee cd. give me power to compass such an
extension of absence.
——″—— Thou askest me of Wysham.   We are on fair terms,
he cometh to my room every afternoon and we have duos, or
trios when Dr. Cockey droppeth in.   But, My Child, 'tis the
smallest, wee-wee-est tiny soul! 'Tis a mouse that by pure
imitation, and by a certain cunning wh. inhereth in the rodent
species, hath learned to squeak at least in the rhythm of a lion's
roar: but squeak he never so bravely, a mouse it is, and a
mouse shall remain.   This discovery gave me much pain, at
first: and to speak of it now, is not without a certain twinge :
but life is too short, and sorrow too plentiful to indulge such a
sentiment.   Not that the little man hath not some good qualities: but alas, the fly in the ointment-pot. —— Doth this
sound cool, and hard and relentless, – for *me*?   It *is* not so, –

even if it sound so, – Dear Wife: my heart groweth tenderer
every day, indeed, since I have *thee* so firmly and fairly in my
heart, I begin to have faith in it as it were a woman's heart,
I am not afraid of its judgments, it seizeth the right by
womanly instinct, and it is as pity-full as The Nonne's Herte: –
thy work, all.

I have a pleasant letter from Mrs. Boykin [47] in response to
some programmes I sent her. Will not thou and I, in May,
draw her heart out of her, with Silvertongue, and the piano,
what time we breathe Schubert's Songs forth upon the sweet
air of that dear old hill?

———————— Thus have I gabbled to thee all the gossip
and scandal and love I now have in store; Go to, I love thee
divinely, thou art a rose done in sweet flesh, and in the spring
God will set kneeling by thee a

lover.

To Mary Day Lanier [48]

[Baltimore,] April 3rd 1874.

I am just come from Venice, My Child: and have strolled
home through the moonlight, singing serenades to thee, – to
thee, Excellent and Heavenly Spirit, floating high before me.

—— In plain terms, – Sweet Heaven, how I do abhor these
same plain terms — I have been playing (in the Orchestra at
the Concordia Theatre,) Stradella, and I am full of gondel-
lieds, of serenades, of balconies with white arms leaning over
the balustrades thereof, of gleaming waters, of lithe figures
in black velvet, of stinging-sweet coquetries, of diamonds,
daggers, and desperadoes –

Truth to say, the performance was but indifferent good,
saving a lovely tenor :– but I had never heard the Opera before,
and I can not tell thee the intense delight which these lovely
conceptions of Flotow gave me. The man has put Venice,

[47] Laura Nisbet Boykin was a Macon friend who played the piano. With her,
and Professor Vincent Czurda of Wesleyan playing the violin, Lanier had spent
many musical evenings during the years of his law practice (see Starke, p. 137).

[48] Excerpt previously published, *Scribner's*, XXV, 746 (June, 1899); reprinted, *Letters* (New York, 1899), pp. 98-99.

lovely, romantic, wicked-sweet Venice, into music, and the melodies breathe out an eloquence that is at once honied and spicy, at once sentimental and powerful, at once languid and thrilling.

—— But ah me, ah me, thou, thou, – when will thou and I know, together, the exquisite fascination of these things ?

———— Uncle Clifford has written me a wondrous loving letter, saying that Judge Cole's place in the Law Faculty of Mercer University will soon be vacant and that I can have it, if I want it.[49] Now, the present aim of my heart is to get the Chair of Metaphysics in the great Johns Hopkins University, wh. is soon to be built in Baltimore with an endowment of two million dollars left for that purpose by Johns Hopkins, recently deceased.   It will likely be a year, ere the appointment is made, to this chair: and if meantime I cd. have some *prestige* from delivering good lectures to the law students of Mercer, and cd. put forth my Jacquerie, and a book on Metaphysics wh. now giveth me the headache until it be *out*, – I think I cd. altogether compass it.   Heavens, what a life thou and I wd. have of it, My child, betwixt the music and the poetry, – if I cd. manage this matter !   To conciliate and concentrate influences towards this end, – hath been my aim for a couple of months past. Canst thou give me yet a year, – to bring thee to Baltimore ?   I might have brought thee, dear Wife, ere now : – but sometimes I wd. walk, in the quarters where live the respectable poor, —— and wd. see some poor lady, with thin arms and a careful pinched face, on a door-step, watching Johnny playing down the street, and wondering how she wd. ever get the house swept, with no nurse to mind that youth : —— and a thousand other sights, of infinitely-sorrowful sort : —— and I vowed, finally, by all the prudent loves of time, that I

[49] C. B. Cole was judge of the Superior Court, Bibb Co., Ga., at the time of Lanier's admission to the bar in 1870. Mercer University, to whose law faculty his Uncle Clifford Anderson suggested his appointment, was a Baptist college in Macon.

In the following sentence occurs the first of many references in Lanier's letters to his desire to become affiliated with the Johns Hopkins University. It was five years before this hope materialized with his appointment as lecturer in English Literature.

The "book on Metaphysics," never published, was probably a revived interest in the volume of essays he had been working on since 1868 (see V, xlix, note).

wd. not have thee here, and go " picking up a living " for thee. Painful as it is to me, to bide my time, – dost thou know how poor a soul mine is to *wait* ? – yet every consideration of tenderness to thee and of worldly prudence as well, urgeth me to have a certainty, – and a dignified certainty — upon which to rest thy comfort when I bring thee here.

—— I do not mean to say that I am determined to spend a year in Macon. I am not determined upon anything : I still hope I may find, in the next two weeks, some speedier method of harmonizing all the delicate and complex requirements of my " situation ": and write thee of these matters simply because I think thou hast been an Angel of Patience hereanent, and doubt if I shd. make such strains upon thy stock of that virtue.

—— Well hereupon thou mayst think. Thou and I will shortly, if God be willing, talk these matters over.

O God, — My Heart, it is incredible that time hath been when I have actually talked with thee, looking into thy corporeal eyes, and hearing thy veritable sweet tongue doing its eloquent office.

—— Bring back this time, O Master-of-Life, – crieth a

lover.——

To Mary Day Lanier [50]

Bo.   April 9th 1874

Thou art my Soul's heart, — and yet it is I know not how many days since I have written thee. 'Tis the same number of days since I have prayed, or worshipped.

—— In these last days of my stay here, come invitations and engagements of all sorts, and no minute of the day is mine, nor of the night.

[50] Previously published, *Scribner's*, XXV, 746 (June, 1899) ; reprinted, *Letters* (New York, 1899), p. 99.

A surviving program of the Liederkranz Concert, Apr. 9, 1874, mentioned at the end of this letter, lists Lanier and a Mr. Green for Titl's *Serenade*, for flute and violoncello. Another indicates that Lanier had also played " Blackbirds " at a Concert of the Brotherhood of the Church of the Ascension on Apr. 7, 1874. (Both programs are in the Charles D. Lanier Collection, Johns Hopkins University.)

Last night I won thee much glory, playing thy Sonata of Kuhlau (which thou broughtest me from Savannah) to the most critical audience in town, viz. at a private Concert of the Germania Club.

I have now to rush down to the Concordia [Theatre], to rehearse with an Orchestra there. Tonight I am going to play that lovely serenade (dost thou not remember ?) which thou and I heard at Theo. Thomas' Concert in Macon, for flute and French horn. I play it with a noble 'Cellist, the horn-part having been arranged for violoncello. I also play first flute tonight in the Orchestra which is to accompany the Liederkranz in bringing out Mendellsohn's " 42 nd Psalm." I dare not say how I long for thee. If I *cd*. say it, my heart would break in the act.

— Now God keep from thee all things, rougher than the tender longings and worshipful aspirations of thy

lover.

To Mary Day Lanier

B^o April 11th 1874.

'Tis a fair-looking boy, and a rare comical, – with his mouth open and awry. What a big broad forehead the fellow hath; and what a general magnanimus nobleness and simple grandeur showeth through his baby's-face! [51]

Du Mutterchen, I thank thee for this man, his face is great and tender like thine. I have ordered thy shoes: and thine other commissions will be fulfilled.

— I should be glad to play for Mr. Habersham *now*, – to redeem the wretched showing I made there, on our last visit. I must tell thee something wh. made me laugh. Some time ago, Wysham rec^d a letter from Mr. Habersham, in wh. allusion was made to me. " Lanier " (quoth'a) is a good player: – BUT (!) he is a wild colt, and needs some one to regulate him." This *but* was in reference *not* to my playing, but to my general behavior in life, – as was evidenced by the context of Mr.

---

[51] The reference is to a photograph of Lanier's third son, Henry Wysham Lanier; it was apparently sent to him by his wife, but none of her letters between Apr. 1 and 29 have survived.

Habersham's letter. – What *cd.* have given the good gentleman such an idea of me? Can it be possible that any human being cd. be less *coltish* than thy (now fearsomely hurried)

lover?

To Mary Day Lanier

[Baltimore, Apr. 14, 1874 ?] [52]

Is it that thou dost really and truly desire to see me, thou, My Queen, thou My One Sweet ?

— See me then ! o' both sides, frontwise and laterally: and if thou canst pierce through the mere flesh, thou wilt see in these two *eidola*, that I am simply and humbly thy lover. My God, how I long to gaze into thine eyes, – into thy *very* eyes, — as I *tried* to gaze into thine *imagined* eyes while these pictures were being wrought.

— Well, in a few minutes, I start a-tootle-too-ing to the West: and then I haste to thee. Write me here as usual, meantime: for I find I must come back through Baltimore, – and have asked them to keep my letters for me.

— This profile picture pleaseth me (–it was the photographer's idea) particularly, because it beareth some faint resemblance to my master and dear reverend poet, Robert Browning.

God hold thy heart in heavenly rest, dear Lady.

S. L.

To Mary Day Lanier [53]

Wheeling, W. Va, April 16th 1874

Wdst. thou see Mammon, dear Soul, thou wert needs be in this place. By Heaven, he *is* as black as he is painted : there be no earthly pigments so inky as this veritable face of Trade

[52] Conjectural dating from the evidence of Lanier's letter of Mar. 25, 1874 (above), where he said that he was to start on a concert tour to the Middle West on Apr. 14.

With the present letter Lanier sent copies of the Cummins cabinet photographs of himself (the profile one is reproduced in the present volume, frontispiece).

[53] This letter is mentioned by Mims, p. 160, as the origin of Lanier's poem, " The Symphony " (I, 46).

that grinneth out from these blaring furnaces and flaming chim-
neys and pitchy smoke-clouds. Not a wall in the town but is
like a chimney-back: a sickish odor of kerosene pervadeth the
whole atmosphere: and an eternal shower of soot drizzles
downward a dismal disgust (wh. alliteration well-nigh temp-
teth the writer thereof to supplement the same with two more
d's connected by a dash).   Add to this a bleak range of
bare and wondrous scraggy mountains which completely doth
wall in this dirty spot: intersect the same with the vile red-
muddy stream of the Ohio river: and cover the whole with a
mean soiled-looking pall of smoke wh. overhangeth all things,
– a pall not even large enough to be sublime! — and thou hast
Wheeling.   O how I do abhor these trade-matters, as they
are carried on here.   God, to see the great stalwart men, in
these acres of rolling-mills, sweating, burning, laboring, with
only enough time betwixt tasks to eat in and sleep in, – far too
little time to wash in !   Why should this be so ?   The men
who own these mills do not so: they have plenty.   It is not
well, it cannot be well, that a hundred men should die in soul
and body, in order that one man should live merely in body.
If I lived among these people, – but I cannot contemplate such
a thing, so why say further.

——   Our first concert was given last night.   It went off
beautifully: and the audience, though quite small, was very
enthusiastic.   My solo was heartily encored, and I responded
with good effect.   I send thee two programmes, the second
of which we play tonight.   Notice the Rubinstein trio for flute,
'Cello, and Piano, on tonight's programme.   It was written
for Violin, 'Cello and Piano: but I have arranged the violin
part for flute, and it is thus finer than the original, the different quality of the instruments producing a lovely effect.   O,
to play this for, and with thee !   The piano part is of course
difficult: but thou wdst. render it grandly.   God hasten this
time.

——   I do not think I am going to make any money on the
trip.   Our manager already proves wretchedly inefficient: and
is far too full of whiskey.   He has done nothing rightly, nor
well.   If I had the strength I would take his part and my own
too: but am afraid of breaking down.

— So, now, thou Compound Sweet, thou Result and Last

Success of God's experiments in fair women, pass thou through
this night as a star through heaven, looking down upon clouds
and seas, – and looking down also upon thy steadfast upgazing
true

lover.

To Mary Day Lanier

Zanesville, Ohio,
April 19th 1874

My Heart of my heart, I have been talking about thee to Miss
Jenny Busk, (our Prima Donna), all the morning, and, dilating
with my rhapsodies, meseemeth that my soul is as large as all
life and all time, and that thou fillest it with a rosy atmosphere
in which sail as sunlit clouds all the cares of existence.
How dear thou art, Large eyes! How dear thou art, Broad-
brows! How dear thou art, How dear thou art, thou Ovalface,
thou Soul-in-lips, thou Fineheart! How loyally, how joyfully
even in absence, how faithfully amid all turmoils, how peacefully amid all disappointments and resultless labors, kneeleth
my soul before thy loveliness, and draweth strength and rest
and hope and glory out of the kind glances which I dream
from thine imagined eyes !
Gentle and spiritual and bright and earnest and tender and
faithful and generous and patient and magnanimous and trustful and loving and passionate and warm and sweet and true-
womanly, – so thou art! – being so, thou art my Heaven-before-
death, and I pray God thou mayst be my Heaven-after-death.

I will not make a cent on my trip. Our agent, as I intimated to
thee, has developed into a perfect marvel and world's-wonder
of stupidity: to which he addeth the wretched climacteric of
drunkenness, having been in a beastly state of semi-intoxica-
tion ever since we started. I find that everything, in these
matters, dependeth on the acts and doings of the Agent: – and
consequently we have played to poor houses. My playing is
always well-received: but, *du Himmel*, what sort of music do I
find myself obliged to play, in order to tickle the ears of
the groundlings!

The " Favorite de Vienne," is my *pièce de resistance* : I
have cut it up, and interpolated a strain from my Swamp Robin,
as also a movement, from a lovely *Concertino* of Briccialdi.
Thus doctored, it seemeth a good prescription, and " taketh."
I also come in in the " Echo Songs " thou seest on the programmes I sent thee :   Miss Busk calleth therein most lustily
for " Sweet Echo ", (with much dwelling upon the "-o") and
I, from far behind the scenes (sometimes from under the
stage) reply in dulcet strains, wh. always bring down the house.
O, how thou wdst. at once laugh and weep, sawest thou mine
agony at this clap-trap. *Basta* ! I compensate myself for it
by inflicting on the groundlings that lovely " Serenade " for
flute, 'cello and piano, and the Rubinstein trio.[54]
    Altogether 'tis a gay experience.   The rain poureth wearily
tonight, and there is prospect of a dismal house tomorrow:–
but I am the Mark Tapley of the Troupe; – or, indeed I
should say, *thou* art the Mark Tapley of the Troupe: for I
think of thee, – – – and then straightway I go and make the
Prima Donna laugh, and stir up the 'cello man, and poke the
baritone in the ribs : – and so thou carriest us through.
—   God in Heaven, – how I love thee, dear Heart !   I cannot become otherwise than good and strong, – it is no credit
to me to be so – because I am thy
                                                            lover.

To Mary Day Lanier [55]

[Baltimore,] April 26th 1874

Soul, Soul, on Tuesday I start toward the holy land, the sweet
land, where thou dwellest.   My head and my heart are main
tired, I wd. fain have some rest, open the great gates of the

[54] Surviving programs for the two concerts in Zanesville, Ohio, Apr. 19 and 20,
1874, list Lanier for the following pieces: *Andante and Allegro, Opus 15,*
Rubinstein; *Fantasie on Gute Nacht,* Popp; *Fantasie on Themes from Lucia,*
Liede; *Allegro from Etoile du Nord*; *Serenade,* Titl; *Allegro from Fille du
Regiment,* Donizetti; *Andante from Opus 104,* Briccialdi; and *Finale from La
Favorite de Vienne,* Terschak (Charles D. Lanier Collection, Johns Hopkins
University).   See Lanier's poem on Miss Busk and this concert tour (I, 199).
    " Mark Tapley," alluded to in the following paragraph, was a character in
Dicken's *Martin Chuzzlewit.*
[55] Lanier had returned to Baltimore two days before.   In his letter of Apr. 24,

Monastery of thy love and pity, my spirit cometh in the winter rain, soaked and cold and hungry, craving the cheerful fire that burneth in thine eyes and the vital food that thy very presence spreadeth before me.

I love thee far more than I did an hour ago, and yet far less than I shall an hour hence. If I live long, with love growing thus by the hour, what shift will I make for words to tell thee about it ? I already foresee the time when I shall be able to speak to thee of my love in music: . . . . when I have run through that, I pray thee die with me, into some Heaven whose strong sweet language may save me from being merely thy love-dumb

lover.———

To Clifford A. Lanier [56]

Brunswick, Ga, May 11th 1874.

My dear Clifford:

I've been trying to write you every day since I arrived here; but the intrinsic *dolce far niente* of the place, a thousand times intensified by my sudden plunge out of the depth of winter into this enervating climate, and aided and abetted by those agreeable distractions of wife and children which a seven months' absence has rendered at once novel and ravishing, – has proven too much for me, and it is only after a sharp struggle with my wife, – in the course of which that admirable lady has set before me considerations of the gravest moral character why I *should* write you, if no one else– that I

1874 (here omitted), he had written: " I can not now tell thee of my adventures, on the musical trip. Suffice it; I made no money, the agent was a drunken ass. . . . Miss Busk is greatly enamored of my playing. She wisheth to take a short trip into Pennsylvania, (to give five concerts) and, with a change of agents, she hath good chance to make some money. I am now going there, to hear what she hath finally determined to do: it may hap that I will go, and so be five days longer from thee. How cooly I say this, with my heart afire." This second concert tour did not materialize, and Lanier left Baltimore for Georgia on Apr. 28.

[56] Lanier had arrived in Macon Friday morning, May 1, and left the next morning for Brunswick. R. S. Lanier wrote to his son Clifford, May 5, 1874: " Sidney . . . is stouter (weighing 145 lbs) than I ever saw him. But he is not strong– can't walk as he used to– had a cold from travelling. . . . Sid has improved in music greatly & is magnificent on his silver flute."

have been able to seat myself at the pen-ink-and-paper, fairly forced into this laborious attitude by circumstances beyond my control.

— The main one of these circumstances beyond my control, —beyond control indeed even of adverse Fate, it would seem! — is your own sweetness, my dear Galahad, which, efflorescing into poems and speeches and deft acts of knightly devotion to the brave dead, has filled my heart with a thousand fair messages to you, — messages of the sort which prefers to sing itself in poetry or play itself in music, but which, denied these methods, finally demands with irresistible imperiousness that utterance, of whatever nature, shall be accorded it.

How beautiful your speech [57] is; how large and graceful and strong the sentiments which compose it; how glowing its knightly fervor, how true and simple and majestic its knightly faith, — how gracious its knightly forgiveness; how solemn its memories, how valiant its tenacious hopes; in fine, how lit the whole piece with a certain serene glory which unites all the brilliance of the light of youth with all the calmness of the glow of manhood, — all this I can not dilate upon, — without writing another speech thereupon as fine as yours! That it should be the speech of a gentleman is, in these days when the world is given over to stealing, glory enough; and that it should be also the speech of a knight, is, in these days when the world is given over to trade, more than glory.

— Thou, my poor Galahad, that art also an inn-keeper, thou that keepest " books " and knighthood along together, — how shalt thou know the tears that have rained in certain long and lonesome nights in thy behalf, — tears not dried save by one thought, — that God is fond of His diamonds, and if He choose to set them in jet, to show off the lustre and sweet coruscations thereof, who shall say Him nay?

— I wd. be glad to send yr. speech to some Baltimore friends, and to that end ask that you will forwd. me two or three copies, if you have them to spare.

— The poem [58] is charming, and full of a genuine realism which will be very taking, in print. It needs a little remodel-

---

[57] Clifford Lanier had delivered the Confederate Memorial Day Address at Montgomery, Apr. 26(?), 1874.

[58] See note 61, below.

ling, and some lopping-off of verses which hinder the dramatic effect. The metre, too, is faulty, but can be easily made perfect. May I turn it over, and re-shape it, in these particulars? The idea is one of rare pathos and exquisite humor combined. With a little practice, and a little study of the pure *machinery* of poetry, such as would conjoin the craftsman's hand to your artistic soul, – I think you would cut a figure among the poets, my dear.

Mary and I start to Macon tonight, on a week's visit. I do not know what my plans are for the summer, yet. I have a partial engagement to go on a concert-tour with Miss Busk, in June. If I cd. only have one free year, unhampered by the necessities which now take all my time! – But these matters are managed Elsewhere.

Where is Aunt Jane? Tell her I long to embrace her, if she is with you. I send a multitude of kisses and greetings to Wilsie, and Grandmother, and Aunt Lucy, and Sissa and all. Hold me in remembrance, as always

Yr. faithful

Sidney

To Paul H. Hayne [59]

Macon, Ga.   May 23rd 1874.

My dear Mr. Hayne:

Your letter gave me sincere pleasure; and I would have sent you some expression of my gratification at hearing from you by a much earlier mail than this, had it not been for my Arabian eccentricities and unreliablenesses of movement, which have kept me on the wing for a month past. I am now in Macon, and shall remain here for three or four weeks, – then Northward again. I am truly rejoiced to see, by occasional evidences in the Magazines, that you are again active in that delicious business of Creation.

My brother has just sent me your " Cloud-Star " which he

---

[59] Previously published, *Critic*, VIII [o. s], 89 (Feb. 20, 1886); reprinted, *Letters* (New York, 1899), pp. 238-240. It was a reply to Hayne's letter of Mar. 21, 1874, and was in turn answered by Hayne on June 1.

has clipped from some paper. I am charmed with it, and am not sure but I shall come presently to think it the strongest thing you have done. To die, consumed by these heavenly fires: – that is infinitely better than to live the tepid lives and love the tepid loves that belong to the lower planes of activity: and I would rather fail at some things I wot of, than succeed at some others. Is not that the secret that lies hid in the bosom of this rose of a poem?

Pray send me immediately the long poem you speak of. I shall take the greatest pleasure in looking it over, and if I find anything in the way of flaws will yell it out to you. Nothing in the world like little niggers and idiots, for finding things, don't you know? Send the poem to me at Macon.

The Review of your " Legends & Lyrics " was sent to Lippincotts', and declined. I afterwards mentioned to Browne that I had written it (tho' I did not offer it to him in terms): who told me that a review of the book had already appeared in the Southern Mag. So my piece lies bleeding, and I don't know what to do with it.

Tell me what you are doing.

In answer to your kind enquiries as to myself: I spent my winter in Baltimore, pursuing Music and meditating my " Jacquerie." I was *Flauto Primo* of the Peabody Symphony Orchestra, and God only could express the delight and exultation with which I helped to perform the great works brought out by that organization during the winter. Of course this was a queer place for me: aside from the complete *bouleversement* of going from the Court-house to the footlights, I was a raw player and a provincial withal, without practice, and guiltless of instruction – for I never had a teacher. To go, under these circumstances, among old professional musicians, and assume a leading part, in a large Orchestra which was organized expressly to play the most difficult works of the great masters, – was, (now that it's all over) a piece of temerity that I do not remember ever to have equalled before. But I trusted in Love, pure and simple: and was not disappointed, for, as if by miracle, difficulties and discouragements melted away before the fire of a passion for music which grows ever stronger within my heart, – and I came out with results more gratifying than it is becoming in me to specify. 'Tis quite

settled that I cannot practice law: either writing or speaking
appears to produce small hæmorrhages which completely sap
my strength: and I am going in a few weeks to New York, –
without knowing what on earth I am to do there – armed only
with a Silver Bœhm flute, and some dozen of steel pens.

Happy man, – you who have your cabin in among the hills
and trees. You who can sit still and work at Home, – pray a
short prayer once in a while for one as homeless as the ghost of
Judas Iscariot.

Write me straightway: and write, as to one who is always

Your faithful friend

Sidney Lanier

To Virginia Hankins

Macon, Ga, May 26th 1874

No, dear Ginna, it will never be, that, – in your own beautiful words – poetry and you will cease to walk hand in hand.
On the contrary, a thousand necessities, – necessities born of a
beautiful soul, of a beautiful person, of a beautiful life full of
beautiful loves – constrain the hand-clasping of you and the
Divine Maid and your two palms will never be unloosed.

—— Verily, morever, it was *too* queer, – to begin your
letter with the declaration that you and Poetry had parted
company, – and end it with a poem which offered confirmation
strong as Holy Writ of the very sweetest intimacy betwixt
you! [60]

Or do you, My dear Child, write poetry without the help of
the Muse, – being yourself at once Inspirer and Inspired?

Whoever was its inspiration, I care not, the poem was simply
lovely, and I would to heaven you would write me some more
of them. Will you not?

I picture to myself each day how ravishingly beautiful are
your trees and flowers, there, in this spring, and how my heart
would ascend into a pure heavenly withdrawal from this earth,

---

[60] Virginia Hankins's letter of Dec. 31, 1873, to which this is an answer,
concluded with a sonnet entitled "Madonna Mia," probably of her own
composition.

if I could but pace down the green woods with you to the church, and hear the stream sing away the afternoon as if a day were simply a tune to be hummed. Friend, Friend, you, leaping the fence, while the fair leaves were waving, the sun shining, the world dreaming; – that is a picture which my heart keeps always alive and breathing, and for which I thank you and God unspeakably.

——   I came here from Baltimore about three weeks ago. The northern winter had so far restored my health that I thought myself able to come back and resume my profession; and I took my old place in the firm immediately on arrival here – But the terribly warm weather has completely wilted me, already: and it is now definitely and irrevocably decided that I am to quit the law.

Behold then, dear Friend, (I know not what caprice it is that makes me tell you this, but somehow I desire to do so; you are so fair and noble and large that sympathy – which I despise, from the balance of the world – from *you*, I think would be sweet, I have no recollection of ever inviting it from any other person in my life) a man, thirty two years of age, so crippled in his right lung that he can neither write nor speak without wretched and dangerous consequences, broken in health and fortune, compelled to abandon the only business he knows, obliged to gather up some three thousand dollars a year, gifted with no resources therefor save a pen which he has to use (thanks to Monsieur Lung) fifteen minutes at a time only, and which, when so used, produces poetry that is mostly unsaleable being too strong for the milk-drinking babes that feed on (and pay for) the Magazines, – and a flute (resource no 2!) which he must agonize his soul by playing to publics who would rather be startled by the high D on it than thrill to his most beautiful compositions!

So! This being my first bid for sympathy in my whole life, – I already realize some benefit, even before you have heard my tale of woe; for now that I have for the first time put the situation on paper, 'tis so desperate as to be unspeakably ludicrous, – far *too* ludicrous to weep over, and not too much so to laugh at.

Don't imagine for a moment that I'm sad or dispirited about it: I hope to have my Jacquerie ready in a couple of months, and to go to New York within that time (possibly in a few

weeks) to seek some musical engagement. You will be glad
to know that I won many signal triumphs during the season in
Baltimore, against such odds as would make you smile were I
to recount them to you, – as I will some day.

— Let me know, by letter addressed here, what are your
movements, and everything you're willing to tell me about
yourself. Convey my warm remembrance to your friends.

Ah, if there were any way for me to tell you how utterly I am

Yr. friend

S. L.

To Clifford A. Lanier

Macon, Ga, May 28th 1874

My dear Clifford:
    I send you and Willie my most loving con-
gratulations upon the recovery of the splendid little boy. I
would give half a nights receipts to toss the fellow up and
have a bout with him on all fours.

I came back here from Baltimore, at the close of the musical
season, with the idea that my health was sufficiently restored
to permit my resumption of my old place in the firm, which
had been kept open for me. A few days of law-work and of
this dreadful climate have demonstrated the absolute impossibility of my being a lawyer, with the most mournful decisive-
ness. The strength I had built up by a year of laborious and
careful and expensive nursing and travelling, has been swept
away in a few days by this overpowering and (to *me*) poison-
ous atmosphere.

In short, I am again all afloat, and must mature some plan by
which to get back to the Northern air, which seems the only
one where life is possible.

— I've shed all the tears about it that I'm going to;– and am
now vigorously engaged in pumping myself full of music and
poetry, with which I propose to water the dry world. I suppose it may now be finally said, that God has cut me off inexor-
ably from any other life than this. So, St. Cecilia to the
rescue ! – and I hope God will like my music.

— I think, now, to carry my wife and chicks to a certain

farm-house about ten miles from Griffin, where board is cheap, and where there is great store of eggs, chickens and milk, – there to finish my Jacquerie and a lot of music wh. I have nearly ready for the press: then to New York – in a couple of months from now – to seek flute-engagements for the winter.

Mary has been here with me until yesterday, when she returned to Brunswick. Your invitation to visit you – – – simply gave us a beautiful dream. I should rarely like to sit with you under a tree, somewhere, in this bountiful spring-glory, and get a good eye-full of you. But alas, – 'tis two hundred miles, and five cents a mile for grown persons and children above three years of age: – that is to say, 'tis impossible.

Tell Aunt Jane I have a photograph of myself which I propose to send her. It is said to be very fine – though much better-looking than I am.

I have heard many commendations of yr. speech, and kind inquiries about you. Received the copies you sent: and forwarded one to J. F. D. Lanier, of New York.

Will you leave Montgomery during the summer ? If so, when, and to what place?

I send an assortment of kisses and squeezes which I beg you to distribute, placing them " where they will do most good."

I hope soon to polish up de ole blind darkey.[61]
Write me.

Yr. Bro.

S. L.

[61] This reference makes it clear that Clifford Lanier's poem mentioned in Sidney's letter of May 11 as needing revision was " The Power of Prayer" (I, 215). Though conceived and first drafted by Clifford, it was so completely revised by Sidney (see his letter of Aug. 7, below) that it came to be considered their joint composition and was later published as such in *Scribner's*, May, 1875.

Strangely enough, Lanier makes no mention in this letter of the fact that he was appearing on the same night (May 28) in the concert of the Harmonic Society, a program of which survives (Charles D. Lanier Collection, Johns Hopkins University). According to a notice in the local paper: " Mr. Sidney Lanier's solo was the most exquisite music it has ever been our good fortune to hear on the flute. Under his graceful and artistic management his instrument becomes a human voice, most beautifully modulated, with a tone and power such as we deemed impossible. An artist in every sense of the word, Mr. Lanier held his audience in rapt attention, and a persistent encore was the only means of relieving everybody." (See the Macon *Telegraph and Messenger*, May 31, 1874.)

Lanier apparently joined his wife in Brunswick a few days later (see his letter to her of May 28, here omitted).

To Robert S. Lanier

Brunswick. June 9th 1874

My dear Father:

Yours of 7th is here, and I write a line by re-turn-mail, to say that I will be very glad to be of service, and will start up tomorrow night, arriving in Macon Thursday afternoon at five o'clock.

For various reasons I have persuaded Mary to let me bring Charley and Sidney with me: so tell Eddy to put himself in training for a wrestler.

We are all in tolerable condition, barring the awfully hot weather.

Love to all.

Yr. Son

S. L.

To Mary Day Lanier

Macon, June 12 th 1874.

So: again is thy face torn out of my daily life: – making the same as it were a flower from which the petals and whole coronal of beauty have been plucked away.

———— We arrived, – as I today telegraphed thee. The boys were dreadfully tired from the long journey: as well they might be, Mrs. Fitzgerald and I being completely worn out. The poor little men were silent and open-mouthed, and had naught to say, until night came on, when they thawed, and ere long were in a prodigious frolic with Eddie and Pringle. This morning they are all merry as larks. Both the rascals slept in my bed. I had arranged to take Charley with me, (on account of his condition) and to let Sidney sleep with Pringle. But on attempting to carry out this last arrangement, the little Soul howled so dismally and long that I finally bore him upstairs and chucked him crosswise at Charley's feet; – where he slept like a log all night. I was up with Charley once dur-ing the night: and once before breakfast: which, with two performances yesterday afternoon (*none* on the cars), consti-

tutes his *diary* up to this present writing. Uncle C's. foot is
much better, and he is to be out by Monday. I am to go there
in a few moments, to talk of some law papers. Sissa has taken
hold of the boys, and will not hear of my getting any one
else ;– wh., indeed, I wd. find it difficult to do. I washed and
dressed Charley this morning, in a manner wh. I fancy wd.
have done credit to Mammy in her most unrheumatic days: –
tho ' , privately, betwixt me and thee, what with his head, his
ears, his hands and between his toes, I thought I would never
get through, and I have all day been moving about in a maze
of marvelling admiration of thee, in that thou has had four of
these beings, and hast not ere now died of the mere multi-
plicity of things-to-be-thought-of.

That thou *has not*, God be praised: – thou art far too sweet
to exhale thus. –   Here is a letter wh. I opened thinking it
was anent board: receive my humble apologies.

Be thou as happy as thou art beloved, prayeth thy

lover.

To Mary Day Lanier

Macon, Ga, June 15th 1874.

All day long hath thy lover been diligently digging pits, under
the guidance, and instigation of Messrs. Lanier & Anderson
those cunning men, piously and prayerfully hoping that certain legal brethren will fall therein, so that we may capture
them in behalf of our clients.

O that this good right arm, which might otherwise have been
employed this day in tenderly sustaining thee, or a flute, or
beautiful-hearted young Hal, – might be weary at some better
work than the work of this same law.

For by The Law is Sin, and by Sin is Death.

I am main tired, having scratched unnumbered words with
the pen in the last few hours.   I have not yet had time to say
anything to either of the firm anent my project for staying with
them a little while: and will not yet commit myself thereto,
feeling great repugnance against the same.

I do well in health, and thy young men are much improved.
I think thy Charles will be much civilized by contact with

Edward & Pringle. He can throw Edward, after the fashion of wrestlers : tho' Edward is his better in climbing and running, being a rare monkey withal.

Sissa will stay to see thee, leaving on the train which departeth at seven O'clock, two hours after thine arriveth. It appeareth by the Atlanta papers that thy train goeth a little later than formerly, towit: at 8.10 instead of 7.30.[62]

Hath any letter come yet from Mr. Gray? I wrote him, thou rememberest, asking if we cd. have both the large rooms. 'Tis time he were replying, so that we cd. make all final and definite arrangements.

A letter from Miss Busk saith she goeth not on her trip, the weather is too warm. I am to go to Gussie's tonight to meet Mr. Bukowitz, the new pianist, and will determine about my concert.

Tell Hal I note Gov. B's letter and his, and will write thereanent. Now may the Night clasp thee about, like the longing arm of thy

lover.

To Mary Day Lanier

Macon, June 16th 1874.

Aye, with what sighs and prayers and tears I read the " Amorum " of André Ampère [63] I cd. never tell thee. Julie must have been like thee; full of sweetness, of wit, of intelligence, of woman-wisdom, of loving-heartedness.

If only I had such prospects as Ampère, and cd. work like him!

Dear Heart, my heart is so sore, I am not well in the spirit,

---

[62] Mary Day Lanier was planning to pass through Macon on June 23 on her way to Griffin, Ga., where Lanier had engaged room and board for the summer in the home of a farmer, H. M. Gray, mentioned in the following paragraph. In her letter of June 14, 1874, Mary Day Lanier had written: " Mr. Gray writes that they cannot well let us have the other large room but his wife ' ses, tha will be no trouble abought rume, as she will make you and your familey comferttable.'— — *Litteratim*."

[63] In her letter of June 14 Mary Day Lanier had spoken of reading this in the *Eclectic Magazine*.

I need thee with great need, where be my eyes to make my
faith live again, to call back my bird to me? [64]

        "
————————
————————
      "

I wd. have telegraphed thee today, – inasmuch as thou art to
be away tomorrow and next day – that I quite agreed with thee
as to the inexpediency of stopping here: were I not sure thou
wdst. have my letter by this time, wherein I have written thee
that Sissa wd. meet thee at the depot, to go by the train which
precedeth them a few moments.

Stay, an thou like, till Tuesday: fret not thyself about a day,
but stay on till Wednesday, if it suit thy convenience. I think I
can keep Sissa over. Gussie [Lamar Ogden] will drive to the
dépôt, and bring little daughter up to see Mrs. Lamar.

I was there last night. Found Herr Bukowitz to be a tolerably good musician, but not much of a pianist. We played
several Schubert's Songs, wherein I melodiously broke my heart
for want of thee. I do not know about my concert. Gussie
will not sing at the coming concert of the Harmonics, (next
Thursday week), and as she said nothing last night when I
spoke of mine incidentally, I rather fancy she hath abandoned
that idea.

I have no business news to report to thee. Father & Uncle C.
have been head over ears in a case for a day and a half, and
will be for some time longer. Meantime I keep office.

The young men are a little husky-voiced this morning, –
Eddie more than all – from the singularly-cold weather. Charles
maketh me to pause and consider, with certain curious products
of his alimentaries o'mornings, yet he goeth upon the even

[64] This obscure reference to Lanier's depression at this time is clarified by a
passage in Mary Day Lanier's reply of June 18, 1874:

" I am all alive with thy feelings, thy thoughts– thy difficulties and barriers.
And the bird flown again? Sweet flutterer! 'tis scared by John Doe and Richard
Roe with their traps. If the bright one but realized his strength of wing, and
his power to float far out of *their* reach while still within hearing, he might
peacefully content thee. 'Tis no snake-charming– this Law-work– and the traps
can draw him with no sweet compulsions. . . .

" Whatever thou mayst choose I crave for thee, my Life, this thing: that thou
mays: choose and pursue it in peaceful persuasion that it is God's path for thee.

" Without that persuasion I could not bear to see thee in that weary tread-
mill again."

tenor of his way. I have thy blessed letter. Have seen Mrs.
[Flora] Smith and got her in proper trim.

Thou poor heart, art thou jaundiced indeed? My soul is all
quivering to minister to thee.

Thou art the one need of thy

lover.

Mrs. Seymour's piano is come.

To MARY DAY LANIER

[Macon, Ga., June 17, 1874?] [65]

I wonder, – thou poor Heart whose hungry letters revealeth to
me that thou must be ill indeed and greatly support-needing, –
that mine have not reached thee sooner. I have written
promptly, each day, I think, but one. Doubtless thou hast
them ere now. If love be a medicament for thine indisposition,
thou wilt find in them some helpful draughts. I have written
that thou must consult thine own pleasure as to the time of thy
departure. Let not any hesitation as to my necessities distress
thee: I live in thine eyes, but I wd. not see them drooping for
weariness.

The case is not yet over which hath detained the firm in the
Court-house, and I am still keeping office, – nominally – for I do
little else than dream of thee. I am going to play " Blackbirds " at the Concert of the Harmonics; and I am determined
to have thee here, if it suit thy will, that night. We can run
down and make a pleasant jaunt of it.[66]

——— I have been in the Court-room listening to the
wrangle, a little. Kind heaven, how I hate it, how the jury
smelleth of tobacco and vile humanity, how outrageously unjust is the judge, how innumerable are the small arts to make
impressions on the jurors outside of the real merits of the case,
how abominably Unchristian is the whole business ! Christian
Civilization: bah, let us play some music.

[65] Conjectural dating from the evidence of the accompanying envelope.

[66] In his previous letter (June 16, above) Lanier said that the concert would
be " next Thursday week "—i. e., June 25. By that time he planned to have
his family settled at Sunnyside, near Griffin, whence it would be only a short
run down to Macon.

The boys seem well today, and have thy messages. Distribute an extra one of thy "sugar-lumps" to thy father and Hal for thy

lover.

To Mary Day Lanier [67]

Macon, Ga.   June 25th [26th] 1874

Heart of My Soul, I have but a few moments wherein to say to thee that I am making preparations to quit this: that then will delay me until tomorrow-night, when I shall depart, hoping to kiss thee at two O'clock in the morning; and that, once with thee, I shall stay for some weeks at least.

I am so happy in this thought that I now say no more than that I am thy true knight and faithful

lover.

Yet I do now remember that I ought to tell thee that my throat is much better and that I played last night very successfully.

---

[67] The date of this letter has been corrected from the reference in the postscript to Lanier's participation in the concert of the Harmonic Society. A surviving program (Charles D. Lanier Collection, Johns Hopkins University) is dated June 25, 1874, Harmonic Hall. The Macon *Daily Telegraph and Messenger* reported, June 26, 1874: "The flute solo, ' Blackbirds,' was performed in highly artistic manner by its composer. His playing is above criticism, and words fail us when we attempt a description of the playing of this master of the flute." The Macon Harmonic Society had been organized in Jan., 1874; this was its sixth concert.

The letter itself is somewhat obscure, but it seems to reflect Lanier's final determination to sever his connections with Macon and the practice of law, including the plan he had been considering of teaching for a year at Mercer University. Another scheme which came to naught is reflected in a letter of July 8, 1874, from George Price, President of the Huntsville (Ala.) Female College, replying to Lanier's note of July 2 and a letter from Macon earlier in the summer (both lost): "The main point of your note, my dear Mr. Lanier, interests me more than I can tell you, yet I am compelled honestly to inform you at the outset that my Faculty [of Music] is filled up to overflowing. . . . Your suggestion as to combining practical teaching with a lectureship is a most happy conceit and pleases me greatly. I think you have the germ of an ideal Music-Professorship, and deeply regret that I can not 'see my way to aiding you in developing and maturing the conception."

To Clifford A. Lanier

Sunnyside, Aug. 7th 1874.

My dear Clifford:

The enclosed poem entitled " Corn " [68] (please *acknowledge* it) is the principal reason why your " Plantation Ballad " has not been returned to you ere now, revised.[69]   I hope you will like both. You will observe that I have changed the metre of yr. poem.   This was done for several reasons. In the first place, the metre in which you had cast yr. poem was in itself unsuited to the tone of the piece; being dactyllic and not at all " niggerish."

In the second place, tho' generally dactyllic, it was not consistently so, nor indeed were there many lines wh. were not faulty either in accent or in metrical numeration.   I only mention this in order to say further that you should post yr.self in this mere craftsman's department of poetry, particularly as I think an hour's instruction from some one who understands it wd. be ample for that purpose.   If I were not quite disabled by a recent return of some old troubles, (brought on by writing), and if I were not obliged to make exhausting draughts upon the capacities and endurance of the " lovely amanuensis " – (who has been betrayed into this shocking statement) – who is now writing this for me, in copying some poetry and music which I am getting ready for the press,[70] I wd. myself,

---

[68] " Corn " (I, 34), Lanier's most important poem to date, had been composed some time in July (receipt of a copy is acknowledged in Paul H. Hayne's letter of July 30, 1874). No account of its composition appears in Lanier's letters, this being the only one that has survived from his residence at Sunnyside, June 23-Aug. 19; but some of the circumstances are recounted in the reminiscences of a friend and neighbor (J. M. Kell, *Recollections of a Naval Life,* Washington, 1900, pp. 296-297).

[69] " The Power of Prayer " (see note 61, above).

[70] The MS of this letter is entirely in the handwriting of Mary Day Lanier, dictated to her because of her husband's difficulty in writing which resulted from his recent illness. In a letter of her own (begun Aug. 7, continued Aug. 12, but not finished until Sept. 15), she wrote to Clifford Lanier: " [Sidney's] trouble was a slight bleeding from the right lung: so slight as to seem unimportant, *per se,* but leaving a soreness of chest and a *thorough* prostration which would alarm me had I not before seen in his case the healing power of Time and Nature. The inaction wh. it compels is, alone, sufficiently distressing in view of the sore *need* to be at work. . . .

" Dearest, it is ludicrous to send you such a patch-work letter! Yet it is in some small sort a picture of my life– and its feelings continue true. I tried to send you a small dissertation upon English prosody wh. I think wd. enable you to pursue yr. poetic career more satisfactorily to yr.self and less invitingly to savage critics.

You will observe further that I have changed yr. poem into the purely dramatic – (from the narrative form in which it was written) although I have endeavored to make " Old Jim " express pretty nearly the same ideas which you had embodied in the narrative portion.   Where this can be properly done it is always much the most energetic form of composition: moreover, people now-a-days have somehow conceived a particular passion for this sort of thing –   I being free to confess that there are, in my judgment, some artistic objections to it as a poetic form wh. I have not time to detail in this writing.

The metre in which I have rearranged yr. poem, you will find to be absolutely faultless in every line; a perfection which I took pains to attain particularly in order that you might scan the poem and in that way possibly catch the idea of rhythm in general.

Your letter came day before yesterday.   Its enclosure must have been inspired above.   Pray don't expect me to say anything more about it.

S. L.

TO MARY DAY LANIER [71]

Wytheville, Va.
Aug. 20eme 1874

Le matin est divine.

Autour de moi les montagnes s'élèvent au ciel: ainsi, les sentiments de mon coeur s'élèvent a toi.

Ce jour-ci, ce nuit-ci, sois tu tranquille, sois tu libre, sois tu pleine du soleil et des étoiles, – toi, qui est mon ciel plus doux que l'autre!

---

write it in intervals of Sidney's music-dictation, and just as I would get down three words I was sure to hear in those dear tones, ' Well!– C an octave below', for the bass– ' and so on. Sweet work it was, you may believe– but leaving no chance for letters."

[71] This note was written on a postal card. Lanier had left Sunnyside the day before for a three months stay in New York (see Mary Day Lanier's letter to Clifford Lanier, Aug. 7-Sept. 15). One-third of the sixty-odd letters from this period have been omitted from the present edition.

To Mary Day Lanier

Bo. Aug. 22nd 1874.

I called on the Youngs last night, who received me with effusion, and showed themselves the same good and christian folk : – also on the Martins, whom I found sitting on the sidewalk, in the moonlight. They knew nothing of Wysham's movements.

Cockey has just left me, having come while I was at breakfast. He is to return at midday. I leave tonight, I think, for New York. Nothing is to be done, now. Hammerik is in Denmark, and will not be back for a month, probably.

I am much better than when I left home. The beefsteaks tell upon me, instantly. Dear Soul, my heart will quite break if thou get not a beefsteak ere long !

I pray thee make me a fair copy of the enclosed, – which was scribbled over the margin of my poor maltreated " Berlioz " betwixt Bristol & Lynchburg – and send the same to Clifford, with my compliments. – Do you know that much of Chaucer's poetry was of exactly similar style to this, *i.e.* written in the vernacular ? I'm really not sure but this is about as *strong* a thing as I've done.[72]

"

"

When I remember all thy wifely lovingkindness, I am dumb. How thou hast grown, Little Woman ! How good was God, to give thee to me ! if He wd. but also give me what my

---

[72] This poem is identified as " Civil Rights " (I, 40) in Mary Day Lanier's letter of Aug. 7-Sept. 15 to Clifford Lanier. A note in her handwriting comments on the postscript to the present letter as follows: " *Civil Rights*: published by Atlanta paper, but not paid for– no one of the three editors avowing responsibility for disregard of terms of offer." (See also Lanier's letters of Sept. 17, Oct. 7, Nov. 2, and Nov. 3, 1874, and notes 113 and 135, below.)

Another of Lanier's experiments in the use of dialect, this poem was printed in several contemporary newspapers but has not been previously collected. It was apparently first printed early in September in the Atlanta, Ga., *Daily Herald,* but unfortunately no file of this newspaper has been located for this period. (The *Union List of Newspapers* credits the Georgia State Library, Atlanta, Ga., with a complete file for 1874, but there is a gap from Aug. 26 to Dec. 6.) It was reprinted in the Savannah *Morning News*, Oct. 28, and the Macon *Daily Telegraph and Messenger*, Oct. 29, 1874.

worship longs ever to give *thee*, – how happy a heart wd. mine
be ! My craving to cover thee with all manner of soft lady-
luxuries groweth and groweth. I stand before the shop-
windows, and say, how fairly wd. my beautiful one shine in
that: I sigh before the picture-stores, and breathe hard upon
the Jewelers' windows, thinking of thy Sweet needs.

Thou patient Sweet. God array thee in His peace, prayeth
thy

lover.

"
_____
"

I send this poem to Col. Avery, of the Atlanta Herald, -- if
peradventure he might buy the same.
Address, " 195 Dean St,

Brooklyn,

N. Y."

To Mary Day Lanier [73]

Brooklyn, Aug. 25th 1874.

O why did I not kiss thee every minute in every hour of every
day, during that heavenly time that God allowed me to be
within kissing-reach of thee!

And yet, what a foolish cry is this ; – for if I *had*, then would
I have been no whit less famished than I now am.

I do now foresee that eternity is not going to be long enough
for me to make love to thee in : – therefore I will e'en tack
Time on to it, and will employ the now remainder of my moiety
thereof in twisting up life into kiss-packages, – with a little
poetical couplet in each, minutely descriptive of thy brows,
eyes, and the like ravishments, – and tossing the same into thy
lap .

"
_____
"

Meantime, I have embraced and been embraced by my jovial
Mr. Horace Ripley, and have wrung hands with the girls and

[73] Lanier did not leave Baltimore until Aug. 24 because, as he wrote his
wife on Aug. 23 (here omitted): " I wanted a day of perfect quiet." In Brooklyn
he made his home once more with Salem Dutcher's sisters.

answered a thousand questions anent thee and the young rose-
buds and have been installed in a splendid front-room, where
everything is marvellous white and bright and comfortable and
thoughtfully-arranged, and out of whose windows in the brilliant morning-sun I behold a superb stretch of hills, trees, ships,
factories, dwellings, churches and sky.
I have slept all night, without waking: and am very well. Dear
Love, if I cd. know that *thou* art very well, this morning !

No more ! saith the Arm, and I have yet some business-
letters that must be written. What will ever I do without thee,
that wert at once my Heart and my Arm and my Hand !

O God of all hearts and arms and hands, I pray thee instill
all delicate sweet thoughts, all tender strengths, all loving
deftnesses, into her who hath been all these to me, looking
upon her as if thou, also, and not alone I, wert her

lover !

195 Dean St, Brooklyn N. Y.

To Mary Day Lanier

Brooklyn, Aug. 26th 1874

My faithful Cockey, – although he had just returned to Baltimore from New York – got himself sent back here in order
to be with me, for a few days: and last night we met by appointment at Thomas' Concert.

But, being there, he dissolved away out of my ken immediately. There was nothing in the universe to me but thee, and
God, and Music, and my heart. If I cd. have looked into thy
face, during some of the pieces, it wd. have been Heaven, pure
and simple. I cannot speak of my delight in this music: it is
so beautiful, Little Heart! It turneth me into one tear of joy.

In the *entr'acte* came Stovasser, mine ancient Comrade, *quon-
dam* First Oboe of the Peabody Orchestra, now Second Oboe
of Thomas', and we drank beer together. He brought also Mr.
Wehner, the new First Flute, of Thomas': a fine player, just
from St. Petersburg, Russia, and we had such talk as my limited
German and Stovasser's more limited English cd. compass by

being put together, Wehner speaking not a word of English.[74]

I met also Mr. Denniston, with whom I played in concert here last winter.

Yesterday morning, I heard my name called vigorously as I was mailing a letter to thee in the Post Office; and turning found my friend Mr. Yzquierdo, with whom I had some fine " blows " last fall. We are to have another, with Pasquale and Cockey, on Friday or Saturday night.

I called on Auntie McDonald yesterday. She was out, but Mr. Ronald and I had a two hours' talk together. Am to go again today. Mr. Ronald thinks the poem—" Corn "—wondrous fine: I have never heard him express himself with so much enthusiasm before.

— Kiss for me *thy* father, and *my* sons – I am improving daily: how much can a week of beefsteaks do! Thou art being starved to death, – God help the bitter, bitter poverty of thy

lover.

To Mary Day Lanier

Brooklyn, Aug. 29th 1874.

Thy commands being law, I herewith inflict a left-hander [75] upon thee.

Thine of 26th is here, and hath much relieved my heart. I believe I have answered most of thine enquiries heretofore. I have not yet seen Latham; he hath just returned to New York.[76]

I pray thee hand to the Pirate $40.00 of the fifty thou hast recd. He hath been paid some ninety ($90.00) dollars hitherto.

---

[74] Carl Wehner and Lanier became close friends. None of their correspondence has been found, but two photographs of Wehner have survived (Charles D. Lanier Collection, Johns Hopkins University), one with an inscription to Lanier dated May 3, 1880.

[75] In her letter of Aug. 26, 1874, Mary Day Lanier had cautioned her husband to save his right arm " to fight the life-battle for us all " (his right lung being the one principally affected by tuberculosis) and to practice writing with his left hand in his letters to her. This accounts for the marked variation in Lanier's autograph from this date on. The facing illustration shows Lanier's left-hand and normal script of 1874, compared with that of 1867-1868 (top).

[76] Latham was a musical friend Lanier had met on previous visits to New York. The " Pirate," mentioned in the following paragraph, was H. M. Gray, with whom the Laniers boarded at Sunnyside.

Specimen Pages of Lanier's Ledger, 1874

"*Poem Outline*" (left), *Prattville Academy accounts* (top), "*In Absence IV*" (right)

Henry W. Lanier Collection, Johns Hopkins University

Yesterday I sent thee a novel called "Nancy," by Rhoda Broughton. Read it *through*: spite of the wretched crisis, all ends happily, and the book leaveth a better taste in one's mouth than any of her previous novels.

I have not yet seen Mr. Bee, who is the writer of the letter " in beautiful handwriting " to wh. thou referrest.[77] I am to spend the afternoon with the McDonalds.

I am doing well in health.

And now God keep thee in His Heart, dear Wife, fervently prayeth thy

lover.

To Mary Day Lanier

Brooklyn, Aug. 30th 1874

Good morning, Little Maydie. How many times has thou waked, and risen, during the past night, in behalf of Lulu, or Rinda,[78] or Hal, or Charlie, or thyself? Art thou tired and sleepy? My heart is *so* full of love and tenderness for thee this day ! I *so* desire to do somewhat for thee, that might perchance lighten a care, or assuage a pain. It is incredible that I have been by thee in time past, for hours, without doing aught to help thee, nay, even increasing thy cares with some flight or other of my dyspeptic folly.

I yearn for thy letters sent to Baltimore, and have written Wysham to have them forwarded to me. I know not whether I told thee that he is at the Highland House, Garrisons, (on the Hudson) and hath written urging me to come and visit them there. I wd. greatly like to go, for I cd. then visit thy Mrs. James, (whom I love because she loveth thee); but I cannot now spare either the time or the money.

Mr. Bee hath just called on me, with all manner of cordial greetings and invitations. I am to go to his house tomorrow night.

I hope to meet Latham tomorrow at two O'clock. If he

[77] Mary Day Lanier had asked in her letter of Aug. 26: "What is the name of the flutist friend in N. Y. who wrote thee a long letter in such beautiful writing– making mention of Yzquierdo & others?"
[78] Nurse-maid to the Lanier children.

does not offer fairly, I think I will take my pieces [79] to Scher-
berth, or Schirmer.

What a pother thou must be at, to read my left-handed
iniquity! Can'st make it out at all?

My fine little Charley! Tell him Papa saith he hath left Mama
in *his* charge, and he must take the best care of thee in the
world; and that Papa loves him for being so manly about
Jeff's pond.[80]

Thou are in my heart as the little drop of distilled sweetness in the bottom of a flower-bell, and thou constitutest the
whole essence-of-all-loveliness to thy

lover.

To Milton H. Northrup [81]

Brooklyn. N. Y.
Sept.1st 1874.

My dear Milton:

I do not like for the earth to go around the
sun more than one time without a line from you to assure me
that you, and the wife and the baby, are well.

After a thorough and (I suppose) final break down of health
at the law, I am here armed with a lot of poetry and music
which I've written, and proposing henceforth to fight the Wolf
in that way, though without any definite plans as yet.

---

[79] In her letter of Aug. 26, 1874, Mary Day Lanier identified three of these
pieces. One of them, a setting for Tennyson's poem " Break, Break, Break "—
a MS copy of which survives in the possession of Henry W. Lanier, photostat
in Johns Hopkins University Library—had been composed three years before
(see Mary Day Lanier's letter to her husband, Sept. 20, 1871). A second, " Wind
Song," had apparently been conceived during Lanier's winter in Texas but revised
and completed during the summer of 1874 at Sunnyside (a one-page musical
MS survives in the Charles D. Lanier Collection, Johns Hopkins University,
dated Dec. 27, 1872, San Antonio, Texas, entitled " The Song of the Lost Spirit. /
Heimweh Polka / Bird Song / Wind Song "; another undated MS entitled " Wind
Song " survives in the possession of Henry W. Lanier, photostat in Johns Hopkins
University Library, facsimile in Starke, opposite p. 184). The third piece was
Il Balen (" From *Il Trovatore*. Air and Variations for Flute, with Piano
Accompaniment "), printed posthumously by A. G. Badger, New York, copyright
1888.

[80] In her letter of Aug. 26, 1874, Mary Day Lanier had told of Charley's
voluntary confession that he had been to Jeff's pond: " No excuse and no pre-
amble– but a straight, manly confession, with a face of genuine grief."

[81] Previously published, *Lippincott's*, LXXV. 314 (Mar., 1905).

Pray tell me what you're about; and, if you come to New York, give me the pleasure of shaking your hand. I am at " 195 Dean St, Brooklyn," where letters shd. be addressed to me.

Convey my hearty remembrance to Mrs. Northrop, and keep me in mind as always

your friend

Sidney Lanier.

To CLIFFORD A. LANIER

195 Dean St.
Brooklyn, N. Y.
Sep. 2nd 1874.

My dear Clifford:

        I write a short note—in defiance of my strange epistolary disability—to beg that you will see [Ben] Screws (if he is still Editor of the Montg'y Mail & Advertiser) and ask him if he has any occasion for the services of a Correspondent in New York. You might tell him I did some work of that sort, while in Texas, for The World,[82] wh. was favorably received. I should like to write him (say) one letter a week, filled with lively descriptions of men and things and events in New York: making them alternately chatty, musical, literary, political, social, descriptive, and even *fashion* after a fashion. I shall be much with newspaper men in N.Y. during the entire winter, and will have some facilities for this sort of thing.

Pray ask him his terms for such service.

I'm pretty well. Am staying at my old friends' the Dutchers', whose kindness and care exceed all precedent. My plans depend much on events wh. will transpire in a week or ten days from now, and you shall hear further of them at that time.

Kiss everybody for me. I long to see you all with great longing. Ask Aunt Jane to send me Aunt Molly's (Sid's) address: or perhaps you have it yourself.

Pardon such a dreadful scrawl: you can't know with what labor I write at all. As soon as possible I must send for my

---

[82] Mentioned in numerous letters during the winter of 1872-1873 (see also VI, 187-201).

sweet Amanuensis.   Address me as at head of this letter: and hold me always in your heart for yr. loving

S.L.

To Mary Day Lanier [83]

[Brooklyn,] Sep. 3rd 1874.

I think I have invented a flute wh. will go down to G below the Staff, and wh. will entirely remedy the imperfections which now exist in that part of the flute that extendeth below D.   I have stirred up Badger about it – with infinite labor: for the old Satyr is far more concerned about silver dollars than about silver flutes, and is almost inexpugnably conservative.   He is always wonderfully kind to me, however, and gazes on me with a half amused smile when I am talking, as if I were a precocious child whom he was showing off.   I have some good hopes of the new flute.   O My Child, dream with me that some day thou and I will listen to an Orchestra in which shall be as many first flutes as first violins and as many second flutes as second violins !   And why shd. it not be so ?   What reason is there in the nature of things why the violins should be the Orchestra, and the flutes and other instruments mere adjuncts ?   I say this not out of my foolish advocacy of the flute: thou knowest that I love the violin with my whole soul.   No, I speak in advocacy of pure music.   No one can hear an orchestra constituted like Thomas' (e.g.) without being convinced that, with all its perfection of handling, its material is *not* perfect.   The *Tutti* in fff is always a grief to me: I defy any musician to extract anything out of such passages, unless he have the score before him, or is otherwise familiar with the theme.   Then he can faintly discern the idea: but to those who are not musicians it is as sound and fury signifying nothing.

—— But, thou, dear Lady, art to me at once flutes and violins and reeds and brass; yea, thou art all harmonies and all melodies melted and clarified and morphosed into one warm crystal, that Sunneth the soul of thy

lover .

[83] Previously published, *Scribner's*, XXV, 746 (June, 1899) ; reprinted, *Letters* (New York, 1899), pp. 99-100.

To Mary Day Lanier

Brooklyn, Sep 4th 1874.

My poor Sweet, how worn thou needs must be, with so much care and heart-strain and fatigue and sleeplessness over our sick ones!

When I go to bed each night in my quiet and orderly room, I hurl a thousand reproaches upon myself that I bear so little of the dreadful brunt of the battle wh. falleth upon thee. Of course, I know that I cannot help it:— I wd. kill myself if I thought I cd.—and *did* not, yet I *must* be angry with *some* one about it!

Dr. Holland, Ed. of Scribner's Magazine, declareth that he is really sorry he cannot print " Corn," because it is too long for the Magazine.[84]

I think I will adopt a suggestion of Col. Barnett's; [85] and have it illustrated with thee or four first-rate wood-cuts, then publish it in book-form on fine paper, as a sort of *bijou*-book, at about seventy five cents a copy. I think I cd. certainly rely upon selling a thousand copies, which would pay a handsome profit on the cost. Tomorrow, after an interview wh. I hope to have with Dr. Holland, I will see the publishers about it.

Sep. 5th

I was unavoidably prevented from finishing my letter last night. This morning cometh thy postal card saying that my fine young man is better, and that thou thinkest always upon thy lover: for both of wh. things I do humbly thank God.

But O my Sweetheart, I do so long for thee, in these days! My heart is so full of all manner of poems, in words and in music, which I wish *thee* to write, thee and not another, because when thou writest them, then I lay at thy feet my flowers with the dew on them. Moreover, all is bitter which thou dost not taste simultaneously with me. My Child, I do love thee so

---

[84] J. G. Holland had also rejected " June Dreams, In January " when it had been offered to him by Ronald MacDonald, acting for Lanier, the previous spring (see MacDonald's letter to Lanier, Apr. 9, 1874).

[85] A friend in Marietta, Ga.

dearly: I am rapt away into love: I am a small white cloud
melting away into the great blue heaven of love-of-thee. I
pray thee think therefore often, and gently, upon thy

lover.

To Mary Day Lanier [86]

Brooklyn, Sep. 7th 1874.

I have not yet seen Dr. Holland, nor received from him the
note wh. I expect, appointing an interview. This will probably
be arranged today.[87]

Latham had not the money to buy my music outright, and I
do not care to publish on shares until I exhaust the probability
of selling.   Tonight I am to see Mr. Cornell [88] and play with
him: from whom I hope to learn something that may be useful
in this behalf.

Badger worked for me like a Trojan all Saturday afternoon,
experimenting on my new long flute. We were much put to it
for some time to get a certain motion that was essential: but I
kept him at it, in spite of the most dismal croaking on his side,
until our efforts were crowned with brilliant success.   I am
going over now to recommence work on it.

I enclose a letter from Father (written on the inside of Aunt
Jane's,) in order that thou mayst see the invitation therein contained to visit them in the early fall. About the same, exercise
thine own sovereign will: if it please thee, go: if not, not.

I have written thee every day but one (the day occupied in

[86] Excerpt previously published, *Scribner's*, XXV, 746 (June, 1899); reprinted, *Letters* (New York, 1899), p. 100.

[87] In a letter of Sept. 8, 1874 (here omitted), Lanier wrote to his wife:
" Cometh this morning a note from Dr. Holland, written at Boston, saying that
he is gone to Maine, to be away for two weeks, and that when he returns ' he
will be glad to see me and more glad to serve me.' Meantime I will take my
poem up town and see what the publishers will do with it."

[88] John Cornell was the Organist of St. Paul's, whom Lanier had known since
his first prolonged stay in New York in 1870. In a letter of Sept. 8, 1874 (here
omitted), Lanier wrote to his wife: " I spent last evening with Mr. Cornell,
winning I believe some glory. He is to take me to see Dr. Dammrosch, who
appears to be the coming man at present; and advises me to try Heuser
(successor to Schuberth & Co), with my music, wh. I will do."

coming hither from Baltimore) since I left thee. Dost receive all my letters?

O, to see thy gray eyes, O to see my little elf Sidney cut a caper!

I wish to hear that thou hast been to Marietta. Go, as soon as thou canst.

God keep thee full of light whereby to see His glory, — prayeth thy

lover.

To Robert S. Lanier

195 Dean St.
Brooklyn, N. Y.
Sep. 8th 1874.

My dear Father:

Your kind letter, annexed to Aunt Jane's is here. I'm glad she is coming on, tho' I fear I shall not have time to escort her about, as much as I cd. wish. However, I believe she is pretty independent, in the matter of beaus, and understands New York well enough to keep out of the labyrinths.

I am trying to find a publisher for some music which I have written: flute-and-piano pieces, and songs. I also am endeavoring to find the most advantageous form in which to issue my poem " Corn," just written. This last has received great commendation from many sources. I am now gravitating towards the idea of getting it printed in book-form, — though it wd. not occupy more than fifteen or twenty pages—, with three or four illustrations of the principal topics in the poem, towit, 1st a man walking meditatively through a fine old Georgia forest of oaks and beeches, towards his corn-field, just beyond

> " The zig-zag wandering fence
> Where lissome Sassafras and brambles dense
> Contest with stolid vehemence
> The march of culture, — setting limb and thorn
> Like pikes against the army of the Corn."

— 2nd a magnificient big stalk of Corn

> " That stands
> Advanced beyond the foremost of his bands

And waves his blades upon the very edge
And hottest thicket of the battling hedge."

3rd   An old red hill of Georgia, deserted by its non-corn-planting tenant who has fled Westward,

" That bares to heaven its piteous, agèd crest
And seamy breast,
By restless-hearted Children left to lie
Untended there beneath the heedless sky,
As barbarous folk expose their old to die.

. . .   A gashed and hairy Lear
Whom the divine Cordelia of the year
– E'en pitying Spring – will vainly strive to cheer,
– King, yet too poor for any man to own,
Discrowned, undaughtered and alone":

– and 4th,   this same hill under the culture of some better man and sounder system, for (so the poem ends)

. . . " Old Hill, old hill,
For all thy low estate
Thou still art rich and great
Beyond all cotton-blinded estimate,
And long I marvel through the August morn
What largesse rich, of oil and wine and corn
Thou bearest on thy vasty sides forlorn.
To render to some future bolder heart
That manfully shall take thy part
With antique sinew and with modern art,
And tend thee
And defend thee!" [89]

—   I sent the poem to Col. Barnett, who suggested this method of publication, averring that he thought it wd. pay, by a large circulation through the South.   Dr. Holland wanted to print it in Scribner's Magazine (of wh. he is editor) but it was too long. I will see the publishers in a day or two.

——   I have forgotten the exact date of a note I have at Nutting's bank. Will you please step in there, ask Mr. Goodall the date, and write me at once?   My address is on the first page of this letter.

[89] The passages here quoted are from an early version of " Corn " (I, 34, note). In answer to his father's enthusiastic reply Lanier wrote on Sept. 17, 1874 (here omitted): " I send a copy of ' Corn ': it is the one that I sent for Mr. Hayne to read and the pencil-comments are his."

I am gratified to hear of Mama's improved health; she was looking so thin when I was last in Macon that I was really concerned about her. My own health is tolerably good. I'm a little worn by work: it takes so much labor to get anything done in New York! I have invented a flute which goes down to G, upon a new principle of fingering: and after two weeks of incessant battering and maneuvring and talking at old Badger, have only just got him aroused and at work upon a trial tube to test the matter. So far as we have gone, it works beautifully: and I hope for some good things from it.

I fear it will be quite impossible for May to accept your pleasant invitation to stay in Macon. Her father has at considerable trouble, arranged a place at Sunnyside where he can stay with her through September and October: and just at this critical period of (little) Harry's and Lulu's teething, it would be extremely dangerous to change milk.[90] May has a sort of music-class, too, wh. she is teaching and wh. I suspect she would not like to leave, after having engaged to teach until Novbr.

I hope yr. business will soon be looking up. When does Uncle C. go to the Springs? I looked at the dear old mountains longingly the other day as I passed by the Allegheny station on my way here, and thought them more beautiful than I had ever seen them.

Kiss Mama for me, and give love to Uncle C. & family. Write me soon,

Your Son

S. L.

To Mary Day Lanier

[Brooklyn,] Sep. 12th 1874.

Latham expecteth to revive his music-publishing business, and hath proposed to me to print three of my flute-pieces, giving me the *first* hundred copies of each. This is a very

---

[90] Harry was Lanier's third son, and Lulu (Mary Louise) was the daughter of Harry Day, temporarily in Mary Day Lanier's care.

On Aug. 26, 1874, Lanier's wife had written that by giving music lessons to her landlord's daughters, she expected to be able to pay part of the board bill.

liberal offer—better than Heuser's, and I will probably accept it.[91]

Suppose I shd. get a job of translation from the publishers, to bring out Jean Jacques Rousseau's book on Music,—cdst. not thou help? Thou wdst. translate his French so beautifully, my Bright-Soul! I do not know that I can do it, (I mean, get the job); but am going to try.

I must now run over to Badger's, and then up town.

Fare thee well, May Lilian, until I again comfort my heart by writing that I am thy

lover.

To Mary Day Lanier

[Brooklyn,] Sep. 13th 1874.

Last night I won great favor in the eyes of Mr. Cortada, – a noble musician, Pianist of the Oratorio Society of New York and of the Handel & Haydn Society of Brooklyn. We played a Sonata of Kücken, one of Kuhlau, Tercschak's *Babillard*, & Fürstenau's Nocturne, together. He declareth that I can do great things with a little study: and volunteereth to introduce me to Dr. Dammrosch, (under whom he saith I must study), who is Conductor of both the above-mentioned Societies.[92] He also volunteereth to endeavor to get me the place of Professor of the Flute at the Brooklyn Conservatory of Music. God speed him.

I have sent the poem to Geo. McDonald & Co. Publishers,

---

[91] In a letter of Sept. 10, 1874 (here omitted) Lanier had written to his wife: "I saw Mr. Heuser yesterday. He looked at my music, was much interested in it, declared that he wanted to help me get it before the public, and finally made me an offer, the details of which I have not time to write thee now. It involved no *cash*: wh. is what I want,– and therefore I will try elsewhere before accepting it."

Rousseau's "book on Music," mentioned in the next sentence, was either his *Dissertation sur la musique moderne* or his *Dictionnaire de musique*.

[92] Leopold Damrosch (1832-1885), violinist, composer, and conductor. A friend of Liszt and von Bülow, he had already made his reputation in Europe with the orchestra at Breslau, when he was invited to conduct the Arion Society Orchestra in New York, 1871. Here he introduced the newer German school of composers, Wagner and Schumann as well as Liszt. In 1873 he founded the New York Oratorio Society; in 1878, the New York Symphony Society.

of Chicago, with my plan for publishing same in book-form, illustrated, – wh. I think wd. be vastly popular in the South. This was Col. Barnett's suggestion: – he thought it wd. be a pecuniary success.

I have writ thee of Latham's proposition.

I am to see Heuser again about the songs, and the "Gnat-dance" ["Danse des Moucherons"]; when I hope to bring him to better terms.

I have written to The Atlanta Herald, the Savannah Musical Magazine, the Baltimore Gazette, the "Musical Eclectic" of Atlanta, the Montgomery Advertiser & Mail, – to know if they desire a N. Y. correspondent, either specially *quoad* Music, or generally. The two last have replied, declining– I have not heard from the others.

I have sent the Article "Peace" (Eddy & Charley) to "Southe[r]n Mag:" – it is accepted.[93] I have sketched a lot of articles on The Curiosities of Music, – in which I mean to lead up, by degrees, to my theory of barbaric music, and of those queer tunes wh. thou wert to copy for me from the Pirate's (and Abe's) "Sacred Harp": – wh. said articles I mean to offer, by letter, tomorrow, to Dwight's Journal of Music. I remember that the editor of this Journal wrote me for my auto-graph just after "Tiger-Lilies" came forth.[94]

I have also sketched a series of articles in the style of Isaac Bickerstaff, (Addison) on certain phases of modern life, – which I will offer, – as soon as I finish the first one for a sample – to "the Nation".[95] I am also arranging a programme and some music for a series of "Soft-Tone concerts" wh. I wish to organize in N. Y.; giving Beethoven's great Octett for Oboes, Clarionets & Flutes, some quartets & trios for flutes, solos on Bass-flute & Concert-flute, &c.[96]

---

[93] This essay had apparently been composed four years previously (see note 84, 1870, and VI, 247). It was published in the *Southern Magazine*, Oct., 1874.

[94] Lanier was mistaken. It was Theodore F. Dwight of Auburn, New York, who had written requesting his autograph (see Lanier's letter to Mary Day Lanier, Oct. 18, 1868, above). The editor of *Dwight's Journal of Music* was John Sullivan Dwight (1813-1893) of Boston. No trace has been found of the articles on "The Curiosities of Music" which Lanier mentions in this paragraph.

[95] Three surviving MS fragments (Charles D. Lanier Collection, Johns Hopkins University) seem to answer to this description: (1.) "Tatler, No .268," 6 pp.; (2.) "The Tatler, No. —," 3 pp.; (3.) "Mr. Querry," 4 pp.

[96] These "Soft-Tone concerts" never materialized. But a number of **frag-**

I am also superintending, by daily visits to Badger's, the experiment of the long flute, wh. is now nearly done.

—— Here, then, Dear Heart, thou hast (as thou requestedst in thy last) pretty nearly all the plans and hopes wh. now occupy my time. I know thou wilt breathe thy soft wifely prayers that they may finally come to some accomplishment. If they do not, – then I am content, for I will have done all that I possibly cd.: more than this, God will not require. Of course some of these plans must needs involve much preliminary failure, trial, patience, and hard work. But I am growing used to these: and they season a man.

And, then, – most blessed of sweet consolations ! I undergo all *for thee*, who art my Darling, and my One-Love, and my Silver Star, and my Perfect Sweet, and my Heart-Of-a-Rose; for thee whom I love each day with new and finer love, as if I were each day born into a larger heaven, a stronger

lover

To Mary Day Lanier [97]

[Brooklyn,] Sep. 17th 1874.

Heart of my Soul, it is true that yesterday I had not time to write thee, from other occupations wh. I knew thou wdst. wish me to pursue in preference.

I hope thou hast by this time the wherewithal to appease thy hungry pirate.

The long flute is nearly done, and I think it will work. It hath revealed sundry hitches wh. have taxed my ingenuity severely; but I have managed to overcome them all, and the final prospect is now good.

---

mentary bits of music survive in MS in Lanier's copy books (Charles D. Lanier Collection, Johns Hopkins University) which were apparently sketched for this purpose: (1.) " Mem. Soft-Tone Concerts. / ' Lâ Rêve ' for four flutes: air & fantasy "; (2.) " Mem. for trio. Fl. B. F. & 'Cello "; (3.) " Bass Flute (To tickle the ears of the groundlings) "; (4.) " Mem. Quartette "; (5.) " Mem. for Trio: Song "; (6.) " Mem. Concert-flute "; (7.) " Mem. for long flute."

[97] Excerpt previously published, *Scribner's*, XXV, 746 (June, 1899); reprinted, *Letters* (New York, 1899), p. 100.

Little's letter is a refresher, and I wish I cd. shake his hand.[98]
I wonder what those leftenants of his have to do, and how
[much] pay they get for doing it? Cdst. find out in any
accidental way?

I have a letter from my father, who is greatly pleased
with some specimen of " Corn " wh. I sent him. I have just
enclosed him a full copy.

My poem on " Civil Rights " appeared in the Atlanta
" Herald " (to wh. I had offered it at $25⁰⁰.).[99] I have not
yet seen it: hast thou? Do not mention that *I* wrote it, to any
one else: – reasons for wh. I will tell thee when I have more
time.

Of wh. I now have none at all: so fare-thee-well, dear Wife,
till tomorrow; and God sail thee over the calm bosom of today,
as thou wert a tube-rose petal floating over a quiet lake, –
prayeth thy

lover.

To Mary Day Lanier

[Brooklyn,] Sep. 19th 1874.

Yesterday, again, I wrote thee not, being over head and ears
in moil and turmoil, and today I must hie me straightway up
into Jerusalem to meet a lady (whose name is Bonner, but who
fought in the Confederate army as " Lieut. Buford ") who is
going to lecture at Atlanta during the fair, and who *may* desire
to read my " Jones " [100] and " Corn " in one of the lectures. I
go now to see whether she has cash to pay for the same.

The long flute cometh on apace, and I make little doubt I
shall bring it to final success.

[98] George Little, one of Lanier's oldest friends, had tried to persuade him to
accept a position at Oakland College, near Port Gibson, Miss., in 1867. The
college had closed shortly after that time, and Little taught for a while, apparently, at the University of Mississippi.

In Sept., 1874, he came back to Georgia as State Geologist, living in Atlanta.
Mary Day Lanier saw him there on Sept. 8 (see her letter to Lanier, Sept. 9,
1874).

[99] See note 72, above. (Lanier's reasons for wanting anonymity are given in
his letter of Nov. 2, 1874, below.)

[100] " Jones of Jones " (the poem more generally known as " Thar's More in
the Man than Thar is in the Land ") treats in humorous dialect verse the same
economic theme as " Corn."

The music standeth in *statu quo*, awaiting the result of certain negotiations which Latham is carrying on.

I have a fair chance to become Musical and Dramatic Critic for the Baltimore Gazette; of wh. I shall know more definitely in a few days.

Heavens and Earth, what an abominable pen this is!

— Thou art always with me, dear Heart, art thou not? O that I had some words to tell thee how light and sweet-companioned thy wise and beautiful face doth make my long rides and my lonesome hours and my strange diverse labors,—as it cometh floating ever into my soul's ken, sweetest *eidolon* that ever was, of Wife, of Comrade, of true

lover!

To Mary Day Lanier [101]

[Brooklyn,] Sep. 21st 1874.

Well then, (in response to thy tender and oft-repeated inquiries, and particularly in rebuttal of thy pretty reproach that thou canst not confide in me *quoad* my reports of health as thou dost in all other matters) I will inform thee that I have not been so well as might be expected, for a couple of weeks past. The weather was very warm, and I was greatly fatigued each day, insomuch that presently came something like a nervous breakdown, followed (even as Aurora by the trooping Hours) by indigestion, inflamed eye-lids, weak eyes, and general good-for-nothingness. I believe I am now much better. My eyes are still weak, and the lids are sore and constantly itching: but otherwise, save some general weakness, I am recovered. I will doubtless improve rapidly, now: this morning, after four days of warm rain, openeth bright and cool, and there is a certain sting in the air wh. braceth the nerves wonderfully.

I wdst. thou hadst it, thou poor overworn Sweet ! Thy little-dainty letter cometh this morning, and sparkleth in my heart like a drop of dew in the velvety-hollow of a heart's-ease. Thy letters are too beautiful: they show God's rarest soul.

[101] Previously published, *Scribner's*, XXV, 747 (June, 1899); reprinted, *Letters* (New York, 1899), p. 101.

The long flute will succeed, in time. It is near enough finished for me to see that. Dost thou know, everything I do or write is so new and upturn-y of old mouldy ideas, here, that I have infinite trouble. E. g.: old Badger has been making flutes for forty years, and when any luckless wight maketh suggestion to him thereanent, he smileth a battered and annihilating smile, wh. saith plainly enough, *pooh*, I exhausted all that a half-century ago. Now this Satyr fought me at every stage and up every step of my long flute. He declared in the very beginning that it was impossible: that a tube so long cd. not be filled by the human breath, that a column of air so long could not be made to vibrate &c, and that he had long ago tried it thoroughly, and satisfied himself it was physically non-achievable. This last of course staggered me: yet, with fool-hardiness (as it is called) I worked at him until I got him to draw out a long tube, upon which in a few minutes I demonstrated to him that the G. was not only a possible but a beautiful note. He then retreated to his second line, and entrenched himself behind the C key, avering that a key cd. not be constructed wh. wd. make C and at the same time hold down the four keys of the right-hand. Then I proved to him it cd. be done, by good logic, and he finally made the key I wanted and it *was* done. Thus from breastwork to breastwork hath he been driven: in three days more I expect him to surrender at discretion.

— Well, dear Comrade, repose thou now, like any white cloud, upon the peaceful blue infinite of God's love, – prayeth thy

lover.

To Mary Day Lanier

[Brooklyn,] Sep. 24th 1874.

I cannot tell thee how I have *been* driven for the last two days in any more impressive way than to say that I have not had time to write thee, save when I wd. come home at night and when I wd. be too utterly exhausted to sit up longer.
I saw " Lieut. Buford ": – and did not think it to my advantage to transact any " Corn " business with her.

I had quite set my heart upon getting the place of musical and dramatic critic to the new newspaper which is about being started here: but the vacancy was filled before my application was received.

Thou wdst. never dream the depth and heart-breaking stupendousness of the wooden-headedness of many people here who are leaders in literary matters. I walk in a continually growing glamor of amazement that such persons conduct things; – until I remember that it has always been so, that the new man has always to work his way over these Alps of stupidity much as that ancient General crossed the actual Alps, – splitting the rocks with vinegar and fire, that is, by bitterness and suffering.

D. V., I will split them.

I must tell thee somewhat, not, I am sure from any immodesty, but because I know that thou wilt be glad to hear it: and that is; the more I am thrown against these people here, and the more reverses I suffer at their hands, the more confident I am of beating them finally. I do not mean, by " beating ", that I am in opposition to them, or that I hate them, or feel aggrieved with them: no, they know no better, and they act up to their light with wonderful energy and consistency: I only mean that I am sure of being able, some day, to teach them better things and nobler modes of thought and conduct.[102]

Thy French cards are so beautiful ! [103] The lovely sentences actually curve with the same graceful redness that thy lips have when thou art speaking.

God be, in His good way, – as I am, in mine, – thy

Lover.

---

[102] In a letter of Sept. 15, 1874 (here omitted), Lanier had written to his wife: " So many great ideas for Art are born to me each day; I am swept away into the Land of All-Delight by their strenuous sweet whirlwind; and I feel within myself such entire, yet humble, confidence of possessing every single element of power to carry them all out,– save the little paltry sum of money wh. wd. suffice to keep us clothed and fed in the meantime."

[103] Several of Mary Day Lanier's notes to her husband during this period were written in French on postal cards.

To Robert S. Lanier

195 Dean St.
Brooklyn, N. Y.
Sep. 24th 1874.

My dear Father:

When the note was made (to wh. yr. letter
of 21st, this moment recd, refers) you were sick, in bed, and it
was impossible to see you, and consult you about it. It was a
sudden thought, and done in a day. You had been sick several
days, and I was unable to talk with you about money: and I
felt myself on the eve of a haemorrhage (wh. I afterwards
had) from the dust of Macon: so that I suddenly resolved, in
duty to those who have claims upon my welfare, to get into the
country, out of the dust and heat of Macon, which were
making the most serious inroads upon my health.[104]

I have had just expectations of being able to pay off a part,
or all of the note, at maturity: but a series of delays has
rendered either impossible, and I enclose another at 60 days,
which I beg you will sign, as you propose, for Uncle C., and
use your influence with Mr. Goodall (he is the party with
whom Uncle C. negotiated) to get the renewal, or some
arrangement. I think I can pay the note in 60 days. The bank
is perfectly secure: it has in its vault near a thousand dollars
worth of silver, deposited by me. Please write me the result
of yr. negotiations: I shall be anxious to know, of course,
though have no doubt you and Mr. Goodall can arrange it.

I have some charming prospects, here: and will realize
some of them in a short time. I find no obstacles to my success
save those which arise from the entire *lonesomeness* of my
previous artistic life: I mean, from the want of that atmosphere
which is only to be found in a great city. These obstacles I
am rapidly levelling, by much study and hard work: and I am

---

[104] The reference is to money Lanier had borrowed from Nuttings Bank,
apparently at the time when he left Macon for Sunnyside the previous June. In
a letter to his father, Sept. 17, 1874 (here omitted), he had said: " It is to
meet this note that I am pushing so hard to sell my poem [" Corn "] outright.
I think from present appearances that my long flute is going to work: and I hope
to sell the patent for something."

determined to win. If only I can get along over the shallows, for a month or two, I believe the easy sailing will begin.[105]

I have a fair prospect of becoming musical and dramatic critic for a large Baltimore paper, – to reside in N. Y, the criticisms to be in a style suggested by me. My poem Corn has made a profound impression upon all who have read it, and can easily be made to net some hundreds of dollars, during the next Sixty days, by circulation even among the friends I have in the places where I am known.[106] I am only delayed in getting it out, by my efforts at finding the cheapest way to do it: which, although this required some time, are now nearly completed.

My music will also sell, in a little while. It is so original, that I have, as all original writers must, to " make my public "; and this I am rapidly doing, by various influences which I have brought to bear, but which it would take me too long to detail.

I have a half dozen other irons in the fire: and it shall go hard but some of them will do some good work.

I beg you therefore to do whatever can be done, in deferring the note. It was only made in a desperate emergency which I knew not otherwise how to meet.

Kiss Mama: and believe me always

Yr. Son

Sidney L.

P.S.

I have left the date blank in the note, so that you can fill it up properly.

S. L.

[105] In a letter of Oct. 2, 1874 (here omitted), Lanier wrote in answer to his father's inquiry: " You must not trouble yourself about me, now. It is true that if I had my family provided for I wd. be greatly better in health and spirits: but . . . I am better in general health than for years past: I am fairly embarked in what is to be my career, and am free from the dismal incertitude of the last two or three years in that particular: I meet with gratifying successes, particularly in music, almost every day, which slowly . . . advance me in the road I wish to travel: and, above all, begin to feel within myself a quiet and restful consciousness of doing my very best, in the vocation for wh. I am sure nature intended me."

[106] In a letter to his father of Sept. 17, 1874 (here omitted), Lanier had written his father apropos of publishing " Corn " by subscription: "I feel confident that with all the friends I have in Macon, Savannah, Atlanta, Milledgeville, Columbus, Montgomery,– and a dozen other places, at least a thousand copies cd. be sold instantly."

To Mary Day Lanier [107]

[Brooklyn,] Sep. 25th 1874.

All things remain *in Statu quo*, and I have not a word of news to tell thee. I have set a good many traps, and must now wait a day or two to see what will come to them. Today I will try to get up town to Judge Herring's. I have not yet seen any of the Laniers ! and I know not what they will think of me. Mr. John Winslow, Mr. Lanier's Son-in-law, is recently dead, after a very short illness. He was the Winslow of Winslow Lanier & Co., and was greatly loved and respected by all who knew him.

I met Mrs. Bill and her husband some evenings ago. He is now stationed in New York; whereat she seemeth vastly pleased.

— My poor little big-eyed Charles: doth he walk still with his hand to his side? I pray thee give my yearning love to him, and to my elf. I never pass a park, nor a toy-store but I heave a great sigh to-them-ward, and dream how happy I would be if I cd. take their little hands in mine, and carry them one merry tramp through the great city.

And little Daughter? I look anxiously for news of her.

I am better since cold weather hath set in. Today I have some sore throat. I touched the same with Iodine last night.

I am going to move heaven and earth for ways and means to take lessons from Dr. Dammrosch, who is leader of the Arion Society and of the Oratorio Society of New York and of the Handel & Haydn Society of Brooklyn. He is a beautiful violinist, and is considered at the head of fine music in New York. A slender blue-eyed man, with a broad forehead, is he: and a man of culture withal.

And now may God write a ravishing harmony of circumstance to the melody of thy life this day, – prayeth thy

husband.

[107] Excerpt previously published, *Scribner's*, XXV, 747 (June, 1899); reprinted, *Letters* (New York, 1899), pp. 101-102.

To Mary Day Lanier

195 Dean St.
Brooklyn. N. Y.
Sep. 28th 1874.

Thy packet, full of matter domestic, friendly, brotherly, wifely, is here this Monday morning, bright and early.

First in response to thy rare sweet reproachful enquiry I must tell thee that for three days I have had a most huge sore-throat, on account of which I have kept my room most of that time; but what with my Bromide of Potassium, my Chlorate of Potassa, my Iodine & Glycerine, my Bronchial Trochees, my Congress-water and the like medicaments and amelioratives, I am today much better, and shall fare forth into Babylon presently.

I rejoice thou hast secured so good a nurse.

How I love to read these letters like Mrs. Logan's, wh. bear testimony to thy loveliness and to thy friendly value !

I like not thy Fanny Bean.[108] This kind of gush in a woman of her age maketh me to think of Mr. Micawber's two aged daughters in short dresses and wide pantalettes: or, on the other-hand, if she *is* quizzing, why, it is motherhood and wife-hood and Love that she is thrusting her poor little frivolous sting into, and she meriteth a worse fate than the other gnats because they are gnats by necessity, she by choice. Therefore were I thee, (and I *am* thee, *nicht wahr?*) I wd. straightway develope which one of these two characters she really is: whether she is really an old-young woman practicing the gospel of Gush, or a mere gnat. And in order to give her a possibly-profitable example of straightforward dealing, I wd. ask her the question in so many words.

Thou dear Dorothea Brooke, thou Large-in-Soul, thou Sincere Heart, how I do thank God for thy sweet heartsome contrast to this indescribable sort of woman that flits by a man

---

[108] Mary Day Lanier had written, Sept. 24: " I enclose thee . . . one of Fanny Bean's characteristic ' effusions '— well-named. . . . I think I shall in my reply playfully recommend to her a less florid view of *things* when connected with myself."

The allusion in the following sentence is to Dickens, *David Copperfield*.

in such an indeterminate twilight way that he cannot tell for the life of him whether it was an old cat or a foolish hare.

— I have written to my father, and to Mr. Goodall (lest the first might miscarry) a plan of arrangement for the note, which I hope will postpone it for two months. In that time I can pay it, I am confident.

- The music hath been waiting upon Latham, whose arrangements hang fire. I have some hope he will be definitely informed on Wednesday next, when he cometh to play duos with me. I have not yet called on Miss [Alice] Fletcher, but hope soon to do so.

In response to thy dread for my arm, know two things: 1st that it is only one, or perhaps two, letter a week, & 2nd that, while by no means perfectly free, I am much better in this particular, and can write three or four pages at a time with but little inconvenience, by alternating each page with a few minutes of flute-practice.

I have not yet called on Miss Fletcher, for lack of time. If all goeth well with me, I will move over to New York in a few weeks, whereby I shall save four to five hours a day of time and an infinity of fatigue and exposure.

Dr. Holland, (ed. of Scribner's Magazine) writeth that " it (the Plantation Ballad, by Clifford and me) " is as well done as it can be, and if the story is not taken from Mark Twain, or if it is drawn from the same source as his version, he (Dr. H.) will very gladly take it." I have promptly replied that the poem is wholly our own production, neither of us being aware of anything like it in Mark Twain. I await his answer.[109]

I will try to call on the Herrings today, and will convey the information thou desirest. I cd. not call on Friday or since, on account of the aforementioned sore-throat.

I return Miss Bean's letter. Dost desire the others?

I pray thee kiss thy good Father for me, and tell him how I pray, labor and hope, for the time when we shall all be together under brighter skies.

Meantime, Thou Tuberose, Mayst thou be the best-tended Sweet and very show-flower of God the Gardener, – prayeth thy

lover.

---

[109] " The Power of Prayer " (here referred to as " The Plantation Ballad ") bears a faint resemblance to Mark Twain's *The Gilded Age,* Chap. III, " Uncle Daniel's Apparition " (see the following letter).

To Mary Day Lanier [110]

[Brooklyn,] Oct. 1st 1874.

Thou wilt scarcely credit that after two days of waiting, I have still no news to send thee. Latham still skirmisheth for money: I do not hear from the Gazette: "Corn" is in the hands of the Philistines: The Atlanta Herald replieth not to my fourth letter, in wh. I have presented my bill for $25.00: Badger is full of orders, and I have not the magical money necessary to make him go on with the long flute.

Cliff's and my "Power of Prayer" will come out in Scribner's; probably in the "Etchings" at end of the Magazine. I wrote thee what Dr. Holland said anent its resemblance to something of Mark Twain's, in plot. Day before yesterday I called, and asked Dr. Holland what work of Mark Twain's he referred to. "Well" said he, "I knew nothing about it, myself: I read the poem to a friend, and *he* suggested that the plot was like something of Mark Twain's. But yesterday I read him your note; and he then recollected that in Twain's version it is God Almighty that is coming up the bend. In yours, it is the Devil:—which certainly makes a little difference!" and here he broke into a great laugh.

"Yes," I rejoined, "a difference *toto cælo*," whereat he laughed again: and told me he had already ordered a check to be sent me for the poem.

This by the way has not yet arrived

I called on our dear old Judge Herring on Monday. He seemed better than when I saw him last year, and was as genial and merry as possible. He made many loving inquiries anent thee, and the babies, and Father and Harry. Miss Mary joined in these; and seemed really joyful at learning that it was my hope at some time to bring thee and all of us back to live in New York. The Judge is really better, I learned from her, than for a long time past. The sweet old gentlewoman! How I love these stately people: and how they dwarf the flippant new people!

[110] Excerpt previously published, Morgan Callaway, Jr., ed., *Select Poems of Sidney Lanier* (New York, 1895), pp. 69-70.

Well! Thou art a Rose open all the year round; in this present climate of my life, there fall frosts of bitter disappointment pretty nearly every day: but they touch thee not, there thou art always, warm, red, heartsome, lovely, a divine Constancy of Love and Hope and Greatness, breathing the wide air full of heavenly solaces to thy

lover.

To Mary Day Lanier [111]

[Brooklyn,] Sep. (no, no) Oct. 2nd 74.

A letter from father just recd advises me he has renewed the note for sixty days, as I desired: whereby I have another lease of life; and whereof I straightway write thee that thy mind may not be troubled in my behalf.

I have just had a very cordial and friendly call from Milton Northrop, of Syracuse, who is here for a day or two with his wife.

On Tuesday I went, by invitation, to Pasqual's rooms to play flute quartetts. They made me take the 1st part: and placed before me a terribly difficult quartette of Walckier's, which I had never seen before. I cd. never tell thee how beautiful it was: such long-drawn chords with sweet thoughts in them like flowers hid in green leaves. I went through it in a great ecstasy, without a break: when we finished Pasqual cried out to me, "Well, Sir, you are the best sight reader I ever saw: Haslam would have broken down at every second bar." Thou wdst. be pleased to know how greatly I have improved in this particular, by a little practice in it, which I have just had for the first time in my life. During the last two weeks Latham has been coming twice a week to my room, and playing for an hour old-fashioned duos which I never saw before. This has set me up greatly in reading. Last night, Mad. Arozarena gave a little *musicale* in order that Dr- Crane, an amateur flutist of Brooklyn — might hear me play. He brought a lot of music, wholly new to me, for me to play; and, although embarrassed at playing at sight before so many people, and with an accom-

---

[111] Previously published, *Scribner's*, XXV, 747 (June, 1899); reprinted, *Letters* (New York, 1899), p. 102.

panyist who was also reading at sight, I went through in grand style amidst such showers of applause and of compliments as quite reddened my face.

My throat is much better. The weather is like winter: it is too cold, but the brace of it is like fire in my veins.

—— And thou art a Fire in my soul; a holy Blaze of passion, wherein burn forever, yet are never consumed, all the hopes and thoughts and substances of thy

lover——

FROM WILLIAM D. HOWELLS TO M. M. HURD [112]

EDITORIAL OFFICE OF
THE ATLANTIC MONTHLY

The Riverside Press,
    Cambridge, Mass.

Oct. 3, 1874.

Dear Mr. Hurd:

    With the greatest wish to like Mr. Lanier's poem, I am sorry to say that I don't find it successful. The reader would be mystified as to its purpose and meaning; and would hardly know how or why to connect the final bit of narrative with the preceding apostrophes. Neither is striking enough to stand alone.

Perhaps you'll be kind enough to show this note to Mr. Lanier, whom I should be glad to count among our contributors. His worst danger is a vein of mysticism running through all he writes.

yours ever

W. D. Howells.

[112] Howells's letter declining " Corn " for the *Atlantic Monthly* was forwarded by Hurd, to whom it was addressed, to Lanier. The effect the letter had on Lanier is recounted by him in a letter to Edward Spencer, Apr. 1, 1875, and is referred to again two years later in a letter to Bayard Taylor, Feb. 25, 1877. The hurt was apparently so great that Lanier could not bring himself to mention it to his wife. Howells had earlier rejected " June Dreams, in January " and had apparently rejected " My Two Springs " when it was submitted to him in Apr., 1874, by Ronald MacDonald, through Hurd. Later he rejected some sonnets and " The Bee." (See A. H. Starke, " William Dean Howells and Sidney Lanier," *American Literature*, III, 79-82, Mar., 1931. For Lanier's letters to Hurd, Sept. 24 and Oct. 7, 1874, discovered too late for inclusion here, see Appendix A, vol. X of the present edition.)

To Mary Day Lanier

[Brooklyn,] Oct. 7th 1874.

Thou wdst. never dream that I have *still* no news to tell thee: but so it is, and I am as bare of interesting novelties as any *Modiste* late in the season. I cannot get any answer from the Gazette. in Baltimore: and every thing else is *in statu quo.*

I sent my account to Hoge, of Atlanta, a lawyer and friend of mine, to collect of the Atlanta Herald.[113] I feel completely outraged at not hearing from them. I hope thou wilt have twenty-five dollars from Macon, by the time this reaches thee. I am invited to meet Mrs. Wysham and Miss Isabel at the house of Mr. Chase in 17th St. on Thursday night.

My Heart, thy letters are so dear ! I think God surely was thinking of me when He fashioned thee.

I have not told thee, I think, that Mr. Cornell was at Ryder's House, at Tarrytown a few days ago, and having told Mr.-Rider [114] that he had met me in New York, the same went off into convulsions of affectionate inquiries about thee, and *Mrs.* Rider even compelled Mrs. Cornell to read Tiger Lilies, – a thing which Mr. Cornell should not have allowed save across his dead body. Seriously, they sent a thousand messages of remembrance and love to thee: and Cornell says Mr. Rider descanted upon thee in most extravagant terms.

I joy to hear that my fine Charley waxeth ruddy in the face and big in the legs: and sorrow to learn of Mrs. Gray's low state of health. What a ministering angel must thou not be to this poor upward-struggling soul !

Thy French cards are so exquisite, I scream over them.

Dost thou not like my *Laus Mariæ* ?[115] 'Tis the only thing I

---

[113] E. F. Hoge was the classmate with whom Lanier had shared First Honor at the Oglethorpe Commencement, July, 1860. On Oct. 8, 1874, he wrote in reply to Lanier's letter (not found): " Col Alston and Henry Grady knew nothing of the Poem till it appeared in print. Col Avery caused it to be published and avers that he did so in utter ignorance of the fact that any price whatever had been put upon it." (See also note 72, above.)

[114] Mary Day Lanier had been a pupil at the Rev. G. J. Rider's school at Poughkeepsie, N. Y., in 1860-1861 (see Appendix B (7), vol. X).

[115] The name originally given to the sonnet sequence, " In Absence " (I, 42) ; later reserved for one particular sonnet (see note 134, below).

have ever done for thee that satisfies me. They leave me almost content. How many of them there will be, I know not.

God distil thee some heavenly draught out of the over-flowing love and praises of thy

lover.

To Logan E. Bleckley [116]

195 Dean St.,
Brooklyn, N. Y.
Oct. 9th, 1874.

My dear Sir:

I could never tell you how sincerely grateful I am to you, and shall always be, for a few words you spoke to me recently.

Such encouragement would have been pleasant at *any* time; but this happened to come just at a critical moment when, although I had succeeded in making up my mind finally and decisively as to my own career, I was yet faint from a desperate struggle with certain untoward circumstances which it would not become me to detail.

Did you ever lie, for a whole day, after being wounded, — and then have water brought you? If so, you will know how your words came to me.

I enclose Ms. of a poem in which I have endeavored to carry some very prosaic matters up to a loftier plane. I have been struck with alarm, in seeing the numbers of deserted old home-steads and gullied hills in the older counties of Georgia; and, though they are dreadfully commonplace, I have thought they are surely mournful enough to be poetic.

Please give me your judgment on my effort, *without re-*

---

[116] Excerpt previously published, with Bleckley's reply of Oct. 14, Morgan Callaway, Jr., ed., *Select Poems of Sidney Lanier* (New York, 1895), pp. 60-61; in full, Mims, pp. 153-154. Logan Edwin Bleckley (1827-1907), an Atlanta attorney, was appointed the following year (1875) associate justice of the Supreme Court of Georgia, where he was to have a distinguished career cul-minating in a long term as Chief Justice. His contemporary reputation was based as much on his unconventional personality and engaging literary style (displayed in poems and essays) as on the unusual quality of his judicial decisions. Lanier had apparently met him in the summer of 1874.

serve; [117] for if you should say you do not like it, the only effect on me will be to make me write one that you *do* like.

Address me as at head of this letter: and believe me always

Your friend

Sidney Lanier.

To Clifford A. Lanier

195 Dean St.,
Brooklyn, N.Y
Oct. 14th 1874.

My dear Brother:

Your poem "The Power Of Prayer" is accepted by Scribner's Magazine. Dr. Holland (Editor Scribner's) thought it "as well done as it could be." I did not feel the right, exactly, to a half-interest in the poem: but your solicitation to me to father it was so earnest, —and our two names look so brotherly in print!—that I signed it "Sidney and

[117] On Oct. 14, 1874, Bleckley wrote Lanier a long letter containing many detailed criticisms of "Corn," some of which Lanier followed in his revision. In conclusion he said:

"Now for the general impression which your Ode has made upon me. It presents four pictures; three of them landscapes, and one a portrait. You paint the Woods, the Cornfield, and a worn out hill. These are the landscapes. The portrait is a likeness of an anxious, unthrifty Cottonplanter, who always spends his crop before he has planted it, borrows on heavy interest to carry himself over from year to year, wears out his land, meets at last with utter ruin, and migrates to the West. Your second landscape is turned into a Vegetable person, and you give its portrait with many touches of marvel and mystery in Vegetable life.

"Your third landscape takes for an instant the form and tragic state of King Lear; you thus make it seize on our sympathies as if it were a real person; and you then restore it to the inanimate, and contemplate its possible beneficence in the distant future.

"As an Artist you seem to be Italian in the first two pictures, and Flemish in the latter two. In your Italian vein you paint with the utmost delicacy and finish. The drawing is scrupulously correct, and the colors soft and harmonious. When you paint in Flemish, you are clear and strong, but sometimes hard. There is less idealization – more of the realistic element: your *solids* predominate over your *fluids*.

"On the whole you give me very decided satisfaction, and I shall always read you with avidity. . . . I think no writer not safely sheltered among the *dead* poets can show finer lines than some of these. . . . I have faith in you as a true Poet." (This encouragement apparently went far in restoring Lanier's confidence.)

Clifford Lanier." I do not know when it will appear: the
Magazines usually buy a long way ahead, of their issues, particularly in the article of poetry.[118]

A squib by me appears in the October number (just out)
of The Southern Magazine, called " PEACE." Browne has
written me a very pleasant letter about it, and I hope it will
make you laugh.

Latham has made me a good offer for the four flute-pieces
I had brought with me; and I hope soon to see them in print.
His publishing arrangements are temporarily disjointed, but
he is every day expecting to get to work again.

I am to see Messrs. Hurd & Houghton tomorrow about
" Corn." I am going to make a neat little book of it, – somewhat like Carleton's " Betsy and I are out ", issued by Harpers—
and sell it by subscription at about seventy five cents a copy. I
am sure of selling at least as many copies as " Tiger-Lilies "
sold, viz. 800: wh. wd. net me about three hundred and fifty
dollars. I think however that the Granger agitation wd. sell
at least a thousand more.[119]

I want some help, dear Clifford. I'm living so far from the
chief places I have to go to, that at least one-half of every
working day is taken from me. For example, it takes me an
hour and a half to go to 14th St. New York; wh. not only con-
sumes my time but tires me so, and exposes me so much to the
weather, that I often cannot do it at all, and so must let opportunities fly wh. are of the utmost value. I know, for instance,
some of the great musicians of New York; with the slightest
chance of prosecuting my acquaintance with them, I could in a
month or two take rank among the very foremost of them, –
(for, you know all professions have ins and outs, and in New
York this is particularly the case: one must have the crust
broken for him by some of the *Ins*, or he will remain forever
out, if he were Beethoven & Wagner in one): but I live so far

---

[118] It did not appear until the following May (see note 61, above). For the
essay mentioned in the following paragraph, see note 93, above.

[119] Will Carleton (1845-1892) had first published " Betsy and I Are Out " in
Harper's Weekly; included in his *Farm Ballads* (1873), it sold over 40,000
copies.

The " Granger agitation," which Lanier hoped would promote the sale of his
" Corn," is a reference to the activities of the National Grange of Patrons of
Husbandry, which reached a peak in 1874-1876.

that we cannot go to see each other, and it takes me months to accomplish what I cd. otherwise do in a few days. As it is, my compositions have made a splendid impression on some of the foremost musicians of New York: but you know that in this remorseless whirl, one must follow up closely every advantage gained, or one is whirled out and must do all one's work over.

Again, my long flute, in which I take a great deal of interest, (for I'll never rest until I lead an Orchestra with twenty flutes sitting opposite twenty violins) has come to a dead stop for want of a little money to put the finishing touches on. The keys are all made; but my funds gave out just as a couple of long levers were to be constructed, which completed it.

Now, if I could get a hundred dollars in hand, I would feel authorized to move over into 14th St. and board there: – wh. I can do for about 12 or 13 dollars a week: cd. have my long flute finished immediately: could get some winter things, of wh. I'm greatly in need, the weather here being now dreadfully cold: and carry out some other arrangements, –wh. I won't detail for my sword-arm is giving out. Can't you manage to borrow a hundred, or a hundred and fifty, on some time, say six months? I hope to get home for a little while in November and to make a couple of hundred there with a concert: after which I trust the receipts from " Corn " will be coming in.

I have made many applications to the country papers; but they all with one accord say they cannot afford it. Only the papers in large cities ever pay for letters. I have a letter pending with the Baltimore Gazette: they seem inclined to make an arrangement for a correspondent here, but I don't know how it will turn out.[120] Mr McDonald (Aunt Helen's husband, one of the " Times " staff) is only waiting for me to come over into town in order to finish with me (he doing the writing, and I dictating) the Flute Method I have designed. The only method for the Bœhm Flute now published in this Country is wretchedly imperfect; yet about 500 copies of it have been sold, at $7.50. Mine will be sold at only $2.50 and will be complete in every particular.

---

[120] Lanier wrote two brief notices for the Baltimore *Gazette* (see notes 11 and 33, 1875), but never achieved a regular position as correspondent.

No trace has been found of Lanier's " Flute Method," mentioned in the next sentence.

If I only had my sweet Scribe, here! To carry about such a load of unwritten music and unsung songs as are in my heart, and to be only able to scratch one down occasionally, with laborious lung-hindrances, –is almost intolerable.

Pray write me, as soon as you can, if you can borrow the $150 at six months, or even four.

Send my "Peace" in Southern Magazine to dear Little Sissa, – who laughed over it greatly, when I read her the Mss. some year or so ago.

Kiss Will, and all my dear ones, for

Your brother

S. L.

To Mary Day Lanier [121]

[Brooklyn,] Sunday. Oct. 18th 1874

I have been in my room all day: and have just concluded a half-dozen delicious hours, during which I have been devouring, with a hungry ferocity of rapture wh. I know not how to express, "The Life of Robert Schumann", by his pupil, Von Wasielewski. This pupil, I am sure, did not fully comprehend his great master. I think the key to Schumann's whole character, with all its labyrinthine and often disappointing peculiarities, is this: that he had no mode of self-expression, or I shd. rather say, of self-expansion, besides the musical mode. This may seem a strange remark to make of him who was the founder and prolific editor of a great Musical Journal, and who perhaps exceeded any musician of his time in general culture. But I do not mean that he was confined to music for self-expression, though indeed the sort of critical writing which Schumann did so much of, is not at all like poetry in its tranquillizing and satisfying effects upon the soul of the writer.

What I do mean is that his sympathies were not *big* enough, he did not go through the awful struggle of genius, and lash and storm and beat about until his soul was grown large enough to embrace the whole of life and the All of things, that

[121] Previously published, *Scribner's*, XXV, 747-748 (June, 1899); reprinted, *Letters* (New York, 1899), pp. 103-105.

is, large enough to appreciate (if even without understanding) the magnificent Designs of God, and tall enough to stand in the trough of the awful cross-waves of circumstance and look over their heights along the whole sea of God's manifold acts, and deep enough to admit the Peace that passeth understanding. This is, indeed, the fault of all German culture, and the weakness of all German genius. A great Artist should have the sensibility and expressive genius of Schumann, the calm grandeur of Lee, and the human breadth of Shakespeare, all in one. Now in this particular – of being open, unprejudiced, and unenvious, – Schumann soars far above his brother Germans: he valiantly defended our dear Chopin, and other young musicians who were struggling to make head against the abominable pettiness of German prejudice. But, withal, I can not find that his life was great, as a whole: I cannot see him caring for his land, for the poor, for religion, for humanity: he was always a restless soul: and the ceaseless wear of incompleteness finally killed, as a maniac, him whom a broader Love might have kept alive as a glorious artist to this day.

The truth is, the world does not require enough at the hands of genius. Under the special plea of greater sensibilities, and of consequent greater temptations, it excuses its gifted ones, and even sometimes makes " a law of their weakness ". But this is wrong: the sensibility of genius is just as much greater to *high* emotions, as to low ones: and whilst it subjects to stronger temptations, it at the same time interposes — if it *will* — stronger considerations for resistance.

These are scarcely fair things to be saying *apropos* of Robert Schumann: for I do not think he was ever guilty of any excesses of genius, – as they are called: I only mean them to apply to the *unrest* of his life.

— And yet, for all I have said, how his music does burn in my soul ! It stretches me upon the very rack of delight: I know no musician that fills me so full of heavenly anguish, and if I had to give up all the writers of music save one, my one should be Robert Schumann.

— Some of his experiences cover some of my own as aptly as one-half of an oyster-shell does the other half. Once he went to Vienna, – that gay New York of Austria –; and writes back to his Sister Theresa: " . . . . So my plans have as yet progressed but little.   The city is so large that one needs double time for everything ----- -But to tell you a secret, I shouldn't like to live here long, and *alone*: serious men and Saxons are seldom wanted or understood here. ----- In vain do I look for musicians: that is musicians who not only play passably well upon one or two instruments, but who are cultivated men, and understand Shakespeare and Jean Paul ----. I might relate all this at full length.   But I don't know how the days fly, here; I've been here three months today: and the post-time, four O'clock, is always just at hand. ------ Clara goes the 1st of January to Paris, and probably to London later.   We shall then be far apart.   Sometimes I feel as if I could not bear it.   But you know the reason: she wants to make money, of which we are indeed in need.   May the good God guard her, the good faithful girl ! "

— And herewith, dear Lady, thou lovely and constant-hearted Wife, mine eyes are dim with love and solicitude for thee, and I can not see to write more than that I pray Almighty God for thy sake to send some great Angel of happy Result to alight on the labor of thy

lover.

To Mary Day Lanier

[Brooklyn,] Oct. 21st 1874.

All things move on, dear Heart, in their customary channels, and I have no news to tell thee.

I do not now think at all of getting into any Orchestra here: for the very good reason that there is really no Orchestra to get into.   Thomas' is the only one in New York, (except the Theatre Orchestras, which of course would not suit me for many reasons) and he had imported a flutist from Russia to fill his only vacancy, some three months before I came here.   I have made several attempts to get permanent employment, but without success.   I have several plans however, in process of negotiation from which I hope something will arise finally.

I continue to improve.   The weather hath been lovely beyond description, and I think I would have given a year of ordinary life for an hour's walk with thee under the tender skies of this last week. Will not some day come when thou and I will see all this beauty together ?

When wilt thou return to Brunswick, dear Love? I have some dim idea of making a flying trip home in early November. But I only hope it as yet; since it dependeth on other events. I will tomorrow see that thou art provided with wherewithal to make thy move whenever thou desirest.

I have not time now to write more. When all else seemeth hell, thy love remaineth pure Heaven to thy

lover.——

To Mary Day Lanier [122]

[Brooklyn,] Oct. 23rd 1874.

My poor Heart, hast thou suffered for thy undervests in this nipping air? They start to thee tomorrow: not having been sent before for reasons wh. thou shalt know some other time.

Thy letter telling of my little Prince's happy birth-day hath come, and giveth me infinite pleasure. What would I not give, to see him cut a caper!

I pray thee do not be sorrowful on account of *me*, in the matter of the disappointments which thy wifely heart hath divined. It is true, they have come; but they have been of great value to me. I will make to thee a little confession of faith; telling thee, My dearer Self, in words, what I do not say to my not-so-dear self, except in more modest feelings.

Know then that disappointments were inevitable, and will still come until I have fought the battle which every great Artist has had to fight since time began. This, – dimly felt while I was doubtful of my own vocation and powers – , is clear as the sun to me, now that I *know*, through the fieriest tests of life, that I am, in soul, and shall be, in life and in utterance, a great poet. The philosophy of my disappointments is: that there is here so much *cleverness* standing betwixt me and the public. The " Readers " of the publishing-houses, the editors of the magazines, are quick to discover cleverness in writing, for it is an article in which they have dealt all their

[122] Previously published, W. H. Ward, " Memorial," *Poems* (New York, 1884), pp. xxii-xxiii.

lives, they know it as well as Mr. Stewart [123] knows silk from
woollen. But works of Art are quite out of their line (as they
would say, in their abominable trade-dialect), they are incredu-
lous of genius, the keenest of them can recall bitter mistakes
in this behalf. Dost thou remember " The Galaxy " and Walt
Whitman ? [124] Or – for further example – read in the November Scribner's wh. I will send thee, the poem " Mildred in the
Library ", from Dr. Holland's (the editor's) new book. This
poem is merely a clever piece of joinery; it is put together, as is
the whole book from which it is taken. But its author believes
it to be a great work: and he is one of the very best of the
Magazine-editors, besides being, as I gather from some little
personal interviews I have had with him, a man of unusual
generosity, warmth of heart, and goodness. Now, as I said,
there is absolutely no method by which an Artist can get to the
people, save through these men: except by money, which I
have not: and therefore I know, and am adequately prepared
for, all the disappointments that await—not *me*, but thee,
dear, loving Heart, in my behalf. If I were like Bret Harte, or
Mark Twain, and the others of this class of wonderfully clever
writers, my path would be easy: but what would I give for
such success? I can not dream any fate more terrible to me,
than to have climbed to their niche, – the ledge where Lowell,
and Holmes, and that ilk, rest – and to find *that* my highest
and ultimatum. If I had such success in my hand, I would
throw it out of the window, and live a quiet life. And I am
sure, withal, that none of these writers has had a warmer
admirer, or a keener enjoyer, than me.

[123] The proprietor of a large department store in New York.

[124] The reference is not entirely clear, but Lanier's implication must be that
the *Galaxy's* mistake consisted not in failing to recognize Whitman but in treating him as a genius. C. J. Furness (letter to the present editor, July 26, 1943)
says of the relations between Whitman and the *Galaxy*: " I find only the
friendliest testimony in all records," the most significant of which he lists as
follows. It was in this magazine that the first long article by John Burroughs
about Whitman was published in Dec., 1866, and two essays by Whitman:
" Democracy " in Dec., 1867, and " Personalism " in May, 1868. (See also
Clara Barrus, *Whitman and Burroughs, Comrades*, Boston, 1931, pp. 43, 48-53,
56, 80, 87, 133-135, 159.) Whitman himself testified to Traubel: " The GALAXY
was hospitable to me " and commented on the editors " opening their doors " to
his work (Horace Traubel, *With Walt Whitman in Camden*, Boston, 1906-
1914, III, 454-455). Lanier's own conversion to Whitman's importance as a
poet did not come until nearly four years later when, apparently, he read him
seriously for the first time (see Lanier's letter to Whitman, May 5, 1878).

Richard Wagner is sixty years old and over, – and one-half of the most cultivated Artists of the most cultivated art-land, *quoad* music, still think him an absurdity! Says Schumann, in one of his letters to a friend: " The publishers will not listen to me for a moment." And dost thou not remember Schubert, and Richter and John Keats, and a sweet host more?

Now, this is written because I sit here in my room daily and picture *thee* picturing *me* worn, and troubled, and disheartened: and because I do not wish thee to think up any groundless sorrow in thy soul. Of course, I have my keen sorrows, momentarily more keen than I would like anyone to know: but I thank God that in a knowledge of Him and of myself which cometh to me daily in fresh revelations, I have a steadfast firmament of blue in which all clouds soon dissolve. I have wanted to say this to thee several time of late: but it is not easy to bring oneself to talk so of oneself, even to one's sweeter self.

Have then, dear Wife, no fears nor anxieties in my behalf: look upon all my " disappointments " as mere witnesses that art has no enemy so unrelenting as cleverness; and as rough weather that seasons timber. It is of little consequence whether *I* fail; the " I " in the matter is a small business; *Que mon nom soit flétri, que La France soit libre!* quoth Danton: which is to say, interpreted by my environment: let my name perish, – the poetry is good poetry and the music is good music, and beauty dieth not, and the heart that needs it will find it.

I pray thee burn this. It is meant for thine eye alone: and is writ, for thy comfort, by thy

true-lover.

To Mary Day Lanier

[Brooklyn,] Oct. 25th 1874.

And now, having dispatched a host of unanswered ghosts who have been uneasily standing on my table " waiting for a reply ", – I spring to thee.

The wild animal that hath gnawed through the cruel boy's trap, and leapeth out towards his sweet woods, – he knoweth the desperate delight with which I come to thee-ward.

In obedience to thy strait command, I send thee Hoge's letter anent the Herald's reply to my " claim." I have written him not to sue, though of course I could recover at law. Tis a small business: not worth thinking of.

I am trying to get a hotel here, for Clifford: of wh. say thou naught. He thinketh that if the State-election goeth against the decent people, there will be little prospect for the Exchange: tho' I suppose he would still retain the management of that and engineer both institutions. I learn that The United States Hotel, corner of Fulton and Pearl streets, might be leased. It is a good old hotel, depending on much the same sort of custom as the Astor House, and is now very poorly kept. I think Clifford could make money there: and will run over in the morning to see about it. I heard of it only last night. How charming would it be for dear Father to be there, just in the scenes of his boyhood! [125] If I cd. but tell thee what lovely dreams I have anent thy being in New York with me ! To us two together this wd. be fairy land. I feel so sure of its some day happening. Do not connect these with the hotel project, though: save that of course we wd. be there a great deal.

I have a charming long letter from Col. Bleckley, of Atlanta, to whom I sent a copy of " Corn ". His criticisms are wonderfully minute, and penetrating : and his praises judicious and weighty. I have recast the whole poem ; have added much to it, simplified the opening – which was too labyrinthine – and removed several crudities which did not satisfy me.

I charge thee to like my sonnets beyond measure. These are only the beginning of a great series in which I hope to set out the true relations of man and wife. I sent the first two to Hayne . He did not like them: thinking them " over ripe " in tone, and " too *luscious* in suggestion." [126]   So ! Is it then

---

[125] Sterling Lanier had been proprietor of a hotel in New York for a brief period during R. S. Lanier's boyhood.

[126] On Oct. 10, 1874, replying to a lost letter by Lanier of Oct. 3, Paul Hayne had written: " I have read your *Sonnets* very *attentively. Parts*, I *like well*; but frankly, the *general effect* does not impress me pleasantly. A certain exaggeration of tone, & imagery; an over-lushness, & over-ripeness, (so to speak) of sentiment–, *ultra* Tropical, somewhat clog one with sweets. . . . Drop the *Sonnet, my boy*, (*it don't pay*), and compose more pieces like your glorious ' *Corn.*' " A MS with Hayne's annotations survives (Charles D. Lanier Collec-

wrong for a man to long for the kiss of his own wife; is it
lusciousness to compare the unremitting joys of heaven to an
eternal kiss upon the never-withdrawn lips of one's Mate ? –
Doth not the holy writer, when seeking the type of highest
union and purest intermingling, call the Church the Bride Of
Christ ? Is that lascivious ? – How little the impure heart
knoweth of purity, and how fearfully men err about this matter
of love !

I send thee Scribner's.

Goodnight, thou who by faithful love hast made thyself ever
with increasing passion the eternal Bride of thy

husband.

To Mary Day Lanier

[Brooklyn,] Oct. 28th 1874.

Dear loving Soul that thou art, I rejoice thou hast had a
little holiday, and I desire thee to take more of them.[127]

Do not write my Father yet about stopping in Macon. There
is just a possibility I may meet thee there – in Macon – and
stay a week. A letter is come from Hammerik begging me to
take my old place again at The Peabody; and I may get a
teachers place which my faithful Cockey is going to vacate at
Christmas; [128] which together with a permanent engagement on
the Southern Magazine wd. enable me to contribute my share
to the Brunswick establishment during the winter, and still
leave me time to write some of the poetry and music with wh.
my heart is bursting.

Life seems so rich to me, My Child. These late hot fires
have set the gold a-running out of my deepest quartz. An I
get not hold of a scribe ere long, I shall actually sweat poetry.

Thy package of undervests went to-thee-ward by Express on
Monday last. I have shopped in vain for the lutestring ribbon.

---

tion, Johns Hopkins University) containing two sonnets, entitled " Laus Mariæ,"
being early versions of the first two sonnets later published as " In Absence."
(See also Lanier's letter of Feb. 7, 1875, below.)

[127] Mary Day Lanier's letter of Oct. 24, 1874, tells of a day she spent in
Atlanta at the State Fair.

[128] See note 35, above.

I cannot find either the quality, nor anything near the size: What shall I do? As for Mad. Julie,[129] she shoppeth not: she goeth about to be a mother, near Xmas time.

I cannot write more now. God keep thee in good heart, dear Moll, fervently prayeth thine

husband

To Mary Day Lanier [130]

[Brooklyn,] Oct. 29th 1874.

Today I played for the great Dr. Dammrosch: – and won him. I sang the Wind-Song to him. When I finished he came and shook my hand, and said it was done like an Artist: that it was wonderful, in view of my education: and that he was greatly astonished and pleased with the poetry of the piece and the enthusiasm of its rendering. He then closed the door on his next pupil, and kept him waiting in the front parlor a half hour, while giving me a long talk. I had told him that I wished to pursue music. He said: "Do you know what that means? It means a great deal of work, it means a thousand sacrifices. It is very hazardous."

I replied, I knew all that: but it was not a matter of mere preference, it was a spiritual necessity, I must be a musician, I could not help it.

This seemed to please him: and he went on to speak as no other musician here *cd*. speak, of many things. He is the only poet among the craft here: and is a thoroughly cultivated man, in all particulars. He offered to do all that he could, in my behalf: and was altogether the gentleman and the wise artist.

Thou wilt share with me the pleasure I take in thinking that I have never yet failed to win favor with an artist. Although I am far more independent of praise than formerly, and can do without it perfectly well: yet, when it comes, I keenly enjoy it: particularly from one who is the friend of Liszt, of Von Bulow, and of Wagner.

[129] Julia Dutcher (Mrs. Horace Ripley).
[130] Previously published, *Scribner's*, XXV, 748-749 (June, 1899); reprinted, *Letters* (New York, 1899), pp. 105-106. (For Dr. Leopold Damrosch, see note 92, above.)

Moreover I played abominably: being both tired, weakened by the warm weather, and excited.

I am pleased that Hammerik shd. have so cordially invited me back to my old place: and anticipate a winter in Baltimore full of substantial work. I find I need Thorough-Bass sorely: and am studying it with might and main.

Dear Heart, thou art an ever-present solace to me. I have often to ride for an hour and a half at a time in the cars; then I sit still, and bury myself in dreams of thy love and loveliness, wondering how unerringly thou hast pointed my long-doubtful way, how faithfully thou hast endured the long trial of illness, of the commonplace, of repression, of poverty; – and presently I am at the journey's end. I am very well in all particulars save languor from the warm weather.

Tomorrow I think to go and look up thy Mr. Reese, and fetch him here to dinner. 'Tis the first day I have had time to do it: and I have to put off another engagement to accomplish it.

May God be in thy dreams this night like a generous sun in a blue heaven, — prayeth thy

lover.

To Mary Day Lanier

[Brooklyn,] Nov. 1st 1874.

Art thou not the sweetest little Frenchman that ever breathed? Thy brief French notes are as if violets exhaled in that language.

Thou hast a genius in letters quite beyond that of any letter-writer, living or dead. Thine are pure and worthy and altogether unconscious works of art: not gossipy like De Sevigne's, not smart like Mary Montague's, not stiff like Chesterfield's, not heartless like Prosper Merimèe's, but with the virtues of all these thrown in one, and the sweet whole suffused with the subtle light of thine own wifehood, motherhood, womanhood. Surely, if thou mightst see the measure of my delight in these thy blessings, thou wdst. feel some sense of pleasant achievement, in reward for the sweet faithful remembrance of my needs wh. in the midst of thy thousand cares so often carrieth thee to thy desk in my behalf.

I dare not say anything positive as to my trip home: tho' I really feel almost certain that I shall go. It is likely I will know by the end of next week. My God, – to see thee again !

Clifford has the fever again – of printing things– and is going to send me his " Two Hundred Bales " [181] to engineer. It will have to be rewritten, I am sure: it is full of good things but they are not put together in the way to take the popularity-worshipping publishers.

I have a letter from Wysham, which informs me it is likely he will also play in the Peabody Orchestra. I am lost in wonder how he will dispose of *Mrs.* Wysham. H. will needs send her out of town: for she would think nothing of marching down the aisle in the middle of a symphony and snatching his flute out of his hands. Wh.–, now that I think of it, – probably he *has* done, – I mean, sent her out of town: for I hear he has rented his house. Mrs. W. may still be at the Grand Hotel in New York: where she was staying some weeks ago. I have been quite unable to call, for lack of either time or strength.

I have the *Libretto* of Wagner's great " Trilogy ", and am going to try to make a contract for translating it during the winter. It is a book of more than four hundred pages.[182]

– No, in truth, the Sonnets are *not* finished. I intend to take my time about them, as about my *magnum opus*.

That I may some day write something worth thy beauty, ——— fervently prayeth thy

lover.

---

[181] A Reconstruction novel begun in 1868 and apparently completed in 1871 (see the following letter and note 23, 1868). It was published posthumously under the title: *Carpet-baggery* (Montgomery, Ala., 1939). The MS has survived in the possession of Clifford Lanier's daughter Wilhelmina (Mrs. John Tilley) of Montgomery.

[182] Lanier's letters of Nov. 8 and Nov. 11, 1874, below, indicate that he proceeded as far as making sample translations of *Das Reingold*. In his surviving copy of J. C. Oehlschläger's *German English and English German Pocket-Dictionary* (Phila., 1872) there are translations of some forty lines of the libretto of this opera, faintly pencilled on the back fly-leaves. Nothing further is known of this project, which apparently did not materialize.

To Clifford A. Lanier

195 Dean St.
Brooklyn, N. Y.
Nov. 2nd 1874.

My dear Clifford:

Yr. novel is just arrived, and I have fallen-to at reading it.

I find that it must be greatly altered: and am going to take all manner of liberties with it in cutting out some things and changing others. Its fault is only that of every young writer of talent: *i. e.* a waste of raw material in redundancy of figurative expressions. Sometimes I find that these detract from the interest of the story, by interrupting it unduly: and – with yr. permission – I shall mercilessly excise a great many of them. I think perhaps I can sell it to Browne, of The Southern Magazine, to be published serially. I should call it " The Carpet-Baggers." If Browne is otherwise supplied, there are a couple of weekly papers in Baltimore to one of which I might dispose of it. I doubt any success with Bonner: [133] he is hedged in by a certain wall of people difficult to penetrate: and, besides, this is not the sort of thing called a Ledger story, and is worth a far better fate than that–The action is a little slow at the beginning, and I think to hasten it materially there. It is not until after one gets a name that one can indulge in these details in the beginning of a book.

I have received a letter from Mr. Hammerik, Director of the Peabody Conservatory at Baltimore, inviting me in very cordial terms to return and take my old seat in the Orchestra. I think it likely I shall do so; as, although the pay is small, it is still a substratum, and my last winter's experience will make the work a great deal lighter to me. – Your kindly and gentle advice to me, to endeavor to find some permanent occupation, made me smile. My dear little Boy, –if you only knew the applications, the letters, the traps, I've made, written, and laid, to get work! — Within the limited range of employments wh. my unfortunate disabilities render feasible, I've made as

---

[133] Robert Bonner (1824-1899), editor of the New York *Ledger.*

many variations of endeavors as Beethoven made on the Waltz of Diabelli: –and, for all that most of them have been as curiously unsuccessful as if some special imp had been set to untune every note I made, still I think some music will come out of them yet.

Scribner's has accepted a sonnet by me:[134] – but I don't know when it will be out. I've just rec^d a paper from home, –The Telegraph & Messenger, – with my " Civil Rights " copied from the Atlanta Herald. The rascals have put my name to it, – when I expressly instructed the Herald *not* to do so. Not that I'm ashamed of it all, –but May is still in the country and I did not want the negroes to have any ground for twisting me into an enemy.[135]

I have delayed acknowledging yr. letter containing the check for $100, – for wh. I cannot at all thank you as I desire– because I was " on track" of a hotel for you, and wished to write of both at once. I have made several attempts to see the owners, but they have been out of town. They are to return on Wednesday, when I hope to get some information from headquarters. The hotel is " The United States," at the corner of Fulton & Pearl Sts: a house with an old reputation, and at which several fortunes have been made. It is now very inefficiently kept; but I am advised by some friends who boarded in it for years, that if it were at all well cared for, it could be quickly made exceedingly profitable. Why cd. you not keep both the Exchange and this?

I will write you more of it when I see the owner.

Kiss Aunt Jane for me and tell her that I do not write simply because it is out of my power.

Your novel is full of good things. How I wish we might be together for a few weeks! I cd. show you so many methods

---

[134] Presumably " Laus Mariæ " (I, 44), published in *Scribner's*, Nov., 1875. Since it is referred to in the following letter as " No. III of the Sonnets," it was apparently composed as part of the " In Absence " sequence, the whole of which had originally been named " Laus Mariæ " (see Lanier's letter of Oct. 7, 1874, and note 115, above). A musical composition bearing this same name has survived in MS (Charles D. Lanier Collection, Johns Hopkins University).

[135] Charles Sumner's " Supplementary Civil Rights Bill," though not passed until Mar., 1875, was being agitated throughout 1874; the South considered it as tantamount to conferring social equality on the negro, and riotings occurred in protest. Lanier's poem " Civil Rights " (see note 72, above) was a denunciation of the pending bill.

of making its points more telling, and of generally improving its form. You need practice in writing, so as to see *the effect on the reader*, just as the painter gets a little distance *away* from his work, and sees how it will look from there. One has to learn to write at this little *distance from one's work*: for there is a perspective in writing as in painting, and the proportions of things vary in a way wh. can only be caught artistically after a great many studies, a great many failures, and a great deal of patient work. *You* wd. require less than most writers: but all require much.

God bless you, dear Boy, I never lose hope that He will some day bring us at least within yearly reach of each other.

My love to Sissa & Will, and Aunt Lucy & Aunt Jane, and all,

S.L.

To Mary Day Lanier

[Brooklyn,] Nov. 3rd 1874.

I look to see thee in print ere long. Scribner's has accepted No. III of the Sonnets: tho' when it will come out, I know not. It pleaseth me to think that thou wilt make thy first appearance in this daintiest of all the world's Magazines.

The Macon Telegraph has been sent me, containing a copy of " Civil Rights," with my name blazoned in full at the head thereof: as also the Savannah " Sun," this latter with a marked editorial notice, comparing the poem to the " Heathen Chinee," —wh. it is *not* like at all.[136]

I am awaiting with some impatience letters from Baltimore, whose contents will quite determine my movements both with respect to that place and Macon. Prof. [J. H.] Rosewald—

---

[136] " The Heathen Chinee," by Bret Harte—first published in the *Overland Monthly*, Sept., 1870, as " Plain Language from Truthful James "—was a dialect poem dealing with the " Pike County " type of poor-white, resembling Lanier's poem in these two characteristics only. In 1871, Harte's *East and West Poems* and John Hay's *Pike County Ballads* had initiated this new genre and given it national popularity. The evidence is not entirely clear, but Lanier seems to have hit upon this same literary type independently in his first dialect poems, at about the same time or shortly before the appearance of these volumes. The first evidence of his acquaintance with the writings of Bret Harte is in his letter of Oct. 23, 1874, above. (No file of the Savannah *Sun* has been found).

formerly Concert-Meister of the Peabody Orchestra (*i.e.* leader of the violins) is getting up four Symphony Concerts there on a grand scale. I have written him today, to know if he wants a first flute. If he does, that will give me employment until the 2nd of January, when the Peabody season opens. In that event, I should start for home *within* ten days from now: and might take thee up at Marietta, if thou wert there. Do not therefore make any final plans for two or three days, I pray thee: in which time I hope to have written thee something definite.

Thine of 29th is come. Thou givest me quite too much praise; yet it is sweet, being fresh out of thy loving heart. Of course thou canst do what thou willest with my letter.

I have had a bad cold for three days, wh. by vigorous treatment is now growing better. The dust here is almost intolerable: and on Saturday came a fierce smiting of cold wind, wh. in combination with the pulverulent horror wrought grief upon many a proud nose. Mine ran quickly into that low state wh. regards the whole Universe as made of mucus. I had also a villainous sore-throat by way of baker's-dozen. But I straightway constructed me a swab, and swabed with Iodine & Glycerine; and I gargled with Chlor. Potassa: and I absorbed Gelseminum in the day-time, and either Bromide of Potassium or a hot Jamaica Rum toddy at night: keeping myself strictly indoors withal: so that I now see the Universe in a less viscid consistency, and shall be running about tomorrow.

— And now God ferry thee softly over this night to the fair silver shore of the morning, prayeth thy

lover.

To Edmund C. Stedman [137]

195 Dean St.
Brooklyn, N. Y.
Nov. 5th 1874.

Dear Sir:

May I beg that you will appoint some hour, – of any day next week, – when I may call and present a letter of introduction from Dr. J. G. Holland ?

[137] Stedman's reply of Nov. 6, 1874, naming hours when he could be found **at**

Pray allow me to say, in explanation, that I desire to see you specially, and that my engagements oblige me to economise time.

Very respectfully

Sidney Lanier

E. C. Steadman Esq
New York.

To Mary Day Lanier

195 Dean St.
Brooklyn, N. Y.
Nov. 6th 1874

Heart of my Soul, I have but a few minutes in wh. to breathe thee a little prayer and blessing; and to tell thee that I have written and finally accepted the place of first flute in the Peabody Orchestra, at the enormous *stipendium* of $20 per week, wh. is $5 a week more than last year. The season does not commence until Jany 2nd, but:—just here it comes to my ass's-brain that I told thee all this in my last letter!

Therefore I will pass on to say briefly that I wish to meet thee in Marietta on the 18th of this month, if God be willing,—and O God, be willing!

Will this suit thee? If thou desirest to go earlier, do so, and I will call for thee at Sunnyside, and take thee on to Macon where I desire thou shdst. spend a little time with me.

If any changes shd. occur in my plans, thou shalt know in ample time through telegram which I will send to Nathan Munroe to be forwarded thee immediately.

Write me all thou desirest hereanent.

There is no news. I wait to hear from several little ventures. I wrote some time ago to have seventy-five dollars sent thee. I hope it has arrived.

God keep thee bright-eyed, dear, dear Wife, crieth thine

husband.

his home and at his office, indicates that a meeting probably took place at this time. But the first positive evidence of their acquaintance is in the following autumn.

To Mary Day Lanier [138]

[Brooklyn,] Nov. 8th 1874.

My poor long-suffering Sweet, hast thou again been nursing the sick? And my generous Hal, my darling Big-Soul, – was he so very ill? I am glad that thy letter and card, – the one announcing his sickness and the other his recovery, – came together, else should I have been most anxious in the interim. I will take pains to find some method of expressing my gratitude to thy good Mrs. Gray: whom I hope to see ere long, when I come.

I have spent the whole Sunday in my room, in reading, with slow labor, – for my German is but limited – Wagner's "Rhein-Gold", – the first part of his great Trilogy, or rather Tetralogy, for it has four parts – which I am going to translate unless some happy mortal gets ahead of me. The conception is very fine: – but, there is a something in it, or rather a something *not* in it, which I detest in everything that any German has yet done in the way of music or poetry. I know [not] exactly what to call it, or indeed how to define it. It is that (if I may express it in a very roundabout way) sentiment lying deep in the heart of the author which wd. produce on his face a quiet wise smile all the while he was writing, – a sort of consciousness underlying all his earthly enthusiasms (wh. are not at all weakened thereby), that God has charge, that the world is in His hands, that any bitterness is therefore small and unworthy of a poet. This was David's frame of mind: it was also Shakespeare's. No German has approached it, except perhaps Richter.

Have I written thee what glory and sweetness is in Shakespeare's sonnets? I long infinitely to read them with thee. They have been my food and my daily care-destroyers for two months past.

Ere long I will see thee. The *moving* trouble wh. thy poor overworked heart wd. have had to engineer, will be naught to me.

[138] Previously published, *Scribner's*, XXV, 749 (June, 1899); reprinted, *Letters* (New York, 1899), pp. 106-107. "Hal," mentioned in the opening paragraph, was Lanier's son.

God support thee on His broad power, as it were a drooping violet on its leaf, – prayeth thy

lover.

To Mary Day Lanier

[Brooklyn,] Nov. 11th 1874.

There is one thing, My dear Heart, wh. makes me mainly sorry for thee: it is, that thou canst never, never know how lovely thou art. Thou art ever too far off from thyself to see thyself at all. Inasmuch as all the beautiful things which I see do make me long inexpressibly for thee,—with what an unspeakably-double passion of longing-within-longing must I yearn, when I not only long for thee in thy sweet self, but also long for my dear wife to know thee with me in thy capacity as being the most beautiful thing I have ever seen!

As the time draweth near for me to see thee, I dare not think upon the intolerable moments which must pass ere mine eyes behold the dear miracle of thy face: I keep myself at desperate work.

I have been to see Holt, the publisher, and found him altogether the best specimen of that genus I have yet encountered. He is disposed to entertain my proposition to translate Wagner's *libretto*, and desires me to send him samples of my work: wh. I am now engaged in preparing.

Browne was pleased with the Hayne review, and has accepted it for the Southern Magazine. It will likely come out in January.[189]

I notice that the "Georgia Musical Eclectic" ("Eclectic" in this connection always means *thief*) reports me as having "accepted a position in Theo. Thomas Orchestra."

---

[189] Printed in the *Southern Magazine*, Jan., 1875, as "Paul H. Hayne's Poetry" (V, 322). In his letter of acceptance, Oct. 23, 1874, W. H. Browne wrote: "Your genial criticism of Hayne so stirred up my sympathies that I seized Legends & Lyrics and read all the best pieces over. Hayne has great tenderness and delicacy, and often rare beauty of expression: what he lacks (entre nous) is strength. He rarely lets fly a thought that strikes to the heart like an arrow, or sticks in the memory like a fish-hook."

No file has been located of the *Georgia Musical Eclectic* mentioned in the following paragraph.

Dear Heart, I can't do it—my heart will break for love of thee if I do not get it appeased with some distraction, I will to my Wagner, Good-night, Thou for whom, and to whom, arise perpetual prayers from thy

husband.

To LOGAN E. BLECKLEY [140]

195 Dean St.
Brooklyn, N. Y.
Nov. 15th 1874.

My dear Sir:

I did not know any method of showing you my thorough appreciation of your criticism on my " Corn " better than sending you a printed copy of the poem thoroughly amended & revised so as to avoid nearly all the flaws which you found in it; & I delayed answering your kind & valued letter in the hope of being able to do so.

But things go slowly here in Babylon, – with all the hurry & bustle: & I have not yet made such arrangements for publication as I wish.

My idea is first to get it printed in a magazine of influence, & then to issue it in the form of a small book. I have your cry of jubilation,[141] & it makes my heart light up all manner of torches.   The War is over.

What a fight it has been! We had to grip religious fanaticism & frantic patriotism for four years & rascality for ten.

If there are any other three Devils that are harder to wrestle with than these, they have not yet made their appearance in terrene history.   I have been wondering where we are going to get a *Great* Man that will be tall enough to see — over the

---

[140] Excerpt previously published under the title " A Great Man Wanted," *Acorn* (Towson, Md., ed. Edwin L. Turnbull), II, 1 (June, 1887); reprinted, *Critic*, VII, 309 (June 18, 1887), and elsewhere. Given more fully in Morgan Callaway, Jr., ed., *Select Poems of Sidney Lanier* (New York, 1895), pp. xlvi and 65, and nearly complete in Starke, pp. 195-196.

[141] Bleckley's letter here referred to has not been found. Apparently, from the echoes in Lanier's letter, it reflected the growing optimism in the South that Reconstruction was coming to an end. Popular risings had added Arkansas and Alabama to the southern states in which the Democrats had ousted the carpet-bag governments and regained control during 1874.

whole country, & to direct that vast un-doing of things which has got to be accomplished in a few years.

It is a situation in which mere cleverness will not begin to work. The horizon of cleverness is too limited, it does not embrace enough of the heart of man, to enable a merely clever politician – such as those in which we abound — to lead matters properly in this juncture. The vast generosities which whirl a small revenge out of the way as the winds whirl a leaf; the awful integrities which will pay a debt twice rather than allow the faintest flicker of suspicion about it; the splendid indignations which are also tender compassions, & which will in one moment be hurling the money-changers out of The Temple, & in the next be preaching Love to them from the steps of it:— where are we to find these? It is time for a man to arise, who is a man.

If you write me in the next three weeks — & I am sure you *would* if you knew what a genuine pleasure your letters are to me — direct to me at Macon.

After that I shall be in Baltimore, where I am again invited to play first flute in the orchestra of the Peabody Conservatory of Music; I shall spend the rest of the winter there.

Your encouraging words give me at once strength & pleasure. I hope hard, & work hard to do something worthy of them some day.

My head & my heart are both so full of poems which the dreadful struggle for bread does not give me time to put on paper, — that I am often driven to headache & heartache purely for want of an hour or two to hold a pen. I manage to get a little time tho' to work on what is to be my first *Magnum Opus*, — a long poem, founded on that strange uprising in the middle of the 14th Century in France, called " The Jacquerie." It was the first time that the big hungers of *the People* appear in our modern civilization: & it is full of significance.

The peasants learned — from the merchant-potentates of Flanders – that a man who could not be a lord by birth, might be one by wealth: & so Trade arose & overthrew Chivalry. Trade has now had possession of the civilized world for four hundred years; it controls all things, it interprets the Bible, it guides our national & almost all our individual life with its maxims; & its oppressions upon the moral existence of man have come to be ten thousand times more grievous than the worst tyrannies of the Feudal System ever were. Thus in the reversals of time, it is *now* the *gentleman* who must arise & overthrow Trade. That chivalry which every man has, in some degree, in his heart; which does not depend upon birth but which is a revelation from God of justice, of fair dealings, of scorn of mean advantage; which contemns the selling of stock which one *knows* is going to fall, to a man who *believes* it is going to rise, as much as it would contemn any other form of rascality or of injustice, or of meanness;– it is this which must in these latter days organize its insurrections & burn up every one of the cunning moral castles from which Trade sends out its forays upon the conscience of modern Society. — This is about the plan which is to run through my book: though I conceal it under the form of a pure novel.[142]

I must beg you to pardon such a long sermon: it is not writ with malice prepense only you seem to be an earnest man, & I know so few of them to whom one can talk of such things.

Your friend

Sidney Lanier.

Hon. L. E. Bleckley
Atlanta, Ga.

To Mary Day Lanier

[Brooklyn,] Nov. 16th 1874.

O Heart, ere three days be past, this hand that now writeth thee out of the solitude where thou art not, will be in thine own very hand, and these eyes that now see nought but a dream-of-thee will see thee.

Of whatever will bring me soonest to be kneeling at thy dear worshipful feet, – may the loving Almighty God have charge, prayeth thy

husband.

[142] " The Jacquerie," which Lanier described elsewhere as a novel in verse, was never completed (I, 171).

To Robert S. Lanier

Sunnyside, [Ga.,] Nov. 21st 1874

My dear Father:

Mary and I arrived here last night and found our little ones pretty well. Mary met me in Marietta, and we spent the night as guests of our friends the Earles, who seemed not able to do enough to show their kindness towards us. In the morning our friend Little, (The State Geologist) who had already been twice to Marietta for the purpose of seeing me, came by on his way back to his camp in Bartow County: but seeing Mary and me at the depot he jumped off the train, and carried us to Atlanta, where we spent a charming day at his house.

We are now in the midst of packing, here. You will be invaded by the Goths and Vandals on Monday next; we reach Macon some time in the late afternoon, — I do not know the exact hour, – leaving here at 3½ P.M. We will get off at St. Paul's, and I will thank you to engage a drayman to meet us there; also to get Uncle Mose Elder, with his one horse hack (he is to be found at Dishroon's, over against your Office) to be on hand.

We rejoiced over your letter giving such good news of Uncle C. I write very hastily, being in great business. All join me in great love to you and Mama.

Yr. Son,

S. L.

To Clifford A. Lanier

Macon, Ga. Dec. 1st 1874.

My dear Clifford:

I met May in Marietta some days ago, and brought her and the children to Macon with me.[148] I had formed a resolution to come home somewhat suddenly, – in consequence of financial pressures – which was hastened by

[148] Lanier and his family arrived in Macon on Nov. 23.

Father's writing me that Uncle Clifford was not expected to live, and desiring my presence here very earnestly. I have only about three weeks to spend, being obliged to attend our first rehearsal in Baltimore on the 28th Dec^br. Your letter mentioning a rumor that I was in Thomas' Orchestra was forwarded to me from New York. No, I am first flute of the Peabody Orchestra: – a much better place in many respects. It does not pay quite so much, but it only occupies two hours a day of my time, besides one concert-night in each week: thus leaving me some time to engage in other matters. I hope to get a position now held by a friend of mine, as teacher in a night-school (from seven to nine P. M. each day except Saturdays and Sundays) which augments my salary (eighty dollars a month) by forty dollars a month: and this will still leave me some time to pursue my daily-growing dream of authorship in music and poetry.

Scribner's has accepted another of my poems, a Sonnet: and Lippincott's has accepted my " Corn ": and the Southern Magazine will print next month a somewhat elaborate paper by me on Hayne's Legends & Lyrics. I do not know when the two poems will be out.

Meantime: I'm trying to employ my little *interregnum* in raising some funds: not having yet even paid up my score with our kind Mr. Gray at Sunnyside, for our last month's board. Will you do me the favor to call on the party in charge of the Theatre at Montgomery, and see whether the engagements run thickly for the next fifteen days, – so that I may judge whether it would pay for me to come there and give a Concert ? – And will you also write me immediately what other *Materiel* I could find in Montgomery, to give a Concert *with* ? I expected to arrange one immediately on my arrival in Macon, but found that other engagements of Troupes rendered it impossible for at least ten days yet: and there is such a run of them that I'm not at all sure it would pay, even when I can get the hall: but shall probably try it, for a sort of remedy *lege artis*, – as the Doctors say in a desperate case.

I telegraphed you yesterday for the piano part of Faust: I have the flute part: & want to play it in concert.

Mary went down to Brunswick this morning with the children. It seemed unspeakably cruel for us to part so soon, and still

be so near: – but money considerations were in the way, – and
she is the loveliest Soul in the world.

And so, – leaving the world to go its own dreary financial
way – how glad, my dear Heart, would I be to clasp your
hand ! It seems a long time since I saw you. Kiss fair Will
for me: and all the host of the dear ones. If some wave of
duty may dash me in yr. direction I shall be your happy

Bro.

S. L.

To Mary Day Lanier

[Macon, Ga., Dec. 3, 1874?] [144]

Thy silver-cup is as it shd. be: and the " di-ders " have been
conveyed to Ellen: and Mama and I are going to the Harmonics tonight: and tomorrow-night I am to play Faust at
Ralston's Hall, having received the same from Clifford, minus
one page: and I have written Cliff. anent the Montgomery
Concert: and my Father is gone to Griffin to try a case: and I
am in sole charge of the office, and have now to draw a mortgage and other papers from the Hebrew Congregation " Kohal,
Kadosh Beth Israel " to The Loan Association, surveying their
Synagogue with all its members and appurtenances thereunto
belonging or in any wise appertaining, and I wonder what the
Loan Association would do with the Ephod? and I have but
time to do the same before night, and to say that I am thy
faithful loving and longing

husband.

[144] Conjectural dating of this and the following letter from the evidence of
Mary Day Lanier's letters of Dec. 1 and 2, 1874, to which these are answers.
Hers of Dec. 2 makes it clear that the entertainment at Ralston Hall in which
Lanier was to play a selection from *Faust* was scheduled for Friday, Dec. 4;
the present letter mentions it as " tomorrow-night," the following letter as
" tonight."

The allusions in the opening sentence of this letter are clarified by Mary
Day Lanier's letter of Dec. 1, en route to Brunswick, in which she wrote that
she had left her silver cup in Macon, and some of the children's diapers to be
taken to the laundress.

To Mary Day Lanier

[Macon, Ga., Dec. 4, 1874?]

I would I might have been by thee through that enchanted day, and we might have together walked through the Cedars to the water. I can dream how unspeakable was the sweet open sunshiny Calm down there: and I was adoring thee all day.

My father remaineth in Griffin. Last night Mama and I sate out the Harmonic Concert, wh. was not very interesting though we enjoyed seeing the people.

The entertainment at which I was to play tonight is [postponed?] on account of the death of a relative of one of the main performers – Jamison, whose Cousin was killed in Bibb County some days ago.

I have just had a long talk with Ogden about a concert here. He is very much afraid it wd. not pay: says the Once-a-month of the Harmonics, with their weekly rehearsals, has rather surfeited the Macon people, and adds that Nillson herself could not fill the house now. Nevertheless, I will try it, if I can get any material.—

I enclose Clifford's letter, anent the Concert there. It is possible I may run over to Montgomery on Monday or Tuesday.

I note all thou sayest anent thy visit here: and will write thee more definitely on that topic soon. I will be sure to come to Brunswick: so be not anxious thereanent.

Uncle Clifford rode out for an hour, nearly, yesterday. This morning he is complaining of a sleepless night.

I know no brighter wish for thee than to wish that thou might'st be as happy as, if he were by thee or within eye-reach, wd. be thy

husband

To Mary Day Lanier

[Macon, Ga.,] Dec. 8th 1874.

Thy daily cries come to me with the sweetness of invitations into Paradise and with the power of commands out of Heaven. Keep crying thus, – and ere long thou wilt be heard above the stars, and we will be together.

I did not get off last night for Montgomery. Father was compelled to be at Wilkinson Court today, and I could not well leave the office unprotected. A paper just recd from Clifford announces a Reading by Mrs. Goodwin, *tonight*, at the theatre, for the benefit of the Good Templars; wh. I suppose effectually puts a quietus upon my project. But I will run over anyhow tonight, and be back to kiss thee here on Saturday night. I learn that the return train from Montgomery this way comes in day time, reaching here about 7.30 P.M.

I will try to send the x x x today, and a x x x brought in thereamongst, x x x [145]

So: hast thou thy " sad failures " in daily life? Thou wert needs, – as all of us must – pray God every day when thou risest up and when thou liest down, for a light heart in the surety of His love, and for a wise brain in the direct enlightenment of His unforgotten and unobserved Presence. Being human, thou wilt fall myriads of times, as do we all; but being rare-sweet and large-in-soul and passionate-hearted for all that is warm and charitable and beautiful, thou wilt each time rise again and strive again.

How I long for thee ! As the one half of the earth clingeth to the other half to make a perfect globe, so fast to thee clingeth thy

lover.

---

[145] Several words have been deleted from the MS at this point.

To Clifford A. Lanier

Macon, Dec. 17th '74.

My Darling Little Boy:

My brief and happy dream with you came to a sad end on reaching Macon, where I learned that my dear life-long friend Gussie [Lamar] Ogden had just died, under peculiarly distressing circumstances. She had been expecting confinement: and, had been ill with bronchitis some days, but was thought to be better, and was sitting on her sofa, after having walked into her room from the tea-table. She was then taken with a sudden faintness, and died in ten minutes, before all of her family even could reach her. She and her child were buried on Friday. There is no describing the peculiarly tender relations which have existed between her and me ever since I was a boy, and I feel her loss inexpressibly.

May met me here on Saturday night, and we are trying to look at each other enough to last us through the long months that will part us soon. I give a concert here on Wednesday night next,[146] and will leave for Baltimore on Christmas day, being obliged to get there on the 27th. Tomorrow I run down to Brunswick to kiss the babies and cheer up poor Hal who is very drooping; – returning here on Monday.

How gratefully I think of my dear willowy Wilsie! She grows more like the tube-rose that I likened her to, in a certain poem I wot of: [147] and her tender and graceful cares of me while I was with you have sunken full deep into my heart. I

[146] Lanier's concert at Harmonic Hall, Macon, on Wednesday, Dec. 23, 1874, according to the Macon *Telegraph and Messenger* of Dec. 20, was given "to accumulate a fund to defray the expenses of . . . some extensive experiments, designed to apply a modern acoustical invention to the purpose of greatly enlarging the powers and resources of the flute and all similar wind instruments." In the issue of Dec. 23, 1874, the program was printed under the heading "Flute Fund Concert." Lanier was listed for the following pieces: *Sounds from Home*, a duo for flute and zither, played with Mr. A. Huber; *The Singer and the Nightingale*, a song by Miss Carrie Boifeuillet with flute obligato; *Canta d'Amore*, a song by Mrs. Cora Hunter with flute obligato; *Happy Birdling*, a song by Miss Jessie Hardeman with flute obligato; and *Fantasie on Airs from Faust*. The tickets were sold at $1.00.

[147] The reference is to a poem Lanier had written in 1866, "To Willie Clopton" (I, 158).

pray God to bless you both as much as I love you. Kiss Auntie
for me, and all the balance of the good people.

Bro.

Sid.

To Mary Day Lanier

[Macon, Ga., Dec. 24, 1874?]

It is quite worth while, dear Wife, to go through adversity,
if only to see for once in a lifetime, so exquisite a picture as
was thy face today.[148] Such elevation of soul, such an outburst-
ing of the sweet lights that dwell in thy heart, I have not ever
seen before, and I walk about in a maze of admiring warmth
and loving exultation, companioned by the clear radiance of
thy remembered last smile.

According to promise I write thee that the concert cleared,
over all expenses, – which were much heavier than I thought –
sixteen dollars and twenty cents: whereof I turned over fifteen
dollars to the faithful and still headachy Bukowitz.[149]

Thou will be glad to know that I send to-day by express
balance due Mr. Gray: and that I am also enabled to pay off
another debt whose existence (thou knowest it not) had given
me great pain.

I also send to Brawner & Co, at Griffin, $10.50, amt due them
for the Organ, which cleareth up our record hereabout.

Tis now late and I must run and see Mrs. Wallen: when I
have a thousand matters to look after before night.

God water and shine on the sweet flower of thy bravery, dear
Love, prayeth thy

Lover.

[148] Mary Day Lanier, who had joined her husband in Macon on Dec. 12,
returned to Brunswick Dec. 24; Lanier left Macon for Baltimore the next day.

[149] Professor J. R. Bukowitz, a local piano teacher who assisted with the
concert.

To Mary Day Lanier

Bristol, Tennessee
Dec. 26th 1874.

Thy little heavenly note came to me through Little. He met me at the cars in Atlanta and had me forth quickly towards his house, where I ate a merry dinner. His present residence being some distance from the depot, I only had time to dine, and hurry back, so could not get any chance at all to write thee. I wrote thee from Macon.

Thine absence at the Littles' table was often and much lamented by them; – and I – was at point of death for thy bright holy face. No, I have no heartaches at all. How can I? I have thee: and I have done my best: – thus my heart, at rest from itself, and lit by thee-light, is full calm and full happy.

— Here have we missed connection, and I must spend the balance of the day. But I hurry this off for the mail.

God be ever about thy heart and thy hand, for thine inward and outward fashioning, prayeth thy   lover.

To Mary Day Lanier [150]

64 Centre St.
Bo.
Dec. 29th [28th?] 1874.

O my dear Soul, Hast thou not felt somewhat falling upon thee for three days, as it were a gentle rain out of a perfumed sky; being indeed the multitudinous loves and yearnings which my heart hath showered to-thee-ward, in that time?

I am come back so entirely into my last winter's life, here, that I find it doubly difficult to persuade myself that I have not had a long delicious night's dream of thee, until I look deeply

[150] The date has been corrected from the evidence of the following letter and from Lanier's previous statement that the first Peabody Orchestra rehearsal was scheduled for Dec. 28 (see his letter to Clifford Lanier, Dec. 1, 1874). Lanier had returned to his previous lodgings at the home of the Misses Mary Ann and "Tina" Young.

into my heart and find there how much stronger I am in soul
by reason of thy very presence and of the teachings I have
drawn from the actual sight of thy great love.

We had our first rehearsal today, and my heart was quite won
with the vigorous hand-shakes and cordial greetings of my old
comrades.

Hammerik was particularly graceful and courteous in his
salutations, and I felt quite like one who had come to his own,
as I took my old chair in Erste Flöte's place. Wysham is playing second flute: and had quite a jubilation over our reunion
as he took his seat on my right.

But my hands were cold, and my heart in a flame, immediately. We played first Gluck's *Iphigenia in Tauris* Overture:
I had played in it before, and so had no distraction from the
heavenly ideas of the great genius who wrote it. It is pure
marmoreal music: it is a keen-white, naked statue of Greek
pain, cut in music.

My faithful Cockey has called and had a talk: and Wysham
has just left me, after playing some of our wonderful Kuhlau
duos. His tone and execution are much improved, and I
wished greatly that thou mightst hear us breathe forth some of
poor old Kuhlau's melodious heart-aches.

I find my room here charmingly fitted up, and the ladies are
wonderfully kind and homelike.

My journey, though tiresome, was a real physical rest, and I
have been bright as a lark all day, with an appetite astounding
to behold. I wish for thee at every mouthfull of the plain,
substantial, well-cooked, un-larded food. I can almost feel it
imparting new life and strength as I swallow it.

Kiss my dear old Cubbie [151] for me: tell him Little spoke
of him in the most affectionate terms the other day and longed
to see him.

I will write him in a day or two.

—   Over the nest that holds thee and my darlings, forever
flutter like unwearied wings, the prayers of thy

husband.

[151] Harry Day.

To Mary Day Lanier

64 Centre St. [Baltimore]
Dec. 29th 1874.

Today again we played the " Iphigenie " Overture, and its crystalline marble grief was set in my heart like a statue in a shrine.

And if thou cdst. but hear the " Nordische Suite ", by Hamerik, (our Director) with me. The first movement " Im Walde " (" In the woods ") is just that famous day of thine and mine at Mrs. Fulton's, done into music. It is so beautiful that the mere physical trituration of the tones against the eardrum becomes distinctly delicious, and goes near to make one scream with delight.

Heart of my Soul, how I dote on the memory of thy heavenly eyes, and the smooth fall of the last kiss thou waftedst to me as thou faredst out of sight around the curve. Thou art surely the loveliest lover that ever hath been: who in all the world hath loved like thee?

I grieve to learn from Cubbee's letter that Charley (*Uncle* Charley)[152] is not well, and that my poor little Harry is stuffed with cold again. Write me of Charley's goat: and if the boys had a fine Xmas.

Now can I not say more than my little prayer that God's blessing in thy heart may be as fair as thine own sparkle in thine eye when thou last lookedst upon

lover.

To Mary Day Lanier

[Baltimore,] Dec. 30th 1874.

So, thou hast had to be nurse, and to do some more waiting, for thy Xmas? My poor little boys! And my poor Sweet! My heart is so full of all of you, that I can with difficulty bring

---

[152] Charles Taliaferro, brother of the late Janie Lamar Day. He had been spending Christmas in Brunswick (see Mary Day Lanier's letter of Dec. 27, 1874).

myself to my work: and, what with loves and loving solicitudes and the agitations of daily music, I am persuaded that my soul casts upon the screen of each day a figure much like that of a vibrating prong of one of Tyndall's big tuning-forks.

— I have not any news to tell thee. I have made no calls yet, and seen no one but the musicians. After rehearsal I have dined,– at three; then here have come Wysham, and one Stobbe, and we have played Kuhlau's trios for an hour: then Mr. Winterbotham, a very remarkable young pianist, called: then tea, then my letters, of which this to thee is the last: and now I must get me to the " Physics of Music." [153]

Kiss thy good Father and Cubbee and Charley for me: and herewith, dear Moll, thou Sweet Violet that the wind hath whirled up and lodged in the beard of Adversity,—May God find thee warmer harborage, prayeth thy

husband.

[153] This essay was written as a reply to a current magazine article, but was not published until after Lanier's death (II, 251).

1875

To Mary Day Lanier [1]

[Baltimore,] Jan 1st. 1875.

A thousand fold Happy New Year to thee, Sweetheart: and I would that thy whole year may be as full of sweetness, as my heart is full of thee!

— All day I dwell with my dear ones there with thee. I do so long for one hearty romp with my boys again. Kiss them most fervently for me, and say over their heads my New Year's prayer that whether God may color their lives bright or black, they may continually grow in a large and hardy manhood, compounded of strength and love.

Let us try and teach them, dear Wife, that it is only the small soul that ever cherishes bitterness; for the climate of a large and loving heart is too warm for that frigid plant. Let us lead them to love everything in the world, above the world, and under the world, *adequately*: that is the sum and substance of a perfect life.

And so God's divine rest be upon every head under the roof that covers thine this night, – prayeth thy

husband.

To Mary Day Lanier [2]

[Baltimore,] Jany, 3rd 1875

Doth not this enclosed programme show a feast of glory? And how we did play it! We were forty four in Orchestra: and we all played as if our souls' welfare hung on each note. How *can I* tell thee the Heaven of it, to me?

---

[1] Previously published, Mims, p. 308.

[2] Excerpt previously published, *Scribner's*, XXV, 749 (June, 1899); reprinted, *Letters* (New York, 1899), pp. 107-108.

A surviving circular (Charles D. Lanier Collection, Johns Hopkins Univer-

Then after the Concert, Mr. Sutro [3] and his wife invited Hamerik, [Emil] Seifert (Leader of the violins, just from Berlin) Wysham, & myself to take Champagne with them at their rooms: where we sat until far into the morning, talking music. My playing is greatly improved: and my flute now fits upon the Oboe like the down upon a peach.

My head is all full of my " gnat-dance " [4] which I am going to turn into a symphony, for orchestra with flute *obligato*. If I but were by thy sweet side, that we might write it together: dost thou remember those exquisite days last summer?

— So the whole *posse* of you have failed to work the lantern? –Directions for using: Hang up a white sheet next the wall so that it will present a smooth surface: having filled the lamp with oil (*not* kerosene, of course), light the wick, put out all the other lights in the room (– the figures will only show at night,) set the lamp in its place in the lantern, and close up the lantern so that the room will be quite dark; then, holding the lantern at such a distance from the screen that the light shining through the lens forms a large disc thereon, push one of the glass plates containing the figures endwise through the slide, so that the figures will come in succession between the light and the lens. [5]

I have not seen thy books, and they are not among my traps.

Now God close thee up, dear Sweet, this night, in some sphere of strong music where no dissonant harm can enter, prayeth thy

husband.

sity) gives the programs and dates for the eight Symphony Concerts and four Chamber Concerts that comprised the Peabody Orchestra season for 1875, on successive Saturday nights from Jan. 2 to Mar. 20.

[3] Otto Sutro (1833-1896), proprietor of the leading music store in Baltimore, was the founder of the Wednesday Club, which grew out of informal gatherings at his rooms beginning in the winter of 1858, and of the Oratorio Society of Baltimore.

[4] A fragmentary orchestration of Lanier's " Danse des Moucherons " survives in the Charles D. Lanier Collection, Johns Hopkins University, entitled " Gnats." (See also note 34, 1874.)

[5] In her letter of Dec. 27, 1874, Mary Day Lanier had written for instructions in using the " Magic Lantern "; and to ask if Lanier had taken with him her " infant Speller, Arithmetic and French book " (referred to in the following sentence), with which she was attempting to instruct their oldest son Charles.

To Laura N. Boykin [6]

64 Centre St.
Baltimore, Md.
Jan'y. 3rd, 1875

My dear Friend:

I intended to call and thank you in person for your exquisite flowers; but was compelled to leave Macon early on Christmas morning, in order to meet my engagement here, and so could not possibly find time, in midst of many delayed preparations for departure, to carry out my wish in this regard. Your kindness however was so particularly grateful to me on that funereal night,[7] that I cannot resist the temptation to send you this brief note, which shall bear to you my sincere acknowledgement of your thoughtfulness.

– Last night we played the enclosed programme, in magnificent style. The success of our Orchestra last year has induced the Trustees to enlarge the resources of it; we are now forty-four good men and true; and I wish you could hear one of our fff's ! Did you ever see, – could you imagine – a more beautiful selection of music than appears on this Programme?

Pray convey my regards to all your family, and believe me always

Your friend

Sidney Lanier

To Mary Day Lanier [8]

[Baltimore,] *Jany 6th 1875.*

Tis simply marvellous how full my days are, and yet how little of actual work-result I can see when each one is finished. I know, however, that much of the time has gone in a thousand

---

[6] Previously published, Macon *Telegraph*, Feb. 4, 1932. For the identity of Mrs. Boykin, see note 47, 1874.

[7] The reference is to Lanier's "Flute Fund" Concert in Macon on Dec. 23, 1874 (see note 146, 1874).

[8] Excerpt previously published, *Scribner's*, XXV, 749 (June, 1899) ; reprinted, *Letters* (New York, 1899), p. 108.

little domestic arrangements incident to settling into my room, negotiating with washerwomen &c. These are now pretty well finished.

Here is just come a fair long home-letter from that sweet saint Cubbie; for whose tender and thoughtful words I pray thee render him my hearty thanks.

I had a talk today with Mr– [Philip R.] Uhler, Librarian of the Peabody. He tells me that there is a full set of apparatus for the physics of music lectures now at the Institute; and that they are not even unpacked ! I have the strongest hope of being able to accomplish my project anent the establishment of such a chair in connection with the Conservatory. I am working hard at all the books I can find in the Library on the subject: and I am going over in a few moments to spend the balance of the evening there.

Yesterday Harry Wysham brought me two reserved seats for Ernani, at The Opera House where The Kellogg Troupe are playing: so I sallied forth and took Mrs. Bird, and we had a merry frolic of it, the little lady going into ecstasies over the handsome tenor, and winding up all with wine and a late supper at her house. Thou wdst. love this good soul cdst. thou see her genuine cordiality to me.

And now Good-Night, Little Maydie: and may God make small the number of nights when this must be written, rather than spoken, to thee by thy

lover.

Pray regard the silly zigzag-ness of this letter as purely accidental: for so it is.[9]

To Mary Day Lanier [10]

[Baltimore,] Jany 9th 1875.

Are there any Forms into which I can mould the love's-yearning for thee, wh. for these three days hath had complete mastery of me? Nothing satisfies me: I cannot write my heart

---

[9] Lanier's postscript was meant to allay any fear on the part of his wife that his right lung and arm were paining him.

[10] Excerpt previously published, Scribner's, XXV, 749-750 (June, 1899); reprinted, Letters (New York, 1899), p. 108.

into a sonnet, my flute's breath is too cold; neither music nor
sweet words bring me comfort: I am all at unrest, I cannot
work quietly. If I could but have one sight of thy true eyes, if
I could but kiss thy hand once ! I lack thee, My soul works as
it were with the left hand when I am away from thee, I am
yet too fresh from thee to have grown used to this sinister-
dextrous labor. If I cd. only tell thee how absolute-sweet thou
art, I might gain a little ease: but alas, thou thyself art the
only thing in the world that is as sweet as thyself, and thine
own sweetness is the only sweetness in the world to which I
have ever found thy heart insensitive.

Our second concert comes off tonight, and we are to play
such beautiful music as makes my heart tremble even to think
of. First comes Beethoven, second Symphony: one written
before the dreadful deafness had come upon his ears and
pierced into his heart. The whole three movements are ravishing melodies from beginning to end: and the Second Movement, a Larghetto, is as if the wind-instruments and strings
were having a game of Hide-and-Seek in Heaven. Then Mad.
De Ryther, a lady in form and manner and stage-appearance
much like our dear departed Gussie, is to sing, with a glorious
Contralto voice, a noble aria from Handel's little-known opera
Rinaldo. Then we play Bernhard Scholz's Overture *Im Freien*
(" In the free Air "), an exquisite embodiment of tender sky,
of birds, of joyful green leaves and lush grasses and brilliant
flowers. Then we have some English Songs by Mad. De
Ryther, and conclude all with Carl Reniecke's lovely Overture
to Calderon's *Dame Kobold.*

I took Isabel Wysham out last night to "Faust" at the
magnificent new Academy of Music: and the notice of the
Opera in today's paper was written by me for Wysham.[11]

I will not get the night-school: there is a failure of funds.
A letter from Mr. [Horace] Ripley apprises me of a fine son

---

[11] A paragraph of 24 lines in the Baltimore *Gazette*, Jan. 9, 1875, p. 2, col.
3-4 (see II, 328).

    In reference to the "night-school," mentioned in the following sentence,
Lanier said in his letter of Jan. 14, 1875 (here omitted): "There was a failure
of funds, and Cockey had to resign in order to save the other incumbent from
losing his place by a discontinuance of the school, the salary only being enough'
for one" (see also note 35, 1874).

("with as much hair on his head as I've got" he says) who
came to Julie Dutcher on New Year's day.

– Now, dear Love, God be thy Dream this night, prayeth
thy

lover.

O, – about *that* goat: I would by all means buy the trained
One! for 'tis a long job to train one, and Charley is almost too
young for it.

To Mary Day Lanier [12]

[Baltimore,] Jany 12th 1875.

I have a nice piano, just arrived, for wh. I pay $ 6. a month.
I found I could not write my Gnat Symphony without it. I am
going [to put?] into the slow movement of the Gnat Symphony
my No. 1 [13] wh. thou didst admire so long ago: taking the
melody first for the flute, then for the violins. The melody
seems fairly ravishing to me.

My article on Hayne is out in the Southern Mag. It does not
cover as much paper as I expected.

I will pray thee to take this hasty kiss. The fury of Creation
is on me today, and I am just going down for some score-paper,
and to mail thee this Caress, – then to the pen.

Hamerik is interested in the project of the Chair of physics, and
will take me to see Mr. Eaton who is chief among the Trustees
in the Conservatory department.[14]

Wert thou but by me, Thou My inspiration, thou my Spirit of
Sweet woods and green leaves, thou that on the hill-side with
thy gray eyes first startled me into the consciousness of of
beholding the flesh-and-blood satisfaction of all the Dreams of
my life : – then were I thy contented as I am now thy most
yearning,

lover.

[12] Previously published, *Scribner's*, XXV, 750 (June, 1899); reprinted,
Letters (New York, 1899), p. 109.

[13] " Song Without Words " (see note 28, 1873).

[14] The department of the Peabody Institute concerned with musical instruction.

To Mary Day Lanier

[Baltimore] Jany 13th 1875.

My heart-brokenly wished-for Heart, thou art in pain and in
midst of many troubles, and I am not by thee; yea, moreover
thou has gone two days without any spirit-of-a-kiss being des-
patched from me to thee ward: yet, thou hast not been a
moment out of my thought: for in meditating out my Gnat-
Symphony I have been again living over the sweet unearthly
glory of being with thee in the woods, under the leaves, by
running water.　Is there not a passionate deliciousness in all my
joyful meetings with thee (wh. is quite beyond all expression,)
arising from the half-mournful intensifying influence of a sense
of the necessary briefness of the same?　Have we not snatched
our meetings, *malgré* the stern opposition of our two fathers, –
thine, Life, mine, Death : whereby we have added to the
already heavenly sweetness of lawful kisses the subtle tang of
stolen ones ? – All this runs through my Symphony, underneath
the more material translations of trees, water, and little winds :
– that is to say, thou, and thou only, art all my music.
———— I wrote thee several days ago, to buy Charley the
trained goat: he will find plenty of work to *keep* him trained.

I have no news: here is my absolute whole heart and soul
in this kiss, which I pray thee, most dear lovely Wife, receive
into thy soul's warmest centre, from thy humble faithful

husband.

To Mary Day Lanier

[Baltimore,] Jany 17th 1875.

Yesterday came a note from Minnie Machen,[15] inviting me
to a state dinner, at 5 O'clock: to which I of course duly went.
The company was pleasant, the wine was good, the feast gorgeous, and the merriment uproarious; but I went through all
in a longing dream of thee, and I did not get my heart free

[15] Mrs. Arthur Machen.

enough from longing to do more than a mere private soldier's duty in the general charge.

My dear Tube Rose, what shall I do to win some way of being with thee? I should think I had battered down God's last objection to my having a little money, and swept away the very débris thereof with secret tears and sorrows that no eye hath seen.

—— I have written to M^r. Jefferson Davis and to Dr. Tucker,[16] for letters of introduction here, which I hope may help me in my Peabody scheme. Hamerik is to call on me tomorrow night, and I will then find out some method of approaching the trustees on the subject. I have spoken of the plan to several persons, who heartily concur in it.

—— Dost thou not feel or hear my heart hanging about the little house there where thou art, dear Love, this night? Upon the wings of a tender and restless solicitude, I fly hither and thither, from thee to my little sleeping sons, and daughter, and from them to dear Father and my sweet old Cubbie:— the fair Rest of God keep all your hearts tranquil this night,— prayeth thy

husband.

To Mary Day Lanier

[Baltimore,] Jany 18th 1875.

So: there is some sign of day, at last : here comes a brave flush in the Eastern sky.

— In this following, wh. is a copy *verb. et. lit* (for I know thou wilt desire to see it, and I must use the original) of a letter received yesterday.

" Office Lippincott's Magazine
&c &c &c.
Philadelphia, Jany 16"/75.

My dear Sir:

Your poem ("Corn") was published in the Feb'y number today, and a check for *fifty* dollars will be sent to you when the accounts are made up next week.

---

[16] H. H. Tucker, Chancellor of the University of Georgia.

Some good judges have already expressed to me their appreciation of the poem, and Mr. Gibson Peacock, editor of the Bulletin, begs me to tell you of his great admiration of it. He goes so far as to call it " the most poetic of American poems." You see I am not afraid of turning your head by repeating such praises. I have only to add that it will give me much pleasure to receive further offerings from your pen.

Very truly Yours

J. F. Kirk

Ed. Lippincott's."

Sydney Lanier Esq.

Dost thou not think this very pretty, dear Comrade ? I have just seen the poem in the Magazine: 'tis much changed, since thou and I wrote it, under the trees: oh, dost thou remember the summer days ? I have been through them again, – as I went through the poem. Midst of this dream comes thine of 15th , with *thy* too-sweet dream of the woods: and so thy soul and mine, proxied by our dreams, as Kings wed by ambassadors, marry till such time as our royal affairs shall permit us to meet in our sovereign proper person.

That God speed the next wedding, thou too-dear Always-Bride, – is the prayer of thy

lover.———

To Mary Day Lanier [17]

[Baltimore,] Jany 20th 1875.

On Monday Night came Hamerik to spend the evening with me. At seven came he: and at two A. M. left he. Such another music-talk have I never had. The fellow is a rare genius ! his music is the most poetic subtlety of tone-combination that could be imagined.

This morning a hasty note came from my friend Mr. [Horace] Ripley, saying that he would pass through today so after rehearsal I rushed out to the depot. As the cars rolled in, he jumped out, & saw me at the other end of the dêpot; at

---

[17] Excerpt previously published, *Scribner's*, XXV, 750 (June, 1899); reprinted, *Letters* (New York, 1899), p. 109.

the same moment I caught sight of him, whereupon we both
took a running start, and caught each other in each other's
arms, and so remained locked in an embrace which must have
been very affecting to the numerous witnesses of the same.
The baby was well, and Julie recovering.

For the first time in my life, I am going to call the attention
of some literary friends to my own work, I've written to
Anderson Reese [18] telling him of " Corn ".

O dear Love, my heart is just one round tear of longing for
thee.

Tomorrow I will send thee thirty dollars, from the Lippincott fifty which is just come.

— This morning I have had a little trouble of the old sort
from. too much writing: and my shoulder is now a little stiff.
The damage is but small though.

Art thou not pleased with Mr. Kirk's letter, a copy of wh. I
sent thee yesterday?

Now, dear Sweet, through this night mayst thou float upon the
Peace of God, as a flower-bell sailing on a river, – prayeth thy

lover .

To Milton H. Northrup [19]

64 Centre Street,
Baltimore, Md.
Jany. 21st 1875.

My dear Northrop:

I have been intending a long time to write
you, particularly in order to say that severe illness prevented
me from enjoying the pleasure of calling on you and Mrs.
Northrop when you were in Brooklyn. I sometimes think I
have more than my share of the downs, and less of the ups.

I send you herewith a copy of Lippincott's Magazine for
February, containing a poem by me. Although only published
a few days, the piece has brought me some charming messages
from people of letters: and I hope you will like it.

[18] Editor of the Macon *Telegraph.*
[19] Previously published, *Lippincott's,* LXXV, 314 (Mar., 1905).

Pray let me have a line, to assure me that you and Mrs. Northrop and the bairn, – to both of whom I beg you to convey my compliments – are well. I shall be at above address until the last of March.

Your friend

Sidney Lanier

To Mary Day Lanier

[Baltimore,] Jany 22nd 1875.

Thou too-beautiful Sweet, thy poem [20] lies in my heart as the blush-spot lies in an opal: wherever I look, I see it, turning the grey into rose.

— I keep it there, just as thou has sent it, for my private delight.

— The desire seized me last night to write something *with* thee: so I melted thy poem with my love, and poured it into my soul, and presently drew it forth again, when I thought that it had absorbed about enough of substance and of form from me, to make it equally mine and thine.

Is it not dainty: and may I send it to some of the magazines with thy name and mine signed thereto?

I sent it up-stairs to Josephine Seaton; here is her note.

An Atlanta Constitution is just come, containing a delightful notice by Col. Bleckley, of my Hayne review. Tell my father to send it to thee. 'Tis the Constitution of the 19th. Comes also – a few moments ago –, a noble and beautiful letter from Paul Hayne, thanking me for what he calls my " wonderful critique ". After writing details, he says: " *Au reste*, that any work of mine should have been made the text for an article so profound in insight, so suggestive, and altogether able as this of yours, must ever yield me a keen delight: " and so on.[21]

[20] Mary Day Lanier had sent her husband a copy, transcribed by herself, of a poem that had appeared in *Appleton's*, Oct. 24, 1874, entitled " Sometime "; Lanier, assuming that it was a poem of her own composition, made a " revised version " of it which survives in MS in the Charles D. Lanier Collection, Johns Hopkins University. (See Mary Day Lanier's letter of Jan. 27, and Lanier's reply of Jan. 31, 1875, below.)

[21] In his letter of Jan. 19, 1875, after lavish praise of the review, Hayne took

Hayne also mentions having just seen " Corn " in Lippincott's, with which he is greatly charmed, and about which he makes very fair prophecies. He is going to review it.

–   I notice by the way that the paper with Col. Bleckley's article is sent me by Sam. Earle, from Marietta: which gives a pleasant coincidence, as it was written under his trees: [22] Ah, thou wast there, also; dost thou remember?——I have dozens of letters to write: and am a little disabled from my trouble: how surely writing brings it on !

Ah, my too-dear Darling – I feel that Sometime is coming, when thou shalt be at once my pen and my inspiration, and I shall be thy contented happy

husband.

To LOGAN E. BLECKLEY

64 Centre St., Baltimore, Md.
Jany. 23rd, 1875.

My dear Sir:

I send you a copy of Lippincott's Magazine for February, on page 216 of which you will find my " Corn."

The poem has had a delightful recognition everywhere, and I have been particularly pleased to find it so cordially taken by the hand among the Northern people, in spite of its being so distinctly Georgian. You will observe that I have only changed it where I thought your criticisms were right: where I thought them wrong I have let it stand so. I hope you will like it.

Some friend has sent me a paper from Atlanta — The Constitution — in which I find marked a communication of yours,

issue with Lanier on one or two points, chiefly the implication that Hayne had been too much influenced by William Morris.

Of " Corn " Hayne said: " It *ought* to make you a name; aye: many a poetic reputation has been founded on single compositions *far far* inferior to this."

[22] The article on Hayne had been put in final form at Marietta in the summer of 1873, when the Laniers boarded at the home of Mr. Earle.

L. E. Bleckley wrote to Lanier, Jan. 17, 1875, supplementing his praise in the *Constitution*: " I declare to you there is no doubt of your ability to write. . . . I do not believe a better Article has appeared, or will appear, this January." A brief notice of Lanier's article on Hayne, signed by Bleckley—presumably the one here referred to—has survived in an unidentified newspaper clipping (Charles D. Lanier Collection, Johns Hopkins University).

over your own signature, calling attention to my review of
Hayne.   I wish I knew some method of conveying to you
my appreciation of so signal a compliment.   I am particularly
pleased with your heartiness and directness.   The best acknowledgement I can make, for your praise, is to tell you that its
effect is twofold upon me: first, it makes me a more humble
and pious artist, by filling me with pure delight at finding that
I am going to be able to pursue an artistic career (which I had
resolved to do, martyrdom to the contrary notwithstanding)
without the necessity of being a martyr, and without having to
fight off bitterness all my life; and secondly, it comes to me
just in that time when the rebuffs (with which I suppose every
young artist must meet) of the world are likely to make my
hand tremble with sheer loss of blood, — it is brandy and a
styptic both at a critical moment.

I write in great haste.   Believe me always your obliged and
grateful friend

Sidney Lanier.

To Mary Day Lanier [23]

[Baltimore,] Jany 24th 1875.

Our Concert last night was magnificently successful.   In
particular, a certain gentleman whom thou out of pure graci-
ousness hast deigned to bend thy gray eyes upon with favor,
won great honor and applause.

Our first number was the greatest of modern works, – the
Symphony by Svendsen.   The third movement is a long and
intricate Scherzo, of indescribable lightness and beauty: and
is, throughout, a solo for the First Flute, supported by a multitudinous accompaniment of the Reeds and Strings.   The instant
I had finished, the audience furiously demanded an encore, the
Director smiled his congratulations over upon me, and we
plunged into it again, like a flock of butterflies drunk with
sunlight swooping upon a flower-bed.   The whole Symphony
gave me immeasurable delight.   I am so much improved now
in playing, that I can pr[e]serve my internal dignity in great

[23] Previously published, *Scribner's*, XXV, 750 (June, 1899); reprinted,
Letters (New York, 1899), pp. 109-110.

measure free from the dreadful distractions of solicitude, and thus my soul revels in the midst of the heaven of these great symphonic works with almost unobstructed freedom.[24]

After the concert, Mr. Knabe (the piano-maker) invited Hamerik, and the Concert-meister, and Courlaender (the pianist), and the Danish Consul, and another Dane (whose name I knew not) and a German gentleman and myself, to oysters and Champagne; and we drank " Skald " many times. Hamerik complimented me in the highest manner: and I was quite feasted with congratulations from others whom I met afterwards.

But I did not like the supper; the men told smutty stories, and abominations out of the Opera-bouffe; and I wished myself away.

Did I tell thee that The Philadelphia " Evening Bulletin ", in reprinting " Corn ", had also an editorial in the " leader " column, slashing at the Boston Illuminati, and declaring that Mr. Longfellow had not written anything to equal " Corn ", together with various other things? I will send thee the paper after a while.[25]

— Letty Wrenschall is out, looking like a daisy at daylight,

[24] Referring to the performance of Svendsen's Symphony, the Baltimore *Gazette*, Jan. 25, 1875, remarked: " Mr. Lanier, the first flute, and Mr. Stubbs, the oboeisto, sustained their parts with great artistic ability, and succeeded in gaining an enthusiastic encore."

Knabe, referred to in the following paragraph, was either Ernest or William Knabe, both sons and successors of the famous piano manufacturer Valentine Wilhelm Ludwig Knabe (1803-1864). The concert-master was Emil Seifert (see Lanier's letter of Jan. 3, 1875, above).

[25] The Philadelphia *Evening Bulletin*, Jan. 20, 1875 (clipping in Charles D. Lanier Collection, Johns Hopkins University), in addition to reprinting " Corn," remarked editorially: " There is a poem in the February number of *Lippincott's Magazine* . . . which is far superior to any recent American magazine poem, and especially superior to those of three of Mr. Emerson's chosen Parnassians in the February *Atlantic*. It is called simply ' Corn '; and its author, Mr. Sidney Lanier, is not a New Englander. In fact he is a Southerner and lives now in Baltimore. . . . But if his poem of ' Corn ' had had Mr. Longfellow's name appended to it, all the world, including the little part outside of New England, would have applauded it, and it would have been copied all over the country. Among judicious critics it would have been rated much higher than Mr. Long-fellow's new, bookish and rather commonplace verses on ' Monte Cassino,' in the *Atlantic*." (For an earlier and fuller notice in the Philadelphia *Evening Bul-letin*, see note 28, below. That Peacock's discovery of Lanier was totally on the merits of the poem is indicated by the fact that he thought " Sidney Lanier " was a *nom de plûme* at first.)

I met her on the street yesterday; and she went into a very pretty rapture of words upon the beauty of thy letter.

—   I believe I have had the good fortune to discover a very curious fact in relation to the vibration of strings, which will exert an important influence in explaining the difference of *timbre* between stringed instruments and wind: and perhaps in other directions wh. I have not had time to think toward.   I have communicated the substance of the proposition to Prof. F. H. Smith, of the Univ. of Va, – a very eminent authority in such matters – and he replies that my idea is unquestionably correct.[26]

– Since last Monday morning, – wh. brought me Mr. Kirk's letter – through the whole week I have had almost uninterrupted success in all my undertakings of each day: and for this I have thanked God with such fervor as could only be born of the hope that erelong it will all lead to the actual kneeling at thy dear actual feet, of thy then-too-happy

S.

To Mary Day Lanier

[Baltimore,] Jany 26th 1875.

Well then, thou wdst. have been proud indeed of thy comrade, cdst. thou have been by, – Ah– cdst. thou have been by —— today.

Early this morning came a message that Charlotte Cushman " desired to make my acquaintance "; – from Mrs. Bird, who had been applied to, as one known to be my friend, to bring about this consummation.   So at twelve O'clock we sallied forth to the Carrollton, and sent up our cards.   After sitting a few moments the great actress came in, and we sat down to a charming conversation which Miss Cushman opened by firing straight at me. She said she had read my poem: that it was the

[26] The reply is printed entire in *Letters* (New York, 1899), pp. 110-111. Francis Henry Smith (1829-1928) was professor of Natural Philosophy at the University of Virginia from 1853 to 1907. Although he was the author of several books (including two on the relation of religion and science and a college textbook of physics), there is no evidence of any distinction in the field of the physics of music. (Information through the courtesy of Harry Clemons, Librarian, University of Virginia.)

greatest American poem: that I wrote like the poets of Shakespeare's time: and a thousand things of a similar tenor: to which I endeavored to make some suitable answer though I found this most difficult, for her praises were so hearty, – and in the meantime the addition of other callers had made so much of an Audience to listen to them — that I was quite put to it to parry with any manner of grace her friendly thrusts. I however managed to say that I was particularly touched by praises coming from one who had so identified herself with the dramas of Shakespeare – when she interruped me and declared that though this was a contemplative poem, yet it was written with the spirit of Shakespeare, and made her think of his vigorous time. Then she quite abandoned all the other callers, made me come and occupy a place on the settee by her, and talked to me, much as an admiring mother would have done. She knew the Brownings well, in Rome: and liked Mrs. Browning better than her husband. She also knew that wonderful Sydney Dobell, and many other celebrities; and told me many fair things of her own art, of herself, and her adventures. She desired that I would write something for her to read in public: and wanted to know where I had been all this time, and what I had written. After much of this, Mrs. Bird got her ear, and proceeded to give her a confidential account of me &c &c. Finally we took our leave, Miss Cushman pressing my hand a long time and saying all manner of handsome things to me, closing with writing her New York address for me and asking that I would always send her everything of mine.[27]

Good Mrs. Bird was quite beside herself with pleasure and friendly exultation.

I was particularly pleased: because all this confirms what I think I wrote thee once from New York, – that the best artists

[27] Lanier followed up this meeting by sending her the next day a poem entitled " To Miss Charlotte Cushman (With a Copy of ' Corn ')," previously uncollected (I, 44). Apparently Gibson Peacock, editor of the Philadelphia *Evening Bulletin,* had read " Corn " to Charlotte Cushman and had urged her to seek out the author in Baltimore (see Starke, p. 199). Peacock, whose meeting with Lanier came two weeks later (see Lanier's letter of Feb. 11, 1875, below), soon proved to be one of Lanier's most valuable friends. He sponsored Lanier editorially, introduced him to Bayard Taylor (through whom he made his first acquaintance with successful literary men), gave him financial aid, and opened his home to him. More than any other one person he helped Lanier achieve a national reputation.

are always most pleased with my work, whilst it puzzles those
critics whose canons of criticism have been evolved in passing
judgments on the productions of mere cleverness. These latter
persons are worse judges of a real work of art just in proportion as they have become good judges of works of cleverness:
they are tasters with *blasé* tongues, the large and pious simplici-
ties of the true artist are not piquant enough for their palates.

— I have written Mr. Peacock my thanks for his bold stand
in my behalf. I would be pleased if the *critique* (which I
herein return, with thanks to Mrs. Westmoreland) [28] could be
republished in the Macon Telegraph: for it really contains
more insight into my artistic faculties and aims than anything I
have seen. To be " John Keats at his best " with " an American
fibre " in him: that is just my desire.

I am so disabled, from having written a multitude of letters,
that I will beg thee send my account of Miss Cushman's kindness to my father, as I think it will give him pleasure; and also
to Clifford: thou canst make an abstract of it, in thine own
words, for them.

Thou art then suffering, My poor One? Do my sweet gray
eyes ache so that thou must needs lay down thy pen? – I could
swear that thou and I will be together ere long ! For it is
always *near the end* of a journey that my longing for thee

---

[28] Gibson Peacock was brother-in-law to a Mrs. Schlatter, who (with her husband and daughter, Mrs. Fannie Westmoreland) lived in Brunswick, Ga., and
was a friend of Mary Day Lanier. On Jan. 22, 1875, Lanier's wife reported
that Peacock had written to Brunswick for news of him and had sent his sister
a copy of his notice of " Corn "—which Mary Day Lanier had borrowed to send
to her husband. This critique said that Lanier's " Corn " was " the best magazine poem we have seen for years . . . full of the marks of poetic genius and
poetic art. The opening passage recalls Keats at his best; but the later ones
show a more virile but not less poetical strength, with an American fibre in it
that makes it all the better." (Philadelphia *Evening Bulletin*, Jan. 15, 1875—
clipping in the Charles D. Lanier Collection, Johns Hopkins University. No file
of the *Bulletin* for this period has been discovered.) A longer passage is quoted
in Lanier's letter to his father, Jan. 26, 1875, below; and the entire notice was
reprinted in the Macon *Telegraph and Messenger*, Jan. 29, 1875. Earlier notices
of " Corn " had appeared in this newspaper on Jan. 22 and 26, 1875.

In a letter of Jan. 25, 1875, Mary Day Lanier added: " The Schlatters have a
second letter from Mr. Peacock loud in thy praises, and a second editorial from
his pen, in the same strain, in a later number of the Bulletin [see note 25,
above]. They say he is devoted to music. In fact, says *Col. Schlatter*, ' he is
everything he should be– except that he is a Radical,– and *he* can't help *that* ! ' "

begins to grow intolerable as it is now, and that the minutes stretch into interminable hours, as now, which I have to cheat with all manner of devices.

– Well, dear Lady, God soothe thy brows, and cool thine eyes, with such tendance of sweet spirits as would be the fairest labor in all the world to thy long-unministering

lover.

To Gibson Peacock [29]

64 Centre St.
Baltimore, Md.
Jany 26th, 1875.

My dear Sir:

A very lovely friend of mine,–Mrs. Fannie Westmoreland—has been so gracious as to transmit to me, through my wife, your first comments on my poem " Corn " in Lippincott's, which I had not seen before. The slip appears to be cut from the " Bulletin " of 16th, or 17th.

I cannot resist the impulse which urges me to send you my grateful acknowledgments of the poetic insight, the heartiness and the boldness which display themselves in this *critique*. I thank you for it, as for a poet's criticism upon a poet.

Permit me to say that I am particularly touched by the courageous independence of your review. In the very short time that I have been in the hands of the critics, nothing has amazed me more than the timid solicitudes with which they rarify, in one line, any enthusiasm they may have condensed in another,– a process curiously analogous to those irregular condensations and rarefactions of air which physicists have shown to be the conditions for producing an indeterminate sound. Many of my critics have seemed—if I may change the figure—to be forever conciliating the yet-unrisen ghosts of possible mistakes. From these you separate yourself *toto cælo*: and I am thoroughly sure that your method is not only far more worthy the dignity of the critical office, but also far more helpful to the young artist, by its bold sweeping-away of those sorrowful uncertain

---

[29] Previously published, *Atlantic Monthly*, LXXIV, 18-19 (July, 1894); reprinted *Letters* (New York, 1899), pp. 9-10.

mists that arise at times out of the waste bitterness of poverty and obscurity.

— Perhaps here is more feeling than is quite delicate in a communication to one not an old personal friend: but I do not hesitate upon propriety if only I may convey to you some idea of the admiration with which I regard your manly position in my behalf, and of the earnestness with which I shall always consider myself

Your obliged and faithful friend,

Sidney Lanier

TO ROBERT S. LANIER

64 Centre St.
Baltimore, Md.
Jany 26th 1875.

My dear Father:

The success of my poem is complete: and I am very grateful to the Powers Above that so much encouragement has come to me, even earlier than I could have expected when I reflect how many years have elapsed with several great singers before they could obtain recognition. From many quarters the most gratifying messages come to me. I send you, the Bo " Gazette " of this morning, containing a notice of " Corn ".[30] All the notices of it are similarly hearty. I wish particularly you might see a long Editorial in the Philadelphia Bulletin. It is so enthusiastic that I will copy the close. After some opening remarks, he quotes a quarter of a column full, and then says: " Is not every line of this a picture? Is not the whole a picture of a midsummer scene in American woods, such as has never before been limned in language? But this is only the prologue, for the poem is long and it has a moral as well as a poetical intention that is well maintained. Seeking some-

[30] The Baltimore *Gazette*, Jan. 26, 1875, remarked that Lanier's poem had achieved " a striking success at the North," quoted long extracts from it, and concluded: " ' Corn ' is the best American poem written in praise of agriculture—a homely subject, but in Mr. Lanier's hands treated with fine artistic effect." (The quotation which follows in Lanier's letter is from the Philadelphia *Evening Bulletin*, Jan. 15, 1875—see note 28, above.)

thing to find fault with, we can find it only in the wrong emphasis that the verse requires in the words " harrass " and " Empyrean ". The poem, with these little and easily remediable defects, is a great and noble one. And now that a new and true poet has made his *début* in Lippincott, its readers have a right to ask who he is and where he belongs. After the trash and sensationalism of the " dialect " poets, the Walt Whitmans and the Joaquin Millers, we have a right to bid welcome to a new poet who is a gentleman as well as a genius, &c &c &c. . . . In England such a poem would make a fame for the Magazine that contained it, worth a fortune. Let us see whether it will be appreciated by the people of culture in America, who do not require to get their hints from England or Boston: and whether such appreciation will lead to fame or fortune." In a subsequent issue the same paper republished the entire poem.

Hayne's letter came, and is full of grateful compliments to my review of him, and of praises of " Corn ", which he is going to review in the Augusta papers.

I had a fine musical triumph on Saturday night: my solo in the great Symphony of Svendsen (a Scandinavian writer) being warmly encored, so that we had to give it again.

I write in haste: my right arm, too, is demoralized by a slight trouble. Uncle C.'s letter has arrived. I wish he *could* come here. Your letter and papers arrived. – If I only had *my* wife, to dictate my letters to! It is a rare cosy picture that you paint.

Love to mama, and all, from

Yr. Son

S. L.

To Virginia Hankins

64 Centre St.
Baltimore, Md,
Jany 28th 1875.

My dear Friend, when your letter came to me last Spring in answer to my Jeremiad, I said to myself, Now I have made a precious fall from my high estate in her heart, and I will be utterly still to her, until I have some pretty success or other to

lay before her in token that this is really but the whimsical
despondence of one who is a man, and who has never dreamed
for any serious moment of being diverted from his chosen path.
So, though many times I have had messages for you out of the
depths of a great friendliness, I nevertheless have refrained
from sending them until my ship of success should come home.
———   It has come. My poem " Corn ", in Lippincott's for
February, has met with such a generous recognition all over the
land that I may have no hesitation in saying, to your friendly
ears, that your friend's *status* as a poet is fixed, – and he will
not go on the farm to plough and reap waste memories of
failures.

As soon as I learn where you actually are, – for I shall direct
this, at a venture, to Scotland Neck, – I will send you a copy
of the poem, and some critiques thereon which will please you.

Therefore, pray write me at once: telling me how you are,
where, and what doing with those sweet gracious hands. Give
me news also of your brothers, and of Mary: and of brilliant-
eyed Miss Smith, and all whom I met when I last visited you.

God bless you, my dear Child: I am quite worn down with
writing, and cannot now say more than that I am always

Your faithful

S. L.

To Mary Day Lanier

[Baltimore,] Jany 31st 1875.

Here comes a little note from Miss Seaton: she commences
(anent thy note to her): " It is just the sweetest thing in the
world, the dear little wifely womanly note. No wonder that
you are a poet ! " &c &c &c.

There, then ! Behold thyself confronted: thou art ever
bringing against me most heinous charges of flattery and of
love's-blindness, when I tell thee that *thou* art the poetry of
which *I* am but a poor translator to the world: art thou not a
most guilty Sweet to accuse me thus, when this good Josephine
Seaton, after the mere reading of one brief note of thine,
exclaims, no wonder that *thy husband* is a poet? Answer me
that.

— In reply to thine underscored command, I have the pleasure to inform thee that no human eyes save Miss Seaton's (and perhaps Martha's, – our colored housemaid, who often in my absence does me the honor to read any letters or bits of writing that may be lying about, – as I judge from certain appearances which I will not detail) saw the amended poem " Sometime ",[31] besides mine own, and thine and such as thou permittedst. Without sentimental superstition, it really does seem as if the goodness of God kept me from sending it to APPLETON'S,– which I was on the very point of doing, a few hours after it was finished, and which I did *not* do purely in obedience to a vague yet decisive reluctance, that I now look back to with reverence, as to the voice of an Angel.

But thou shalt not feel pain to tell me that the little poem was not thine. Thou canst write a far sweeter one, if thou wilt. Perhaps sometime it may give thee a little satisfaction to do so: and I can still write a poem with thee.

Yesterday, I dined at Mrs. Bird's; in honor of Edgeworth's birthday: and the night before was given to a *musicale* at the Machado's, where I won great fame with the flute, Wysham and I playing a couple of duos with immense effect. I have now far outstripped W. in technique: and execute with ease passages where he flounders and splutters in a way that would go near to make thee die of laughing.

Thou wilt be glad to know that Prof. [Alfred F.] Mayer, whose discoveries in the Physics of Music have gained him much fame both abroad and at home, is now here delivering a series of four lectures on Sound, and that we have become friends, mainly through my poem. He is professor of Physics in the Stevens Institute of Technology, at Hoboken, New Jersey: and has offered me the free range of his laboratory there, and any such special course of instruction in acoustics as I may desire. In pursuing his researches, he is greatly hampered by the disadvantage of knowing nothing about music. He was in my room for an hour on Friday, and told me at leaving that he thought my qualifications fitted me, in a very peculiar way, for success in this science. I hope to get an opportunity in the Spring, of accepting his invitation to Hoboken.

[31] See note 20, above.

One month of daily service in his well-appointed laboratory
would suffice to give me that manual dexterity in experimenting
which I lack.

I have not deemed it prudent to make any advances to the Trustees in relation to the establishment of the Chair, yet: deeming
it wiser not to make any of them commit themselves to opposition, until I can bring all my forces to bear.

Didst thou receive my P. O. order for $30 ?   Thou has not
mentioned it.

What did the Tel.-Messenger say the second time about
" Corn " ?

—   Ah – *Pobrita Mia*, dost still suffer?   How unspeakable
is my longing to be by and tend thee !   How many weary days
and nights hast thou spent in ministrations at my bedside, during those long illnesses which now seem like dreams !   And
what poems can I ever write that will compare in sweetness
with these impromptu stanzas-in-act of thine ?

—   Dost thou know where my June-Dream [32] is?

I send thee a letter from Miss Seaton. 'Tis a lonesome soul,
and mostly a sad one. She lives in the top of the house, and
her meals are sent to her, – she being inordinately averse to
coming among people because of her great deafness.

If I shd. succeed in having the Chair established, I will not
commence my duties before next October. My plan wd. be to
go to Hoboken immediately on the termination of my engagement here, – Mch. 20th – for a month: then to Boston for ten
days, to investigate some methods of teaching sight-reading of
music to very large classes,– wh. I design to suggest as part of
the duties of my Chair: then, about May 1st, to secure the use
of the Apparatus here for a short lecturing tour in the main
cities of Georgia and Alabama, which I shd. undertake only
upon guaranteed receipts, arranged beforehand.

—   And during which, – Ah, kind Heaven ! – I shd. pick
thee up, and carry thee with me, and be thy divinely-content

                                                                        lover.

---

[32] A reference to Lanier's poem " June Dreams, In January " (see Mary Day
Lanier's reply of Feb. 14, 1875). Written seven years earlier, it was not
published during Lanier's lifetime.

To Virginia Hankins

64 Centre St.
Baltimore, Md,
Feb. 3rd 1875.

Your letter, dear Friend, does not tell me who it is that has gone from you: but it must needs have been some one very dear, to wring from you such profound pain. How can I speak to you the solicitude with which my heart hovers about you? You know. Yes, you know. I will beg you to assemble in your memory all the sunsets we have seen together, all the trees we have ridden or walked under, all the waters we have gazend on in silence, all the fair broad stretches of fields and uplands and meadows that have wrought their subtle wonder of delight-and-pain in our hearts when we have loved them to-gether: and when you have done so, to compress into one all the tendernesses and sympathies which are forever distilling in my own heart out of these lovely hours of bygone companion-ship. So shall you have some sense of the intense desire which I feel to be near you, and to give you such comfort as might come from the entire devotion of a friend who is sure that the passion of his friendship is at once wonderful and unique.

Dear Child, why can you not run here, to your friends', the [Reverdy] Johnsons', a little while? Give me the comfort of being *your* comfort, – if ever so little! – Why not? – Come.

—— I send you a copy of Lippincott's Magazine contain-ing my poem. It is called " Corn ". I have every day the most gratifying evidences of its success. I enclose a couple of notices. I also send you a " Southern Magazine " for Jan'y, containing a review of Hayne by me, which has been almost as successful as the poem.

God house you in His love, dear Ginna, as you are in the heart of your friend

S. L.

To Mary Day Lanier

[Baltimore,] Feb. 5th 1875

Thou Rosebud, whose rough calyx, I, has been torn away from about thee, canst thou dream how empty of all glory my life is, thou being out? Not music, not poetry, not ambition, not charity, not labor, will go into the vacancy of thee: my soul is all a hollowness left sweet by thee, as a heaven with its stars gone out, still half-warm and half-lighted; what can I longer do without some sight of thy sweet eyes?

—— The notice of the lecture on Sound, (at the Peabody last night) in this morning's Gazette,[33] is by me:— for Thomas " Lung " pray read Thomas *Young*. My days are mostly devoted to making friends who will aid my project of the Chair: and I have to record some very charming successes in that direction. I have now made a tolerably good survey of the situation, and ere long shall issue the signal to storm the works. One of the " works " is a wondrous dictatorial old official who thinks he knows everything but who really knows nothing: and I anticipate a great pile of killed and wounded at *his* particular part of the defenses. But I have got a mine under him, whereof he wotteth not: and when I touch it off, I really think he must go down.

A friend tells me that the St. Louis " Globe " has copied " Corn " in full, with a very complimentary notice: and I hear of many other papers that have done likewise.

Wysham has come for me to go out with him, to fill an engagement.

Dear Rose, God's Love be Calyx, stem and growing-place for thee this night, prays thy.

lover.

[33] A critique of 52 lines in the Baltimore *Gazette*, Feb. 5, 1875, p. 4, col. 6 (see II, 329).

To Mary Day Lanier [34]

[Baltimore,] Feby. 7th 1875.

I am in a rage of delight over the enclosed poem, which is just now hot from the mint: of delight, not because it satisfies *me* any better than the No. 1 of the *Laus Mariæ* series, – of which it is a re-coinage – but because I know that it will express to *others* the pure hunger and thirst of my heart for thee in a form which will not (as the first No. 1 *does*, – alas, for the *impure* to whom all things are impure) set the thoughts of fleshly-minded readers in a direction which I never meant at all.[35] The first No. 1 was criticised by one person to whom I sent it,– a poet, too – as " exquisitely beautiful " *but* too " ripe and luxuriant." This cut me like a knife, with the sheer cruelty of its Swinburnian misconception; for my heart was never exalted higher in unearthliness than when I wrote that No. I. But in the enclosed, what with the pure and keen stress of salt seas, and the grey hunger of the appeal of a lonesome heart to God, I have managed to cast a different color over the whole, which I do not think can be mistaken. Tell me, very freely, if *thou* thinkest so: and all that thou thinkest about it.

Our Concert last night – whereof I send thee the beautiful programme – was brilliantly successful. We had only rehearsed the Mozart *Concerto* once, Mr. Hoffman not arriving until Friday: but it went off nobly on the part of the orchestra, and Mr. Hoffman played it with a subtle delicacy of touch and of expression of which I had never dreamed him capable. The Proch variations were sung charmingly by Miss Thursby: I standing with her and playing the flute *obligato*: all with such effect, that I had twice to lead her back in response to vociferous encores.[36] The third movement of the Hiller Symphony

[34] Excerpt previously published, *Scribner's*, XXV, 750 (June, 1899); reprinted, *Letters* (New York, 1899), p. 111.

[35] The first sonnet of the sequence soon to be published under the title " In Absence." Paul H. Hayne (see note 126, 1874) was the poet who had criticized the sonnet mentioned in the following sentence as the " first No. 1." The published version of this sonnet differs radically from the original version submitted to Hayne.

[36] Referring to the performance of this number, the Baltimore *Gazette*, Feb. 8, 1875, said: "The chief feature of this was a very lovely cadenza with the flute.

was full of lovely flute-effects: and my playing won me many compliments from the stolid Germans of the Orchestra.

Thou art the sweetest Heart in the world – to tell me thy piano-news for my birthday gift.[37]   Thou could'st have given me nothing, short of a sight of thine eyes, that cd. have pleased me more.   Pray do not higgle upon the $5 difference betwixt 25 and 30: it were shame if I cannot write a poem for this last amount, in the next three months.   Practice, I beseech thee at least two hours every day: particularly scales, and sight-reading. In this last (sight-reading) take some piece thou dost not know, and play it through *very slowly*, WITHOUT STOPPING FOR MIS-TAKES OR DIFFICULTIES: but note these, and then when thou hast finished the piece, take the difficulties separately, conquer their *technique*, and then play the whole piece over again; but always *without* STOPPING OR FALTERING, – dost thou hear, my dear Sweet-Fingers ?

Thus thou wilt quickly acquire the habit of reading.   At which I remember thou wast formerly skillful: – dost thou recall the time when thou and I practised the Fürstenau Nocturne at Clare [de Graffenried]'s ?

I dined at Mrs. Bird's today, with a very jolly company.   Thy name was often mentioned, and I had a fair opportunity to sing a song in thy praise, wh. I did improve.

I will have to abandon the title *Laus Mariæ* for my sonnets: it wd. be misleading, as every one wd. take it to be praise of the Virgin.   Perhaps I will head them *Laus Uxoris* (" Praise of a Wife"), for I wish to preserve the pious tone of the *Laus* form of expression.

Miss Cushman has sent me a second photograph, better than the first one.

Three weeks ago I sent Mr. Rees [38] a reed for the Oboe, accompanied with a letter.   I have not heard from him, and fear he has not received it.   Nor have I heard from Mamie Boifeuillet: and I also fear she failed to get my letter.

Mr. Lanier's exquisite tone and finished technique upon this instrument was exhibited in this cadenza in a marked and beautiful way, the voice and flute blending in perfect accord."

[37] Mary Day Lanier had written, Feb. 3, that she was planning to rent a piano if she could get it for three months for $25.

[38] The rector of Christ Church, Macon, who had performed the marriage ceremony for the Laniers.

Thy tooth-brushes and hair-pins have been sent.

And now, dear Love, mayst thou have this night as many fair dreams as there be fair loves in thy most fair soul, – prayeth thy

lover.——

To Clifford A. Lanier

64 Centre St.
Baltimore, Md,
Feby. 8th, 1874 [1875]

My dear Clifford:

They marred the dramatic effect of the close of " Corn " most dreadfully, by a misprint, and a transposition: instead of " *So* " it should read " Lo, through hot waverings &c ": and it should end:

> " To render to some future bolder heart
> That manfully shall take thy part
> With antique sinew and with modern art,
> And tend thee
> And defend thee! " [39]

You have carried out the story of the Surgeon [40] with admirable poetic ingenuity, and I enjoyed your mss. keenly. You will observe that I have entirely stricken out the first address, in regard to the time of the " action " of the story, and the reading of it &c: and that I have materially shortened the preface. Most of this shortening has been done either to sharpen up the contrasting force of the antitheses, or to prune away the overload of outgrowths which is common to all young writers of talent, but which the experience of every successful writer leads him to excise with unsparing hand, no matter if the sweep of his scythe cuts down flowers he particularly wanted to live.

[39] For the several variant versions of " Corn " see note thereto in vol. I.

[40] In his letter of Jan. 28, 1875, Clifford Lanier had sent his story, " The Doctor's Legend," asking his brother's criticism and commenting: " I send you today the child of your suggestion, dashed off in a few days after you left us, and while I wrote it, my mind and heart were filled with the conviction that you had inspired everything I had ever accomplished." (Lanier had made a brief visit to Montgomery in Dec., 1874.)

Your story is simply charming, and is beautifully worked out. You are quite too good in giving any tribute to me, in connection with it. Nobody has ever thought of considering Shakespeare under any obligations to the old story-tellers who preceded him: yet he took whole plots from them, while you have only received from me the bare suggestion of uniting heads to bodies. Your story ought to make an admirable entertainment for the Arlington.[41] You were better re-write the preface, making the indicated changes: and you shd. so familiarize yourself with your mss. as to read it with proper intonations. Do not read too fast: and read with a certain dignity, even in the comedy-parts.

If some good wave might throw us together for a little while next summer, we could, by somewhat changing the form of the story, and throwing in a little more of such epigrammatic French wit as would not stand reading *aloud* to your audience – make it a very pretty Magazine paper.

" Corn " is now making quite a triumphal progress over the West. Have any of the Ala. papers noticed it?

God bless you my dear Little Boy: and all the balance of you,

Your

S. L.

I return your mss. by – Express.

To Mary Day Lanier [42]

[Baltimore,] Feb. 11th 1875.

My poor much-burdened Heart, thy letter yesterday is all one cry of an outworn body and soul; less in what it saith, than in what it refraineth from saying;— and I would to God thou might'st have some rest from so much hand-work and so much helpless heart-sympathy, wh. is more wearing than all. And thou hast not the piano after all! —*Canst* thou not find another, through the whole of Brunswick? I had so rejoiced in the thought that thou wdst. be doing *something* besides mere drudgery.

---

[41] Presumably a literary club in Montgomery.
[42] Excerpt previously published, W. H. Ward, " Memorial," *Poems* (New York, 1884), p. xxvii.

I feared you wd. be all be sick during this terribly cold weather. As for me, I have not suffered at all. I go out every day, and splash through the ice and snow and " slush "; but although I get very cold when outside,—having really no clothing at all suitable for this climate—yet as soon as I get into my room I am in a warm dry atmosphere that seemeth to be proof against cold.

— Well, then,–if thou wilt not write me a poem! – I have written one *to* myself *for* thee. In this little song,[43] I have begun to dare to give myself some freedom in my own peculiar style, and have allowed myself to treat both words, similes and metres with such freedom as I desire. The result convinces me I can do so, now, safely. Dost thou not like it? It is a song, to go in *Jacquerie*. It is to be read *aloud*, in a round-lipped, tender, passionate voice.

I had a charming dinner on Wednesday with Mr. & Mrs. Peacock *en trio* at their hotel. After dinner we went to the Gilmore Band concert. I was greatly pleased with the Peacocks. They are quiet, cultivated, earnest people, such as thou wdst. like to know. They pressed me with cordial invitations to make their house in Ph^a my home when I come there.

If my yearning had power over space as it hath over my heart, how instantly, dear Love, wdst. thou find at thy feet thy

lover.

To Mary Day Lanier

[Baltimore,] Feb. 17th 1875.

It is an Æon – of four days – since I have written thee: and here comes thine of 14th, bringing me violets, and a note from my dear Mrs. Wallen; and pray who is this " Miss Sallie " that writes to her so fairly of thy lover? And why, My Child, hast thou dyspepsia? Art thou not too much given over to household and infant-tending avocations? *Canst* thou not manage in some manner to go away for a few days? I beg thee to run off. – Go to some of thy Savannah friends. I am so sure this would help thee greatly. Go to Savannah and see Charley

---

[43] " Special Pleading " (I, 45) according to Ward (see note 42, above) and by implication from Lanier's letter of Feb. 26, 1875, below.

[Taliaferro], and present my regards to Mr. Habersham, and tell him how greatly I am improved in my playing, insomuch that I daily get compliments even from these stolid old German workhorses in the Orchestra; tell him moreover how much I should like to forgather with him and ha' a twa-handed crack (as Jamie Hogg used to say) at Kuhlau, and Handel, and Beethoven. Dear Heart, do go: I ask it: I look every day for some money whereof I will send thee a part *instanter*, and thou shouldst have by this time a second reinforcement from Macon, for wh. I wrote a little while back. Go, Little Maydie: not for a mere couple of days, but for a week, or ten days *at least*. It is for my sake: thine account of thy health gives me sleepless nights: I think all the time of thy sufferings, and I wear my heart with vain reproaches that I can not do better for thee. Things move slowly with me: often the weather is so cold (they say it is the worst winter in years) that I have to postpone visits which are absolutely necessary to the success of my plans. Yet for all the slow movement of affairs, time dashes by with fearsome speed: I have but about a month to play, longer, at the Peabody.

A very fine editorial has appeared in the AUGUSTA CHRONICLE AND SENTINEL, quoting Mr. Peacock's and adding comments of the Editor of the C. & S. Have none of the Sav^h papers noticed the poem?

Nirvâna is of course still mine, for they never paid me a cent for it. I wish however to relieve it of some of my earlier crudenesses, and to re-write it ere it shall again be printed.⁴⁴ I looked for the June song, but found it not; thou knowest, however, that I am not a good looker, – and therefore I will look again.

Is not this a sweet note of Miss Seaton's? I met her on the street yesterday and told her I was not very well; hence her offer.⁴⁵

⁴⁴ In her letter of Feb. 14, 1875, Mary Day Lanier had suggested in reference to " Nirvana," which had been published four years previously: " Is there any objection to having it republished? Has the Southern Mag any rights in the matter? It is worth bringing forward prominently: *even* after Corn! ' "

She added that she had not ⸢een the MS of " June Dreams, In January " (referred to in the next sentence) since 'it was returned with annotations by Paul Hayne – in the spring of 1873.

⁴⁵ Josephine Seaton had offered to help Lanier with library research work (undated note in the Charles D. Lanier Collection, Johns Hopkins University).

– Well, God be thy strength, and Love by thy health, – crieth thy

lover.

To Mary Day Lanier

[Baltimore,] Feb. 24th 1875.

In the cruelest press of business I have but a moment to enclose thee a " Martha Washington Court Journal ", in the upper corner of the first page whereof thou wilt behold a sonnet [46] by thy lover. I purpose tomorrow to give thee the account thou desirest of a week of my life; sending it thee in instalments.

O hast thou yet gone to Macon? I beg thee to go immediately when this cometh, – if it suit thine *other* arrangements and conditions, caring not for money, wh. shall be handed thee *there.* Let me know straightway all thy needs in this behalf. I yearn unspeakably to know that thou art *in manibus Buncombii.*[47]

Now cannot I say more, — though full with a year long communication for thee — than farewell, dear Lady, and may God soon send thee a

lover.

To Mary Day Lanier [48]

[Baltimore,] Feb. 26th 1875.

Well then, installment No. 1 shall relate to thee in how wholly unorthodox a manner,– yet to me how devout! – I spent last

[46] " Martha Washington " (1, 46), published in a brochure entitled *Martha Washington Court Journal*, Baltimore, Feb. 22, 1875, by the ladies of the Martha Washington Tea-Party, to raise money for certain local charities.

[47] The reference to " Cousin Buncombe " in several of Mary Day Lanier's letters and in this one by Lanier seems to be an allusion to " the doctor " in general, not necessarily to any specific one. The expression seems to be part of a special language used by the Laniers to refer to some matter connected with her health.

[48] Excerpt previously published, *Scribner's*, XXV, 750-751 (June, 1899) ; reprinted, *Letters* (New York, 1899), pp. 111-112.

Sunday: and I shall then bring thee along with me through this week to next Sunday.[49]

—   At half-past ten I was ready for action, and proceeded to meet my colleagues of the wind-quintette,– with whom I was to play at the Concert that night,– for a rehearsal of our piece;– which by reason of short notice and of the exactions of our Orchestral rehearsals, we had not been able to rehearse before. This occupied until after one o'clock: when I rushed back to my room, made some changes of toilet, and repaired to the Perots', where I was promised to dinner. After dinner, Mr. Perot and I looked over a magnificient bound collection of colored prints representing the progress of Art in all times and countries: till half-past five, when I returned to my room, fell on the bed and rested an hour; then tea, then a hasty arrayal in dress-coat and white tie, and a flight to the Germania Hall where we were to play the Quintette. Which having played, I rushed, at nine O'clock, to the house of M. Rabillion [50] where I had been engaged to play in a string quintette of Haydn, – for three strings, Flute, and Piano; Mad. Rabillion playing the piano part, and her daughter playing the violoncello part. Arriving here, found the violin and viola men had not arrived: so played trios with mother and daughter (violincello, flute and piano) and chatted (with the father, of course) until eleven, then took leave of these charming, cultivated, un-affected, simple-mannered French people, (whom I hope thou shalt know some day) and got me home to bed, tired as thou mayst imagine. Of course this was an exceptional Sunday. I usually spend the day until dinner-time, in my room writing to thee, and meditating upon God. I then dine at Mrs. Bird's and spend my evening alone in my room, bringing my life up.

—   So: on Monday at half-past ten I fared down into the city, in order to discover if I might see a proof-sheet of my Sonnet to " Martha Washington," which I feared would else prove full of errors. Calling at Turnbulls, learned that I was just in time for my purpose: and at same time met Col. Johnson

[49] In her letter of Feb. 19, 1875, Mary Day Lanier had asked for "a brief diary, . . . hour by hour, through *one* week."

[50] Léonce Rabillon (1815-1886), French Consul and teacher of romance languages in Baltimore. Upon the opening of Johns Hopkins University in 1876, he was appointed Lecturer in French Literature, a position held until his death.

(Richard M.) and Wm Hand Browne. Engaging the former
to call on me at two on his way back to Waverley (where he
lives), I repaired to the printing-office, found my poem full of
errors, corrected them, hastened home, got my little half-hour
of practice, and then to the Peabody, at twelve, rehearsing there
with Orchestra until two. Returning at that hour, found Col.
Johnson and Mr. S. Teackle Wallis [51] in my room, and had an
agreeable talk with them until three. Mr. Wallis then leaving,
Col. Johnson remained some time, asking me of my plans, and
requesting to hear any poems I had on hand; whereupon I
read him "Pleading," and the Martha Washington Sonnet, at
which he expressed many tokens of great pleasure. Finally he
left, after making me promise to visit him next week. Then
dinner: after which I sought to rest a little before dressing to
go to the Martha Washington Tea Party at the Academy of
Music.[52] Rested, and arrayed, I arrive at the Academy, and
find even the vestibule packed. I calmly wait: presently some
individual in the struggling mass grows desperate, the crowd
heaves, he plunges forward, I follow in his wake and gain a
few feet. Thus, by alternately waiting, and taking advantage
of the gap which strong impatience make in front, I gradually
mount the stairs, and finally emerge into the Concert-Room of
the Academy, (a room distinct from the theatre-room, and one
of the loveliest concert-rooms in the world) where the tea-
tables are set. I encounter Innes Randolph, and we go together to take some supper, I being villainously hungry. Cir-
cling round the room, I find my good friend Miss Rebecca
Perrine presiding at her table in a big white mobcap of the
style of 1790, (—as are all the other ladies at the tables) and
here Randolph and I sit down. By Miss Rebecca's direction,
the waiter brings us some cold turkey, some *pates*, ham, and
(successively) four cups of coffee, for which we are previously
admonished we shall have to pay the sum of thirty five cents

[51] Severn Teackle Wallis (1816-1894), a lawyer and local literary figure in
Baltimore.

[52] The Academy of Music had been formally opened only a month before, at
its new hall on Howard Street (now the site of the Stanley Theatre), though
plans for it had been formulated as early as 1870. (Not to be confused with
the Conservatory of the Peabody Institute, which was at first known as the
Academy of Music also.)

apiece. Miss Rebecca now hastens away into the theatre-room, to see the pageant which is to be revealed at eight O'clock, first bidding us join her in her *loge* when we have finished. We absorb vast quantities of nourishment, and repair towards our friend's *loge*. Arriving at the passage leading past her door, we find the crowd so densely packed that there is no advancing a foot. Randolph despairs, and commences to retreat: I hold him and say wait; presently a stockholder of the Academy who owns a box and cannot get to it by reason of the press, arrives with a couple of policemen who force him a lane through, we deftly glide behind, and in another moment are safely in the *loge*, relating our adventures. Presently the curtain rises, and reveals a magnificient sight; about two hundred persons, in the costumes of Gen. Washington's time, (many of them lineal descendants of the characters they represent, and wearing actual dresses and jewels which have come down from that time) advance in couples, and are presented in slow succession to Gen. and Mrs. Washington, who stand upon a dais to the left: which presentation being concluded, certain notabilities – of both sexes – gravely advance and dance a stately minuet; with great applause from the people. By this time I am half dead with the heat, and the much-breath'd air, and I sally forth, and, after wandering round the lobbies and meeting a few friends, I buy a " Martha Washington Tea-Cup ", and get me home. Here after awhile arrive Mr. Charles Young, Uncle of the ladies of the house, who has won great honor as the Marquis de Lafayette during the evening; as has also our Miss Mary Ann, who has gone in the character, and in the actual old brocade dress, of her ancestress, Mrs. Charles Young. We have a lively discussion of the events of the evening, relate our individual adventures, and finally part for the night.

— As now I must from thee, dear Love; praying that God may be in His Greatness, as I am in my littleness, thy

Lover.

To Edward Spencer [53]

64 Centre St.
Baltimore, Md,
Feby. 26th 1875.

Dear Mr. Spencer:

Last night during a rehearsal of the quaint and sorrowful " Good-night Symphony " of dear old Papa Haydn, a friend handed me your letter: and while I had a few bars rest, I read it.

Several times, I have been on the point of sending you a copy of Lippincott's Magazine for February, in which " Corn " appeared first: but each time my heart failed me. In the wonderful scope and range of your own literary country, — extending from your statistical papers to " Mother Peablossom " — I had found so many varied climates, bracing or soothing: so many springs and streams of purity: such strong and (in this age) picturesque mountains of integrity: such arable lands of learning and cultivation; and such lovely forest-forms of imagination, that I could not bring myself to see how any little landscape of mine could add to that agreeable prospect which you must continually enjoy within.

I cannot, therefore, (–indeed I do not strongly attempt to–,) repress the pleasure I feel in having from your own hand your commendation of my poem. It is doubly grateful to me: first, because it comes from you, whose approval I set more estimation upon than that of any person I can name; and, second, because it comes just at a critical time when, after a few amateur attempts, I have been driven by irresistible circumstances to devote the rest of my life to poetic work, and am naturally

[53] Previously published, *Studies in Philology*, XXVII, 463-464 (July, 1930). Edward Spencer (1834-1883), of Randallstown, Md., was an author and journalist, who contributed to the New York *World* and the Baltimore *Bulletin*. On Feb. 22 he had written Lanier of the pleasure he had found in reading " Corn," which had been reprinted in the *Bulletin*: " If I were to say how thoroughly I admire that very perfect and very powerful poem, you would suspect me of designs upon your modesty. . . . The gashed hillsides and deserted old fields of your Southern country owe you a debt of gratitude indeed, and ' corn ' should testify its spirit of appreciation to you in a cask of choice old Bourbon."

anxious to know whether the artistic career, which is to *be* whether or no, is to be with or without sympathy. Your letter, which crowns a very pleasant number of hearty recognitions with which " Corn " has been honored, gives me great comfort on this point, and, with that comfort, much firmness of hand and humble piety for future work: and you can in this view understand an enthusiasm of thanks that might under other conditions appear to you as the effusive extravagance of one unbalanced by praise.

Can you really not manage to unclasp the handles of those envious pincers of hard work wh. your letter informs me you are held by,–and run over here for a little while? You know *so* many things that I wish to know: and your imparting of the same to me wd. not have the slightest flavor of a commercial transaction, for I cd. not offer you the least *quid* for any of your *quo*, – unless, it might be, you wd. consider a cigar in that connection.

Seriously, come, Mr. Spencer. This is the season for charity: and there is much distress among the poor, *quorum magna pars.* I am sure that your friend and gossip, Gaffer Browne,[54] wd. join me in this appeal very fervently, if he knew thereof. It is only the other day that he and I were chanting a pæan over yr. University article: and at the close of the same, he plucked from his pocket some well-thumbed letters of yours, declared that you were the only personal correspondent whose letters he preserved, and bade me observe, with a vehemence not to be expected from a person of his great age, how fair a spectacle was the regularity of your handwriting.

Finally I vow and protest that if you do not come to see me, soon, – I will come to see you.

Has menace any higher climacteric ?

Most truly yours

Sidney Lanier

---

[54] Spencer was a friend of William Hand Browne and mentioned in his letter that Browne had often spoken to him of Lanier.

To Mary Day Lanier [55]

[Baltimore,] Feb. 28th 1875.

O lame and impotent conclusion ! – Here have I sate me down to take up the thread of my week's life,– and cannot remember, if I were to be hanged for it, what I did o' Tuesday: nor o' Wednesday. But if thou wilt take my Monday or Sunday, and vary the same with a journey to the P. O. with a letter to thee, the mailing of a paper to Father, the answering of much correspondence on many topics, the paying of a visit to some Trustee or other, (or to somebody that knows somebody that &c &c knows a Trustee), a delicious hour in the Peabody Library where I go twice or thrice a week and feed with such hunger and such yearning for a little free time as God only knows, a painful and laborious sewing on of buttons, drawer-strings and the like (wherein I am beset by ten thousand devils,– (the vigor of this expression is due to the fact that I have just been doing some sewing, (by the way, *can* you tell me what makes the accursed thread.double up into about two hundred thousand loops on the other side when I pull the needle through? (Perhaps it is because I do not use a thimble, and therefore sew with a pull instead of with a push ? I seriously wish advice for this point.)))) An occasional little luxurious peep into my Shakespeare, my Chaucer, my Spenser, my Tyndall on Sound, my Lucretius,[56] a semi-occasional playing of Schumann's Songs, or Schubert's, or Rubinstein, with Winterbotham, the pianist, who dashes in, in his shy way, plays his face in a glow then dashes out; – and then if thou wilt fancy these and a thousand other minute details moving like *fantoccini* in front of a vast twilight background of utter yearning for thee who art the only companion I have ever had in my whole life:– so wilt have my daily existence with tolerable distinctness.

[55] Excerpt previously published, *Scribner's*, XXV, 751 (June, 1899) ; reprinted, *Letters* (New York, 1899), pp. 112-113.

[56] The surviving volumes of Lanier's library (Charles D. Lanier Collection, Johns Hopkins University) include the following, which are apparently the books here referred to: *The Works of William Shakespeare* (Cincinnati, 1857) ; *The Canterbury Tales and Faerie Queene with other poems of Chaucer and Spenser* (Edinburgh, 1872) ; John Tyndall, *Sound. A Course of Eight Lectures* . . . (New York, 1867) ; and T. Lucreti Cari, *De Rerum Natura* (New York, 1861)—all with Lanier's annotations.

I enclose a beautiful letter just received from Edward Spencer. He is the "heavy" writer of the New York "World": and I value his praise more highly than that of any man's I can name. We had a beautiful Concert last night, The Seventh Symphony of Beethoven, the great Concerto of Schumann for Piano and Orchestra, the Marriage of Figaro; winding up with the dreary old "Good Night" Symphony of Haydn, in which each of us had a candle attached to his stand (the hall being in total darkness) which he blew out as his part was finished (the parts come to an end successively), until finally naught was left but a lonesome old fiddler who dismally sawed away, but at last left, the leader beating time for a few bars longer, then sadly blowing out his solitary candle and moving away.

Dear Lady, God bless thee as utterly as I am utterly thy

> lover.

To Gibson Peacock [57]

> 64 Centre St.
> Baltimore, Md.
> Mch. 2nd 1875.

Dear Mr. Peacock,

　　　　　　I write a line to say that business will probably call me to Philadelphia in a day or two, and that I particularly desire to go with you and Mrs. Peacock to Theodore Thomas' Symphony Concert on Friday night.

If you have no other engagement for that evening, pray set it apart graciously for me: who am already tingling with the anticipated double delight of *yourselves* and of music.

Many thanks for the BULLETIN containing the Sonnet.[58] I am gratified that you should have thought the little poem worth republishing.

I have not now time to say more than that I am always

> Your friend
> Sidney Lanier

---

[57] Previously published, *Atlantic Monthly*, LXXIV, 19 (July, 1894); reprinted, *Letters* (New York, 1899), p. 11.

[58] "Martha Washington" (see note 46, above).

To Mary Day Lanier

[Baltimore,] Mch. 3rd 1875.

I have but a moment to scrawl thee a kiss in. Thy wood-bines came, and sent a breath of love into my heart, fresh out of the Day at Mrs. Fulton's.

Josephine Seaton sends me a note full of sweet enthusiasm anent thy letter to her: but vows and protests I shall not see it. I enclose her communication.

I have a most fair letter from Dr. Tucker, containing wondrous compliments to the poem, and to me.[59] Thou shalt see it sometime.

Also letters of similar purport from Ginna,[60] and from Mr [Ronald] McDonald.

Also thine from Macon, whereof, poor, suffering Heart, I dare not speak, lest my heart turn into a tear.

    x   x   x   x   x   x   x [61]

I pray thee stay in Macon as long as may be. Is it *absolutely* necessary that thy luminary shd. send thee home? 'Tis but an uncertain light at best: and if it shone, – why thou mightest make shift to get along anyhow. However, thou knowest best, my dear Mistress.

I have secured permission from the Board of Trustees of the Peabody Academy to use their apparatus in my musical experiments: wh. is parallel No. 1 towards taking the fort.

In measure as thou are sweet so may God be tender, – prays thy

                                            lover.

---

[59] In a letter of Feb. 25, 1875, H. H. Tucker, Chancellor of the University of Georgia, offered to aid Lanier in his effort to secure the establishment of "A Chair of the physics & metaphysics of Music," presumably at the Peabody Institute, by writing to the "Rev. Dr. Sears of Staunton Va, the agent of the Peabody Fund."

[60] Of Lanier's success Virginia Hankins wrote on Feb. 27, 1875: "I have believed in your genius, always."

[61] A half page has been cut from the MS at this point. Mary Day Lanier had gone to Macon to consult a doctor.

To Mary Day Lanier

[Baltimore,] Mch. 7th 1875.

Thine from Macon, enclosing thy long-missing letters and cravat,[62] is but now read,— and I would I had this same caitiff Distance (whose dull bulk lieth betwixt me and thee) under my foot so that I might smite off the head thereof and even hew his carcase into innumerable small fragments to be quickly devoured of the birds utterly away. For here is such gracious woman's-wit, such tender play of roguish-eye-sparkles through cunning-sweet words, such large wife's wisdom, such divine and quiet height of love: and all uttered (as I full well remember) in that most sad summer when life seemed really nothing but a sort of dreary amplitude to be sick in; that my heart seemeth as it might not brook to be longer in any other place than at thy dear feet.

—— I am just returned from Philadelphia, where I have spent two days with the Peacocks. Such a rush,— of all manner of friendly expeditions and charming undertakings,—as they did carry me upon! Their house is lovely, and their domesticities in admirable taste. Last night they had Mr. [J. F.] Kirk (Ed. Lippincott's Magazine), and Mr. [Charles Heber] Clark, *alias* " Max Adeler " to meet me at dinner: with whom I had a pleasant three hours. Then we went to the famous " Saturday Night Club ",— whose meeting was held, (as my good fortune wd. have it) in the magnificent house of Col. Tom Scott, the Railroad magnate. There I was presented to untold· millions of money, to vast and imposing amplitudes of comfortable stomachs and port-winey noses, to Dr. Pancoast, to Howard Furness (who is a rich man of letters, now editing a great *variorum* edition of Shakespeare, and who was pleased to say some very charming things· anent thy lover's poetry) to Governor Hartranft, to the Mayor of Philadelphia, to the British Consul, to George W. Childs, and a host of others, besides mine host himself, Col. Scott, with whom I had a pleasant little

---

[62] On Mar. 1, 1875, Mary Day Lanier sent two letters written by her to her husband in 1872, which R. S. Lanier had forgotten to mail, and which she found in a bureau drawer. One of them contained a cravat.

interchange.   On the same day, Mr. McClellan,[63] (who, curiously enough, proved to be a dear friend of the Peacocks)
came over and lunched with me, and gave me a pleasant two
hours, which he mostly filled with affectionate inquiries after
his friends, and with confidential disclosures about the Baby,
with whom he been up promenading most of the preceding
night.

Mrs. Peacock begged me at parting to give her love to thee.

—— And now must I leave thee.   May Sleep bear thee upon his
wing even as tenderly as thou art borne upon the desirous
heart of thy

lover.

To Mary Day Lanier

[Baltimore,] Mch. 12th 1875.

Today, dear Comrade, I am very much better, and will soon be
in brave condition again.   My shoulder-pain is almost entirely
gone, and I can draw something like a decent breath.[64]

— Wh. last is joyful: for the tender air of this day is heavenly.
The morning is perfect Brunswick.   I can not hear any birds,
but I have a distinct sensation that they are about.   On the
opposite sidewalk a lovely little girl in white and blue has just
bounded out of the door with her dog, and her merry cries,
as the little black-and-tan leaps up at her face and then dashes
off in a wavy circle around her, echo up and down the quiet
narrow street, like a bird's song in a glade.   By all the buds
in the woods,– if I might but spend this day with thee there
among the trees !

[63] Apparently R. Miller McClellan, mentioned several times in Lanier's
letters from West Chester, Summer, 1876.

[64] In a letter of Mar. 9, 1875 (here omitted), Lanier had written: "On
Monday mine ancient tiger, the Pleurodynia, leaped upon me from out of the
jungles of the brambly inscrutable,– and gripped me by the left shoulder-blade
in a manner full perilous and painful.   I have been fighting the same for three
days, with the help of a homœopathic doctor, and am today much better."

In a letter of Mar. 11, 1875 (also omitted), he added: "My sickness came
in the worst possible time: and interferes with my projects in a manner which I
wd. regard as bitterly vexatious,– were I not perfectly sure that God is . . . .
confident of His own doings."

————   Thine account of our poor little Elf's illness [65] — — — — — leaves me quite unable to allow myself to think on aught but the greatness of God: – for if I let my yearning contemplate my own powerlessness even but an instant, my reason begins to stagger.   I suppose it will be arranged, Above, and arranged well : – but I wish I could hold the boy in my arms a little. — Meantime, to do what we can : I strongly advise giving him a small *hourly* dose of whiskey. Watch closely to find if it should produce any headache, or other such disturbance, and if so, reduce dose.   But continue for a week or two, even if no immediate effect should follow. Well, some day I shall see thee.   I wish thee, dear Love, as much happiness as these words contain for thy

lover.

To Clifford A. Lanier

64 Centre St.
Baltimore, Md.
Mch. 14th 1875.

My darling Little Boy, I've been in bed for some time with a severe attack of one of my old enemies, – the Pleurodynia, – and what with the keen pain thereof have not been able to write you. Along with this bruise, comes your balm, your Sonnet: [66] whereof I know not well how to speak.

Truly, however, the world's nomenclature is not by any means correct.   Poetry is simply a collection of poetic things: these " things " may be words, or they may be deeds: and he who *lives* poetry is not less, (but more,) a poet than he who speaks it or writes it.   Why, then, sink you yourself, who are the poet-in-act, below me who am but a poor stammerer in song? *Doubtful mint*, quotha! *sun and rain*, quotha! Well,

[65] In her letter of Mar. 8, 1875, Mary Day Lanier had reported the illness of their son, Sidney, Jr.
[66] The reference is to the first of several sonnets to his brother sent from time to time by Clifford Lanier and published many years later in *Sonnets to Sidney Lanier and Other Poems*, ed. E. H. Griggs (New York, 1915), p. 17. The following paragraph echoes the substance and even the phrases of this sonnet.

sun and rain you are; but there is more poetry in a ray of the one and a drop of the other than I will ever sing. It is to feed you act-poets, that we song-poets grow; I am your Corn, you must eat me: alas, that I am a sickly stalk whereupon you must waste much strength and substance, – to get, I fear, but an absurd and altogether preposterous small nubbin of result.

The " help " came. I have been almost entirely prevented from work by much bodily worthlessness.

May has the poem on Wilsie,[67] and will send you a copy; – but I would like to do a better one, for my recollection of it is, it was shamefully unworth so much loveliness.

I do not know whether I have told you that I have been engaged for two months past in laying plans to cause the establishment of a chair of the " Physics of Music " (embracing all that is very cursorily treated in the " Tyndall on Sound " which you loaned me) in connection with the Peabody Institute of this place. The circumstances are all unfavorable, but I hope to succeed in time, and, if I do, I will have effected a very charming settlement for life, here, in a position which of all others I would desire. I should deliver about twenty lectures on the physics of sound; twenty more on the metaphysics of music: and superadd a continual instruction of large classes of people in sight-reading and simple part-singing.

If I succeed, my plan contemplates a short lecture-tour through the South this spring, – if I can arrange the same on a safe basis beforehand. I should deliver a couple of lectures at each place so arranged, on the physics of music: these would be copiously illustrated with wonderfully-beautiful experiments, of which few persons in this country have any conception. The lectures would be in the highest degree *popular*: they are really almost like a fairy-land of wonders, in their revelations of things which have for many ages been dark. Would the Arlington Club be willing to contract for two of these lectures @ $150 ($75 apiece)? Please ascertain for me. I rather think I could draw that amount to the house, without difficulty: and the probabilities are, that Club would have something over. The Club to furnish Hall, lights &c: and the lectures to be delivered sometime in May. I cannot now make a definite arrangement; but would be glad for you to find out

[67] " To Willie Clopton " (I, 158), written in Mar., 1866.

the possibility of it and let me know immediately if you can.
The lectures would be illustrated musically by the flute, and
scientifically by apparatus constructed for that purpose: and
would be much like those which Mr. Tyndall delivered to
such crowds of people.

Kiss all my dear people for me. I have many things I
would talk to you about; but my sword-arm is now clinging to
my side.

God bless you,

Your bro.

S. L.

To Mary Day Lanier

[Baltimore,] Mch. 16th [17?] 1875.[68]

Good-Morning, My Sweetheart: art thou better of any of
thy maladies, spiritual or bodily, this morning? I would I
were there, to nurse thee. I have never had thee, sick and
deliciously helpless, all to myself, as thou hast had me!

The Ladies' Literary Club desire a piece by me to be read at
their meeting tomorrow afternoon: and I am going to send the
Laus Mariæ.

I have had a talk with Mr. Eaton, one of the active Trustees of the Peabody, in relation to the proposed Professorship.
I do not think it *can* be carried out now as I desire it. They
have just torn down the building in which the musical department of the Institute had been carrying on its operations, to
build a handsome new structure which will require a couple of
years to complete. Until that time they propose to get along
as best they may, and I do not well see how my plans can be
executed,— for want of room. He did not express any more
opposition to the idea than I expected: he belongs, by nature,
to the Opposition: and I think that the other Trustees might be
carried in the way they should go,—if it were not for the
building business. I am to confer further about it, however;
and we may hit upon some plan. Failing in that, I think I

---

[68] Date corrected from the evidence of another letter dated Mar. 16, 1875
(here omitted).

shall attempt some lectures, independently. Whereof I will speak to thee hereafter. Dear Comrade, may God make thee a special Spring, beyond the setting-back of these March-winds,– prays thy

lover.

To Mary Day Lanier

[Baltimore,] Mch. 21st 1875.

Hast thou been such a *very* bad girl? – *I* will forgive thee: how much easier God!

From thine own account of thyself, I judge thou art not a proper person for me to associate with: and as for small Charley and Sidney and Hal and Lulu,— I tremble to imagine the effect upon their morals of one so utterly given over to all manner of evils as thou describest thyself. Dost thou teach Charles to be a Ghoul and rob graveyards? Dost thou privately incite Sidney to clap Hal on the gridiron at first opportunity and roast him and eat him? Art thou suckling Lulu upon the Black Arts? Thy letter makes me fancy thee standing with one foot upon the prostrate forms of thy father and brother, thy hair waving in the breeze which comes from the sighs of mankind, and thy hands setting a torch to the world to complete the grisly desolations thou hast brought upon it.

—— My dear, most sweet Gentle Heart, how well I know all the wretchedness and the pain thou sufferest? Thy physical illness is of the sort that quickly spreads to the soul and makes that sick. It will not be long ere thou art better.

The *Laus Mariæ* [69] made a profound impression on the Literary Club, and I had many fair compliments and felicitations thereupon, last night, from some ladies, who, after hearing the same read, had asked my friend Miss Jones to present me to them. They declared it to be at once " strong and tender ": thou shdst. have heard Miss Florence Locke—a magnificent girl, whose hand and foot were the rage and the despair of the sculptors in Rome, where she has mostly lived,—

[69] Apparently the " In Absence " sequence and not the single sonnet " Laus Mariæ," though that may have been included with the others.

discoursing thereupon, what time she seemed trying to look me through with her brilliant eyes. This last I allowed her to do: because I knew she would see *thee* at the back of me: and I wanted her to see thee. How I love to hear them praising these poems! – for it is praise of *thee*, of whom the poems are but a simple translation.

I am much better. My shoulder is not yet quite free from pain: but I can get a very fair long breath, and this is to me as one of the delights of the Gods.[70]

Thou wilt find the money awaiting thee at Macon. I am indescribably anxious for thee to get there, and be relieved from the body of thy present death.

So: God is great: with Him can I leave thee, and to His love can I commend thee, for I am sure He is at once my and thy

lover.

To Mary Day Lanier

[Baltimore,] Mch. 23rd 1875.

Here comes a letter from Clifford filled with Sonnets, addressed to—O Beauty of Beauties—to *me*. He lays it on with such a hand, to be sure: slap-dash, and never mind the spattering. They are really lovely: and, barring some artistic crudities, due only to want of practice and craftsman's experience, would make a pretty show by the side of gentle Edmund Spenser.

Here comes also a fair letter from Mr. Peacock, begging me to come over again, and sending me Max Adeler's love. I do not know if I told thee that I fell quite in love with this latter when I was in Philadelphia: — a fine broad fellow with no nonsense about him.

[70] In a letter of Mar. 18, 1875 (here omitted), Lanier had written to his wife: "I am better this morning, than in several days. Have been suffering greatly from obstruction of that expectoration which seems to keep me safe. Today the ice seems broken, and I hope my internal trade will revive." But in a letter to L. E. Bleckley, Mar. 22, 1875 (also omitted), he wrote: "My Ne'er-do-well of a lung is in a contrary fit just at present, to such a degree that I cannot write a line without injury and pain."

I have not any news to tell thee. How I know each long sickening of thy heart for some indication of thy future! Dear Comrade I will have somewhat to tell thee, of trust in God and prayer, when I meet thee.

And Oh, how many things have I not to tell thee! Meseems I grow away from my old self, and I am part stranger to thee, and thou to me, and we must meet again and fall in love anew and have over again the old delicious unfolding. Kind Heaven, if thou and I could only be together, in any state approaching tranquillity as to the mere means of life, what a happy mortal were I!

Well, well:— we will not understand, I suppose, till we overstand.

Thy word being Law, I write by this mail to Mrs. B.[71] In truth I had thought not to answer the letter at all: it did not require one, and I did not know that she wd. expect it.

I am buried, deeply interred, and utterly entombed in a little poem,–wh. thou shalt see in a day or two.

God distill thee without more crushing, – – – prays thy

lover.

To Gibson Peacock [72]

64 Centre St.
Baltimore, Md.
Mch. 24th 1875

My dear Mr. Peacock:

A thousand thanks for your kind and very thoughtful letter. I should have gone to Philadelphia in acceptance of your invitation, to meet Miss Cushman,– although much tied by engagements here, and in ill condition of health to go anywhere– had I not expected to meet her here in April. Your announcement of her illness gives me sincere concern, and I will be thankful to you if you will keep me posted as to her progress in recovery. I wrote her a short time ago, to care

[71] Mrs. Bostwick, a Brunswick friend who had nursed Sidney Lanier, Jr., when he was ill, during Mary Day Lanier's absence in Macon.

[72] Previously published, *Atlantic Monthly*, LXXIV, 19-20 (July, 1894); reprinted, *Letters* (New York, 1899), pp. 11-12.

of her bankers in New York: but fear she has been too ill to read my letter.

I have the delightful anticipation of seeing you again, for a day or two, ere long: but cannot now tell whether it will be in two or three weeks. My plans depend on the movements of others: and as soon as they become more definite, you shall know them.

Pray tell your good Mrs. Peacock that I am much better, and, though in daily fight against severe pain, am hard at work. About four days ago, a certain poem which I had vaguely ruminated for a week before, took hold of me like a real James River Ague: and I have been in a mortal shake with the same, day and night, ever since. I call it " The Symphony ": [73] I personify each instrument in the Orchestra and make them discuss various deep social questions of the times, in the progress of the music. It is now nearly finished: and I shall be rejoiced thereat for it verily racks all the bones of my spirit.

Did you see Mr. Taylor? Tell me about him.[74] I can not tell you with what eagerness I devoured " Felix Holt ". For perfect force-in-repose, Miss Evans, (or, I should have said, Mrs. Lewes) is not excelled by any writer.

Pray convey my warm regards to Mrs. Peacock: and keep that big heartsome " Max Adeler " in remembrance of his and

Your friend

Sidney Lanier.

To Mary Day Lanier

[Baltimore,] Mch. 24th 1875.

Small favors thankfully received.

Here hath come a letter from one A. Pope, the same being a high functionary in the net-work of railroads running (happy roads !) towards thee, towit, the " Great Atlantic Coast Line

[73] See I, 46.
[74] The reference is undoubtedly to the poet Bayard Taylor, whose friendship with Lanier, through the medium of Peacock, began the following summer.

Felix Holt, mentioned in the next sentence, was a novel by George Eliot, who had long been a favorite of Lanier's.

&c&c&c ", asking me to call on a certain day at the Office of said Roads in Baltimore: and I have called: and he wisheth me to write, – By Homer and Lucretius, By Dan Chaucer and John Keats and Will Shakespeare, — he wisheth me to write a — . a ———– (Choke, choke, choke) a – ch —. (gulp, gulp, gulp) a Guide book To Florida Travellers. He proposeth, By Pegasus, to pay my hotel-bills and travelling expenses, and to give me One hundred and twenty five dollars a month – By Crœsus, in addition thereto: and I am to take from April to the last of June for the work.[75] I am to do Norfolk, Richmond, Petersburg, Wilmington, Raleigh, Charlotte, Columbia, Augusta, Charleston, Savannah, Jacksonville, St. Augustine, and Florida generally: I am to relate their histories, recount their products, immortalize their great men, describe their topographies, and depict their " points of interest ": and am–, according to the instructions of my patron and Mæcænas, to get up a Guide-book, which shall at once be a literary attraction and a statistical thesaurus. I owe all these honors to my Mæcænas' having read " Corn ".

Well, Apollo was a swineherd: By Gog and Magog, shall I twist my nose at bread and meat?

My frame of mind is, as thou perceivest, expletive. In fact, I have accepted the offer.

Mr. Pope goes to New York to see the publishers: and will return early next week, to make the final arrangements.

Dear Heart, dear Love, dear Wife, if nothing go wrong, I shall see thee within three weeks from this time: it may be earlier. For this grace, Laus Deo, ten thousand times : and I will arise and play me a heart's-relief on my piano.

I wrote Mrs. Bostwick.

Mayst thou sleep and dream that thy heart beats double, – prays thy

lover.———

---

[75] *Florida* (VI, 3-183) was published in Nov., 1875, by J. B. Lippincott & Co. The work on this pot-boiler consumed nearer six months than three.

To Mary Day Lanier

[Baltimore,] Mch. 28th 1875.

I am just from St. Paul's Church where they have had a small orchestra – *quorum pars* – to play with the organ and chorus for Easter services. How wondrous pathetic are these boys' voices: there is a saintly tenderness, and yet a depth of human passion, in them.

–   If my plan with Mr– Pope hold, – and I am to know tomorrow or next day, finally – I am going to do Florida first, and I intend to take thee there with me. Thou and I, alone, for a month, in among the beautiful rivers and leaves ! It doth soberly seem to me that God hath arranged this matter, both for thee and for me: and I feel sure it must be accomplished, in some way.

Laus Mariæ, my poem " The Symphony " is finished. I have just sent a copy up-stairs to Miss Seaton: here is her note anent the same. In the last sentence of her note she refers to going to the Catholic service,– which she doth today for the Easter music. It was lovely that she should have referred the poem to *thee*. It is nearly twice as long as Corn, I believe: and it says some things I have very long wanted to say.

I am bathed in the blissful sweetness of the hope of seeing thee very soon: insomuch that although I am tired to the verge of paralysis with the writing which I have *had* to do, yet I am like a lark midway betwixt the sun and the dew: and I am going forth presently to the Park, – where I have never yet been – to sit and build thy face in among the trees, and fill the heavens as full of thee as my heart is.

So, dear Wife, may shaggy-maned Life bear thee along to the morrow, even as the lion bare Una,[76] – prays thy

lover.——

---

[76] The allusion is to Spenser's *Faerie Queene*.

To Mary Day Lanier

[Baltimore,] Mch. 31st 1875.

My Heart of my heart, Mr. Pope has not yet returned, and I
have no news to tell thee, and I do but scratch this little note
to kiss thee at Macon.

Thy slipper is not with the shoes: *sois-tu tranquille*, I will
bring thee a pair of dainty ones for thee to wear in Florida.

Here has come a charming letter from Mr. Spencer, mostly
in the nature of hints and instructions, as from a veteran soldier to a raw recruit. " Eschew versatility ", he says. " Take
your one motive judiciously, work it industriously, stick to it
faithfully. If you have chosen poetry, be a poet and nothing
else – so you will be a great one. I never did anything passing well in my life but I tired of it immediately and so have
disappointed myself and everybody else. I have made margins of success in many fields – editorial – verse – novellette –
tale-writing – stage – but I never worked the gold-veins I have
discovered down to the quartz, – and the prospector never gets
rich. The discoverer of the Comstock Lode died in the alms-
house." And much more he saith in the same vein.

Now can I not write more. May God quickly unite the
threads of me and thee, – prayeth thy

lover.

To Edward Spencer [77]

64 Centre St.
Baltimore, Md.
April 1st 1875.

Dear Mr. Spencer:

That you speak of yourself, at once honors
me and pleases me: and I find your letter altogether delightful.
You are like a road through the woods, that often turns: as
one achieves each bend of you, one has not only the glade that
is immediately about one, but there is the curve ahead: – in

[77] Previously published, *Studies in Philology*, XXVII, 465-466 (July, 1930).

which one knows there will be revealed something at once
good and unexpected. Do you know, one of the most difficult adjustments I have had to make in life has been the pre-
serving of my friendships sacred from that sort of weakening-
of-force-according-to-the-square-of-the-distance which appears
to obtain as well in the inner as in the outer world. Almost
all my friends have been men immersed in business, whilst I
was compelled, a year or two ago, to leave my trade (by a
scalawag lung) and to betake myself to the other side of life.
Hence a certain divergence betwixt me and these friends: I
was conscious as it were of having to raise my voice, to communicate with them, – of an empty space intervening. Of
course, the sacredness of friendly faith made me careless of
the small trouble of speaking a little louder: and so I have
learned to continue to love them with all my heart, at the
same time without sacrificing the desire that we might not be
too far apart for whispering. It is loving, with a sigh : not
less in intensity, only less in the pleasure it yields.

— Wherefrom, as Jean Paul says, important inferences are
to be drawn: and I advise the reader to draw them.

—″— From what I know of your writings, I can easily see
how great must have been your temptations to " versatility ":
and I thank you for the warning, in that behalf, though I obsti-
nately refuse to see that your own example points your moral,
for your success in so many fields is rather a seduction thereto
than a repulsion therefrom. Fortunately for me, a decisive
limitation of faculty has prevented me from the disasters which
must have ensued if I had attempted to caper over such an
enormous playground as you breathe yourself in.   Things
come to me mostly in one of two forms, – the poetic or the
musical. I express myself with most freedom in the former
modus: with most passionate delight in the latter. Indeed I
ought to say that, *apud me*, music is, in my present stage of
growth, rather a passion than a faculty: I am not its master,
it is mine. It is only within a few months that I had the least
glimpse of my own relation to Art. May I tell you how I got it?
It was through a chagrin. I had sent " Corn " to the Atlantic
Monthly. It went under exceptionally favorable auspices. Mr.
Hurd (one of the owners of the Atlantic Monthly) had read
the *ms.* and sent it himself to the editor, with his commenda-

tion. Mr. Howells wrote back, that "with every desire to
like" the poem, he "did not find it successful," that readers
would be mystified by it, that there was no "connection between the apostrophe in the beginning and the bit of narrative
at the close," and that "neither was striking enough to stand
alone": – and declined to put it in the Magazine. He finished
by coolly asking Mr. Hurd to show the letter to me: – which
Mr. H. had done, through the mail.[78]

—   I took the letter to my room, – it was a high room, in
Brooklyn, N. Y. from whose window I could see many things –
and there, during a day whose intensity was of that sort that
one only attempts to communicate to one's God, I led myself
to an infinite height above myself and meditated: and when
evening came I found myself full of the ineffable contents of
certainty and of perfect knowledge and of decision. I had
become aware,– not by reasoning, I could only reason about it
afterwards, I know not what the process was – that my business
in life was to make poems. Since then it has not occurred to
me to doubt about my sort of work. Why should one disquiet
oneself with asking whether one is to sing solos, or to come
on only in the concerted parts? God must have His chorus.

—   I please myself with believing you will be glad to know
that the martydom which has preceded the heaven of so many
finer singers than I am, is not likely to be mine. "Corn" has
met with a recognition all over the country far beyond my
utmost hope, I am still all in a smile at having been sent for,
the other day, by Miss Charlotte Cushman, who kept me
a-blush for an hour with big generous praises, enough to make
a man a pious and humble workman for the balance of his life.

So !   I have told you what I have not dared to speak of, to
any man. In so doing, my desire was to show you how sensible
I am of your goodness in writing me as you have, and how
glad I will be to call myself

Your friend

Sidney Lanier.

[78] This letter (dated Oct. 3, 1874) is printed above, p. 96.

To Mary Day Lanier

Philadelphia, April 7th 1875.

Well then –, hast thou thought thy lover was dumb? I have
not been able to write thee: I have been here with Miss Cushman for three days, and what time has not been taken up with
business has been completely given to her.   We are at Mr.
Peacock's house.   Yesterday I read her " The Symphony ": she
requested it and took me off alone into a lovely little room in
the house called " The Brown Study ".   I wish I might describe to thee all her exclamations and manifold expressions
while I was reading: or tell thee one-half the handsome things
she said with eye, with tongue and with hand, when I had
finished. This afternoon,– while I was out – she read the poem
to the others: Mr. Peacock and wife, and Miss Stebbins: [79]
so when I came in I was greeted with effusion, and their honest
and hearty praises pleased me mightily: they all appeared to
have seen exactly what the poem *wants* its readers to see.
—   I also read Miss Cushman the " Power of Prayer ",
which I have rewritten and much enlarged with special reference to her dramatic recitation of it.[80]   It seemed to fill her
with pleasure: and she is to read it in her next tour, in public,
beginning at New York.   How she does seize good ole blind
Uncle Jim !   It is a miracle of acting.
(While this is being written she has come in, and sate down
by me, and, exclaiming at my writing with my left-hand, I have
told her it is for thee, to thee, and through thee originally,
that I so write; then we have discussed Michael Angelo's
Sonnets, and Shakespeare's, and *others*: and presently she rises
to go, and I kiss her hand, and she presses mine and declares
that thy lover is " a very dear fellow and she is very fond of
him; " whereupon he continueth to write to thee, to the effect
that Mr. Kirk has been completely conquered by the Symphony
(K. is a fine musician) and has received me with many smiles

[79] Emma Stebbins, a sculptress, was the companion of Charlotte Cushman,
who became a good friend of Lanier's.
[80] In a letter to his brother Clifford, Apr. 12, 1875 (here omitted), Lanier
said: " I have written four more verses to it, in order to intensify the climax
by postponing it a little."

and great cordiality.[81]   I came here specially to get an estimate
from Lippincott & Co, of the cost of the book I'm to write for
my Mæcænas Locomotive.   I leave here tomorrow for New
York, then to Boston for a day, – on the same business – then
to Baltimore by Sunday, and to thee-wards on the Tuesday
following.   Heartsease, my heart can scarcely contain itself at
all, either with the joy of seeing thee again, or the ineffable
desire to have my route fairly turned in thy direction.

So now dinner is come.   God have thee in His love as it
were a Rose in some Heavenly South,–crieth thy

lover.——

To Mary Day Lanier [82]

[Boston,] Mass
April 10th 1875.

My Heart: It is seven O'clock in the morning, – I am just
come from the sleeping-car in which I have groaned and tra-
vailed all night with the too-much-humanity therein and the
heart-breaking air thereof; have ridden down through a brilliant morning – a most rare and lovely opposite to the drear
easterly rain through which I splashed all day yesterday in
New York; have come to the Revere House, and passed up to
my room betwixt long rows of honest broad-footed Boston
boots, the toes that should inhabit the same being yet asleep,
and God knows what wrigglings of the same will be accomplished under these leathern hidings ere this " business-day "
be done: – and so I am finally at a table, to send thee one little
kiss before I get me in to breakfast and start forth on my round.

I had a running day of it in New York: saw Foster & Park-
man for a few minutes, talked with Mr. [J.F.D.] Lanier &
Charles about Florida, (they have just returned from there)
had a pleasant interview with Mr. Gilder (of Scribner's Maga-

---

[81] On Apr. 4 J. F. Kirk had sent Lanier a check for $100.00 in payment for
" The Symphony," published in *Lippincott's* in June, 1875.

[82] Lanier had gone to Boston at Pope's request to secure an estimate for the
printing of the Florida guide book from H. O. Houghton & Co. and Rand,
Avery & Co. (see letters from both firms dated Apr. 10, 1875). Lanier's
letter is written on the stationery of the Revere House, Boston.

zine) and obtained permission for Miss Cushman to read the
" Power of Prayer ", saw Hurd & Houghton about the Florida
book, had a talk with the McDonalds, rushed over to Brooklyn
and got hugged and kissed by Anna Mary and dined with the
Ripleys, – and how proud the old gentleman is, of the success
of Corn ! he has had it circulated among all his friends and
thinks it wondrous fine himself —: then back to 42nd street
dêpot where I took cars for Boston.

This afternoon at five I start back to New York, reaching
there tomorrow morning, and returning to Baltimore tomorrow
afternoon. On Tuesday I hope to start to thee.[83]

I would, O my Too-Sweet, that my yearning were some soil
and climate wherein thou grewest for a heartsease: so should'st
thou be fed forever from the unending desire of thy

lover.

To Mariquita Peacock [84]

Brunswick, Ga.
April 18th 1875.

My dear Mrs. Peacock:

Such a three days' *dolce far niente* as
I'm having! With a plenty of love, wife's bairn's and brother's
—and no end of trees and vines. What more should a work-
battered man desire, in this divine atmosphere which seems
like a great sigh of pleasure from some immense Lotus in this
vague South? This little house, by one of whose windows I
am writing, stands in one corner of an open square which is
surrounded by an unbroken forest of oaks, of all manner of
clambering and twining things and of pines—not the dark
gloomy pines of the Pennsylvania Mountains, but tall masses
of vivid emerald all in a glitter with the more brilliant green
of the young buds and cones: the sun is shining with a hazy
and absent-minded face, as if he were thinking of some quite

[83] Lanier spent Apr. 11 in New York and Apr. 12 in Baltimore, leaving for
the South the next day (see his letter to Mary Day Lanier, Apr. 12, 1875, here
omitted).

[84] Previously published, *Atlantic Monthly*, LXXIV, 20 (July, 1894); reprinted *Letters* (New York, 1899), pp. 12-14.

other star than this poor earth: occasionally a little wind comes along, not warm but unspeakably bland, bringing strange secrets rather of leaves than of flowers: the mocking-birds are all singing, but singing *sotto voce*, and a distant cock crows as if he didn't *mean* to crow, but only to yawn luxuriously: an old mauma over in the neighborhood is singing, as she sets about her washing in her deliberate way, something like this

persistently rejecting all the semitones of the D minor in which she is singing (as I have observed all the barbaric music does, as far as it can) and substituting the stronger C♮ for the C♯: and now my little four-year old comes in from feeding the pony. and the goat, and writhes into my lap, and inquires with great interest "Papa, can you whistle *backwards*?" by which I find, after a puzzled inquiry, that he means to ask if I can whistle by drawing my breath *in*, instead of forcing it out, – an art in which he proceeds to instruct me with a great show of superiority: and now he leaves, and the whole world is still again, except the birds' lazy song and old Mauma's monotonous crooning.

I am convinced that God meant this land for people to rest in,–not to work in. If we were so constituted that life *could* be an idyll, then this were the place of places for it: but being, as it is, the hottest of all battles,– a man might as well expect to plan a campaign in a dream as to make anything like his best fight here.

My wife and I are to meet the Schlatters this afternoon, when I expect to discuss you and your other half *in extenso* with Madame Fanny.[85]

Pray write me how Miss Cushman seemed on the morning after the reading. She was so exhausted when I helped her from the carriage, that I fear her strength must have been severely taxed. My address, for a month hence, will be at Jacksonville, Fla–: I leave for that place on Wednesday, (day after tomorrow) and shall make it headquarters during all my ramblings around the flowery State.

[85] See note 28, above.

These lonesome journeys—which are the necessities of my unsettled existence— make me doubly grateful for the delightful recollections which form my companions, along the tiresome miles, and for which I am indebted to you. Believe, my dear Mrs. Peacock, that they are always with me, and that I am always your and Mr. Peacock's,

Sincere friend

Sidney Lanier

To Clifford A. Lanier

Brunswick, Ga.
April 21st 1875.

My dear Clifford, Your no. 6 would make a dumb man scream; if I didn't have any arm at all I would be obliged to write you about it; it makes me think of the time when our dear reverend Master Will had the quill betwixt his fingers. I am marvellous anxious to talk to you about it, and about these others, scarcely less beautiful. You need but the least bit of a hint, calling your attention to certain inward and subtle matters of *tone*, of a certain *pervading atmosphere* which a great artist exhales through his work, – such a hint as indeed our same Will Shakespeare (without blasphemy be it spoken) would have been all the better for—in order to *hasten* you forward on your growth; – for you would quickly find out for yourself what I mean, if your mode of life allowed you to go through with all those odd and seemingly unoccupied hours of scribbling and apparent trifling, which have usually earned for artists in their early life the reputation of being but lazy and trifling chaps. If life allowed you time to pass through this strange formation half-calm-before-a-storm, this doldrums of the artist, I would not say a word in the way of hint to you: but I only come in to supply the want of time, I am but a substitute for the trifling moments when hints are born.

Without time to detail my admiration, I say in general that your sonnets surprise me and delight me. I see what a revelation has come to you out of Shakespeare's Sonnets: – and the fullness and the glory of it shine in your writings since then.

I really think it would be a good test of the great artist (as distinguished from that host of merely *clever* culture-poets who now deluge the world with smug verses and keen conceits) to note what effect the reading of Shakespeare's Sonnets wd. have on him. If they transported him, – as they have you – into a fervent world where even the dreariest commonplaces of life put on the tenderness of a new and unspeakable religion, and where the devout soul, walking about among his former blasted trees and scaly mountain-sides, is continually breaking out into fresh songs of delight as he finds them flashing into leafage and verdure and spouting springs; – I say if this were the effect of them, it may be finally set down that he is an artist and no mere product of cleverness and education.

Pray write as much as you can, without any reference at all to the use of what you write. You will find that with every poem you step up to a higher outlook and to a freer use of your powers. – How hard it is to me, not to be impatient of this disability which prevents my eager pen from saying all I *would* say to you, now!

– The " weary night of march " continues, my dear Boy; and now presents us in different relations, – for it is *you* who are now pulling *my* boat out of the mud, and helping *me* along, – with these strangely-named " Checks," of yours.[86]

Well – there is nothing to *say* about it.

I will write you from Jacksonville, where I go tomorrow, after my three happy days here with the wife and the bairns. If I can find a place for private board at all within reach, I shall send for May to come to me for a week, at some point not far from Jacksonville, so that she may give me a lift in the writing I have to do.

I send a kiss to anybody that wants one, from your

S. L.

[86] The phrase ("weary night of march") is from the sonnet sent by Clifford Lanier. The reference to a check is to a seven line verse, dated Apr. 17, 1875, above which Lanier himself wrote: "From my dearest Clifford, accompanied by a ' check ' for money. S. L." (MS, Clifford A. Lanier Collection, Johns Hopkins University.)

To Mary Day Lanier

Jacksonville, Fla
April 27th 1875

Heart of My Soul, there is just a moment ere too late for the mail to write thee that I find many reasons leading me to come back to thee, instead of bringing thee to me,— tho' this last I wd. greatly prefer. I must sigh and give it up, therefore; and the joy of seeing thee will be great enough wherever it may be.

I will return to thee on Wednesday, reaching Brunswick D. V. on Wednesday night.

God keep thee and all mine till then, prays

thy

lover.

To Mary Day Lanier

J[ackson]ville, May 11th 1875.

I came safely here, dear Comrade, this morning, in company with Col. Thomes, who joined me at Jessup. We have jogged along into a very social companionship, and I find him very pleasant, abounding in stories of Western life, – he has been on the surveys of all the Pacific railroads from Texas to the most Northerly one – and quite orthodox on the subject of Brunswick. We had a lovely sail in a small yacht this afternoon, and my sighs for thee and the boys were intense enough to have driven the sail if the breeze had failed.

I found letters from Mr. Pope, containing what I expected, and stating that he had telegraphed me: – tho' I have never rec'd the telegram. Also find I have a couple of charming epistles from Miss Stebbins (the sculptor who did the beautiful fountain in Central Park, and now Miss Cushman's inseparable companion)[87] and from my faithful Mr. Peacock. Thou wilt see how the inspiration which rayed out from thee as thou

[87] Emma Stebbins mentioned in her letter of May 2, 1875, the project under way in New York for the establishment of an American College of Music—a project which was of much concern to Lanier during the ensuing year.

sat'st by me while I wrote the letter to Mrs. Peacock, did fill
the same even to such a degree that she calleth it a poem.

I am better today. Strange to say, for two days I have had
no expectoration at all. I don't know what this means, but I
feel very well; and I suppose it will return gradually.

Thou wilt kiss all my dear ones from Grandpapa to grand-
son; and wilt be always the sweet heaven out of which comes
poems to thy

lover.

To Mary Day Lanier

St. Augustine, Fla.
May 13th 1875.

I have had my rage of delight over the old Fort, I have paced
the sea-wall, I have had a fair draught of the glory of the
water, I have lounged along through the 16th century, I have
struggled through a night of fleas and mosquitoes, I have
shaken hands with Col. Thomes, (who left this morning,— and
I'm rather glad he's gone, for he isn't a bit sentimental in my
way): and so now I am abandoned to an agony of yearning
that thou mightst be with me in this lovely solitude of a city.
I cannot get myself to be satisfied, I wander about, I do
nothing, I resist work with enough energy to *do* it, my heart
calls and cries like some one lost in the night, it is intolerable
that I should be bereaved of thee so soon, what shall I do?

The hotels here are all closed; I board at Mrs. Gibbs', and
had a pleasant meeting today at dinner with Lieut. Hubbell,
and a couple of other army-officers, one of whom was " the
captain " that figures in the Harper's articles on " The Ancient
City." [88]

The air is languid and sleepy and sweet to the last degree, if
thou wert here it would be heaven.

Pray apply this enclosed to such of thy little woman's-wants
as the same may suffice for. To send thee such a sum!

[88] Two articles on St. Augustine by Constance Fenimore Woolson were published under this title in *Harper's*, L, 1-25 (Dec., 1874), and 165-185 (Jan.,
1875).

— I will likely stay here five days and thou mayst write me *here*.

May Comfort come to thee up out of the sea, and fall upon thee down out of the heavens, and steal into thy heart from every tree that stands, yea every happy tree that stands there, about thee and near to thee,— prays thy

lover.

To Mary Day Lanier

St. Augustine, Fla.
May 14th 1875.

Thine was forwarded me from Jacksonville today. How piteous is thine appeal! I am half in the mind, as I read thy longing words, to rush back to thee. Thou art the sweetest-hearted Sweetheart that ever went unkissed. I cannot but believe that some day will come when I will be by thee always. The immensity of love often accomplishes itself.

— Every day I find new books about Florida. I have written the first fifteen pages of mine.[89] I put on great airs, therein, as if I were going to sum up and conclude the whole business, and forever remove the necessity of any more being said anent this country:—but 'tis hard work.

I am much better: there is scarcely a tinge of blood. This climate is heavenly in May. How blind are the people that leave it in March for the villainous nose-blowing North!

Here have I met Richard Armstrong, originally of Macon. He has a glorious large house, in a few feet of the water, and leads a careless life, with a sailboat and a gun. He was with John Kell on the Sumter and the Alabama.

I pray thee send back, to this place, Miss Stebbin's letter. I must read it again ere answering.

I manage to write, better than I expected. —Here are three army-officers, who are very pleasant companions. Lieut. Hubbell,— who is a violinist, is greatly taken with the flute: and last night I played piece after piece to a very enthusiastic audience at Gen. Sprague's house. One of the most ardent ap-

---

[89] Probably part of the section entitled "Historical," eventually published as Chap. XIII of *Florida* (VI, 116).

plauders was a very pleasant Miss Worth, daughter of Gen.
Worth.

If thou cdst, only stand with me this night, and look from
the sea-wall at the brave steady light over yonder! – But thou
art at once light, landscape, water-sheen, sweet breeze, and
starry heaven, to thy

lover.

To Mary Day Lanier

St. Augustine, Fla.
May 19th 1875.

Thine of 16th bringeth me both rejoicing and grief: rejoicing
in the fact, grief in the scant measure of the same.

Thou art a born letter-writer: and I would I had thy
powers. I would be fain to leave scribbling verses and betake
me to epistolary works.

Thy letters are honey-sweet, and full of vast loves and com-
forts that help my heart marvellously.

I linger here, being in midst of my second chapter, " On
the Climate of Florida." [90] I have now about got the book in
my head, I believe, in a general way: and am in a fair way to
accumulate particulars. It has been the hardest work I ever
did, to evolve the matter in any method satisfactory to myself:
and I don't yet quite dare to read what I have written.

The flute hath taken many captives here, and I have to steer
away from musical engagements, in order to get time for my
pen.

Thou wert better write me to Jacksonville. I will likely go
up the river on Saturday, and know not where I will stop. It is
not probable I can easily get across to Tampa, from Mellon-
ville: and I now think to come back to Jacksonville by
steamer, and go thence by rail to Cedar Keys, for a look at the
Western Coast: then on a flying visit to Tallahassee: and
then—to Heaven— which thou art, to thy

lover.

---

[90] Actually published as Chap. XII (VI, 101).

To Mary Day Lanier

St. Augustine, Fla.
May 22nd 1875.

Thine enclosing Miss Stebbins' and the Prof.'s [91] letters
hath reached me. Thou art a good lady and a sweet, and I
am much famished for a kiss.

I will leave this place on Monday morning, to go up the
river. I know not how long the journey will take me: but I
hope not more than four or five days. Thou wert best write
me at Jacksonville, where I will be circulating for some days.

Tell Sidney and Charley I saw Seventy two big Indians
yesterday: proper men, and tall, as one would wish to behold.
They were weary, and greatly worn: but as they stepped out of
the cars, and folded their ample blankets about them, there was
a large dignity and majestic sweep about their movements that
made me much desire to salute their grave excellencies. Each
had his ankles chained together; but managed to walk like a
man, withal.   They are confined, – by some ass who is in
authority – in the the lovely old Fort, as unfit for them as they
for it. It is in my heart to hope sincerely that they may all get
out.[92]

I am very well: and have written some eighty five pages
of ms. which I find will make forty or more pages of my book.
At this rate, I shall get on very well.

God build thee a little special Florida about thy soul,
my dear Heart, – is this day's prayer of thy
husband.

To Mary Day Lanier

Polatka [Pilatka,]
May 27th (I *think*) 1875.

I have to stay here all day, in order to take a boat tonight
going up the Oclawaha. I now think I will not go up to
Enterprise at all: there is nothing to be seen at that point, of

[91] Prof. A. F. Mayer had written to Lanier, inclosing a pamphlet on "Acoustics" (see Mary Day Lanier's letters of May 19 and 21, 1875).
[92] Treated at some length in Chap. III of *Florida* (VI, 25).

different character from what I have already seen. My Oclawaha boat returns on Saturday, and I hope to be back in
Jacksonville on Monday morning.

As soon thereafter as I can telegraph to Mr. Pope and get
an answer, I will forward $125 to Harry: and there is no rea-
son why it cannot be all done on Monday. There is a banker
in Jacksonville, through whom I can draw as soon as Pope
lets me know by telegraph upon whom to make my draft.

Travelling is slow, here, and all things move somewhat
languidly. I am very well.

I have had just a glimpse of " the Symphony ", in Lippincott's. It looks lovely; in a somewhat hurried though careful reading, I did not find a single error of any description.
The Power Of Prayer is also out in Scribner's.

Lippincott writes me, agreeing to Pope's arrangement, about
the Florida articles for the Magazine.[93]   But heavens and earth,
what shall I do, I have but two hands, if I could write with
both of them simultaneously I would scarcely be able to make
ends meet, now. I'll think of it. But meantime, thou must
meet me at Jacksonville. Do not come by the boat, but take
the first train after this reaches thee,—either the B. & A. or
M. & B. as thou shalt find on inquiry to be most convenient; I
will be sure to meet thee at the cars in Jacksonville. I will
greatly need thee, then, to do some writing which thou canst
do even better than I could: being short descriptions of a list
of towns which I wish to prepare in order to make my book
complete. I pray thee stop not for aught, but come immediately; as for clothes thou canst have nice washing done in
Jacksonville, and as for appearances thou wilt see no one there
half so lovely as thou habitually art. Herein fail not: and
telegraph me, at Jack'ville, when thou startest.

So God have thee in His holy keeping, thou sweetest Heart
that e'er He hath set throbbing,— prays thy

husband

---

[93] " The Ocklawaha in May " and " St. Augustine in April," published in
Lippincott's, Oct. and Nov., 1875, were also included as chapters in the book
itself (VI, 13, 25).

To Clifford A. Lanier

Pilatka, Fla,
May 27th 1875.

My darling Little Boy,

     I had hoped to write you some short method of meeting me somewhere in Florida; but I have found all my movements so entirely beyond prophecy that I have been wholly unable to appoint a place or time, – and so I must give *that* up, too.

Our Power of Prayer is out in Scribners'. I got just one glance at it before leaving St. Augustine, in a copy belonging to another person. From that glance I think the villain of an editor has changed the brogue: *e. g.* I observed he spelled " Marster " *Mah'sr* – which is simply abominable, and I hope life will sometime put me in position to polish him off some time. The amount of pure jackass-ism which exists among these editor people is a thing that no man can credit until he has had a little to do with them. You will scarcely believe that this same fellow wrote me a letter, – when he sent me the pro[o]f-sheets of The Power of Prayer – desiring me to change the dialect in one or two points: and that I replied at length giving him a fair and full exposition of the negro brogue which ought to have convinced even himself that *quoad* this matter he was an ass: and yet he changes it, again, of his own motion.

My " Symphony " is out in the June number of Lippincott's, and is beautifully printed. It looks better in print than it did in ms.; and I hope you'll like it.

I've had a somewhat rough experience here, and am in great stress to get my work done in time.

If you write me at Savannah, I will get your letter. I'm going up the Oclawaha river this evening and will be back in Jacksonville on Monday. By the way, if you should write immediately, a letter would reach me addressed to Jacksonville, Fla. Perhaps you'd better write me there, anyhow; I'd like to know how the poems strike you, as I haven't had a fair look at either yet, and can't get the magazines for some days.

Where is Aunt Jane? I will have to spend a day or two in Charleston, soon.

Tell Sissa I shall write her the minute I get time, and that I have by no means forgotten her sweet little letter to me in Baltimore. Pray explain to this dear little girl how small my chirographic capacity is.

Kiss everybody for

Yr. bro.

S. L.

To Robert S. Lanier

[Jacksonville.   June 4th 1875.] [94]

My dear Father:

I found my work here assuming such proportions that I sent for Mary to help me, and she joined me on Tuesday morning at this place. This gives me the first opportunity I have had—to write you:– an opportunity I have been vainly trying to secure for a month past. Besides the book I am to write for the Coast Line, I have a commission from Lippincott's for a couple of Magazine articles about Florida, which I wish to execute if possible.

Until the last two days I have found the climate of Florida very delightful: and I' should enjoy it now, though somewhat warmer, were I not beginning to get a little bilious, I suppose from my sudden change in climatic surroundings, from cold to warm.

My " Symphony " has brought me some gratifying messages. I regret I am so busy that I have not had time to attend to it properly. The " Power Of Prayer," in spite of the prejudice against the over worked vein of dialect poems, is having a fine run over the West.

Harry forwarded your letter here, and we got it this morning. I will try and run over to Macon from Augusta, (which I think I can do at night), and see you. I am glad to know that Uncle C. is better, and shall be rejoiced to see him again, as all of you. I hope to be in Augusta about the twentieth, next.

[94] The date is in Mary Day Lanier's handwriting.

I enclose notice from the Ph^a Bulletin, about the Symphony.[95] Please return it to Mary at Brunswick.

We leave here this evening for Cedar Keys; will spend a day at Gainesville, and one at Tallahasse, besides two at Cedar Keys: and then to Brunswick, whence after one day's stay I must get on to Augusta and Savannah.   I sent Harry my first month's wages today– $125– but I am still greatly behind-hand with him, and he is hard pressed: so that if you can send (as you mention in your letter) some money to Brunswick next week, it will be of great service.   You had better send it to Harry, directly.

Convey a great deal of love to all, from

Your Son

Sidney L.

To Virginia Hankins

Tebeanville, Ga.

June 15th 1875

In the almost weekly hope of clasping your hand, dear Friend, – your own very hand – I have forborne to write you, pleasing myself with delicious vaticinations of arriving at a Richmond hotel, of dispatching you a line to ask if I may see you and when, and of receiving from you some brief expression of that friendliness upon which I have reposed so profoundly for so many years; but I find that my Richmond appari-

---

[95] The Philadelphia *Evening Bulletin*, in May, 1875, gave a running account of the poem with excerpts, but declared: " No description can give an idea of this remarkable production, the conception of which is original even to audacity, but the execution is a complete vindication of the author's boldness. Being a musician as well as a poet, and a student of human nature as well as of art and letters, Mr. Lanier has thrown his whole soul into this poem. . . . The poem is, like all works of art, to be judged of as a whole.   It gives new laurels to Mr. Lanier, and strengthens his position among the very first of American poets."   In a subsequent issue the entire poem was reprinted, accompanied by an editorial pronouncing it the " finest American poem ever written on an aesthetic subject."   (From an undated clipping in the Charles D. Lanier Collection, Johns Hopkins University, and Mary Day Lanier's letters of May 23 and May 26, 1875.   No file of the Philadelphia *Evening Bulletin* for this period has been found.)

tion postpones itself yet for something like ten days or two
weeks, and this morning something or other, in the nature of
those inward voices which I have learned not to disobey, tells
me to write you.

    —   And yet I am so near talking to you that the pen gives
off its ink but coldly.

Write me, at *Savannah, Ga*, I pray you, if you remain in
Richmond yet some weeks longer, indeed your whole summer
programme.

The success of my " Corn " brought me several engagements,
among others one to go and roam over Florida and write a
book about it. I am now just returning Northward in order
to superintend the printing of the book which has resulted from
a long ramble over Florida that I've been prosecuting ever since
I left Baltimore in May.

A copy of Lippincott's for June will be sent you, containing
a long poem of mine called " The Symphony ". Of course I
know that you will like it: but I *hope* that you may love it
immensely. I have dared *almost* to write quite at my ease in
the matters of rhythm, rhyme, and substance, in this poem.
You will be glad to know that it has had a grand success.

There is also a poem by Clifford and me, in Scribner's for
June, called the " Power Of Prayer." The villainous editor,
without our knowledge, changed the spelling of some of the
words (notably *Marster*, which he, ignorant Yankee soul, con-
verted into " Mah'sr ") and so has saddled us with an appearance of artistic untruthfulness. The brogue of the piece was
perfect when we sent it to him.

You are not one who, tired of *poor* dialect poems, condemns
all dialect poems? One must remember that Burns wrote
almost wholly in dialect: and that the strongest poem of
Tennyson [96] is in dialect.

                         "
————————————————————————————————————
                         "

My Friend, I long to see you. Write me quickly, as I am to
be in Savannah only two or three days.

                                        S. L.

[96] The reference is to " Northern Farmer, Old Style " (see also Lanier's letter
to Charlotte Cushman, June 17, 1875, below).

TO EDWARD SPENCER

Brunswick, Ga,
June 16th 1875.

Dear Mr. Spencer:

Herewith should reach you a copy of Lippincott's Magazine for June which contains a poem by me called "The Symphony." I wish I could tell you how fervently I hope that you will like it! It has so much of my heart in it, that I feel a personal fate as inhering in it.

Why have you not written me? Was the screed I sent you from Baltimore some months ago too much for you; and did you lose desire to land a fish that bit so easily at your friendly bait?

I don't believe it, – and I won't believe it.

A friend from Philadelphia has sent me a World of June 7th containing an editorial, in the tail-end of wh. there is a pleasant enough allusion to me.[97]

Did *you* write it?

These be grave catecheticals: I pray you answer the same, and send the answer to me at Baltimore, to the special care of Gaffer [W. H.] Browne: begging moreover that in your said reply you may forget the wit of Heinrich Heyne, while you remember the affection of

Sidney L.

---

[97] The editorial, "Literary Aspects of the Centennial," New York *World*, June 7, 1875, was inspired by the appointment of Longfellow to write the ode for the centennial celebration at Philadelphia in 1876. The writer suggested that open competition might produce a better ode, and named various poets from whom an able one might be expected. The concluding paragraphs of the editorial read:

"The South has always had its poets— few, but choice and lyrical, too dainty, perhaps, for great occasions, but capable of fervid dithyrambic strains. PAUL HAYNE, last of the faithful, still courts the muses like a lover in the pine woods of GEORGIA, and has come prosperously to a second volume since the war, while that new and happy singer, SIDNEY LANIER, rapidly mounts the wave of recognition like a strong swimmer as he is.

"With all these opportunities before it for getting something fresh, we cannot but regret that the Centennial Commission should have designated a poet for the celebration next year, even though the poet designated be Mr. LONGFELLOW himself."

To Gibson Peacock [98]

Brunswick, Ga.
June 16th, 1875.

My dear Mr. Peacock:

I am just stopping here a day, after the woods of Florida.

I have all your letters. Out of what a liberal sky do you rain your gracious encouragements upon me! In truth, dear friend, there is such large sweep and swing in this shower-after-shower of your friendliness, it comes in such big rhythms of generosities, it is such a poem of inner rains,—that I cannot at all get myself satisfied to meet it with anything less than that perfect rose of a song which should be the product of such watering. I think I hear one of these growing, now, down in my soul yonder, somewhere: presently the green calyx of silence shall split – – – – and you shall see your flower.

Your notice of " The Symphony " has given a great deal of pleasure to my family, as well as to me. It has been extensively copied in the Southern papers, and adopted by editors as expressing their views of the poem.

Mr. [Bayard] Taylor's letter [99] brings me a noble prospect of realizing an old dream. I had always a longing after him: but I never dared indulge it, more than one indulges what one considers only a pet possibility; so that now when I behold this

[98] Previously published, *Atlantic Monthly*, LXXIV, 21 (July, 1894); reprinted, *Letters* (New York, 1899), pp. 14-16.

[99] Peacock had written to Bayard Taylor, May 21, to ask that Taylor get the New York *Tribune* or some other New York " authority " to notice " The Symphony "—" in praise or dispraise. Either would' be better than total silence about [Lanier], when they praise and quote from others whose work is trash in comparison." Taylor thanked Peacock, June 3, for sending him a copy of " The Symphony " and added: " I hail in the author a new, rightfully anointed poet, in whom are the elements of a great success. . . . He has an unusual instinct of rhythm; but, what is best and most encouraging, it rests on a rich basis of underlying ideas." Taylor called " The Symphony " a more important poem than " Corn," declaring that " it reveals deeper, stronger and more original qualities." He concluded: " I fully share your interest in Mr. Lanier's literary future," promising that he would meet him and be of whatever service he could. Peacock acknowledged Taylor's letter, June 6, thanked him for his " generous praise " of Lanier's poetry, and asked Taylor to write to him at Brunswick. Apparently he then sent Taylor's letter on to Lanier (here referred to).

mere shadow of a meeting assume the shape of an actual hand-
shaking in the near future, it is as when a man wakes in the
morning and finds his Dream standing by his bed.

After August, when my present engagement will terminate,
my motions will entirely depend on whatever income-bringing
work I may succeed in finding. Within three weeks from this
time, I will however be *en route* to New York, and you
must write me, as soon as you receive this – addressing me at
Macon, Ga. – your programme for that time, if you're going
to be out of Philadelphia. I shall look you up *ubicumque in
Angliâ*, wherever you may be.

May I beg that you will cause Mr. Taylor to address me to
your own care,–or, if you are to leave town before I get there –
to care of *The Bulletin*? I will write my own plans more
definitely in a few days.

Pray accept this photograph. Of course you will see that
instead of being an *average* of my phiz., it is the best possible
single view thereof and is for that reason much better-looking
than I am: – but it will serve to remind you and my dear Mrs.
Peacock of

Your friend

Sidney L.

To Charlotte Cushman [100]

Brunswick, Ga.

June 17th 1875.

It is only seldom, dear Miss Cushman, that I can bring myself
to such a point of daring as to ask that you will stretch out
your tired arm merely to take one of my little roses — you
whose hands are already filled with the best flowers this world
can grow.

Does she not (I say to myself) find them under her feet and
wear them about her brows, may she not walk on them by day
and lie on them by night, nay, does not her life stand rooted
in men's regard like one pistil in a great lily ?

— But sometimes I really cannot help making love to

---

[100] Previously published, Mims, pp. 184-186.

you, just for one little intense minute: there is a certain Com-
munistic temper always inhering in true love which *will* occasionally break out and behead all the Royal Proprieties and
hang Law to the first lamp-post: it is even now so, my heart is
a little '93, *aux armes* ! where is this minister that imprisons
us, away from our friends, in the Bastille of Separation, let
him die, – and as for Silence, that luxurious tyrant that collects
all the dead for his taxes, behold, I am even now pricking him
to a terrible death with the point of this good pen.

– When one is in a state of insurrection, one makes demands:
mine is that you write me, dear friend, if you are quite recovered from the fatigues of Baltimore and of Boston, and if
you have not nourished yourself to new strength in feeding
upon the honies the people brought you there so freely.
And in the second place you shall straightway inform me where
you are, how long you're going to be at Newport, and when
you will move to Lennox. For I am surely going to find you,
at one place or t'other, – provided heaven shall send me so
much fortune in the selling of a poem or two as will make
the price of a new dress-coat. Alas, with what unspeakable,
tender care I would have brushed this present garment of mine
in days gone by, if I had dreamed that the time could come
when so great a thing as a visit to *you* might hang upon the
little length of its nap!

Behold, it is not only *in* man's breast that pathos lies, and
the very coat-lapel that covers it may be a tragedy.

Pray write me at Philadelphia, care of Mr. Peacock: or of
The Bulletin Office, when I shall call for letters if Mr. Peacock
should be out of town. I hope to be in Philadelphia in two
weeks from now: and will be occupied, either there, or in
New York or Boston, for a month or so longer, in superintending the printing of the Florida book; when my present engagement will terminate.

Copies of " The Symphony " have been ordered sent to you
and Miss Stebbins: and I have the *Ms.* copy which you desired, ready to transmit to you. You will be glad to know
that The Symphony has met with favor. The " Power of
Prayer " in Scribner's for June, – although the Editor cruelly
mutilated the dialect in some places, turning for instance
" Marster " (which is pure Alabama negro) into "Mah'sr "

(which is only Dan Bryant [101] negro, and does not exist in real life) – has gone all over the land, and re-appears before my eyes in frequent heart-breaking yet comical disguises of misprints and disfigurements.   Tell me: *ought* one to be a little ashamed of writing a dialect poem, – as at least one newspaper has hinted?   And did Robert Burns prove himself no poet, by writing mostly in dialect?   And is Tennyson's Death of the North Country Farmer, – certainly one of the very strongest things he ever wrote– not a poem, really ?

Mr. Peacock's friendship, in the matter of the Symphony, – as indeed in all others – has been wonderful, a thing too fine to speak of in prose.

Tomorrow I go to Savannah, and hope to find there a letter from Miss Stebbins.   Tell me of her, when you write, and tell *her*, from me, how truly and faithfully I am her and

Your friend

Sidney Lanier.

To Mary Day Lanier

Savannah, Ga
June 19th 1875.

Heart of My Heart, I will but take time for one little kiss to thee this morning, wherein I wd. thou mayst find compressed the very essential and perfect ultimate of all the All of me.

The whole work of my life is like the water of a certain Lake whereof thou knowest, upon whose surface sits one white water-lily, thou—as it were the culminant transfiguration and final spirit of all the sheens and sky-reflections and heavenly splendors that the bosom of the waters had ever held.

I have written to Gov. Walker,[102] and to every one else that I am owing. I requested Gov. W. to forward my over-

[101] Leader of the famous Bryant's Minstrels which played in New York almost continuously from 1857 to 1866. It was while with this troupe that Dan Emmett wrote *Dixie*.

[102] The Laniers had been guests of ex-Gov. David S. Walker and his daughter Florida in Tallahassee earlier in the month (see Florida Walker to Mary Day Lanier, June 21, 1875).

coat to Brunswick by Express. I will advise thee how to send
it from there as soon as thou shalt let me know that it is come.

Pray ask Cubbee to make special enquiry at the P.O., if
there be any letters for me in the General Delivery, not addressed to his care.

I do not find any letter from Miss Stebbins, nor my supply
of Magazines from the publishers. Here is a very pleasant
letter from Innis Randolph, anent the Symphony; he says a full
notice of it will appear in the Baltimore " Bulletin." [103]

I now think to stay here until Tuesday. No letter has come
from Pope, mine having probably been delayed in reaching him
by the run-off on the J. P. & M. R. R.

I will attend to the debts due in Macon, when I get there.
On Monday thou canst enclose the two bills to me at Macon.

I am very well: and quite strong.

God keep thy heart light, dear Moll, saith thy

husband.

The Morning " News " [104] has a pleasant personal notice
of thy

husband.

To Mary Day Lanier

Sav^h June 22nd 1875.

Here have I been, dear Soul of my heart, waiting on my
friend Pope. Yesterday his letters came, late in the afternoon.
I have thought it better to go to Macon before Augusta, and
therefore leave at 7.30 this evening for that point. Have
telegraphed Father that I was coming.

I have written up my account of the Oclawaha river,
while here. I think I will go from Augusta immediately to

[103] Randolph's letter has not survived. No file of the Baltimore *Evening
Bulletin* for this period has been discovered.

[104] The Savannah *Morning News*, June 19, 1875, said: " Mr. Sidney Lanier,
whose recent poems, ' Corn ' and ' The Symphony,' published in Lippincott's
Magazine, have attracted such wide attention, is at the Pulaski House. Mr.
Lanier, as we learn from our Florida exchanges, is engaged in compiling
a guide-book of the principal points of interest in that favored State. We con-
fidently predict that it will be something more than a mere professional guide-
book.''

Wilmington and see Pope there: then straight on North, to wherever we shall determine to have the book printed: my aim being to start the printers and engravers and have them working while I am finishing up the book. Then I will come back and do Charleston, and the other places to the north of it, more at leisure. I do not *know* that I shall carry this out, but think it now probable.

Tell Harry I will send the $20 back as soon as I draw in Augusta. I expect to spend two days in Macon, to try and locate thee for the summer.

Called on the [Wm.] Duncans, and found they had all gone to Marietta. Mr. Habersham called on me – and yesterday we had a twa-handed crack wi' Mr. Lessing. We played Kuhlau's grand Trio for two flutes and piano, in great style. Then Mr. Lessing and I played thy Fürstenau Nocturne,— and it was voted very beautiful. Then they put me to work at playing Beethoven's Violin Sonatas,—transcribed for flute – with Mr. Lessing. We played two I had never heard before: and although I scratched along through them in a very lame way, I thought them beautiful beyond measure. Mr. Lessing inquired particularly of thee: and I told him of thy remembrance.

I am very well, tho' the weather is fearfully warm. Charley T[aliaferro] has been with me several times. He looks very thin.

I am anxious to get to Macon, where I will expect one of thy love-letters.

To think thee, to dream thee, to live through the time when I will again see thy face,—that is the life of thy

lover.

To Mary Day Lanier [105]

Macon, Ga. June 23rd 1875

Thou art in the midst of sickness, and I am not with thee. I know how tired thou must needs be. What *can* I do, to send thee some rest?

[105] This letter and the following one are written on the stationery of Lanier & Anderson, Hill & Harris, Attorneys at Law.

– I now think to go up to the Indian Springs either tonight or tomorrow night, and make arrangements with The Elder House for thy summer board.   This has been suggested by Uncle Clifford, and strikes me as being the best arrangement I could possibly make.   Thou wouldst be near the Sulphur Spring, and I believe it could be of immense use to thee: and thy father could recruit there very greatly.   I think I can get board there at the rate of $20 per month, by making an arrangement for all summer: and excursion tickets are sold cheaply, so that thou couldst come to Macon at will.   Of course I will not *conclude* any bargain until I hear from thee anent the same.   Pray write me therefore, at *Wilmington, N. C.* thy full views of this project so that I may immediately communicate with Elder.

I am to see Mrs. Wallen this afternoon, and find out what Mr. Jamison has learned.[106]   But I fear these fried-ham places: and am told that Elder, who is an old resident of Indian Springs, has in time got quite comfortable, raising most of his own provisions &c, and that thou wdst. likely fare well there.   It is but a very short walk to the Spring: and the boys would have fine play-ground, and fishing-ground in the creek,– where I fished when I was a boy.

A letter from Salem brings me a charming notice of his, printed in the Chronicle & Sentinel, praising "Corn" and "The Symphony".[107]

[106] Concerning a summer boarding place for the Laniers at Howard's Station, Ga., about 50 miles southwest of Macon (see Mary Day Lanier's letter of May 28, 1875).   Indian Springs is a resort about 30 miles northwest of Macon. Neither plan materialized.

[107] A notice in the Augusta, Ga., *Chronicle and Sentinel*, June 11, 1875, reads in part as follows: "In *Lippincott's Magazine* for this month Mr. Lanier has a magnificent poem, 'The Symphony,' which reflects new lustre alike upon the author and his State. Excellent as the idyll 'Corn' is, this later production casts that entirely in the shade and rings as sweet and steady as the sound of a silver trumpet." The notice was signed "Tyrone," a pen-name frequntly used by Dutcher. In his letter of June 11, 1875, concerning "Corn" and "The Symphony," Salem Dutcher had written: "After the hideous verse-deifications of r.r. engineers, scuttled prostitutes, frozen beggars, brats, 'sass garden farmers etc which has been so much belched out of late years, I rejoice, yea am mightily upborne, to hear the sound of a knightly clarion with no taint of scum upon its notes. Damn the sausage-grinding school."

At least one unfavorable notice of "The Symphony" appeared. The *Nation*, XX, 362 (May 27, 1875)—one of Lanier's severest critics throughout his life and a journal that looked favorably upon the very school of poets disparaged by

Uncle Clifford now walks down to the Office every day, and seems greatly improved; though he has not yet gone into active business, and is going off this summer, somewhere.

I could go North with a much lighter heart, if I had thee comfortably fixed at Indian Springs for the summer. Write me *what time* thou cdst. go, – in thy Wilmington letter.

I telegraphed from here this morning.   Embrace all my dear ones. I yearn so, for all of you, today: my heart is unquiet about you all.

So God be thy Friend, –   prays thy

lover

To Mary Day Lanier

Macon, Ga.   June 24th 1875

My Child: Mammy surprised me delightfully yesterday afternoon with thy messages, and the Golden Age: [108] and I now remember that I have not hitherto acknowledged thy two letters which I found waiting here for me.   This morning comes Harry's telegram anent the coat.   Mammy tells me she is not going to Louisville, and will betake her to the Indian Springs next week early.

I am going up there tonight.

I have been spending an hour and a half at Mrs. Wallen's. I had previously gone down to Roosevelts' to pay off their bill: (which I *did*) and the little Doctor coming in afterwards, followed me up to Mrs. W's, so that I saw them all together

Dutcher and Peacock—said of his poem: " It is fluent, fanciful, and sweet, not over-sensible, and hurt by mannerisms both of expression and sentiment, some of which seem to be original and some caught in Mr. Morris's school.   But it is better than most magazine verse, and is worth reading for the sake of the fancy it displays."

[108] Mary Day Lanier had sent her letter of June 22, 1875, to her husband— and various papers received from Gibson Peacock— by Mammy Lucy, who had gone from Brunswick to Macon.   One of the papers was an appreciation of Lanier in the *Golden Age*, V, 4-5 (June 12, 1875), by George Henry Calvert (1803-1889), a Maryland author then living in Newport, R. I.   Introduced to Lanier's poetry by Gibson Peacock, Calvert became at once an admirer and shortly thereafter a friend.   (See Calvert to Peacock, May 25, and Peacock to Mary Day Lanier, May 28, 1875. See also Ida G. Everson, *George Henry Calvert*, New York, 1944, pp. 206-207.)

and we had a very jolly talk, the Doctor and I dividing the two ladies, – he taking Mamie while I took Mrs. Wallen, and then reversing, so that we could both do our love-making alone – They both seem mightily pleased with the poems, and said many fair things in that connection.

A pleasant letter comes from Mr. Peacock this morning, inviting me there on my way through Philadelphia.

I am exceedingly anxious to get forward, in order to see Miss Stebbins and move in the matter of the Musical College. I pass on through here tomorrow night, and will stay but one day in Augusta.

I am greatly pleased with the Indian Springs prospect. I think thou wilt lay on some sweet flesh, there, and grow me some roses, and that thy father and the boys will prosper. Mrs. Wallen tells me that we could not get board at the place Jamieson was inquiring about.

Mrs. Cosby Smith has been very ill for two months. Somewhat better now, Mr. Smith tells me. Everybody asks for thee, and appear to do so with a loving heart.

How I long for thee, little Lady: hast thou seen a man that hath lost his arm in the wars, how lop-sided he goeth through life? It is thus my Soul walketh, without thee.

I am rejoiced to hear that my fine old Cubbie is better, and that my boys improve.

Embrace them all for me. I am very well.

I pray that Heavenly winds may quickly drift about, and drive thee to thy

lover.

To Mary Day Lanier

Augusta, June 27th 1875.

Thy two letters of 24th and 25th are here, dear Sweetheart; I met them, and the telegram, and Salem, almost simultaneously as I was walking to the Post Office yesterday afternoon.

I lost a day, in coming here, by the running off of our tender; and had the pleasure of spending a whole night at Gordon, and part of a day at Millen, before I arrived here.

As for the Indian Springs, I'll kiss thine answer, be it yea or nay. I did not go to Howards, — as " agreed "— because the only family I cd. hear of thereabouts had refused to take boarders, — as Mrs. Wallen informed thee, and I cd. not bear the idea of spending my only available day in so forlorn a hope as was presented there. Thou knowest it is only a railway station. And so, in pure desperation, I went to the Springs. But I shall not at all insist on thy going there. I have just now thought that Frank Nisbet lives at the Mims Place, a short distance from Howards. I do not know how to get a letter to him: but if thou wilt send one to Mrs. James T. Nisbet (the Mims Place belongs to Mr. James T.), she will forward it to him. Thou canst write to Frank, asking him to inquire for board for thee and thine, describing thy *dramatis personæ*: and enclose thy letter in a note to Mrs. James T., asking her to forward immediately to Frank. Thou wert also better make inquiries of some one in Forsyth. Would it not suit dear Father to make a little trip to Forsyth, and look at whatever places he could hear of in that neighborhood? I wish sincerely that it might. Uncle Clifford knows many of the prominent men about Forsyth and could give Father letters securing their aid in his quest : and I doubt not Father has also acquaintances there.[109]

He will find the Pye house a pleasant enough place to stop at for a day or two.

Pray urge Father to try this: I am sure the trip wd. do him good, and wd. result in finding thee some place on the R. R. The moving consideration wh. took me to the Springs was the Sulphur water,— for which I had heard thee express a longing: but I wd. much rather thou wert near the Doctor.

So get thee to work, little Lady,— thou and thy Father— and find thee some place, anywhere between Forsyth and Macon, on the R. R. I long to know that thou art near Dr. D[unwoody] and that thou art out of the warm airs of B'k. How I wish that my good old Cubbee cd. go, also!

I am very well indeed: Salem is much thinner than I ever saw him, but full of friendliness: he and Randall [110] were in my room most of this morning.

---

[109] In her letter of June 25, 1875, Mary Day Lanier had listed her objections to Indian Springs. The eventual solution was that she stayed in Brunswick until the end of July, spent August in Macon, and then went to board in the country a mile above Forsyth, Ga., with the family of S. D. Mobley.

[110] James Ryder Randall (1839-1908), editor of the Augusta *Constitutionalist*

I go to Wilmington tomorrow afternoon. Cannot now tell how long I will stay there.

My Little Heart, how am I ever to pass these long weeks without once seeing thy face? God send thee some perpetual dream which shall be as lovely to thee, as is thy countenance to me,— is the prayer this day of

thy

lover.

To Mary Day Lanier

Wilmington, June 29th 1875.

Why, my Sweetheart, I am ready to fly back to thee, in reading thine which thou thoughts't I wd. miss.

Hath Laura [111] also joined the ranks of the enemy? But hers was a beatitude wh. cd. not last alway, and wh. had already endured longer than I hoped. I pray thou mayst find some way to bring matters back to the old sweetness, — or to quietly get rid of her.

I wrote thee from Augusta, urging thy Father to go at once to Forsyth, and try to seek out a place for thee somewhere in that neighborhood, or anywhere between there and Macon. I hope sincerely he has found this idea a pleasant one. I so long to know thee and him out of the flat-lands, and among the hills. Thou wilt find a new spirit in both of your bodies.

Here am I stranded for three days to wait for Mr. Pope, who is today going towards Atlanta, but will be here about July 2nd. Meantime I am writing for life and death.

Salem was all kindness to me in Augusta, and quickly furnished me with the items I wished to have anent that city.[112]

As I got on the train, yesterday afternoon, I found an old

---

and a poet, best known for his "Maryland, My Maryland." Both he and Dutcher are mentioned in the account of Augusta in "Other Winter Resorts," Chap. XV of Lanier's *Florida* (VI, 147).

[111] One of the negro nurse-maids for the Lanier children. In her letter of June 27, 1875, Mary Day Lanier had reported trouble with her.

[112] Dutcher was apparently already something of an authority on matters of local history. This interest culminated some years later when he completed and published in 1890 the *Memorial History of Augusta*, begun by Charles C. Jones, Jr.

Allegheny Springs friend,— Miss Annie Adams – who recognized me first. She introduced me to her mother, and, on telling her that I was Mary Day's husband, that good lady's face lighted up, and she said she had known thee when a little child, and thy mother.

I did not say to thee that I recd the overcoat safely. Thou mayst keep the Maury book [113] for me, until further advices.

Now must I cease. May God beguile all the hearts about thee, dear Heart of my Soul, into such tenderness as may faintly shadow that which burns in the heart of thy

lover.

TO VIRGINIA HANKINS [114]

Savannah, Ga. July 3rd 1875

Your arrangements will likely suit me very well, dear Friend; though my business obligations are such as to render my movements for the next month quite beyond anything like exact prophecy. I am, strange to say, Poet-in-Ordinary to a long line of Railroad Corporations: – which will make you stare till I get a chance to explain it to you.

At any rate I would to heaven I might write you – according to your request, which is always law to me – the precise day after the sixteenth when I will be able to meet you. I will have to make a journey to New York in a week from now, and on the way there I will likely learn some facts which will probably enable me to fix my programme exactly: as soon as I do so, I will communicate with you. The flute shall come, too: and we will have a duo with Mr. [Leo] Wheat.

— Dear Little One, *where* is this "Varina" [115] from

[113] M. F. Maury's *Physical Geography of the Sea* (New York, 1857), an authority used by Lanier in his *Florida*. A copy given to him by ex-Gov. D. S. Walker in Tallahassee on June 14 survives in Lanier's library (Charles D. Lanier Collection, Johns Hopkins University).

[114] Virginia Hankin's letter to which this is an answer has not survived. No explanation of Lanier's sudden change of travelling plans appears in the letters; but it seems likely that, finding it impossible to get in touch with Mr. Pope for the next two weeks, Lanier returned to Brunswick (via Savannah) to spend the interim with his wife. The present letter was written on the stationery of the Pulaski House.

[115] The flag of truce ship that brought Lanier back to the Confederacy in Feb., 1865, discharged the exchanged prisoners at Varina, Va. (see Appendix C, vol. X).

which your letters come? It sounds exceedingly familiar: yet,
– puzzle as much as I may – I cannot locate it.

How I long to see you. I scarcely know why, – I *always* long
to see you – but just now I seem to have a special uprising of a
certain Ginna-want, – I do not know what else to call it.

I am going to be at Brunswick about a week: – where you
can address me, if you have occasion to write. Your letter will
be forwarded if I shd. have left.

In a great hurry, – and in a great repose of steadfast and
faithful affection –

Your

S. L.

To Gibson Peacock

Brunswick, Ga.

July 10th 1875

My dear Friend:

I had fully expected to shake your hand, and
kiss Mrs. Peacock's, before this time: but man proposes, rail-
road-man disposes: and I have been chasing my Mæcænas about
through the country for a week in order to have a final conference with him and show him the Florida book, which is
about written. I am to meet him in Columbia S. C. on Tuesday next: and expect to go immediately northward after two
days there. But there isn't the least reliance to be placed on
my motions there being none on *his*: and so I don't know
really when I'll be through Philadelphia. Of course I'll miss
you, as you're going to leave town on the 14th: but you must
leave a note at THE BULLETIN office for me (where I will call
for my letters) telling me where you go, and your general programme as far as possible. I will find you, somewhere, if
you don't go *too* far out of my tether-length.

I was glad to read the account of Sidney Dobell, and I do
not wonder at the affection of Miss Cushman for one who
could evolve such subtle and delicate loveliness as these poems
display. I promise myself the delight of reading Dobell,
through, as a poet *ought* to be read, when my rest-time comes
in September.

I long to see both of you: and my lovely comrade here joins

me in all manner of affectionate messages to you, declaring that she is, no less than I am,

Your faithful friend

Sidney Lanier

To Mary Day Lanier

Columbia, S. C.

July 13th 1875

My Heart of My Soul, I have but one little moment in which to send thee a kiss.

Mr. Pope and I were together all the morning: I read him much of the book,— here and there – and he seems greatly pleased with my handiwork. I go on tonight to New York to make the final arrangements.

I am so sleepy I can scarcely hold open my eyes to write this: and the dust, whereof I have never known the like, is not yet out of those hiding-places where it insinuated itself during my yesterday's ride.

Tell Harry I have not had time to go to the Office for the money-order today and will send it from Baltimore, where I will stop over a part of a day.

What a scrawl! But thou art as dear and as sweet as this chirography is vile, and I each day grow to be a thousand-fold more thy

lover.

To Mary Day Lanier

Philadelphia, Pa,

July 18th 1875.

O, my too-dear Heart, I would rather than forty million pound that I might sit by thy sweet side for one little half hour this day, and drink me a draught of pure love out of thy loveliness that is in thy face; for thou hast in the two gray ellipticals of thine eyes more true-love and more faith in faith than is in the great ring of all the world besides.

Here am I working night and day to get my mss. in shape,— wh. I am to hand to the publishers tomorrow that they may give me answer on Wednesday— copying here, pruning there, altering this, adding to that, paging the whole. My lord Pope desires that the publisher shall take some interest in the book – which I advise – and so they are to commence the examination tomorrow.

I am tolerably well, and have now no more time than to tell thee I am lonesome for thee to the very verge of despair, and wishing, wishing, wishing all the day and all the night that I might be in thy presence a perfect happy, as I am now in thine absence a perfect unhappy

lover.

To Mary Day Lanier

Continental Hotel
Phila. Pa. July 22nd 1875

I am just returned, dear Soul of my Heart, from a flying visit to New York, where I was detained two unnecessary days by matters at once vexatious and trifling. I ran by the Bulletin Office and received there thy last two letters, – one with enclosures – which I have read.

The publishers propose that they will print the Florida book, in a sort of partnership with Mr. P[ope]: Lippincott & Co. paying all expenses of printing, binding, materials, and advertising, and giving all their facilities for selling: while Mr. P. is to pay for the stereotype plates· and the illustrations, and to receive twenty five per cent of the wholesale price of all copies sold. Besides this they desire to print two of my chapters (The " St. Augustine In April ", and " The Oclawaha River ") in the Magazine, Mr. P. paying half of the cost of the illustrations. This plan contemplates postponing the publication of the book till cold weather sets in: the preliminary Magazine articles coming out in the October and November numbers. I think to set out tomorrow night southward, to see Mr. Pope about the proposition, and have a final determination. I suspect it is about as good as I could get elsewhere.

Tomorrow I hope to send thee some funds, to get to Macon
on.   The four Sonnets to thee [116] are in type for the September Number of Lippincott's: and I will try to collect what
is due for them, and forward to thee immediately.   I think
thou wert best buy a "thousand mile ticket" for $30.00 :
though if that seem not best to thee, do as thou likest.   I dread
thy stay at the Vineville house: [117] 'tis far warmer in those
up-stairs rooms than thy Brunswick habitation.   I will procure that further funds come to thee in a few days. – My
Child, My Child, this business of funds is so hard on one's
heart ! – To think of sending thee, thee, My sweet tender
Stalk-of-a-lily, thee, My Lady-heart, _____ indeed

to think of it is not good, and I will on, and tell thee that I
saw no one in New York but Miss Florida Walker, whose
father had gone off and got married to a young girl in Virginia,
to the utter and tearful discontent of the former young lady.[118]
She told me, after some hesitation, the whole story, and seemed
to feel a little better after weeping over it.   I met her this
morning, tripping along through the sunlight past the Fifth
Avenue Hotel, where I was standing waiting for a down town
car.   I joined her and walked with her a little way down the
street.   "She was going" she said, with a very pretty shame-
facedness, "to do some extra devotions; she was setting out to
attend four different churches a day, for fifteen days: by the
expiration of which time, if the duty were well done and faithfully, the laws of Holy Church gave remission for certain sins,
and full pardon therefor: and " – on my enquiry what crimes
she was now expiating – " she had been *so* selfish in refusing
to go to Papa's wedding, and in other matters connected with
the same, that she must not rest until she had obtained indul-
gence: " and much more the like artless prattle.
     Dost thou remember the telegram we sent Father when
Charley was born? ——   Yesterday, while I was in the Telegraph Office in New York, a German came to me in some distress, and begged in very broken English that I would write

---

[116] "In Absence" (I, 42).
[117] Mary Lanier was planning a brief visit with the R. S. Laniers.
[118] Mary Day Lanier had written to her husband, June 30, 1875, that Gov.
Walker and his daughter had left Tallahassee for New York on June 28.

out plainly a telegram which he desired to send but which the
telegraph clerk was unable to make out.   He handed me his
attempt at a message.   It was about this:

> " To J. Jacob,
> Rundouht:—(Rondout,)
>   J. Rosentein ist confint widht a
> buoy.   You are invided to the party tomor nein Oglock.
>
>   L. Rosenstein " :

and I will wager thou makest out the important fact it com-
municates, in three winks.

I have letters from Miss Stebbins (enclosing a letter of introduction to her brother, the Chairman of the Board of Trustees
of the Musical College) Miss Cushman, the Peacocks, Mr.
Spencer, and a host of others anent business.

Those that interest thee I will send soon.

Perhaps I may have the quiet month with thee, in the cool
woods, towards September.   What a delicious dream it is,
Sweetheart !   Dost thou know, I thought I loved thee to the
full measure, yesterday: but I love thee more today than then,
and I shall love thee infinitely more by tomorrow.   Sometimes
when I am not as bad to thee as usual, thou hast a sort of
brown faithful-spaniel look out of thine eyes, a look at once
wise, tender, faithful, dumb, pathetic, and immortal: – and I
have had it looking straight into my eyes for a week past,
shining quite through those *fantoccini* of Lippincott, Pope and
Kirk.

—   In truth, dear Comrade, I am quite worn with longing
for thy companionship: I am too lonesome: and somehow
there is no one but thee with whom I am *not* lonesome: thou
art all the company there is for me: — and what a diatribe I
am sending thee, to be sure, to make thy heart full !   —But it is
a comfort to tell thee that in the whole world thou art the sole
desirable Sweet, – to thy

                  lover.————————————

To Mary Day Lanier

Wilmington, N. C.
July 26th 1875.

Dear Heart, Sweetheart, Roseheart, I am all steeped in longing for thee as the great sea out yonder is steeped in sunshine.
— It grows always harder and harder for me to live away
from thee, I am so much in love, and thou art so dear, dear
Wife.
— I have just had an interview with Mr. Pope. He
thinks Lippincott's terms are fair and accepts them.

I go this afternoon again to the dreadful cars, on my way
to Charleston where I will stay two days, and then fare back
to Philadelphia. Thou mayst write me there, care of the Ev'g
Bulletin, as usual.

Much work is yet to be done on the book, and I think to
find me some quiet boarding-house in N. Y., and do it there.
I will be employed until the end of August when my engagement will terminate. I hope to find me something else ere
that time.

I sent thee $35.00 from Phila. More soon. Write me imme-
diately what amt thou receivest from Father.

Thief that I am, I brought away thy Coleman letter.[119]

I stopped in Richmond a day and a half and had a wondrous fair meeting with Ginna.[120] She sends thee a multitude
of sweet messages.

And now, thou dear worshipful Wife, may my devout
wistful longings go and surround thee as the rose-glow sur-
rounds a rose — cries thy

lover.

To Mary Day Lanier

Phila. Pa.   July 30th 1875.

So: again I am off the dreadful rails, and for a couple of days
shall inhale somewhat besides car-dust and the fumes of axle-
grease. Here came I from Charleston today, having left Aunt

---

[119] Concerning a boarding place for the summer at Howard's Station.
[120] See Lanier's letter to Virginia Hankins, Aug. 15, 1875, and note 131,
below.

Willie [121] in mourning for my short stay at her hospitable board — I could never tell thee how they petted me there. On the day I arrived it got bruited about that I was come: and in the evening the entire neighborhood poured in, until the house was full. Presently the flute was brought: and after the first piece, nothing else was thought of: the evening was all flute, and I played, in response to call after call, until eleven o'clock. They made me go into the light, and all gathered round to see my fingers move. It quite touched my ever-prurient vanity — to see these people's faces when I played my bird-songs for them: they grew solemn and tender, and gazed at me with earnest and half wondering eyes as at one bringing news from other worlds. Aunt Willie was quite in raptures at the evening's success: she appears to have been bragging upon my fluting to an alarming extent among her neighbors. We had some long talks about thee, and she told me of all the sweet things which other members of the family had told her of thee: whereat being loosed, I let my love give her a brave account of thy loveliness.

Mr. Pope immediately accepted the Lippincott proposition. I will remain here probably through tomorrow, re-writing my St. Augustine Chapter so as to make it available for the Magazine. Then I think to go to New York and spend a month in revising and finishing the Florida book,— upon wh. I have not been able to put a stroke of work in ten days past, by reason of my nomadic movements. If I shall succeed during this New York month in some plans I have, I will come and have a heavenly September with thee somewhere.

—— I have just gotten thy letter 27th from The Bulletin Office. My poor Heart: how ever wilt thou get to Macon with one nurse? Of course thou wilt find another as soon as thou canst, after arriving: send for Sally and make her help all she can, until thou securest a permanent nurse. I tremble to think what thou wilt endure tomorrow on the long hot journey, worn with sleeplessness and fatigue. How I long to hear that thou and the good little Doctor have come together and entered upon some healthful course!

I sent Harry fifty dollars today: and will send thee fifty about the seventh of August.

---

[121] Wilhelmina Lanier Eason, usually referred to as "Aunt Mina."

I have such an array of correspondence accumulated during my journeyings as makes me a very coward to face it. I was glad to read Clifford's letter, and father's.

Pray get me a copy of this " Constitution " in which Mr. Hilliard'[s] letter appears.[122]

Thou wert better write me after receiving this, to my old *195 Dean St. Brooklyn.*

Now, thou dear lovely Wife, may thy heart be this night as full of peace as my heart is full of thee, – prays thy

lover.

To Gibson Peacock [123]

Philadelphia, Pa.
July 31st 1875.

If you have ever watched a shuttle, my dear friend, being violently knocked backward and forward in a loom — never settled for a second at this end before it is rudely smacked back to the other— you will possess a very fair idea of the nature of my recent travels.

I do not know how many times I have been from North to South in the last six weeks: the negotiations about the Florida book, and the collection of additional material for it, have required my presence at widely-separated points often: and as my employer is himself always on the wing, I have sometimes had to make a long chase in order to come up with him. I believe my wanderings are now ended, however, for a time; and, as the very first of the many blessings which this cessation of travel will bring to a tired soul, I count this opportunity to send a line which will carry my love to you and to your *other* you.

Lippincott has made what seems to be a very fair proposition

---

[122] H. W. Hilliard (1803-1892), a prominent lawyer and literary man of Augusta, had written a letter to the editors of the Atlanta *Constitution* (published in the issue of July 22, 1875), eulogizing " The Symphony." Lanier's letter of appreciation (not found) was answered by Hilliard on Aug. 12. He wrote in part: " I agree with you perfectly in regard to the time, the tendency of the age– and the true office of Art."

[123] Previously published, *Atlantic Monthly*, LXXIV, 21-22 (July, 1894); reprinted, *Letters* (New York, 1899), pp. 16-18.

to print the Florida book, taking an interest in it which I think practically amounts to about one-half. I am going to add to it, by way of appendix, a complete Guide-book to Florida: and as this feature ought of itself to secure some sale among the fifteen or twenty thousand annual visitors, I am induced to hope that my employer may be reimbursed for his entire outlay, – though I keep in mind, what they all tell me, that the publication of any book is a mere lottery, and baffles all prophecy as to its success. Two chapters of the book, one on " *St. Augustine In April* ", and one on " *The Oclawaha River* ", are to appear in the Magazine, October and November numbers.

I will probably leave here today, and my address for a month hence will be " *195 Dean St, Brooklyn, N. Y.*"

Your package of letters was handed me duly at the Bulletin Office. I was ready to murder somebody, for pure vexation, when I learned there that I had just missed you by about two hours: it would have been *such* a comfort to have seen your two faces before you left.

Many thanks for Mr. Taylor's letter.[124] I do hope I may be able to see him during this next month. Do you think a letter from me would reach him at " Mattapoisett "? For his estimate of my " Symphony " seems to me so full and generous, that I think I will not resist the temptation to anticipate his letter to me. I will write also to Mr. Calvert tomorrow: his insight into a poet's internal working—as developed in his kind notice of me in the *Golden Age*– is at once wonderful and delightful.

The next number of Lippincott's will contain four sonnets of mine, in the Shakespearian meter. I sincerely hope they are going to please you. You will be glad to know that " the Symphony " meets with continuing favor in various parts of the land.

My month in Brooklyn will be full of the very hardest work. I will be employed in finishing and revising the Florida book, many of the points in which demand very careful examination. In August my railroad engagement terminates.

My friend Miss Stebbins has sent me a letter of introduction to her brother, who is chairman of the Board of Trustees of

---

[124] See note 99, above.

the New College of Music in New York. I am going to see if they will found a chair of the Physics Of Music, and give it me. I can scarcely describe to you how lively my life would seem, if I could devote the balance of it to such lectures as would properly belong to a professorship of this nature,–and to my poetry.

——So now, You know all about me: tell me in return how you and Mrs. Peacock fare through the summer. What is Cushing's Island? A small one, broken, with water dashing up all round you, and a clean sweet wind airing your very souls? I wish it might be for your sakes: and I hope you are both getting strong and elastic. Write me straightway all about yourselves.

I beg that each one of you will deliver a loving message for me to the other: and that you will both hold me always as

Your faithful friend

Sidney Lanier

To Charlotte Cushman [125]

Philadelphia, Pa.
July 31st 1875.

It was so good of you, my dear friend, to write me in midst of your sufferings, that it amounts to a translation of pain into something beautiful; and with this thought I console myself for the fear lest your exertion may have caused you some pang that might have been spared.

I long to hear from you: tho' Miss Stebbins' letter brought me a good account from your physician about you. If tender wishes were but medicinal, if fervant aspirations could but cure, if my daily upward breathings in your behalf were but as powerful as they are earnest, – how perfect would be your State !

– I have latterly been a shuttlecock betwixt two big battledores – New York and Florida. I scarcely dare to recall how many times I have been to and fro in the last six weeks. It has been just move on, all the time: car-dust, cinders, the

---

[125] Previously published, Mims, pp. 186-189.

fumes of hot axle-grease, – these have been my portion: and
between them I have almost felt sometimes as if my soul would
be asphyxiated. But I now cease to wander for a month, with
inexpressible delight. Tomorrow I leave here for Brooklyn,
where I will be engaged at hard labor for a month, mainly in
finishing up the Florida book. My address will be " *195 Dean
St. Brooklyn*, N. Y.".: and I beg you will make somebody
about you send me a line to let me know whether you are well,
and what time you go to Lenox. I hoped beyond all measure
that I might be able to run to Newport and see you and my
good Miss Stebbins, – and that fine Mr. Calvert, whose generous exposition of me in the Golden Age, as it had already gone
to the bottom of my mind, naturally found no difficulty in
going to the bottom of my heart when I read it. Possibly the
heavens may yet relent: – but I do not know.

I am very glad to find my " Symphony " copied in full in
Dwight's Journal of Music: [126] and I am sure you will care to
know that the poem has found great favor in all parts of the
land. I have the keenest desire to see some English judgment
on this poem: but not the least idea how to compass that end.
Can you make me any suggestion in that behalf?

I am full curious to hear you talk about Tennyson's " Queen
Mary ". Nothing could be more astonishing than the methods
of treatment with which this production has been disposed of,
in the few criticisms I have seen upon it. One critic declared
it was a good poem but no drama: another avers decidedly that
it is a fine drama but not a poem: while the Nation man thinks
that it is neither a poem nor a drama, but a sort of didactic
narrative intended to be in the first place British, and, in the
second place, a warning against the advancing powers of the
Catholic Church. There is but a solitary thread of judgment
in common among these criticisms: every one of them contains some sort of excuse for it, more or less hidden in
commendation.

I cannot tell you with how much delight I read the account
of Sydney Dobell: nor with how much loving recognition I
took into my heart all the extracts from his poems given in the
review. I am going to read all his poems when my little
holiday comes – I hope in September – and I will send you then

---

[126] *Dwight's Journal of Music*, XXXV, 41-42 (June 26, 1875).

some organized and critical thanks for having introduced me to so noble and beautiful a soul.

When you see Mr. Calvert next will you not do me the favor to convey to him my earnest thanks?

I will write Miss Stebbins as soon as I shall have seen her brother, to whom I intend to present her letter sometime next week.

As for you, My dear Queen Catherine, – may this velvety night be spread under your feet even as Raleigh's cloak was spread for *his* queen's, so that you may walk dry-shod as to all pain over to the morning, —   prays

Your faithful

Sidney Lanier

To Mary Day Lanier

195 Dean St.
Brooklyn, N. Y.
Aug. 3rd 1875.

Here am I again, dear Heartsease, at my old quarters in Brooklyn, though things are somewhat changed –   Julie Ripley and older sister are down at Canarsie for the sea-air, – the baby being a long time ill nigh unto death.   Mr. Horace goes down this evening to see them, leaving my Anna Mary and myself in charge of the establishment.

I am in my ancient apartment, and here sit I by the hour gazing, gazing, gazing to the Southward whereupon my window opens, and fluttering about thee yonder so far off, so far off, even as the gray sparrow over my head is fluttering about her velvety dear ones.   All day Saturday my heart was toiling with thee along the weary hot road to Macon, and feebly trying to help thee with Lulu and Harry.   Last night when I laid me down here, and drew two blankets and a thick coverlet over me, I was ready to weep with thinking of thee wearily sweltering in the hot Vineville house.

And all the time, all the time, I am so piteously lonesome for lack of my dear Comrade that I do not make a good battle, my heart is so heavy with longing for thee that I scale the wall of fortune with but laborious and lagging sinews, I spend in vain yearning the strength that should be all consecrate to climbing.   I pray thee sit down and write me off some of the loving gray that is in thine eyes, some of the tender encouragement that is in thy wonderful warm hands, some of thy sweet and cunning tongue's comfort, some of the heaven of thy kiss.

So shalt thou mayhap abbreviate by half some whole sigh of thy

lover——

TO BAYARD TAYLOR [127]

195 Dean St.
Brooklyn, N. Y.
Aug. 7th 1875.

My dear Sir:

When a man, determined to know as well what is under as what is above, has made his plunge down to the bottom of the great Sea Doubtful of poetic endeavor, and has looked not only upon the enchanted caverns there but upon the dead bodies also: there comes a moment as his head re-emerges above the surface, when his eyes are a-blink with salt water and tears, when the horizon is a round blur, and when he wastes strength that might be applied to swimming, in resolutely defying what seems to be the gray sky overhead.

In such a moment, a friendly word — and all the more if it be a friendly word from a strong swimmer whom one perceives far ahead advancing calmly and swiftly — brings with it a pleasure so large and grave that , as voluble thanks are impossible, so a simple and sincere acknowledgement is inevitable.

I did not know that my friend Mr Peacock had sent you my " Symphony " until I received his letter enclosing yours in reference to that poem: your praise came to me therefore with the added charm of surprise.   You are quite right in supposing the *Makamât* of Hariri of Basrah to be unknown to me.   How earnestly I wish that they might be less so, by virtue of some

[127] Previously published, *Atlantic Monthly*, LXXXIII, 791-792 (June, 1899); reprinted, *Letters* (New York, 1899), pp. 120-122.

account of them from your own lips ! I could never describe
to you what a mere drought and famine my life has been, as
regards that multitude of matters which I fancy one absorbs
when one is in an atmosphere of art, or when one is in con-
versational relation with men of letters, with travellers, with
persons who have either seen, or written, or done large things.
Perhaps you know that with us of the younger generation in
the South since the War, pretty much the whole of life has
been merely not-dying.

I will be in Brooklyn about a month, and if you should come
to New York in that time I beg you will send me a line to
above address telling me where I can find you, – and *when*, so
that I may not miss you.

I remember how Thomas Carlyle has declared a man will be
strengthened in his opinion when he finds it shared by another
mortal: – and so enclose a slip which a friend has just sent me,
from the Boston Transcript, containing some pleasant words
about my poems by Mr. Calvert.

Pray believe that I shall always hold myself, and always
rejoice to be held by you, as

Your friend

Sidney Lanier.

To Gibson Peacock [128]

195 Dean St.
Brooklyn, N. Y.
Aug. 10th 1875.

My dear friend:

Your letter of 8th, enclosing McClellan's,
reached me a few moments ago. Accept my thanks for both.

Your syren-song of the beauties of your Island is at once
tempting and tantalizing. When you say you " think I would
be tempted to come, if I could imagine the enchanting views
from this house ", –you make me think of that French Empress
who *wondered how the stupid cannaille could be as obstinate*
as to starve when such delicious pâtés could be bought for only

---

[128] Previously published, *Atlantic Monthly*, LXXIV, 22-23 (July, 1894);
reprinted, *Letters* (New York, 1899), pp. 18-19.

five francs apiece. Cushing's Island,[129] my dear friend, is as impossible to me, in the present state of the poetry-market, as a dinner at Venz's was to a *Chiffonier*: all of which I wouldn't tell you—both because it is personal and because poverty is not a pleasant thing to think about at Cushing's Island—except for the single controlling reason that I cannot bear your thinking that I *could* come to you, if I would.

—And all of which you are to forget, as soon as you have once taken in the whole prodigious conclusiveness of it, and only remember so far as to consider yourselves charged to breathe enough sea-air-heavens, how I long for it!—for all three of us: as Arséne Houssaye's friend with the big appetite said, on sitting down and finding that the gentleman who had been invited to dine with him was unavoidably absent, " well, I will eat for us both," and then proceeded actually to do it, helping himself twice at each course.

I will probably see you, though, in Philadelphia when you come; and that is some consolation.

Pray kiss each other, for

Your friend

Sidney Lanier.

To Charlotte Cushman [130]

195 Dean St.,
Brooklyn, N. Y.,
August 15, 1875.

I did not dream, my dear friend, of giving you anything in the least approaching the nature of a worry, – in asking you for a suggestion as to the best method of piercing the British hearts of oak; and you must not " think about it " as you declare you are going to do – for a single minute. Indeed, I had, in mentioning it to you, no more definite idea in my head than that perhaps you might know somebody who knew somebody

[129] The Peacocks were spending the summer on Cushing's Island, Casco Bay, near Portland, Maine.

[130] Previously published, Mims, pp. 189-190, and reprinted here from that source, the MS not being found.

that knew somebody that – – – etc., etc., *ad infinitum* – – – that might – – – and then my idea of what the somebody was to do, completely faded into a vague nothing.

It isn't *worth* thinking about, to you; and I have not the least doubt that what I want will finally come, in just such measure as I shall deserve.

The publishers have limited me in time so rigorously, *quoad* the Florida book, that I will have to work night and day to get it ready. I do not now see the least chance for a single day to devote to my own devices before the fifth or sixth of September.

And I do *so* long to see you and Miss Stebbins!

Out of the sombre depths of a bottomless sea of Florida statistics in which I am at this present floundering, pray accept, my liege Queen, in art as in friendliness, all such loyal messages and fair reports compacted of love, as may come from so dull a waste of waters; graciously resting in your mind upon nothing therein save the true faithful allegiance of your humble knight and subject,

Sidney L.

To Virginia Hankins [181]

195 Dean St.
Brooklyn, N. Y.
Aug. 15th 1875

Dear Bettina, how much lovelier you are than the first Bettina!

— For you *say* things more beautifully than she dreamed

---

[181] In Virginia Hankins's letter of Aug. 5, 1875, which Lanier's letter answers in some detail, she had said: " ' Grasshopper, fly thou away, and know that thou did'st one day, in midst of Summer's greenery, light upon the hand of a Poet! '– In some sort, were not these your words– There– under the trees?– then, forgive me, that I only remembered it was the hand of a Friend;– and now, having ' flown ' do remember your poethood and so, greet you. . . . I like your Symphony, beyond praise. Yet you say I never really like your poetry! The truth is, I have not been able to watch the slow, gradual onward-moving of Art. I still believe in the masterhood of Tennyson and William Morris. There is a something in your poetry only for the Few– not the All; and it may be I am not content that you should be any lower than the highest."

The allusion in Lanier's salutation is probably to Elizabeth Brentano, Countess von Arnim, who used this name in her publication entitled *Goethe's Letters to a Child* (1835).

them, and you *do* things more nobly than she ever thought them.

I had been in much anxiety for your health – for I saw that you were ill – and had (for much the same reason that I did not visit you that last forlorn day) refrained from writing inasmuch as I knew no address whereby to reach you save that of the people who might misconstrue the quick succession of a letter to a visit. Your letter therefore crowned all its exquisite goodness with a much-desired relief from my suspense in your behalf.

—— No, Tennyson and William Morris are not the masters; indeed, My Child, they never were: and it is the goodness of your heart, together with the poetry of your own which you unconsciously put between their lines, that have made you think so. Chaucer and Shakespeare – these are the Masters.

—— And the time will come when your wish that I should not be any less than the highest will be not so vain. What you think to be something not for the masses – " something only for thet few," you call it — in my poetry, is only an evidence of its perfect newness, its absolute unlikeness to what has been before said. Because it *is* uncommon, – is not a reason that it will be unpopular. Its originality is not in its words or forms: – *outré* poetry is a shallow device: – it is in its ideas, which have not been heretofore advanced.

And the *facts* are, that Smith and Jones like it as well as Miss Cushman and Bayard Taylor. Hereof come daily evidences. —— To whom could one say such things about one's own work, but to *you*, who understand so clearly, and who trust so largely!

The September number of Lippincott's is just out: I will try to find one tomorrow and send you. It contains four sonnets of mine, in the Shakespearian Sonnet meter, which you are politely requested to like infinitely.

Write me hereafter to the address at head of this letter. Pray let me hear soon that you are entirely well.

How lovely you are! —— This, which I said in the beginning of my letter, say I also in the end thereof: so binding all that comes between in a sacred circle of the faithful and tender admiration of

Your friend

S. L.

To Bayard Taylor [132]

195 Dean St.
Brooklyn, N. Y.
Aug. 19th 1875

Dear Mr. Taylor:

It would give me a great pleasure to hear you read your Goethe ode, and – though trembling a little at the idea of giving trouble to a busy man – I cannot resist the temptation to avail myself of your kind offer to intercede for an invitation.

I thank you for the fair words your letter brings, and am always

Your friend

Sidney Lanier.

To Robert S. Lanier

195 Dean St.
Brooklyn, N. Y.
Aug. 19th 1875.

My dear Father:

I have just received your letter from Blount Springs, and am truly glad to get some news from all of you.

I'm sorry May should have suspected my health: she's a keen one. I *had* a wretched cold for several days, and was in great discomfort: but am now free from that, and only worn by overwork. My time for getting the Florida book ready grows short,[133] and the reappearance of ever-new matter in all direc-

---

[132] Previously published, *Letters* (New York, 1899), p. 123. Taylor had written to Lanier, Aug. 17, 1875, inviting him " to attend the celebration of Goethe's 126th birthday " in New York on Aug. 28. He wrote in part: " I am heartily glad to welcome you to the fellowship of authors, so far as I may dare to represent it; but, knowing the others, I venture to speak in their names also." (Printed entire in *Letters*, New York, 1899, pp. 122-123.)

[133] In a letter to his wife, Aug. 15, 1875 (here omitted), Lanier had said: " The publishers only give me a few weeks more (until the middle of September) to finish the book."

tions, together with the intrinsic labor involved in the very nature of the undertaking, give me as much as I can do by working all day and much of the night. I am however upborne marvellously under the circumstances: and I hope to be through in two weeks.

My poem " In Absence " is out in the September Lippincott's and has already provoked a couple of very charming notices, one from the N. Y. Commercial Advertiser, and one from the Pha Bulletin.[134] Mr. Hilliard has written asking permission to print a letter I sent him thanking him for his little notice; and I have just replied, consenting provided he does not think it will subject me to the accusation of being too much in print.[135]

If you can manage to let Mary have thirty dollars, as soon as you get home, it will be great assistance to me. I do not get my salary until the last of this month. My Florida engagement then terminates.

What has become of Uncle Clifford?

One account of him is that he has gone to New Holland Springs: another, to Saratoga.

I hope to see you sometime late in September and long unspeakably for a little rest, with you all

Love to Mama and Pringle. I write May by this mail. Will try to find out poor Aunt Mollie,[136] soon.

Your Son

S. L.

[134] In a latter to his wife, Aug. 19, 1875 (here omitted) Lanier reported: " The N. Y. Commercial Advertiser says: ' Sidney Lanier's new poem, " In Absence " is very beautiful and powerful, and if it were a little more regular in its force and expression would be called a perfection of the highest order of poetry.' — Which makes me thankful that a blind ass can see, if but dimly, *sometimes.*" (No file of the Philadelphia *Evening Bulletin* for this period has been found.)

[135] If H. W. Hilliard printed Lanier's letter to him (see note 122, above), it has not been located; nor has the MS been found.

[136] The widow of Lanier's Uncle Sidney C. Lanier. She had remarried and was living in New York; her second husband seems to have deserted her (see R. S. Lanier's letter to his son, Aug. 15, 1875).

To Mary Day Lanier

195 Dean St.
Brooklyn, N. Y.
Aug. 24th 1875

On Saturday night I learned that Uncle C [137] and wife were at the St. Nicholas, and so went over on Sunday and spent most of the day with them.   Uncle C. was in the high noon of that disgust which a stranger usually passes through in the course of his initiation into the ways of the big rude Babylon: he had not been able to get the hotel-clerks to converse freely with him upon many subjects whereon he desired information, the hackman had overcharged him, he had made two or three attempts to get away to Saratoga but had been unsuccessful owing to various annoying causes, the ticket-agents were surly, the newspaper schedules were unreliable, upon interrogating a lot of Southern friends he had met he had received as many different accounts as there were individuals inquired of, and finally he was sick from a slight return of palpitation brought on by over-exertion and worry, and with disordered digestion.   After giving me, however, a minutely accurate account of these matters I think he felt better, and we had a pleasant afternoon together.   They left for Saratoga next morning, where they think to spend two weeks, then back here for two more, then home.

——   After great labor tribulation I begin to see the beginning of the end of my book, and look forward to that consummation with unspeakable longing. I am all in a flame with another " Symphony " and I shall die of inward heat if it be not soon quenched in the tears of expression.

What doest thou, dear Love?   I am fain to hope that thou art settled somewhere, and that Father's trip to Monroe Court will be of service to thee in some way.[138]

I pray thee embrace my two young men for me. I have been thinking of them with a full heart of late.   There is a book of

[137] Lanier's Uncle Clifford Anderson had been seriously ill for some months (see R. S. Lanier to Mary Day Lanier, Apr. 22, 1875).

[138] Forsyth, where Mary Day Lanier expected to go for the rest of the summer, is in Monroe County, Ga.

Gail Hamilton's called " Nursery Noonings ", wh. I happened to pick up and dash through the other day, wherein among some sentimentality and a little down-east flippancy, I found a noble vein of right-thinking, of good sense, and of sound logic. The outcome of it all was: that amidst all the rough-nesses and rudenesses and apparent heartlessnesses of a boy, one should nevertheless persistently " spoil " him, in a judicious way, one should never be angry with or in the least loud-voiced to him, one should not-see a great many of his peccadilloes, and when he does something very wrong one should wait until next day, and then gently discuss it with him alone.

If I might but read it, and talk it over with thee, my Heartsease!

If God may but bring me to thy feet, soon ! – then will I be as a stray wind-blown seed that hath found his own country again, – being elsewhere thy stint-leaved and unflowering

lover————

To Mary Day Lanier

[Brooklyn,] Aug. 28th [29] 1875.[139]

My too-dear Heartsease, what can thy " dear banker " say to thee? Day by day have I been hoping to get off thy funds to thee so as to be in full time for thy projected move on the 2nd; but the salary is not yet drawn. I hope to get it tomorrow: but it may not come till Tuesday. My locomotive gentleman is sometimes hard to reach. I think of thee morning after morning looking for the letter to come from me, with thy relief:– and the thought is , – – – – as thou knowest.

A day or two ago Bayard Taylor sent me an invitation to occupy a seat in the box which had been assigned to him at the Goethe Festival to be held in Gilmore's Garden on the occasion of Goethe's 126th birthday; and last night I went up town in accordance therewith. I found Mr. Taylor in the box when I arrived: he was to deliver the ode, written by himself, for the occasion: and presently Wm Cullen Bryant

---

[139] Date corrected from reference to Goethe festival, second paragraph, and evidence in Taylor's letters of Aug. 23, 26, printed in *Letters* (New York, 1899), pp. 123-124.

came in, and sate with us until time came for him to ascend
the rostrum from which he was to deliver the oration of the
evening.   I am sure thou wilt be glad to think of thy poor
sweetheart in such good company. We had an open box, and
we fairly reviewed the twelve thousand people who were
present, for they filed by in a continual throng to look at Mr.
Bryant, whose long white hair and white beard made him
easily recognizable to all.   Among others, presently came Gov.
[David S.] Walker and Miss Florida by: and the latter sent a
beaming smile to me.   Soon the poets were conducted to the
stand, after some noble music: and I then joined the Walkers.
In a few moments the Governor left me to take charge of Miss
Florida, while he went away to look for some friends.   She
looked hard at me: I was in full evening dress, as per command of the invitation; presently she burst out " Do you know
who you are?   " No " I said, wondering.
She fairly shouted, in her excitement; " Seraphael ! " [140]

—— Which I call a triumph of mind over matter: for thy
poor lover is as peak-snouted a poet and starveling as thou
shalt see in a summer's day.

Mr. Taylor read a beautiful ode.   He invited me to spend
today with him, as we parted: and I have just returned, after a
charming six hours.   Mrs. Taylor was out of town: and we
had our quiet dinner *en duo* , then a long delicious afternoon
in his study, both whose windows looked out upon a great
stretch of trees and flowers and grass in Central Park.   We
compared notes upon a great many points, and agreed to a
marvel.   That in which we were most completely at one was
our adoration of our wives.   I told him of thee: that thou wert
at once my constant inspiration and my perfect critic: and with
this we both set off, tilting valorously in praise of our ladies
in the friendliest joust was ever ridden.

He gave me one of his books at parting: and I am to see him
again next Wednesday.

I had also a charming little hour with the Peacocks on
Wednesday last.   I had to go to Pha on business, and took an

---

[140] Seraphael is the character generally recognized as Mendelssohn in Elizabeth Sheppard's novel, *Charles Auchester*. Mary Day Lanier replied, Sept. 12,
1875: " The very name which I gave thee twelve years ago. . . . Didst thou
know that Georgia Shackleford and I wrote *always* of thee as Seraphael? "

hour after it was finished to see them. They were just returned from Maine where they have been spending the summer; and were as cordial and heartsome as could be. They made many inquiries anent thee: and they think thy sonnets in the September Lippincott are " exquisite."

And now may the great love of God this night be thy flower-bell, wherein thou shalt lie as any bright dew-drop till the morning,– prayeth thy

lover.

To Bayard Taylor [141]

195 Dean St.
Brooklyn, N. Y.
Aug. 30th 1875

Dear Mr. Taylor:

The three numbered sonnets [142] enclosed are in continuation of those in the magazine which I mail herewith. Any criticism you may make on them, when we meet again, I will take as a special grace: for they form the beginning of a series which I will probably be writing all my life, knowing no other method of heart's-ease for my sense of the pure worshipfulness which dwells in the Lady they celebrate.

The other two [143] are only a couple of little snatches which were both born last Thursday: and I don't know any other reason for sending them to you, save that they're curiously unlike – for twins.

Sincerely yours

Sidney Lanier.

---

[141] Previously published, *Atlantic Monthly*, LXXXIII, 793 (June, 1899); reprinted, *Letters* (New York, 1899), pp. 124-125.

[142] " Acknowledgment " (I, 56); the accompanying magazine was undoubtedly *Lippincott's* for Sept., 1875, containing the " In Absence " sequence.

[143] Conjecturally identified in the note to " A Song of Love," vol. I of the present edition.

To Mary Day Lanier

Brooklyn, N. Y.
Sep. 4th 1875.

Dear Heartsease, I can but send thee a longing word today, being quite disabled from writing by an unusually severe return of mine ancient enemy. He came five days ago, in small force: but next day stronger, and next still stronger, until yesterday I summoned a homaeopathic physician, who has been treating me, with good results. I am better today: but will be quite incapable of the pen, or of my work, for several days.

Uncle C. and Aunt Annie are in town, much delighted with Saratoga, and in better humor with New York. The former has called to see me twice: inasmuch as I feared the jar of the long ride over to see *them*.

I have had another charming day with Mr. Taylor.[144]

Now write I no more. Thou shalt have a little bulletin each day from thy *too*-lonesome

lover.

To Mary Day Lanier

Brooklyn, Sep. 5th 1875

I think of nothing but thee all day, and I dream of nothing but thee all night. What a strange thing is Distance.

I am better today: and will be writing again in less than a week. I have but about five days of steady work, more, in order to be freed from the dreadful bonds of the Florida book.

Harry Wysham popped in this morning, fresh and tidy as a dear little Sunday school boy, and paid a pleasant visit. He is just from Saratoga: and was going to Pascual's this (Sunday)

[144]Lanier had been with Taylor on Wednesday, Sept. 1. Taylor's note of Sept. 2, 1875 (printed in *Letters*, New York, 1899, p. 125), refers to the meeting and to Lanier's projected visit to Boston. Lanier had on this occasion presented a copy of the Cummins profile picture of himself to Taylor (reproduced with autographic inscription, dated Aug. 31, 1875, in Marie Hansen-Taylor's *On Two Continents*, New York, 1905, facing p. 258); and Taylor had given Lanier his own photograph, by Kurtz, New York, dated Sept. 1, 1875 (facing).

BAYARD TAYLOR IN 1875

Charles D. Lanier Collection, Johns Hopkins University

afternoon for a grand quartett, Wehner playing first flute. Alas, alas, I could not go.

— And I see and sigh over so many people going along the street out yonder, in the very vigor of health, and apparently not knowing what to do with it.

Thou shdst. see my sonnet to Charlotte Cushman.[145] She says " it is the sweetest thing was ever said to her in all her life."

I *must* stop. God sometimes give me strength enough to tell thee with a pen truly how I am thy

lover.

To Mary Day Lanier

195 Dean St.
Brooklyn, N. Y.
Sep. 9th 1875.

My too-sweet Heart, I have had no further set-back in the way of hæmorrhage, and I improve in strength.[146] It is likely I will go over to Phª some time next week, when I have to meet Mr Pope at Lippincott's. I hope to be quite in working trim in a week from now.

I long to know that thou art safely housed and homed among the Oaks.[147] If thou seest e'er a jaybird, or a brown thrush, or a tomtit hopping in the fence-corners, I prithee convey my most tender compliments to the same, and my longing that I might also be there where thou comest along the road. Yet I cd. not sing but just our little song: towit, how that I am thy

lover.

---

[145] " To Charlotte Cushman " (I, 58).

[146] In a letter of Sept. 7, 1875 (here omitted), Lanier had written to his wife: " I have had but little hæmorrhage since yesterday morning. I am quite debarred, however, still from speaking or writing." And in a letter of Sept. 8, 1875 (also omitted), he added: " I am still improving, . . . and have good hope to be again at work before a great while." In her reply of Sept. 10, Mary Day Lanier said: " I marvel now that I could have hoped for thee to escape it in this long strain of writing. The wonder is it did not come sooner."

[147] Mary Day Lanier and her children had left Macon on Sept. 8 for the home of S. D. Mobley, near Forsyth.

To Gibson Peacock [148]

> 195 Dean St.
> Brooklyn, N. Y.
> Sep. 9th 1875.

My dear Friend:

Will you be in Pha about the 12th or 14th next?
Business calls me there at that time: and I wish to know if
I'm going to have the pleasure of seeing you.

I can only scrawl a line. My work has been rudely interrupted by a series of troublesome hæmorrhages which have for
some time prevented me from reading or speaking, as well as
from writing.

I'm crawling back into life, however, and hope to be at work
in a few days.

I send my loving remembrance to you both, and am always

> Your friend
>
> Sidney Lanier

To Mary Day Lanier

> Brooklyn. Sep. 10th 1875

I continue to improve, My *Mia*, and now suffer from nothing
more than the pain and feebleness usually consequent upon
such attacks. These diminish daily.

Everything is desolate, here. Poor Julie Ripley has been
nursing her baby at Canarsie [N. Y.] for many weeks, with a
tender desperation endeavoring to stave back death from him:
this morning at two the little fellow died, and they are all just
arrived at home, with his body. The poor girl seems wild
with grief: and to hear her calling upon the child in cooing
tones, with the half-conscious attempt to coax him back by the
mere sweetness of her voice, is enough to woman any man.
The poor old gentleman, too, seems quite crushed.

[148] Previously published, *Atlantic Monthly*, LXXIV, 23 (July, 1894); reprinted, *Letters* (New York, 1899), p. 19.

I am rejoiced to be able to tell thee of steady improvement. How farest thou, My poor Heart, with the tooth? Thou suffering one! Hast thou indeed been again worn with this pain, to reinforce all thine other cares?

God send thee quiet of body, soul and heart, fervently prays thy

lover.

To Mary Day Lanier

195 Dean St.
Brooklyn, N. Y.
Sept 12th 1875.

My heart's Heartsease, My sweet Too-sweet, My Heaven of My Heaven, if I could wrap thee in a calyx of tender words still would they seem but like the prickly husk in respect of thee, thou Rose, within.

—— — I dream thee all this day, going in and out among thy little ones, dear Motherkin: now it is Hal that calls thee, as King Arthur might have called when he was a baby: now it is my Charles, with the gray eye that is like Wakulla under the sky of dawn; now thou must needs do somewhat for Sidney, that frail dear Incomprehensible; now thou tiest a shoe for Lulu, a witch and a beauty.

Art thou indeed among the trees? I fancy thou must be; and hence,– in the midst of the cares of new settlement – thou hast not written. But I will hear tomorrow.

Here have we had the funeral today, and poor Julie with a broken heart is gone with the little casket to the steamer that carries them northward.[149]

[Monroe] Ogden called to see me this morning. Coming to the door in midst of the funereal signs, he was for a time stricken, and turned to go away; he thought it was I who had gone: but Anna Mary happened to see him, and told him better.

---

[149] To "Cherry Valley (near Sharon Springs, in Northern N. Y.) for interment"—according to Lanier's letter to his wife, Sept. 11, 1875 (here omitted). Cherry Valley seems to have been the family home of the Dutchers.

Which reminds me to tell thee that I am doing marvellous well, in view of my recent stroke. I grow stronger day by day.

Now God make thee also stronger day by day, in body, in mind, in heart, devoutly prays thy

lover.

To Robert S. Lanier

Philadelphia, Pa.
Sep. 15th 1875.

My dear Father:

I ran over here yesterday on a flying business trip, to see the Lippincott's and to meet Mr. Pope. I've been staying at Mr. Peacock's house, and they seem unwearied there in their kind ministrations to my feebleness.

Pope was to meet me here today. He has not yet arrived, however. I return to Brooklyn this afternoon.

I have got the publishers to give me a week more on the Florida book, – which was entirely suspended during my illness– and I'm going to work in the morning on it, with the most fervent hope of being able to finish it.

The October number of Lippincott's, just out, contains one of the chapters of my Florida book: it is called " the Ocklawaha in May." The illustrations are mostly poor; – but they are about as usual so the experts say.

I find it will be absolutely necessary for me to rest. I'm quite tired out, in body and mind. A couple of weeks would set me up wonderfully. I can manage this, if you can send me thirty dollars. Please send to *195 Dean St, Brooklyn*, N. Y. I should be glad to have it as soon as possible.

I am improving, daily, in strength though suffering considerable pain from what seems sometimes a toothache, sometimes neuralgia, sometimes a sympathetic affection with the lung trouble.[150]

---

[150] In a letter to his wife, Sept. 15, 1875 (here omitted), Lanier wrote: "I continue to improve, suffering now with little save the painful tooth-disorder. I think probably an abscess has formed under my gold-tooth, and this seems to ramify into eye and ear and throat. It is now getting much better, though, and will probably wear away in a day or two."

I wrote you a few days ago. Your letter reached me. Cannot write much now.

Love to Mama, and all, from

Your aff. Son

S.L.

To Sarah C. Bird [151]

195 Dean St.,
Brooklyn, N. Y.
Sep. 17th , 1875.

My dear Mrs. Bird:

Your proffer is so intrinsically sweet, and so sweetly made, that one could wish one were back at the gates of death, in order that one might avail one's self conscientiously of your ministrations.

—But, alas, I am better: so much so that I have not now the least excuse to call you over here through the multitudinous perils of Fulton Ferry. The only consolation I can offer myself is the hope that I will be able to see you in a few days, at your New York lodgings. Though little able to travel, I was compelled to go to Philadelphia on imperative business last Tuesday, and find myself quite knocked up on my return. The delay in answering your letter is due to this journey.

I am too delighted to hear from you, and shall be more so to see you. Pray send me a little line to tell me how long you'll be in New York.

Perhaps you'll care to know that the September number of Lippincott's has a poem of mine; and that the October number, now just out, has an article which constitutes one of the chapters in the Florida book I'm writing, called " The Oclawaha in May."

Your kind remembrance of me goes — where indeed you led the way yourself long ago — to my heart, and I am always

Your friend

Sidney Lanier.

[151] Mrs. Edgeworth Bird, a Baltimore friend, formerly of Macon.

To GIBSON PEACOCK [152]

Brooklyn, N. Y.
Sep. 24th 1875.

My dear friend:

How bright you made my little visit to Philadelphia, a sort of asteroid to circle round my dark.

—But I haven't more than just time now to thank you for
the letter and papers which you forwarded: and to tell you to
address me henceforth at the *Westminster Hotel*, New York
City, where I go presently, being now in the bitter agonies of
moving, packing and the like dreadful bores.

A letter from Miss Stebbins informs me that they are all
safely at Lennox and our dear Miss Cushman improving.

One can entrust one's message to a blue sky like this morning's: consider this lovely day to be the salutation of

Your friend
Sidney L.

To BAYARD TAYLOR [153]

Westminster Hotel
New York City.
Sep. 25th 1875.

My dear Mr. Taylor:

For some time after my last charming
day with you, it really seemed as if the ghost of Dr. Sangrado –
him of bloody memory – [154] had obtained permission to work
his will upon me, as the Devil did upon Job: I was unmercifully phlebotomized: hæmorrhage came upon hæmorrhage.

— Which I would not mention, except that I can not bear
you should believe any light cause able to prevent me from
immediately acknowledging a note so thoroughly kind and

---

[152] Previously published, *Atlantic Monthly*, LXXIV, 23 (July, 1894); reprinted, *Letters* (New York, 1899), pp. 19-20.
[153] Previously published, *Atlantic Monthly*, LXXXIII, 793 (June, 1899);
reprinted, *Letters* (New York, 1899), pp. 125-126.
[154] The quack physician in Le Sage's *Gil Blas*.

heartsome as your last to me.[155]   When it came I was not allowed the privilege either of speaking or writing.

But I'm getting in prime condition again: and anticipate with keen eagerness the pleasure of seeing you when you return.

Pray send me a line, to let me know when that will be.   I've moved over to New York: and my address is at The Westminster Hotel, this city.

My illness has deprived me of the pleasure of seeing Mr. Hassard: [156] but I hope to call on him in a day or two.   If you should see him before I do, I will thank you if you will say as much to him.

An accumulation of work keeps me at my desk the whole of each day and much of each night.   I pray you therefore, invert the littleness of these words, and therewith measure the scope of that affection wherein I am

faithfully your friend

Sidney Lanier.

To Mary Day Lanier

Westminster Hotel
New York City.
Sep. 26th 1875.

My dear adorable Comrade, today is Sunday but I have been writing Florida during the whole of it, verily believing that if ever an ox hath been in the ditch, mine is: it is now night and bedtime, and I send thee this little word by way of prayer before I sleep.

Thou wilt see from the heading hereof that my location is changed.   Julie Ripley is just moving into her new house, and I have come over here to spend a couple of weeks.   After which, I know not what I will do, or where go.   Thou must address me as this letter is headed.   Thy sweet motherly letter anent my young men came to me yesterday.   Thou art the prettiest writer in the world and thy delicate unconscious fancies continually charm me.

---

[155] Apparently Taylor's letter of Sept. 2, 1875, referred to in note 144, above.
[156] J. R. G. Hassard, music critic of the New York *Tribune*.

I wish I might kiss thy hand.

I cannot give thee the least news. I am marvellously upborne through such labor as I cannot describe to thee. I have now come to the last job of the Florida book – the list of the towns &c, on which I start tomorrow. Thy dear pages, full of thy very hand marks are before me now, and I see thy gray eyes bent thereupon with the heavenly helpful look thou wearest when thou laborest for me.

Give my love to thy Father. I am charmed to hear of his improvement. My poor Charlotte Cushman has been very ill, but is now better. Hast thou seen the Oclawaha article in Lippincott's and dost thou like it?

Whether thou dost or not thou art the sweetest Sweet God hath yet made, and thou hast a very faithful true

lover.——

Be sure thou dost not address any more letters to *Brooklyn*, from force of habit.

To Clifford A. Lanier

Westminster Hotel,
New York City,
Sep. 26th 1875.

My dear Little Boy: I'm sure I can't give you the least idea of the desperate run I've been making for the last two months, in the attempt to get my Florida book finished in the time set me. Finally, about three weeks ago, my flues collapsed: I had a half dozen exhausting hæmorrhages in succession in the course of a week, which brought me down to a point where I could only lie on a bed and look up, without being allowed the privilege of even speaking. I worried through, however, and for a week past have been again going, night and day, with the interminable pen. I never dreamed the book was going to ramify into such unearthly directions. Besides all the travelling I've done between Boston, Mass, and Silver Springs, Fla, since the middle of last April, I've written about a thousand pages of Ms., read innumerable books on or connected with Florida, and conducted a business correspondence frightful to think of.

All of which I mention, to let you know how it is that I've had to neglect you so. Your last letters, with the dear Sonnets, came when I was bleeding and quite incapable of aught but the bed. And now my time is so limited—I have to finish the Florida book in a very few days, under dire consequences of failure—that for a week hence I do not expect to do aught but what I have done the week past, towit: write at my best speed all the time betwixt waking and sleeping that isn't wasted in eating.

Have you seen the "Ocklawaha in May," by me, in the October number of Lippincott's, now just out? The next number (for November, which will come out about the middle of October) will contain another illustrated article of mine on "ST. AUGUSTINE IN APRIL." Both these are chapters out of the early portion of the Florida book.

These articles appear to have pleased the Editor, and he offers me another job for the first four numbers of 1876.[157] He has also engaged me to write the Centennial Poem for the Magazine. About this latter, do not say anything: I don't want it to get in the papers.

After the next week I will take up this matter of the sonnets, and see what can be done. I am sure they will need treatment, before offering them for sale. How I wish I might see you and talk over these things. I wish you would sketch another negro poem, and let me do my half with it. I have a project to make a great comedy out of the Doctor's Legend: and wish to detail some ideas for it to you, when we meet, so that we may write it together. But it will have to be incubated a long time: and there's no need to hurry now. All the hurrying men, who have shot up like rockets recently, are coming down like sticks.

I am to push, as soon as my week of work is over, my plan for a chair of THE PHYSICS AND METAPHYSICS OF MUSIC, to be attached to the New York College of Music. I have some valuable introductions to start on; and the thing may succeed. If it does, – life will have permanently arranged itself for me: and I won't have anything to do for the balance of it, save to talk of music and write poetry.

---

[157] "Sketches of India" (VI, 254). The poem mentioned in the following sentence was "The Psalm of the West" (I, 62); it was published in *Lippincott's* for July, 1876. (See also Lanier's letter of Oct. 4, below|)

I wish I had time to tell you what a faithful and large friend I have found in Bayard Taylor. I spent two charming days with him, here, a month ago; and have had great edification from his companionship.

My last two weeks has thrown me behind a little, financially. I have much need of some thirty dollars. If you can, pray let me have it. Address me here; "*Westminster Hotel, New York City.*"

I'm *too* lonesome, and yearning for some sight of dear faces. I *hope* to run home soon: but can't tell. If I do, you must come over and meet me. But more of this hereafter. Kiss sweet Will for me: and keep me in remembrance of all who are with you. Will dear little Sissa stay at her home all winter?

Your bro.

S. L.

To Bayard Taylor [158]

Westminster Hotel, N. Y.

Sep. 29th 1875.

My dear Mr. Taylor:

Your note comes flushed with good news. For bringing me within two blocks of you I will in the most sublime manner forgive Fate a dozen heinous injuries.

I will eagerly await you on Friday evening; and will be delighted to go with you to the Century Club.

I write in the greatest haste, today not being long enough by some six hours for what I have to do before it ends.

— Which makes me realize how glorious is Friendship, to whose immortality the poor necessities of night and sleep do not exist.

Your friend

S. L.

[158] Previously published, *Atlantic Monthly*, LXXXIII, 793 (June, 1899); reprinted, *Letters* (New York, 1899), p. 127.

Taylor had written to Lanier on Sept. 28 (*Letters*, New York, 1899, pp. 126-127) that he was moving to the Stuyvesant, 142 East 18th St., within two blocks of Lanier's hotel. He invited Lanier to the monthly meeting of the Century Club on Saturday, Oct. 2, and stated that he would also call to see him on Friday evening.

To Bayard Taylor [159]

Westminster Hotel
Friday noon.
[New York, Oct. 2, 1875?]

My dear Mr. Taylor:

Pray tell me if I must go in full dress tonight, – or only in a black frock.

Also, behold, in this I Sonnet,[160] how this morning the idea which you were good enough to present me, last night, *would* sing itself in me till I cd. do no less than put it on paper.

Also, tell me when we meet tonight, if you have now any objection to the II and III, – which you have seen before.

Your friend

S. L.

To Robert S. Lanier

Westminster Hotel,
New York City.
Oct. 2nd 1875

My dear Father:

Many thanks for your prompt response to my request.

Night before last, after an incredible burst on the last heat – as the jockeys would say – I finished the dreadful Florida book: and yesterday and today I have devoted to absolute rest.

Tonight Mr. Taylor is going to take me to the Century Club, and I expect to meet many of the *illuminati*. His kindness to me continues in extraordinary measure, and I have formed the greatest attachment for him.

---

[159] Previously published, *Atlantic Monthly*, LXXXIII, 793-794 (June, 1899); reprinted, *Letters* (New York, 1899), p. 128. Conjectural dating from the evidence given in note 158, above; Lanier's dating " Friday noon " is apparently a slip for Saturday.

[160] Probably the first of the " Acknowledgment " sequence, as published in *Lippincott's*, Nov., 1876. Lanier had previously sent Taylor three sonnets of this series (see his letter of Aug. 30, 1875, and note 142, above)— not just the " II and III " referred to in the last paragraph of this letter.

My movements are utterly undecided: but I hope that the end of next week will give me some definite notion of my plans for the winter. The date of my home-coming will depend much on this. I long to see you all.

I am getting quite well, again: and marvel when I think of the state I was in, a couple of weeks ago, to see myself so well. A week more of life at this charming hotel will make me, I believe, as good as new.

Love to Uncle C. and Mama and yourself,

from

Your Son

S. L.

To Bayard Taylor [161]

W. Hotel.
Sunday morning.
[New York, Oct. 3, 1875 ?]

My dear friend:

Any time between now and tomorrow night, won't you please look over this Cushman stanza,[162] and tell me when we next meet if you do not think it more consistent than formerly? I think to send it to Scribner's, if peradventure it may find favor in their eyes.

— And won't you accep[t] the ms. of this little Song? [163]

I hope you're quite well today. Don't trouble to answer this.

Hastily: (and yet not hastily)

Your friend

S. L.

---

[161] Previously published, *Atlantic Monthly*, LXXXIII, 794 (June, 1899); reprinted, *Letters* (New York, 1899), p. 128. Conjectural dating from the sequence of Lanier's letters to Taylor and from the partial dating "Sunday morning."

[162] "To Charlotte Cushman." It was published in *Lippincott's*, Mar., 1876.

[163] Possibly "A Song of the Future" (I, 59). Lanier was paid $10.00 for this poem by *Scribner's* on Nov. 9, 1875; it was published in the issue of Aug., 1876.

To Mary Day Lanier [164]

Westminster Hotel, N. Y.
Oct. 4th 1875.

From longing for thee there is no rest: if I am sunken in work I desire thee infinitely, if I am enjoying my rest I desire thee more infinitely—for, in love the Infinite hath degrees—and if I am well I desire thee most infinitely. Picture to thyself, then, thou that hast so bright wit, how much I long for thy good company, now when I have combined the last two of these conditions, when I am given over to the long-dreamed of luxury of rest, and am at the same time in great pomp of riotous health – – for *me*. O, might'st thou but share my State, for only one little day, dear Love. My heart is torn, sweet Heart, My Gray One, My little Girl of Dawn, with perpetual wakings to thine absence, out of perpetual dreams of thy presence.

—————— Saturday night was to me an Arabian Night. My good Caliph Haroun Al Raschid Taylor took me to the Century Club and there for the first time in my life I had the delight of meeting and of conversing with thoughtful men and artists of many sorts. I wish I might tell thee the keen pleasure of it all.

I had also in the course of the evening some special individual warmths of greeting from here and there a man to whom my little ventures had come to port, which were very charming. Among others I was presented to David Huntington, whose picture of Miranda inspired the poem that was printed in the Evening Post.[165] He had seen the poem there when it first appeared, and had preserved it and spoken specially to Mr. Bryant about it. He was very gracious in warm expressions of his sense of the compliment to his picture, and of his appreciation of the poem which he said had completely caught his idea of the Miranda creation, and had pleased Mr. Bryant as well as himself.

---

[164] Excerpts previously printed in the circular announcing the Centennial Edition of Sidney Lanier, Baltimore, Feb. 3, 1942.

[165] See note 2, 1874. The painter's name was Daniel (not David) Huntington.

I was pleased more than all with a hearty and wholly un-expected offer of assistance from Mr. Stedmen,[166] who late in the evening came to me and after many pleasant things about myself informed me that Scribner's would probably have some book-reviewing to do, that I was the man to do it, and that if I would consent he would see the editors and endeavor to make the arrangement. Of course I consented.

In the course of the evening I met Gov. Tilden, Whitelaw Reid (with whom I was greatly struck), Stoddard, Ward (the Sculptor), Charlton Lewis, Holt, Putnam,[167] and many others. I found Ward a splendid fellow: and had a pleasant talk with Stoddard.

Yesterday morning my dear old Mr. Calvert [168] called, on his return from Washington; and presently took me out for a long drive in the Park, after which I dined with him and Mrs. Calvert — a charming little old lady with profuse tight curls of gray hair in front on each side of her face, and with man-ners and speech like thy father's when he is happy. Moreover we dined at the Everett House; I had a sense of thee, all about: constantly wondering whether mayhap thou hadst sate in the very spot I was sitting and other the like particulars, whereby

[166] Edmund Clarence Stedman (see note 137, 1874). It was probably with Stedman's and Taylor's kindnesses in mind that Lanier wrote to his father on Oct. 9, 1875 (Here omitted): " I am sure you would be gratified if you could know all the pleasant things which my very meagre poetic accomplishment has brought me, here. I have only to get something large before the public, in order to take, before it, the pleasant position which I seem to have won among the literary men here. I was really touched by some offers of assistance which were made to me at the Century Club the other night, where I was carried by my constant friend Mr. Taylor: offers so warm, and so wholly unsought and unexpected, could not have come from any source but hearty appreciation."

[167] Samuel J. Tilden (1814-1886), Democratic Governor of New York, 1874-1876; Whitelaw Reid (1837-1912), editor of the New York *Tribune* since 1872; Richard Henry Stoddard (1825-1903), poet; John Quincy Adams Ward (1830-1910); Charlton Thomas Lewis (1834-1904), lawyer and classicist; and probably the publishers, George Haven Putnam (1844-1930) and Henry Holt (1840-1926).

[168] George H. Calvert (see note 108, above). The friendship here begun continued throughout Lanier's life, though it lacks a proper representation in these volumes since none of his letters to Calvert have been found. From seven surviving letters written by Calvert, however, the warmth of their devotion is apparent. Several years later, for example, hearing indirectly of Lanier's straight-ened circumstances, he sent financial aid; and on another occasion he offered to help pay the costs of stereotyping a volume of Lanier's poems so that the author could retain control of the copyright. (See Calvert to Lanier, Mar. 22, 1879, and Oct. 13, 1880.)

I fear I was *distrait* enough. But the dear little gentle lady talked evenly along: and we had a smoke, graciously allowed by her, in their parlor after dinner: and then the good gentleman (he is over seventy three) must see me home, so out with me into the night: and arrived at my house, he comes up to my room, and we discuss many matters and I read him a poem or two, writ on Saturday: [169] and finally he sighs and declares he *must* go: and I walk back to the Everett House with him: where, arriving, in midst of some interesting talk or other, he vows I shall not return alone to my lodgings and actually walks all the way back with me, and after standing in the office a little while to finish our talk, finally gets him home to Mrs. Calvert.

Mr. Kirk has given me a job, of four ten-page articles on India to be richly illustrated from French plates sent over by J. B. Lippincott from Europe. I will have about $300 for the four papers: the first one to come out in January next. He has also engaged me to write the Centennial Poem, for the July Magazine of 1876, which he proposes to illustrate, — and for which I shall charge him a round sum. The whole idea of the poem has come to me in a whirlwind of glory, and I am thirsty for the time to arrive when I can sit daily by thee and write it.[170]

My Caliph Bayard Taylor, has made me some suggestions in the matter of the College of Music Professorship which induce me to wait some three days before approaching the Chairman of the board to broach the subject. There is really a possibility of the thing's success: not more, now.

Thou shalt have money in a day or two for board. My God, I fear thou art destitute: — but it really begins to look, now, as if there were some sign of steady and profitable employment for me in the work that I love: and my heart grows daily dry and hot with praying God to hasten the time when my love can put somewhat else about thee besides his arms, for I think daily upon thy needs — ah, my beautiful shining hair, canst thou not keep it from falling? [171] and I am not the least jot or title of anything in the world over and above thy

lover.

[169] See notes 160, 163, above.
[170] " The Psalm of the West " (see note 157, above).
[171] Mary Day Lanier had several times written that her hair was getting thin.

To Edmund C. Stedman [172]

Westminster Hotel [New York].
Tuesday, Oct. 5th 1875.

Dear Mr. Stedman:

Won't you sometime or other – if only for your sins – read my " Symphony " in the Magazine sent herewith?

Although written in a mere lawless gust – a sort of little whirlwind originating at a point when the passion of music and the passion of pity, blowing different ways, happened to converge — yet, since it has cooled a little, and I have called myself to account for it, so many and great extensions of the artistic principles underlying it occur to me that I feel a strong desire, in beginning to exemplify them in new works, to do so with at least the hope that better embodiments of them than this very crude one might find favor in the eyes of so keen a critical faculty as that which reveals itself in your " Victorian Poets ".

When we meet again, which I hope may be soon, you shall abuse or praise my poem just as much as you like, knowing that in either case I'm going to remain

Your friend

Sidney Lanier.

To Mary Day Lanier

New York, Oct. 12th 1875

My too-dear Heart, my Sweetest Child, thy letter sent out thy sighs mingled with the sweet-briar's to me a few minutes ago, and the world seems to have turned into a tender throb. If I might only take thy head on my breast and thy hands in mine and thine eyes in mine.

If God shall be willing, soon I will.

I am sure that life is come to the point with me where I

[172] Previously published, Atlanta *Journal*, July 6, 1931.

have the right to hold thy soul by mine and to possess the continual comfort of thy neighborhood, and I am quite resolved that we shall soon unite, not to be parted again with these long heart-break partings. Moreover, I find it simply impossible to endure the thought of thy physical condition, and thy subjection to ———— that Terror. I *know* that a bracing climate, proper food, a larger outlook for thy mental and artistic faculties, the superior skill of physicians here (which has made great advances), and the nursing which my love is too-eager to give thee and which my improved health will render possible to me, — will altogether make of thee in a wonderfully short time a new creature in the flesh.

I go over to Phil^a tomorrow morning. I hope to persuade Mr. Lippincott to give me some employment — possibly as assistant-editor of the Magazine [173] – which will afford a definite basis of support, besides the irregular monies that I can get by music and magazine-contributions. I saw Col. Stebbins the other day, – the Chairman of the Trustees of the Musical College – and learned, in a very pleasant interview, that that matter postpones itself until Spring, in consequence of legal complications which have intervened. The donor of the fund has not yet made a deed: there is nothing so far more than a bequest: and I rather fancied from what he said that the gift is going to be disputed, but of this *say thou naught*. He however expressed his confidence that the matter would come through safely, invited me to his house, and closed by desiring that he might have further communication with me as soon as any active steps could be taken.

I wrote thee that I had a job from Mr. Kirk worth some $300, for next year. That and the poem will come to about

---

[173] In a letter to his brother Clifford, Oct. 14, 1875 (here omitted), Lanier wrote from Philadelphia, where he was staying with the Gibson Peacocks:

" I ran over here yesterday in order to set the printers to work on the Florida Ms; and they're hard at it today. We are trying to rush the book through, so as to have all ready to publish by Dec. 1st. I will likely be here about two weeks longer. . . .

" I have just been talking with Mr. Lippincott about getting the place of assistant-editor of the Magazine. There is no such position at present, and has never been: but both the other rivals,– The Atlantic and Scribner's– have taken unto themselves assistants and the idea seemed to strike him very favorably. He is to think it over and let me know."

$500: and the Baltimore music-season (if I shd. *have* to come down to that in the last resort) will bring some $300 more: which with the amount I could draw – and usually do draw – from Father, would keep us from starvation for at least a year; by which time, with my present outlook, I feel perfectly sure I can manage matters. In truth, I spend considerably more money, in my present manner of life, than I would if we were together: for now I have to keep, as it were, two establishments, which have been particularly galling of late in a financial way.

So that thou mayst conclude we will winter together. I cannot yet tell whether in Baltimore, Phila, or here: but in one of the three.

I have not yet been able to get any rest. The papers on India are terribly troublesome, for *me*, who had to begin from the very beginning, and they involve a great range of matters. If we were together thou couldst be of infinite service to me, herein: there is a great French book, of a thousand pages, to be read. The worst of it is that the first paper – wh. will take about eighty pages of my Ms.– must be in Mr. Kirk's hands by the 10th of next month, wh. only gives me about three weeks for the whole preliminary preparation. During this three weeks I must necessarily be in reach of libraries. I have too some other things to do, in this time. Were it not for these latter considerations I wd. come immediately home: but that is now impossible *within* two weeks. After that I hope to be sufficiently armed and equipped to venture.

Thus, thou hast now my plan and hope, in the rough. Of one thing, I am thoroughly satisfied: I must be by thee . I cannot longer contemplate thee there, alone for months, ill, and worn by the very patience which thou art so sweet in.

O True Heart, cd. I only tell thee some little hymnlet of the devout and tender worship wherewith I revere thee, wherewith I tremble in even writing on this cold page that I am thy

lover.

To Bayard Taylor [174]

1425 Walnut St.
Philadelphia, Pa.
Oct. 15th 1875.

My dear Mr. Taylor:

I hope you'll like this little song,[175] which is but lately an inhabitant of this planet.

We – we is Mr. Peacock and I – were too sorry you couldn't come over last night: though of course neither of us *hoped* much from the mere possibility that you *might* be able to come. It is likely I will be here a week, or perhaps ten days longer. Did I not hear you say that you would be leaving New York next week?   Pray tell me how long you'll be away.

I will miss my Saturday-night tomorrow: [176] and I would be strongly inclined to consider this a *very* cross-purpose indeed, if I did not feel myself so indebted to Purpose already.

And perhaps it is well enough for me to be away for a week or two.   I want to digest Mr. Stedman and Mr. Stoddard.   I find that spiritually we are cannibals, all: we feed upon each other, soul assimilates and makes tissue of soul.

I haven't time to *write* you.

God be praised that you exist, – is a frequent ejaculation of

your friend

Sidney Lanier.

---

[174] Previously published, *Atlantic Monthly*, LXXXIII, 794 (June, 1899); reprinted, *Letters* (New York, 1899), pp. 128-129.

[175] "Rose-Morals. Red " (I, 59), as evidenced from the quotations in Taylor's answer of Oct. 16, 1875 (*Letters*, New York, 1899, pp. 129-130).

[176] A guest card, extending to Lanier the privileges of the Century Club, had been issued Oct. 9, 1875, "at the request of Messrs. Taylor, Stedman, and Stoddard," and sent to Lanier by Taylor the same day with the brief injunction: "Please come around at once. B. T." This letter indicates that Lanier took advantage of the courtesy when he was in New York. (The card is preserved in the Charles D. Lanier Collection, Johns Hopkins University.)

To Paul H. Hayne [177]

Philadelphia, Pa.
Oct. 16th 1875.

My dear Mr. Hayne:

Your note – which has followed me about and finally reached me here – gave me a great deal of pleasure, and I hasten to assure you that I have for months only been putting off from day to day the actual committal to paper of the letter which has been lying really written within me. This "putting off" has been due, not to laziness, but to its opposite. I believe I wrote you sometime ago that I had been employed to make a book on Florida. I commenced the travels preparatory thereto in April last: the thing immediately began to ramify and expand, until I quickly found I was in for a long and very difficult job: so long, and so difficult, that, after working day and night for the last three months on the materials I had previously collected, I have just finished the book, and am now up to my ears in proof-sheets and wood-cuts which the publishers are rushing through in order to publish at the earliest possible moment, the book having several features designed to meet the wants of the winter-visitors to Florida. It is in truth only a kind of spiritualized guide-book.

– This it is which has prevented me from writing you. With a nervous employer and a pushing publisher behind me, I have had to work from ten to fourteen hours a day; and the confinement to the desk brought on my old hæmorrhages about a month ago which quite threatened for a time to suspend my work forever on *this* side of River.

I'm thus minute in detailing the reasons for my failure to write you, because all along through these last three or four months when gratifying things have been happening to me in connection with my little artistic efforts, I have had constantly in mind the kindly help and encouragement which your cheering words used to bring me when I was even more obscure than I am now. Even in my insignificant experience I have seen so much of the hue-and-cry sort of criticism – that which waits until it finds how the big-mouth'd dogs are running and then

---

[177] Previously published, *Critic*, VIII [o.s.], 89 (Feb. 20, 1886); reprinted, *Letters* (New York, 1899), pp. 240-242. Lanier's *Florida* (first paragraph) contained forty wood-engravings by Van Ingen-Snyder (see illustration).

"A Landing on the Ocklawaha"

From the First Edition of Lanier's *Florida*, 1875

squeaks in chorus without the least knowledge of, or regard for, the game or the course of the hunt – that I have learned to set a high value on genuine and independent judgments. These *you* gave me, and I will always be grateful to you for them.[178]

I fully expected to go to Aiken, and to have sight of you, there; but the devious current of work bore me to New York, and although I had to run back to Charleston for two days, about a month after I wrote you,[179] I was never able to get to Aiken. I met Dutcher and Randall in Augusta, but had only one uncertain day there, and they agreed it was impossible to get hold of you in the limited time I had.

– Now, then, let me know upon what you are engaged, and how you are faring. I have not yet had a moment to look into your last volume [180] – a pleasure I've been promising myself as soon as these dreadful proof-sheets are finished.

Write me " Care of Gibson Peacock Esq
1425 Walnut St.
Philadelphia
Pa."

I will be glad to hear from you, and of you; being always

sincerely yours

Sidney Lanier

[178] In his reply, Oct. 23, 1875, Hayne expressed himself as deeply touched by this testimonial given in " the bright morning of your fame," so different from the way most men repudiate their old associations " the moment they begin to rise in the world." He added: " With *pride* no less than *pleasure*, I hail your really brilliant success in Literature. Some fools in this quarter of the world have thought proper to express *surprise*, at your waking up one morning (after the publication of ' Corn ') and ' finding yourself famous.' . . . They can't understand that *Lanier*, being a Georgian, *has*, or *could* have any *real* claim to artistic distinction! " He concluded by saying that he wanted Lanier to do for him what he had done for Henry Timrod— edit his literary remains after his death so that his memory " would not wholly die out." (But Hayne outlived Lanier by five years.)
No letters from Lanier to Hayne for the next five years have been found. But seven surviving letters from Hayne show that Lanier continued to write him, though at longer intervals, and that he sent him copies of his *Florida* and *Poems* (1877).
[179] The reference is to a lost letter by Lanier of June, 1875; for he was in Charleston at the end of July, 1875, but no letter to Hayne earlier in this year has been found. (Hayne's letter of Apr. 7, 1875, acknowledged receipt of another lost letter from Lanier of Apr. 3, 1875.)
[180] *The Mountain of the Lovers. With Poems of Nature and Tradition* (New York, 1875).

To Clifford A. Lanier

Philadelphia, Pa.
Oct. 16th 1875.

My dear Little Boy, This came from Ginna yesterday, and I send it to you because she seems so touched by your friendly greeting.[181] It is a fine soul, and a long-suffering; and I know you will do all you can to give her the support and sympathy she has so long done without.

I'm quite tired out, and am only making a desperate spurt to get through with my Florida proofs – the publishers are now carrying the book through the press in a tremendous hurry – and to get ready the first India paper, when I'm going to run home for a couple of weeks rest.

These hæmorrhages of mine have been dreadfully expensive luxuries. I have great necessity for some $25.00 now. That this is my only method of helping you to pay your $4000 debt,[182] – is not a thought for a sick man to indulge in.

Address me " care of *Gibson Peacock Esq*
1425 Walnut St.
Philadelphia,
Pa."

Kiss all the dear ones for

Yr. bro.

S. L.

To Charlotte Cushman

1425 Walnut St.
Philadelphia, Pa.
Oct. 29th 1875

I dreamed about you all last night: and here, a few moments ago, comes Fulfilment dropping on a come-true dream in the

---

[181] Virginia Hankins had accepted a position in a Montgomery school and had taken her sister Mary with her (see her letters of Sept. 22 and Oct. 10, 1875).
[182] Apparently the result of a bad year in the hotel business (see Lanier's letter

shape of your perfect letter.[183] This I should have had, more than a week ago, but for some reason it lingered at the Westminster Hotel, instead of being forwarded to me here, as have been several others in the meantime.

Dear Friend, your letter goes so deeply into my heart, and I find myself so lovingly drawn to you that it is impossible for me to stay away. I am coming, to accept your good invitation. I am in the midst of a most absorbing piece of work (The India Papers), but I will bring this with me, and so I will gain some time with you. I am limited to the 10th of Nov. as the last moment at which my first paper can be in the hands of the printers; and have not as yet written a word, for lack of time, through the extensive nature of the preliminary studies.[184] These papers are not to appear over my name: so you need not mention my writing them.

—   But, I am coming, in a day or two: I can not now say exactly *what* day; don't look for me until I am there.

I suppose one has a right to feel complimented when one's poems are made *texts* for others: and so here is a little one Mr. Peacock has just brought me, by a lady I do not know personally—from the GRAPHIC of 27th *inst*.[185]

I commend you, with all devout loyalty, to God: if I but had the moiety of His power to piece out the humanity of my love, I wd. make you a sky out of my heart wh. shd. be as blue as this one that shines today, and as large, – but shd. not cover any pain, nor any separation betwixt you and your

faithful

S. L.

to his brother, Oct. 14, 1875, here omitted, and Clifford Lanier's letter of Dec. 28, 1875).

[183] Charlotte Cushman's letter of Oct. 21, 1875, invited Lanier to come to Boston and pay her a visit at his first opportunity.

[184] In a letter to his wife, Oct. 29, 1875 (here omitted), Lanier said: " I start today to writing my India article for which I have long been studying. I hope in four days to finish it."

[185] "What the Violin Said," by Elizabeth Stuart Phelps, New York 'Daily Graphic, VIII, 910 (Oct. 27, 1875). Beneath the title was printed:
"'We're all for love,' the violins said."—*Sidney Lanier.*

To Bayard Taylor [186]

1425 Walnut St.
Phila Pa
Oct. 29th 1875.

My dear Mr. Taylor:

I have just received a letter from that lovely Charlotte Cushman, which invites me with such lavish goodness to come to her that I cannot at all resist; and so I'm going there (Boston: Parker House) for a few days, before returning South. I will stop in New York a day or two on my way back – probably about a week from now – to see you. Will you be there ?   As I will remain in Boston about a week I will be glad to avail myself of your kind offer of letters to Mr. Longfellow and Mr. Lowell. These will reach me if sent to the Parker House, – where Miss Cushman is staying, and where I will stop.

On second thought, as her letter contains a message to Lord Houghton [187] (who, it seems, went to Newport to see her, but missed her) which you will much more likely be able to deliver than I, I'll enclose it herein.   Her disease renders her unable to sit at a table: hence she writes in pencil. Pray read her letter, if only to see what a fair large Soul it is.

I sent you a paper (The Graphic of 27th) which contains a very pretty compliment to me, in the shape of a poem by Elizabeth Stuart Phelps based on a quoted line from my Symphony. The same paper contains an extract from my paper on St. Augustine, which unfortunately the scissors-wielder clipped off just as the climax was reached. The Nation takes occasion to give me some pain, anent this poor St-Augustine article, by first making a statement which is grossly inaccurate, and next basing on it a criticism which would be unjust even if its foundation were not untrue, and finally dismissing the subject with a comparison of my merits and Mrs. Rebecca Harding Davis's, which is as pure a piece of gratuitous ungentlemanliness as a vulgar

---

[186] Previously published, *Atlantic Monthly*, LXXXIII, 794-795 (June, 1899); reprinted, *Letters* (New York, 1899), pp. 130-132.

[187] Richard Monckton Milnes (1809-1885), statesman and poet; he visited America for the first time in 1875.

soul could well devise.   Not that I care in the least for
the judgment, or that I shall change my " foible " — foible !
of seeing God in everything: but the point where the pain
comes in is simply that it may interfere with one's already
very short allowance of bread, by making the magazines shy
of giving employment to one who fails to please the Nation.[188]

What a diatribe I've written !   But such indignation as you
detect herein is wholly impersonal, and entirely due to that
repugnance with which one sees a really strong newspaper
turning over artists to be " criticised " by persons who do not
even understand the usages of gentlemen.   How differently
come *your* criticisms, which I always receive thankfully whether
unfavorable or otherwise !

Mr. Peacock sends messages of friendly remembrance to you.

Pray make my compliments to the ladies of your house, and
believe me always, my dear Mr. Taylor,

Your faithful friend

Sidney Lanier.

To Mary Day Lanier

Parker House, Boston, Mass.
Nov. 2nd 1875

My Too-Sweet I arrived here this morning at six, and on step-
ping from the cars plumped into the snow !

I was nigh frozen in getting to the hotel: but found that my

---

[188] The notice in the *Nation*, XXI, 277 (Oct. 28, 1875), read in part: " ' St.
Augustine in April,' by Sidney Lanier, . . . is more historical than descriptive,
and Mr. Lanier's poetical licenses in prose are accordingly fewer than usual. He
has an agreeable style when it is not surcharged with imagery.   Even here his
rhetorical-poetical foible of seeing ' God in everything ' displays itself once too
often, in the passage where he speaks of ' a morning which mingles infinite repose with infinite glittering, as if God should smile in his sleep.' . . . Mrs.
Rebecca Harding Davis is a much more restrained and artistic writer, and her
descriptions in ' Qualla ' of the natural scenery of North Carolina are excellent
in point of taste and effectiveness."

In his reply of Nov. 1, 1875 (*Letters*, New York, 1899, pp. 132-133) Taylor
wrote: " As for the *Nation*, be calm! that is nothing, and will have no effect
whatever. . . . When you consider that for eight years the *Nation* has snubbed
me and sneered at me in the most vulgar way, and ' I still live,' you will not
allow so flippant a notice to trouble you."

good Charlotte Cushman had caused my room to be prepared
for me beforehand, and everything in it was glowing with a
great coal-fire. I rolled up in the blankets, and snuggled away
into a wondrous dream till nine: then, just as I was all soap-
lather as to the face and beard, a merry tap at my door — and
on opening the same, the face of my veritable Charlotte –
whom I had expected to find all propped up with pillows –
glowing, and radiating friendly auroras.   Presently I joined
her at breakfast in her own parlor, – where I also found Miss
Stebbins – and we had a merry time until the Doctor came,
when I took my leave until twelve, at which time I must return.
We have not *commenced* our talk, yet: and poor I have to
write and write, every day, with no heart for aught but thee.

I saw Mr. Taylor a few moments in New York yesterday:
and find here this morning a note from him enclosing letters
to Longfellow, Lowell, and Aldrich.   How good every one is
to me ! Except " The Nation ", which has done its best to
wound every rising writer of the United States. It says (apropos
of my St. Augustine in Lippincotts,) " He (Mr. Lanier) has an
agreeable style when not surcharged with imagery " : – and then
goes on to dilate upon what it calls my " rhetorical – poetical
foible of ' seeing God in everything '."   Foible ! of seeing
God in everything !

— And yet the price of mules still keeps up to $350 a pair.

I will be here likely until Friday. I enclose Charlotte Cushman's letter.[189]   God keep thee, dear Love. Hast thou received my fifteen dollars, sent thee from Pha three days ago ?
Thou may'st write me at Westminster Hotel, New York, where
I will stop a day or may be two, ere starting to thee.

I cannot sleep for thinking on thee. God in His good Mercy
bring thee quickly out of all thy great sufferings and send thee
quickly the loving ministration of thy

lover .

---

[189] Forgetting to send it, Lanier inclosed it the next day in a note to his wife
(here omitted), in which he said: " My good Charlotte is all love and sweetness, and I am getting fearfully pampered with praise.—Is it not strange, I feel
so thoroughly at home with a great Artist, when the clever writers scare all the
wit out of me? " (Clara Louise Kellogg, who was present at one of Lanier's
evenings with Charlotte Cushman, records a pleasant account of it in her
Memoirs of an American Prima Donna, New York, 1913, pp. 50-51.)

To Gibson Peacock [190]

Parker House
Boston, Mass.
Nov. 4th 1875.

My dear Friend:

On arriving here at Six O'clock in the morning, half frozen and very sleepy, I found a pleasant room with a glowing fire, ready for me, and so tumbled into bed for another snooze before the world should rise. About nine, I rose again; and while I was *in puris naturalibus*, – 'midst of the very crisis and perilous climax of ablution, came a vivacious tap at my door; I opened the same, with many precautions: and behold, my eyes– which were all in lather, what time my beard was in strings that shed streams around my path, and as it were " writ my name in water " wherever I walked—rested on the bright face of my good Charlotte Cushman, shining with sweetness and welcome.

I had expected to find her all propped up in pillows; and was therefore amazed to see how elastic was her step, and how strong and bright she is in all particulars. She sleeps " beautifully " (she says) and, as we met at the breakfast-table each morning she is fairly overflowing with all manner of bright and witty and tender sayings, although in the midst of them she rubs the poor swollen arm that gives so much trouble.

Altogether, there can be no question as to her temporary benefit, nor as to the permanent gain resulting from the good digestion, the healthy appetite, the sound sleep, and the control of pain which her physician has secured for her. I believe that she is at least half-convinced that he is going to cure her: he tells her so, continually, and does not seem to entertain the shadow of a doubt about it. I have seen him twice for a few moments: and can say that he interests me very much, because his theory—which he makes no concealment of, whatever—is, as far as he has been able in our very short talks to expound it to me, at least new, bold, and radical, while I do not perceive that he gives any sign of being a mere charlatan. I heard last night, at the Wednesday Night Club, (where Mr. Coolidge was kind

[190] Previously published, *Atlantic Monthly*, LXXIV, 23-24 (July, 1894); reprinted, *Letters* (New York, 1899), pp. 20-22.

enough to invite me) all sorts of stories about him, many of which I do not doubt to be true. So that on the whole, I am still waiting for a little further drawing-out which I intend to bring to bear on him, before I allow myself to make a final judgment about him.

Meantime there can be no question of Miss Cushman's genuine improvement: and her intercourse with the young physician seems to have been satisfactory to her.[191]

I have not yet written a line of my India papers: and am going at it this morning, tooth and nail. Will you take the trouble to ask the Librarian of the Pha Library, if I may keep the two books [192] I have, for a couple of days longer? If he refuses, I will ask you to telegraph me, so that I may get them back in time.

Mr. Taylor, whom I saw for a few moments in New York, asked after you both very particularly: Miss Cushman is now secluded with the physician, else I am sure she would send messages to you.

As for me, dear friend, my thoughts go to you as thickly as these snow flakes which are now falling outside my window, – and alas, as silently, for lack of expression. But I feel sure that you know I am always

Your friend

S. L.

To Henry W. Longfellow

Boston, Mass.

Nov. 5th 1875

Dear Sir:

　　　　I would be glad to know at what hour I might call, without infringing upon matters having better claim to your time, in order to present a letter of introduction from my friend Bayard Taylor.

---

[191] G. H. Calvert had written Lanier, Oct. 23, 1875: "You will be glad to hear that Miss Cushman is better, is in good spirits and full of hope. She is in the hands of an *ir*regular physician in Boston, who has the reputation of having cured Cases of her disease. He is a young Englishman, Dr. Thornton, 29 years of age, with a practice worth $60,000 a year."

[192] Probably two of the authorities Lanier was using in the preparation of "Sketches of India," listed in the notes to the present edition (VI, 254 ff.).

I am further driven to make this somewhat unusual request by the circumstance that I am here only for four days (guest of Miss Cushman, at the Parker House), and that I might miss you – which I would greatly regret.

Very respectfully

Sidney Lanier.[193]

To Thomas B. Aldrich

Boston, Mass.
Nov. 5th 1875.

Dear Sir:

I called at Messrs. Osgoods' yesterday, in order to present to you a letter from my friend Bayard Taylor; but failed to find you or to get any notion of your probable movements in this direction.

A sincere desire to meet you makes me write to beg you will let me know if you should come to town at any time between now and Tuesday, until when I am at the Parker House.

Very respectfully

Sidney Lanier.[194]

[193] Longfellow replied, Nov. 6, 1875: "I shall be at home tomorrow (Sunday) at four in the afternoon, and in the evening at eight; and shall be very happy to see you at either hour." On Nov. 12, he wrote to Taylor: "I was much pleased with Mr. Lanier."

[194] Aldrich replied, Nov. 8, 1875, from Ponkapog, Mass.: "I very much regret that I cannot have the pleasure of receiving Bayard Taylor's note from your own hands. I shall not be able to go to Boston until the latter part of this week– when it will be too late. However, I shall visit New York sometime this winter, and perhaps Mr. Taylor will be good enough– he is good enough for anything– to bring us together." There is no record that a meeting between them ever took place.

Lanier also sent a note to Lowell (not found) and received this reply, dated Nov. 6, 1875: "I shall be at home during the afternoon of Monday when it will give me great pleasure to see you if it will suit your convenience." Years later Lowell wrote to D. C. Gilman (Jan. 27, 1888): "I had the pleasure of seeing [Lanier] but once, when he called on me . . . at Elmwood, but the image of his shining presence is among the friendliest in my memory." (Printed in *The Forty-Sixth Birthday of Sidney Lanier*, ed. Gilman, Baltimore, 1888.)

Charlotte Cushman's letter of Dec. 12, 1875, indicates that Lanier just missed meeting J. T. Fields, the publisher, while in Boston. She added: "Fields came to see me yesterday– Why did you not go to see him in Baltimore? He is a very useful man! . . . You made a very agreeable impression here & are remembered."

To Gibson Peacock [195]

Boston, Nov. 10th 1875

My dear friend:

I scrawl a hasty note, just as I am leaving, to beg that you will hand the two books which I have today sent you *by Express* to the Librarian, with my thanks for his kind permission to keep them over the time. They were very useful to me.

Our friend Miss Cushman is suffering a good deal of pain every day, but appears to keep up her general health steadily. I've had several talks with her doctor:—and I would not be surprised if he really cured her. I find him not at all a quack, at least not an ignorant one: he is quite up to the most advanced ideas in his profession.

But I have not time now to say more. I go directly to Macon, except one day in New York: and will be at home for two weeks, then to Baltimore for the winter, to resume my old place as first flute in the Orchestra.

God bless you both,—says

Your friend

S. L.

To Bayard Taylor [196]

Macon, Ga.
November 24, 1875.

My dear Mr. Taylor:

Poets understand everything: I doubt not you well know a certain sort of happiness which at the same time locks up expression and enlarges fancy, and you will therefore easily comprehend how it is that thirty days have passed

---

[195] Previously published, *Atlantic Monthly*, LXXIV, 24 (July, 1894); reprinted, *Letters* (New York, 1899), p. 22.

[196] Previously published, *Atlantic Monthly*, LXXXIII, 795-796 (June, 1899); reprinted, *Letters* (New York, 1899), pp. 133-135 (reproduced here from the latter source, MS not being found).

On Nov. 13 Lanier met his wife in Macon, and on Nov. 15 they rejoined their children at Forsyth. By Nov. 16 it had been decided that Lanier would

without any message from me to you, although there has been no one of them during which you were not constantly in my mind. This happiness of which I speak – which freezes one's pen and tongue while it melts one's heart – means in the present instance that I have been at home for ten days past, joyfully reunited with the other – and far sweeter – Moiety of me. My three young men – one of seven, one of five and one of two years – keep me in an endless labyrinth of surprises and delights: nothing could be more keen, more fresh, more breezy, than the meeting together of their little immense loves with the juicy selfishness and honest animalisms of the dear young cubs. What a prodigious Candor they practise! They're as little ashamed of being beasts as they are proud of being gods: they accept themselves at the hands of their Creator with perfect unreserve: pug nose or Greek, blue eyes or gray, beasthood or godhood – it's all one to them. What's the good of metaphysical moping as long as Papa's at home and you've got a Mama to kiss and a new ball from now till dinner and *then* apples!

This is their philosophy: it is really a perfect scheme of life, and contains all the essential terms of religion, while – as for philosophy – it is perfectly clear upon points which have remained obscure from Plato down to George Lewes.[197]

How I wish my lovely two-year-old boy – my royal Hal – could look you in the eyes for once, and put his arms deliberately round your neck and give you one of his fervent kisses! Fancy that your big Lars was also a baby, and also a poet; and you'll have a whiff of it.

take his oldest son Charles to Baltimore for the winter; that Lulu, Harry Day's daughter, would be returned to her father in Brunswick; and that Mary Day Lanier and her two younger sons, Sidney, Jr., and Harry, would accept Clifford Lanier's invitation to spend the winter in Montgomery. (See Mary Day Lanier's letter to Clifford Lanier, Nov. 16, 1875, which also reported: " [Sidney] has been through so much heat of strife, so many nights of sleepless labor, so many varying scenes and exciting emotions that there has come upon him for a month or two some irregular action of the heart: a disorder so annoying in its action as to keep sleep from him when everything else invites to it. Miss Cushman's famous young physician in Boston (who begged to examine and prescribe for him,) says it is a thickening of the valves of the heart and attributes his hæmorrhages to that cause: without, however, denying that there is lung disease.")

[197] Lanier had apparently been reading recently George Henry's Lewes's *Problems of Life and Mind*, which he refers to in *Florida* (VI, 52).

Your letters came to me while I was with Miss Cushman, and were the means of procuring for me two delightful afternoons with Mr. Lowell and Mr. Longfellow. I was sorry to miss Mr. Aldrich. I wrote him a little note, to find out when he would be in town. He replied that he could not come until after I had left Boston, but added that he would be in New York during the winter, "when perhaps Mr. Taylor would be good enough – he is good enough for anything – to bring us together."

I'm sure you'll care to know that I had a charming visit to Miss Cushman, and that each day was crowded with pleasant things which she and her numerous friends had prepared for me.

I leave Macon for Baltimore on Friday next. My address there will be 64 Centre St., and I will hope to hear from you very soon after my arrival. I resume my old place as first flute of the Peabody Orchestra, which lasts until March; though hoping all the time still to find some opportunity for getting my longed-for chair of The Physics and Metaphysics of Music established in some college or other.

My pretty Comrade here begs that she may be allowed to join me in grateful and affectionate messages to you, – for she knows in detail all your thoughtful kindliness in my behalf. Pray let me not quite drop out of the recollection of Mrs. Taylor and of your daughter.

> Your friend,
>
> Sidney Lanier.

To Mary Day Lanier

> 64 Centre St.
> Baltimore, Md
> Nov. 29th 1875

So, dear Sweetheart, we are safely arrived – at ten last night – and are now fairly settled at my old quarters in Centre St., though not in my old room, which I found occupied by others. Charles has been a very good little man on the journey, and has uttered a great many *whoo – ee's* today over the manifold new sights and sounds of the large busy city.   He begs me in a very sleepy tone to tell you that he saw the mountains, and was greatly pleased with them.   We also had quite a steamboat ride on the Potomac, at the point where the B. & O. barges receive the cars and are towed across the river near Washington.   This operation – of sending a couple of passenger-cars bodily on a boat – astonished the small man very greatly.

After we parted with thee in the dépôt at Macon, he crawled into the berth, and wept there a long time, finally falling asleep with the tears in his eyes.

The ladies here have already begun to pet and coddle him, and I foresee great bespoilment for the youngster.   We are close to Jack Wrenshall, and are going to hunt him up tomorrow.

Our rehearsals are now at five P. M : lasting till seven.   This is a good hour.   If I could but even hint to thee my delight in the first one, which I have but left an hour ago !   We played the " Jewish Trilogy ", by Hamerik ; the Poet's Curse, by Von Bülow; and the overture to Oberon, by Von Weber.   I found myself in great tune, and got along admirably.

Wysham has called; and I found Col. R. M. Johnston'[s] card at noon, whom I was sorry to miss.   I've met Wm Hand Browne in the street, and Norah Fulton,[198] and hosts of other friends.

And now, dear Moll, mine eyes are quite given out.

—— But I must tell thee that in opening my hat-box, I find Oodie's [199] bonnet – or hat – therein esconced.   I will send it thee, some way, soon.

In thinking of thee, I become sure that thou art the most forgiving angel that God has yet made.   That I should have gone home and fretted and put on airs around thee,[200] thou dear beautiful suffering One !   How lovely thou wert, as thou

---

[198] The daughter of Lanier's Macon friend, Harriett Freeman Fulton.

[199] Lulu (Mary Louise Day).

[200] In her reply of Dec. 3, 1875, Mary Day Lanier remarked: " And much am I entertained by thy repentance for having ' put on airs,' ' around me,'– when, in the next moment I open and read a tender letter from Lily, part of which runs thus: ' Sid has been keeping such high company of late that I am sure he will not condescend to speak any more to plain, matter-of-fact country people. Indeed, I was told that when he was last here " he was putting on a great many airs! " I wonder if they would scare me?' So, thou seest, I am not the only aggrieved party. Thou hast been finding some one else ' provincial ' – Mr. A. la Mode! Pity for them that they cannot have my compensations."

wast walking along with our departing train; I was ready to leap off, and stay by thee, all the world to the contrary notwithstanding.

That God will soon send me this heavenly thing:– to stay by thee:– is the fervent prayer of thy

lover.

To Mary Day Lanier

66 Centre St.
Baltimore, Md.
Dec. 2nd 1875

My darling Sweet Angel, I have been waiting each day to get an expected remittance from Philadelphia for my India paper (which they write me is in type), so as to send the same away to thee. It should have come today, and as I see there is a new postman, I am afraid it has been delayed by him.

We found our room at 64 not altogether desirable; and so, discovering that we could get much roomier apartments at the next door, we moved yesterday. We still eat at the Youngs'. We have a very pleasant little sleeping-room and parlor, on the first floor; and there is a back piazza communicating with the Youngs'. Nothing could have been more opportune than our finding the rooms.

The little man dances down town with me every day: and while I am at rehearsal the Youngs take charge of him. He is quite a belle: and has spent a day with Jack Wrenschall. He bids me tell thee, while I am writing, that he likes Jack very much, and that they slided on the ice in the street. He also sends thee a kiss and his love. He scarcely ever sees anything beautiful without wishing that Mama was here.

Lippincott has just sent me two copies of the Florida book. It is very handsomely printed, bound and illustrated:– but I hate it with intense hatred, and I have no pleasure in it.

I hope to send thee money tomorrow, and therewith a hat and other things.

My delight in the Orchestra is *too* fair and ravishing sweet. I have wonderfully improved in tone: wh. is strange since I have had no practice.

— I long for thee as if I had never seen thee, as if thou
hadst been always a dream, and I alway only a famishing

lover .

To Mary Day Lanier

66 Centre St.,
B⁰ Dec. 4ᵗʰ 1875

Dear Love, dear Love, I have been fairly choking with impatience for two days at the non-arrival of my money, – for which
there is no reason in the world save the forgetfulness of Mʳ
Kirk, – or some other equally trivial matter. I think of thee
hour after hour needing everything, – and it is hard to hold my
heart. Pray forgive me, and try to do what thou canst in the
way of looking with some patience upon the ineffectualness of
thy poor lover, – who is indeed just now sore beset in many
quarters and in unexpected ways.

— Our little man fares well, and will make a man I think.
Thy sweetnesses, – thine own peculiar ones – continually pop
out on me from him, in the most delighful way: and I find
everyday some new evidence of all that thou hast taught him.
I think he has a great turn for figures. Last night we had a
long conversation on the subject of gravitation : and then I
read him some passages from Shakespeare – *Henry V* and *Tem-
pest* – with which he seeemed immensely taken. We are both
agreed that if we had the two rooms above these, thou and
Harry and Sidney could live charmingly herein with us. My
God, if I could sit here quietly with thee, for the rest of this
dark afternoon ! This is one of my Limbo days. I seem to
have weights on my soul though I have done nothing wrong,
everything hangs, life is limp, I wish to see thy two faithful
eyes which are like religions to me and contain my whole creed
within their two lovely ovals.

To day there is no rehearsal, our first concert coming off
tonight.[201] Next week we play at Von Bülow's concerts.

[201] The season consisted of a series of eight Peabody Concerts on alternate
Saturday nights from Dec. 4, 1875, to Mar. 18, 1876, with a recess at Christmas.
A circular containing the programs survives in the Charles D. Lanier Collection,
Johns Hopkins University. Hans von Bülow, referred to in the following
sentence, gave two concerts, Dec. 6 and Dec. 10, 1875, at the Academy of Music,
assisted by the Peabody Orchestra (program in the Charles D. Lanier Collection,
Johns Hopkins University).

I have not yet seen Josephine Seaton. She has just arrived –
yesterday – from Atlantic City.
Charley and I called on Mrs. Bird yesterday, and had a very
cordial reception. We are to dine there tomorrow.

Now God take thee in His loving Arms, thou well-beloved
Soul that art the sweetest He hath made in all the ages of
time, – prays thy

humble faithful

lover.

To Mary Day Lanier

66 Centre St.

B⁰ Dec. 5th 1875

My Sweet Angel, My Heart of all Good, this is Sunday, the
rain is pouring, Charley and I have been to dine with Mrs. Bird,
and have gotten us back into our rooms, the small man has
whittled a while with my knife and has then fallen asleep on
our bed – a great wide old-fashioned bed that makes my heart
leap with thinking of the Great Bed of Ware at Mrs. Earle's –
and so here sit I, to send thee a little prayer and loving worship. I think the world has never seemed so lonesome as since
I have left thee this time, my longing for thy sweet company is
unspeakable, my heart refuses to be comforted with friend or
child or music or work, thee I need, thee I desire, thee only.

Today is Sunday, we have had no letters. If my funds come
not tomorrow, I will raise some another way, and send thee,
for I am in agony with fear that thou hast had inconveniences
on this head.

Our little man is very sweet. I have quite loved him into
perfect accord with me, and I think he is already very fond of
me. He is thoroughly confidential : and a simpler and chaster
soul never was in flesh, I am sure. This gives me infinite
delight. I am surprised at the number of things thou hast
taught him, and thy groundwork has been so thorough – a most
sweet thorough Heart I know thee to be, indeed – that I have
little trouble in carrying him along. He goes through thy
precise forms of prayers each night at my knee,– only thy name
is put for mine in the last petition, – a proceeding which quite

breaks my heart anew each evening with fresh longing for thy welfare and for the blessing of God upon thy beloved head. – Then I tuck him away, and kiss him; and he falls asleep in three breaths. I have no difficulty in amusing him, or rather in getting him to amuse himself: he has a small box of tools, and he works busily for hours, constructing impossible tables with very wild legs and always split in the tops, – and the like. When he tires of this he paints, or plays with Dixie, – the shaggy poodle of our neighbors, – or converses with me, or walks with me. I find him, in short, a rare companionable little soul, and have great joy in him altogether.

I long to hear what thy Buncombe says of thee, and that thou art safely invested with thy help.

Thy letter [202] is come, and gave our man a great deal of pleasure. Enclosures also.

And now, dear Silver Star, may God be about thee as it were a soft encompassing Halo of love and glory, and mayst thou shine thus environed through this night, – prays thy true

lover.

To Mary Day Lanier

66 Centre St.
Bo. Dec. 8th 1875

This day have I sent thee by express, dear Moll, two hats,– being a lavender and a black – which, albeit I say it who should not say it since they have been evolved as to their furbelowing out of my own consciousness, are nevertheless as fair and perfect a pair of shelters as ever have been superimposed upon the female head.

I worked two days ere I cd. find me a milliner that would understand what I wanted: – not that the hats are not in style, but that the wretched misguided souls wanted to smear them all over with flowers and wings and velvet monstrosities; till finally I found one quiet and gentle lady who caught my conception instantly, – and *voila*, two angels of hats. When thou shalt put one on thy head, dream thou it is a Cornucopia out of which descend upon thy sweet brows a thousand blessings and kisses from thy true

lover.

[202] A letter from Mary Day Lanier to her son Charles, Nov. 28, 1875.

P. S.

I have not yet found any dress to suit : but I will send thee
some stuff to Montg'y, and then Wilsie will tell thee of some
good sewing-woman, and thou shalt have it made as I will
write thee.   Meantime thou shalt wear thy black: or thy yellow
and black calico.

I think thou art simply Obedience done into sweet flesh,— to
stand all this from me.

Tell Clifford I have written to the Hotel man,[203] but without
reply yet: and kiss Ginna for me.

To Mary Day Lanier

> 66 Centre St.
> Baltimore, Md.
> Dec. 15th 1875.

My dear Soul, I have been toiling night and day over my second
India paper – for which I found the Magazine was waiting –
and after an infinity of labor got it off this morning.   Although
it has been written under many distractions and depressing
influences, I like it more than the first paper, – which is probably out by this time, though I have not yet seen it.

Thy note is come, telling me that the hats had come.   I hope
they fit thy sweet round head.   How I envy them.

Our little man does well.   Every night as I kiss him after I
have tucked him in, he cries " Now if Mama were only here, to
kiss me good-night ! "   He is at this moment out in the snow
in front of the house, dressed in his long ulster overcoat and a
pair of India-rubber boots, and looking like Napoleon in Russia.

Now must I tell thee farewell till tomorrow.   Thou didst
[not] say whether thy funds suffice for thy needs.   I long to
hear that thou art safely in M[ontgomer]y.   Kiss Cliff and
Ginna for thy longing

                                        lover.

[203] Clifford Lanier was still trying to find a hotel in the North to manage.

To Gibson Peacock [204]

66 Centre St.
Baltimore, Md.
Dec. 16th 1875.

My dear Mr. Peacock:

Yours enclosing three dollars came to me safely and I should have immediately acknowledged it had I not been over head (literally) and ears in a second instalment of my India papers for which the magazine was agonizedly waiting.

Possibly you may have seen the January number by this time: and it just occurs to me that if you should read the India article,[205] you will be wondering at my talking coolly of strolling about Bombay with a Hindu friend. But Bhima Gandharva (Bhima was the name of the ancient Sanskrit hero *The Son of the Air*, and *Gandharva* means *a heavenly musician*) is only another name for Imagination — which is certainly the only Hindu friend I have—; and the propriety of the term, as well as the true character of Bhima Gandharva and the insubstantial nature of all adventures recorded as happenning to him and myself, is to be fully explained in the end of the last article. I hit upon this expedient, after much tribulation and meditation, in order at once to be able to make something like a narrative that should avoid an arid encyclopedic treatment, and to be perfectly truthful. The only plan was to make it a pure *jeu d'esprit*; and in writing the second paper I have found it of great advantage–

I haven't heard a word of the Florida book beyond what you sent me;–God have mercy upon its soul,–I suppose it will be (as the Judge says when the black cap is on) hanged by the neck until it is dead, dead, dead.

I have with me my Charley, *aetat*. seven, the sweetest, openest, honestest little man was ever built. I find him splendid company: and I wish you might see him at this moment, with

---

[204] Previously published, *Atlantic Monthly*, LXXIV, 24-25 (July, 1894); reprinted, *Letters* (New York, 1899), pp. 22-24.

[205] The first installment of "Sketches of India" (VI, 254).

his long lashes fringing the full oval eyes, profoundly slumbering in bed where I have but ten minutes ago tucked him in
and kissed him good-night.

I have a charming letter from C[harlotte] C[ushman]; but
through all the fair things she says to me I can detect the note
of physical pain, and the poor sweet soul is evidently suffering
greatly.

It does not now look like I shall be able to see you as I had
hoped at Xmas.

I wish I had some method of telling you with what deep
satisfaction I reflect upon you both, and with what delight I
would find myself able to be to you, in one fair act as well as in
all fair words.

Your faithful friend,

S. L.

To Henry W. Longfellow [206]

66 Centre St.
Baltimore, Md.
Dec. 17th 1875.

My dear Sir:

I send you today by express three magazines containing the poems [207] you were kind enough to speak of during
my recent visit to Boston.   I have the less hesitation in sub-
mitting them to you since I know that upon your own theory
of criticism – as you expounded it to me – you will give yourself no trouble to say anything about them in the event you
shall find them having no effect upon you as poems.

Very truly yours

Sidney Lanier

---

[206] Previously published, Starke, p. 221. No reply has been found.

[207] Probably " Corn," " The Symphony," and " In Absence." (" Laus Mariæ "
had also been published by this time, in *Scribner's* for November.)

To Mary Day Lanier

66 Centre St. [Baltimore]
Dec. 19th 1875

My darling: I have just tucked the small man in his bed, and read him some chapters in his little " Picture Bible " (for which he calls nightly). The evening has so far been entirely devoted to him: I have read several stories from the Xmas number of St. Nicholas (which I will send thee for Sidney when we have finished it) and he has been greatly pleased with Bayard Taylor's story of " Jan of Iceland ": – then we have had a monstrous romp in the course whereof I have discovered that the little rascal is well-nigh as strong as I am: – and so now I come to send thee a worshipful kiss ere I take my place at thy child's side. This is the dearest boy, thou hast brought me, in the world: he quite flowers out under the new stimulus of unfamiliar scenes, and all the ladies are fond of his open and simple nature. My little experience with him quite convinces me that no word of harshness, of impatience, of peevishness ought ever to be said to a child, that incalculable harm is done by every the least querulous syllable, that no desirable effect comes from any reproof administered hastily, that the only method is to save the teaching – when wrong is discovered – until such moment as one finds oneself entirely large and grave and free from even disappointment and conscious of the immense number of mistakes one has oneself made even in maturer years and thus able to *teach* in the purely loving way. Unlimited exhibition of tenderness, unlimited reliance upon rightly-made appeals to the young sense of right, unceasing interest in the small sports and toys, – that is the sesame which opens these little hearts so that they cannot quite close against us.

I have so longed for a little quiet talk with thee today: thou art so dear, my heart leans on thee so freely, thou hast such marvellous understanding, thou lovest a man as genius loves its art and thou lovest art as woman loves man, and there is no change in thy faithfulness, and thou art like a rose-bush all green and red whereunder my head hath lain and wherethrough I have seen the blue heaven.

In many hours of solemn meditation the Angel of Foresight
appears to tell me that thou and I will sometimes come to have
a sore heart as regards our beloved arts of music and poetry,
unless we start wisely prepared to find the general world very
crude of ear and very unskillful in discriminating the heavenly
Song from the earthly imitation. When I think for example
how little the mass of the audience to whom we played last
night were able to draw from the divine concords of the flutes
and the reeds and the violins which were to me – and would
have been to thee – simple Heaven; when I think how divided
are the opinions even of people of culture upon contemporary
poets – Rosetti in England (for example) swearing that Whitman is the greatest American Singer and Lowell declaring that
Arthur Clough was the finest poetic exponent of modern life –
and how intolerant the great ruling power of modern literary
thought – Cleverness—is of all that rough-shod riding with
which Genius tramples along over the little laws of dilet-
tantism; when I perceive how the literary Clubs become
" rings ", and how the people read Dr. Holland's poetry rather
than Mr. Taylor's and abandon Thomas' Orchestra for Gilmore's and forget what a large criticism might be while they
applaud the dyspeptic accuracies and clever mistakes of the
" Nation "; – then I become aware that thou and I have a long
and mayhap sometimes dismal battle for art in our front.

I scarcely believe I could undertake it without thee. Although
every poet desires fame by his nature, yet if he is great, he can
do without it; but unfortunately this usually involves the heart-
break; so that when I remember that I have thee, whose praise
is sweeter than fame to me, I feel as one who starts across the
desert with a mighty Angel bearing water by his side. My
God, – who knows the Thirst of the Artist ! It comes often
suddenly; the hand, the head, the heart, all burn; it is the flaming out of his love toward his kind, – for the artist is essentially
the Forlorn Hope that marches ahead of mankind and the
wounds which he receives from his own as well as from the
enemy, from behind as well as in front, cannot be bandaged till
one side or other is victorious.

—But thou, thou lovely Double, thou art at once my sweet
Surgeon that tends all hurts and my Sweeter I that art hurt along
with me being the artist that is within me: thou art at once

the Angel that carries water, and the Strength of him that needs it; thou art at once Glory and that which wins glory.
———— I enclose a letter, from a lady of whom I have not heard before, which seems earnest, and to which I have replied in such a preachy way that if she *is* earnest she will be pleased and if not she will discover that there is absolutely no flirtation left in me.[208]

I send also a programme of the concert last night. Thou wilt care to know that my rendition of the famous flute-solo in the William Tell Overture won much favor, insomuch that Papa Metz (as he is called, the old long-hackneyed First Violin) came and said afterward he had never heard it done so well; – which considering that the Germans love neither the silver flute nor American players, was a triumph indeed.

Tell me that thou hast met Ginna, and how thou art circumstanced; and God bless thee, dear Moll, that art God's blessing to thy

lover .

To Clifford A. Lanier

66 Centre St. [Baltimore]
Dec. 21st 1875

My darling Buddy, It has seemed as if the time would never come when I cd. quietly sit down and write you: and indeed it has not yet come, but I won't postpone sending you anyhow a little kiss for Xmas. In truth my Comrade who, as I learn by her letter recd this morning, is now with you, will tell you all that is to be told about me. I have been quite hard run with the India papers, finding them involving a very great amount of labor.

I can not tell why I do not hear from Edwards the hotel man, to whom I wrote soon after arriving here. Perhaps I will write to Mr. Peacock in Pha to stir him up. Let me know what further thought you have had about the matter we spoke of, and how your mind now stands.

My Florida book is out, and I hope you'll like it. I've just

---

[208] No letter has been found which fits this description.

seen my first India paper, in a copy of the January Lippincott's wh. the pubs. have sent me. I see they have also put in a little poem of mine called " Special Pleading " [209] by which I set considerable store and which you are newly commanded to like immensely.

I hope to let you know in a few days about " In de Grass " [210] which is as good a poem as has been writ in many a day.

In a week from now I will be in receipt of some $75. for my second India paper which has gone forward. I fear May has nothing left from the instalment of the first wh. I sent her; so please hand her twenty dollars as soon as you get this, and I will reimburse you in a short time. She will need funds for Xmas.

God bless you and all my dear ones. How I wish I cd have a kiss from my little Sissa, this lonesome night; pray be my proxy and give her a brother's most loving salutation in my behalf.

And now, my dear sweet Clifford, may the blessing of God come out of Heaven even as fragrance comes out of a rose, and be about you and possess your spirit, –

prays

Your bro.

S. L.

To Mary Day Lanier

[Baltimore,] Dec. 22nd 1875

O Heart that enclosest my Heaven as a calyx encloses its rose, if I could compress the whole Desire of the whole Love of Man into each word I still could not tell thee the mournful — because unavailing — longing for thee wherewith I drag through my days. Companioned by this sad and beautiful ghost which is yet my only reality, I move among people and things which are so far off from me that they are as if they were not, and the world is but a desolate desert of love.

---

[209] Composed the previous February (see I, 45).

[210] " Uncle Jim's Baptist Revival Hymn " (I, 217), by Sidney and Clifford Lanier.

I seem to have been calling for thee ever since eternity was, and I cannot hear anything about time but my own cries for my dear mate.

The days sparkle upon the nights as snow upon the trunks of the trees: I flit about through these wintry woods of life, and find thee not, and the boughs are cased in ice, and everything is too cold to rest on.

—— I think thy love must have quite won access to me with some sweet persuasions past the grim miles that stand guard betwixt us, on last Sunday. I did not once dream — thrice-sodden dolt that I am — that it was the anniversary of the dear day when thou and I got leave from the world to be one; yet I felt somewhat moving about my heart all day unwontedly, and finally sat me down and made my worship to thee in a long letter which thou wilt have read ere now, I hope. I too had my grape from the good friend that lives in Eshcol and my violets from her that dwells in Sunnyside [211] — and these were very fair tokens and loving.

I think thou wouldst rejoice in thy young man couldst thou see him. He is as bright as any lark, and full of affection and simple goodness. I could have smothered him with kisses last night for his behavior to Mr. Taylor.[212] I went with the latter to his lecture at the Peabody Institute (on Schiller), and after the lecture he came and sate with me in my cosy study until late in the night. Soon after he came Charley came over from the other house. I introduced him, Mr. Taylor took him in his arms and kissed him, and they fell a-talking about painting, during which conversation Mr. T. drew him a very awe-inspiring Guyascutas. Charley then slipped down, brought the " St. Nicholas " and opened it at Mr. T.'s story of Jan of Iceland. Mr. T. then asked him if he knew who wrote the story; he looked at the name a moment, then into Mr. T.'s eyes with a lovely smile and spoke out very bravely " Bayard Taylor." He

[211] Mary Day Lanier had written, Dec. 17, 1875: " Perchance, sweet Heart of mine, this will reach thee upon our wedding-day! Happy letter! Unhappy—scribe! Already there cometh to me a little cluster of violets from ' Sunnyside ' [Mrs. Wallen] with ' Dec. 19th ' attached; and from ' Eshcol ' [Mamie Boifeuillet] this ' Grape.' "

[212] Bayard Taylor had written Lanier on Dec. 13, 1875 (*Letters*, New York, 1899, p. 135), that he would be in Baltimore to lecture before the Peabody Institute on Dec. 21 and 23.

then asked me if he might paint a picture in a little book one of the ladies has given him to paint: and proceeded to do so, holding very confidential conferences with Mr. T. on the questions of the mixtures of colors to produce certain effects, and the like. He was, in fine, simply charming, and the complete absence of shyness, with the perfect frankness and confident opening of heart which he exhibited gave me great delight. I have read him thy letter, enclosed in mine, and he is committing all the verses. I saw Mrs. Jones to-day about the kindergarten. It resumes operations next Tuesday week: and if I can possibly get together the cash which has to be paid down (some thirty dollars, to begin with, and thirty more in Feb'y: wh. pays for the year) I will certainly send him.

I have not yet received the money for my second instalment of India, and desiring that thou shouldst be provided in time to enable thee to make some little provision for such Xmas gifts as thou wishest to distribute, I to-day telegraphed Clifford to hand thee twenty dollars, which I will send by mail as soon as my funds come.

I like not that Ginna will not allow thee to love her: [213] but I half-fancy that I can understand it, and will tell thee sometime. I like still more *not* that thou hast no time to play the piano: why is this? – But never mind: if thou canst laugh thyself into a few more dear pounds of most sweet flesh, I care not,— or at any rate, I can wait.

I have had the pleasure of seeing my good Mr. Taylor a great deal yesterday and today; and have just now returned from dining with him at the Carrollton.

— No, I am not ill. The heart-trouble is much less than formerly. I have not had quite enough sleep for a week or two: but beyond this there is no special cause for complaint physically. I know not why it is exactly that my heart feels sore and unusually lonesome, — unless it is simply my daily increas-

---

[213] Mary Day Lanier had written, Dec. 19, 1875: "There have indeed been some special blessings on our anniversary. For one, I had thy letter of 15th this morning. . . . Next, I went to church with Ginna. . . . I think, however, that she does not intend to let me love her. I shall not give up my own intentions for all that, and perhaps her manner is more proud than her heart. It is quite the same with Willie, and likely if we cared for her less we would not notice any barrier at-all.

"Her eyes and her voice match her letters."

ing need of thy presence which gives me no rest: thou art so
sweet and fine a spirit, I am so much at home with thee, there
is naught but the bitter sense of exile when I am away from
thee.

And now, thou dear Home-land, God tend thy sun and
sky,— prays thy true

lover.

To Mary Day Lanier

[Baltimore,] Dec. 26th 1875.

Yesterday thou hadst the lonesomest lover that ever loved or
was ever lonesome. I did nothing all day but sit about my room
and cry out in my heart for thee.

Thy young man was a very happy one indeed: but he too
longed constantly and articulately for thee: and once we both
broke out into desires after thee and he came and put his arms
around my neck and we embraced in silent token of the empti-
ness of our arms.

—— The boy had a great table-full of Xmas presents, which
I collected on the night before Xmas, and arranged in gorgeous
dispositions upon the marble slab under our mirror, near which
he sleeps. There were a couple of very pretty games, a lovely
large paint-box, a white palette with thumb-hole and colors
already arranged thereon, a case of many-colored lead pencils,
and a mass of miscellaneous items sent in by the fellow-
boarders. In addition to these, the lady who lives above us
had petitioned for a stocking, wh. she had hung up in her own
room, and to which he repaired early in the morning, finding
there a lot of oranges, apples, and other things. From Saida
(Bird) Smith came a large lace stocking filled with bon-bons;
and Jack Wrenschall sent a ball.

Thy lover had two presents: a pretty blue-and-gold edition
of Praed's poems, from Josephine Seaton: and a fur cap and
collar from Mrs. Bird, whose note I enclose.

I dined with the latter, quite en famille, at six last evening:
and after dinner we went over to Minnie Machen's, where Clare

is staying.[214] Thou wilt be glad to know that I made energetic love to Clare, – in whom a certain unwonted appearance
of gentleness and of very-tired-ness, was pathetically lovely –
and that she returned my demonstrations of affection in a
simple, confident, heartsome manner as if the fellow-sense of
common exile drew us together. We were like two long lines,
which parallel at the observer's place, come together in the
distance. She has conceived a monstrously fine estimate of my
poetic faculty.

I pray thee give a sweet Xmas kiss for me to all those who
are in kissing-reach of thee, especially to my dear little Sissa,
after a sight of whom I do constantly long.

O Heart of my Soul, when thou art far away there remains
but an un-nourished and unbeating shell of a soul to thy

lover .

To Bayard Taylor [215]

66 Centre St.
Baltimore, Md.
Dec. 29th 1875

My dear Mr. Taylor:

If it were a cantata upon your goodness,
– – – I'm willing to wager I could write a stirring one and a
grateful withal.

Of course I will accept, – when 'tis offered.[216] I only write a

---

[214] Clare de Graffenried, who had long been a friend of the Laniers, and a
bride's-maid at their wedding, was teaching mathematics in Miss Lipscomb's
school in Georgetown, D. C. She was spending her Christmas holidays with
Mrs. Arthur Machen in Baltimore.

[215] Previously published, Marie Hansen-Taylor and H. E. Scudder, eds., *Life
and Letters of Bayard Taylor* (Boston, 1884), II, 677; reprinted, *Letters* (New
York, 1899), p. 137.

[216] Taylor had written Lanier, Dec. 28, 1875 (*Letters*, New York, 1899, pp.
136-137), that Gen. J. R. Hawley, President of the U. S. Centennial Commission, had asked him to name a poet *not* of New England to write a cantata for
the grand opening ceremonies of the exhibition at Philadelphia, and that he
had named Lanier:

"I write in all haste to say– you *must* accept, if it is offered. The Cantata
should not be more than from 40 to 50 lines long, of unity of conception, yet
capable of being divided easily into three parts– an opening chorus, a bass solo,
and a finale, either general or alternating chorus. The measure ought to be

hasty line now to say how deeply I am touched by the friendly forethought of your letter.

Charley joins me in love to you: and I add a hearty wish that the New Year may be to you a friend no less loving than will always be

S. L.

To Charlotte Cushman [217]

66 Centre St.
Baltimore, Md.
Dec. 30th 1875.

If this New Year that approaches you (more happy than I, who cannot) did but know you as well as I (more happy than he, who does not) he would strew his days about you even as white apple-blossoms and his nights as blue-black heartsease; for then he should be your true faithful-serving lover – as am I – and should desire – as I do – that the general pelting of Time might become to you only a tender rain of such flowers as foretell fruit and of such as make tranquil beds.

But though I cannot teach this same New Year to be the servant of my fair wishes, I can persuade him to be the bearer of them, and I trust he and these words will come to you together; giving you such report, and so freshly from my heart, as shall confirm to you that my message, though greatly briefer than my love, is yet greatly longer than I would the interval were, which stands betwixt you and your often-longing

S. L.

irregular, yet sufficiently rhythmical. My additional suggestion is– and I think you'll pardon it– to make the lines simple and strong, keep down the play of fancy (except where it may give room for a fine musical phrase), and aim at expressing the *general* feeling of the nation rather than individual ideas– though the latter might be much finer.

"I have just had a visit from Theo. Thomas and Mr. Buck, and we talked the whole matter over. Thomas remembers you well, and Mr. Buck says it would be specially agreeable to him to compose for the words of a Southern poet." (Dudley Buck had been chosen to compose the music; Theodore Thomas was in charge of the performance of the cantata. The official invitation was sent to Lanier on Dec. 31.)

[217] Previously published and reproduced in facsimile, Mims, p. 191, from which the present text is taken, the MS not being found.

1876

To Mary Day Lanier

> 66 Centre St. Bo.
> Jany 1st 1876

So: I have counted and put away the clean clothes: I have read Charley his Bible, and said my prayers with him, and tucked him away, and kissed him good-night: and there is now no duty lying betwixt me and thee. Would God there were no distance, either. For it is with me, always, *O dear Love,* and *O dear Love,* and *O dear Love*: this is the list and perfect registry of my heart-beats: this is the song which the current of my life sings, this is the ripple of it against obstacles, this is the plash of it against the banks thereof: as a strong tone draws into its own speed all lesser vibrations, so into this tune melt all the lesser melodies of my life.

Thy lovely Mercury – who, coming from thee, would seem to have gone into *the* service of the Queen of the Gods – is here; as also thy hankerbushes [?]: together with thy most dear loving messages. I have also a very fair and comforting letter from Clifford. – So it was thou that didst send the Chicago Tribune notice ?[1] And where pray didst thou get it ? Have

---

[1] A brief notice in the Chicago *Tribune,* Dec. 18, 1875, objected to Lanier's " exaggerated style " and " frenzied raving " over everything romantic in Florida, but admitted that the volume was a serviceable guide-book. Clifford Lanier had written on Dec. 28, 1875: " ' Florida ' charms me and I have devoured the whole state, Saurians and all. Maydie and I have had our laugh, mixt with indignation, over the notice of it contained in the Chicago Tribune which she has sent you *via* Macon."

In her letter of Dec. 27, 1875, Mary Day Lanier had reported that on Christmas night Clifford read *Florida* aloud to the family group in Montgomery–Virginia Hankins also being present: " Clifford is in a land of pure delight in reading ' Florida.' I think it is a noble work and will live when ' Florida travel ' has passed away. In it I review our happy journey and sojourn in that land, and thus have a double delight in it."

290

the Southern papers noticed the book at all ? I have had no
time to think of it.

Tout le Monde has been paying New Year's calls today.
As for me I had not the heart for it. I went and captured
Clare [de Graffenried] (the Machens not receiving today) and
we spent most of the day in a long aimless stroll in the Park.
I was quite sore-hearted to see some woods and open country:
and this good child was tender to my lonesomeness, and was
altogether sweet to me.   Late in the afternoon I took
Charley – having written his name on some tiny cards, and
gotten him into his kid gloves – to pay a few informal visits
with me. He enjoyed these very greatly: and was greatly
amazed at the magnificence of the dresses and the houses, particularly at the Perots', who have recently moved into a very
grand mansion, where we found a most dazzling blaze of light
flashing over ladies in full dress and bewildering mirrors and
lofty ceilings and the like.

I love not to read that thou art not well. Here have we had
a strange succession of warm days, and the small man is a little
disgusted that the snow has not come.

I have a monstrous yearning after my little Sissa, and I pray
thee brew thy kiss extra-sweet and strong and give it her for
me.

So, dear Moll; this is the first day of the year: I wonder if
the new king will be so good a friend to my fame as was the
dead one: I was up last night when he breathed his last, and I
wrung his Majesty's hand with grateful devotion as of one
heartily sorry to see him go, for, with many trials, he brought
me also many sweet possessions and gifts which remain: I am
trying, this night, to curry some favor with the now Monarch,
in Thy behalf: Gracious One, – I have cried unto him – she
is so lovely and so dear, be thou unto her, even as I am, a true
faithful

lover.——

To Bayard Taylor [2]

64 Centre St.
Baltimore, Md.
Jany 4th 1876

My dear Mr. Taylor:

Gen. Hawley's invitation has just arrived and I have sent my acceptance. I will probably see Theodore Thomas here on Monday next, and will try to arrange a meeting with Mr. Buck in N. Y. soon.

There isn't the least use in my trying to thank you for this pleasant surprise; but I *do* wish I could tell you the delight with which I find my name associated with yours in this way.[3]

Are we at liberty to mention our appointment in this behalf to our friends? I only ask, remembering that the name of the Centennial poet has not yet been officially announced, – at least so far as I know.

Charley sends you his love.   I write in much haste, but am no less – always your faithful and grateful

S. L.[4]

To Dudley Buck [5]

66 Centre St.
Baltimore, Md.
Jany 4th, 1876

My dear sir:

I am requested to communicate to you immediately my acceptance of an invitation to write the text for a Cantata to be composed by yourself and sung at the opening of the International Exhibition.

[2] Previously published, *Atlantic Monthly*, LXXXIII, 796 (June, 1899); reprinted, *Letters* (New York, 1899), pp. 137-138.

[3] Taylor had said in his letter of Dec. 28, 1875 (*Letters*, New York, 1899, pp. 136-137) that he was to write the Hymn for the Centennial Exhibition for which Lanier was to write the Cantata.

[4] Taylor replied on Jan. 7, 1876 (*Letters*, New York, 1899, p. 138): " Don't overvalue my friendly good-will, nor ever let it impose the least sense of obligation upon you. I am very glad when I can be of some encouragement to a man in whom I have faith."

[5] Dudley Buck (1839-1909), having become assistant conductor of Theodore

Pray give me all your ideas freely as to the conditions you would desire to control the form of the poem. I hope to see Mr. Thomas here next Monday or Wednesday: and probably I could arrange to meet you in New York soon. I will trouble you to write me immediately what will be the latest time at which you must have the text.

I beg you will let me express the pleasure with which I find myself engaged with you in this work.

Very truly yours,

Sidney Lanier.

To Mary Day Lanier [6]

B°

Jany. 8th 1876

Well then : God be praised that giveth us the victory. I have late this afternoon finished my third India paper, which was a great labor and strain: and tonight we have played a divine Concert of Scandinavian music whereof I enclose herein the programme; and my heart is so full of this heavenly melody that I cannot find me any rest till I have in some wise enlarged me by the addition of thee .

Moreover I have a charming piece of news which – although thou are not yet to communicate it to any one except Clifford – I cannot keep from thee. The opening ceremonies of the Centennial Exhibition will be very grand: and among other things there are to be sung by a full Chorus (and played by the orchestra, under Thomas' direction) a hymn, and a Cantata.

Thomas's Orchestra in 1875, had just begun his long career as composer and church organist in New York and Brooklyn after an apprenticeship of twelve years as organist in other cities. His greatest reputation came as composer of religious music and concert cantatas — a reputation that was first established on a national basis by his Centennial Cantata.

The originals of Lanier's letters to Buck have not been found. The texts in this edition are taken from copies (now in the Duke University Library) made by the historian John Spencer Bassett, a colleague of Edwin Mims at Trinity College, presumably from the MSS at the time Mims was preparing his biography of Lanier in 1904.

[6] Excerpt previously published, M. M. Baskerville, *Southern Writers* (Nashville, Tenn., 1899), I, 200-201; reprinted, Mims, pp. 167-168.

Gen. Hawley, Prest of the Centennial Commission, has written inviting me to write the latter (I mean the *poem*; Dudley Buck, of New York, is to write the music). Bayard Taylor is to write the hymn. This is very pleasing to me; for I am chosen as representative of our dear South; and the matter puts my name by the side of very delightful and honorable ones, besides bringing me in contact with many people I would desire to know.

Mr. Buck has written me that he wants the poem by Jany. 15th: which, as I have not yet had the least time for it, gives me just seven days to write it in. I would much rather have had seven months: but God is great. Remember, thou and Cliff, that this is not yet to be spoken of, at all.

Tell that King Arthur, my Sweet Liege, that Scribner's has accepted the Revival Hymn of old Uncle Jim.[7] I altered it considerably in shape, little in matter.

Thou feedest me, dear Heart, upon such distillations of dear honey in thy last letter that I am grown at once full of love and humility. All that thou sayest of thy doings and goings pleases me, save that thou canst not practise the piano. But thou shalt erelong. I like (to answer thy question) that thou shdst. have the insatiable longing to utter thyself musically: and I would wish thee to be inordinately desirous of such a consummation. It is the way that thine *I* speaks, which is very strong: and thou needest much out-going of thyself. There are many — I and thou are two that I know — who do not prosper under self-repression: it deadens the elasticity of our souls: and self-denial is only good when one's self desires what is wrong, — which neither of us do. In music one finds an immense compensation for all the necessary repressions which come in daily life. In music the Hope — the divine indescribable enthusiasm towards that formless Sweet which scarcely any soul has even named for itself — blossoms again, through the dusty coverings and heartless snows of daily life. I find it growing more and more necessary to me. What will I ever do without the Orchestra?

But I must sleep. For the next seven days I am to be buried in my Cantata. God send that I shall find time to write thee:

---

[7] "Uncle Jim's Baptist Revival Hymn" (I, 217), originally written by Clifford Lanier.

but an I do not, thou wilt think that I am underground forging gems to hang about the sweet neck of that Most Sweet to whom I am true

lover.

To Bayard Taylor [8]

66 Centre St.
Baltimore, Md,
Jany. 9th 1876.

Dear Mr. Taylor:

Yesterday I impressed myself with these following principles:

1st That the Cantata was to be sung not only at our Centennial, but at a festival where the world was our invited guest, to be welcomed:

2nd That spread-eagleism would be ungraceful and unworthy:

3rd That something ought to be said in the poem:

4th That it afforded room to give the musical composer an opportunity to employ the prodigious tone-contrasts of sober reflection, the sea, lamentation, a battle, warning, and magnificent yet sober and manly triumph and welcome:

5th That it ought to be not rhymed philosophy, but a genuine song, and lyric outburst.

Having put this offering on my altar, I waited; and this morning I saw that the Fire had come down from a gracious Heaven, and that it was burning.

Here is the result. Pray read it, and send me word immediately, – and with perfect candor, – as to such parts of it as strike you unfavorably.

– I wish I could hear you intone it, *ore rotundo* !

Your friend

S. L.[9]

[8] Previously published, *Atlantic Monthly*, LXXXIII, 797 (June, 1899); reprinted, *Letters* (New York, 1899), p. 139.

[9] Taylor's reply, Jan. 12, 1876 (*Letters*, New York, 1899, pp. 140-142), contained detailed criticisms of Lanier's poem, some of which influenced the final revisions. (For an account of this and of the several surviving versions of the " Centennial Meditation of Columbia, 1776-1876 " see vol. I of the present edition.)

To Bayard Taylor [10]

66 Centre St.
Baltimore, Md,
Jany 12th 1876

Dear Mr. Taylor:

Being cool next day, I found some flaws in
my poem: and having made out a working-copy of it (by reading the analysis of movements written in the margin, you will
see what immense resources it offers to the musician)   I send it
to you.   Pray let me know freely if it the whole is worthy.

Always your friend

S. L.

I have not yet sent it to Mr. Buck.

To Bayard Taylor [11]

66 Centre St.
Bo Md.
Jany 13th 1876

My dear Mr. Taylor:

I agree with your main points of objec-
tions: and I will change the stanza about which you are most
apprehensive.   I'm particularly charmed to find that you don't
think the poem *too* original.   I tried hard to think – – – in a
kind of average and miscellaneousness.

I read and explained it to Thomas [12] last night; he said " I
think Mr. Buck ought to be delighted with the musical conceptions of the poem ": adding that of course he would not dare
to pronounce upon the poetic merits of it beyond saying that
the ideas seemed to him very beautiful.

[10] Previously published, *Atlantic Monthly*, LXXXIII, 797 (June, 1899); reprinted, *Letters* (New York, 1899), p. 139. Taylor's reply, Jan. 13, 1876, is
printed in *Letters* (New York, 1899), p. 143.
[11] Previously published, *Atlantic Monthly*, LXXXIII, 798 (June, 1899);
reprinted, *Letters* (New York, 1899), pp. 142-143.
[12] Theodore Thomas, whose orchestra gave two concerts in Baltimore, Jan.
10, 12, 1876.

I sent you the copy showing the movements, before I had
rec^d yr. letter. I'll send a final copy when I've finished it.
You see, I had to compose for the musician as well as the
country: and had to cast the poem into such a form as would at
once show well in music (where contrast of movement between
each adjacent part, in *broad bands of color*, was, from the
nature of the art, a controlling consideration) and in poetry.
I wished indeed to make it as large and as simple as a Symphony of Beethoven's. If it does not come up to this, I've
failed: – but your commendation confirms my own cool feeling
about it, which is that it will do.

I thank – – — but I won't either, for it's simply absurd.
Your criticisms on the piece are invaluable to me; for though I
don't agree with all of them, the sharp re-examinations which
they compel me to make develop many things which otherwise
wd. *not* be developed.

Charley sends love, and mine is always sent before.

Yr. friend

S. L.

To Bayard Taylor [13]

66 Centre St,
B^o Md –
Jany 15th 1876.

Dear Mr. Taylor:

You are so far responsible for me as the
writer of this Cantata that I don't intend to feel satisfaction
until I am sure that you think the poem absolutely worthy of
the country and of poetry as an art. Therefore, having after
two days cooling found many faults with it myself, I have quite
rewritten it and send it to you, hoping that you will let me
know if it seems to you entirely large, simple, and melodious.
For it is to this that I have directed all my efforts in it: I have
had constantly in my mind those immortal melodies of Bee-

[13] Previously published, *Atlantic Monthly*, LXXXIII, 799 (June, 1899); reprinted, *Letters* (New York, 1899), p. 144.

thoven in which, with little more than the chords of the tonic and dominant, he has presented such firm, majestic, and at the same artless ideas.   Of course, with the general world – especially in a Swinburnian time [14] – I do not expect to obtain the least recognition of the combination of child-like candors and colossal philosophies which I have endeavored here to put in words: but I do wish to know whether to *you* the poem as you now see it comes near this ideal.   I don't believe there is the least necessity for me to beg you not to have the least regard for *me* in pronouncing upon anything that you still find wanting.   I desire the poem to be perfect.

I put the *Farewell dear England* into the Mayflower strophe because Mather relates that the people on the vessel actually stood up and cried out these words as they were departing.   I also entirely rewrote the stanza you did not like: and then inserted a whisper chorus, (of the Hugenot and Puritan, in dactyllic measure) to prepare, by its straining pianissimo, for the outburst of jubilation.

Always your friend

S. L.[15]

---

[14] This phrase probably reflects Lanier's resentment at an unfavorable criticism of his poetry by Swinburne.   On Jan. 11, 1876, Emma Stebbins, Charlotte Cushman's companion, wrote in a letter from Boston which he must have received by Jan. 15: " You remember that at C's request I sent out your two chief poems, to a mutual friend of ours in London– an intimate of Swinburnes, asking that they might be shown to him, with a view to future contingencies.   Well I have an answer from this friend– the poems were shown to Swinburne, and she sends me an extract from a letter– in which he gives his opinion of them– it is English– it emanates from one of a clique who welcome Joachim Miller and call Walt Whitman our ' *one* great poet '. – You perhaps may prefer to get all opinions and hold them for what they are worth.   I suppose an Artist should stand ready to profit by all winds that come– favorable or unfavorable.   Shall I send you this extract? "   (The extract has not been found.)

[15] Taylor replied, Jan. 20, 1876 (*Letters*, New York, 1899, pp. 145-146): " The revised *Cantata* . . . is in every way better than the first draught.   It is what it purports to be– a *Cantata*, not an Ode– with the musical character inherent in its structure and not to be separated.   If the composer seconds you properly, the effect cannot be otherwise than grand and satisfactory."

To Dudley Buck [16]

66 Centre St.
Baltimore, Md.
Jany 15th, 1876

Dear Mr. Buck,

I send you herewith the complete text for the Cantata. I have tried to make it a genuine Song, at once full of fire and of large and artless simplicity befitting a young but already colossal land.

I have made out a working copy for you, with marginal notes which give an analysis of each movement (or rather *motive*, for I take it the whole will be a continuous progression; and I only use the word "movement" as indicating the entire contrast which I have secured between each two adjacent *motives*), and which will I hope facilitate your labor by presenting an outline of the tone characterizing each change of idea. One movement is placed on each page.

I also send a continuous copy of the poem, in order that you may read it without the disadvantageous breaks of the working-copy.

Mr. Thomas was kind enough to express himself very cordially as to the ideas of the piece; and I devoutly trust they will meet your views. I found that the projection which I had made in my own mind embraced all the substantial features of the Scheme which had occurred to you, and therefore although greatly differing in details I have not hesitated to avail myself of your thoughtful warning against being in any way hampered.[17]

[16] Previously published, Mims, pp. 168-169.

[17] On Jan. 5, 1876, Buck had written: "It . . . pleases me that I am to join partnership with a Southerner on this truly national occasion. Now as to 'my ideas' respecting the Cantata— I do not want you to hamper yourself in anyway. As I am so fortunate as to have a musician for my poet we shall doubtless understand each other. I will however give you the few points which now occur to me." He then stated that the Cantata was to be limited to twenty minutes, that he preferred irregular verse, and that he and Theodore Thomas had decided that it should consist of "three movements or rather one continuous movement including three episodes": (1) An opening chorus of rejoicing and thanksgiving; (2) a short recitative and solo in which "an old man of the people . . . looks back & recounts what he has heard of the early trials & tribulations of the

It will give me keen pleasure to know from you, as soon as you shall have digested the poem, that you like it.

God send you a soul full of colossal and simple chords,— says

Yours sincerely

Sidney Lanier.

To Gibson Peacock [18]

66 Centre St.

Bo. Md.

Jany 18, 1876.

My dear friend:

For several weeks past all my minutes have been the property of others, and I have in vain tried to appropriate a little one to you.

The enclosed will show you partly what I have been doing. I am not at liberty to mention the matter: but you will keep it, until the interdict against publicity is removed. The Centennial Commission has invited me to write a poem which shall serve as the text for a Cantata, (the music to be by Dudley Buck, of New York) to be sung at the opening of the Exhibition, under Thomas' direction. All this is to be kept secret.

I've written the enclosed. Necessarily I had to think out the musical conceptions as well as the poem, and I have briefly indicated these along the margin of each movement. I have tried to make the whole as simple and as candid as a melody of Beethoven's: at the same time expressing the largest ideas possible, and expressing them in such a way as could not be offensive to any modern soul. I particularly hope you'll like the Angel's song, where I have endeavored to convey, in one line each, the philosophies of Art, of Science, of Power, of Government, of Faith, and of Social Life. Of course, I shall not expect that this will instantly appeal to tastes peppered and salted by

---

Republic . . . & then, if you will, prophecies its future glory"; and (3) "Finale– The Chorus take up the above prophecies of the future perhaps with some repetition of the thanksgivings of No. 1."

[18] Previously published, *Poems* (New York, 1884), pp. 251-252; reprinted, *Atlantic Monthly*, LXXIV, 25 (July, 1894), and *Letters* (New York, 1899), pp. 24-25.

Swinburne and that ilk: but one cannot forget Beethoven, and somehow all my inspiration came in these large and artless forms, in simple Saxon words, in unpretentious and purely intellectual conceptions: while nevertheless I felt, all through, the necessity of making a genuine Song – and not a rhymed set of good adages – out of it. I adopted the trochees of the first movement because they *compel* a measured sober and meditative movement of the mind: and because too, they are not the genius of our language. When the troubles cease, and the land emerges as a distinct unity, then I fall into our native iambics.

I am very anxious you should think it worthy. If your Maria shall like it, I shall not feel any fear about it. Pray kiss her for me, and assure her, as yourself, of the unfailing regard of

your friend

S. L.

To Dudley Buck [19]

66 Centre St.
Baltimore, Md.
Jany 19th, 1876

Dear Mr. Buck:

I'm glad you like the poem: and I hope you will exercise the most confident freedom in calling my attention to any verbal alterations which may render the sounds more singable.

To answer your points *seriatim*.

1. The " weltering flow " is only meant to symbolize the remote Past breaking like a sea against the firm existence of our Republic. The word " weltering " is meant to be sung (as well

---

[19] In his letter of Jan. 17, 1875 (error for 1876), Buck had written: " Your poem arrived safely early this morning and I hasten to express to you the pleasure its perusal has afforded me. It is certainly original both in thought and expression and I should have no trouble in setting it worthily I think were it not for one thing– viz: this miserable writing against time. . . . I am only too much delighted to find [it] . . . so thoroughly *en rapport* with myself." He then listed the four criticisms which Lanier's letter answers in detail.

In his letter of Jan. 19, 1876, Buck added: " The poem is splendid– I am quite in love with it as it sinks in deeper & deeper."

as read) in two syllables, *i. e.* welt'ring. If you find it bad for singing, of course I'll change it: but I hang to it because it is a maxim among poets to vary the vowel-sounds as much as possible in every line, and you will observe that this line contains a different (and pleasantly-contrasting) sound for every syllable.

2.   Your difficulty on this point (about the " dear in vain " of the Mayflower stanza) arises solely from my indistinct chirography, through which you have mistaken the " v " in " vain " for an " r ": it is not *Rain* but *Vain*: the reply of the winds *but dear in vain* referring simply to the hopelessness of that affection for England which is expressed in the sigh of the fugitive.

3.   I do not at all like the line " Toil e'en when brother-wars new-dark " &c and am sure that in a poem written at a speed less like lightning than this I wouldn't have let it go forth at all. I'm going to beg that you'll let me alter the end of the Huguenot-Puritan stanza, so as to make it read thus:

> Toil through the stertorous death of the Night,
> Toil through the riotous birth of the Light,
> Toil when wild brother-wars grasping at Right
> Sunder his head from his heart in despite,
>   Toil through the after-wars,
>   Scorn-wars and laughter-wars,
> Toil, and forgive, and kiss new, and o'er-plight.

Several reasons, aside from euphony, impel me to make this little addition: and as the movement is a very rapid one, and the extra time not above a minute, I will ask so much liberty.[20]

4.   I will dispose of this objection by altering the whole stanza of four lines which closes the poem. It does not at all suit me, for lack of majesty. In its place therefore, please put this, which has a larger-rolling rhythm:

> O Music, from this height of time my Word unfold:
> In thy large signals all men's hearts man's heart behold:

---

[20] A marginal gloss by Buck opposite this passage on the MS of Lanier's letter read: " Original [version] the best." In his letter of Jan. 11 (error for 21), 1876, Buck wrote that the time limit for the performance of the Cantata made it imperative that not a single line be added to the poem. Consequently, Lanier withdrew this addition, as the following letter reveals.

Mid-Heaven unroll thy chords as friendly flags unfurled,
And wave the world's best lover's welcome to the world.

Pray make these corrections on your copies, – provided you
find no other euphonic alterations desirable.

I have been careful to say nothing about the poem except to
a few friends confidentially. Do you suppose it will be published by the Centennial Commission before the ceremonies?
I will be glad to know immediately if it now quite suits you.

Yes: I am from Georgia.

Pardon this unconcionably long screed: for I
had only three real days to do the whole poem in, and that
isn't enough to allow it to cool, after it is finished, down to
the point where one gets a view of its true color.

Very truly yours

Sidney Lanier.

To Dudley Buck

66 Centre St.
Baltimore, Md.
Jany 22nd, 1876

Dear Mr. Buck:

1. Agreed, about the two lines you wish
lengthened: only, substitute the words " oft-granted " in place
of " Almighty ", so as to make them read:

" Now Praise to God's oft-granted grace,
Now Praise to Man's undaunted face," &c.[21]

2. Agreed also, as to omitting the two lines " Ghosts of Goods
&c &c ", for, —though it's like chipping a notch in the leg of a
statue—yet when you tell me that the poem is encroaching
upon the time alloted it, I am ready to do any amount of cutting, being quite resolute upon keeping it fully within bounds.
For this last reason, I withdraw the addition (in my letter which
probably crossed yours on the way) to the Huguenot and Puritan
stanza, and you may let that stand just as it is, except that I

---

[21] This revision was retained in the final version, as were also the two lines
which Lanier agreed in the following sentence to omit.

don't like the word " e'en " in the next to the last line, and beg therefore that you will alter that line, to read thus: " Toil when wild brother-wars new-dark the light ".

3. The last four lines of the poem must flow a little more majestically than the five-foot verse allows, and therefore I will ask you to alter them as indicated in my last letter, towit:

> " O Music, from this height of time my Word unfold:
> In thy large signals all men's hearts Man's Heart behold:
> Mid-Heaven unroll thy chords as friendly flags unfurled
> And wave the world's best lover's welcome to the world."

This carries out much more satisfactorily to me my favorite practice of three-fold metaphors, e. g. the idea of Music, of friendly banners, of welcome, each holding the others within itself, and the words " unfold ", " signals ", " unroll ", " flags ", " wave " &c all converging mutually upon the metaphor.

I am sincerely pleased at knowing that you like the poem. Perhaps you will care to know (one always likes to have one's judgment backed up) that Mr. Gibson Peacock, of Philadelphia,—the only critic to whom I have submitted the poem— writes, in a letter just received: " You have succeeded amazingly well, better I believe than any other living man could have succeeded in a poem written to order and for music. . . . The Angel's song is simply divine. . . . . can't you get an Archangel with a bass voice to sing it? " [22]

Pray let me have a line when you receive this, to let me know that all is now finally to your perfect liking.

In great haste, yours very truly,

Sidney Lanier.

To Mary Day Lanier [23]

[Baltimore, Jan. 22, 1876?]

Thou inquirest of the 3 concerts upon the alternate weeks and askest why I have not written of them. There are none. As for the little side-playing I used to do, there is none now

---

[22] Quoted from Peacock's letter to Lanier of Jan. 20, 1876. A marginal gloss by Buck opposite this passage on the MS of Lanier's letter read: " Yes– Myron Whitney of Boston."

[23] This letter is Lanier's answer to his wife's letter of Jan. 12, 1876, the MS

to be done; music is quite dull, as yet; and if there were plenty I do not see how I could find time for it at all. The India papers appear to have found favor: Mr. Peacock writes me that they " are praised everywhere ": and I have just had a letter from Mr. Kirk asking that I will run them into five numbers instead of four as originally intended.[24] There are thus still two more to write, and they have to be done within the next two weeks. Besides these I must also write the promised Centennial poem for the Magazine: which will be a long one, and is already rending me and tearing my heart for liberation. In addition to this I have quite a voluminous correspondence with Mr. Buck (who is now in all the agonies of *his* part of the Cantata) to conduct almost daily: an introduction to the poem of Clifford's for Scribner's to write, in pursuance of a request from Gilder " for the illumination of the secular reader " upon some of Uncle Jim's idioms: [25] a long article on the Physics of Music [26] to re-write for the Southern Magazine: negotiations to carry on anent the chair in the N. Y. College of Music: frequent letters to my poor sweet Cushla (which has come to be my name for C[harlotte] C[ushman]) who is suffering dreadful tortures and seems to take a little comfort in my love-making: as well as my rehearsals, Charley's demands, and a

of which has been mutilated, apparently to destroy a reference to the writer of a note mentioned in a previous letter by Lanier (see Dec. 19, 1875, above).

The first part of the present letter is missing, and the opening words have been copied on the remaining portion of the MS by Mary Day Lanier. Her reply of Jan. 26, 1876 (which furnishes the evidence for the conjectural dating here given), contains a hint of the contents of the missing portion of Lanier's letter: " And well! – how thou hast ' run off ' in thine of 22nd! When I spoke of ' Caesar's Wife ' I but referred to ' paths ' that I saw some *other* people treading— (for, in this town, heavy flirtation is quite irrespective of previous marriage-bonds) and had no wonderful stories at all to tell thee. Some two or three gentlemen have seemed to like my company more than the others, in my social evenings outside, but they all find out too soon that I love best to talk of *thee* to dream of any amusement of the popular kind with me."

[24] Only four installments of " Sketches of India " were published (*Lippincott's*, Jan.-Apr., 1876), though Lanier's letter of Mar. 20, 1876, to Bleckley, below, seems to indicate that a fifth was written.

[25] When "Uncle Jim's Baptist Revival Hymn" was published in *Scribner's*, XII, 142 (May, 1876), it was accompanied by a headnote explaining some of the dialect phrases (reproduced in the notes, vol. I of the present edition).

[26] This article was rejected by R. W. Gilder of *Scribner's*, July 2, 1878, after apparently being turned down by the *Southern Magazine*. It was first published posthumously in 1898 (II, 251).

thousand miscellaneous matters.   I have to refuse nearly all invitations to visit, and am much put to it for practising-time in order to gain the *technique* I desire upon my instrument.   I do not know whether I wrote thee that there is a probability of Thomas' Orchestra being enlarged, and that Mr. Thomas has in the most unexpected manner offered the additional flute to me, if it should be so.

I have, beyond these matters, the keenest desire to put Cliff's novel of two hundred bales [27] in thorough order, so as to put it in for the prize of $500 offered by the " Sun ", of this city, for the best American novel.   I have only recently learned of this, and the idea struck me immediately: but I have in vain struggled for a single minute to give to it: and it must be sent in within a few weeks.   But I will not give over trying.   It needs an immense reduction (the novel), and unsparing cutting away: I should want a good month's work on it, and it has to be sent in in just that time.

So: thou hast in brief a little of what I am doing.   I could not in many letters tell thee all: life is very full with me just now.

For this reason I doubly need thee.   It is *too* full, for one.

Write me of all thy lovers.   Kiss my sweet little Sissa for me.   O if I could only drop in upon all of you, and have a good month of utter freedom from racking thought !

I wish to know how thou art.   God be thy Health, prayeth thy

lover.

To Dudley Buck

66 Centre St.
Baltimore, Md.
Jany 25th, 1876

Dear Mr. Buck:

I wrote you yesterday of my desire to keep the poem well within the limits of time assigned to it, and withdrew the proposed addition to the Huguenot stanza.

---

[27] Published posthumously under the title *Carpet-baggery* (see note 131, 1874).

I believe I anticipated all the points in yours just received, except your wish concerning the last two lines of the poem.[28] You will observe that the first two lines of this quatrain consist of six *iambi*, and this would make it quite impossible for the last two to have less than six. I gave some additional reasons in my letter of yesterday which will probably have weight with you. There are no *immediately*-consecutive " w's " in the last line: between " wave " and " world's " comes " the "; between " world's " and welcome come two words " best lover's "; and between " welcome " and the last " world " also two words " to the ". So that if you *can* possibly get along with these just as they stand, I'm going to beg that you do so, —particularly as this is the only point I've been *mean* about. Of course if you *can't*, you have only to speak and I'll alter until you are thoroughly satisfied. Pray don't feel the least hesitation in asking for anything of the sort: it would be too absurd for me to be " touchy " in a matter requiring such close conjunction of judgments and fancies as this; and then, moreover, I'm not at all one of the " touchy " sort.

As for your proposition to hand the poem to the Tribune, I will beg you to hold all that over until you hear from me again. I hope to see you next week, early: and we will then talk of it.

Truly yours,

Sidney Lanier.

[28] In his letter of Jan. 11 (error for 21), 1876, Buck had objected to the new version of the closing couplet as given in Lanier's letter of Jan. 19, above, saying that he preferred the original version which had only five iambic feet instead of six: " The shorter lines give me a chance to develope musically just that majesty you want— but the many words of the last two, as changed, compel shorter values in notation within one & the same measure, & work against what you desire— besides— excuse me— but they are *tough* to pronounce in an *Allegro* movement— Would not the following combination of the two versions satisfy the poet— they would gladden the heart of the composer. . . .

> Roll forth, broad tones as friendly flags unfurled
> And wave Columbia's welcome to the world!

For my use " Columbia ' is better than *w*orld*s w*ishers *w*elcome— or *w*ave *w*orld'*s* lover'*s w*elcome. I don't want *repeated* ' w's ' & s's if I can help."

In his answer to the present letter, dated Jan. 27, 1876, Buck withdrew his objection to the closing couplet and Lanier retained the longer alliterative lines that he preferred. Apropos of Lanier's other concessions he added: " You are the Prince of Poets to be so accomodating. . . . I consider the poem perfect now."

To Gibson Peacock [29]

66 Centre St.
Baltimore, Md.
Jany 25 / 1876

My dear friend:

Your praise, and your wife's, gives me a world of comfort. I really do not believe anything was ever written under an equal number of limitations: and when I first came to know all the conditions of the poem, I was for a moment inclined to think that no genuine work could be produced under them.

As for the friend who was the cause of the compliment, it was, directly, Mr. Taylor.[30] I knew nothing of it whatever until Mr. T. wrote me that it had been settled to invite me. *Indirectly*, I fancy *you* are largely concerned in it: for it seems from Mr. Taylor's account that Gen. Hawley was very glad to have me do the work, and I fancy this must have been owing much to the reputation which you set a-rolling so recently.

If you should see anything about the India papers, I particularly desire to get it; for I fancied that Mr. Kirk was not quite as pleased with them as with other works of mine, and I would therefore hail any sign of their popularity. I do not have time to read any papers: life is getting so full to me that I scarcely know how I am going to win through the next two months' work. After that, though, there is a charming *possibility* ahead of me, which holds the frequent sight of *you* among its delights. (None of this is to be mentioned yet.)   When Theodore

[29] Excerpt previously published, *Poems* (New York, 1884), p. 252; reprinted, *Atlantic Monthly*, LXXIV, 25-26 (July, 1894), and *Letters* (New York, 1899), pp. 25-28.

[30] A note appended at this point in the previous publications of this letter consists of a letter from Gen. J. R. Hawley to W. R. Thayer (?) on the subject of Lanier's appointment. Hawley stated that he invited Lanier to write the Cantata because Taylor had recommended him so highly: "We were all of us always glad that we had done so. The Cantata was somewhat unusual in style and character: that is to say, it was original, but it was charmingly so, and both Buck and Thomas thought it very remarkably adapted to our needs. I saw something of Mr. Lanier, but not much. What I did see impressed me very favorably, and I have a very kind and tender recollection of that gentleman."

Thomas passed through here a few days ago, to my great surprise he told me that his orchestra would probably be increased
during the summer, and that he would like me to take the additional flute in it. I had played several duos with his first
flute – Wehner – and it is to his voluntary recommendation that
I owe the offer. It would be very charming for me: and is such
a compliment to a player wholly untaught as I am, and but
recently out of the country, that I'm indulging myself in considerable gratification over it.

Mr. Buck writes me that he has now completed his sketches
for the Cantata, and is going at once to the work of scoring it
for orchestra and voices. He seems immensely pleased with the
text, and we have gotten on together with perfect harmony
during the process of fitting together the words and the music,
which has been wholly accomplished by letter.

By the way, there are two alterations which I think I have
made since your copy was sent you. They are

> Now praise to God's *oft-granted* grace,
> Now praise to man's *undaunted* face

the two underscored words having been added; and the last
four lines – which did not roll with enough majesty to suit me –
have been entirely remodelled, to read thus:

> " Then Music from this height of time my Word unfold:
> In thy large signals all men's hearts Man's Heart behold:
> Mid-heaven unroll thy chords as friendly flags unfurled,
> And wave the world's best lover's welcome to the world."

Pray make these alterations in your copy. Also in the Huguenot
stanza instead of " Toil e'en when brother-wars " write " Toil
when wild brother-wars &c."

So, God bless you both.

Your friend

S. L.

To Dudley Buck

66 Centre St.
Baltimore, Md.
Jany 29th, 1876

Dear Mr. Buck:

I have been unavoidably prevented from making my visit to New York this week, and it is now probable I cannot come before week after next.

Meantime, in regard to printing the poem, let me submit to you these considerations.

1. No official announcement has yet been made by the Centennial Commission of the appointment of myself or of any other person. This being so, will not the publication of the poem be premature if made in advance of such announcement?

2. The fate of the Centennial Bill in Congress reveals—in spite of its passage—a good deal of opposition. All this will die out in a couple of months, and *then* every one will be in a temper to receive a poem of reconciliation. I fancy that to print the poem *now* will be much like making a dinner-speech before the wine has been round. Whether or not these considerations shall strike you with the same force as me, I will at any rate ask as a personal favor that the poem be not handed to any papers for publication until you hear further from me. I hope to see you in ten days, at least, from now.

Let me know how you progress in scoring the Cantata. I'm quite keen to see your sketches.

Sincerely yours,

Sidney Lanier.[31]

---

[31] Buck replied, Jan. 31, 1876: "I have nothing to urge against your idea of withholding the poem if it *can be* withheld. . . . I find the best judges of the real sentiment of the country consider the opposition to the Centennial bill a purely (miserable) political party affair. The reconciliation *sentiment* is already as good as universal.

"I shall do nothing in the way of communicating your poem to the press before you say the word, but T[heodore] T[homas] may desire it on his return from Phila."

To Dudley Buck [32]

66 Centre St.
Baltimore, Md.
Feb'y 1st, 1876

Dear Mr. Buck:

I have been so intently engaged that I have not had time to read the papers, and I did not know our appointment was " out " in the Tribune until your letter, received this morning, informed me.

I will leave the whole matter of the publication of the poem in the hands of Mr. Thomas and yourself; only begging that the enclosed copy be the one which shall go to the printer.— The truth is, I shrank from the criticisms which I fear my poem will provoke, — not because I think it unworthy, but because I have purposely made it absolutely free from all melodramatic artifice, and wholly simple and artless; and although I did this in the full consciousness that I would thereby give it such a form as would inevitably cause it to be disappointing on the first reading to most people, yet I had somewhat the same feeling (when your unexpected proposition to print first came) as when a raw salt spray dashes suddenly in your face and makes you duck your head. As for my own private poems I do not even see the criticisms on them, and am far above the plane where they could possibly reach me: but this poem is *not* mine, it is to represent the people, and the people have a right that it should please them.

—Pray pardon such a screed about myself:—but I did not want you and Mr. Thomas to think me finical.

— I have to beg one last little touch of alteration. Please make the *seventh* and *eighth* lines of the *first movement* read thus:

> " Yonder where the to and fro
> Weltering of my long ago."

instead of as they are. This is far better for many reasons which I will explain to your satisfaction when I see you soon.

Finally: whenever you *do* think it adviseable to publish the poem please send me a line a day in advance, notifying me.

[32] Previously published, Mims, pp. 169-170.

Business will probably call me to New York in a week or two.

Truly yours,

Sidney Lanier

P.S. I thank you for your suggestion as to the title, and you will see I have changed it to " The Centennial Meditation of Columbia ",[33] which enables me to impress a sense of soberness at the start, upon the reader.

To Mary Day Lanier

Bo Md,
Feb. 7th 1876

So, – dear Nourmahal, Light of the Palace – thanks be to the God of the laboring-man, I have at this moment finished p. 113, being – O Joy – the last, of the remaining India papers. The burden of it has been on my back so long that I still perceive it though it is now off, and I do not expect to feel otherwise than hump-back'd for several days.

Yet I intend now to rest profoundly during the next week, for I am greatly wearied in spirit after so much strain. It is not that the quantity of the work has been so great: but the nature of it has been such as would try the stoutest brain, for it has all been *tours de force* executed under the greatest imaginable disadvantages and under the leaden weight of limited time. When I think of the numbers of minute facts with which I have had to make myself thoroughly acquainted in this India business, I feel grateful to God that I still have my mind. Which I have, and 'tis in perfect working order; there isn't the least sense of confusion or of overwork, only it feels tired just as your muscles do after a long walk: and this sensation is not unpleasant now that I have reached a point where I can rest a little, though it has been for many days,

---

[33] Buck had written, Jan. (30?), 1876: " I write now in regard to the title. . . . Are you fully satisfied with ' Centennial *Song* of Columbia '? The word ' Song ' seems to me hardly worthy of the calibre of the poem, altho' this may be simply a notion of mine. From your notes to my working copy (' a colossal Figure on a height, meditating on the Past ') it occurred to me that perhaps, on second thoughts, you might prefer Centennial Musings or Meditations (or the like)— of Columbia." The title given in Lanier's letter was the one retained.

while I have been working, a desperate drawback, forcing me to whip up the jaded intellect most unmercifully. The hardest difficulty of all has been thine absence, this keeps me in a mournful dream which half paralyses my energy: and the desperate thought of picking up a living in this way is always nagging at the other half.

—— Well ! The very last thing I expected to write was this Jeremiad and arraignment of obstacles; but thou hast a forgiving soul,—and so let it go.

I am much better than when I last wrote thee, and there is today only the least little roughness of the throat to remind me of past soreness. Our concert last night was very successful. My centennial poem will probably be printed in the New York papers before long. I have given up the idea of trying to get in Cliff's " TWO HUNDRED BALES " for the Sun prize, as I find it would have to be entirely rewritten, and this would be a sheer physical impossibility in the time allowed. But I think I can sell it to Dr. Brown for the Southern Magazine: which is probably better than the other arrangement for the conditions are that every novel sent in is forfeited to the paper whether taking a prize or not. I have not seen the Telegraph & Mess. notice of Florida,[34] father's papers never having come to hand. The Oriental Annual arrived safely, and I have made good use of it in my last paper.[35] Charley's stockings and vest arrived safely also and he hath worn the latter today. We have had a great snow and he has been coasting with much vigor for two days: though now all's over, the rain is freezing as it falls. Thou shalt thank my dear little Sidney for the charming birthday message, and tell him how I do long to hear him say these same letters which he has learned so manfully for my sake. Inform him also that Charley was sliding on his sled yesterday

---

[34] The reviewer in the Macon *Telegraph and Messenger*, Jan. 26, 1876, paid Lanier glowing tribute as " Georgia's gifted son. . . . A poet essentially by nature, taste and the cast of his intellect " and praised his book as " brilliant and charming . . . even the most methodical prose, as it emanates from his teeming brain, bears about it the delicate tracery of a vivid imagination, and fanciful and weird delineations which startle, amuse and attract the reader." In conclusion it was announced that the book had already gone into a second edition.

[35] Lanier's father-in-law, Charles Day, had sent him an Oriental Album which he thought " might contain some ' India ' suggestions " (see Mary Day Lanier's letter to her husband, Jan. 12, 1876).

when three loafers asked him to let them ride. Charley said *no*, when they proceeded to take it from him: whereupon Charley struck one of them, but still they would not let go and were carrying it away from him when one of Charley's friends came up and rescued it.

In answer to thine inquiries about Jack [Wrenschall]: we see not much of him. I fancy Charley is almost too much *boy* for him, Jack being still in long dresses and being correspondingly kept at the apron-strings of his pretty mama. But Charley has made acquaintance with a number of other boys who often come to see him, or meet him up at the square and play with him. He goes out freely alone, and has even been down among the busiest streets on errands for me. 'Tis a queer little soul, compound of the rude boy and of somewhat else which I have not yet had time to study out. I will say here that I do much long for thee in the matter of buttons: such a set of no-buttons as we have thou wdst. not find in a summer's-day, and I am mostly dressed with pins, like a doll-baby in cut-paper patterns. I do not expect that these matters will be remedied until thou shalt superintend the same: for I have not had time, and tomorrow when I *will* have it, I protest I won't think of it for it is a burden more wearisome than writing another India paper. So all hail, Pins: and I pray heaven that when my breeches fall, it may not be when I am playing a solo at a Concert, – and when it is inconvenient to spare either hand. As for Charley, I have in vain endeavored to keep him decently sewn up in the seam of his trousers, he splits them out daily with his big stretches, and I do not know what to do unless I have the place plated with boiler-iron and riveted at a machine-shop.

My birthday brought me some charming little bouquets and a bottle of cologne from the people about the house.

—— And if there is anything else to tell thee, I'll write it tomorrow.

Kiss my pretty little Sissa for me. Continually do I yearn for her: it is like recalling one's mother: and I would give, I think in my great longing, a year of life for an hour with my dear Saint's hand on my head.

So God have thee well tended, Scheherazade, Rose of the West, prays thy

lover.

To Dudley Buck

66 Centre St.
Baltimore, Md.
Feby 11th 1876

Dear Mr. Buck:

On returning from Washington, I find that a
letter which came yesterday during my absence has been mis-
laid, and I fancy from the description that it was one containing the proofs of the Cantata. If this be so, I will beg you to
mail another one to me.

I saw Gen. Hawley in Washington last night. On communicating to him your proposition to hand the poem to the
newspapers, he seemed decidedly opposed to it. He said he
would write you on the subject, and I presume it would be best
therefore for you to suspend all action in that regard until you
hear from him.

Very truly yours,

Sidney Lanier.

To Mary Day Lanier

B⁰ Md.
Feby 12th 1876

My sweetest Soul, this has been what can only be called an idle
week, – for there is no tangible outcome of it, – and yet somehow when I look back over it I seem to have always had something or other to do. I had intended – among many other
sweet things to devote a great deal of it to thee; but somehow
it has been one of those vile weeks which come along occasionally when one's whole existence outwardly is at odds with
one's heart, when one says the things one had firmly resolved
not to say, does the things one despises, and compasses the ends
one hates. It is therefore with a certain eagerness that I devote
the last hour of these seven days of cross-purposes – for it is
now nearly Sunday morning – to a purpose which not all the
contrary devils can twist cross, namely, to making love to thee,

my sweet straightforward Soul and my truthful Heart wherein
Love keeps all things in well-ordered agreement. It is among
my chief delights to reflect on the constancy and superb surety
with which I have always known thee loving true love and I
am always constrained to believe that Love must of necessity
love thee in response to thy so sweet and unwavering passion
for him. This being so – thou being in the good grace of
Love – I please myself with believing that nothing very cross
of purpose can ever happen to thee.

Day before yesterday I was in Washington, where I ran over
to see Gen. Hawley, and hoping also to see Gen. Morgan. I
could not find the latter, – and I *did* long to behold palpably
some eye that had so lately beheld *thee* palpably.[36] I went in
my search to the Capitol, where the Senate and House were in
session. It was the first time I had been there. Thou wilt not
laugh when I tell thee there was here such an atmosphere of
rascality, such an odor of scoundrelism floating about all the
corridors and arising from every sight one sees, – that I came
away sick, and my heart has had no comfort since.

Hereby hangs a tale. In these days a curious struggle sometimes occurs in my spirit. The times are out of joint: – and I
seem to hear a certain voice from far off (within) calling me
to set them right, the gray martyrdoms of Luther and Savonarola pass clothed in serge before my eyes, I hear myself asking
myself across a noise like that of crackling flames and falling
timbers whether the mild ministry of poetry and of music which
I love is the only work I am entitled to do or commissioned to
do, a fierce sense of spiritual battle against the sins of the
Church and the state blares like a trumpet in my heart, – and
then I awake, exhausted and trembling, and am ill with pure
weakness for days.

— In my wiser and calmer moments I seem to know full
well that these are simply intensities which will reappear in my
artistic work hereafter. I seem to recognize clearly that there is
no ghost of a chance in these days for Luther or Savonarola,
and that poetry and music – particularly music, – must do their

[36] Gen. John T. Morgan (1824-1897), Senator from Alabama, was a friend
of Lanier and an admirer of his poetry– having quoted " Corn " in a political
speech the preceding year. (See Mary Day Lanier's letters of Jan. 3 and Feb.
5, 1876.)

work; – and I only tell thee of these things because – – because thou art my dear wife and thy loving intelligence is entitled to the deepest moments in the life of thy

lover .

To Laura N. Boykin [37]

66 Centre St.
Baltimore, Md.
Feby. 12th, 1876

Dear Mrs. Boykin:
It was a very fair and gracious inspiration that impelled you to write me about my " Florida." The book has been like a wound to me ever since I was engaged to write it; for, aside from the inherent difficulties of the commission (my instructions from my employers were simply to write them a guide-book which should be also a poem), I did not wish ever to appear before the public again save in the poetic character, and it was like being stabbed with a dull weapon to be compelled to put forth any more prose. You can therefore fancy that it is balm to my hurt when anybody finds poetry in the book – as your kind letter tells me you do; though after all, perhaps it is the old sweet scent of those orange-blossoms in your hair which filters through my words and gives them a grace due at bottom to your own recollections of your early home in Florida.

At any rate I thank you heartily for all that you say. In truth a certain sense of exile – which I feel would seem maudlin to most people and which nevertheless grows stronger with me every day – makes me prize any words from those dear old Macon hills. It seems a particularly hard cross-purpose that I – who love them surely better than any other of their children – must remain away from them in order to sing about them.

I often think of you in the midst of my orchestral work here. The delight of this I cannot at all describe; and now that I have tasted the divine intoxication I do not know how I shall ever do without it. I have a dream of leading an orchestra, and doing what I like with it some of these days; and there is

[37] Previously published, Macon *Telegraph*, Feb. 3, 1932.

so much promise in the present condition of music that I even hope this consummation may not be far off.

I am always charmed to have anything from your hand, being always your friend

Sidney L.

To Edward Spencer [88]

66 Centre St.
Baltimore, Md.
Feby. 12th 1876

Dear Mr. Spencer:

I have read MATERNUS [39] with a great deal of interest, and should have acknowledged your kindness in sending it to me earlier but for a severe attack of illness which quite disabled me for several days.

I am not possessed of sufficient skill in the playwrights' craft to have much confidence in my own judgment as to an acting play which I have only read, and not seen: – but this one seems to me full of intensely interesting action, and unusually abundant in effective situations. I think you have admirably depicted in Commodus that cruelty which is naturally the last resort of satiety, in Lucilla that love which having given its all has not even reserved to itself the strength to withdraw when it discovers itself loving unworthily, in Zabol that treachery which has in its very nature what must finally in some sense or other result in a certain suicidal death *by* treachery, and in Maternus that extremity of outrage where the impossibility of Justice seems to legitimate the frenzy of revenge. Judging by the manner in which I found myself drawn on from one page to another by the plot, in reading, I should argue that in actual representation it would be exciting enough.

By the way, a little grammatical error has escaped your attention in the first line on p. 28 – where the word "which" is without relation in the sentence. Perhaps you will also care to note that the first line on p. 55 seems to have six iambi.

---

[88] Excerpt previously published, Starke, pp. 205-206.

[39] A tragedy in blank verse by Spencer, printed in Baltimore, 1876 (copy in the Lanier Room, Johns Hopkins University).

I hope very heartily that the play will meet with all the success you can desire; and will be glad if you advise me of its fortune whenever it shall be produced.

I met with a line in one of Shakespeare's sonnets some time ago which seems to me so completely a nutshell judgment on my side as regards the possibility of interpreting – within limits – one sense by another through the forms of art, that I can't help sending it to you. – It is:

> " To hear with eyes belongs to Love's fine wit."

In my " Symphony ", Love's fine wit – the love of one's fellow-men – attempts (not to hear with eyes, but precisely the reverse) to see with ears.

A short time ago – I may also say in this connection – I found Heinrich Heine doing exactly what the Symphony does, *i.e.* interpreting a musical work through the form of a vision. It is in one of the Florentine Nights, – I think the second or third of those translated by Simon Stern of Philadelphia and published a year or two ago by Henry Holt.[40] I had never seen it however until long after " the Symphony " was written.

I am always glad to hear from you and of you, and will be delighted if you will sometimes come and have a quiet talk in my lodgings here, wh. are often lonesome enough to me.

Sincerely yours

Sidney Lanier.

To Mary Day Lanier

66 Centre St.
Baltimore, Md,
Feb'y 13th 1876

"God bless dear Mama, and Sidney, and Hawwy ! " So hath just run our nightly formula up to Heaven, wherewith we conclude our prayer of The Lord and our Now I lay me: and

---

[40] The volume referred to by Lanier was apparently *Scintillations from the Prose Works of Heinrich Heine*, translated by Simon Adler Stern, and published by Holt & Williams, New York, 1873. It includes the *Florentine Nights*; "Night the First" (pp. 38-40) fits Lanier's description.

the small man is in bed and hath made his nightly wish that he
might see thee, and been kissed good night, and urged his usual
outcry that he does not feel at all like going to sleep, where-
after he is usually as now – slumbering profoundly in three
minutes; and here am I alone with my pen which I love because thereby I come nearest to thee – In the way of gossip
about mine own goings and comings thou wilt care to know
that I was at a pleasant little party in honor of Clare [de
Graffenried] given by Minnie Machen on Friday night; that I
dined today at Col. Edgar Dawson's, – one of the Georgia
colony in B°; that I afterwards went to bid Clare good bye at
the Machen's, and having so done strolled home with a dear
little girl of thirteen to whom I have taken a huge fancy, by
name Edith Gittings: that I have then repaired to my own
house and spent the remainder of the day and evening in reading to Charley the words of St. Matthew whereof he eagerly
absorbs Chapter after Chapter though I am sure he cannot
understand the half nor the tenth of the same.

Thou wilt also care to know that the boy says to me his
lessons every day, giving the two hours betwixt one and three
to study. His daily round is a reading-lesson of some four
pages, a column of spelling, a column of the multiplication-
table, and a page of writing. He has been through the table,
having yesterday recited the twelve-column successfully, and is
now practising the capital X's in writing. His main hopes and
energies are nowadays concentrated upon laying up money
enough to buy a velocipede. I sometime ago established a
system of financial rewards and punishments which has seemed
to work well. He receives, by the terms of our contract, fifty
cents a week to be applied to his own devices, but he is fined
one cent each for a great number of lapses and misdemeanors,
such as leaving a toy about the room, going to a meal without
cleaning his hands and nails, allowing water to stand in the
bowl, letting the door remain open, and a long catalogue of
the like felonies. Under the mulcts and losses of this scheme,
he usually accumulates some thirty cents nett each week, and
what with other little odds and ends of income he seems likely
to have his velocipede in a month or so, though he sometimes
bewails the snail-pace of his riches with much pathos. I could
not find just the place to suit him in the way of kindergartens:

and there were some considerations in favor of my present plan which seemed to make it preferable.

Tomorrow I must go at hard work again, on the Centennial poem [41] for the magazine. I could wish very much that after that I might not be compelled to write any more for several months. I have now achieved a position where I can rest for a while with great advantage, and I greatly need a few months in which to gather the ends of my thoughts together, as well as to refresh a much-worn physique. I desire also to read many things which are of necessity to me in both my arts. — I have just been thinking that this is February, and that it is now exactly a year since " Corn " came out. How much I have been granted by the good God of the success an artist loves, in that time, and what immense strides I have made within my heart beyond the artistic crudeness and babyhood of this same February a year ago !

–   Tell little Sissa that Minnie Machen took me off into a corner this afternoon and asked me all manner of affectionate questions about her and discoursed most sweetly of the fair old days of their friendship at " Miss Gay and Melville's ".[42] We both agreed that Sissa was a person who had no Original Sin in her disposition.

I write these left-hand letters for pure fancy – and not from the old trouble, as thou wilt be surmising.

Loving, and in great need of love, I am, dear Wife, thine

Husband .

To Dudley Buck

66 Centre St.
Baltimore, Md.
Feby 14th 1876

Dear Mr. Buck:

      I hasten to say in reply to yours just received that I thoroughly understood— and explained to Gen. Hawley —your idea that the poem would probably find publicity

[41] " The Psalm of the West " (I, 62), written by request for *Lippincott's Magazine,* where it was published in July, 1876.

[42] The reference is presumably to Lanier's uncle, Melville Anderson, and his wife.

through some member of the chorus and that it was better to forestall that by a previous authentic publication. I was careful to do this because I thankfully recognize that the forethought was purely a friendly one on your part, since you had no personal interest in the printing of my poem.

I return the proof. After seeing the thing in print I am thoroughly satisfied that for many reasons which I have not now time to detail it is better that *all* the exclamations in the early part of the proof of the poem should be *in italics without any marks whatever*: and I have so corrected the proof. I hope there will be no trouble in getting in all the corrections, and will be glad if you can call the printer's special attention to the punctuation-marks as they stand corrected, inasmuch as the intelligibility of the poem depends in an unusual degree upon them, in consequence of the great compression of matter in it.

Thanks for the message from Mr. Cornell, to whom I beg you will convey my pleasantest remembrances when you meet him again.[43]

I'm very glad you are instrumenting the Cantata fully: the orchestra is my dream and my delight; — and I wouldn't mind playing one of your three flute-parts myself at the opening! This is indeed, seriously speaking, a charming hope which Mr. Thomas held out to me when I last saw him, — that his orchestra would probably be increased at Philadelphia and that in such event he was going to offer me the additional flute. –But I've heard nothing more of it, and only fear that it is quite too nice to be carried out.

I congratulate you on your progress. You must be a good worker.

Very truly yours,

Sidney Lanier

---

[43] Buck had written, Feb. 12, 1876: " Mr. John H. Cornell spent an evening with me lately — alluded to having seen the ' Tribune ' article & spoke in very pleasant terms of you."

To Mary Day Lanier

Bo. Md.
Feby 16th 1876

My dear Heart, This is only to carry thee a kiss. How long it seems since I have kissed thee ! I am working on the Centennial poem, and go in a few minutes to our rehearsal which is from five to seven P. M.

The sonnet to Charlotte Cushman is in the March Lippincott (now just out) as also my third India paper. Mr. Peacock writes that they both are "charming". Charlotte Cushman does not know I have sent the poem to the printer, and it will be a pleasant surprise to her. Mr. Peacock writes of many pleasant allusions in the current papers – *apropos* of the cantata appointment, – to "the new poet, S. L.".

I wrote some days ago to have some funds sent thee from Macon, and these will be supplemented in a day or two by more from the last India installment wh. I will receive certainly within a week. I am full of concern over thy statement of health. Here is some colder weather which I greatly hope will be of benefit to thee.

I sent the tooth-brushes two days ago.

God be thy Strength and Refuge and Patience, dear Wife, prayeth thy

lover and husband.

To Mary Day Lanier

Parker House
Boston, Mass.
Feb. 21st 1876

My Sweet Child, Thou wilt have seen in the papers the sorrowful telegram which explains my presence here.[44] Mr. Cushman (Charlotte's nephew and adopted son) telegraphed me to come as his guest, and I knew it was her wish, so I came. Charley is with me.

[44] Charlotte Cushman had died on Feb. 18, 1876.

I have just seen in the papers that Judge Herring is dead, and his sister very ill. I will hasten to New York tonight, and write thee again tomorrow, more fully, from there. Of course I will go immediately to Judge H's house to find out all.

I write in the greatest haste. The whole city is pouring through the rooms where dear Cushla is lying with the largest, calmest, most majestical face I ever saw, to get a last look at her. The funeral is in a half hour.

God bless thee and keep thee, prays thy

lover .

To Mary Day Lanier

New York.
Feby. 23rd 1876

My dear Heart. It is late at night. I have been running through the bitter cold all day on many errands, and I will but send thee my worship in this brief hymn wherewith I close my labor. I have written thy Father a letter containing such details of Judge Herring's death as I have been able to gather. Miss Mary is now dangerously ill, though better than on yesterday. I will communicate with thee more fully when I get back to my desk at Baltimore, where I long to be, tired wayfarer as I am. Charley has been with Russell and Aunt Mary Sid [45] all the afternoon, and evening, and I have still to go for him (up to thirtieth street) before I get me to bed. He is in love with New York and begs that I will buy a house near the city and live there so that we can come in every day. God answer his childish petition! I love thee much more than I did yesterday, though not so much as I will tomorrow. Thus forever grows in love

thy
lover.

Clifford should hand thee twenty dollars herewith: I hope the twenty five from Macon is come. I leave here so as to get to Philadelphia on Friday, and to Baltimore on Saturday.

[45] A nickname for Lanier's Aunt Mary, widow of Sidney C. Lanier.

To Robert Lanier

66 Centre St.
Baltimore, Md.
Feb'y. 26th 1876

My dear Father:

I reached home last night after a week's absence, and found your letter. Mr. Cushman (Miss Cushman's nephew and adopted son) telegraphed me on Saturday that a room was ready for me at the Parker House, and I felt constrained to do this last act – all I could ever do– in honor of one whom I loved so dearly and who was so fond of me. So I started off on Saturday night, spent Monday in Boston – where I was treated altogether as one of the family and participated with them in the funeral services – and on Monday night returned to New York. Business kept me there, and in Philadelphia, until yesterday. I had a great deal of wearisome running about to do in New York, and as the thermometer was within some ten or twelve degrees of zero, with a raw wind blowing people off their legs, I caught a violent cold which took complete possession of me, body and spirit, yesterday. Today, here in Baltimore, is as bland as Florida, and I am greatly better, though much worn by a hard week's work.

Mary has enclosed me your letter to her, and I note what you say as to rest. I will try to go a little slower; but it is very difficult.

I found also the Telegraph & Messenger with notice of " Florida ", and am very much obliged by Mr. Jones' kindly appreciation. I saw Lippincott yesterday: he told me the book was selling very well. He had filled some orders for California. I noticed also, in Trübners' (of London) " Centennial List of Guide Books ", an advertisement of " Florida ", as by me, with title in full: but don't know whether it is an English reprint or not.

I saw Mr. Taylor at his house in New York, and had a charming two hours' talk with him. Also Aunt Helen and husband, who sent their love to you and Uncle C: also Aunt Mary Sid and her two boys, who did likewise.[46]

---

[46] The people mentioned in this sentence were: the Ronald MacDonalds, Clifford Anderson, and the family of Sidney C. Lanier.

Charlotte Cushman died without knowing of her approaching dissolution, indeed thinking that she was better only a few hours before the end.   She was wholly unconscious for two hours before death.   It seems that, several days before this, she had spoken of giving me a certain antique ring – a jacynth, with the tragic and comic masks cut in intaglio – which had been presented to her in Rome: and this Miss Stebbins handed to me.   It is said to be very rare and valuable.

I am in great strait for money.   If you can send me forty dollars it will be of great service to me.

Charley unites with me in loving messages to you and Mama, and all who are near you.

Your Son

S. L.

Tell Uncle C. I saw Uncle Melville [47] in Phª yesterday.   He sent love: and was very well.

To Mary Day Lanier [48]

Bᵒ.   Feby 26th 1876

My poor Heart, In all thou sayest of thy pleasure and exaltation over Booth I see so many things that I scarce know where to begin saying all the sermon that unfolds itself from this sweet text of thee.

First: I see that, as I have always told thee, thou hast the true artist's need to mingle thy Self with whatever Art is toward: and also the other true artist's need to say thy Self in some way.   What I said to thee upon this topic some weeks ago was merely confined to musical considerations because thou hadst spoken of it in that connection.   Thou art, without regard to Music or any other Form, a genuine Artist: and speakest never a word but showeth the same.   Hereof I have thought much, of late times: and I have quite settled with myself that thou art to be a noble and beautiful violin player.   Thou art

---

[47] Melville Anderson was at this time living in Philadelphia.

[48] In her letter of Feb. 19, 1876, to which this is a detailed answer, Mary Day Lanier had told her husband of seeing Edwin Booth in *Hamlet* the night before.

to begin thy lessons as soon as thou comest to me, here or in Ph^a : and art to be spoken of in the future as a great player. Thy hand, thine arm, thine eye, thy nature, these all belong to the violin: an it please God, thou shalt carry out all these sweet functions. Thou art now just ripe for the violin.

Secondly. I see, with my heart breaking for very tenderness, how greatly thy life as to art hath been repressed, and to what a savage hunger thou art brought by long starvation in this behalf. To a poor famished Castaway, a hunk of mouldy ship's bread would taste like food from Heaven: and so it is (partly) to thee that thou art quite ravished away with Booth. I say *partly* so it is: because it is partly from another cause, towit, that thou attributest to Booth the majesty and the wonder of the words which he speaks, – whereas these are Shakespeare's and thy passion is, in very truth, for the latter.   For indeed Booth is not a great artist at all, and thou wouldst be wofully disappointed in his presentation of Hamlet if thou shouldst see it three years hence. I saw it, here, just before he started South: [49] it is most faulty in several grave particulars; indeed Booth is well-known among the artists and art-lovers as a man not nearly tall enough in soul to be a great Hamlet or a great anything. Whereof are many evidences, which I cannot now detail to thee. For three reasons I am mainly glad thou didst not send thy note. It is much too fine and high for him, and he would not have understood it.

I started, – to find thee saying that after seeing the Hamlet thou didst "walk home on air." So, exactly, did I, a month before, after seeing this same Hamlet. But it was not Booth's acting that gave me this lightness and exaltation of spirit: I found it not at all satisfactory, with its epileptic sinkings and weak frenzies. It was the pure force of this divine composition, which attains to such a height as the reaching hand of man has not touched before or since. Do you know what Hamlet means? He is Man without Belief. Polonius is Orthodox Religion after it has ceased to be persecuted, and has become fashionable and pliant and as it were place-hunting.

[49] Lanier had also probably seen Booth in *Richard II* when it was played in Baltimore on Jan. 14, 1876. Charlotte Cushman had sent him on Jan. 11 a letter of introduction to Booth, but there is no record of a meeting between them.

The Grave-scene is the most immense conception of all Tragedy, to me: it is the Apparition of Death upon a world which has not yet learned the meaning of Life: how bleak it is, it is only Skulls and Regret, there is no comfort in it.

But Death, my God, it is the sweetest and dearest of all the Angels to him who understands. -- If thou coulds't have seen the face of my dear vanished Cushla the other day !

Now can I not write thee further. With unspeakable devout worship and longing I am thy

husband .

To Bayard Taylor [50]

66 Centre St.
Baltimore, Md.
Feby. 27th 1876

My dear Mr. Taylor:

Pray tell me how you are. I wished for you all day yesterday with special fervor, thinking how the bland and sunny air that bathed us all here would have soothed your malady. I was grieved to miss your call, and would have run round to inquire about you but was entirely occupied by business until six when I quitted New York for Philadelphia.[51] It has been but up-hill work with me to struggle against the sense of loss which the departure of my beloved Charlotte Cushman leaves with me. She and you were the only friends among the Artists I have ever had: and since she is gone I am as one who has lost the half of his possessions. The passion to which my devotion to her had grown takes it hard when sight and hearing are both become forevermore impossible. Today, though keenly desirous to rest after a week of great strain, this little poem [52] teased me till it was on paper. I hope you will think it not wholly unworthy. As I read it over now, a disagreeable fancy comes that the last two lines of it are

---

[50] Previously published, *Atlantic Monthly*, LXXXIII, 800 (June, 1899); reprinted, *Letters* (New York, 1899), pp. 146-147.

[51] A card in the Charles D. Lanier Collection, Johns Hopkins University, bears Taylor's pencilled note: " For S. Lanier, Esq. Bayard Taylor. A little better, but must go home— too much wind."

[52] " At First (To Charlotte Cushman.)" (I, 200).

somewhat like something of somebody else, and these vague
" somes " are intolerable.   Pray tell me if this is so.[53]

Make my compliments to Mrs. Taylor.   I hope Miss Taylor
is quite recovered.

Charley joins me in love to you; and I am always

Your friend

S. L.

To Mary Day Lanier

B° Mch. 5th 1876

All the world has a Cold, dear Heart, during this last week:
and I have not yet had the pleasure of bidding farewell to mine.
Today I have mostly spent lying on the bed, though I have
attended table. I have great misery from a kind of feverish
irritation in the face which I suppose is catarrhal. Tonight,
however, driven by uncontrollable desire to look out upon
some larger prospect than my cracked walls, I have wandered
out alone into the warm moonlight, and shuffled about – in a
gait which I fear would have compromised my reputation for
sobriety in the day time – past the churches where I saw happy
men worshipping with their wives, and past the blessed lights
in home-windows revealing genial libraries and cosy family
parties. I have tried to still the cries of my heart by stretching
out my hands and laying them as it were on these house-roofs
for the imposition of the blessing of the homeless: and this
has not been difficult, for somehow when one walks under the
stars one feels taller than houses, one can patronize that which
in lower moods one might envy.

But I am withal more empty-hearted than ever for thee and
I must even go sleep and win the exquisite chance that some
dream of the night will be more piteous than the dream of
today and bring me where I may at least see thee.

[53] Taylor replied, Mar. 4, 1876 (*Letters*, New York, 1899, p. 147): " Your
poem is strong and full of feeling, with which the occasional roughness entirely
harmonizes. The idea is a little similar to a poem of mine, ' The Mystery,' but
is very differently expressed. I notice no resemblance to anything in the last
lines."

Thy small man is better of his cold, and hath been to church – today with Eleanor Latrobe. He had a field-day yester-day, – with his first visit to the Negro Minstrels. A rehearsal prevented me from going with him: he came back however in great feather and expounded to me many wonderful things. He has such a consuming passion for companionship as I have never seen: and the boys with whom he has scraped acquaint-ance are sighed for, as a mistress by a lover, when he is not with them. What will be the final outcome of a soul so plastic as this, – is more than now can be revealed.

God be thy Sleep, and I thy Dream, tonight, dear Love, cries thy

lover.

To Mary Day Lanier

[Baltimore, Mar. 9, 1876?] [54]

My Sweetest Soul, The picture is thine, only the outline is but bold: wit, grace, genius, these thou hast liberally; and many more sweetnesses, such as I would I might have beheld beaming under thy white cap. I fancy thou must have been simply ravishing in this costume, and I make no doubt I would have been plunged in the same low state with this newspaper-writer if I too could have stood " in the door-way ".[55]

I have been in bed for three days with such a cold as the gods do not probably brew more than once in a man's lifetime. I should have gone to bed on Monday morning: but had promised Leo Wheat [56] to play at his two concerts here, and there were

---

[54] Conjectural dating from the facts of Lanier's three-day illness (beginning Tuesday, Mar. 7) detailed in the second paragraph.

[55] Mary Day Lanier had written, Mar. 5, 1876, of a Centennial costume party in Montgomery which she had attended " in Martha Washington cap and kerchief and stately flowing black silk and velvet." Lanier apparently refers to a newspaper account of the party sent with her letter.

[56] Leo P. Wheat was a pianist who directed a series of charity concerts for the benefit of the Ladies' Relief Association at the Academy of Music on Mar. 6-8; Lanier is listed as playing the flute obligato to *The Shepherd's Lament* sung by Miss Jenny Busk at the last concert (see the Baltimore *Gazette*, Mar. 7 and 9, 1876). Wheat was apparently a friend of Virginia C. Clay and Virginia Hankins, through whom he was known to Lanier.

reasons (he thought he had been badly treated by the Germans in Balt°) why I should make extraordinary exertions to fulfill the engagements. But they were very hard on me, and so on Tuesday night I fell into bed after the concert and have not since been out. My homoeopathic doctor attends me: he says it is catarrh, coming upon a system long needing rest. I will be up on Sunday, and out on Monday: it is very fortunate for Solomon Grundy that this week is not a concert-week.

But next week is: and the last. I know not what I will do then. Whatever it be, it will tend towards thee directly. I am very tired, and my spirit hath need of thine. I must finish my Centennial poem in order to get money enough to do anything. Now am I lean-pursed beyond description. I do not hear anything further from Thomas: but will write to Mr. Buck when I get well.[57]

I am rejoiced to think of thee at the Tea-parties and the like—.

My catarrh does not seem to have materially affected aught but my head: and I am much better today, suffering more from pure prostration than otherwise. I will write thee again to-morrow. Miss Dunbar and the Youngs [58] are unceasingly kind and attentive.

My little Hawwy, how I ache for his fervent arms round my neck. God keep thy heart and thine eyes so that the former shall be full, until the latter also are, of thy

lover.

---

[57] In a letter to his wife, Mar. 2, 1876 (here omitted), Lanier had written: " I am all undecided as to my plans . . . and will be so until I hear finally from Thomas. I have procured a wooden flute which I think will answer my purposes.
" I am in midst of my Centennial poem for the Magazine. I hope to finish it in three weeks' time. If all should turn out well with Thomas, I would either come for thee, or send for thee, in a month from now, or thereabout. Were it not for lack of funds, I should like amazingly to come to thee, then, in Montg'y, and spend a month among all the people, in absolute rest from work. I am desperately tired."
[58] The family next door, with whom Lanier had formerly roomed; he and his son still boarded there.

To Mary Day Lanier

Bo. Md.
Mch. 10th 1876

My Too-Sweet One, Charley has gone,—from early after
dinner—to seek his beloved " boys ": and Wysham has been in
for an hour, letting off little watery puns (which he pathetically
entreats me not to consider very wicked, but only the mis-
chievous element in him) and drooling dismal tunes out of
Terschak and the Italian Opera on the flute: and now he is
gone, and in the twilight a hand-organ has waked the lyre
again, sounding loud as the crack of doom in the stone-paved
street: and now he too is gone, and I am in such a helpless
blank of longing for thee that I am for all the world but
another gray twilight done into scant flesh: and here have I
crawled out of bed to sit at my desk and tell thee how dear
thou art—nay, but to begin to stammer to thee how dear thou
art—to thy lacking-thee-lacking-all

lover.

To Bayard Taylor [59]

66 Centre St.
Baltimore, Md.
Mch. 11th 1876

My dear Mr. Taylor:

I've only just crawled out of a sick-bed
where I have been spending one of the most unsatisfactory
weeks of my existence — a week whose place in the General
Plan of Good I find as much difficulty in justifying as croton-
bugs or children born idiots or the sausage-grinding School of
poetry.

I have particularly desired to write you about The Hymn.[60]

---

[59] Previously published, *Atlantic Monthly*, LXXXIII, 800-801 (June, 1899);
reprinted, *Letters* (New York, 1899), pp. 147-151.

[60] In his letter of Mar. 4, 1876 (*Letters*, New York, 1899, p. 147), Taylor
had sent Lanier a copy of his Hymn for the opening ceremonies of the Centennial Exhibition, saying: " I ask you to be as frank with me about it as I am
wont to be with you."

Of course the value of a friend's criticism in this kind is simply
that when one has to write in a hurry, the friend is in the nature
of one's own Conscience of Beauty (as you have beautifully
called your wife) *as that conscience will be after the coolness
of time has come.*   The friend is a mere anticipation of time, –
oneself-after-awhile.   Purely upon this theory I acquire boldness enough to say what follows.

1st, generally.   Inasmuch as the opening verse presents a noble
Tema, or motive, of triple design, in the ideas of

$$\text{The God of} \quad \left\{ \begin{array}{l} \text{Peace} \\ \text{Toil} \\ \text{\& Beauty} \end{array} \right\},$$

would it not be best to carry on this motive entirely through
the poem, making (say) the II verse converge upon the idea
of Peace, the III upon Toil, IV upon Beauty (or Art) and (–if
you choose) V re-gathering the whole by means of some common tone, – the whole thus gaining perfect unity of impression ?
In looking down the poem with this view, one easily sees that
with a very small change of phraseology it can be perfectly
carried out.   In the III verse you have indeed returned to the
original motive in a very beautiful manner: – the oak of toil,
the rose of art &c.   The II verse ought on three accounts clearly
to be stricken out: (1) it is a departure from the whole plan
of the poem; (2) it is explanatory of what all the parties to the
hymn thoroughly understand already to be the situation: (3)
it is below the plane of the other conceptions.   Conceding
these views for a moment (and I think there can be no doubt
that your cool judgment after a while will estimate the poem
precisely according to the success with which it carries out the
general scheme indicated), the following will be an outline of
the poem as it will finally appear:

I

(Just as you have it; or with any transposition, of the lines
that may seem desirable to facilitate the new arrangement).

———"———.

II

(For this you can take your number IV, and with a slight change of idea make the whole refer to PEACE, as for example a general supplication that, although our eras are but as dust, yet dust may become fruitful, and Peace may be vouchsafed as the climate favorable &c &c).

III

(This is nearly ready, in the number III of the poem, which closes with the lovely reference to the oak of Toil and the rose of Beauty (or Art). The opposition of these two is so fine that it suffices to authorize the consolidated treatment of the ideas of Toil and Beauty in one and the same verse.)

IV

(For this your number V can easily be made to serve by directing its general tone upon the three prominent ideas already treated, having reference to the exchanging of each with each, and the relation of each to the God of the three, thus making a perfect return to the I and ending as it were upon the tonic.   This would make the poem perfect in four stanzas: and it can all be done without altering the structure of the sentences at all, and with only changing here and there a noun, a verb, or an adjective, so as to make the sense point always towards the thematic ideas.

2nd.

If, however, this does not happen to meet your fancy, and you decide to retain the poem as it is, there are one or two minor matters to which your attention should be called.

1st. I am clear that the II should either disappear entirely, or be replaced, – for the reasons hereinbefore stated.

2d   In III the sounds of " *thy guidance* " (y and long i), and of " made failure " (two long a's), seem bad, particularly as they come so close to each other.

3rd. In IV, the idea in the two lines which come after the first two should be a more closely logical *sequitur* upon them.

4th The fourth line of V (I mean " Thyself in *him* " only; the rest of the line is perfect) can be justified in one's thought, but it compels one to think hard in order to do that,— and this is a disadvantage. Can you not make it a little more transparent? Again: the last two lines might *so* easily be made to re-affirm and point the first stanza as well as the whole poem: e.g.

All conquering PEACE thy gift divine,

All Toil, all Beauty, { shadowing / meeting / imaging / based on &c ? } Thine !

I think further, in reference to these last two lines, that it would be well to give them either a stronger hold by a verb of some sort, or some turn more precisely parallel with the rest of the verse. The first two couplets commence with

Let each with each,

& Let " in " , which is fine: – it is somewhat weakening the force of these to close with a grammatically independent couplet which has no verb at all.

— Of course you understand that I like the poem (except the II verse): all the ideas are noble, and there is a simple grandeur in the expressions which is fine. All my suggestions are made simply with a view to concentrate the impression. The shot are all good: let them not scatter, but strike like one bullet.

Pray let me see the poem again, as soon as you put it in final form.

Charley sends love. I am rejoiced to know that you are quite recovered: bronchitis always scares me. Let your two ladies know that they are held in good remembrance: and believe me always

Your friend

S. L.[61]

[61] In his reply, Mar. 17, 1876 (*Letters*, New York, 1899, pp. 151-152), Taylor agreed with Lanier's detailed criticisms, but declared: " I don't entirely agree with you in regard to a rigid architectural structure for the hymn. . . . [This] would give a too conscious air of design. Here, again, is an instance where you cannot apply the laws of Music to Poetry."

To Clifford A. Lanier

Bo Mch. 11th 1876

My dear Clifford:

Do not you want my silver flute? I have an opportunity to get two wooden Boehm flutes, which would admirably answer my purpose in the Orchestra (better than the silver) for $85.00; and if you can advance that amount I will send you the silver one (which cost $240. and will readily be saleable at $150 for the next ten years) to use for your own playing.[62] So much of my heart is in it that I don't mind giving it up to you. I will send also an Instruction Book which I have, and which will enable you in a couple of weeks to play with much satisfaction to yourself.

I am so anxious you should not waste the beautiful talent you have for music, that I do not hesitate to urge you to make this little investment in the eternities: and when I think of playing duos with you (if you only could hear some of Kuhlau's!) through some of the long happy days I hope to spend with you, it seems like a duty for you to practice. You could learn with great ease; and would be master of the instrument soon. You have the true *pathetic* tone: – and I have not heard any one else among the flutists who has.

If you should prefer, I could send you one of the wooden flutes, which are made exactly like the Silver; and I rather think you will like the tone better. It is broader, and fuller, and more suave than silver.

I have the refusal of this arrangement for about a week. I will make it immediately if you shall send the money. The condition of my own purse scouts such an idea.

God bless you, my dear, and all yours, says your hurried

Bro.

S. L.

[62] Clifford Lanier bought the silver flute. It is now in the possession of his daughter Wilhelmina (Mrs. John Tilley) of Montgomery, Ala. The wooden flutes are in the possession of Henry W. Lanier, New York City.

To Mary Day Lanier

Bo. Mch. 14th 1876

My dear Heart, Thy card announcing Sidney's convalescence is here, and several most sweet letters for which I would I had time to make adequate love to thee. My sickness has thrown my work much behind, and I have to make double time. The engravings with which the publishers wish to illustrate my Centennial poem will require some months for preparation and I must have the poem ready early in April. This gives me as much as I can do in the next three weeks.

I have been attacked with a lot of painfully-delicious dreams of MARIETTA, during the last two or three days. The thought of a long sweet summer in that free air with thee, when I would feel (as I have never been, there) that I had the right to rest and to thoroughly enjoy everything; the thought of the music we might have, the strolls we might have, the love-making over the valley to Kennesaw, the birds in the Earle-yard, the trees, the blackberries, the brook over towards Rood's,—ha! what a dream is here!

— But I must to other dreams. Wherever thou art, there will be summer, and all summer's contents, to thy

lover.

P.S. Curiously in consonance with this Marietta dream comes a pleasant letter from Mrs. Carter [63] (thou rememberest her, with the little lame son, Robbie, and the small Mr. Edmunds, both from Massachusetts?) making affectionate enquiries anent thee. She had seen some notices of my poems and extracts therefrom, and desired to remind me of a promise that I would let her know of my writings and our general welfare &c. I will send thee the letter when I have answered it.

Thine

---

[63] Apparently Mrs. Carter Edmunds. A surviving letter from Lanier to " Mrs. Edmunds," Mar. 20, 1876 (here omitted), fits the facts in this paragraph; no letter by her has been found.

To Mary Day Lanier [64]

Bo   Mch. 18th 1876.

My Sweetest Heart, I have just come from the last concert, whereof I send thee herein a programme. A certain sense of melancholy is upon me – the last of anything is *per se* not joyful – but I quite kill it with the thought that I am now entirely free to be with thee as soon as I shall have finished my Centennial Ode. I do not know how soon this will be: it *ought* to be in the hands of the printers and engravers early in April: but it has been so much interrupted by illness and a thousand little extraneous matters that I fear it will be late. However the God of the humble poet is very great, and I have had so many signal instances of His upholding grace that I do not now ever quite despair of anything. Thomas is to be here next Wednesday, and I hope then to have some final report from him whether he will be able to put in another flute upon his Orchestra.

I have received a copy of the piano-score of the Cantata, which I will send to Father on Monday, with word to transmit to thee when he shall have read the poem, – which appears on the first page in connected shape, as well as in its proper place along the music. This piano-score is only written for the purpose of drilling the chorus: the full Orchestral score will soon be printed and I will then send thee a copy of that.

Thine enclosing C. C.'s letter and convoying thy father's and Cubbie's to Charley, are in my hand. I think by all means Cubbie should have the full advice of Mettauer in Macon after an examination with ether-treatment.[65] When I wrote him approving of his coming on to New York, I was under the impression that the Savannah examination had been full and satisfactory: but from his further account I am sure it could not have been decisive.

[64] Previously published, *Scribner's*, XXV, 751-752 (June, 1899); reprinted *Letters* (New York, 1899), pp. 113-114.

[65] Because of the serious illness of his daughter, Mary Louise, Harry Day was planning to take her to St. Luke's Hospital in New York for treatment (see Mary Day Lanier's letter of Feb. 26 and Lanier's answer of Mar. 2, 1876– here omitted).

Delia Roberts had written me of her engagement, in reply to a letter I wrote her some weeks ago. It goes to my heart that I never find time to write Mrs. Wallen or Mamie, – or indeed any one of a score of others to whom I [am] desirous of sending messages. I am continually and increasingly amazed at the intense rate of life at which I have to live here. There is never a moment when I have what cd. be called leisure: a duty of some sort is always ready. I am always pressed for time, and that too at the total neglect of scores of visits which I ought to pay here. I do not even have time to think out why it is so.

I hope thou wilt like my dactyls: I am greatly interested in them: they do roll most fairly upon the tongue when I say them aloud *ore rotundo*.[66] If I were only fresh, to write this poem ! – but it is done with a laggard spirit. I am tired, with much vain desiring of a sight of thy true eyes. I am sure I shall soon have this: upon this surety I have patience to bid thee good-night from this cruel distance, Dear Love, and to write myself, with not wholly paralyzed hand, thy

lover.

To LOGAN E. BLECKLEY [67]

66 Centre St., Baltimore, Md.
Mch. 20th, 1876.

Dear Judge Bleckley:

I've been ill ever since your letter came — the general result of a year of frightful overwork — and what with the accumulation of matters that *had* to be done (the Magazines *must* come out, you know, at the appointed time, though the heavens fall) I have not had, in the times when I have been able to write, the ten minutes to acknowledge your kind messages which I received a month ago.

[66] The reference is to a part of " The Psalm of the West " which Lanier had sent to his wife. In his letter of Mar. 11, 1876 (here omitted), he had written: " tell me what impression this succession of spondees and dactyls makes: it forms the invocation to my Centennial poem for the magazine."

[67] Previously published, Morgan Callaway, Jr., ed., *Select Poems of Sidney Lanier* (New York, 1895), p. xxx; excerpts reprinted, Mims, pp. 163-164.

It is a striking commentary on the vanity of fame, — that you say you "have not seen anything from my pen for a long time." I have been working at such a rate as, if I could keep it up, would soon make me the proverb of fecundity that Lope da Vega now is, ever since last June. In December last Lippincott's published a book of mine on Florida. It has been very successful; but I did not send you a copy because, although the book is written with just as rigid a conscience as any of my poems, yet from the nature of the subject it could not be upon such a plane as I desire everything to be that I send you. There was no possibility of making it a great book. I was employed to write it, by some persons who were interested in having a more elaborate presentation of Florida made to the world than has been heretofore given.

Besides this, five [68] papers in Lippincott's Magazine, beginning with the January 1876 number, called " Sketches of India," are by me. They purport to be written by a traveller in India (of course, the nature of the *jeu d'esprit* is explained at the end of the last one), and the collection of the multitudinous particulars involved in them cost me such a world of labor among the libraries of Boston, New York, Philadelphia and Baltimore as would take a long time to describe.

In addition to these I've written a number of papers not yet published; a dozen small poems which have appeared here and there; a poem for the Centennial Exhibition opening in May, at the invitation of the Centennial Commission, to be sung as a Cantata under the direction of Theodore Thomas; and part of a Centennial Ode, upon which I'm now engaged, to be published with illustrations in Lippincott's Magazine for the Fourth of July, 1876.[69]

All of which has been done outside of my regular duties as first flute of the Peabody Orchestra.

Thus, at the risk of boring you, I have made this enumeration in the way of indignant protest against your atrocious suggestions anent the flute.

[68] See note 24, above.

[69] In a letter to Mrs. Carter(?) Edmunds of the same date (Mar. 20, 1876, here omitted), after a similar review of his recent work, Lanier added: " I have not had time to collect my poems; but I hope to do so in time to print a volume next autumn."

No. I don't work for bread. In truth, I suppose that any
man who, after many days and nights of tribulation and bloody
sweat, has finally emerged from all doubt into the quiet and yet
joyful activity of one who *knows* exactly what his Great Passion
is and what his God desires him to do, — will straight way
lose all anxiety as to what he is working *for*, in the simple
glory of doing that which lies immediately before him . As
for me, life has resolved simply into a time during which I
want to get upon paper as many as possible of the poems with
which my heart is stuffed like a schoolboy's pocket. He would
indeed be in pitiable case who would write nowadays, if any
one can write so, from without — for the hope of any reward.
It is now even as when dear old William Drummond of
Hawthornden said, in that simple and powerful sonnet:

> I know how all the Muse's heavenly lays,
> With toil of Sprite * which are so dearly bought,
> As idle sounds, if few or none are sought;
> And that naught is than airy praise.
> . . . .
>
> *Know what I list, this all cannot me move,*
> *But that, O me! — I both must write and love.*

I am rejoiced to know that you find your station [70] congenial
and not taxing your strength. Where are you going to dispose
of yourself for your rest this summer? I have a mighty yearning for the Marietta woods and old Kennesaw, — but I fear a
vain one until the price of poetry rises.

Let me hear from you. I am always

Your friend

Sidney Lanier.

* Spirit: old form. [Lanier's note.]

---

[70] Bleckley had been appointed Associate Justice of the Supreme Court of
Georgia in 1875.

To Bayard Taylor [71]

66 Centre St.
Baltimore, Md,
Mch. 20th 1876.

Bravissimo, dear Mr. Taylor: why, this is the very Fitness of Things: the appointment matches, as a rhyme matches a rhyme: nothing can be more evident than that God has temporarily taken the direction of matters into His own hands. I think with all honesty, and apart from friendly preference, that you will do the Ode far better than either of the three other gentlemen could: and I send you my congratulations and fair wishes with a certain sense of indignant triumph in the coming-to-pass of what ought to have been.

I see, from what you say in reply to my letter on the Hymn, that my musical associations have put me under a certain general suspicion, with you, of a propensity to impart the principles of musical construction into poetry.[72] But this was a principle far larger than any peculiar to music or to any one art. I am so much interested in it that I am going to beg you to let me plead the case with you a moment.

Permit me first to say that I came at it, not by any reasoning *prepense*, but by examination, afterwards, of wholly unconscious procedure. It revealed itself clearly to me in thinking about a little poem I wrote a few days ago. Perhaps I can best illustrate it by first quoting the poem, which is a pendant to a little song you have already seen, being No. II of " Rose-Morals " : [73]

---

[71] Previously published, *Atlantic Monthly*, LXXXIII, 802-803 (June, 1899); reprinted, *Letters* (New York, 1899), pp. 152-155. In his letter of Mar. 17, 1876 (*Letters*, pp. 151-152), Taylor had said that he had been asked to write the Ode for the " grand national celebration of the 4th of July " instead of the Hymn for the opening ceremonies. In his reply to the present letter, Mar. 23, 1876 (*Letters*, p. 155), he added that Whittier was to write the Hymn to be sung on the same occasion as Lanier's Cantata. And in his letter of Mar. 26 (*Letters*, pp. 156-158) he concluded: " The appropriateness of the two selections is admitted by everybody. You can now easily make yourself (as you are) the representative of the South in American Song."

[72] See note 61, above.

[73] See I, 60.

Soul, get thee to the heart
Of yonder tube-rose, hide thee there,
There breathe the meditations of thine Art
Suffused with prayer.

―――――――――

Of spirit grave, yet light,
How fervent fragances uprise
Pure-born from these most rich and yet most white
Virginities !

―――――――――

Mulched with unsavory death,
Grow, Soul, unto such white estate
That art and virginal prayer shall be thy breath,
Thy work, thy fate.

Now it seems to me – as a mere extended formulation of the
thoroughly unconscious action of the mind in this poem – that
every poem, from a Sonnet to Macbeth, has substantially these
elements, – (1) a Hero, (2) a Plot, and (3) a Crisis: and
that its perfection as a work of art will consist in the simplicity
and the completeness with which the first is involved in the
second and illustrated in the third. In the case of a short poem
the hero is the central Idea, whatever that may be: the plot
is whatever is said about that idea, its details all converging,
both in tone and in general direction, thereupon : and the
crisis is the unity of impression sealed or confirmed or climax'd
by the last connected sentence, or sentiment, or verse, of the
poem. Of course I mean that this is the most general expression of the artistic plan of a poem: it is the system of verses,
which may be infinitely varied, but to which all variations may
be finally referred. I do not think that there is, as you feared,
any *necessary* reason why a poem so constructed should present
" a too-conscious air of design ": that is a matter which will
depend solely upon the genuineness of the inspiration and the
consummate command of his resources by the artist.

Is not this frame-work essentially that of every work of any
art ? Does not every painting, every statue, every architectural
design owe whatever it has of artistic perfection to the nearness
with which it may approach the fundamental scheme of a

Ruling Idea (or Hero), a Plot (or involution of the Ruling Idea
in complexities related to or clustering about it), and a Denoue-
ment, or Impression-as-a-whole?

I don't mean this for a theory: I hate theories, I intend it
only to be a convenient synthesis of a great number of small
facts: and therefore I don't stickle at all for calling the elements
of a work of art " Heroes ", or " Plots ", or " Crises ", and the
like–, only using those terms as the shortest way of expressing
my meaning.

Any way, fair fall the Ode.   I hope that God will let you
into Heaven, with no limitations as to walking on the grass or
picking the flowers, – till you've got all you want.

Mr. Buck has sent me a copy of the Piano-score of the Cantata, but I have not yet had time to examine it thoroughly.
Anything will go well, though, with a large chorus to sing it
and Thomas' Orchestra to play it.

If it will not trouble you I will be glad if you'll send me
whatever announcement of your appointment shall be made.

Charley joins me in fair remembrances to you and the ladies
of your house.

Write me soon, as to your always desirous

S. L.

To Bayard Taylor [74]

66 Centre St.
Baltimore, Md.
Mch. 24th 1876

Dear Mr. Taylor:
Don't trouble to write me any elaborate reply.
I only sent you this continuation of my thought about the
centralization of ideas in poems because I have been studying
your work within the last two or three months and have become
clearly satisfied that *that* is the direction in which you should
grow. You tend *from* it by reason of the very stress and crowding of the multitudinous good things which you give to the
world. I find poems of yours in which every sentiment, every

[74] Previously published, *Atlantic Monthly*, LXXXIII, 803 (June, 1899); reprinted, *Letters* (New York, 1899), pp. 155-156.

thought every line, — *as* sentiment, thought, or line — is exquisite, and yet which do not give a full white light *as poems* for want of a proper convergence of the components upon a single point. Sometime we will talk of this: I am not at all sure that in my hasty letters — for I am worked almost to the annihilation of sleep and of meals — I have given anything like a clear idea of what I mean.[75]

— But this *do* write me: what do you mean by your " Tribune-work "? Are you officially connected with the paper: and how?

Interrogatory 2d : Please state why Longfellow, Bryant, & Lowell declined the Ode.

I am going night and day on *my* Centennial Ode for the Magazine, which is to be illustrated and made the feature of the July number. It has to be furnished early in April, and I am only about half through.

Some people will put their hands to their ears at the doctrine it preaches.

My musical engagement here is now completed, and as the poem is the only piece of work I have, I suppose God intends me to feed on blackberries all the summer.

Charley sends you his love, with which also goes that of

your friend

S. L.

To Dudley Buck

66 Centre St.
Baltimore, Md.
March 26th 1876

Dear Mr. Buck:

I think it will *go* admirably. Your procedure in keeping the voices to the utmost simplicity of movement quite fulfils my idea of fitness. The melody seems grave, large, and

[75] In his reply of Mar. 26, 1876 (*Letters*, New York, 1899, pp. 156-158), Taylor wrote: " You are quite right in your application of your scheme of Song to many of my poems; I am well aware of the deficiencies of my early work." But he added: " Poetical ideas have a wilful being of their own, and there are cases where they are best expressed through an apparent disregard of form."

worthy: and I am pleased with the progressiveness of all the voices. I think it ought to be thoroughly successful when brought out, I hope you have given everything in the orchestra plenty to do:—for I find that Wagner is to have a march in the beginning, and you know how gloriously full are his scores. By the way, can this march be that magnificent Huldiguns March I heard Theodore Thomas play here on Wednesday night last?

Pray cause them to send me as many copies of the final edition of the full score as can be spared: indeed, I suppose the Commission will not object to do us the grace of giving us a dozen or two of their copies. I want some for my friends. Have you sent one to Gen. Hawley? I did not send him any ms. of the poem, expecting to have it in print, and I do not know whether he has yet seen it.

As to your proposition that I write for you, sometime, the text of some large work; it would give me great pleasure to co-operate with you in this way. I take an interest, much too deep to *say* anything about, in the problem (not yet completely solved) of the proper relation of articulate to inarticulate tones, and desire to contribute towards its solution the result of many humble, but very loving, meditations.—I hope we may talk of your project, sometime.

I write in the greatest haste, being chained night and day to a piece of magazine work which is much behind time in consequence of my illness.

I am always glad to have a line from you.

Sincerely yours,

Sidney Lanier.

To Mary Day Lanier

66 Centre St.

B⁰ Md.

Mch. 26th 1876

My poor Heart, Hast thou suffered so wretchedly? I am ready to quit all and fly to thee. Alas, that if I did, I could not give thee complete ease ! But thou has not the right to abuse my

Darling as thou dost ! What am I worth to thee if I cannot receive the overpourings of thy too-full discomfort ? Thou must not chide thyself that thou writest me of thine ills : – thou art my Sweetest One and I will not have thee chidden by anybody !

— Tomorrow, – this being Sunday, when I cannot – I will cause to be shipped to thee a dozen botles of Hathorne Water. 'Tis much like Congress, being a recent spring found near that, at Saratoga. But the effect is the most delightfully complete and satisfactory I have ever experienced, – in two or three trials I have given it. Thou art to drink a bottle *immediately* before breakfast, taking coffee thereat. I think thou wilt be greatly relieved with the first experiment.

I have been on the divine heights of my art for several days and nights, and the poem has grown fast. I hope to finish it in ten days. I work about fourteen hours out of twenty four. I think Charley has his own private idea that I am mildly insane.

But all my song is sung just above a strenuous set of sweet longings for thee, – even as a solo on the stage wherebelow sits the Orchestra in heavenly commotions of harmony.

God grant that my aspirations may soon find thee, prays thy

lover .

To Mary Day Lanier

Bo. Mch. 30th 1876

How it is, dear Soul, that four times twenty four hours have wedged themselves in between this day and that on which I wrote thee last, — is a matter into which I dare not enter for I shd. consume the same time in explaining it.

I sent the bottles of Hathorne water on Monday – ½ dozen – consigned to Clifford. My experience is: that one must *go* immediately after breakfast: any delay, although there be no intimations, is hurtful: after taking one bottle, endeavor to do without any more as long as possible: and do not take more than two bottles consecutively.

Here comes a fair letter from Emma Stebbins, with much

about the project for a Life of Charlotte Cushman.[76] I will be
full proud and happy to do this work, and I judge from E. S.'s
letter that it will be likely the matter which will occupy the
last half of my summer and the early fall. But of this we will
talk soon.

We will talk ! — — I begin to see the end of my poem. I
do not dare to say when I will see thee, in this chaos: but it
will not be very long first.

Poor Heart, poor Heart, how wretched thou art ! Thy
piteous letters are wrought into the tissue of my soul, as the
sorrow that goes on nightly unweaves itself with the night, —
for even as Night is Grief's Lover,   so   am   I

Thine .

To Bayard Taylor [77]

66 Centre St.
Baltimore, Md.
April 1st 1876

My dear Mr. Taylor:

Will you do me the favor to read this [78]
and send it back to me, if you do not find it objectionable? I
am going to offer it to the Tribune. If they print it, so: if they
do not, I will try some one else. I have endeavored to speak

[76] Emma Stebbins had written on Mar. 1, 1876, that Helen Hunt (Jackson)
wanted to write the official memoir of Charlotte Cushman, but that she " could
not accept her as the right one for the task " even if she had not had a conversation with Miss Cushman about Lanier. And on Mar. 27 she wrote that Edwin
Cushman, her nephew and adopted son, wanted Lanier to come to Newport to
make plans for the memoir.

[77] Previously published, *Atlantic Monthly*, LXXXIII, 803 (June, 1899) ; reprinted, *Letters* (New York, 1899), pp. 158-159.

[78] A letter by Lanier addressed to the Editor of the New York *Tribune*. It
was an answer to the notice of the " Centennial Cantata " in the issue of Mar.
31, 1876, by the *Tribune's* music critic, J. R. G. Hassard, who confined himself
for the most part to a detailed analysis of Buck's composition. He praised the
score generously, saying that the music was " simple and clear in expression,
while Mr. Lanier's language is sometimes obscure." He then pointed out some
of the pitfalls Lanier had set for the composer, who, however, " escaped them
all with great skill "—especially lines 17-22 which he called " a tough morsel."
Lanier's defense of his poem was finally published in the *Tribune* on May 20,
1876 (II, 266). The controversy is discussed at length in the letters of the
next two months.

with the utmost justice towards the Tribune's critic, and modesty as regards myself. If you can make any suggestions to me which will enable me to see it otherwise than a duty *to speak at all*, I will be profoundly thankful to you. In any case of a poem of my own private giving forth, I would never dream of rebuking the most brutal critic for mistaking my artistic purposes as artistic ignorances: but many of the people who will read this Tribune attack are not only incapable of judging its correctness but will be prevented from seeing the whole poem for yet six weeks, and will therefore come to its final perusal with the prepossession that the author of it was stupidly ignorant of the first principles which should guide a writer of text for music. This prepossession is a wrong on the public, and without reference to its wrong on me should be immediately and decisively overturned.

Before I send the paper to the Tribune, I will submit it to Mr. Buck.

I'm hard at my Ode, and see the beginning of the end. Tell me how you fare with yours. I fervently pray the God of the Poet to give you all such fire as you shall want.

Charley joins me in love to you.

Your friend

Sidney Lanier.[79]

[79] In his reply, Apr. 3, 1876 (*Letters*, New York, 1899, pp. 159-160), Taylor wrote: " I don't wonder you were annoyed at the notice of your Cantata in the ' Tribune.' I was surprized when I saw it; but I have since ascertained how it came there. It is published by Schirmer, and was sent to Mr. Hassard to be noticed. The advertisement to-day says it will appear *shortly*. Mr. Buck must explain this: I cannot. Mr. Hassard, of course, supposed it was a legitimate subject to write about; and in talking with him about it to-day, I learned incidentally that he meant no special criticism of the text, but only used what he thought necessary to illustrate the music.

" This does not lessen your grievance, but it ought to modify your expressions. I have marked with a pencil certain things which I earnestly beg you to omit. In such matters the man who betrays his exasperation puts himself at a disadvantage: the reading public *never* fully apprehends an author's position, and there are not fifty readers of the ' Tribune ' who would comprehend your annoyance sufficiently to sympathize with your rejoinder. Were it my case, my first thought would be, to reply as you have done; my second thought would be, not to reply at all. One result will be the publication of the whole text at once, by other papers; since they can now so easily get it."

To Bayard Taylor [80]

66 Centre St.

Bo. April 4th 1876.

My dear Mr. Taylor:

It suddenly occurs to me – *apropos* of your connection with the Tribune – that in sending you the article to read I may have rendered myself liable to a fancy on your part (for you have not known me very long) that I was trying in a roundabout way to secure some sort of interference by you in its, or my, behalf.

But, no ! My only reason for sending you the piece was that I quite distrust my own judgment in such matters; I live so utterly alone, that just as a deaf person forgets the proper intonations of voice in speaking so I forget how matters look, and go, among men; and I therefore sent my article for your judgment and advice to me upon its propriety, knowing that you are more among men than I am. I never asked, and will never ask, help in such a matter; and, were this not so, I would ask it *directly*, or not at all.

By the grace of God my Centennial Ode is finished. I now only know how divine has been the agony of the last three weeks during which I have been rapt away to heights where all my own purposes as to a revisal of artistic forms lay clear before me, and where the sole travail was of choice out of multitude.[81]

---

[80] Previously published, *Atlantic Monthly*, LXXXIII, 804 (June, 1899); reprinted, *Letters* (New York, 1899), p. 161.

[81] In a letter to his wife of the same date (Apr. 4, 1876, here omitted) Lanier wrote: "With fervent gratitude and unbounded wonder I find that I have finished my poem. It is much the longest I have written, covering forty one pages of this paper— about three times as long as The Symphony, I shd. think. It has been a sheer matter of inspiration: each morning awaking worn and weary with many physical discomforts and some spiritual ones— for my fight with the inartistic world begins— I have found myself presently rapt away into a Heaven of Invention where all the artistic principles which I wish to infuse into the old veins of poetry lay clearly defined before me and where the procession of thought was so crowding that the agony was not one of composition but of analysis and choice only."

The surviving MS of "The Psalm of the West" (Johns Hopkins University, gift of Mrs. Sidney Lanier, Jr.) covers exactly forty-one pages. It bears the early title: "TO / THE UNITED STATES OF AMERICA."

I hope to see you on Thursday, being called by business to New York. Of course you won't care to see my Ode until after you have written your own, – wherein may the God of the Artist detach His best Angels to your service.

Your friend

S. L.

To Robert S. Lanier

66 Centre St.
Baltimore, Md.
April 4th 1876

My dear Father:

I have been so completely engrossed by the necessity of having my poem ready for the Magazine by the appointed time,– as well as by the inspiration of the poem which has quite had possession of me for some three weeks past – that I have failed to send you a copy of the piano-score of the Cantata which I had obtained for you. As it is, I now expect to run to Montgomery, – and of course to see you– in the next ten days, and will bring it. I have finished my poem by the grace of God. It is about three times as long as the Symphony, and embodies a great many pet ideas of mine, relating to poetic forms, which I have not hitherto dared to venture. It will make a stir: and I will have a sharp fight about it: but it will conquer in the end. The first gun has already been fired by the Tribune man in a notice of the Cantata, – which he had no right to " notice " at all, it having been printed (*not* published) solely for the purpose of drilling the Chorus. He objected to my use of certain syllables, on the score of their unsonorous effect: stupidly failing to see that the passage – in which I am describing the freezing, hunger, and starvation of the early colonists – was filled with these very syllables – (double *e*'s) as *i.e. freeze, thee,* &c— in order to produce a certain ghastly effect with the voices, not to be attained by any other vocable.

I rejoice in the prospect of seeing you before long, and I shall enjoy a rest with such zeal as is not to be described.

It is probable that I will have a noble commission to write the Life of Charlotte Cushman, in which I should take the greatest delight. I fear that Thomas will not be enabled to enlarge his orchestra as he expected, and that my prospect of that engagement is swept away.

Please send Mary twenty five dollars as soon as you get this, if possible. I have to wait until I can draw on my poem, before I can get funds enough either to pay up board or go South.

I send love to Mama, and Pringle. Charley is out.

Your loving

S. L.

To Bayard Taylor [82]

66 Centre St.

Baltimore, Md.

April 8th 1876

My dear Mr. Taylor:

From indications at Philadelphia yesterday I deem it of very great importance to me that some intelligent criticism of my poem should appear in a journal of standing. Without wishing to *guide* or in any way *direct* criticism, I am keenly desirous that the poem might be judged *on the plane of its principles,*—leaving the critic the utmost freedom in pronouncing how far it has succeeded in carrying them out. I have not yet been able to tell *you*—in all our correspondence about the poem—what were the main considerations leading to its substance and form. Please let me do so now.

1st. The principal matter over which the United States can legitimately exult is *its present existence as a Republic*, in spite of so much opposition from Nature and from man. I therefore made the Refrain of the song—about which all its train of thought moves—concern itself wholly with the *Fact of existence*: The waves cry " IT SHALL NOT BE ", the powers of nature cry It shall not BE, the wars &c utter the same cry. This Refrain is the key to the whole poem.

[82] Previously published, *Atlantic Monthly*, LXXXIII, 804-806 (June, 1899); reprinted, *Letters* (New York, 1899), pp. 162-166.

2nd. The poem was limited to sixty lines: in which space I had to compress the past and the future of the country, together with some reference to the present occasion. This necessitated the use of the highly-generalized terms which occur, – as for instance where, in the Good Angel's Song, the fundamental philosophies of Art, of Science, of Power, of Polity, of Faith, and of Social Life, are presented in the simple Saxon words, and in one line each.

3rd. I wished that the poem might belie the old slanders upon our tendency to Fourth of July uproariousness, Buncombe, Spread-Eagleism, and the like. I tried therefore to make it the *quietest* poem possible.

4th. A knowledge of the inability of music to represent any shades of meaning save those which are very intense, and very highly and sharply contrasted, led me to divide the poem into the eight paragraphs or movements which it presents, and to make these vividly opposed to each other in sentiment. Thus the first movement is reflection, measured and sober: this suddenly changes into the *agitato* of the second: this agitato, culminating in the unison shout "No! It shall not be", yields in the third movement to the *pianissimo* and meagre effect of the skeleton voices from Jamestown &c: this *pianissimo*, in the fourth movement is turned into a climax of the wars of armies and of faiths, again ending in the Shout, "No! &c": the fifth movement opposes this with a *whispered* chorus – Huguenots whispering *yea* &c : the sixth opposes again with loud exultation "Now Praise &c": the seventh opposes this with the single voice singing the Angels' song: and the last concludes the series of contrasts with a broad full chorus of measured and firm sentiment.

5th So far, I have spoken of the main circumstances determining the substance of the poem. The metrical forms were selected purely with reference to their descriptive nature: the four trochaic feet of the opening strophe measure off reflection, the next (Mayflower) strophe swings and yaws like a ship, the next I made *outré* and bizarre and bony simply by the device of interposing the line of two and a half trochees amongst the four-trochee lines; the swift action of the Huguenot strophe of course required dactyls: and having thus kept the first part of the poem (which describes the time *before* we were a real nation) in metres which are as it were exotic to our tongue, I now fall into the iambic metre – which is the genius of English words – as soon as the Nation becomes secure and firm.

6th. My business as member of the Orchestra for three years having caused me to sit immediately in front of the bassoons, I had often been struck with the possibility of producing the ghostly effects of that part of the bassoon register so well known to students of Berlioz and Meyerbeer, – by the use of the syllable *ee* sung by a chorus. With this view I filled the ghostly Jamestown Stanza with *ee's*, – and would have put in more if I could have found them appropriate to the sense.

$$\frac{''}{''}$$

Now let me ask your friendship two questions.

1st. Is there any *proper* way in which you could call the attention of the Tribune *literary* Critic – whenever my poem as poem is to be noticed – to these considerations I have above enumerated? Would it be trespassing either upon his, my, or your position, if you should hand him what I have written above?

2nd In view of the fact that the poem is now printed with the piano-score and is liable at any time to be copied – and copied badly by other papers, would it not be well for me if it were printed by the Tribune, properly ?

In fine, I am convinced that if one influential paper would take the initiative in judging the poem from the above standpoint, all the loose opinion would crystallize about it: and, if not, I shall be cruelly misjudged and mistreated.

Two reflections make me bold enough to ask this of you: first, that I would so gladly embrace any opportunity of giving you my love in this or any other way: and second, that I feel as if the great wrong done me by Mr. Hassard's criticism gave me a half-right and claim upon the paper. If the enclosed letter of Dudley Buck's [83] would be of any service in this connection, – *let* it be.

---

[83] In his letter of Apr. 4, 1876 (*Letters*, New York, 1899, pp. 165-166, n. 1). Buck had written: " I am sorry that the ' Tribune ' article gave you pain, but after you have been dissected, flayed, and otherwise disposed of as many times as I have been, you will not wince at one newspaper article. No, I did not find the poem so difficult to set as it strikes the critic of the ' Tribune ', whose

Buck showed me Mr. Whittier's hymn yesterday, wh. was just received. I noticed *the* two lines.[84] It is good.

I trust with perfect confidence to your candor in this matter, – if my request seem bizarre, or in any the least wise improper.

God bless you,

Your friend

Sidney Lanier

P. S. I should like it to be stated that I have been a member of the Peabody Orchestra for three years, under Asger Hamerik.

S. L.[85]

---

article was as great a surprise to me as to yourself. The 'pitfalls' referred to were rather godsends in my case." He added that the more intelligent the reader the better he would like the poem; but all would find that it would grow on them with several readings. He then concluded: " It was this which made me so desirous to have the poem printed in advance of the music. Then it would have been studied and analyzed *per se*, and they would have gotten at the merits of it quicker. Why this was not permitted has always been beyond my comprehension. In a word I think the intelligence of the country will be on your side, and about the rest I would not trouble myself. Be therefore comforted and write me a dramatic cantata! Have you any ' bits ' lying about that would do for songs? "

[84] Whittier retained two lines from Taylor's Hymn, which had been withdrawn (see S. T. Pickard, *Life and Letters of John Greenleaf Whittier*, Boston and New York, 1894, II, 618-619).

[85] In his reply, Apr. 11, 1876 (*Letters*, New York, 1899, pp. 166-167), Taylor wrote that he had spoken to Whitelaw Reid, editor of the *Tribune*, and that with his approval the full text of the Cantata would be published: " I shall . . . write an appropriate and explanatory introduction. . . . I cannot go quite as much into technical details as you may desire. . . . But I shall do my best to set other papers upon the track of a right understanding."

The *Tribune* of Apr. 12, 1876, printed the full text of the Cantata, with Taylor's introduction. In the opening paragraph he gave a brief sketch of the pertinent facts in Lanier's life, with a tribute to the two poems that had brought him national prominence ("Corn" and "The Symphony") and to his exceptional qualifications for the present task by reason of his connection with the Peabody Orchestra. The cantata form, Taylor reminded his readers, presents peculiar difficulties because it has to acknowledge the double sway of poetry and music: " Mr. Lanier's verses, therefore, must be read with constant reference to the inevitable restrictions of his task." Then, after a resumé of the contents of the poem, he declared in conclusion: " It is both simple and original in character. Contrasted with the Cantata written by Tennyson for the opening of the International Exhibition in London, its greater freedom and freshness are very evident, while in earnestness and absence of self-gratulation it will doubtless harmonize with the spirit of Whittier's hymn." (The entire article was copied in the Macon *Daily Telegraph and Messenger*, Apr. 18, 1876.)

To Mary Day Lanier

Bᵒ   April 9th 1876

I arrived late on Friday night, dear Sweetheart, from my flying visit to New York and Philadelphia. I expected to come back with all preparations quite complete, but must return to Philadelphia tomorrow, to spend a few hours. I hope to reach here again tomorrow night, and then to be fully ready to start to-thee-ward on Tuesday night: yet a day more may very likely be consumed in the great heat of my hasty movements. I have to do everything, as thou knowest, without means, and by mere invention: and the workman who has no tools but his hands is necessarily slow.

Mr. Kirk was not able to read my poem with such attention as he desired before making up his mind about it until today, when he will do so and give me his final answer tomorrow. Of course he will accept it, but its great length is in the way and will necessitate some talk between us. Moreover it is new, and as of old so now there is much stoning of the prophets who preach new Gospels.

I had a long talk with Emma Stebbins on Thursday, mostly about the Memoir of Charlotte Cushman which we are to write – if suitable arrangements can be made – together. The only difficulty in the way is my bread, which has to be made while the book is being written: and it is therefore a matter of simple impossibility for me to give all my time to the book without advances from somebody to sustain me in the meanwhile. I have just written her that if Mr. Cushman (Charlotte's heir) can see his way clear to advance a couple of hundred a month for six months, trusting to the sale of the book for his remuneration, the thing can be done so far as I am concerned.

My Cantata poem is going to provoke some criticism; there is so little expectation of aught but crude art among the critics of our country that when a work *not* crude comes before them they are mightily tempted to charge its prominences and innovations to ignorance rather than to that seeming roughness and half-shock which the new in Art always produces in the minds of those accustomed to judge it by old canons. I have wholly departed from the Conventional Cantata-poem, and have made a work of utter simplicity and quietness, wholly out of the plane of the Fourth-of-July extravagances. A strong clientelage of people who think will be in my favor, but the local editors who get up the news about bar-rooms and join to this the department of art-criticism will likely put much superb advice and instruction upon me from on high.

Which I will not mind if so be I may look into thine eyes a little, soon: and therefore God bring me soon where that is to be compassed, prays thy

husband .

To Gibson Peacock [86]

Baltimore, Md.
April 11th 1876.

My dear friend:

By a miraculous burst of hard work since early this morning I've managed to get ready a few minutes before time for me to start, and I devote those to sending you a line which may convey to you how sorry I was to miss you yesterday. You will care to know that Mr. Kirk gave me three hundred dollars for this poem:—but that includes book-copyright and all.

Write me at " Exchange Hotel, Montgomery, Ala."

If you only knew what an uplifting you have always been to your friend,

S. L.

To Robert S. Lanier

Montgomery, Ala.
April 13th 1876

My dear Father:

Charley and I arrived here safely last night, both of us a little demoralized by the heat and dust of a trying journey. The luxury of rest is however a great restoration and

[86] Previously published, *Atlantic Monthly*, LXXIV, 26-27 (July, 1894) ; reprinted, *Letters* (New York, 1899), p. 28.

I am in a state of lazy enjoyment quite remedial to all my ills. I am indeeed in fine condition, as to all my old more distressing ailments, and do not suffer from aught save long overwork. May looks wretchedly: she has had a hard attack, of more than a month in duration, and I must adopt some vigorous measures to bring her back into anything like health.

My plans are to be governed much by letters which I hope to receive in the next week: but if not materially changed thus, I hope to come over to Macon in about ten days from now, bringing May (who ought to see her good homœopathic Doctor), but leaving all the children here.

I write in Cliff's office, and the train is just come with disturbing passengers. As soon as my letters come, I will more fully post you. I long to see you all. You will be glad to know that my Centennial poem (for the Magazine) has found great favor with the Editor: and Mr. Peacock says it's the greatest poem ever written in America!

Kiss Mama, for

Your Son

S. L.

To Virginia Hankins

[Montgomery, Ala., Apr. 13, 1876 ?] [87]

Dear Little One. It has always happened with me that Life has adopted some large and generous method of heaping coals of fire on my head whenever I have dared to limit its possibilities in advance by despairing of any sweet consummation; and I have come to know, certainly, that in some life or other all the desires of one's Soul that are worth satisfaction will win it.

— So that, although I still find it a strange and not easily realizable sensation that you *are* here, nevertheless I discover in the bottom of my heart that I always knew it would be so, – –

[87] Conjectural dating from the following facts: Lanier was in Montgomery from Apr. 12 to Apr. 26, as evidenced by the preceding and following letters; the accompanying envelope indicates that the present letter was delivered by hand (it bears no postmark and is addressed simply "Chez Mrs. Chilton"); hence it must have been written in Montgomery, where Virginia Hankins was living– in all likelihood shortly after Lanier's arrival.

and I can even recall prophecies to that effect made among the woods of your sacred old Castle.

Yes, it is well that your very self as you are now should have become known to those here, for in you the real and the ideal live no divorced life, and there is always a benign influence – which people about you will rather feel than perceive – flowing from this rare unity of spirit and act which you present.

Those dreadful involutions of existence which necessitate life-long concealments and which offer to one's soul a ceaseless hypocrisy as the highest duty — God has kept you from these; and in so doing He has excused Himself for all the strokes He has given you, and has left you still His debtor.

———— The only reply to a flower is a song; and as you are out of song-reach, this fair morning, there is no help save to beg you listen in your own heart for the unceasing " ditty of no tone " which is perpetually hymned in your praise by

" The Friend and The Friend's Wife."

To Gibson Peacock [88]

Macon, Ga.
April 27th 1876.

My dear Mr. Peacock:

May and I ran over here yesterday from Montgomery Ala. where I have been spending the time since I saw you with my brother's family and my own. My father lives here: and we are to remain about five days, when May returns to the children at Montgomery, and I hasten back to Philadelphia. I therefore hope to see you within a week.

I've been such a subject and helpless victim of ovation among the good people of these regions that the time has never seemed to come when I could answer your good letter. The Southern people make a great deal more of my appointment to write the cantata-poem than I had ever expected, and it really seems to be regarded by them as one of the most substantial tokens of reconciliation yet evinced by that vague *tertium quid* which they are accustomed to represent to themselves under the general

[88] Previously published, *Atlantic Monthly*, LXXIV, 27-28 (July, 1894); reprinted, *Letters* (New York, 1899), pp. 28-30.

term of " The North ". I am astonished, too, to find what a hold " Corn " has taken upon all classes. Expressions come to me, in great number, from men whom I never supposed accessible by any poetry whatever; and their recognitions arrive hand [-in-hand] with those from persons of the highest culture.

The *Tribune* notice of the Cantata has been copied by a great many Southern papers, and I think it materially assisted in starting the poem off properly; though the people here are so enthusiastic in my favor at present that they are quite prepared to accept blindly anything that comes from me. Of course I understand all this; and any success seems cheap which depends so thoroughly on local pride as does my present position with the South; yet, in view of the long and bitter struggle which I must make up my mind to wage in carrying out those extensions of poetic Forms about which all my thoughts now begin to converge, it is pleasant to find that I have at least the nucleus of an audience which will be willing to receive me upon the plane of mere blind faith until time shall have given a more scientific basis to their understandings.

I have seen a quotation (in the Baltimore *Bulletin*, which indignantly takes up the cudgel in my behalf) of one sentence from *the Nation* which makes me suppose that I have had a harsh reception from the New York papers generally, in the matter of the Cantata-text. The *Bulletin* represents *the Nation* as saying that the poem is like " a communication from the Spirit of Nat Lee through a Bedlamite medium ".[89] Nothing

---

[89] The *Nation*, XXII, 247 (Apr. 13, 1876), said: " An injury has, we fear, been inflicted on the Centennial celebration by the acceptance, as a portion of the opening ceremonies, of a ' Cantata ' written by Mr. Sidney Lanier." After quoting from the opening lines, the critic declared that this and much more " reads like a communication from the spirit of Nat Lee, rendered through a Bedlamite medium. In one sense, perhaps, it is suitable to a commemoration of the Declaration of Independence, as it is a practical assertion of emancipation from the ordinary laws of sense and sound, melody and prosody. Seriously, but that the music is already composed for it, we should hope it was not too late to save American letters from the humiliation of presenting to the assembled world such a farrago as this as their choicest product."
Since no file of the Baltimore *Bulletin* for this period has been found, the defense in that newspaper cannot be given. But a surviving clipping (Charles D. Lanier Collection, Johns Hopkins University) shows that in a previous issue, Apr. 15, 1876, the *Bulletin* had printed the full text of the Cantata, accompanied by a detailed and highly favorable critique of the poem and the music. In alluding to the special difficulties of the Cantata form, the critic remarked:

rejoices me more than the inward perception how utterly the time, and the frame of mind, are passed by, in which anything of this sort gives me the least disturbance. Six months ago this would have hurt me, even against my will. Now it only seems a little grotesque episode,– just as when a few minutes ago I sat in my father's garden, here, and heard a cat-bird pause, in the midst of the most exquisite roulades and melodies, to mew — and then take up his song again.

What a fearsome long screed, and all about Me!—But it is not with the least malice prepense: you are to reflect that I've just stolen away, from a half-dozen engagements, to my father's office, in an unspeakable Spring-morning, to send you a little message out of my heart—wherein, truly, whenever I think of you, there is always instantly born a Spring full of gardens— and of song-birds that never *mew*.

I hope so soon to kiss the hands of your two ladies that I send no further messages now save the old one that I am always their and your friend   S. L.

To Mary Day Lanier

Pha May 8th 1876

Well, Sweetest Heart in the World, I am finally in mine inn. My whole afternoon—for I arrived here at 1.20 P.M.—has been employed in looking up my baggage, which had become involved in such a maze of stupidity and carelessness as rarely falls to the lot of man to unravel. It has finally arrived,— though I have not yet had time to make a toilet. I have seen

" Such poetry must lie on the borderland between thought and melody; and it is in that region that Mr. Lanier is most happy and at home . . . , a poet who is himself a musician, and keenly alive to musical ' motives ' as well as poetic thoughts." He then added: " In saying that this poem was written with a special view to musical treatment we do not intend to slight its great poetic beauty. Its tone is elevated and noble; it is full of condensed thought, and its artistic treatment is original and striking. . . . In fact Mr. Lanier has sought to compress so much thought into this small compass that the poem is not caught in a rapid reading, and does not reveal its full beauty until one has become somewhat familiar with it. . . . He has made scores of friends here who appreciate his genius and admire the man, and no work of his could fail to excite an interest in Baltimore." Both notices were probably written by Innes Randolph (see Lanier's letter of June 19, 1875, and note 103, above).

Mr. Kirk, and gotten from him a proof of the poem. I have until Friday to make such emendations as I desire. I have also seen the Peacocks; who have a house full of company and lament that they cannot take me in. I am domiciled temporarily at Pétry's European House, a few doors from Mr. Peacock's residence. Thou wert best write me care of Mr. Peacock, 1425 Walnut St., as usual. I learn that Thomas opens his Garden here on Thursday night, with a repetition (mainly) of the programme of the Wednesday festivities at the Exhibition Grounds.[90]

I found Major W. L. Lanier, of Selma, on the sleeping-car wh. I took at Atlanta and wh. brought us all the way to Baltimore without change. Our journey was straight and without incident.

Might I but tell thee, poor suffering Heart, poor Dear Heart, how utterly all that is I hath remained behind, there, with thee! I leaned from the departing train at Vineville and watched thy form until the remorseless curve swept thee far out of sight,— and then sank into a passion of inward weeping not to be comforted nor dried till I see thy true eyes again.

This, from a lonesome late-in-the-night, from a lonesome

lover.

To Robert S. Lanier

Philadelphia, May 12th 1876

My dear Father:

I have in vain tried to get time for even a note to you. I have found all manner of vexatious little matters revealed by the proof of my long poem, and these have required all the moments I could spare from what seemed pressing duty. I am still at work on the poem, but will finish tonight.

You will have seen accounts of the great success with which the Exhibition opened, and I send you herewith Bayard Taylor's account in the TRIBUNE, and a more detailed notice of the Can-

---

[90] Theodore Thomas's Orchestra was officially employed to furnish the music for the Centennial Exposition in Philadelphia.

W. L. Lanier, mentioned in the following paragraph, was an Alabama cousin.

tata performance in the Philadelphia PRESS.[91] I sat by Mr. Taylor during the ceremonies – both of us being a few feet from President Grant and the Central group which surrounded him. We had the best position of the whole multitude and often congratulated ourselves on the good fortune which caused us to meet on the platform and to witness this great scene in company. I wish I had time to give you some idea *how* great it was; probably nothing like it has ever been beheld or heard. The Cantata was sung with immense effect, and the great volume of tone from the chorus surprised and delighted the whole assemblage. The Bass Solo,[92] commencing " Long as thine Art &c " was heard by at least twenty five thousand people, and was encored, – both of which circumstances are probably without parallel on an occasion of this kind. Mr. Taylor and I joined in the procession, after the final speech, and moved through the vast buildings in company with the *other* dignitaries, before the public was admitted.

At night I went to Mr. [George W.] Child's reception, where I was presented to the President, Secretary Fish and other eminent personages. I stood near Dom Pedro for some time,

[91] The grand opening ceremonies of the Centennial Exhibition on May 10, 1876, included the performance of Wagner's *Centennial Inaugural March*, Whittier's Hymn, and Lanier's Cantata– sung by a chorus of 800 voices and accompanied by an orchestra of 150 musicians. In his account of the occasion in the New York *Tribune*, May 11, 1876, Bayard Taylor declared: " I wish some of the critics who were made so unhappy by Mr. Lanier's cantata could have heard it sung to Mr. Dudley Buck's music. The words suffered ' a sea-change ' into another tongue; the stanzas relieved each other, and unexpected dramatic felicities were recognized by the mind through the ear. . . . It was original in the perfection of the execution no less than in the conception of both poet and composer. The effect upon the audience could not be mistaken." The Philadelphia *Press*, May 11, 1876, gave the full text of Lanier's Cantata, followed by a detailed analysis of the music. It spoke of " the multitude of eager listeners," the " well-trained chorus," and the admirable solo, concluding: " Protracted and most appreciative applause greeted this performance."

A further account of this occasion has been preserved by D. C. Gilman, President of Johns Hopkins University, who was present on the occasion: " From the overture to the closing cadence it held the attention of the vast throng of listeners, and when the Cantata was concluded loud applause rang through the air. [Buck was called out and the chorus rose and cheered.] A noble conception had been nobly rendered. . . . Lanier had triumphed. It was an opportunity of a lifetime to test upon a grand scale his theory of verse. He came off victorious." (" Sidney Lanier: Reminiscences and Letters," *South Atlantic Quarterly*, IV, 116, Apr., 1905.)

[92] Sung by Myron Whitney of Boston.

and studied his face while he was talking with my friend Mr. Peacock. I did not care to be presented to his majesty – though this was offered – for I saw that he was quite overrun with presentations, and knew that Mr. Peacock's conversation was in honor of his wife's old friendship with the emperor.[93] Mr. and Mrs. Peacock called on him by appointment next day and had a charming visit.

Many of the papers have renewed the most bitter abuse and ridicule upon my poor little Cantata, and have displayed an amount of gratuitous cruelty and ignorant brutality of which I could never have dreamed.[94] I am glad to know however that Gen. Hawley is pleased with the work. He remarked to a friend some nights ago that he thought the papers had been very unfair to me about the poem and that he quite agreed in the view of it published in the TRIBUNE.

I am going to run over to New York in the morning. Expect to return Monday. Received the letter forwarded by you. After I get back will have more leisure to write.

Meantime, and always, God bless you, and all my dear ones. I write May a little note tonight.

Your son

S. L.

[93] Dom Pedro II, Emperor of Brazil. Gibson Peacock's wife was the daughter of the Marquis de la Figanière, at one time Portuguese minister to the United States.

[94] According to the New York *Herald* of May 11, 1876: " Mr. Lanier is an intelligent poet and his verses have ideas and melody. But he seems to have made the common mistake of supposing that verse should be itself musical to be sung. Verse written for music should be simple, clear, direct and brief in its statements. . . . He has written a beautiful poem, but it is obscure to the eye and must be unintelligible to the ear. . . . The argument of the poem is not easily to be comprehended, and the language is harsh." Even more critical was the editorial in the New York *Times*, May 11, 1876. After a favorable review of Whittier's Hymn, came the following comment: " We wish we could say as much for Mr. Lanier's Contata. A more bewildering collection of rhymes we do not ever remember to have seen, or one more entirely at variance with the taste of the American people."

To Mary Day Lanier

New York, May, 15th 1876

Thy poor Heart, My Sweetest Heart, how tired must be thy heart and thy body with this new stroke upon our dear Elf.[95]

—— I have much ado with myself to be quiet in these days, and when I think of thee there struggling with thy damnable imp of disease I find the conception too strong for my endurance unless I straightway think upon myself as made in the image of God, and then I try to be like God, and it would seem as if He came down and met me half-way.

I have just arrived here. A letter reached me from Hal this morning, from which I infer he will be here tomorrow. He seems greatly disappointed at failing to meet thee in Macon. I have also thy last anent my darling Sidney, whose sweet lips I would give a world to press at this moment.

My Cantata has met with a storm of abuse from many quarters, and thou wouldst find it hard to conceive the ignorant brutality which has been poured upon the little poem by some of these people.

Dost thou remember a long letter I sent thee from Baltimore just about the time of writing this poem, prophesying my struggle with the Beasts ? It would seem as if the veritable shadow of the battle must have hung over me that night. Of course I will win, finally: but my God, how bitter is the heedless hurt of this hoofed Stupidity which one cannot allow oneself to hate ! [96]

Meantime, here and there a sweet voice is heard in my favor. The Bulletin had a strong article vindicating me: and I enclose a paragraph from the new paper called " *The New Century for Women.*" [97] Others also defend me. – But, bitterest of all,

---

[95] Mary Day Lanier had been called back to Montgomery because her son, Sidney, Jr., had been suddenly taken ill with pneumonia.

[96] In a letter to his wife on May 12, 1876 (here omitted), Lanier had said: " 'Tis a long and bitter fight I have to fight with some of these poor crude people who pretend to judge my art;– but Time is a better critic than they and the prophets of my God are stronger than the soldiers of theirs."

[97] The favorable notice in the Philadelphia *Evening Bulletin* appeared on May 13, 1876. Referring to the " vast amount of very stupid and unmeaning abuse " that had been heaped upon the Cantata, Gibson Peacock declared editorially:

there is no comfort in the praise of my friends:– they do not know what I am about, and the cheap triumph of wrong praise is but a pain to the Artist.

I have been hard at work on a thousand little matters revealed by the proof-sheets of the long poem. I am to see a final proof on Monday next when I expect to be back in Philadelphia. I have no news for thee – I am all one prayer for thee who art the one Love of thy

lover .

TO ROBERT S. LANIER [98]

New York, May 18th 1876

My dear Father:

I got yr. letter this morning. Mr. Peacock forwarded it to me here.

I see from reading it that you are in some concern over the

" Mr. Lanier's experience is only that of all who have gone before him. No man ever yet lifted himself up, or was lifted up by the spirit that is in him, and proclaimed a new idea . . . without setting loose upon himself the whole pack of critics and cynics, honest and dishonest, intelligent and stupid, high and low, who either hunt him down to his death or drive him forward and upward until he rests in safety upon the heights to which his pursuers cannot reach. . . .

" In the particular instance of the Centennial Cantata, there is needed neither apology nor defence; and yet there is one fact about it that the most obtuse and the most ill-disposed should bear in mind. . . . Mr. Whittier, with his great fame forever established, could well afford to sing his simple fervent hymn of praise, in vernacular verse; but the younger poet, with all the stirring of original conception alive within him, could not dare to be anything on such an occasion that was not wholly true to his own genius, his own idea of art." He then concluded with a prose paraphrase of the poem " because we believe that the wholesale abuse that has been so hastily and foolishly lavished upon it will naturally attract much attention to it, and because it only needs the slightest clue to the poet's purpose to enable any intelligent reader to realize how admirably he has done his appointed work." (Clipping in the Charles D. Lanier Collection, Johns Hopkins University.)

The Philadelphia *New Century For Women*, No. 1, May 13, 1876, printed the text of the Contata on p. 8, and commented on it editorially (p. 1), speaking of " its strikingly original cadences, its thrilling questionings, its abrupt and stern responses." Then, referring specifically to the performances, it said: " Criticism of the words, so freely offered upon their reading merits, was disarmed and taken captive at the outset. The cantata is the century itself, two centuries in its bosom. Those who have not heard it sung, have not begun to spell its meaning."

[98] Excerpt previously published, W. H. Ward, " Memorial," *Poems* (New York, 1884), p. xxv, misdated May 8, 1876.

maltreatment of my poem, and I confess that it is difficult to regard this mountain of stupidity and injustice without indignation. But on all sides come to me signs of a reaction, and I am assured by many friends here that this will probably leave my poem finally where I desire it to be. I have written a letter to *The* TRIBUNE which has been accepted,[98] and will probably be out tomorrow, though it may be crowded over until Monday or Tuesday, as Mr. Taylor told me forty columns of other matter would be. This afternoon a letter comes out in the EVENING POST (the one enclosed) which is genuinely good for my side: the Baltimore GAZETTE and the Ph[a] BULLETIN have editorially defended me in admirably-written papers, and I think it likely other friends will turn up.[100]

As for the CONSTITUTION article wh. you enclose, nothing could be more plainly the offspring of that Stupidity against which Schiller has declared that the Gods themselves are powerless. In the first place the idea that this was " a magnificent

---

[98] " The Centennial Cantata " (II, 266), published in the New York *Tribune*, May 20, 1876 (see note 78, above).

[100] A letter signed " Z " and dated " New York, May 16 " appeared in the New York *Evening Post* on May 18, 1876. It consisted of an even more detailed prose paraphrase of the Cantata than had been given in the Philadelphia *Evening Bulletin* (see note 97, above), with the following introductory paragraph: " Sydney [*sic*] Lanier may or may not be a well known writer; but certain it is that his lines sung at the opening exercises of the Centennial Exhibition have found an echo in many hearts, calling forth no little admiration and praise from those who felt the spirit in which he wrote. The ode has been severely criticised; one of our morning journals gave its readers the pleasure of a laugh by analyzing the lines in a mocking vein, and pretending to find resemblances between it and the ' Jabberwocky ' ballads. Many intelligent persons have read the poem by the aid of the article referred to, and have said that it seemed all ' jabberwocky ' to them; it is to these persons I appeal . . . to make Mr. Lanier's meaning clear."

The editorial in the Baltimore *Gazette*, May 15, 1876, also grew out of a burlesque in The New York *Times*, May 12, 1876, comparing Lanier's Cantata to the " Jabberwocky " of *Alice in Wonderland*. Admitting that this was an excellent bit of fooling, the *Gazette* directed its attack against the Baltimore *American*, which in cribbing from the *Times* had missed all the humor of the original. In defense of Lanier's poem it concluded: " There is no obscurity about these lines. Whether or not they are beautiful is a matter of taste, but whether or not they are comprehensible is a matter of fact. . . . There is no extravagance of diction in the verses of the cantata that cannot be paralleled by similar ones from the poetry of Milton, Shelley, Coleridge, Wordsworth, Tennyson, Browning, Swinburne and others; or from the prose of Carlyle, Emerson or Ruskin. There is no phrase in this poem that cannot be understood by those of average intelligence who wish to understand it."

opportunity " for me is indescribably preposterous; for every literary man is perfectly well aware that the writing of such things is without exception the most dangerous and thankless work which can be devised, for success in it is never acknowledged and failure is always overpunished. It is but a day or two ago that one of the greatest poets in America told me he would not have undertaken to write the Cantata text for any considerartion. Such articles as this of the CONSTITUTION's are precisely the sort of things that have rendered it so hard for a Southern man to make any headway in the North: for if you examine it a moment, you find that there is absolutely no coherent purpose in it, the middle does not hang by the beginning, nor the tail by either, and the whole is a mere piece of tobacco-sodden bosh such as the Southern editors are prone to eject from their pen-points.[101]

And I find it really difficult to withhold my scorn, when I read the patronizing interest which these gentlemen take in my efforts and the lofty magnanimity with which such a man as this declares that he is not going to deprive me of praise, and the like. Where was all this patriotic interest, before I had won my way at the North? The Atlanta CONSTITUTION, wretched sheep that it is, waited a long time after the Bell-wether jumped, before it went over the fence. I hope this doesn't sound like a tirade. I do not mean it for that: It is simply the truth.

In short, my dear Father, my experience in the varying judgments of men about poetry has now become pretty large. (An example, which you won't be sorry to hear, is that the very

[101] The writer in the Atlanta *Constitution* said in part: " The expectation was general that upon this magnificent opportunity for fame of the fullest measure Mr. Lanier would devote the richest ministrations of his fancy and the finest exhibition of his poetic art. . . . [But when the Cantata was given out,] it did not meet that enthusiasm of satisfaction which had been promised in advance. There was much to question mixed in with the glittering flashes of song and we are free to say that its high-wrought delineation was of a too advanced art. In this it failed, perhaps very greatly, to adapt itself to the broader and more rugged sentiments of the popular heart. Regret for this is natural to his friends who know his powers and appreciate his genius." Then after a fling at Lanier's northern critics, he concluded: " He deserves, honor for the courage of that attempt and the almost signal success in which it resulted. We shall not essay to deprive him of one jot of that richly deserved, because earnestly aimed at, honor." (Undated clipping in the Clifford A. Lanier Collection, Johns Hopkins University.)

Ballad of Lexington [102] &c about which you are so nervous excited Mr. Taylor's special applause three nights ago, and he thought the poem grew continually better to the very end! this being exactly the reverse of the impression made on you.) It has all converged upon one solitary principle, and the experience of the Artist in all ages is reported by history to be of precisely the same direction. That principle is: that the artist shall put forth, humbly and lovingly and without bitterness against any opposition, the very best and highest that is within him, utterly regardless of contemporary criticism. What possible claim can contemporary criticism set up to respect — that contemporary criticism which crucified Jesus Christ, stoned Stephen, hooted Paul for a madman, tried Luther for a criminal, tortured Galileo, bound Columbus in chains, drove Dante into a hell of exile, made Shakespeare write the Sonnet " when in disgrace, with fortune and men's eyes &c.", gave Milton five pounds for Paradise Lost, kept Samuel Johnson cooling his heels on Lord Chesterfield's door-step, reviled Shelley as an unclean dog, killed Keats, cracked jokes on Gluck, Schubert, Beethoven, Berlioz and Wagner, and committed so many other impious follies and stupidities that a thousand letters like this could not suffice even to catalogue them?

No: do not be in the least dismayed at any reception with which my poems may meet. I will always do my very best to make them thoroughly intelligible. I do not think, by the way, that the Cantata-text is amenable to criticism on that point: it is not transparent, but there is nothing in it which any person of ordinary understanding should not quickly seize. When you come to read the philosophical exposition of mine in THE TRIBUNE on the new relations of poetry to music brought about by the great modern development of the Orchestra, I think you will be thoroughly satisfied with the Cantata in every possible view of it. I myself have not the least doubt that it will finally come to take its place as a pioneer poem in a School whose very fundamental principles have not yet been dreamed of by any English writer besides myself. The beastly jokes will be forgotten in a month: the poem will be recalled, for its very quaintness, at the next Centennial.

[102] A passage in " The Psalm of the West," which Lanier had apparently read to his father while in Macon.

Inasmuch as I am dreadfully pressed for time, I'm going to
beg that you will send this over to May, for I gather from her
last letter that she is just a trifle inclined to fancy me too much
hurt by the senseless babble of the newspapers.   Of course, it
did hurt me: but the feeling is quite gone, and I now understand the whole matter so thoroughly that it is as if it had not
been.   Meantime, there can be no doubt that my personal
interests are on the whole advanced by the commotion; for I
am presented with an audience familiar at least with my name
very much sooner than I could otherwise have been, and there
are already several notable instances of the conversion of persons who were merely neutral into friendly admirers of my
poem, through the double reading they have been led to give
me since the harsh criticism began.

My plans do not develope at all.   I will write you again
soon.   I return to Pha on Monday morning.   Harry is here with
the little girl, and we propose to leave her at the Hospital
tomorrow.

Mary will need considerable money to get her away from
Montgomery, in consequence of my poor little boy's illness. If
you can send her fifty dollars as soon as you receive this, it will
greatly relieve matters.   She wishes to be out of the way by the
23rd, in order that Cliff may have the use of her room for the
Convention which meets on the 24th.

As for me, I am financially *in extremis*, and you would laugh
if you knew where my watch was. If you can send twenty
dollars to me at Pha, I will be much happier.   Address always
" care of

Mr. Gibson Peacock
1425 Walnut St.
Pha
Pa. "

I have seen Mr. J. F. D. Lanier, and he seems to be very proud
of my success, and of the cantata-poem which he saw with The
Tribune's notice.   I have not called on any other friends, for
lack of time.

God bless you all, prays

Your Son

S. L.

To Mary Day Lanier

N. Y. May 18th 1876.

My Sweetest Soul in the world, I have just written my Father a long letter explaining several matters, and have asked him to transmit it to thee, since I wish thee to know some things therein and cannot in any way find the time to write them over.

Thine of 14th & 15th with enclosures reached me this morning, having been ford from Pha. I have enclosed Father a couple of articles defensive of me which he will send thee. The whole matter is now under my feet. As to the Southern papers, their babble is as a child's and unspeakably vain and foolish.

Cubbie and I have been together three days, and it is a great treat to me to sit here in a cosy room with him (we sleep together tonight) and do my work. We are going to carry the dear little girl to the Hospital tomorrow. We had Dr. Taylor —a specialist— to examine the case yesterday. He immediately pronounced it *no* dislocation at all, but a clear case of hip-disease. It will require years for a total cure.[108] They will apply a well-known system of bandages to relieve the pressure at the joint. This will not require any confinement at all, however, and the little patient will move about more freely with it than without it. Julia Carville has been ever so kind, and Loulie will have no lack of attention.

Whereof more another time. I dare not try to tell thee how my heart is about thee. Here is a fair letter from Emma Stebbins. There is now only a remote prospect of my doing the Cushman memoir *soon*. The income of the estate for this year is swallowed up by extraordinary expenses. I return to Pha on Monday. Cubbie will likely go too, and fare on to [R. M.] McClellan's.

Thou wilt kiss my dear Clifford for me a hundred times, fifty being for Will, yea, all for Good Will. I long for my boys unspeakably. As for thee, there is no one who *can* kiss thee for thy

lover.

---

[108] Mary Louise Day remained a cripple through life.

To Mary Day Lanier

N. Y. May 21st 1876

My Sweetest Soul, My dearest Sense, My deepest Thought, My whole Contents of Me,– This entire day hath been passed in a passion of longing for a sight of thy gray eyes, and although I have had much business to transact,—albeit Sunday —my heart and mind have been quite absent there with thee.

I sent thee yesterday a TRIBUNE containing my letter. I believe it has had a good effect. Mr. Taylor tells me of several pleasant expressions which he has already heard about it: and it cannot fail to accomplish the paramount intent with which I put it forth, *i.e.* to saddle the stupidity with which I have been charged upon the chargers thereof.

It now seems probable that I will be soon employed to write the Life of Miss Cushman. Last night at the Century Club Mr. Osgood (of Boston " Osgood & Co ") came to me and said he had been written to by Miss Stebbins in relation to the matter; that he was to see her this morning, and would call on me again this afternoon,— All of which has been done. He called at five, and spent an hour with me, leaving me a most agreeable impression of the Boston publisher. I told him my terms for writing the book would be two thousand dollars, which he could pay if he liked in instalments of two hundred and fifty a month. 'He seemed to think this thoroughly reasonable, and is to let us know his final determination in two days, after consulting his partners. He returns to Boston tonight.

We carried little Daughter to the Hospital yesterday. Contrary to the dismal apprehensions with which we had been groaning all the previous day and night, we had not the least trouble. The dear little thing sailed in among the " pitty babies " as she called them, and soon captured the entire establishment. With the utmost nonchalance she would take away this one's doll, that one's bread, and the other one's book, and appropriate the same to her own use, incontinently pulling the nose of one of the victims who made some show of resistance. Midst of her pre-occupation with this free-booting expedition we slipped Rinda out of a side door,— and the thing was done. Harry and I remained for some time but there seemed no sign of wailing for the lost Dah. The scenes were so novel and exciting—there are about thirty other children in the same room—that her little mind could find no room for old recollections.

Hal saw her today,— but she was asleep. All accounts represent her as doing charmingly.

And now I must leave thee. I have many pleasant *rencontres* which I have not time to write of. I wrote Father to send thee fifty dollars before thy letter came referring thereto. No, I did not pay Gaston's bill for the first illness. It must lie for a little while. I am main tired tonight. I go back to Phᵃ early in the morning. May it then be soon the Morning in which I arrive there, prays thy

lover.

To Clifford A. Lanier [104]

Philadelphia, Pa.
May 23ʳᵈ 1876.

My darling Sweet Boy; This is the sixth letter I've written since nine o'clock tonight, and it is like saying one's prayers before going to bed to have a quiet word with you.

Your letter came today, and I see that you have been annoyed by the howling of the " critics " over the Cantata. *I* was greatly so at first, before I had recovered from my amazement at finding a work of art received in this way sufficiently to think; but now the whole matter is quite plain to me, and gives me no more thought at all.

I enclose a letter of mine to The Tribune which, by all accounts, leaves me master of the situation.

I find I have sent away all the " sweet voices " for which you ask, anent the cantata. They were principally in The Tribune, the Bᵒ Gazette, the N. Y. Evening Telegram,[105]

---

[104] Excerpts previously published in *Literary Life*, III-IV, Supplement (Apr., 1885); Mims, pp. 171-172; Starke, pp. 246-247.

[105] The notice in The New York *Evening Telegram*, May 10, 1876, was only an advance announcement. For the other favorable notices here mentioned see notes 85, 91, 97, and 100, above.

the Ph^a BULLETIN, and the Womens paper called THE NEW
CENTURY FOR WOMEN, — so far as I know, besides the Southern papers. Mr. Taylor tells me that he knows of quite a reaction in my favor, in New York; and my letter completely
demonstrates that the whole body of absurdities called critics
went off half-primed. The poem is not in the least ultimate
danger; and the snarls will have long been forgotten before it
dies. It is really the first English poem written in such a way
that the whole body of it could be genuinely *set* to music.

The EVENING POST (N.Y.) of some days ago had a long and
able communication, from a source unknown to me, in my
defence.

The whole agitation has been of infinite value to me. It
has taught me, in the first place, to lift my heart absolutely
above all *expectation* save that which finds its fulfillment in the
large consciousness of faithful devotion to the highest ideals in
art. This enables one to work in tranquillity. In the second
place, it has naturally caused me to make a merciless arraignment and trial of my own artistic purposes; and an unspeakable
content arises out of the revelation that they come from the
ordeal confirmed in innocence and clearly defined in their relations with all things. I do not hate the people who have so
cruelly maltreated me; they knew not what they did: and my
life will be of some avail if it shall teach even one of them a
consideration that may bloom in tenderer treatment of any
future young artist.

The Columbus " TIMES " article wh. you send is very good.
I had not heard that Randall and Hope were unfavorable to the
Cantata.[106] If it is so, I am sorry for them; for, wholly leaving
aside all question of the truth of their criticism, their position

---

[106] Clifford Lanier had written, May 20, 1876: " The Augusta paper of Randall and the Norfolk paper of James B. Hope are stupidly condemnatory from
the wicked motive (I am told) of envy." James Ryder Randall (1839-1908)
and James Barron Hope (1829-1887) were minor literary figures; both were
friends of Lanier. The Norfolk *Landmark*, May 13, 1876, commented editorially:
" We rarely print poetry, and we don't think we violate our rule in reproducing
Mr. LANIER'S ' Centennial Cantata,' which will be found in another column.
This composition is as hysterical and stunning as one of WALT WHITMAN'S
amazing performances, and makes a sorry show beside WHITTIER'S Hymn, which
itself is unworthy of the occasion. . . . we regret to see [it] put forward as the
literary contribution of the South to the Centennial." (The accounts in the
Columbus, Ga., *Times* and the Augusta *Chronicle and Sentinel* are treated in the
Introduction to vol. I of the present edition.)

as poets who have failed makes it unquestionbly a thing of bad taste to say anything, if not something favorable, in such a case as mine.

The commotion about the Cantata has not been unfavorable on the whole to my personal interests. It has led many to read closely what they would otherwise have read curiously, and I believe I have many earnest friends whose liking was of a nature to be confirmed by such opposition.

There is now a strong prospect that I will be employed to write the Life of Charlotte Cushman. I devoutly hope for it, in the present state of matters. It would keep me near my family for the next Eight months. I expect to hear finally about it on Friday next.

On Thursday I am going over to West Chester, [Pa.,] to make inquiries about board for you.

If I could only kiss my sweet Wilsie for her unspeakable kindnesses to my poor little boy! There is nothing to *say* that does not seem cold.

I suppose my belongings are all starting Maconwards today. I hope to send amount of Dr. Gaston's bill in a few days, tell him.

I have not yet had any chance to talk about the re-purchasing of the copyright.[107] Will do so soon.

And now dear Little Boy may God convoy you over to the morning across this night and across all nights, prays

Your

S. L.

TO MARY DAY LANIER [108]

Pha Pa.   May 27th 1876

My *Mia*,   Cubbie and [R.M.] McClellan have come in from Westchester this morning and I am going with them again to the Exhibition. On our last visit we devoted our time to finding out *where* to go, and what there was we liked to see.

[107] In her letter of May 14, 1876, Mary Day Lanier had asked: " Please tell us why the Lippincotts did not answer the request to buy back half of the copyrights of the 3 poems "– presumably " Corn," " The Symphony," and " The Psalm of the West."

[108] Excerpt previously published, W. M. Baskerville, *Southern Writers* (Nashville, Tenn., 1899), I, 207-208.

I am mostly interested in the pictures, and though there are acres of daubs hanging on the walls yet I saw several as we hastily " did " Memorial Hall the other day which made me long for thee with all the lonesomeness which beauty brings around me when my dear Mate is absent. Yet I took some comfort in thinking that we *will* look on these things together some time this summer.

I do not hear from Emma Stebbins, and am at some loss to account for it. I wrote her, however, yesterday, and will likely get some explanation soon. Osgood was to write in two days after reaching Boston (starting on Sunday night from New York), and she was to send his proposition straightway to me. Inasmuch as she is now fully alive to the necessity of beginning the book, I do not doubt but we will make some satisfactory arrangement with other publishers if Osgood's proposition should not meet our views: and this will ensure our passing the summer together here.

Hal is going back to New York, tonight, for the purpose of having a farewell look at the little girl, and will *probably* leave there Wednesday night for the South. But these arrangements are all subject to change, as he is not particularly limited in time.

The papers are wondrously more respectful in their tone towards me, and it really seems as if my end of the see-saw was now rising steadily. I think the business has been of great value to all my artistic purpose, just at this stage of it: I have been compelled to throw aside every adventitious thing in the way of inspiration, God has been good to show me at the outset in its most repulsive form the fatal figure of Contemporary popularity, and to remind me how far apart from it were Shakespeare, Beethoven, and Bach. Herefrom I feel already resulting an immortal and unconquerable toughness of fibre in the strings of my Harp, insomuch that if the World shall attempt to play me — as it does play all the popular men — it will only get its awkward fingers sore. – – –

— And thou, out of all thy multitudinous destraction and sickness watching, and labors of removal, and damnable personal ill, – thou wouldst sit down and write me thy heavenly sweet words of comfort as " thy dear Poet " and the like ! This made many thoughts in my heart, and many tears in my eyes.

I enclose a slip of two for thy perusal. The NATION is marvellously another NATION than the contemptuous thing which a few weeks ago dismissed my poem in three lines. Of course all it says in this note is simply that sort of nonsense which Stoddard affectionately calls " Rot "; the NATION neither knows nor cares anything with regard to Music.[109]

Thomas stopped me last night and expressed his entire concurrence with my Tribune letter, in very cordial terms.[110]

— I desire deeply to know, dear beloved Wife, how thou art in thy spirit and body. Was it indeed the music which " unlocked thy prison-house ? " These mournful words of thine have affected my soul as nothing else thou hast ever said. I seem to be awaking from some vile infernal dream in which I have treated thee with flippancy, in which I have not been thy large comforter and patient helper. Dear Love, I know thou wilt forgive me, but I will not forgive myself until I have lived [?] thee a sweeter and humbler helpfulness. I look back and see how my selfish grief in thy sufferings was hindrance to

---

[109] The *Nation*, XXII, 336 (May 25, 1876), said that Lanier's letter to the *Tribune* in defense of his Cantata had the same defect that had marred his poem– the failure to use words with precise and definite meaning: " Mr. Lanier's poetic sensibility and serious purpose cannot make up for the lack of clear expression in his writing. This lack is the evidence not so much of want of practice in composition as of discipline in thought. His letter contains much that is interesting in regard to the extension of the capacity of the modern orchestra. . . . But the most important part of it is vitiated by a fallacy prevalent at the present time among loose thinkers concerning music. He affirms that the ideas in every poem intended for a musical accompaniment should belong only ' to that class of intellectual conceptions which is capable of being adequately expressed by orchestra instruments.' But music is not capable of adequately expressing any strictly intellectual conceptions; its function is not that of definite expression of ideas, or even of emotions. At its best, it can do nothing to express ideas; it can but arouse emotions in harmony with certain broad, intellectual conceptions. . . . Mr. Lanier has at least succeeded in showing that the difficulties of writing a good poem for musical accompaniment have been increased by the vast development of the powers of the orchestra, and that, with all his good-will, careful legality, and artistic purpose, he did not succeed in writing one that is universally approved."

[110] Similarly Dudley Buck expressed his approval in a letter of May 29, 1876, saying that Lanier's defense was "extremely dignified and manly. As far as my circle goes it has unquestionably produced a good effect, and elevated the author in their estimation." He added that he had worked out the plan of the music before allowing himself to look at Lanier's marginal suggestions in the working-copy and " on comparing was of course pleased to find that your idea & mine so nearly coincided." In conclusion he again urged Lanier to write him another cantata and some songs to set to music.

thee. Sweetheart, do not despair of me, till I have *one* more
chance of being with thee !

My heart is all tremulous with thee, as is this day tremulous –
through all the wheel-noises and grind of trade – with that
indescribable Sweetness we name The Spring, for I am thus thy

lover.

To Mary Day Lanier [111]

Pha.   May 28th 1876.

Today, dear Wife, I have done nothing save weave my
thoughts and loves about thee in all manner of curves and
traceries, as stars assembled about a tender white Moon.   I
had an invitation from Wehner [112] to come and spend the
morning with him.   I went at half-past ten, flute in hand. His
knowledge of English is even less than mine of German, and
we wasted not a word in talk beyond the usual salutations, but
went immediately to our matters, by a delightful plunge into a
volume of Kuhlau's duos which I had not before seen.   We
were in a cool retired parlor, the morning was sweet, there
was no third person in the room, the music was of the simple
grave religious character of Bach's, and my heart was all crying
for thee.   At the end of each movement, as we played straight
through the book, my big phlegmatic square-bottomed German
cried Goot ! and looked meaningly upon me: I said *wunder-
schön* , and looked meaningly upon him: and at the end of two
hours I made a hasty *adé* with a full heart, and came back to
the Peacock's for dinner.   But as I had played nothing but
thee, so I ate nothing but thee: and thou wilt therefore know
how, at this present moment, I am from soul to lip only a
Yearning-for-thee, – that is, only thy

lover .

---

[111] Previously published, *Scribner's*, XXV, 752 (June, 1899); reprinted,
Letters (New York, 1899), pp. 115-116.

[112] Carl Wehner, first flute in Theodore Thomas's Orchestra.   It was upon
his recommendation that Thomas had offered Lanier a position in his orchestra
whenever it could be expanded—an offer that never materialized.

To Mary Day Lanier

Ph^a May. 31st 1876

Dear Soul, I have still no definite news to tell thee. A letter
is come from Emma Stebbins, but it only brings word that
none has come from Osgood. I do not at all know why his
deliberations are protracted so much beyond their anticipated
duration. Of course I am expecting to hear every day.

I went out to Conshohocken, yesterday with Charles Clarke
("Max Adeler") for the purpose of looking at a boarding-
place of which he had advised me. Conshohocken is a small
town on a commanding elevation overlooking one of the most
[beautiful ?] stretches of the Schuylkill: and Clarke, who lives
there, is very fond of it. I found it a lovely situation. At the
boarding-house,—an old fashioned establishment in midst of a
yard much the same size and appearance of our Mrs. Earles'
at Marietta— I found our only possibility for accommodation
to be in a cottage which the proprietor has recently built in the
other end of the yard from the main building. Here we could
have three apartments, and board for ourselves children and a
servant, at $128 a month. The fare is said by fastidious people
to be perfect: the yard is full of fruit-trees, raspberries &c. and
the country is in midst of dairy-farms.

I made this tentative exploration fearing that Westchester
might prove too far from town for a permanent location. Conshohocken is about a half-hour's journey: while Westchester
is an hour and a quarter. I have not yet been to Westchester,
however. I expected to go today, meeting Harry on his return
from New York and making a joint visit with him. But a
telegram from him this morning postpones that until tomorrow
afternoon.

Thy little card is come, and I am thankful to know that all of
you are *assez bien.*

My heart takes no comfort until I am thy present adoring, as
I am now thine absent adoring,

                                                            lover.

To Mary Day Lanier

Pha.   June 8th 1876.

My Sweetest Soul:

How soon canst thou be ready to come on to me? I am just about to go over to Westchester on an afternoon train, for the purpose of looking at things over there, so as to make up my mind about engaging permanent quarters either there or in Conchohocken. Tomorrow I will run to Boston and find out what is the cause of the delay in Osgood's reply. The firm was in a somewhat shaky condition a year ago, resulting from the failure of Lee & Shepard; and I'm a little afraid the relief which they then obtained by selling off much of their most valuable copyright property may have been only temporary.

I think it best in all respects for thee to keep Rhinda by thee and *bring her on with thee.* She is good, she loves thee, and Mrs. McClellan was much pleased with her. We could retain her here with great advantage, and if we should afterwards see fit to get a white nurse, there would be no difficulty either in securing a good place for Rhinda, or in sending her back, – just as she might prefer. This would enable us to look out for a suitable white nurse at our leisure; it would also give us a month or two of ease from any particular care in that matter (Rhinda much pleased me by the inquiries she made after Harry and by the deep affection which she displayed in her undisguised joy at the idea of seeing him in Macon) for the girl loves thee and Hal devotedly; and it would set my mind free from what, as it approaches, seems to me intolerable, *i.e.,* your journey without a servant. This I cannot endure: and the cost of bringing Rhinda on is trifling,– not *more* than twenty five dollars, and perhaps (if Pope, to whom I have written, replies favorably) less than twenty. I would far rather pay double this sum than think of thee travelling in this warm weather without a nurse; indeed it is thy duty *not* to do that, the long days would weary thee beyond measure.

In three or four days I will send thee money to come with.

Pray, pray, Sweetheart, come in time for – for – this Glory of The Spring which is too much for the One-some heart of thy

lover.

To Robert S. Lanier

1425 Walnut St.
Pha , Pa.
June 12th 1876.

My dear Father:

Yours with enclosure came most opportunely and I thank you for both.

I expected to go to Boston last Friday, but hope to hear from there in a couple of days and to be relieved from the necessity of the journey.

I spent Thursday night with McClellan at West Chester, and we devoted some time to exploring the boarding-places. I do not think there will be any difficulty in finding a place for you and Mama (at 8 to 10 dollars a week apiece) near ourselves, whenever you get ready to come. It is of course impossible to engage board without knowing exactly what day you will come: but this is not necessary, for there is now, and will continue to be, the greatest abundance of room, nothing being crowded except the hotels. It will however be well enough for you to ascertain your day of departure as soon as you can, so that May and I, during our stay at West Chester, may perfect some arrangement by which we can all be near together. I wrote to Pope about rates: and have just received his answer – that the rates are " agreed " (at $26 a single ticket to Pha: $41.75 for round trip tickets) except when parties of more than *fifteen* are made up, in which case only is he entitled to make reductions. I will send Mary, on Wednesday, seventy five dollars, and if you can add fifty to this, it will not only get her here, but will, I have every reason to hope, constitute my last demand on your purse for several months.

I find that McClellan has a charming place, and the West Chester air is as much like that of Marietta as two peas. After we have spent our visit there, however, it will probably suit us better to be at Media, a village half way between Pha and West Chester. I met Bayard Taylor passing through town today, on his way back to N. Y. from Kennett Square (12 miles from

West Chester) where he has his old ancestral farm and where he has just carried his wife and daughter for the summer. We arranged for some happy Saturdays and Sundays (when he gets off from his desk in THE TRIBUNE office) to be spent together. He says that my letter has made a clean sweep of the prickly critics: and tells me that the *Independence Belge's* Correspondent at the Centennial opening gave hearty praise to the Cantata, both poem and music, and of other kindly expressions from various sources. DWIGHT'S JOURNAL OF MUSIC has reprinted my letter in full.[113]

The enclosed little slip from the Burlington HAWK-EYE made me scream: show it to May.[114] The parody which I also enclose has some good points — particularly the Angel's Song — that were very effectively laughed over when I read it at the Peacock's dinner-table the other day.[115]

God bless you all.

S. L.

[113] XXXVI, 242-243 (June 10, 1876). No file of the *Independance Belge* has been found for this period.

[114] An undated clipping from the Burlington, Iowa, *Hawkeye* (Charles D. Lanier Collection, Johns Hopkins University) reads: " Out on South Hill, Sunday evening, a fond young man, inspired by the love which mocks at fears, disobeyed the stern parental injunction ' Never to darken that door again,' and rang the bell. It was answered by paterfamilias in person and the young man, although he had never read Lanier's poem, felt the unseen influence of 178 pounds ' moving about his moveless base far below his resting place.' Thus the discipline of adversity attunes the soul to the loftiest flights of poesy." (The allusion is to lines 9-10 of Lanier's Cantata.)

[115] Two parodies of Lanier's Cantata have been found. One, in The New York *World*, May 13, 1876, was a burlesque letter from " The Grand Lama of Thibet " entitled: " FIAT JUSTITIA. / MR. LANIER'S PLAGIARISM EXPOSED – THE CENTENNIAL CANTATA IN ITS ORIGINAL FORM." After three paragraphs of obvious nonsense the writer said: " Permit me, sir, in this centennial year to lay on the altar of our common country my cantata in its original and authentic form, freed from the puerilities of the hireling jackdaw who would fain have strutted in its peacock plumage."

A second survives in an unidentified, undated newspaper clipping (Charles D. Lanier Collection, Johns Hopkins University) with the prefatory statement: " It is difficult to imagine the feelings of Mr. Sidney Lanier reading this most audacious travesty of his Centennial Cantata. The author is unknown to us; we find it in the New York *Graffic.*" A pencilled annotation on the clipping says: " It is by Richard Scudder." A search of the files of the New York *Daily Graffic* fails to reveal the original printing. (The texts of both parodies are given in vol. I of the present edition.)

To Robert S. Lanier

New York. June 26th 1876

My dear Father:

I met my party of dear ones at Baltimore, and brought them safely into harbor by Wednesday night.[116] May was greatly overcome by fatigue; and, judging from my own sensations after taking the care of the youngsters off her hands during Wednesday, she had cause. What a precious trio of little monkeys they are!

Under Mrs. McClellan's thoughtful nursing May begins to brighten up very greatly, and I think the new atmosphere and surroundings generally will soon make another and better physique for her. How you would delight in the country round about West Chester! It is surely the perfection of pastoral regions. It seems to me that you could come on with Mamma and live here for a month or two without spending any more money than you would if you were at home. I beg that you will do this; May tells me you are overworked, and I can easily believe it. It would seem to be almost like a duty for you to take some rest; and we could have a charming retirement together somewhere among these lovely hills. Don't come before the middle of August, unless it should be greatly more convenient to come earlier.

I expect to go to Boston tonight, on a flying trip, and write hurriedly. Love to Mama & Pringle. You had better address me " *care of R. M. McClellan, West Chester, Pa.*"

Your loving

Sidney.

---

[116] Lanier had met his wife and children in Baltimore on Wednesday, June 21. In urging her to come some ten days earlier than she had planned, Lanier said in his letter of June 15, 1876 (here omitted): "I have been through much that required all my powers of resistance: . . . in short, I must have thy dear company and thy nursing, I am not well, my spirit is sick. . . . I have had *so* many cruel and unexpected disappointments just on the verge of accomplishment, I need thee every hour to get some more strength for work; come to me."

To Mary Day Lanier

Westminster Hotel. N. Y.
June 28th 1876.

My dearest Heart,   I am just off the steamer by which I returned from Boston last night.

I had two interviews with Osgood yesterday. He appeared
to have what the Presbyterians call a realizing sense of his own
exceeding sinfulness in having dilly-dally'd so long, and manifestly tried in various ways to make what reparation he could.

He offers, in brief, to pay me two thousand dollars,– in six
monthly instalments –, and to assume all the other expenses of
the book, commencing to pay Miss Stebbins a copy-right of ten
per cent on the retail price after ten thousand copies shall have
been sold. He is to be in New York tomorrow, and is to call
on me here. Meantime I am going to consult Bayard Taylor,
and, if he agrees, propose a slight modification which Osgood
has already intimated his willingness to accept. I hope then to
hear tomorrow evening from Miss Stebbins – to whom I have
written – and so to conclude the whole business happily and fly
back to thee for whose dear eyes I long every minute in the
day. I will remain here until the matter is finished, and may
not reach thee before Friday.

I have just sent off four little poems to Dudley Buck, to be set
to music (if so be that they shall find favor in his eyes, – or his
ears), in response to a request of his wh. has been several times
repeated.[117] I have also written a long letter to Miss Stebbins,

----

[117] There is no direct evidence of what these four poems were, but the best
conjecture seems to be " A Song of Love," " To ——, With a Rose," and the
two parts of " Rose-Morals " (see note to the last-named, vol. I). On Aug. 21,
1876, Buck wrote to Lanier returning the four poems and saying that although
he liked them as poems they were not suitable for musical settings: " You
refer to their not being ' conventional ' songs– Suppose you try your hand at
one that *you would call* ' conventional '– . . . I want an ' Evening Song,' a sort
of ' Ueber allen Gipfeln ist Ruh ' but longer. Likewise a real bright tripping
jolly one." Apparently Lanier composed his " Evening Song " (I, 88) during September or October, 1876, at West Chester and sent it to Buck. For the
latter wrote on Nov. 7, 1876: " I composed your song last night at ' one heat '
and . . . like the composition very well. . . . Now as to title. Evening Song
is too indefinite– besides– yours is (Hallelujah!) an utterly unconventional evening song." Buck asked him to change the title to " On the Sea Shore " and to

explaining various matters connected with Osgood's proposition. I wrote my father of thine arrival, on Monday. Tomorrow I will go and see little Daughter.[118] Now, I have to go to the Bank, down town. Thus thou has my present, past, and future – as far as I know it – all these however being but phrases which mean at bottom that I am thy

lover.

To Clifford A. Lanier

New York, June 29th – 1876

My dearest Clifford: Enclosed is a check to your order for fifty dollars which I beg you will apply, one-half to *your* fifty, and the other half to Dr. Gaston's account. Please tell Dr. Gaston at the same time that as soon as I get my next month's wages – which will be just a month from now – the balance of his bill will be paid; – and give the same information to Mr. Clifford A. Lanier.

I am just returning from Boston where I was compelled to go for the purpose of completing negotiations in the matter of the Cushman book. Osgood has finally made a proposition wh. I have accepted. I am to get two thousand dollars in monthly instalments. This Mr. Taylor considers very liberal and so do I.

I long to know when you are coming hitherward. My dear ones are now all at West Chester, where I safely convoyed them a week ago. We are guests of our ancient friend Miller McClellan, and our surroundings are sweet and wholesome as can be. Such reachings of green hills, such vasty waves of clover, such brooks down such dells, such all-day mazes of

---

revise the line "Now in the sea's *red cordial* melts the Sun," saying that "the simile seems drawn too much from 'Curaçoa,' or Angostola Bitters!" (Lanier revised the line but not the title.) He continued: "The 'Egypt's pearl' and 'Cleopatra Night' idea is simply lovely and as new as lovely, albeit I fear it will escape the brains of most *singers*. In writing songs for actual composition I think it ordinarily advisable to consider this point, as it will often ensure a better vocal rendering. I have written your Song for Alto or Baritone." He concluded by requesting more poems to set to music, asking that in the future Lanier avoid compound words as much as possible.

[118] Mary Louise Day, who was being treated at St. Luke's Hospital.

robin-melodies, – never have I seen or heard, and I am almost too happy at being amid all these things (as I shall be to-morrow) with my fair four lovers. If *you* and *yours* can also be among them with us, I shall have no more petition to trouble Heaven with in a long while.

You don't know how much esteemed our last little Uncle Jim song is: de Baptissis is quoted right and left.[119] Mr. Taylor told me last night that Whitelaw Reid was speaking to him of it the other day in fine terms, and thinks we shd. write more of them. Cannot we make a general song for Uncle Jim *apropos* of the two equally good presidential candidates? He commences " Good mahnin', Mass John &c :

> – – –Thank you, Sah, I'se powerful weak dis mahnin'.
> Hauh? How I gwine vote?
> Well: Miss Wilsie used to sing a song
> When I was a little nigger 'bout *How happy*

could I be, ef t'other dear Charmer &c," But between these two ends of the poem he discusses Tilden (He's de man what cotch de rogues): & what's Hayes dun? Aint dun nuthin? Dat's better'n some on 'em 'at's done a good deal &c. I'm writing in a flying hurry, and just put down these disjointed words as suggestions to your invention. Let the fundamental aim of the poem be: an example set by dear old Uncle Jim of a *fair* discussion of candidates, and its tendency be to curb the abominable lies and campaign-manufactures which the papers are dealing in about men *either* of whom would be infinitely better than Grant or any of that ilk.[120]

Commend me to Grandmother & Aunt Jane, and my dear

---

[119] " Uncle Jim's Baptist Revival Hymn," by Sidney and Clifford Lanier, published in *Scribner's*, May, 1876. (Their previous dialect poem, " The Power of Prayer," had also dealt with Uncle Jim.)

In her letter of May 14, 1876, Mary Day Lanier had reported: " Clifford wishes thee to perceive that ' Uncle Jim ' has not escaped scoring either, and to that effect sends thee the enclosed answer– out of ' de grass.' Having learned that Mrs. Worth was the perpetrator he has to-day mailed to her the reply on the opposite side of the leaf." Neither Mrs. Worth's answer nor Clifford Lanier's response has been found.

[120] The presidential campaign of 1876, in which Rutherford B. Hayes won by a slender and bitterly contested margin over Samuel J. Tilden. No negro dialect poem by the Lanier brothers dealing with the material here indicated has been found.

waterlily Will.   You had better address me " Care of R. M.
McClellan Esq.   West Chester Pa."

Always

Yr.

S.[121]

To Bayard Taylor [122]

West Chester, Pa.
July 19th 1876.

My dear Mr. Taylor:

I'm just crawling back into some sort of
shambling activity after a very depressing illness; and my congratulations on the success of your ode will therefore not be
considered by you as too late to enter in.

I found that Gen. Hawley had been kind enough to send me
an invitation to the platform; [123] but it did not arrive until
some days after the event, having been sent to Baltimore and
forwarded from several other addresses before finally reaching
me.   I hear, however, the most pleasant accounts of the complete success both of your matter and your manner on the
" stately day ", from Mr. Peacock.   My retired position – we
are boarding at a farm-house about a mile from West Chester,
Mr. Thompson's – has rather taken me out of range of the
newspapers, and I have seen no newspaper-account of the Ceremonies except the Pha BULLETIN'S.   I sincerely hope that the

[121] Since Lanier and his wife were together from this time on until the end
of his life, except for occasional brief periods, the number of his surviving
letters for the next five years is considerably less than for the previous five.

No letters by Lanier between June 29 and July 19, 1876, have been found.
Letters from Emma Stebbins during this period, however, indicate his disappointment and embarrassment over the indefinite postponement of Charlotte Cushman's memoir, because of Miss Stebbin's ill health– after he had accepted one
month's salary from the publisher, Osgood.   Lanier's own illness, referred to in
the following letter, was undoubtedly in part the result of the tension under
which he was living because of these circumstances.   On July 19, 1876, Mary
Day Lanier wrote to Clifford Lanier: " Sidney has left his bed but is not yet
materially better.   He recommenced yesterday his whiskey and flute-playing."

[122] Previously published, *Atlantic Monthly*, LXXXIV, 127-128 (July, 1899) ;
reprinted, *Letters* (New York, 1899), pp. 169-170. (Taylor's reply, July 21,
1876, is printed in *Letters*, p. 170.)

[123] Taylor's Ode was read at the 4th of July celebration of the Centennial
Exposition.

malice which you thought likely might seize this opportunity to vent itself has recoiled before the calm and noble front of your ode. I have not seen or heard any evidences of its activity.

My wife sends you all manner of pleasant messages, which I should detail if I were strong enough to do much writing. Please keep me in fair remembrance with Mrs. Taylor and your daughter.

My address is simply " West Chester ", where I have a box at the P. O. I hope you are not now so busy as before the Fourth and are finding some time to rest.

Your faithful

S. L.

TO ROBERT S. LANIER

West Chester, Pa.
July 24th 1876.

My dear Father:

I fear you are troubling yourself more than necessary about the mutations of my fortunes. I note all you say in this behalf, and regret that you should be taking pains to think so much about it at a time when you must certainly be in need of rest.

Perhaps now — judging from more recent letters of Miss Stebbins' — the Cushman book will be postponed merely : and I have written her today that I would wish to receive two months' salary (*one* has already been paid me), in order to enable me so to arrange matters as to enable me to hold myself in readiness to recommence work with her whenever she was able.

I will also write to Mr. Lanier, though I would much rather starve than do it, if my personal fate were solely concerned.

We have left Mrs. McClellans and are boarding at a very pleasant farm-house about a half mile from West Chester. Our board costs us about a hundred dollars a month, which is considered a very cheap arrangement for these parts. The people of the house are all we could desire, and we are already greatly attached to them. You can address me simply at " West

Chester, Pa." I have a box at the Post Office, and the clerks are very careful.

All are pretty well except me. I've been somewhat under the weather for some days; part of the time in bed. A cool change has brought me up however, and I hope soon to be much better.

I have paid part of my month's board. If the arrangement I propose to Miss Stebbin be accepted, I shall be in funds for this and the next month. Meantime, I will be glad if you can send me sixty dollars, as the balance of my board will be needed by our hosts immediately, while my salary will not be due until the second of next month. When this comes I will return you the sixty. I will hope to get it as soon as you can send it.

We have had the most terrific weather, and I have never suffered from heat nearly so much before. They say here it is wholly exceptional: and I hope it is, – otherwise I shall think of going *South* for the next summer!

Please ask Uncle Clifford to get for me a letter of introduction from Prof. Le Conte [124] to Prof. Gilman, Prst of the Johns Hopkins University, at Baltimore. Uncle C. can give him such information as to my devotion to Art as he may desire: but perhaps Prof. LeC. is not on such terms with Prof. Gilman as would authorize him to do this. You can see.

All send love to you & Mama.

Your son,

S. L.

TO ROBERT S. LANIER

West Chester, Pa.
[Aug. 7, 1876?] [125]

My dear Father:

Yours with enclosure of Sixty dollars came duly and gave great relief in a crisis otherwise difficult to rule.

I made my application for a loan to Mr. Lanier, and yester-

---

[124] Joseph LeConte (1823-1901), professor of geology at the University of California, where he had known Daniel Coit Gilman, recently called to Baltimore to become president of the newly founded Johns Hopkins University. Lanier's aunt by marriage, Mrs. Clifford Anderson (née Anna LeConte), was a niece of LeConte. (See note 139, and Lanier's letter of Oct. 4, below.)

[125] Conjectural dating from the accompanying envelope.

day received an answer refusing it. He "was just about leaving for a prolonged absence: had given up all matters of business, in consequence of feeble health, &c. &c." The letter was written by another person, and stated that Mr. L. had long ago abandoned all attempts to write.

Of course there isn't the least use in regretting this failure.

But I am obliged to ask you to make a negotiation with Mr. Goodall again for me. My box of Silver is still there. It is absolutely necessary for me to raise three hundred dollars immediately. Miss Stebbins's health now quite precludes all idea of the Cushman book, and I must return two hundred and fifty dollars of salary which was paid me by Osgood under the contract more than a month ago. It is to pay this $250 that I want the money from Goodall, – the other fifty serving to start me on next month's board. If you can get this for three months it will be well for me. Should you wish my name on the draft, this will be authority for you to sign it in as full a manner as I could myself.

I am very much better, and as full of fight as e'er a game cock that has struck out. I doubt not to get in some work in a day or two that will keep my pot boiling. I beg you will not let these matters trouble you, my dear Father; if another year send me as much higher above my present state as the last did above its precedent, I will certainly be out of reach of all similar trouble.

A letter has come to me from Terre Haute, Indiana, in which a very enthusiastic gentleman [126] praises the Psalm of the West as a " wonderful poem ", and thinks the people will come to it yet. Have you seen my little song [127] in Scribner's for August?

I hope every day to have certain news of seeing you soon. A letter from Clifford surprises us with information that he is at New Haven.

---

[126] A. H. Dooley, a book-dealer. His letter, dated July 10, 1876, has survived. In his answer of Aug. 15, 1876 (here omitted), Lanier said: " Messrs. Lippincott & Co. of Philadelphia inform me that they intend issuing a volume containing three poems of mine– Corn, The Symphony, and Psalm of the West– during the coming fall. These are my first poems, excepting short songs which have appeared in Scribner's and Lippincott's Magazines." " The Psalm of the West " had been made the feature of the July issue of Lippincott's, with the name of both poem and author printed in bold type across the front cover.

[127] " A Song of the Future " (see note 163, 1875).

—— I hope you will be able to see Goodall immediately and forward me the results thereof.

God bless you,– say all here, including Mama as "you". We hope Pringle is better.

Your loving

S. L.

To Edward Spencer [128]

West Chester, Pa.
Aug. 15th 1876

Dear Mr. Spencer:

A long illness has kept me from complying with your request until I fear the time is past when I can be of service to you. I am not sure, from your letter, whether it is the topography, or the personnel, of the club you want.

The former is simple. The club-building is on 15th St. between Irving Place and 4th Avenue, and looks as to its exterior like nothing but a plain brick dwelling-house. One enters and passes into a room on the right where one hangs one's hat on a peg, most likely alongside of hats that give one a sensation of awe – vast castors, much belled in the crown, with a certain look of the back-rooms of banks and trustee-meetings about them. Opposite this, across a passage, is the newspaper-room, where are files of all the papers. The passage gives presently into a stately room where are knots of gentlemen smoking and talking, the furniture being arranged for those indulgences, and the wine-room opening conveniently into the apartment. Your friend who carried you in asks you what you will take almost immediately; summons a colored waiter, delivers him your order (which if you are wise will be for brandy-and-soda, it being the best tipple of that nature I have ever seen), lights cigars, and points out to you the notabilities; calling them up if he knows them and introducing you in a very easy and informal way. On *my* first night I thus met Gov. Tilden, Mr. Dor-

---

[128] Previously published, *Studies in Philology*, XXVII, 475-476 (July, 1930). Spencer's letter, to which this is an answer, has not survived.

Lanier's visits to the Century Club in New York, here described, were during the preceding October (see notes 167 and 176, 1875).

sheimer, Whitelaw Reid, Ward (the Sculptor) Stedman, Stoddard, McDonough, and many others.   One is likely to see
young Austin Flint (a very fine-looking man), Draper, Gifford
(the painter), Bayard Taylor, Conant (the sleek beast of
Harper's Weekly) Bryant, and many others.[129]   Without ceremony you approach any of the groups formed: at the first lull
in the talk your friend introduces you round, the circle is opened
for you, you are asked to sit down and to have a cigar along
with whatever the people are drinking, – and then the conversation goes on, whatever you may have to say being listened to
with great politeness and respect – though among the familiars
one hears many sharp repartees and the utmost candor of dis-
agreement though always in good taste and gentlemanly respect
for opposing opinion.   Presently folding-doors open (this is
on a Saturday night only) and a table is seen in the centre
of a large room, containing Oysters in various forms, salads,
crackers, sardines, lemons, &c; at one side of the room is another
large table which is a vast plateau of oysters on the half shell,
which you approach and prod up with silver oyster forks, being
very liberal previously with your lemon-juice and salt and
pepper.   This supper is free to all members and guests and is
served each Saturday night during the season.   Both this dining-
room and the room last mentioned have doors open into an
apartment as large as both of them which is hung with valuable
paintings many of them by members of the Club, and around
the base-board of which are shelves containing current numbers
of many reviews and magazines in several languages.   Here
one smokes and reads, or gazes at the pictures, or chats more
en duo with one's friend.   These comprise the lower rooms;
the story above has the rich hall of the Club, the library &c; I
explored it very hastily, and do not remember much of it, the
pleasant talk downstairs being very attractive to me during the

---

[129] Samuel J. Tilden (1814-1886), retiring governor of New York and Democratic candidate for the presidency; Wm. E. Dorsheimer (1832-1888), lieutenant-
governor of New York, 1874-1878; Austin Flint (1836-1915), professor of
physiology at the Bellevue Hospital Medical College; probably John W. Draper
(1811-1882) or his son Henry Draper (1837-1882), both professors at the
University of the City of New York and pioneers in astronomical photography;
either Sanford R. Gifford (1823-1880) or Robert S. Gifford (1840-1905), both
landscape painters; S. S. Conant, editor of *Harper's Weekly*, 1869-1885. The
others here mentioned are identified in note 167, 1875, except McDonough.

four or five visits I made. Soon after my first visit – when I was the guest of Bayard Taylor – a card was sent me, signed by him, Stedman and Stoddard, inviting me to use the privileges of the Club for thirty days.

These items will probably furnish you with what you want. If they do not, I will take great pleasure in supplementing them as far as I am able.

I hope your health is good. Pray give my love to Dr. Browne when you see him or write him. I am here for the summer: address simply, West Chester, Pa. What's the novel you're writing?

Sincerely yours

Sidney Lanier.

To Robert S. Lanier

West Chester, Pa.
Aug. 22nd 1876.

My dear Father:

I was prevented from writing you on Sunday by a junketing in which May and I were engaged all day. Mr. Taylor wrote for us to come and spend that day with him at Cedar Croft, his home near Kennett Square; and we drove over in a buggy (twelve miles) Sunday morning, returning in the afternoon after a pleasant day in one of the most magnificent homes I ever saw. About a hundred yards from the house stand a couple of chestnut trees supposed to be eight hundred years old: and May and I both wished, as we stood under them with Mr. Taylor, that you might see their majesties.

I hope to see you in about a week from now. I fancy however that the cool weather will be soon driving you away from Saratoga: and if this should be so I will meet you in New York. Write me, as soon as you receive this, your movements as far as you know them. I send a letter of Clifford's just received, from which you will be able to calculate so as to meet him, if you desire it, when he comes to New York.

Pray send some twenty five dollars when you write.

May and the children are in tolerable condition: I, not very
well.[130]

I enclose a letter from May to Mama written some time ago
and rescued from the mail just as we heard of your departure
from Macon.

All send love to yourself and Mama. I've been hard at work
for several days on a lot of poems, and am considerably fagged
with writing.[131]

Your son

S. L.

To Mary Day Lanier

St. Denis Hotel, N. Y.
Sunday, Sep. 3rd 1876

My Sweetest Heart. I arrived here safely last night, and
found Clifford just coming in from supper, which he and family
had been taking at the " Quaker Dairy " over against this hotel,
the same being cheaper than the restaurant hereunto appertaining. Father and Mama arrived yesterday morning by boat
from Boston: having been compelled (with Mr. [Monroe?]
Ogden also) to sit up all night in consequence of failing to get
a state-room, there being a great rush of passengers. They are
at Mrs. Watson's, corner of Fifteenth St. & 5th Avenue; but will
move here tomorrow, not liking the fare there. They both
seem well, and have apparently taken a vast deal of enjoyment
from their journey.

This morning we all sallied forth and went over to Green-

---

[130] Mary Day Lanier had written Clifford Lanier, Aug. 17: " S— keeps up,
but his troubles are not checked and develope every few days into some added
forms of suffering. He cannot use his old *supportive* treatment: it increases
pain; so only the flute & cream nourishment are within his power."

[131] One of these was probably " Clover " (I, 84), Lanier's pencilled notes
for which fill the back of a letter from J. R. Osgood dated July 21 and the
three blank pages of Bayard Taylor's letter of Aug. 16, 1876. Another was
probably " The Waving of the Corn " (I, 83), references to which appear in
Lanier's letters of Sept. 21 and Oct. 6, 1876 (see notes 135 and 140, below).
The sentence may also refer to printer's copy of the poems for Lanier's forthcoming volume, which he was presumably working on at this time (see note
126, above).

wood, we all being Clifford and family, Will Chambers [132] and family, Father and Mama, and thy poor lover. In gorgeous weather, and with much talk to exchange, we had a pleasant visit to the dead city, and are but lately back. Tonight we are going to Gilmore's Garden, where they are going to attempt the Fifth Symphony, and give what is called a Sacred Concert.

There has been no talk of plans yet, for lack of time: but Father does not wish to remain here more than two or three days, and I now judge (without *knowing* at all) that next Thursday will see us in Philadelphia. But hereof I will write thee with more particularity tomorrow—if the plans are made by that time.

Enclosed is ten dollars for thy Ph^a trip. I hurry to mail this hoping it may reach thee tomorrow morning.

There has been much inquiring after thee and yearning about thee, among those here: but none so fervent, none so expressed and born out of the deep of perfect lonesomeness as the continual desire-after-thee which runs currently West Chester-ward from thy

husband.

The check is endorsed by me payable to thine order. Write thy name across the back of it, and present it to the bank (any bank) in West Chester. They will cash it for thee.

To Mary Day Lanier

N. Y. Sep. 7th 1876

With the most worthy intentions to tell thee of my condition, Dearest of loving hearts, have I commenced each of the two scrawls that have gone to thee from here: and each time have these intentions been broken up into small bits suitable only for the paving of that fearsome place which is said to be macadamized with these same parlous materials.

In truth, tis no easy matter to tell thee how I am. In the matter of the special trouble whereunto thou wert wont to

[132] William Chambers of Montgomery had married the sister of Mrs. Clifford Lanier.

minister with such heavenly and allowing patience, I am certainly better.

In the matter of lungs I am changed somewhat, but much suffering. The soreness and irritation are not so great as when I left thee: but a continual manufacture of phlegm keeps me in much discomfort and I seem unable to free myself therefrom. I sit and purr, like a cat. This endless internal rattling is hard to endure.

If it were not for thy positive command, thou shouldst not have these details of suffering. But thou assurest me of thy desire for them in such sweet pleading that I find no peace of mind save by doing as thou wishest.

My yearning for thee is mortal. I do nothing day or night save simply wish that I were by thee. Within the small boundary of the belt which maybe thou art at this moment buckling about thy waist, thou enclosest all the world of my wishes.

"
——————
"

Aunt Jane and Mina Eason are here, and both revile the cross-purposes which caused them to miss thee in Pha on Tuesday. They were at the Continental two days, and at the Exhibition on both.

We all leave here (except the two Aunts aforementioned who remain a week in N. Y.) tomorrow for Pha, and I will hasten on to thee by the earliest train after our arrival. I do not know which one, but thou wilt see me on Saturday morning some time. It may turn out I will telegraph thee to come to Pha. Allow all manner of margins for change of plan and be not expectant until I come. – My dear beautiful boys, – I long for them inexpressibly. I commend thee to the God who hath power to make me thy happy present

lover.

To Daniel C. Gilman

West Chester, Pa.
Sept. 18th 1876.

Dear Sir:

May I trouble you to cause to be sent me at above address any Prospectus or other the like paper which may have been issued containing the scheme of Johns Hopkins University so far as now perfected ? I do not know the proper officer to be addressed in this behalf; and beg that you will consider this ignorance a valid reason for venturing to send my request to you.

The particular information which I desire is as to any means which may be offered by the University to those prosecuting special original researches in science.

Very respectfully

Sidney Lanier.[188]

Prest D. C. Gilman
Baltimore,
Md.

To Bayard Taylor [184]

West Chester, Pa.
Sep. 21st 1876.

My dear Mr. Taylor:

In spite of the rejected poem which your letter contained, I was glad – O Might of Friendship (for I fondly expected twenty five dollars instead of this *ms.*) ! – to get your little message.

[188] Gilman wrote Lanier, Sept. 21, 1876, that the facilities for scientific research at Johns Hopkins were " as good . . . as the country affords." He concluded: " I hope that another winter will not pass without my having the pleasure of meeting you personally." (See Lanier's letter of Oct. 4, 1876, below.)

[184] Previously published, *Atlantic Monthly*, LXXXIV, 128 (July, 1899); reprinted, *Letters* (New York, 1899), pp. 170-171.

I don't at all know why they sent it to *you*: the poem contained my address plainly written on the last page. It was making you *particeps criminis*. In order that you may see the unrelieved blackness of their (*i.e.* D^r. Holland's,) guilt, I send you the poem and message accompanying, which you can read in some little by-time when you've nothing better to do.[185]

As to pen and ink, and all toil, I've been almost suppressed by continual illness. I can't tell you how much I sigh for some quiet evenings at the Century where I might hear some of you talk about the matters I love, or merely sit and think in the atmosphere of the thinkers. I fancy one can almost come to know the dead thinkers too well: a certain mournfulness of longing seems sometimes to peer out from behind one's joy in one's Shakespeare and one's Chaucer, – a sort of physical protest and yearning of the living eye for its like. Perhaps one's friendship with the dead poets comes indeed to acquire something of the quality of worship, through the very mystery which withdraws them from us and which allows no more messages from them, cry how we will, after that sudden and perilous stoppage. I hope those are not illegitimate moods in which one sometimes desires to surround oneself with a companionship less awful, and would rather have a friend than a god.

May joins me in begging to be kept in remembrance by the ladies of your house.

Don't take the trouble of returning the poem: I've another copy.

Your friend

Sidney L.

---

[185] Apparently Taylor had submitted Lanier's poem, "The Waving of the Corn," to *Scribner's*, the editor of which had rejected it, and Taylor had returned it to Lanier with a letter that has not been found. (See also Lanier's letter of Oct. 6, 1876, and note 140, below.)

A few days later, on Sept. 25, Lanier submitted another poem to *Scribner's*–presumably "Clover"– with the following remark: "The enclosed grew out of a mood of solemn protest against the doctrine of 'Art for Art's Sake,' which has led so many of our young artists into the most unprofitable and even blasphemous activities." (This letter has not been found; the passage here quoted was printed in *Van Nosdall's List of Books for Sale*, No. 300, June 2, 1929.)

To Gibson Peacock [136]

West Chester, Pa.
Oct. 4th 1876.

My dear friend:

I had expected to be in Philadelphia today, and to answer your kind inquiries in person. But some of those hateful things mildly called circumstances beyond one's control prevented, and I send a note to say how much obliged we have been by your thoughtful communication from Brunswick.[137] Our own advices from Mr. Day, which had been delayed in some way, now arrive regularly.

I returned from Baltimore late on Saturday. Mr. Gilman, Prest of Johns Hopkins University, received me with great cordiality. I took tea with him on Thursday, and he devoted his entire evening to discussing with me some available method of connecting me with the University officially. The main difficulty was in adjusting the special work which I wish to do to the existing scheme of the institution. I found that Mr. Gilman was familiar with all my poems, and he told me that he had thought of inviting me to a position in the University, last winter, but did not know whether I had ever pursued any special studies. He had been greatly attracted by the Cantata,[138] and its defence. It was finally agreed that a proposition should be made to the Trustees to create for me a sort of nondescript chair of "poetry and music", giving me leave to shape my lectures into any mould I desired. He is to choose whatever time may seem suitable to him, in which to broach the project: and will then write me the result. I have no doubt of his sincere desire for the favorable consummation of the business: and inasmuch as the most happy relations have heretofore existed between him and the Trustees, it would seem that the prospect is good.[139]

---

[136] Previously published, *Atlantic Monthly*, LXXIV, 28 (July, 1894); reprinted, *Letters* (New York, 1899), pp. 30-31.

[137] There was an epidemic of yellow fever in Brunswick, where Peacock as well as Lanier had relatives. (Fanny Westmoreland, mentioned at the end of this letter, was Mrs. Peacock's niece.)

[138] See note 91, above.

[139] In a letter to his father, Oct. 1, 1876 (here omitted), Lanier had said:

I am better than when you saw me last, but still suffering much with cough. May is much worn with nursing Harry, who has been quite troublesome of nights.

I hope you are both well. I'm trying hard to get May off to Ph^a again soon, for a day and night; the tonic of seeing or hearing anything beautiful seems to have a wonderful effect on her. She joins in loving messages to you both.

We hear that Fanny Westmoreland was married, on her sick bed, to Mr. duBignon. Harry Day is out: Mr. Day – *pére* – still in Macon forwarding supplies to Brunswick. Your Faithful

Friend,

S. Lanier

To BAYARD TAYLOR [140]

West Chester, Pa.
Oct. 6th 1876

My dear Mr. Taylor:

I've been absent in Baltimore, and this will explain my delay in writing to thank you for the evident trouble you were at in behalf of my poem. Your somewhat

---

" Of course we could do nothing final, the whole appointing power being lodged in an Executive Committee of the Trustees: but Mr. Gilman assured me, in parting, that everything would be done by him which he *could* do to bring about a connection between myself and the University of some description. . . . It is probable that both my work and salary would be small, the first year: but both would increase if the former should prove acceptable."
From the beginning Gilman seems to have been eager to attach Lanier to the faculty of the Johns Hopkins University, probably recalling the success with which the poet Edward Rowland Sill had taught at the University of California.
[140] Previously published, *Atlantic Monthly*, LXXXIV, 129 (July, 1899); reprinted, *Letters* (New York, 1899), pp. 172-174.
In his letter of Sept. 23, 1876 (*Letters*, p. 172), to which this is a reply, Taylor had written: " I've read your poem over several times, and am quite clear about it. The title, ' The Waving of the Corn,' is slightly fantastic, rather than fanciful, and the word, or act, of *waving* is too weak for a refrain. The last stanza is quite unnecessary: it drops out of the tone of the three preceding ones, forces a moral where none is needed, and is in no sense poetical. *Voilà tout!* I don't know that precisely these things decided Dr. Holland; but I feel pretty sure that he would have accepted the poem had they not been. The rest is so sweet, tranquil, and beautiful, that it has the best right *to be*, without a moral. Now, don't take offence, but let me make the changes in your MS. and send with this, just to show you– not how *I* should have written it (our ways are

serious defense of Dr. Holland leads me to fear, a little, that you misunderstood my allusion to his " criminality &c " in rejecting the poem – which I meant for the merest joke. A good deal of experience in these matters renders it quite impossible for me to have any *feeling* as to the judgment of any given person upon the merits of a poem, or its availability for magazine purposes: for I have seen that these judgments depend upon two elements which are infinitely variable: the mood of the person judging, and the particular idea which he may have formed in his mind of that phantasm called the General Public. Certainly nothing can be more striking than the perpetual reversal of such decrees by time and the popular tide; and the day is quite past when I could be in the least disturbed by any contemporary judgment either as to the artistic quality, or probable popularity, of a poem.

I am thus didactically particular for the reason that you really seemed to think I was cherishing enmity against the Scribner gentlemen, whereas the fact is that I feel greatly obliged to them for a general reception of my little offerings far more hearty than I could expect, in view of our wholly different ways of looking at things.

And as for your prefacing your own suggestions with " Now don't take offence, but &c ", – nothing could be more absurd; – offence, indeed!

I find myself agreeing with two of your verbal criticisms on THE WAVING OF THE CORN (the " haply undainty ", and the equivocal " faint "); and though not agreeing at all with your condemnation of the last stanza, I think I will strike it out, as likely to produce a disagreeable impression of moralizing. In reality it is a rigorous carrying out of the idea of *personal* tranquillity: advancing beyond that, to the conception of the larger tranquillity of *Society*.

It's very good of you to offer to try THE GALAXY: but I wouldn't like the poem to win a place in print upon any influence save its own merits; – and, if this objection were disposed

not the same, you know), but how I think *you* should have written it. The feeling of peace and blissful pastoral seclusion is so exquisitely expressed that the poem should be restricted to that only. . . . I think I could get the ' Galaxy ' to take the poem."

of, I could not bear to think of giving such trouble to so busy a man as I know you to be.

Pray tell me of Deucalion and Pyrrha.[141]   Have the world, the flesh and the devil completely crowded the sweet typic Man and Woman to the wall? I hope you manage to escape into their larger realm sometimes.

Will you probaby be lecturing in Baltimore this winter? It now seems likely I will hibernate there.

My wife joins me in warm messages to you and Mrs. Taylor.

Your faithful

S. L.

To Robert S. Lanier

West Chester, Pa.
Oct. 10th 1876

My dear Father:

Your two letters reached me yesterday. I write hastily to say I am sorry you spoke to Mr. Gresham about the J[ohns] H[opkins] matter, – for fear he may be writing to some of his Baltimore friends to interfere in my behalf, which would infallibly ruin all my chances. The poor Trustees have been so badgered and button-holed by the " friends " of innumerable candidates, and so persecuted with " letters of recommendation ", that they are utterly sickened of such processes. The president told me this – and a great deal more than I have time to write you. If you reflect for a moment that these Trustees are absolutely independent, that they have a large sum to dispose of, that they have determined to construct their faculty out of persons of world-wide reputation if possible, – you can easily see how impertinent must seem to them the letters and button-holings of people (like Mr. Gresham, for instance) not known outside of their counties.

Perhaps I may add that I personally know of a strong attempt having been made by Mrs. Bird in behalf of a friend of hers in this very direction, which signally failed; and I think that

---

[141] Taylor's *Prince Deukalion*, published in 1878. Lanier treated this poem at length in his last series of lectures at Johns Hopkins University in the winter of 1881 (IV, 66 ff.).

every single person who had made this kind of attack upon the
Trustees has been disappointed. I knew all this when I went
to see the president personally: if I had *not* known it, I would
have adopted the same course: I do not think they *ought* to
appoint any man to a place in such an institution who had to be
made known by others than himself. The only letter I wanted
was one of *introduction* from Prof. LeConte – such a letter as
any gentleman uses to gain *personal* acquaintance with another
gentleman through mutual friends – so that I might make some
enquiries of the president about the institution. I was as much
surprised as pleased when I found him giving these inquiries a
practical turn.

I am thus full, because I would like you to understand the
importance of immediately asking Mr. Gresham not to mention the matter in any way to his Baltimore kinsmen. I have
myself seen several of them since the matter was pending, but
have been careful to keep it entirely secret from them. I do
not think Mr. Gilman would like it to be spoken of at all, until
the whole is consummated.

As to the Osgood matter; [142] when I wrote you of it last
summer, you replied that you had seen some of the bankers
in Macon, and that not a bank had a dollar to loan, but you
thought there would be no difficulty in the fall. From the
proposition you now send me, I infer that you have offered our
note to the banks at home, and been unable to negotiate it.
Under these circumstances how could I possibly offer it to
Osgood? Of course – as you well know – no northern bank
would take it. Mr. O. might well ask me, of what use to him
would be a paper which no bank here would take, and which
can not even be negotiated in the place where we have lived
and done business all our lives?

But I see, from your making this proposition, that I failed
to make you understand the situation. It is not Osgood who is
in a hurry to be paid: it is *I who am in a hurry to pay* a debt
whose continued existence seriously undermines my health.

I can not possibly offer him anything but money. If you
write me finally and decisively that no bank in Macon will take
our note at four months for three hundred dollars, I will immediately go to work to sell my watch, my flute, and such jewelry

[142] See note 121, above.

as May can spare, and so pay the debt.   Let me earnestly beg that you will cease to worry yourself, – as all your letters tell me you are doing – about this: that you will consider it a mere business-matter: that you will immediately write me, yes or no, whether it is possible to negotiate the note I have described: and that you will then dismiss the whole matter from your mind, whether the answer be yes *or* no.   It is the *delay* which kills me.   If I may know *at once* that there is nothing for me but the last resort, I shall not take five minutes to decide upon my course.   I see that you must have thought it mere excitement in me when I told you all this before: but I wish I knew some way to persuade you that I thoroughly understand the whole business and that I can not possibly offer these gentlemen anything but money, which I am determined to raise in whatever honorable way remains to me.

As for the horseback exercise, and the removal to Baltimore, – I have exactly two pennies in pocket: and find it difficult, while ill and unable to work, to raise money for daily expenses.

But withal I have not the least doubt of my ability to get over my straits, nor of my success in my own line of life; I am never discouraged for a moment, and sincerely wish I knew how to induce you to abandon the broodings and worryings over my affairs of which you tell me.   My career lies perfectly plain before me, and is by no means so encumbered with difficulties as many others have been.   I need nothing in the world but a little money: if I cannot get this from one source, I will from another.

There! This is quite a screed: but your letters reveal to me that you are making yourself far more dismal over my matters than the occasion demands.

Harry is better: May considerably tired, but improving a little. My cough is gradually becoming less troublesome, and I find myself growing stronger.[143] All join in a great deal of love to you and Mama.

Your son

S. L.

[143] On the contrary, Mary Day Lanier had written to Clifford Lanier, Oct. 6: " Sidney has been much worse since you saw him. His cough has been more

To Robert S. Lanier

West Chester, Pa.
Oct. 22nd 1876.

My dear Father:

I am very glad to get your last letter.

I really tried to write mine in such a way that you would find nothing objectionable in it: and I beg you to attribute any expressions which may have seemed brusque or blunt, to the fact that I had to compress a good deal in a small space, — being really not well enough to write much — and that I wished above all to make clear to you a situation which I felt very strongly. I did not *mean*, certainly, anything but the quietest and yet most earnest representation to you of my views.

I fear you think me very obstinate in the Osgood matter: but I can't see it in any different light, after the most strenuous attempts; and every hour will seem a day to me until I get your letter with the check in it.

I do not hear anything conclusive from Baltimore.

Mary has a sore eye, from bad cold. Harry better. I have been suffering with some bleeding from the lungs for several days.[144]

In the November number of Lippincott's — just out — are four sonnets of mine, which I like altogether better than anything I have yet done.[145]

According to your permission, I will probably draw on you for $40.00 tomorrow, though possibly I may be able to postpone it until next day.

All join in a great deal of love to you and Mama. We suppose that if Pringle has kept up his Forsyth rate of increase, he must be as broad as he is long, by this time.

Your loving

S. L.

violent than any I have ever listened to. . . . Two months ago he wd. try nothing; now he is willing to try everything." (See also the following note.)

Lanier's son Harry had been ill with tonsilitis (see Lanier to Charles Day, Oct. 11, here omitted).

[144] Mary Day Lanier had written to Clifford Lanier, Oct 21: " [Sidney] keeps his bed and suffers great pain in the chest, with the weakness which lung-bleeding always brings."

[145] " Acknowledgment " (I, 56).

To Bayard Taylor [146]

West Chester, Pa.
Oct. 22nd 1876.

Dear Mr. Taylor:

I hope you'll like these enclosed sonnets, – from the November number of Lippincott's just out. I believe I think more of the two first than of anything I have done; the last two are redactions of two earlier ones wh. I think you have seen in ms.[147]

I hope you and Mrs. Taylor are well. I suppose Miss Lilian is away at Vassar by this time.

Your friend

S. L.

To Daniel C. Gilman

West Chester, Pa.
Oct. 22nd 1876.

My dear Sir:

Since I saw you I have been several times a little distressed with the fear that some reference made by me to the matter of salaries in the University, during our conversation, may have seemed indelicate to you, until I add – as I then intended to do – that in all my changes I have to think of four other mouths dependent on me. I do not think it would have occurred to me if I had been alone in the world.

I thank you sincerely for your kind note informing me of your intended absence.

In thinking over the skeleton of a department of " Poetry and Music," I find that the whole course of thought which I [have long been] brooding over [would bring both of these arts] within its purview: [which] makes me hope more than ever that the Trustees may see their way clear to entrusting me with it.[148]

[146] Previously published, *Atlantic Monthly*, LXXXIV, 129 (July, 1899); reprinted, *Letters* (New York, 1899), p. 174.

[147] See Lanier's letter of Aug. 30, 1875, and note 142, above.

[148] A corner of the MS has been torn off. Conjectural restorations have been supplied in brackets.

I have taken the liberty of sending you a November number of Lippincott's, just out, containing four Sonnets of mine which I hope you may like.

Pray let me assure you how deeply I am sensible of all your cordial goodness in my behalf.

Sincerely yours,

Sidney Lanier.

From Mary Day Lanier to Clifford A. Lanier [149]

3315 Baring St. Phila.
Nov. 8th 1876.

My dear Clifford:

. . . I have not written because nearly blind , for a month [150] and Sidney has been *ill* for a month: almost all the time in bed.   He crept out Nov. 1st to take me to an occulist in Phila –   We stayed at the Peacocks' two days – had my worst eyelid operated on and then he went to Baltimore, tho' hardly able to sit up, to examine the Johns Hopkins chances.   He found Pres. Gilman warmly on his side but trustees had decided to make no more appointments until Spring. Gilman begs him to come there for the winter and *be on hand*: has no doubt of success in the Spring.   Hamerik begs him to return to the Orchestra.   So, if we can sell some lots I have in Clinch Co. we will go to Baltimore. [151]   But, dear brother, if our darling is not *soon* better, by "Spring" your brother and my *All* will be far from us: – even *at rest*.

(Nov. 9th   Am finishing my letter at W[est] C[hester] depot, & just succeeded in buying a sheet of paper & ink.)

[149] This letter is included because it not only covers a period for which no letters by Lanier have been found, but also furnishes the background for an understanding of later letters. A long passage at the beginning and one sentence at the end– concerning a servant for the Clifford Laniers– have been omitted.

[150] In a letter to his father-in-law, Charles Day, Oct. 25, 1876 (here omitted), Lanier had written: "May is greatly out of sorts, with a catarrhal face, an inflamed eye, and general weariness."

[151] In a letter to Charles Day, Oct. 11, 1876 (here omitted), Lanier had written: "if I had in hand the titles to the two pine lots of Mary's, I could either sell them, or get an advance upon them for a year's time, through a Philadelphia friend. Will you . . . send me a deed to the two lots?"

He is very low; in quite different condition from ever before,
and finding all alcoholic stimulants – as well as cold air – to
disagree with him. Could the heavy pressure in money-matters
have been lifted as early as September I have no doubt he would
have rallied promptly if slowly, but I do not feel confident now
that fullest prosperity could arrest the ebbing tide of life in
time.   I say, " not *confident* " – but as for *hope*, that seems
rooted with my very life.   Yet when I kneel to pray for his
life I find my prayer always turning, instead, in behalf of peace
and a calm, strong soul upon which he may rest throughout
his long sufferings.

O Clifford ! he is too *unearthly* sweet a soul.   If we could
but all go together: the little ones, too !

I have not yet told you how we come to be at Mrs. Roberts'.[152]
I have had two or three pleasant interviews with her since you
left and she invited us each time so cordially to come and stay
there all night whenever we were in the city that I agreed to
bring Harry and Agnes down Monday P. M. – (Agnes needing to come to the city) that I might take Harry to the Centennial on Tuesday morning.   He is still so sick with his throat
and a persistent malarial fever (the doctors say it is) that I
dared not carry him out at 7 in the morning.   The little fellow
had been promised all summer that he should go and has
waited so patiently.   When I reached Mrs. Roberts' I found
Sidney there just from Balt° ill in bed with a hard chill and
high fever together.   There he has lain ever since, this being
the fourth day.   He went down to the parlor sofa at noon
yesterday but seemed worse all night and will not rise — to-day.
Of course I stayed with him and sent Agnes & Harry home.
If he can go out tomorrow he proposes to go down to dear,
kind Mrs. Peacock and tell her he wants to stay with her a few
days and put himself under Dr. Lippe's care – if, upon consultation, Dr. L. is confident of helping him.   Dr. Lippe is an
old, experienced German Homoeopath: the foremost in the
city: the pet physician of Miss Cushman and of the Peacocks.
Mrs. Peacock is always begging me to persuade Sidney to try

---

[152] Mrs. George Roberts, a friend with whom Lanier's children were left
when he and his wife went to Florida in December. Agnes, mentioned in the
following sentence, seems to have been a white nursemaid who had charge of
the Lanier children at West Chester and also at Mrs. Roberts's.

him.   It seems the best thing open to us — — may our merci-
ful Heavenly Father prosper it.   Mrs. Roberts has been as good
to us as she was to you and I am full of gratitude to her.   We
had found some strong ties of interest between us.   She has
two brothers in Brunswick, one of them, Brother's dentist – and
a man whom we have a high regard for.   Then Sidney's friendship with their life long friends, the Taylors of Kennett Square,
has been another pleasant meeting-point.   I am just going up
to West Chester for an hour or two to get clean clothing for
Sidney, see to the dear children, and bring the letters which *we*
hope have accumulated in these three days.
We have been so happy in believing Tilden elected ! but half
of the papers now pronounce it doubtful, & my heart trembles
with fear.   Should Hayes be elected we feel there is no chance
to sell our Georgia lots, and perhaps my darling's life may hang
on having that assured support for two or three months.
Train time approaches. – –   *Think not* that I show my full
fear to Sidney.   Indeed I do not.   I am always as bright for
him as if he were well. . . .

Mamie.

To Clifford A. Lanier

Phil^a Nov. 12th 1876

My dearest Clifford:
                    A very severe attack of ? has caught me
here and prevented me from going home for several days.   I
think however I am now getting better.   The physician is
earnestly advising me to go to Florida, and in thinking over
the possibilities, I remember to have heard either some of our
kinsmen Paines or Ligons speak of the virtues, particularly the
non-mosquito-ness, of a certain spot on St. Andrew's Bay where
I think they had saw-mills, or the like interests.   Will you be
kind enough to make immediate inquiry and find out for me,
1st where exactly is the place and how accessible, (*i.e.* by what
route), 2nd if any hotels, boarding-houses, or private-houses
willing to become such exist in that locality, and what would
likely be terms of board for me and my family, 3rd if fish and
oysters (upon which I wish to live mainly) are to be had, –

together with any other miscellaneous items you can pick up about it. Probably Uncle Bob Ligon could supply all this information.

I will hope to hear from you as soon as possible. The Doctor says I have plenty of vim left – though it has been cruelly imposed upon – and that if I go in time I may recover and have a long life. He adds that my lungs are in such condition that I could not hope to pass through an attack of pneumonia such as would be likely to visit me if I remain here or in Baltimore.

I have not made up my mind to go, at all: but I suspect it will come to that. I have suffered very greatly: and I do not feel myself getting well, as I have heretofore in like attacks.

While I am writing, it occurs to me that an out-door winter at some such place in Florida might be the very thing for our sweet Will; and if *we* went, she might consent to go, to some place where you could see her with a day's journey. I should hope to finish a new volume of poems I have on hand (my first is just published, and you will soon have a copy) and to think out a number of ideas which

x   x   x   x   x   x   x 153

To Bayard Taylor [154]

1425 Walnut St.
Philadelphia, Pa.
[Nov. 13, 1876 ?]

My dear Mr. Taylor:

I write a mere note to say, in answer to your kind enquiry about my volume, that Mr. Peacock brought up a copy yesterday which had just been sent to the Bulletin Office, – from which I presume that the book is now published. I've been here (at the Peacock's) for several days very ill, and have not seen the publishers in a long time – which accounts

[153] The rest of this letter is missing. For Lanier's volume of poems see the following letter and note 155, below.
[154] Previously published (misdated July), *Atlantic Monthly*, LXXXIV, 127 (July, 1899); reprinted, *Letters* (New York, 1899), pp. 168-169. Conjectural dating from the evidence of the conclusion of the preceding letter and the date of Taylor's reply, Nov. 15, 1876.

for my lack of more precise knowledge. The book is called simply POEMS BY S. L.[155] I'll have a copy sent you as soon as I get out.

I'm glad to find that the lectures are swelling your purse. I hope the golden shower will thicken until the Bureau shall represent a substantial Jupiter and you a well-satisfied Danäe.

I found pleasure in learning from your letter that the EVG. POST had copied the Sonnets. I can't tell you with what ravishing freedom and calmness I find myself writing, in these days, nor how serene and sunny the poetic region seems to lie, in front, like broad upland fields and slopes. I write all the time, and sit down to the paper with the poems already done. I hope to have out another volume soon, of work which will show a much quieter technique than this one. A modern French writer has spoken of the works of the great Artists of the world as being like the high white clouds which sail calmly over a green valley on a summer day. This seems to me very beautiful.

If you should write within a week, address me here: afterwards at West Chester, as usual.

My wife would join me, if she were here, in cordial messages to you and Mrs. Taylor. We have been hearing some very fine stories of you from your true friend and admirer Mrs. Roberts (née Anderson), at whose house in West Philadelphia we have been staying, to see the Exhibition.

Your friend

S. L.[156]

---

[155] Published by J. B. Lippincott & Co., Philadelphia. Though issued on Nov. 12, 1876, the title-page bore the date 1877. The volume contained only one poem not previously published, " Dedication. To Charlotte Cushman" (I, 83); the other ten had appeared in *Lippincott's Magazine* during 1875-1876.

[156] In his reply, Nov. 15, 1876 (*Letters*, New York, 1899, pp. 174-175), Taylor wrote: " It's very pleasant to get such good news . . . of your poetic activity. All poets have *periods*, and you are just passing from one into another. I have seen and felt this, but did not say so, because I was not sure whether you quite knew it yourself; but *now* I may freely say that I comprehend the change and rejoice in it for your sake."

To Bayard Taylor [157]

1425 Walnut St.
Ph^a Pa.
Nov. 24th 1876.

My dear Mr Taylor:

A peculiar affection of the side has almost
incapacitated me for any use of the pen, temporarily; but I
must send you a little note in order to share with you – for
I would like you to have half of *all* my good things in
this world – the pleasure which your generous notice in The
Tribune [158] has given me. I recognized it as yours at once;
and I therefore did not stint myself in my enjoyment of its
appreciative expressions any more than I would mar my smoking of your cigars, or my drinking of your wine, with *arrières
pensées,* – for I knew that the one was as free as the other.

I was particularly pleased with the light way in which you
touched upon my faults; and I say this not hastily, but upon a
principle to which I've given a good deal of meditation. The
more I think of it, the more I am convinced: that every genuine
artist may be safely trusted with his own defects. I feel perfectly sure that there are stages of growth – particularly with

---

[157] Previously published, Marie Hansen-Taylor and Horace E. Scudder, eds.,
Life and Letters of Bayard Taylor (Boston, 1884), II, 693-694; reprinted,
Atlantic Monthly, LXXXIV, 129-130 (July, 1899); and *Letters* (New York,
1899), pp. 176-178.

[158] A review of *Poems* (Philadelphia, 1877) in the New York *Tribune,* Nov.
21, 1876; reprinted in Bayard Taylor, *Critical Essays and Literary Notes* (New
York, 1890), pp. 312-314.

Taylor said, in part: "Mr. Lanier's dainty little volume contains only ten
poems, but they embody as much character and thought as are usually found in
the first hundred of a new poet. It is impossible to read them without feeling
the presence of a clear individuality in song – a nature free, opulent, exquisitely
impressible to a great range of influences, melodious, and daring almost to an
arbitrary degree. . . . In poetic aim, form, and choice of themes, Mr. Lanier
has expressed himself so positively that he cannot be mistaken for any one else."
After some praise of individual poems, he designated Lanier's chief faults as
"redundancy" and "apparent *abandon* to the starts and bolts . . . of Fancy."
In conclusion he said: "It is still too soon to decide whether Mr. Lanier's true
course is to train or carefully prune this luxuriance. Meanwhile we heartily
give him welcome, and congratulate his native South on a new poet." (For
a further account of this and other reviews see the Introduction to vol. I of the
present edition.)

artists of very great sensibility who live remote from the business-life of men – in which one's habitual faults are already apt to be unhealthily exaggerated from within and the additional forcings of such a tendency from without, through perpetual reminders of shortcomings, becomes positively hurtful, by proud-fleshing the artistic conscience and making it unnaturally timid and irritable. In looking around at the publications of the younger American poets I am struck with the circumstance that none of them even *attempt* anything great. The morbid fear of doing something wrong or unpolished appears to have influenced their choice of subjects. Hence the endless multiplication of those little feeble magazine-lyrics which we all know; consisting of one minute idea, each, which is put in the last line of the fourth verse, the other three verses and three lines being mere sawdust and surplusage.

It seems to me to be a fact bearing directly upon all this, that if we inquire who are the poets that must be read with the greatest allowances, we find them to be precisely the greatest poets. What enormous artistic crimes do we have continually to pardon in Homer, Dante, Shakespeare! How often is the first utterly dull and long-winded, the second absurdly credulous and superstitious, the third over-done and fantastical! But we have long ago settled all this, we have forgiven them their sins, we have ceased to place emphasis upon the matters in which they displease us; and when we recall their works, our minds instinctively confine remembrance to their beauties only. And applying this principle to the great exemplars of the other arts besides poetry, I think we find no exception to the rule that as to the great artist, we always have to take him *cum onere.*

I have to send you my thanks very often: I hope they don't become monotonous to you. Your praise has really given me a great deal of genuine and fruitful pleasure. The truth is that, as for censure, I am overloaded with my own: but as for commendation, I am mainly in a state of famine; so that while I cannot, for very surfeit, profitably digest the former, I have such a stomach for the latter as would astonish gods and men.

Your last note gave me pain, with hints of calamity in your family, and of your own need of physical rest. You won't laugh if I tell you – *apropos* of my haunting desire to see you at liberty from the shackles of daily bread and free to work entirely upon poetry – that I was yesterday half dreaming alone, in my sick-chair, that my portion of the Jennings estate in England (to which I am really one of the chief heirs)[159] had arrived, and I had just addressed you a little note stating that in a certain bank of New York there was deposited to your credit the sum of ————— thousand (I held over this blank to fill up at my leisure) dollars which I begged you would use, if for no other reason at least to save me the trouble of thinking what else to do with it, – the same to be repaid some time or other in heaven, – where gold would be plenty and cheap – – – when I awoke, without even having had the pleasure of filling up the blank.

– And this is a fearsome long screed, for what started to be a " note ". But you will pardon this, as you would pardon any other fault, in

Your faithful true friend

S. L.

[159] The " great Jennings estate " was the supposed estate of William Jennings (1701-1798), said to have been a cousin of Sarah Jennings, Duchess of Marlborough, a miser, fabulously rich, who had died unmarried and intestate. The real estate passed to a distant cousin, Richard William Penn Curzon, Viscount Curzon, Baron Howe, Earl Howe. The personal property passed to William Lygon, Earl Beauchamp, and Lady Mary Andover, who presented a claim to the property as next of kin.

William Jennings (1676-1775), uncle to the creator of the Jennings estate, had emigrated to America, where by his wife Mary Pulliam he became the father of five sons and five daughters. His great-grandson " Lame " Archer Robertson (1775?-1830) was Sidney Lanier's maternal great-grandfather.

Conventions of American " heirs " to the Jennings estate were held in Nashville, Tenn., in 1849 and in Charlottesville, Va., in 1850, at the latter of which the Jennings Family Association was formed. In 1869 an action was instituted in the High Court of England against Earl Howe, holder of the real estate of William Jennings, the miser; but the Statute of Limitations was held operative against the claimant, an American " Jennings " by the name of Baylis.

Lanier's great-uncles, James H. Robertson and Mallory W. Robertson, persuaded their nephew Clifford Anderson to prepare certain legal documents necessary to a second action, in which Judah P. Benjamin represented the American claimants. This action, instituted in 1880, was an attack on the legitimacy of Earl Howe. Other actions, equally unsuccessful were instituted in 1890, 1893, and 1931.

To Bayard Taylor [160]

1425 Walnut St.
Philadelphia, Pa.
Nov. 29th 1876

Dear Mr Taylor:

I want to try the Editor of Harper's Magazine with the poem in enclosed envelope. I don't even know who *is* the editor: will you be kind enough to address the envelope and mail it for me? [161]

Yours containing the EVG. POST notice came, and was " accepted, with thanks." [162] Who is the Literary Editor of the Post: is it Mr. Geo. C. Eggleston, – as I *think* I have been told?

I'm better, and go to Baltimore on Monday, to fulfill orchestral engagement. Letters will reach me still if addressed to West Chester, where my wife will remain for sometime: my Baltimore address will be

40 Mt. Vernon Place.

I hope you are well. Pray commend me to Mrs. Taylor. I'm writing hastily. I stay with the Peacocks until Sunday afternoon.

Your friend

S. L.

[160] Previously published, *Letters* (New York, 1899), pp. 178-179.

[161] Taylor did more than Lanier asked. In sending the poem (" The Waving of the Corn ") to H. M. Alden, editor of *Harper's*, he enclosed a personal note, dated Dec. 2, 1876, in which he said: " Mr. Lanier sends me the accompanying poem, which he wishes me to forward to you. As he is now generally admitted to be the chief Southern poet, and his name is becoming well-known, I think he will not be unwelcome as a contributor– provided you like his verses." The poem, previously rejected by Holland of *Scribner's*, was accepted by Alden, though it was not published until the Aug., 1877, issue of *Harper's*.

[162] The review of Lanier's *Poems* in the New York *Evening Post*, Nov. 23, 1876, by Geo. C. Eggleston, said in part:

" Mr. Lanier's verse is peculiarly rich, even to luxuriance, in imagery and in poetic suggestion. Every line is packed full, as it were, of suggestions, and some of the lines are whole poems condensed into a single phrase. . . . Condensation, indeed, is the leading feature of Mr. Lanier's work. He carries his habit of compression even beyond the limits of excellence, and at times makes a fault of that which is in the main the chief merit of his work. . . .

" The fault is an uncommon one, truly, and it is a fault born of a virtue.

To Mary Day Lanier

Wednesday Noon
[Philadelphia, Nov. 29, 1876 ?] [163]

Soul of my heart, thou wilt see from the enclosed that I am due in Baltimore by next Monday.

I write this little note to beg that thou wilt come here on Friday. Pray bring with thee my black dress-coat, and the black cloth vest thereunto belonging: also, the thick gloves in my trunk: also the extra flute joint which lieth around somewhere: also my small satchel: also my cards which are in the red Russia-leather pocketbook in the trunk, – bring pocketbook and all. I think I can do without the trunk until I see thee again, and much prefer to do so.

I find no letter from thee in the package, and having failed to see Mr. Thompson [164] myself this morning (he was at dinner and sent the package out by another) do not know how my darlings are. Mr. Peacock is going back to his office however in a moment, and will go down and ask Mr. Thompson if he has any loose letters for me.

I am much better: was out for two hours this morning: without detriment.

God have thee and thy sweet little doubles in His holy keeping prays thine and their

lover.

I sent thee a check for twenty five dollars yesterday.[165]

The tropical luxuriance of this young man's imagination is a source of very great power for the future . . . , and it shows already the beginnings of order and symmetry." In addition to the " rich promise of excellence yet to come," the reviewer concluded that the present volume was " full of genuineness and truth." (See also the Introduction to vol. I of the present edition.)

[163] Conjectural dating by reference to the preceding letter and the partial dating of this one: Nov. 29 was the Wednesday preceding the beginning of the Peabody Orchestra rehearsals on Dec. 4, 1876.

[164] Probably Lanier's landlord at West Chester.

[165] The next day Lanier received an unexpected gift which caused him to change his plans. It was an envelope, postmarked " New York, Nov. 29, [1876,] 4:30 P. M.," addressed to him at 1425 Walnut St., Philadelphia, which has survived (Charles D. Lanier Collection, Johns Hopkins University) with the following annotation in Lanier's autograph: " In this envelope there came

To Bayard Taylor [166]

1425 Walnut St.
Philadelphia, Pa.
Dec. 6th 1876

My dear Mr Taylor:

My physician has become alarmed at the gravity and persistence of my illness and orders me immediately to Florida, denouncing death unless a warm climate is speedily reached. He might as well talk to the stars whose light hasn't yet reached us, as try to persuade me that any conceivable combination of circumstances could induce me to die before I've written and published my fine additional volumes of poems; nevertheless it is decided that my wife is to leave here with me on Monday night next, for Florida, and I'm scratching this hasty note in the possibility that your nomadic habits might bring you to Philadelphia within that time simply to ask that you won't fail – if they *should* bring you here – to give me a final sight of you. I'm still at the Peacocks'.

I hope you didn't take cold at Greenwood the other day. My wife would join me in messages to you and Mrs. Taylor, but she ran over to New York this morning on a flying business-visit for a couple of days.

Many thanks for the Post notice.

Your friend

S. L.

to me, on the morning of Nov. 30th 1876, a five hundred dollar bill, unaccompanied with any writing. I have never been able to obtain the slightest clue to the name of the sender. I was then ill at Mr. Peacock's and this money saved my life, by enabling me to go to Florida, where my physician had ordered me."

With the receipt of this money, which was probably the gift of Gibson Peacock (see Lanier's letter of Dec. 3, 1877, below), Lanier abandoned his determination to return to Baltimore and resume his place in the Peabody Orchestra. Replying to a lost letter by Lanier, Asger Hamerik, conductor of the orchestra, wrote on Dec. 2, 1876: " How sorry I am that you are sick. What shall we do, and how get along without you?

" Indeed I am afraid to direct, without both seeing, hearing and feeling your flute on the wont place.

" But I hope the sun shall improve you, and we will yet see you in Baltimore this season."

[166] Previously published, *Atlantic Monthly*, LXXXIV, 130 (July, 1899); reprinted, *Letters* (New York, 1899), pp. 179-180.

To Mary Day Lanier [167]

Pha. Dec. 6th 1876

Dear Heart, I am scrawling this in the hope that it will carry you a kiss to meet you at breakfast tomorrow morning. I am pleasing myself with so many loving visions of your happiness in meeting your long-unseen friend that the mournful lonesomeness which always settles upon me in your absence is half dispelled. You will be delighted to know that I have been out for an hour, and that the air is like new life to me. I am altogether better than for many days.

You have so many grave matters in hand that I wish to impress you with the wisdom of taking more time if that should seem necessary to the better accomplishment of our purposes. My sweetest *Femme d'affaires*, would all thy projects might come to thy hand as loyally as does thy

husband .

To Mary Day Lanier

[Philadelphia ?] Dec. 10th [1876 ?]

My dearest Soul. It just so happens that I have a check from St. Nicholas for twenty four dollars,[168] which I endorse to you and send hastily, in response to your telegram. I have written Mrs. Roberts, and Emma Stebbins. It is now time to mail this. If I were but going with it to thee ! – for I am as always thy lonesome – if thou art not by –

lover.[169]

---

[167] On the envelope of this letter, addressed to her in care of Mrs. F. P. James, 400 Fifth Avenue, New York, N. Y., Mary Day Lanier made the note: "Dec. 6– 1876– Trying to get money to go to Tampa to heal lung."

[168] Apparently in payment for "The Story of a Proverb. I" (VI, 324), published in *St. Nicholas Magazine*, IV, 468-472 (May, 1877), which is the basis for the conjectural addition of "1876" to the date of this letter.

[169] The envelope shows that this letter was sent to Mary Day Lanier at West Chester. Shortly after this date (Dec. 10) Lanier's wife joined him at the Peacocks, and they left Philadelphia for the South, spending one day in Macon and three in Brunswick, Ga. They reached Cedar Keys, Fla., on Dec. 19, 1876, on which date Mary Day Lanier wrote to Clifford Lanier, giving an account of

To Gibson Peacock [170]

Cedar Keys, Fla.
Dec. 20th 1876.

Through many perils and adventures we are so far safely on our way, in much better condition than could have been expected. We leave for Tampa presently. It is about 125 miles southward; but we stop at Manatee, and do not reach Tampa until tomorrow night,–spending thirty-six hours on the steamer. We have been wishing all the morning that you might pace these white sands with us, in the heavenly weather. Will write you immediately from Tampa.

S. L.

To Charles Day Lanier

Tampa, Fla.
Dec. 27th 1876.

My dear Charley:

When I first opened my eyes on Xmas morning, your mother drew a very mysterious-looking package from under her pillow, and presented it to me with *your* compliments. On opening it I found the charming little silver corkscrew which Mama informs me you had bought for me before we left Philadelphia. I am delighted to find myself thus remembered; and shall drink your health from the very first bottle of wine which I open with this dainty present.

Have you bought your sled? I picture you to myself every day, mounted upon a long rakish-looking gas-pipe runner, flying down the hills of West Philadelphia. I hope you are always careful to make way for the girls' sleds: and don't run over any more boys than you can help. Have you learned how to guide your sled easily, yet? Pray write me all about it.

their trip, concluding: " S has much fresh cold, from sleeping-cars chiefly. It does not seem to attack the lungs pointedly. He bears the journey as well as we had reason to hope."

[170] A postal card, previously published, *Atlantic Monthly*, LXXIV, 181 (Aug., 1894) ; reprinted, *Letters* (New York, 1899), p. 33.

Mama is writing you a long letter: and inasmuch as I am able to use my pen but little, I must let her tell you of all the things you care to know about our surroundings and the like.[171] I am a great deal better than when I saw you last, and have the utmost reason to believe that I will soon be able to write *to* you and *for* you just as much as I like: – though if I should commence to tell you how much I love you and how many times in each day my thought hovers around my brave little boy, I should never be able to finish if I had all the good health in the world.   You must embrace my sweet Sidney, and big-eyed Hal for me: and do not fail to tell our good Agnes how often we have thought of her this Xmas tide, and how heartily we have wished that she has been able to get to her Church frequently and enjoy all its beautiful ceremonies.

Say to Sidney that I will write *him* by next mail.

Remember always to be a brave, quiet and truthful gentleman, my darling Boy; so shall you be ever as dear to others as you are to

your
father.

To Gibson Peacock [172]

Tampa, Fla.
Dec. 27th 1876.

My dear Friend:

On arriving here we find that your friendship has as usual anticipated us.   May and I, strolling down to the Post Office to rent a box and not daring to think of letters, are told by the clerk that he thinks there is something for us,–and the something turns out to be your pleasant budget, which we

---

[171] Mary Day Lanier's letter to her son Charles, dated Christmas, 1876, said in part: " Dear Papa suffered from cold and fog and wind on our long and fatiguing journey and was quite sick when we landed here, nearly ten days after we left you.   It is very warm here and he is getting rested and free from his cold.   Indeed it is too warm for our comfort at present– the thermometer is at 80° on the cool side of the house: as warm as in July and August on Mrs. Thompson's piazza.   They expect a cool change soon though, and if one will sit still there is nearly always a nice sea-breeze."

[172] Previously published, *Atlantic Monthly*, LXXIV, 181-182 (Aug., 1894); reprinted, *Letters* (New York, 1899), pp. 33-36.

incontinently open and devour, sitting down on the steps of the Post Office for that purpose, to the wonderment of the natives. Your news of our dear mannikins is the first we have had and is a fair gift for our Christmas. May calls out to me while I am writing this that *she* does not wonder, either, at Sidney's desire to kiss Mrs. Peacock, and that she would vastly like to do so at this moment, for her own private delectation.

The letters you sent were all pleasant, in one way or another. One is from H. M. Alden, Editor *Harper's Magazine*, enclosing check for fifteen dollars and accepting the poem (*The Waving of the Corn*) sent him by me through Bayard Taylor.[173] Another is a very cordial letter from " Geo. C. Eggleston, Literary Editor *Evening Post*," making tender of brotherhood to me in a really affectionate way and declaring that " the keen delight with which he recently read my volume of poems sharpens the pang he feels in knowing that one in whose work he sees so rich a promise lies on a bed of illness." [174]

The Postal Card is from Gilder, whom I had requested to make a slight addition to my article on *The Orchestra* in Scribner's.[175]

The fourth letter is as you guessed from Emma Stebbins, and I enclose it for you to read. It seems from the last portion of it that she has quite abandoned the idea of writing the life of Charlotte Cushman, substituting for that the project of merely printing a Memorial Volume.

The *Bulletin* with the notice you mention has not yet arrived. I am very much pleased that the Psalm of the West has given Mrs. Champney a text to preach from. One begins to add to the intrinsic delight of prophet-hood the less lonesome joy of human helpfulness — when one finds the younger poets resting upon one for a support and buttress in this way.

[173] See also note 161, above.

[174] Neither Eggleston's letter to Lanier, nor Lanier's reply, Dec. 27, 1876, has been found. But two sentences from Lanier's reply are quoted by Mims, p. 292: " I know you very well through your ' Rebel's Recollections,' which I read in book form some months ago with great entertainment. Our poor South has so few of the guild, that I feel a personal interest in the works of each one." (See note 162, above.)

[175] Lanier's article, " The Orchestra of Today " (II, 291), had been accepted by R. W. Gilder on Nov. 6, 1876; he was paid $80.00 for it, but it was not published until Apr., 1880.

You will be glad to know that we are situated much more comfortably than we could have hoped. Tampa is the most forlorn collection of little one story frame houses imaginable, and as May and I walked behind our Landlord who was piloting us to the "Orange Grove Hotel" our hearts fell nearer and nearer towards the sand through which we dragged. But presently we turned a corner and were agreeably surprised to find ourselves in front of a large three story house, with many odd nooks and corners, altogether clean and comfortable in appearance, and surrounded by orange-trees in full fruit. We have a large room in the second story, opening upon a generous balcony fifty feet long, into which stretch the liberal arms of a fine orange-tree holding out their fruitage to our very lips. In front is a sort of open plaza, containing a pretty group of gnarled live-oaks full of moss and mistletoe. They have found out my public character already: somebody who had traveled with me recognized me on the street yesterday and told mine host. He and his wife are all kindness, having taken a fancy, I imagine, to my sweet Angel May. They have just sent up a lovely bunch of roses and violets from the garden,– a sentimental attention which finds a pleasant parallel in the appearance of a servant at our door before breakfast to inquire whether we prefer our steak fried or broiled.

The weather is perfect summer, and I luxuriate in great draughts of balmy air uncontaminated with city-smokes and furnace-dusts. This has come not a moment too soon: for the exposures of the journey had left my poor lung in most piteous condition. I am now better, however: and May is in good case, except that the languid air takes the spring from her step, and inclines her much to laziness. She had a perfect democratic eye during the journey: the Doctor's tourniquet having pressed so hard that a space as large as a silver dollar under the eye showed first an inky black, then a brilliant purple, like the damaged optic of a prize fighter. It is now much decreased, and bids fair to disappear in a day or two.

We have three mails a week: two by stage from Gainesville (which is on the railroad from Fernandina to Cedar Keys) and one by steamer from Cedar Keys. Address me simply " Tampa, Fla." I have a box (No. 8:– I don't think there are more than twenty five or thirty in all) at the Post office, and the clerk knows me: — as in fact everybody else does, a stranger is a stranger in Tampa.

So: I must stop. Tell my dear Maria Peacock that we should never have gotten along without the blue blanket: and kiss her for me as for one who loved her very dearly even before he owed his life to her. May sends you a kiss, and so does

Your faithful

S. L.

P. S. This is Tampa ink. It has nearly destroyed my reason in one letter.

Dear Mr. Peacock:

Sidney has forgotten my message which entreated Mrs. Peacock (Heaven bless her!) to consider my letters *unanswerable*.

You are *one* in our thoughts and affections and we are content to hear from either one of you. And I am so selfish as to wish that she should always be *glad* when my poor letters come.

When you see Dr. Lippe pray give him our best regards and say that we will write as soon as we have had time to know how Sidney is.

Your loving

Mary D. L.

P. S. No. 15   I enclose the two receipts for the silver: [176] Robbins's and the Trust Company's. We will write about it some future time, meantime as to the set at Robbins, place it wherever you like.

S.L.

---

[176] The reference is apparently to the Laniers's wedding silver, which they had several times tried to use as collateral for a loan. They were now planning to sell it if necessity arose (see Lanier's letter of Jan. 17, 1877, below).

To Gibson Peacock [177]

Tampa, Dec. 31st 1876

My dear Mr. Gibson: I am writing a line to send you both a New Year's kiss from us two. We have had a great change in the weather: a couple of days ago the hyperborean blasts turned our pretty summer quite out of doors, and we have had for thirty six hours a temperature which reminds us very forcibly of a New Year's Day at the North. As we sit over our blazing knots of "fat lightwood" we think with double vividness of your two dear faces, and wish that they were by ours, or ours by them.

We send a thousand congratulations on the triumph in the Libel Suit. From the form in which the jury have drawn their verdict, I fancy the Judge must have charged against you, but that the jury were very decidedly in your favor.

The Magazine has arrived, and your lovely notice of my little Evening Song gives me genuine pleasure.[178] I see too that the poem has smitten the hitherto-invulnerable R. Shelton McKenzie under the fifth rib.[179] This is a triumph indeed. The *Bulletin* with the notice from the *Evg. Post* has also arrived. The letter from Lippincott's which you forwarded was an enclosure of check for ten dollars for the Evening Song.

May is doing well; and I, with some set-backs am on the whole improving. I have found a shaggy gray mare upon

[177] Previously published, *Atlantic Monthly*, LXXIV, 182-183 (Aug., 1894); reprinted, *Letters* (New York, 1899), pp. 37-38.

[178] Lanier's "Evening Song" was published in the Jan., 1877, issue of *Lippincott's*. For an account of the composition of this poem see note 117, above.

Peacock reprinted it in the Philadelphia *Evening Bulletin* with the following comment: "There is no more rich and tender love-song than this in the language, and while the whole construction is artistic, the bold, magnificent simile in the second stanza is especially admirable. . . . This little gem of a poem is enough to glorify any number of any magazine." (Undated clipping in the Charles D. Lanier Collection, Johns Hopkins University; no file of the *Evening Bulletin* for this period has been found.)

[179] An undated clipping in the Charles D. Lanier Collection, Johns Hopkins University, marked "Dr. Mackenzie in the [Philadelphia?] Press" reads: "We have never been impressed, however hard our attempt to be so, with the idea that Sidney Lanier is entitled to the high title of poet; but an 'Evening Song' here [Lippincott's, Jan., 1877], only three four-line stanzas, has convinced us that he *is*."

whose back I thrid the great pine forests daily much to my delight. Nothing seems so restorative to me as a good gallop. We have now only two mails a week, and these take a long time to go and come. If there should ever be any occasion to telegraph us, a dispatch can be sent to TUCKERTOWN (which is on the telegraph line, thirty miles from here) whence the operators will, if so requested, forward it by carrier on horseback to Tampa.

I sent you the two silver receipts by last mail. Forward me whatever you happen to see about the little Song: I wish to send the notices to Dudley Buck, who has set this poem to music. God bless you both,—say May and

S. L.[180]

[180] Evidence of the national recognition that Lanier had attained is found in a squib that appeared in the Cincinnati *Gazette* at about this time: "A NEW AMERICAN POET. Mr. Sidney Lanier, who has been first flute in Asgar Hamerik's orchestra in Baltimore for the past three years, has been ordered by his physician to leave his post and go South for his health. Mr. Lanier has the erect and graceful person and the quiet manners of a gentleman, and he is a man of much general culture. He is tall and slender, somewhat pale, has eyes of a fine gray, and a black beard. The gods have made him poetical, both in temperament and in face, this being of a sensitive and thoughtful character. He is as accomplished in music as in the literary art." This was copied in the New York *Sun*, and probably elsewhere. (Undated clippings in the Clifford A. Lanier and Charles D. Lanier Collections, Johns Hopkins University.)

1877

To Sarah C. Bird [1]

Tampa, Fla.
Jany 10th, 1877.

My dear friend:

I am not yet allowed to use the pen, but I am rebelling against tyranny tonight merely to send you some little loving greeting for the New Year, and to tell you that I am improving in health.

Today has been simply heavenly: fancy me, your poor slave of ice and slush, lying in a hammock from which, as I swing to and fro, I can almost pluck oranges off a tree which is all green and gold and which thrusts its liberal clusters of fruit into the long second-story balcony; while the robins and the mocking-birds and the jay-birds and the jorees are making a clamor which is at once lovely and absurd, and the air comes warm and clean as a baby's breath, and the sun blazes hot as a — as a — well, as a Louisiana Democrat.

But I'm already out of bounds, and May protests. Pray give my love to all yours; and herein May begs to join. We have dined with the Verdiers, and I have had a good talk about you with Mrs. Dr. Verdier, neé Crawford, formerly of Sparta [,Ga.] My address is "Tampa;" we will be here some months, likely.

Your friend

Sidney L. [2]

---

[1] Mrs. Edgeworth Bird, a Baltimore friend, formerly of Macon.

[2] On Jan. 7, 1877, Mary Day Lanier had written to Wilhelmina (Mrs. Clifford) Lanier: " [Sidney] has been riding several days and went twelve miles this morning with great enjoyment. The lung continues to feel & act the same and the hoarseness does not lessen; but freedom from fever, hearty appetite, and good sleep, with increase of strength should mean *something* encouraging.

" He says– lazily, from the bed,– ' Tell Cliffy I'm too hoarse to write to him, tell him my voice is like pale ink.' "

To Bayard Taylor [8]

Tampa, Fla.
January 11, 1877

My dear Mr. Taylor:

What would I not give to transport you from your frozen sorrows instantly into the midst of the green leaves, the gold oranges, the glitter of great and tranquil waters, the liberal friendship of the sun, the heavenly conversation of robins and mocking-birds and larks, which fill my days with delight!

But if I commence in this strain I shall never have done; and I am writing in full rebellion against the laws now in force over the land of Me – which do not yet allow me to use the pen by reason of the infirmity of my lung; yet I could not help sending you some little greeting for the New Year, with a violet and a rose which please find herewithin. The violet is for purity, – and I wish that you may be pure all this year; and the rose is for love – and I'm sure I shall love you all the year.

We are quite out of the world and know not its doings. The stage which brings our mail (twice a week only) takes three days to reach the railroad at Gainesville; and it is a matter of from nine days to any conceivable time for a letter to reach here from New York. Nevertheless, – nay, all the more therefore, – send me a line that I may know how you fare, body and soul.

I received a check for fifteen dollars from Mr. Alden, Editor " Harper's," for the poem you sent to him; [4] and I make little doubt that I owe its acceptance to the circumstance that you sent it. I hear of an " International Review," but have not seen any copy of it: do you think it would care for anything like the enclosed? [5] – a poem which I have endeavored to make burn

---

[8] Previously published, *Atlantic Monthly*, LXXXIV, 130-131 (July, 1899); reprinted, *Letters* (New York, 1899), pp. 180-181, from which the present text is taken, with two obvious errors corrected by reference to the *Atlantic* text (MS not found).

[4] " The Waving of the Corn " (see note 161, 1876).

[5] " To Beethoven " (I, 88). In his reply of Jan. 27, 1877 (*Letters*, New York, 1899, pp. 181-183), Taylor said: " I shall send your poem immediately to the ' Galaxy.' The ' International Review ' is a mean concern,– publishes little poetry, pays its authors next to nothing, and hasn't much circulation. I know Church of the ' Galaxy,' and am free to ask him, not only to publish the poem, but also to pay you properly. If I see him to-night at the Century I can settle

as hotly as, yet with a less highly colored flame than, others of mine. If you do, pray direct the envelope; if not, address it to the " Galaxy," unless you think that inadvisable: in which last event keep the copy, if you like.

I had a very cordial letter from Mr. Eggleston about my volume of poems, which gave me pleasure.

I'm sure you'll be glad to know that I improve decidedly; I see no reason to doubt that I shall be soon at work again. In truth, I " bubble song " continually during these heavenly days, and it is as hard to keep me from the pen as a toper from his tipple.

I hope Mrs. Taylor is well, and beg you to commend me to her; wherein my wife very heartily joins me, as well as in fair messages to you. I wrote you several times before leaving Philadelphia: did you get the letters?

Your faithful friend,

S. L.

To GIBSON PEACOCK [6]

Tampa, Fla.
Jany 17th 1877

My dear Mr. Gibson:

I wrote you immediately upon arriving here, enclosing the two receipts for the silver; and I believe some sort of greeting has gone from one of us to one of you by nearly every mail, since our arrival. I only mention this because our Florida mail arrangements are of the very slowest description, and, as we have yet had nothing from you written since any of our communications reached you, we presume the latter have taken the very uttermost limit of time in getting to you.

We fare slowly on, in health. May has been very much affected by the warm weather which has prevailed for the last

---

the matter in two minutes. If you have anything more, of a simple, melodious quality, send it to me, and I'm much mistaken if I can't get it into the ' Atlantic.' . . . In the ' New Library of Song,' to which Bryant's name is attached as editor,– though he doesn't edit it much,– your Cantata is published beside Whittier's Hymn and my Ode. So pluck up heart, and don't be discouraged! "

[6] Previously published, *Atlantic Monthly*, LXXIV, 183 (Aug. 1894); reprinted, *Letters* (New York, 1899), p. 38.

two weeks and suffers much from lassitude, with some appearance of malarial symptoms. I think my lung is healing gradually: and although I have a great deal of hoarseness, it does
not seem to be attended with any other serious accompaniment.
I certainly improve in strength, though pulled down, as indeed
are all the healthy people about us, by the languorous summer
temperature.

I think we will have to sell the silver; if you can get $350
for it, it may go at that. Possibly we will sell it for old silver,
after awhile, at $200; but I would be glad if you would see
whether any silver dealer with whom you should leave it (after
Robins) can get an offer of $350.[7]

Pray kiss my dearest Maria Peacock for me with a special
fervency in consideration of her dainty cards which greeted us
in due time; and give her these enclosed violets, which will be
crushed, yet I hope still odorous with sweet messages, when
they arrive.

I am writing in haste, having come in from a ride, horseback
just as the mail is about to close. God bless you both, from us
both.

Your faithful

S. L.[8]

To Charles N. Hawkins [9]

[Tampa, Fla., February 4? 1877]
Dear Mr Hawkins:

Mrs. Lanier adds her thanks to mine for the
superb tangle of yellow jessamine. Nothing could have been
more *apropos*: it is the tutelar flower of our old courting days,

---

[7] See note 176, 1876.

[8] On Jan. 20, 1877, Mary Day Lanier wrote to Clifford Lanier: "Our patient
has been better since I last wrote. To-day, a little fresh cold makes him less
bright. . . . He rides daily now, but finds the rides must be short."

[9] Previously published, *American Book Collector*, VI, 203 (May-June, 1935).
Conjectural dating from the pencil notation in another autograph: " Feb. 1877 "
and from the evidence of Hawkins's reply, dated Feb. 4, 1877.

Hawkins was the editor of the Tampa *Sunland Tribune* and lived at the
nearby Tampa Hotel. It was probably at about this time that Lanier sent his
poem " On the Receipt of a Jar of Marmalade " (I, 202) to Mrs. Hawkins, in
appreciation of a gift from her.

and our first love-making was achieved in the overhanging presence of its vines.

Perhaps you'll care to see this copy of Dr. Deems new " Sunday Magazine". We have also the " ATLANTIC MONTHLY " [10] and SCRIBNER'S ", both for February, which we will send if you have not seen them.

Yours truly

Sidney Lanier

Orange Grove Hotel
    Sunday Afternoon, Feb. 1877

TO BAYARD TAYLOR [11]

Tampa, Fla.
Feby 7th 1877.

My dear Mr Taylor:

Your letter, bringing many pleasant words, came *on* my birthday: which I consider a fair reciprocation for mine, written (as you tell me) on yours. My wife had managed to arrange my room, with the help of some cunning female friends, without my knowledge; and when I awoke in the morning I found myself in the midst of a very brave array of flowers; during the day our apartment was further hung with wreaths of gray moss, bamboo vines, and fragrant spruce pine tassels, to such a degree that I felt like a whole Sunday School celebration all by myself: and in the afternoon among a lot of pleasant mail matter came your letter.

I was never able to *stay* angry in my life; and I should meet Stedman without ever letting him know how much pain he had

---

[10] On a fly-leaf of this magazine, loaned to the Hawkinses, Lanier had written the nonsense verses beginning " Our turkey walks across the yard " (I, 202). Mrs. Hawkins copied them, with this information, on the back of Lanier's letter. (See J. S. Mayfield, " An Immoral Bird," *American Book Collector*, VI, 200-203, May-June, 1935.)

[11] Previously published, *Atlantic Monthly*, LXXXIV, 131-132 (July, 1899); reprinted, *Letters* (New York, 1899), pp. 184-185. (The MS of this letter is mutilated in paragraphs 4 and 5; the missing parts have been restored from a contemporary copy—Cornell University Library— made by Marie Hansen-Taylor.)

given me. Indeed, he has quite forgotten the details: it was not at the Century, but on the night when we left your house together: and he did *not* speak " harshly " or " abruptly " to me, — I fear the old Gascon Adam in me would have had an all-too-quick slap in the face ready for that; – but he *advised* me, in a friendly way, " not to be asking poets to dinner lest I might be thought to be pushing my way "! I fancy it only increased the pain of the wound that it was given in this advisory way which would have made me seem very truculent to resent it: and there was nothing to do but get off into some brake of silence, like a deer with a shot in the flank, and lick mine own wound. This seems extravagant: but it is not, compared with the real suffering: it was *such* a fall for my vanity, to think that any human being could have dreamed me capable of such a thought, after having seen me twice! [12]

Voilà tout. – As for forgiveness: the summer and the silence here have been very medicinal to me: since I have been here I've thought over the few people that ever wrong'd me; and I don't find in my heart the least speck of hard-feeling against anybody in the world.

Pray keep the enclosed little poem,[13] and send it anywhere where you think it might be accepted. I should mention that Scribner's, Harper's and Lippincott's, each, has a poem of mine on hand (and you'll care to hear that Scribner's paid me twice as much as ever before for the last one, bought a couple of weeks ago).[14] Don't charge your mind with it: and pray don't be at the trouble of writing any recommendations, or the like. I cannot bear to think of taking your time.

My wife is trying to get off a small box of orange-blossoms to Mrs. Taylor by this mail: but she may have to wait over until the next.

[12] Lanier's reference to Stedman was probably prompted by Taylor's mention of him in his letter of Jan. 27, 1877 (*Letters*, New York, 1899, p. 182): " Last night I spent with Stedman and Dudley Buck, and we talked much of you. Buck played the accompaniment, and Mr. Brown (a barytone) sang your last song in " Scribner's '– ' The Cleopatra-night '; so that I have heard it before you! It is simply superb." (Lanier's " Evening Song " appeared in *Lippincott's*, not *Scribner's*.) Taylor added that the poem had been widely copied.

[13] " The Bee " (I, 91). See the following letter.

[14] In a letter of Jan. 19, 1877, *Scribner's* had sent Lanier a check for $20.00 for " The Stirrup-Cup " (I, 90). (See also note 4, above, and note 28, below.)

Have you seen a somewhat elaborate notice of me in THE GRAPHIC by Orpheus C. Kerr? [15]

I should like to see your " Assyrian Chant," and specially " Peach blossom." If you could only see the plum-trees, the roses, the orange blossoms, here!

God bless you.

Your friend

S. L.

TO BAYARD TAYLOR [16]

Tampa, Fla.
Feby 11th 1877.

My dear Mr Taylor:

In the poem I've just sent you – THE BEE –, it occurs to me that I have carelessly used the pronoun " him " referring to the bee, – forgetting that, although the worker-

---

[15] A review of Lanier's *Poems* by Orpheus C. Kerr (pseud. for R. H. Newell) had appeared in the New York *Daily Graphic*, XII, 560 (Jan. 22, 1877). After a long introductory attack on the feudal caste system of the old South— where " Cotton was a king inciting his nobility to egotisms and extravagances far beyond their real importance and legitimate purses "– the reviewer said: " It is a hopeful sign when we see the present literature of the South boldly attacking this principle by literal concrete illustration of its pitifully ruinous logic and implications. . . . The modest little volume of ' Poems' by Mr. Sidney Lanier . . . deserves much more attention by the Northern press than it has thus far received, if merely for its earnest bearing upon this point." " Corn " was then quoted and paraphrased to show that Lanier saw plainly " the real rottenness of the former South . . . how hollow a delusion its past Kingdom of Cotton has been." Then the reviewer cited his " resonant and large minded ' Psalm of the West' " as proof that Lanier had passed from the old sectionalism to a national viewpoint. In conclusion he declared: " This vigorous strain of sympathy for the young life of our own great continent is novel and brotherly as coming from the lyre of a section hitherto best pleased with attempts to adapt Old World conceits and traditions to itself in numbers not more original. The tenderness, passion, and local sentiment of the South have been musically sounded by Timrod, Hayne, and Flash; but this new singer puts something of the straightforward spirit of the Whole Country even into this passage of chivalry in his fanciful ' Symphony.' . . . He is just the virile, rational, clear-thinking bard to strike the true note of the new South, and begin for her future a· nobler music than that by which she has hitherto been lulled to fatal delusions in peace and marched to hopeless defeat in war." (For a further account of this and the other reviews of Lanier's *Poems*, 1877, see the Introduction to vol. I of the present edition.)

[16] Previously published, *Atlantic Monthly*, LXXXIV, 132 (July, 1899); reprinted, *Letters* (New York, 1899), pp. 185-186.

bees were formerly thought to be sexless, they have recently
been found to be imperfectly-developed females. Pray let me
trouble you therefore to substitute " its " for " his " in the
sixteenth line from the beginning

                    its
(" Thrust up ~~his~~ sad-gold body lustily ") :

                    ∧

and also " it " for " him " in the thirty-sixth line from the
beginning,

                    it
(" Perceived ~~him~~ poising o'er a fresh new cup ").

                    ∧

I am too in some little doubt about the words " *on his wings,*"
six lines further on from the last-quoted: (" He hath a sense
of pollen on his wings "). While I know that the pollen used
by the bee *for food* is carried in the " pollen-baskets " of the
legs, I am not sure whether any of the pollen used in cross-
fertilization is carried *on the wings,* – my impression is that it
mostly adheres *to the body.* Perhaps therefore it would be
better to substitute for this line, the following:

　　" Some sense of pollen every poet brings,"
　　(Of pollen for to make thee fruitful &c &c) ".

—　　To how many sins one sin leadeth – – – – is shown in
all this trouble I'm giving you, in consequence of failing to be
strictly accurate at first.

I write in great haste, to save a mail.

                    Your friend

                    S. L.[17]

---

[17] In his reply, Mar. 12, 1877 (*Letters,* New York, 1899, pp. 189-190),
Taylor said that he would make the changes Lanier desired, but added: " I
must send you a long magazine article I have just written on Tennyson to
illustrate the fault of over-attention to details."

To Bayard Taylor [18]

Tampa, Fla.
Feby 25th 1877.

My dear Mr Taylor:

Yours with the GALAXY check came safely, bringing me heaviness of purse and lightness of heart, – for both of which pray hold yourself thanked.[19]

About the piece for the Atlantic I am afflicted with doubts which I find myself unable to solve. Once— in my very early pleiocene epoch, before the Man had appeared in any of my formations to supplant the crude monsters of earlier periods – I sent " Corn " to Mr Howells: [20] and, upon his refusing it, I tried, some time afterwards, a couple of sonnets, accompanied by a note asking (poor green goose that I was! as if an editor had time for such things, – but I really knew no better) if he would not do me the favor to point out in these a certain " mysticism " of which he had complained in " Corn ". This he did not answer: only returning the two poor little sonnets with the usual printed refusal.

This looked so much like a pointed invitation to me to let him alone that I have never had the courage to trouble him since. I thought his treatment very cold, at that time, and wrote so, once, to Hurd & Houghton, who had been friends of mine. Of course I now see how absurdly callow and unreasonable were my views then: but this does not diminish the mortification with which I remember the ignominious termination of my efforts in that direction: and, while I do not retain the least spark of feeling against Mr. Howells , I do not feel at all sure but *he* may remember *me* as an absurd person whom he was obliged to rebuff by silence. What would *you* do? I'm sure I do not want to be finical.

[18] Previously published, *Atlantic Monthly*, LXXXIV, 133 (July, 1899); reprinted, *Letters* (New York, 1899), pp. 186-188.

[19] Taylor had written Lanier on Feb. 5, 1877 (*Letters*, New York, 1899, pp. 183-184): " I enclose Sheldon & Co.'s ('Galaxy') check for $25, for your ' Beethoven.' I tried hard to get $40 for it, but failed. . . . Send me a poem for the ' Atlantic.' "

[20] For a history of Lanier's relations with the *Atlantic Monthly*, see A. H. Starke, " William Dean Howells and Sidney Lanier," *American Literature*, III, 79-82 (Mar., 1931), and the Introduction to vol. I of the present edition.

We got off some orange-blossoms to Mrs. Taylor, last week, but I much doubt if the buds will open on the way, according to my wife's expectation. They have made a very pretty heaven indeed for the bees and for us during the last two weeks.

I have occasional backsets, due to the warm climate; but there is now no doubt the lung is healing rapidly, and I am much better. – – – I hope your project for the German lectures (which I saw announced in the *Evening Post*) has been successful. What a foolish noise is this about " Deirdrè "![21] It is just a poor dull piece of orthodox verse. I do not find an *idea* in it, from beginning to end: and the imitations of Homer's ideas affect me unpleasantly. Moreover the story is too little for an epic. There isn't wind enough for so much canvass: whereby the latter is pot-bellied, and bags absurdly.

My wife joins me in affectionate messages to you and Mrs. Taylor. I wish I could gossip a little: but mine infirmity of the pen-arm saith, Forbear.

Your friend,

S. L.

To Bayard Taylor [22]

Tampa, March 4th 1877.

My dear Mr Taylor:

I earnestly hope you'll like this:[23] it is written with a very full heart! I wanted to say all manner of fair things about you: but I was so intensely afraid of appearing to *plaster* you, – that I finally squeezed them all into one line,

In soul and stature larger than thy kind,

which in truth has kept saying itself over within me ever since it was written, until I have come to take infinite satisfaction in it.

If you like this well enough to be willing that I should print

---

[21] A book-length poem by R. D. Joyce in Roberts Brothers " No Name Series," Boston, 1876.

[22] Previously published, *Atlantic Monthly*, LXXXIV, 133-134 (July, 1899); reprinted, *Letters* (New York, 1899), pp. 188-189.

[23] " Under the Cedarcroft Chestnut " (I, 93). Cedarcroft was the family home of Bayard Taylor near Philadelphia.

it, pray give me a hint in what direction I had better send it, –
I mean, where you would best like it to appear.

I have just seen the " BEETHOVEN ", in the GALAXY. A queer
mistake in punctuation occurs when it says,

> " When luminous lightnings blindly strike;
>
> The sailor praying on his knees
> Along with him that's cursing God &c ".

The semicolon marked is an error: the verb " strike " governs
" the sailor &c ". in the following line; the luminous lightnings
blindly strike (not only) the sailor praying &c but also the
sailor cursing &c. I speak of it as a *queer* error because I am
amused to see that a sort of dim sense may be evolved out of
it even as it stands.[24] On seeing the poem in print, I find it
faulty: there's too much matter in it; it is like reading the dic-
tionary – the meanings presently become confused, not because
of any lack of distinctness in each one, but simply because of
the numerous, and differing, specifications of ideas.

Did you get a letter from me enclosing a poem called " THE
BEE " ?

But I must stop writing. God bless you.

Your friend

S. L.[25]

[24] Taylor had written to Lanier, Feb. 5, 1877 (*Letters*, New York, 1899, pp.
183-184), that he had read proof on the poem carefully and had made " one
or two necessary changes in punctuation," but there is no indication that he was
responsible for this error. He also said: "I . . . was much tempted to change
a word–' The slanders *told* by sickly eyes '– but it seemed too great a liberty."
This line was omitted altogether in the revised version (see note to the poem in
vol. I) which resulted from Lanier's dissatisfaction with the poem, mentioned
in the following sentence.

[25] In his reply of Mar. 12, 1877 (*Letters*, New York, 1899, p. 190), Taylor
said of Lanier's poem addressed to him: "I must say frankly . . . that the
Chestnut-tree is very fine. . . . I return it, because, as you well understand,
I can't offer it anywhere; yet I am sure Scribner would publish it. Why not
change the title to ' The Chestnut-Tree at (or of) Cedarcroft '? It seems a
little less personal. The line you mention *is* fine, apart from mine own interest
in it,– too good as applied to me. Somehow I feel as if such things might be
said after a man is dead, hardly while he is living. But that *you* feel impelled
to say it now, gives me a feeling of dissolving warmth about the heart. You
must not think, my dear friend, that simply because I recognize your genius
and character, and the purity of the aims of both, that I confer any obligation
on you! From you, and all like you, few as they are, I draw my own encouragement for that work of mine which I think may possibly live."

To Robert S. Lanier

Tampa, Mch. 15th 1877.

My dear Father:

I was glad to get yours of 6th, today, with the Galaxy, and the newspaper. Our mail has now been cut down to a service of *once* a week – twice seemed bad enough – and its arrival is, as you may imagine, an important event with us.

I note what you say of Mr. Day's letter about the place at Brunswick. I think it would be an admirable one for *him*: but am sure the Brunswick summer would finish *me* before it was half over. If I were offered the Macon Post Office, now ! – I think I would bite. – But we can speak of these matters hereafter. I have hardly been able to make up an opinion about them yet.

I find myself gaining in strength, and I think there is general improvement, though slow, in the lung. I have just been able to resume the horseback exercise, and it now seems a benefit to me.[26] May has been suffering much with malarious influences.

I would like to have the hundred and fifty dollars as soon as you can send it. I am anxious to leave here as soon as I prudently can, and go to Brunswick where I shall be at scarcely any expense for the following month. The money in hand from the sale of silver (only a part of which has been yet received) has to be devoted to some doctor's bills, and other obligations necessarily incurred within the past year. In defraying these it lifts a great load from my mind.

I long to see you, and we hope that when we get to Brunswick you and mama can run down and maroon with us for a while. Please tell Uncle Clifford that the *Ms.* arrived safely, and has my attention. I will write him about it by next mail.

May joins me in loving messages to you and our mama. By the way, in answer to the latter's question, tell her " Beethoven "

---

[26] On the same date, Mar. 15, 1877, Mary Day Lanier wrote to Clifford Lanier: " Sidney has been improving for ten days. He was very ill for a week in February, beginning on the 17th, and has not easily rallied– an attack of dysentery. We were compelled to call a physician to administer morphine hypodermically, for three days." But four days later, Mar. 19, she wrote to Mrs. Clifford Lanier: " Sidney has been housed for two or three days with an incipient pleurisy. It is less acute than yesterday and I hope he will escape an illness."

was written mostly on the cars between Baltimore and Philadelphia, in December last.

Your son

S. L.

To Mariquita Peacock [27]

Tampa, Fla.
Mch. 25th 1877.

My dearest Maria Peacock: If Mr. Gibson objects to this warm address, pray explain to him – by way of consolation – that it's *nothing* to what I would do if I were in kissing distance of you. For what an age it seems since that last very miscellaneous caress *à huit mains* which we four took all together in the West Philadelphia depot! And now that I have to make love to you at such long range, it really seems as if the most burning words of affection must necessarily cool before they can reach Philadelphia from Tampa.

But – Blessed be the steadfast heart! – the love which sends them doesn't cool; and I wish we were spending this March day in your dear little Brown Study with you. I have an inexpressible longing to see you when you will not be – as during that last month – anxious at heart on my account. This might now very well be: for although many breaks and exasperating interruptions have checquered my progress since I came here, yet on comparing my present condition with the state I was in when I left you, no room is left for doubt that my lung is certainly healing, and that the rest is only matter of time and warm weather.

We expect to leave Tampa on the 5th April, for Brunswick, where we will remain until May. Our after-programme is to spend the month of May in Macon, and to return to Philadelphia in June. Consider that our address, therefore, is changed to " Care of Chas. Day, Brunswick, Ga."

May has been suffering much with malarial influences, and I am impatient for the time when she may return to the bracing

[27] Previously published, *Atlantic Monthly*, LXXIV, 183-184 (Aug., 1894); reprinted, *Letters* (New York, 1899), pp. 39-40.

northern air which appears to agree with her so well. She sends you all manner of loving messages.

Please ask Mr. Gibson as soon as the rest of the silver money comes in to send for Dr. Schell's bill, and discharge it. I have been more pained about the long standing-over of it than I can tell you.

Did you see my "Beethoven" in the Galaxy? A bad misprint occurred in the punctuation at the end of the 8th verse, where somebody inserted a semicolon. In the original, there is nothing: the two verses (8th and 9th) being intended to run together, i.e. the luminous lightings blindly strike the sailor praying on his knees along with & c. In reading other articles in this Magazine I observe that the proof must have been very badly read.

I have had a very affectionate letter from Emma Stebbins,[28] enclosing a fifty-dollar bill which she wanted to loan me.

My thoughts are much upon my French poem—The Jacquerie outburst—in these days. If Mr. Hayes would only appoint me Consul somewhere in the South of France! ! ! But I must stop writing now,– so says my Missus. God bless you, my dear sweet Soul, prays always your faithful,

S. L.

To Bayard Taylor [29]

Tampa, Fla.
Mch. 29th 1877.

Dear Mr Taylor:

I cut this slip out of an " Evening Post " which comes in the same mail with your letter of 12th. Both tell the same story: that you are overworked.

For this reason I rejoice to learn that you think of running away for a little while from New York, and – without waiting to *answer* your letter – I write a line by return mail to say that at the time you mention I will be in Brunswick, Ga. There is a

---

[28] In her letter of Feb. 18, 1877, Emma Stebbins wrote that she had seen Lanier's sonnet, " To the Red Breast of Tampa " (early title for " Tampa Robins," I, 92), reprinted in the New York *Evening Post* from the March number of *Lippincott's*. This poem is not mentioned in any of Lanier's letters.

[29] Previously published, *Letters* (New York, 1899), pp. 191-192.

route to Florida — perhaps the quickest and pleasantest — which passes through Brunswick. It is called the " Cumberland Route " (from passing by Cumberland Island, on the Georgia Coast, between Brunswick & Fernandina, Fla.) and is the one by which I travelled last time. You take a sleeping-car at New York which brings you through to Danville, Va: there you find another sleeping-car which brings you all the way to Brunswick without change. At Brunswick you take a steamer to Fernandina, forty five miles: and, at Fernandina cars for Jacksonville, sixty seven miles. If you are coming to Florida, you would probably be best pleased at St. Augustine.

Pray write me a line when you receive this, telling me whether you'll come through Brunswick. My address henceforth is " Care of Chas. Day, Brunswick, Ga." We leave here for that place on the 5th of April.

Your friend

S. L.[30]

To Robert S. Lanier [31]

B[runswic]k.   April 18th, 1877.

My dear Father:

Enclosed are the letters for which you wrote. I gave the address of Mr. Taylor in my last, with that of Mr.

---

[30] Taylor had written, Mar. 12, 1877, that he might come to Florida for two weeks in April; but in his reply to the present letter, Apr. 15, he said that he was going to Cedarcroft instead (*Letters*, New York, 1899, pp. 189-190, 192-193).

He added that he had sent Lanier's poem to the *Atlantic*, in spite of what Lanier had said about Howells in his letter of Feb. 25: " Howells returned ' The Bee ' along with my ' Assyrian Night Song,' having no mind for either. But for this fact, I should regret having sent yours. I have several times half resolved never to send him another poem; but now I wholly resolve. He has personal whim in place of clear critical judgment. I shall next try Harper's with a better hope of success."

[31] While Lanier was in Florida, his father made efforts to secure a government position for him. His first project was to have his son appointed Collector of the Port of Brunswick; then U. S. Marshal for Georgia; and finally Postmaster at Macon. He had already written to J. F. D. Lanier, his cousin David Clopton (Clifford Lanier's father-in-law), and Senator John T. Morgan of Alabama. On Mar. 26, 1877, he wrote to his son Clifford: " As for Sid's accepting office you know he is broadly Catholic & non-partisan, – & your Uncle C. & I. & many others, Alek. Stephens &c. &c. feel no hesitancy as to Southern men getting offices wherever they are properly tendered."

Peacock. To save you the trouble of looking up this and other addresses in various letters, I give herein all that you need.

Gibson Peacock
1425 Walnut St.
Philadelphia,
Pa.

Bayard Taylor
142 East 18th St.
New York
N. Y.

Gen. Wm. M. Dunn
Judge Advocate General's Office
War Dep't,
Washington,
D. C.

J. F. D. Lanier Esq
27 Pine St.
New York
N. Y.

Gen. John T. Morgan
Selma
Ala.

Mr. Clopton's letter is not good as it mentions the place of Collector of Br'k, and would be misconstrued. It is better that all the letters should be general recommendations of capacity and fitness, and should avoid mentioning any particular place.

Mary and I returned last night from Waynesville, where we spent a couple of days with the Hazlehursts. We are all pretty well.[32]

Tell Uncle Clifford his last letter was forwarded me from

[32] But on Apr. 12, 1877, Mary Day Lanier had written to Clifford: " Sidney not very well."

Tampa, and that I send the Manuscript by Express today as directed.

Love to Mama,

Your son

S. L.

To Bayard Taylor [88]

Brunswick. Ga.

April 26th 1877.

Dear Mr Taylor:

Pray don't trouble to send The Bee to Harper's. I haven't the least idea of letting you act as poem-broker for me any longer. I'm now getting well enough to write a little, and May (that's my wife) is becoming a capital secretary.

If you should not have sent off The Bee before this reaches you, I'll trouble you to enclose it to me: I've kept no copy, and am not sure that I remember it exactly.

Have you happened to see the illustrations to an *extravaganza* of mine (a sort of story which one "makes up as he goes along", to a lot of importunate youngsters) in the May number of St. Nicholas? [34] They seem to me, who am but little of a critic however in such matters, to be very charming. Mrs. Dodge appears not to have received the proof-sheets, which I returned from Tampa, in time; for in them I carefully corrected some very disagreeable repetitions, and faults of punctuation, which appear in the publication.

I believe there is a little scrap of a poem of mine in Scribner's for May; [35] but I haven't seen it.

I take real delight in thinking of you at Cedarcroft among the leaves. How fares my Master, the Chestnut-tree? If you only had there the infinite sweetness of Spring which is now in full leaf and overflowing song all about us here! I have at

[88] Previously published, *Atlantic Monthly*, LXXXIV, 135 (July, 1899); reprinted, *Letters* (New York, 1899), pp. 193-194.

[34] "The Story of a Proverb" (VI, 324), for which Lanier had been paid $24.00 ca. Dec. 10, 1876. Mrs. M. M. Dodge, mentioned below, was the editor of *St. Nicholas Magazine*.

[35] "The Stirrup-Cup" (see note 14, above).

command a springy mare, with ankles like a Spanish girl's, upon whose back I go darting through the green overgrown woodpaths like a thrasher about his thicket. The whole air seems full of fecundity: as I ride, I'm like one of those insects that are fertilized on the wing, – every leaf that I brush against breeds a poem. God help the world, when this now-hatching brood of my Ephemeræ shall take flight and darken the air.

After the third of May, my address will be " Macon, Ga. "; we will spend a month there. As for further plans, – about which you kindly ask – they will depend entirely on my state of health at the end of May. I *hope* to be in New York during June: – but you will be informed of my motions.

Tell Mrs Taylor I wish we could send her a rose from the little garden of the house where we sojourn: though we don't dare to pick one often, by reason that a mocking-bird is sitting on her eggs in the Spiræa-bush, and we shrink from disturbing the tranquillity of her mind at this interesting period.

Your friend

S. L.

To Gibson Peacock [36]

Brunswick, Ga.

April 26th 1877.

My dear friend: If I had as many fingers as your astounding servant-maid, and each one could wield a pen separately, I still wouldn't be able to write the fair messages which continually construct themselves in my heart to you both. That such a very pitiful fraction of these has actually reached you during the last few weeks is due to mine ancient infirmity in the matter of driving the quill, and to May's constant occupation with her father and brother. These poor lonely men live here in a house to themselves, with no women, or children about them: and when May comes with her bright ways and intelligent sympathies, she has both hands, lips and heart very busy from morning till night.

---

[36] Previously published, *Atlantic Monthly*, LXXIV, 184 (Aug., 1894); reprinted, *Letters* (New York, 1899), pp. 40-41.

I suppose you've seen a little *extravaganza* of mine in *St. Nicholas* for May. The proof-sheets were sent me at Tampa, and I promptly corrected and returned them: but they seem not to have arrived in time, and I desolate myself at finding some miserable repetitions and awkward expressions, which I had carefully amended, appearing nevertheless,—besides some very bad punctuation systematically interpolated all the way through by some other hand than mine. The illustrations are charming, however, and I feel as if I ought to write a special letter of thanks to Mr. [E. B.] Bensell for the evident care he had taken. The story I meant to be only such an incongruous melange as one might "make up as he went along" for a lot of children about his knees: and its very intentional incongruities must have been serious stumbling-blocks to the engraver.

I sincerely regret the continued illness of Mr. Wells.[37] He was so full of life and so overbrimming with his quips and his quiddities, that I can scarcely realize him as a sick man. Pray send him my cordial greetings when you write, with my earnest wishes for his speedy recovery.

I wrote Mrs. Peacock just before we left Tampa. We remain here until the fifth of May: after which our address will be "Macon, Ga." We think to spend a month there: and then, if I continue to improve, to make our way back northward. I can't tell you how famished I am for the Orchestra: an imperious hunger drives me towards it.

We both send a kiss to you both. If Miss Phelps[38] is with you, we'll put in two, mine being particularly by way of response for her kind note. I long to see you all.

Your friend.

S.L.[39]

[37] Editorial assistant on Peacock's paper, the Philadelphia *Evening Bulletin.*
[38] Elizabeth Stuart Phelps (see note 185, 1875).
[39] No letters by Lanier between Apr. 26 and May 25, 1877, have been found. On Apr. 26 Mary Day Lanier wrote to Clifford: "S has been doing poorly for a long while and courage has to be fought for. His journey [to Macon] is likely to be very fatiguing to him and therefore I shall be glad if you chance to decide upon a time slightly later than that of our arrival [May 5]—for meeting us. I want him to be able *to get a great deal out of yr. visit.*" He had improved only slightly when Clifford paid his visit, about May 21.

During this period of inactivity and rest on Lanier's part, there was considerable effort made on his behalf by others to secure him a government

To Bayard Taylor [40]

Macon, Ga.
May 25th 1877.

My dear Mr. Taylor:

Yours with THE BEE – my poor little bee, my humblest of humble-bees – came to me here.

Within two weeks from now I hope to see you, and the anticipation gives me a great deal of pleasure. I seem to be fairly on the high road to health – almost within the boundaries, indeed, of that most lovely state – and am quite agog

appointment. R. S. Lanier wrote to Bayard Taylor, Apr. 21, for a letter of recommendation; and Taylor replied, Apr. 28, inclosing a letter addressed to the Secretary of the Treasury, John Sherman, in which he said: "I know of no man more worthy to be entrusted with a place requiring intelligence, integrity and honor. He is a gentleman who knows how to labor,–a man of distinguished intellect, who is yet practical enough for strict routine duties. . . . I write in ignorance of what has been done by others; but I venture to say that Mr. Bryant and Mr. Longfellow (both of whom know Mr. Lanier personally) would be equally ready to second the application."

Judge L. E. Bleckley addressed a letter to Clifford Anderson, Apr. 22, stating that whereas he could not actively cooperate with Lanier's friends in promoting his advancement, because he was "a member of the Judiciary, . . . bound to abstain from all interference in competition for appointments to office," none of Lanier's friends would be more gratified than himself at the success of any application that might be made in his behalf.

Senator J. T. Morgan addressed a letter to Secretary Sherman, Apr. 23, saying: "I do not know any gentleman who in respect of his character and accomplishments would be better entitled to high consideration."

Gibson Peacock wrote to R. S. Lanier, Apr. 27, that he would make a special trip to Washington to see both Sherman and W. M. Evarts, Secretary of State.

J. F. D. Lanier wrote to Sherman, an old friend of his, on May 18: "I should feel under personal obligation to you for any trouble you may take . . . [in behalf of my kinsman, who is] a most worthy young man, of high character and unexceptionable habits." All of these letters, together with an application for an appointment for Lanier, were filed at the Treasury Department by J. F. D. Lanier's son-in-law, General William Dunn (see Lanier's letter of July 3, 1877, below).

[40] Previously published, *Atlantic Monthly*, LXXXIV, 135-136 (July, 1899); reprinted, *Letters* (New York, 1899), pp. 195-196.

Taylor had written, May 9, 1877 (*Letters*, p. 194): "I return your 'Bee' with a sense of discouragement at my inability to find a place for it. I went to 'Harper's,' meaning to *read* it aloud to Alden, but didn't find him. . . . I read it the other day to [George H.] Boker, who was here, and he said the [*Atlantic?*] doesn't have more than two as good poems in a year."

with all manner of matters about many of which I desire greatly to talk with you.

The talk here is of the advance in corn, and of the failure of our City Bank; and, so far as concerns any man I have yet conversed with, there is absolutely nothing in heaven or earth or the waters under the earth but corn and the City Bank. Perhaps if I had several thousand bushels of the former, or a large deposit in the latter, these topics might interest me more. But I haven't: and when I think how I shall enjoy tackling you about something or other – say Emerson, whom I have been reading all the winter, and who gives me immeasurable delight because he does not propound to me disagreeable systems and hideous creeds but simply walks along high and bright ways where one loves to go with him [41] – then I am ready to praise God for the circumstance that if corn were a dollar a bushel I could not with my present finances buy a lunch for a pony.

I will be here until I start Northward: where you may address me if you should have occasion to write meantime.

My wife would send cordial greetings to you and Mrs. Taylor if she knew I was writing. God bless you.

Yr. friend,

S. L.[42]

To Gibson Peacock [43]

Macon, Ga.
May 26th 1877.

My dear Friend:

They have had a family gathering here to meet me; and what with fondling numerous new babies that have arrived since I last met the parents thereof, and with much talk of matters high and low, I have not found time to send my love to you.

[41] This was apparently Lanier's first serious reading of Emerson, whose influence is traceable in the poems of this period, notably in "A Florida Sunday" (see note 45, below), written during the previous winter, and in some of the poetic fragments mentioned in the following letter, posthumously published as *Poem Outlines* in 1908 (see vol. I of the present edition).

[42] Taylor's reply to this letter (June? 1877) is printed in *Letters* (New York, 1899), pp. 196-197.

[43] Previously published, *Atlantic Monthly*, LXXIV, 184-185 (Aug., 1894); reprinted, *Letters* (New York, 1899), pp. 41-42.

I have gained greatly in strength within the last three weeks, and although I have still much discomfort at times I feel perfectly sure that I have quite got the upper hand of this particular attack at least. We propose to start for Philadelphia within two weeks from now: waiting so long only to be sure of escaping any possible caprice of this very unreliable Spring. The prospect of speedily turning northward gives us, as you can imagine, great delight: for it is a prospect which holds in its "middle distance" you two, and our dear monkeys for whom our arms are fairly hungry.

I long to be steadily writing again. I'm taken with a poem pretty nearly every day, and have to content myself with making a note of its train of thought on the back of whatever letter is in my coat-pocket. I don't write it out, because I find my poetry now wholly unsatisfactory in consequence of a certain haunting impatience which has its root in the straining uncertainty of my daily affairs: and I am trying with all my might to put off composition of all sorts until some approach to the certainty of next weeks' dinner shall remove this remnant of haste, and leave me that repose which ought to fill the artist's firmament while he is creating. Perhaps indeed with returning bodily health I shall acquire strength to attain this serenity in spite of all contingencies.

Address me here, if you write within the next ten days. May would send a kiss to you both if she knew I was writing. Cordial greetings to Miss Phelps if she is now with you. I hope Mr. Wells continues to improve.

Your friend,

S. L.[44]

To ROBERT S. LANIER

40 Mt. Vernon Place.
Baltimore, Md.
June 13th 1877.

At length, My dearest Father, I have come to a sort of breathing-place of which I can avail myself to write you a line. Although we had a charming journey,– the rains having laid

[44] On May 29, 1877, Mary Day Lanier wrote to her sons: " [Papa] has been

the dust ahead of us everywhere,– yet I was greatly fatigued, and had to devote my whole energies to resting for several days.

Mary and I expect to go to Gen. [William] Dunn's for a three or four days' visit next Monday, 18ᵗʰ June. The General has been ordered to West Point during the Examination there, and expects to return next Saturday. Mary and I ran over to Washington yesterday and had a pleasant chat with Mrs. McKee, General D.'s daughter.

We remain here (at Mrs. Bird's) until Monday or Tuesday when we go to Washington. Probably you had better forward any letters that may come, as usual, to this address, until I inform you otherwise. We have received several from you. I'm glad you liked the Florida poem.[45] They misprinted "joys" for jays (*birds*) when I speak of "Live-oaks round heads

Busy with jays (*i. e.* jay-birds) for thoughts": – meaning to describe the jay-birds flitting through the tree as thoughts flit through a man's head: the punctuation is also quite mutilated in some places.

But I am now very tired, having written several other business letters, and must stop. May sends kisses, with me, to you and Mama. I forgot to ask you to send back carefully Uncle C.'s book (the red one by Dʳ. Le Conte,[46] left on the bureau in my room): please, do so.

God bless you all.

Your son,

S. L.

The "Tribune" some days ago had a very cordial notice of my restoration to health and return to New York, which has been copied, in an abridged form, by the Baltimore and other papers.[47]

growing stronger and stouter lately and if he could be free from suffering when he lies down I would feel quite certain he was getting well."

[45] "A Florida Sunday" (I, 94), published in *Frank Leslie's Sunday Magazine*, July, 1877.

[46] Presumably Joseph LeConte's *Religion and Science*, a series of lectures on the relation of natural and revealed religion, published in 1874.

[47] The New York *Tribune*, June 7, 1877, said: "Mr. Sidney Lanier, who has been staying in the South for the benefit of his health, has recovered. He is coming to New-York to work in the ways of literature." (See also the Baltimore *Gazette*, June 8, 1877.)

To Gibson Peacock [48]

40 Mt. Vernon Place.
Baltimore, Md.
June 13th 1877.

My dear Friend:

I am really distressed to know that you should have spent your day at Washington in the unprofitable business of pottering about those dreary Departments in my behalf:—but I won't lecture you for your unearthly goodness to me.

May and I are to go to Washington next Monday, to visit Judge Advocate General Dunn, who is a son-in-law of my kinsman J. F. D. Lanier (of New York), and who has extended a very cordial invitation to us. We will also meet there Gen. Humphreys, Chief of the Engineer Corps, who is an old and intimate friend of May's mother, and has always made a great pet of May herself. It seems like stretching our hearts to stay away from the boys longer: yet we have determined finally to do it, inasmuch as we do not know when we will have another opportunity to meet these friends.

As for the "application": you must know, my dear good Friend, that all *that* matter was gotten up without my knowledge, and has been carried on by my father and Mr. Lanier of New York. When they finally wrote to me of it, I replied (after a great struggle which I have not the heart to detail to you) that inasmuch as I had never been a party man of any sort I did not see with what grace I could ask any appointment: and that, furthermore, I could not see it to be delicate, on general principles, for me to make *personal* application for any particular office: but that I would be grateful if they would simply cause my name to be mentioned to the proper persons as that of a person who might be suitable for certain classes of appointments, and that I would accept with pleasure any result of such an application. This has been done; my name has been mentioned to Mr. Sherman, (and to Mr. Evarts, I be-

---

[48] Previously published, *Atlantic Monthly*, LXXIV, 185-186 (Aug., 1894); reprinted, *Letters* (New York, 1899), pp. 42-44.

lieve) by quite cordially-disposed persons. But I do not think
any formal application has been entered, – though I do not
know. I *hope* not: for then the reporters will get hold of it,
and I scarcely know what I should do if I should see my name
figuring alongside of Jack Brown's and Foster Blodgett's and
the others of my native state,– as would quickly be the case.

But I can speak of all this when I see you. It will probably
be nine or ten days before I have that pleasure,– even if you
shall have returned to Pha. by that time. Pray send me a line
(see address above date of this letter) to let me know your
motions.

Kiss my dear Maria for me. May, I think, is writing her
own messages.

–Meantime, don't think me finical,– and don't think me anything but your faithful

S. L.

To Mary Day Lanier

Westminster Hotel
New York,
June 27th 1877.[49]

This is but a line, dearest Soul, to kiss thee and tell thee that I
am feeling better than when I was last in sight of thy sweet
and wise face.   Charles Lanier has just called, and I have
put in training the business for which I came here. Mr. Taylor
is away at Providence, reading a Poem to the Army of The
Potomac, but will return on Friday.

My name appearing this morning on the list of " Prominent
Arrivals " in the newspapers, here come a batch of polite
requests for my autograph by mail from Brooklyn and New
York.

And this is all the news now. I am all one longing for my

---

[49] Lanier seems to have stayed in Washington about a week. In a letter to
his father, June 16, 1877 (here omitted), he said that he expected to stay there
from June 19 to 22; but a surviving MS fragment– probably an album inscription– bears the date " Washington, D. C. / June 25th, 1877 " (MS, Kenneth
Rede, Baltimore). He must have left there the next day, for according to the
following letter he spent a night in Philadelphia before going on to New York.

sweet boys. Waste none of thy strength in writing me of them: as long as I hear not, I will know that the measles is progressing well.

Every time the sun rises, or sets, I discover anew that I am, and more fully always,

thine

S. L.

To Robert S. Lanier

New York City.
June 28th 1877.

My dear Father:

After a night in Philadelphia with the boys, I ran over here, being under the greatest necessity to do something with the Policy which you entrusted to me in order to raise money.

Charles Lanier called yesterday, and today was kind enough to send his cashier to see the Knickerbocker people about it. I enclose the cashier's note to me. Of course it quite destroys all hope of doing anything with the Policy. You observe they say that it is only after the note of $576 is paid that the Policy can be worth the amount on its face, even at death of the insured: and that it has now *no cash value.*

Of course this is bad, but you must try to work out of it somehow. I owe about $150 for board of the boys, which must be paid immediately as the people expect to leave town: and other little matters, such as washing-bills, and nurse's wages, and summer-clothing for the chickens, demand quick attention.

Mr Peacock was absent from Pha. when I came through there, so that I could not tell what had been done actually with the silver. He has just returned now, and as soon as I get back I will ascertain, so that if the silver is still accessible I may send it South and pledge it with the Loan Association for such amount as they are willing to lend on it. But in the meantime, I wish you would raise me whatever you possibly can,– a hundred if possible, if not, less – and send it to me, at the Philadelphia address which I gave you, as early as may be.

It would take a long letter to tell you the pleasant things which Gen. and Mrs. Dunn said to us and did for us; and we feel that their friendship has become a genuine new possession for our lives. Gen. Dunn says there is no doubt but Mr. Sherman will offer me *something*: and I wait to hear from him. I expect to return to Ph^a. tomorrow or next day. Kiss Mama for

Your

S. L.

To Robert S. Lanier

3351 Baring St.
Philadelphia, Pa.
July 3rd 1877.

My dear Father:

I arrived here late on Saturday night from New York, and found the boys progressing as favorably as could be expected with their measles. Sidney and Harry are both out of bed today, and Charley is going about as usual.

A letter from Gen. Dunn says: " I called on Secretary Sherman yesterday, and you will receive an appointment under him so soon as a place at all suitable to your condition of health can be found for you. He gave such an order to his Chief Clerk in my presence. His Chief Clerk is a personal friend of mine, – an ex-army officer: . . . . he is a man of culture, had read the letters which I filed with the application in your behalf, and was very glad of the opportunity of serving you. He told me, however, they were discharging so many clerks now that it might be a month before he could find a place for you ". Gen. Dunn adds: " Do not get disgusted with these hard business details. . . . I hope you found your dear children well. Your brief stay in Washington drew many hearts warmly to your wife and yourself. Love to her &c."

I believe I wrote you that under the present furor for Civil Service reform, I would have to commence with one of the lowest places in the Department: salary $1200. This seems trifling, but I will accept whatever comes very thankfully, so long as I may be thereby enabled to write my poems without hurry and with that tranquillity of mind necessary to works of pure art.

Gen. Dunn appears annoyed at the smallness of the position he has been able to secure, but insists that I should accept and wait for better things, of whose occurrence he entertains no doubt. It is important that I should go to Washington, and be on the ground ready to confer with Gen. Dunn upon whatever may be offered me. But I cannot do this until I arrange money matters here.

I find that the silver has been really sold, and yesterday received from Mr. Peacock such small balance as remained after paying Doctor's bills &c. This has enabled me to pay about fifty dollars toward the board-bill. But there will still remain about a hundred and fifty due at the time we hope to leave – *i. e.* in ten days from now: and besides that I will need as much more to get the family off to some cheap spot in the country here, for a couple of months, by which time I will hope to provide something for them in Washington.

I found I could do nothing towards raising money in New York. I have evolved scheme after scheme, and tried it without effect: if I think of it any more I shall be ill: I am simply dependent on you.

I was sorry to note the death of Watson in the paper you sent. The same paper stated that argument was to be concluded that day in the City Bank case before Judge Hill. Tell me the result.

Mary joins me in a great deal of love to you and Mama. She seems pulled down a little by the exactions of the boys, who seem never to be able to get enough of either of us, and who show every day a depth of tenderness and love which is wonderful to see in such young people. I am much wearied from hard work in New York, but otherwise I think I have not fallen back materially in special health.

I think of you working in your hot office every day, and utter hundreds of unavailing wishes that I might help. Perhaps the time will still come when I can have that pleasure.

God bless you both.

Your son

S. L.

To Bayard Taylor [50]

3315 Baring St.
Philadelphia, Pa.
July 9th 1877.

My dear Mr Taylor:

I am merely writing a line to enclose the two slips which you will find herein, and which I thought might interest you à propos of what you were telling me the other day. The Philadelphia LEDGER, from which the slip of July 7th is cut, is so reliable in these matters that I suppose there can be no doubt of the substantial fact as therein stated: though it seems wonderful that the originators of such a movement should not have been immediately struck with the propriety of sending the translator of Goethe to Germany, instead of to Russia or to Belgium.[51]

But isn't Russia or Belgium a somewhat queer alternative: something like offering a man either the Presidency of the United States or the Postmaster-ship of Kennett Square?

I sent you today a Boston Magazine containing a portrait of me [52] which I think will amuse you, – particularly the smutched one accompanying the biographical sketch inside. This, this is Fame: to have your "visnomy" transformed into that of a keen blue-nosed New England manufacturer of shoe-pegs.

I have not often seen anything more tragic than my wife's indignation over this wood-cut: – nor have I succeeded in allaying her resentment by my sympathetic assurance that I think it the unkindest cut of all.

My wife joins me in friendly messages to you both. With

[50] Previously published, Atlantic Monthly, LXXXIV, 136-137 (July, 1899); reprinted, Letters (New York, 1899), pp. 197-198.

[51] Taylor's name had been mentioned in the newspapers in connection with an appointment by President Hayes to a diplomatic post abroad.

[52] Earl Marble, "Sidney Lanier," Cottage Hearth, IV, 141-142 (June, 1877). Lanier's portrait— a wood engraving made from the 1874 Kuhn and Cummins profile photograph— appeared on the cover as well as in the article itself (reproduced in Starke, facing p. 294). The biographical sketch is brief, and the criticism chiefly interesting for its long quotation from an estimate of Lanier as a musician, written in a note to the author by Ronald MacDonald of the New York Times (reprinted by Starke, p. 294).

earnest wishes that you may be drawing strength from the dear mountains, as it were from the very breasts and big nipples of our Mother Earth,

faithfully your friend

S. L.[53]

To Robert S. Lanier

3315 Baring St.
Philadelphia, Pa.
July 12th 1877.

My dearest Father:

I have been very hard at work for a week preparing a sketch of the Lanier family which is to be printed in a second edition of Mr. J. F. D. Lanier's account of his own life, as an appendix.[54] His whole thought seems to turn upon this matter, so that, although I had little strength for investigating genealogies and the like, I mustered a desperate courage and plunged in. I sent it, (the sketch)– to General Dunn day before yesterday, for any suggestions he might make. He seems much pleased with it. Today it goes to Mr. Lanier.

I have put off drawing on you until tomorrow when I will in accordance with your last letter draw on you at sight for $100. If you can send the next $100 one week afterwards, I can manage to wait for the third until twenty or thirty days from that time.

Mary and I are going into the country tomorrow to look at a place. If I am called to Washington soon I will leave my family in the country until September. Gen. Dunn saw Assistant Secretary McCormick yesterday, in calling at the Treasury Dept. to look after my interests. He writes: " I find that Mr. McC. is much interested in you. He was one of the Centennial Commissioners ".

[53] In his reply, July 11, 1877 (*Letters*, New York, 1899, pp. 198-199), Taylor wrote: " As for the mission, I think ' Belgium ' must be a mistake for ' Berlin.' It would be singular to offer the choice of a *first* or a *fourth* rate place! In any case the German mission is the only one I am able to take; and if it is not offered, I'll even stay at home."

[54] This article, in the form of a letter dated July 6, 1877, was published in the second edition of *Sketch of the Life of J. F. D. Lanier* (Philadelphia, 1877), pp. 75-87 (see VI, 350).

Mr. Day writes that Dr. Dunwoody told him before leaving Macon that Mama was seriously ill: which makes us rejoice to hear that she is better.   Let us know of her continued improvement.   Harry was quite sick yesterday, and for two days before: but he now seems a great deal better and is playing about.

I am quite tired, but doing my best to be brave and quiet. May has gone out for an airing with the two older boys.

Your loving

S. L.

To Robert S. Lanier

3315 Baring St.
Philadelphia, Pa.
July 16th 1877.

My dear Father:

I write a note to enclose a letter from Gen. Dunn rec'd this morning.   It bears pleasant testimony to his activity in my behalf; though I found it impossible to avail myself of the offer.[55]   Some of the climates we would have to visit would be extremely unfavorable to my disease: and the success of my literary work is, I now believe, quite dependent on my having a settled home for the next two or three years. Please send this enclosed letter down to Mr. Day when you have read it, asking him to return it to us here.

By a Tel. & Mess. which Mr. Day has mailed us, I see that you gained the Insurance case before the U. S. Court at Atlanta. But I have not yet heard from the Bank case.

I am anxious to get my people into the country: and as I can't make the least move till I get my second hundred (I drew on you for the *first* hundred last Friday, Mr. Peacock cashing my draft) I hope to have that pleasure as soon as possible.   It will be some saving to me if I get it the last of this week, as we can avoid some expenses by being able to make prompt engagements of board in the country.

---

[55] The nature of the offer is revealed more fully in the following letter.

I wish you would ask Theo. Ellis to put up a couple of bottles of the Lightfoot Remedy and send me by Express. My cough is become quite hard and painful. The boys are well, and Mary better than usual. I hope Mama is quite recovered. Love to her and you from all of us here.

Your son,

S. L.

To Robert S. Lanier

3315 Baring St.
Philadelphia, Pa.
July 23rd 1877.

My dear Father:

I feel sure that your consultation with Uncle Clifford has been held under a misapprehension as to the facts.

First: if the China voyage were the sole refuge now from my present condition of starvation I would unhesitatingly accept it. But it is not. There is now no doubt that I will receive a position of $1200 a year in the Treasury Dept., as soon as the mere detail of selecting for me a place suitable to my health can be carried out. This would probably have been accomplished before now, had it not been for the absence of Secretary Sherman, who has just returned to Washington. The extraordinary expenses involved by my position as Commodore's Secretary would make the two thousand dollars of that salary really less useful to me than the twelve hundred at Washington. The mess-bills alone of the Secretary amount to $420 a year: and there would be personal expenses amounting to as much more: and it would require the whole of the balance even to have my wife with me, leaving the children at home. In this connection I may further remark that the Secretaryship is only for 2½ years, and when it ended I should be exactly in my present situation: moreover it is not at all in the line of any promotion. Opposed to this, the Treasury position offers employment for many years, in all probability: and Gen. Dunn assures me that if I pass a " First Class " examination, I may look for early promotion to more lucrative places.[56]

[56] In connection with the civil service examination that Lanier was expecting to take, Gen. Dunn had asked a Miss Sarita M. Brady to outline the type of

Secondly. The journey I am to make is not a mere pleasure-voyage such as Uncle Sidney and Mr. Obear took, but it involves prolonged stays at some of the most unhealthy places in the world. I know two persons who were ruined in health by a similar expedition: one died, and the other is a complete wreck in health, though both started as vigorous men in splendid bodily condition.

Thirdly: in two years and a half buried away in Asia, life would rush completely past me in America, and I should have to commence it over again.

Fourthly: I could do nothing in the way of literature. I would have no libraries at hand, and no literary companionship. I could not even write Magazine articles: for the countries I am to visit have been done *ad nauseam* by the magazines.

Fifthly: my longing for a resting-place has reached a point where it must be satisfied. My existence as a nomad for the last five or six years has been satisfactory enough, and I have made a great many friends in various parts of the United States: but I am now tired of living in a trunk, and I must get some kind of abiding-place. Aside from this need, there are other more sternly practical reasons: my boys have reached the age where my daily guidance is imperatively necessary to the proper development of their natures: I need to be near libraries, to complete studies essential to my work: I need occasional literary companionship, and opportunities to make acquaintance with Magazine-editors and publishers: and I might add a half-dozen equally pressing considerations.

In treating of the aspect of matters from the point of view of *healthiness*, I should have remarked, by way of answer to your objections to Washington in this particular, that the idea of its unhealthiness seems to be mostly due to the floating population of Representatives and others, who usually invite disease while there by imprudences in eating or drinking, or by exposures in the unventilated rooms of the Capitol. The statistics of the city show it to be a very healthy place: and that is the only reliable criterion.

examination she herself had taken. Her letter of July 20 to Gen. Dunn was forwarded by him to Lanier. (A copy of *Poems*, 1877, inscribed " To Miss Sarita Brady. With the sincere esteem of Sidney Lanier. Philadelphia, July 23, 1877 " was offered for sale by the Collector's Bookshop, New York, in Mar., 1936.)

Thus in the particulars of financial help, of health, of future success, of facility for work, and of my personal needs, the position at Washington is very much preferable to the other, and for these reasons I had promptly declined it before your first letter came. I have not time to detail all the reasons leading me to do so: they were thoroughly weighed by Mary and myself, and we agreed that there could be no hesitation between staying in Washington together, and going to China under the circumstances proposed. With a regular income of $1200 a year (which is more than I have drawn each year from any outside source since I left Macon) in addition to my income from literary sources, I can live in some way, and, at any rate, with a peaceful mind, which is now the most important of all considerations to me.[57] To leave either my wife or my children for two years and a half, now, would be simply to exchange one anxiety for another.

I feel perfectly sure that you will see this to be the wise course for me.

Yours containing enclosure $100 is here, and most opportunely in hand.

There is great and increasing excitement here over the riots. No one can fail to be astonished at the wretched handling of the troops at Pittsburg.[58] Although the whole of rascaldom is out this morning in Philadelphia,— they have just set fire to an oil train on the Pa. road, a half mile from the station — I think the police, and a strong force of regulars who are either here or on the way, will prevent any repetition of the Pittsburg

[57] In a letter to Clifford Lanier of the same date (July 23, 1877, here omitted), after a similar outline of his prospects, Lanier wrote: "I can at least fight starvation from a fortified stronghold, as it were, instead of in the open field with all the odds against me, as has been the case for the last four or five years. . . .

"Meantime, what with all the poems I can now sell, and with what Father can spare (for he writes that he has great trouble to raise money), I still lack about sixty dollars to finish paying my board-bill here. Please lend me this: perhaps I can return it to you next month, if my pending literary ventures prosper. . . .

"Have you read the letters of John Keats to his brother George (at Louisville, Ky), published in the N. Y. World a couple of weeks ago? They make me think of you and me. But my lot is far brighter than Keats's."

[58] A general railroad strike beginning in the eastern states about the middle of July and extending as far west as Chicago before order was restored about Aug. 1. There was much mob violence and considerable loss of life. (Details are given in the Baltimore *Gazette*.)

terrors.   In three days, or perhaps four, we expect to go into the country, to a charming place which I have found after a long search — a house on a hill, with a fine view from the front porch, and a great green lawn sweeping down to the Brandywine which flows at the foot of the hill.   You had better address me, here, however, until further advices.

All send love to you all.

Your son,

S. L.

P. S.   Your Life-Policy is in my hands, and has been so all the time.   I will send it to you whenever you write for it.   Perhaps you had best take some action about it, in accordance with the suggestion of the actuary.   I find, on re-reading your letter, that you seem to be under the impression that the Policy is somewhere out of my possession.   You have probably misunderstood something I may have written about it.

Aff.

S. L.

To Bayard Taylor [59]

Philadelphia Pa.

July 28th 1877.

My dear Mr. Taylor:

I send a line to say that we will move, on the day after tomorrow, to Mrs. Caleb Brinton's, about a half mile from Chadd's Ford, where we expect to spend the next two months.   We are delighted with the place, which my wife and I have visited and inspected: and we hope that when you return to Cedarcroft you will bless us with the light of your countenance.   My address will be " Chadd's Ford."

I haven't time to write.   My wife unites her cordial salutations with mine to you and all your house.

Faithfully yours,

S. L.[60]

[59] Previously published, *Letters* (New York, 1899), pp. 199-200.
[60] Taylor's reply, Aug. 11, 1877 (*Letters*, New York, 1899, p. 200), was an invitation to Lanier to visit him at Cedarcroft.

To Robert S. Lanier

Chadd's Ford, Pa.
Aug. 1st 1877.

My dear Father:

We left the sweltering city day before yesterday, and are now comfortably domiciled at our new quarters in the country. It was not a moment too soon that we came away: for our drooping frames had begun to suffer great loss by the heat and its concomitants in a large city.

Our new place is very delightful, and seems like a different world from that of Philadelphia. We are about half a mile from " Chadd's Ford," a station on the " Baltimore Central " railroad, not quite two hours journey from Philadelphia. This " Baltimore Central " railroad is now only an offshoot of the Philadelphia, Wilmington and Baltimore Railroad, branching off from the main stem at Chester, Pa. and rejoining it at Perryville, Md, after looping round a considerable extent of country to the westward.

I've been working very hard for three weeks on a lot of poems which I have sent off to various periodicals,[61] and am feeling some unusually severe effects from writing. Did you see my sonnet to " the Mocking-Bird " in THE GALAXY for August? It was sent one day in your office, at the same time with the one to SCRIBNER'S which was answered so promptly.[62] I have just finished another " Story of a Proverb " for ST. NICHOLAS,[63] which I hope they will find available.

[61] The only poems by Lanier definitely known to have been written at Chadd's Ford are " The Dove " and " A Puzzled Ghost in Florida "; another possibility is " A Dream of the Age: To Richard Wagner." (See Lanier's letters of Aug. 7 and Nov. 25, 1877, and notes 65, 85, and 101, below.)

[62] In a letter to his brother Clifford, July 23, 1877 (here omitted), Lanier had written: " The poem in the August HARPER'S called ' The Waving of the Corn ' is by me: and my ' Mocking-bird ' sonnet (which you saw in ms. in Macon) is in the August GALAXY. Did you see my ' From the Flats ' [I, 97] in the July LIPPINCOTT'S? " The first of these had been written the previous summer at West Chester; the second at Brunswick or Macon, Apr.-May, 1877; the last during the winter or spring at Tampa. The poem mentioned as having been sent to Scribner's was probably " Under the Cedarcroft Chestnut " (see Lanier's letter of Mar. 4, 1877, and note 23, above; also note 86, below).

[63] Presumably " The Story of a Proverb: a Fairy-tale for Grown People " (VI, 331). It was finally published in Lippincott's, Jan., 1879.

All send love to you and Mama. You have never told me, yet, about the Bank Case.

Your loving

S. L.

To Gibson Peacock [64]

Chadd's Ford, Pa.
Aug. 7th 1877.

My dear Mr. Gibson: This is but an hour old; and after sending it off to HARPER's,[65] I've made a hasty copy for you, thinking you would care to see it. The poor dove whose sorrow it commemorates wakes me every morning, calling from the lovely green woods about us.

We are charmed with our place: I myself have rather too much pot-boiling to improve much, but the boys are having a royal time.

May sends a kiss to you both, as does your faithful

S. L.

To Sarah J. Farley [66]

Chadd's Ford, Pa.
Aug. 11th 1877.

My dear Sarah:

We have been in a remarkable state of confusion here for several days, and in consequence thereof the messages which ought to have gone to you have remained like

[64] Previously published, *Atlantic Monthly*, LXXIV, 186 (Aug., 1894); reprinted, *Letters* (New York, 1899), p. 44.

[65] The poem inclosed was "The Dove" (I, 99). Rejected by *Harper's*, it was published in a revised version by *Scribner's*, May, 1878.

In a letter to his father, Aug. 8, 1877 (here omitted), Lanier wrote: "I have a considerable amount of poetry 'out' among the magazines: but most of the editors about this time are off on their summer vacations and I cannot look for any returns for a month, or longer." The only one of these poems that can be positively identified is "The Dove." Others were probably "The Bee," written the previous winter at Tampa, and "A Dream of the Age: To Richard Wagner," apparently written at Chadd's Ford (see Lanier's letter to Taylor, Oct. 8, 1877, below).

[66] The Laniers had met Miss Sarah Farley (1838-1914) at West Chester the previous summer. She and Mary Day Lanier were drawn to each other in part

the unplayed music in a violin. You have been lovingly discussed at the table among several of us who have acquired some dim perception into your reserve of sweetness, and between my lovely comrade and myself your name is an everpowerful guide into pleasant thoughts. But:— our nurse went off to New York on a holiday about a week ago: at the same time a cruel influx of work fell upon me out of those regions where matters concerning the boiling of the pot are determined and apportioned: and finally our good host Mr. Caleb Brinton jr, was brought home in a dangerous state of paralysis, occasioned by a fearful fall on his spine out of a wagon, and had to be carried into the library down-stairs which he has occupied ever since: all of which, together with various and sundry little episodes, such as stings of wasps, wettings in showers, movings-in and out of new and old shoals of boarders, and the like, have continually kept the pen out of our hands, as to all correspondence.

Tell my Lady, your mother, that although I missed that fair combination of odors which she had arranged for me, yet the fragrance of her thoughtful care in my behalf has reached me and has brought with it a charm at least superior to the actual sensation in one point—that it does not pass away.

May and I both were filled with regret at learning that you had waited for us in vain on Sunday. There is some misunderstanding between you and her as to an appointment for that particular day.[67] But the nurse is now returned, my work draws near a temporary completion, the new boarders are all arrived, Mr. Brinton is rapidly improving, — and we expect to settle down into some sort of tranquil existence immediately. This is equivalent to saying that we expect to see you soon: for we *couldn't* have any tranquil existence, my dear Child, in being only seven miles from you *without* looking upon your face. We are to run across to West Chester the very first chance.

Of course you are to come over and spend a day with *us*: but don't come before next Monday: because I'm obliged to go to

because both were earnest Episcopalians, but she became also a close friend of Sidney Lanier, and he addressed to her some of his best letters. After his death she was a frequent companion of Mrs. Lanier.

[6.] Sarah Farley and Mary Day Lanier had agreed to take Sunday communion together whenever possible.

New York on business tomorrow, and won't be back before that day.

May sends no messages herein, expecting to write them for herself. And so, till we both see you both:

Your faithful

Sidney L.

TO MARY DAY LANIER

Westminster Hotel, N. Y.
Aug. 16th 1877.

My dearest Soul: I came safely here last night, arriving about eight o'clock. The 12.35 train on which I left Chadd's Ford proved to be a pay-train and did not reach Ph^a until three in the afternoon.

I saw Mr. Lanier and General Dunn [68] this morning; and have my hands full of work for a couple of days. Mr. L. seems to be poorly off. General Dunn's son, – he who was indisposed while we were at his house – goes out on the China voyage to which we were invited.

I expect a letter from my father during the next three days with a check for $100 in it. *Please open any letter from him, (between now and Saturday) and promptly telegraph me at this hotel whether it contains the check or not.* Do likewise with any other letter that *seems* to contain a check. It is now likely that I will return on Sunday, or Monday morning.

Harry [69] and I took lunch together today. He looks quite as well as I expected to see him, and seems very happy at being near Loulie.

He boards at the "Grand Union," in 42nd Street, European plan. Has leave of absence until October. I will write more of him anon.

---

[68] Gen. Wm. M. Dunn had written to Wm. M. Evarts, Secretary of State, Aug. 11, 1877, asking an appointment for Lanier to a clerkship in his department or to a European consulate. With his letter he filed the recommendations previously made in connection with an appointment in the Treasury Department (see note 39, above), all of which are now among the records of the Department of State in the National Archives.

[69] Mary Day Lanier's brother, Harry Day.

Embrace my darling boys for me, and convey my remembrance to the household.   I am tired, and weak, but less so than when I left Chadd's Ford.   I remain at this hotel, where thou mayst write me.

There was never so dear a wife as thou art, nor so devout a worshipper as

Thine.

To John B. Tabb [70]

Address: Chadd's Ford, Pennsylvania.
Aug. 25th 1877.

My dear Tabb:

I heard some years ago that you had moved to Baltimore: and being much in that city soon afterward I made diligent inquiry after you, which was finally closed with the information that you had died there.   I have therefore mourned you, ever since, as one never to be seen again on This Side; and you may judge, herefrom, with what pleasure I read your letter.

I must also tell you that one day, a couple of months ago, in reading HARPER'S, I called out to my wife that I had really found a *poem*, and showed her "The Cloud".   It bore no name, and I had no conception of its author.

You may therefore imagine that it is with double delight that I have heard not only that you are alive, but that you are so wisely and beautifully alive as to produce "The Cloud."

My admiration for it is so genuine that I will not hesitate a moment to give you a little bit of fatherly advice about "An Allegory".   Of course I'm going to send it to Dr. Holland, with a good word, which it deserves: but before I do so, I strongly advise you to change it in two particulars; adding, before I state them that although I know Dr. Holland well and am on the very pleasantest terms with him, he would not accept anything in the world which didn't please him, even if

---

[70] With this letter Lanier renewed his friendship with his companion at Point Lookout Prison in 1864-1865, John Banister Tabb. Tabb, a convert to Roman Catholicism in 1872, was now at St. Charles College, near Ellicott City, Md., where he was studying for the priesthood.   Apparently he had written Lanier that he was the author of "The Cloud," published in *Harper's*, July, 1877, and had sent the MS of another poem to Lanier for criticism.

Homer, Shakespere, Dante and Milton should go down on their eight knees and beseech him, – in which he is, of course, right. The particulars in which I recommend alteration are: first, a change of name; and, second, the omission of the third and fourth verses.

1st The title " An Allegory " is too vague: it would serve for a thousand other poems: and the rule that a title ought to contain something more *particularly* descriptive is apt to be insisted on by Magazine-editors, who lay a good deal of stress upon the attractiveness of their Table of Contents, which of course consists of nothing *but* Titles.

2nd The third and fourth verses, regarded with a cold eye, will not stand, in point of truth. Within the sense of those stanzas, man *does* snatch at the treasures of the sky, as eagerly as at the treasures of the deep. Are we not now gloating over the moons of Mars?

I feel sure you will pardon the freedom of these recommendations. The first one is not so important as the second. Don't think of heeding *either*, if they do not meet your own ideas. I will retain the poem until I hear from you: and will gladly send it as it is, if you finally conclude not to alter it.

Pray tell me something of yourself, your past movements, and your future plans. I retain the liveliest remembrance of our comradeship at Point Lookout: and, independently of that, I take a keen interest in all the young spirits that incline to poetry.

Sincerely yours,

Sidney Lanier.

To Bayard Taylor [71]

Chadd's Ford, Pa.
August 26, 1877.

Dear Mr. Taylor:

Your letter came just as I was starting for New York on a business matter which has occupied me quite closely ever since. I'm now again at home, however, and hope to be at comparative leisure for a week or so.

[71] Previously published, *Atlantic Monthly*, LXXXIV, 137 (July, 1899); reprinted, *Letters* (New York, 1899), pp. 200-201.

I should have been inclined to think you a very shabby
Colossus, indeed – to stay away for a week when there were so
many Rhodes from here to Kennett – if I had not gathered
from your brief note that you were either very busy or very
worried, or both. I do hope you are now more at ease from
whatever may have troubled you.

In truth I particularly longed for one whole free day about
this lovely house with you. Do you know the place – old Mr.
George Brinton's? To the west is a vista running for miles
along the Brandywine; it's so fine that you can fancy, every
sunset, that the sun has gone that way on purpose to see the
country over there. A long green hill in front of the house
slopes down to the river, and within a few feet is a wild ravine
through which a stream runs down to the great rock-built
milldam.

Tell me how fare our friends Pro- and Epi-metheus, as also
Deucalion and Pyrrha, with attendant Spirits and Voices.[72] As
for me, all this loveliness of wood, earth, and water makes me
feel as if I could do the whole Universe into poetry; but I
don't want to write anything large for a year or so, and thus I
content myself with throwing off a sort of spray of little songs,
whereof the magazines now have several.

Mrs. Lanier joins me in hoping that Mrs. Taylor has brought
back some new strength out of the Virginia Mountains.

Faithfully yours,

Sidney L.

To ROBERT S. LANIER

Chadd's Ford, Pa.
Aug. 26th 1877.

My dear Father:

Yours with enclosure came, and brought great
relief.

I have been spending a week in New York, where Mr.
Lanier invited me to meet Gen. Dunn for the purpose of consulting about an Appendix which he desired me to prepare for

[72] In his reply of Sept. 6, 1877 (*Letters*, New York, 1899, pp. 201-202),
Taylor wrote that he had just begun work again on his long poem *Deukalion*.

the second Edition of the Sketch of his life which he wrote and had printed some years ago. The Appendix is in the shape of a letter from me to him – J. F. D. L. – giving some general account of the early history of the family.

I worked away at it for several days, and finally brought forth a satisfactory document. I am now superintending the printing of the book, at Lippincott's.[73]

I believe Gen. Dunn has not yet returned to Washington. I have had nothing from him since I left New York. He tells me that some unknown friend of mine has been to see the private secretary of The President – Mr. Rogers – in my behalf, and that Mr. Rogers had requested the Assistant Secretary of State – Mr. [Frederick W.] Seward – to give me a consulate. I have no idea whatever who this friend is. Gen. Dunn thinks that if this fact were stated – just as I have stated it to you – to Senator Lamar, Senator Gordon, Alexander Stephens, Philip Cook, and Henry W. Hilliard (the latter I think lives now at Columbus), and if they should thereupon write such letters recommendatory as they might see proper in relation to my fitness and to the acceptableness of such an appointment to the Georgia people, it would secure me a good place in the State Department.

These letters should be addressed to " the Hon. Wm M. Evarts, Secretary of State ", but *should be sent under cover to* YOU, at Macon. You could then forward them to Gen. Dunn, in an enclosure. He will make the proper application of them. I will send you his address whenever you get ready to transmit the letters.

If you will attend to this promptly, I do not doubt it will be of great service. I think the applications for such letters will come more properly from you than from me. In writing, you might add that my great desire, in getting such a position, is to secure an opportunity to prosecute my literary labors without being under the necessity, as at present, of selling my poems as soon as written. Perhaps Uncle Clifford would not mind writing to Alexander Stephens, and to General Gordon, for such a letter.

Of course I expect to go and take my place in the Treasury

---

[73] See note 54, above.

Dep^t as soon as I am called: but I wish to press the application, all the same, in the State Dep^t., so that I may be on the road to something better.

We are all about as usual, except Charles, who is a little ailing. Harry Day came yesterday and is to spend a week here with us before going to Charley Taliaferro's place in Virginia for a month. I am glad to learn from your letter that the hot weather does not harm you.

May joins me in a great deal of love to you and Mama.

Your loving,

S. L.

To GIBSON PEACOCK [74]

Chadd's Ford, Pa.
Sept. 8th 1877.

My dear Mr. Gibson:

I am called to Washington for the purpose of prosecuting my affairs —which are delayed much beyond expectation –, and am obliged to anticipate my income a little, being out of funds for a week. Please loan me fifty dollars if you can do so without inconvenience to yourself.

You can send your check payable to my order.

—which takes my breath away, and I can't say anything more, now.

Your friend

S. L.

To JOHN B. TABB [75]

Chadd's Ford, Pa.
Sep. 11th 1877.

My dear Friend:

I enclose Dr. Holland's reply to my letter.

In writing him, I mentioned that a false rhyme appeared in the second verse of " The Swallow," and that I would get you

[74] Previously published, *Atlantic Monthly*, LXXIV, 186 (Aug., 1894); reprinted, *Letters* (New York, 1899), p. 45.

[75] Previously published, Gordon Blair, *Father Tabb* (Richmond, Va., 1940), pp. 55-56.

to change it, if he should find the poem otherwise acceptable. The erring words are " borne " (last word in the 5th line) and   " on "   ("   "   "   " 6th "). This is not admissible as a rhyme   You can easily change one word, or the other, or both, so as to get a perfect assonance.

I feel sure you will pardon me for being bold enough to send him also your " Allegory ". You note what he says of that. I do not agree with him that there is any necessity for a change of form: the poem needs nothing except the striking out of the third and fourth verses, and the change of the word " calm ", or its corresponding word " aim," in the last verse. This – " calm " and " aim " – is a bad rhyme.

I return " The Swallows " that you may make the correction indicated. I hope also that the omission of the third and fourth stanzas of " An Allegory " may recommend itself to your judgment. I wish I had time to present you a number of reasons, in addition to those already stated, which seem to me to make this omission desirable. I think you will be soon struck with the general principle that a poem of this sort ought to be as short as possible: for the reason that its *raison d'être* is always revealed in the last verse, and *that* should be delayed by nothing which does not quickly advance the action of the poem. In this respect every lyric is subject to the strictest rules of the drama.

" The Swallow " is so simple and severe and large and transparent, that its excellence is more than likely to escape the great majority of inartistic readers. Do not be surprised, therefore, that Dr. Holland appears to like the " Allegory " better. Dr. H. is one of the very finest *men* in the world, and is a sturdy thinker upon many topics: but he is not a great artist, nor a very keen searcher after delicate excellence in that particular. He is altogether a loveable man and generous soul, though, and I am glad he has accepted " The Swallow ".

I will take some future letter to tell you about my family and the other personal matters concerning which you are kind enough to inquire; only mentioning now that I have a wife who is every day more adorable, and three of the loveliest boys in the world. As for your adoption of the Catholic form of belief: pray fancy me as far as possible removed from any thought of *that* as coincident with death, or in any way like it.

I long ago outgrew the possibility of such narrowness. An earnest Belief is always beautiful to me: the circumstance that it does not happen to be my own never makes it less so.

Sincerely yours,

Sidney Lanier

To Robert S. Lanier

Chadd's Ford, Pa.
Sep. 11th 1877.

My dear Father:

I have your letter of 5th, and am rejoiced to see how stoutly you keep up under your manifold labors.

The Repudiation clause in the Georgia Constitution gave me great distress.[76] It is atrocious that a great State should display such eagerness to shirk obligation. The whole matter might have been made such an honor to us – instead of the disgrace it will now forever be – by the simple and manifestly just expedient of leaving the matter to some fair tribunal. I had thought of presenting some quiet and sober arguments on the question through one or other of the Georgia newspapers; but, from all accounts the new Constitution will be ratified by an overwhelming majority, and it does not seem worth while to waste time in fighting it. I feel very much like writing an ode to the sixteen members of the Convention who voted against the clause: and yet – I have not seen their names – and they may have had expectations from Judge Lochrane!

So runs this wicked world away.

Various causes have conspired to prevent me from trying the Mullein remedy. In a very short time I hope to be more settled and I will then give it a fair test.

Tomorrow I propose to go to Washington, and make a desperate attempt either to hurry up the Treasury business, or to get a position elsewhere which will yield immediate income.

General Dunn wishes me to come to his house, and I will do

---

[76] The reference is presumably to the repudiation of the State Bonds issued by R. B. Bullock, Reconstruction Governor of Georgia, for which he had been tried on a charge of embezzlement (see note 72, 1871).

so, for a few days, until I can settle myself. I intend to remain there until I get something satisfactory. Meantime: next Thursday (19th) I have to provide thirty-five dollars, for a payment here, ($35.), and it seems as if there was no way save to ask you to send it to me. My address will be:

>" Care of Gen. Wm M. Dunn,
>>*War Department,*
>>>Washington,
>>>>D. C."

As soon as you shall have received any of the letters about which I wrote, please send them to same address.

My health, – about which you ask – does not show much change. I am not so strong as I was in Macon: but I do not think I have lost much flesh. This is saying a good deal, too: for the summer has been a very anxious and painful one to me, and I have used up a good deal of strength in the maintenance of outward composure and inward patience. I find it very clearly demonstrated that anxiety and uncertainty are my worst foes. Even during those periods of the summer when I have been able to see two weeks ahead, I have visibly gained ground. The prescriptions which will cure me like magic are (as I told May the other day) those which are signed by Dr W. W. Wrigley, Cashier.

The Lanier book will be out next Thursday. I am to have fifty copies, and I am prepared to send you as many as you may like.

Mary sends you all a great deal of love: wherein joins

>>>Your

>>>>S. L.

To Mary Day Lanier

>>>Washington. Sept. 20th 1877.

A letter should have gone to thee, dearest Soul, some hours earlier, but I was detained in town. Thine with the enclosures has just reached me— three P.M.

I do amazingly well. When going from thee to Pha yesterday morning, the pain in my neck was so great that I feared I would have to give it up after all: but the Dr.'s *Dulcamara*—" Take every four hours one powder"—seemed to produce a sensible effect within two hours, and the pain was greatly lessened last night, insomuch that I had a good night's sleep. The old pain—the pleurodynia—is quite gone; and, strange to say, I feel better than in months before, as to general condition. Yesterday I had some real long full breaths, and I could never tell thee how much relief each one gave me. Today I am a little headache-y, from fatigue: but otherwise am far better than could be expected. I'm now a little tired, too, with writing, having accomplished a letter to Harry, one to Mrs. Bird, and one to Lippincott.

I am now going to see Clare [de Graffenried], from whom I found a note awaiting me.

There is no news of business. —And yet there is, too: namely, that I love thee infinitely, which is the only business worth that name in the world, to thy

husband.

To Mary Day Lanier

Washington. Sep. 25th 1877.

My too-dear Heart: Herein find P. O. order for thirty-five dollars. Pay Agnes her wages (thine announcing her intention to leave is just received) and hand such balance as thou canst spare to Mrs. Brinton, to be credited on board account. Please say also to the latter that the balance due her up to date will be sent by next Monday, along with such amount as shall be due at that time.

Harry spent two hours here last Saturday night while passing through: but I was in Baltimore. I am sorry to have missed him.

I had a pleasant talk with Mr. Gilman, and he is going to try to arrange some sort of place for me there, though the professorship is now out of the question until Spring.

It does not now seem probable that anything whatever can be done here. There appear to be no vacancies.

Thou wilt pardon a letter written hurriedly at the Post Office on a torn sheet.

I cannot say more now. Here is a sweet letter from Clifford which I will forward. I rejoice that thou hast Mrs. Fleming to lighten thy labors.

My heart is so full that I can neither say anything to thee nor leave off trying.

It is my Refuge from all trouble to remember that I am thy

husband .

P. S, If there is not time to send the money-order to West Chester before Agnes leaves, just endorse it to Mr. Brinton, and get him to give thee the twelve dollars for her. You will see the place on the back of the order for you to endorse.

To Daniel C. Gilman [77]

Washington, D. C.
Sep. 26th 1877.

Dear Mr. Gilman:

From a published report of your very interesting Address I learn that there is now a vacant Fellowship. Would I be able to discharge the duties of such a position?

My course of study would be: first, constant research in the physics of musical tone; second, several years' devotion to the acquirement of a thoroughly scientific *general* view of Mineralogy, Botany and Comparative Anatomy; third, French and German Literature. I fear this may seem a nondescript and even flighty process; but it makes straight towards the final result of all my present thought, and I am tempted, by your great kindness, to believe that you would have confidence enough in me to await whatever development should come of it.

My address is " Care of Gen. Wm M. Dunn, War Department, Washington, D. C."

Sincerely yours,

Sidney Lanier.

[77] Previously published, *South Atlantic Quarterly*, IV, 117 (Apr., 1905); reprinted, Mims, p. 232. This letter was apparently intended as a formal application for a Johns Hopkins fellowship, made at the suggestion of Gilman, with whom Lanier had recently conferred in person.

To Gibson Peacock [78]

Washington, D. C.
Sep. 27th 1877.

Dear Mr. Peacock:

Yours was forwarded to me here.

Just as I received your check, a severe pleuritic attack seized me and kept me in great pain for ten days. I then got up from bed to come here, in the desperate necessity to do what could be done. Last Monday at daylight an exhausting hæmorrhage came, which has kept me confined to my room ever since. In this enforced inactivity, I have had nothing to return to you. This morning a check comes from Lippincott for a little story I sent,[79] and I enclose it, endorsed to your order. Please let me know what your address will be, so that I may send the remaining twenty-five at the earliest possible moment.

There does not appear the least hope of success here. Three months ago the order was given by Secretary Sherman that I should have the first vacancy; but the appointment-clerk, who received the order, is a singular person, and I am told there are rings within rings in the Department to such an extent that vacancies are filled by petty chiefs of division without even being reported at all to the proper officers. You will scarcely believe that, in my overwhelming desire to get some routine labor by which I might be relieved from this exhausting magazine-work so as to apply my whole mind to my long poem on which I have been engaged, I have allowed a friend to make application to every department in Washington for even the humblest position—seventy-five dollars a month and the like—but without success. I also made personal application to several people in Baltimore for similar employment, but fruitlessly. Altogether it seems as if there wasn't any place for me in this world, and if it were not for May I should certainly quit it, in mortification at being so useless.[80]

[78] Previously published, *Atlantic Monthly*, LXXIV, 186-187 (Aug., 1894); reprinted, *Letters* (New York, 1899), pp. 45-46.

[79] " The Story of a Proverb," for which *Lippincott's* paid $25.00 (see note 63, above).

[80] Though it appears but little in surviving letters, Lanier's spirits seem to have reached a low ebb during the summer of 1877. This is echoed in Paul

I hope you will have a pleasant holiday. Give my love to my dear Maria Peacock and say how glad I am to think of her long relief from the household and other cares which give her so much trouble.

Your friend,

S. L.

To Mary Day Lanier

Washington. Sep. 27th 1877.

Thy letter, dear Heart, with Hal's and thy Father's voluminous communications, is here this morning. I had hoped to hear that thou hadst made some arrangement, at least temporarily, for a nurse, and fear from thy " positively" that some insurmountable difficulty has presented itself. My poor sweet Soul, what a labor thou wilt have!

And I cannot send thee now anything very encouraging to help thee along: but I doubt not all will be right finally. As for me, I have been poorly for several days. Last Monday, while in Baltimore, came a hæmorrhage—one of my old friends—and gave me much trouble by disabling me from carrying out some of the plans for which I had gone there. I managed however to see Mr. Gilman and two others. Today the bloody discharge is almost gone, the expectoration being entirely of the " brick-dust" character. I am weak, as usual, but there is every indication that I will be as well as ever by Saturday. I remember that the attack I had in Brooklyn two years ago—which was precisely similar to this—left me feeling better and freer in the lungs than for a long time before: and I think my unusually good sensations of which I wrote thee were the effects of the relief, and that, though temporarily interrupted by the process of lesion and healing, they will return afterwards.

Hayne's reply, July 19, 1877, to a lost letter apparently written by Lanier before leaving Macon in June: " The *whole tone* of your communication shows the natural, the *inevitable* despondency which comes of a diseased physical condition . . .; & *poverty* (accursed poverty!!) being added, as you remark, to physical weakness, *must* produce a general condition of things the reverse of agreeable. . . . Touching *literary* success, it is evident that you take too low a view of your own position, & prospects."

— These details, under stout protest! but I know thou wishest them and I remember my promise.

An opportune check from Lippincott's this morning enabled me to remit half the amount due Mr. P.

I am admirably tended by Mrs. Dunn, and lack for nought.

Hast thou seen a bird with a wounded mate, hovering, caressing, and powerless? It is so that about thee hovers all the thought of thy

husband.

To Mary Day Lanier

Washington, Sept. 28th 1877.

I send thee, dear Wife, a little bulletin to say that I continue to improve in all respects, and that I expect to be in full fighting trim again by Monday. I am quite free today from fever and from a distressing headache which troubled me for three days; and there is less sign of bloody effusion in the expectoration. I went down to the General's Office yesterday, and again this morning, without damage. I have relied much upon milk, lemons, and fruit, to subdue the fever, and they appear to have justified my confidence.

My thought was all day with thee yesterday, engaged in all manner of tender and hopeless speculations and sympathies excited by thy loss of Agnes.

I do charge thee, dearest Einzige, that thou let the little ones go free of much care; any damage done to them can be repaired, they are young: but thou art my Only one, bodily harm *must* not come to thee, all the love thou hast for me must cry continually that the best way thou canst love me is to save thyself for me in all possible manners .

I do pray thee therefore to try with all thy might to keep a tranquil mind, and a gentle spirit, in the midst of all those childish happenings of every day which seem so large at the moment but which will seem so small from the distance of a few happy weeks. As for thy physical labor, I beg thee to spare no pains in finding some one who can at least take the washing and dressing of the children morning and afternoon.

Perhaps from the little settlement clustered about the house where the laundress lives thou might'st obtain some one who would come, mornings and afternoons, to do this work.

It is *so* hard to stop talking to thee ! But I have had business to write upon this morning, and my sword-arm is tired. There is no stronger proof of some prodigious and radical lack of adjustment betwixt the spiritual and physical *me*, than the circumstance that, while my soul seems incapable of fatigue in communicating with thee, my arm so quickly is worn out in the same sweet business ! – But, perhaps, for this very reason, God will soon give thee to the eyes — which do *not* tire of continually sending thee reports of love — of thy

husband .

To Mary Day Lanier

Washington, Sep. 30th 1877.

How devoutly I hope that thou art as well in body and soul as is thy lover, on this pious morn!

That which cometh out of the mouth thereof is no longer incarnadined: and the lungs thereof do play in and out with freedom: as for wheezing and rattling, they are banished into the uttermost parts of the earth, they are gone to dwell in the Lake of Eternal Flame where their Worm dieth not and their Fire is not quenched,— though I wish they might die and be quenched, sincerely.

I am so full of poems in these days that it is a chief torment not to be able to write. I am determined *not* to commence anything until I find some repose in the routine-work that brings bread. Tomorrow I will be well enough to recommence this task: it seems scarcely possible I should finally fail.

I wrote Clifford, yesterday, urging him to come on here at once. I had happened to hear of a chance to lease a small hotel, very charmingly situated near this house: and, upon making more minute inquiries, was struck with the suitableness of the place to his requirements. I hope sincerely he will come.[81]

[81] Lanier's letter to his brother Clifford, Sept. 29, 1877 (here omitted), gives the details of this proposition. (See also his letters to Clifford and Mary Day Lanier of Oct. 8, 1877, below.)

The Express package ought to have been acknowledged earlier: it came duly. Thine with memorandum of the Brinton account is arrived. I hope thou hadst some comfort yesterday in Sarah [Farley]'s devotion, at West Chester.

— But I have only intended this as a bulletin of health: I wish to save all possible strength for this next week's work: for, with the favor of God, it shall bring to thee thy true worshipper and

lover.

To Mary Day Lanier

Washington, D. C.
Oct. 4th 1877.

Dearest Soul, I am just leaving for Baltimore, and there is but time to say that thou must address me there "No. 40 Mt. Vernon Place," and that I am excellent well, and that thou art the one Desire of thy

husband.

To Daniel C. Gilman

Mt. Vernon Hotel
Friday morning
[Oct. 5, 1877?] [82]

My dear Sir:

I fear this note will make you cry out: *Nulla dies sine Lanier*; but in the very face of this ghastly Latin pun, I send a line to say that I am at this hotel until tomorrow, and to ask if you had a letter from me about the Fellowship.

Very truly yours,

Sidney Lanier.

[82] Conjectural dating from its sequence with the preceding letter, Oct. 5 being the first Friday thereafter.

To Mary Day Lanier

Baltimore, Oct. 8th 1877

Dearest Angel, Here is a P. O. order for thirty-five dollars, which will pay part of the demands mentioned in thy last: and by Thursday I hope to send thee the whole of the sum thou wanted'st for thy private needs, *i. e.*, ten dollars more: $25 + $10 + $10.

Clifford came to Washington and I spent Saturday and Sunday with him there. He returned to Montgomery last night. We concluded that the hotel project in Washington would not do. He was heavenly sweet to me, and we both lamented thine absence.

It now looks more likely that we will be *here* this winter: but I hope to write thee more definitely about it in a couple of days. It is not probable that my permanent matters in Washington will reach any final shape until after the assembling of Congress.

My Child, – when ?

I long for my boys unspeakably. Write me at 40 Mt. Vernon Place.

The good God of Heaven make a quiet world of love and set thee in it, prays thy

lover.

To Clifford A. Lanier

Baltimore, Md.
Oct. 8th 1877.

You dear Angel, Ever since you vanished from my longing eyes, as I stood at the car-door, I have felt as much the men of old when the Messenger of God drew up his shining raiment and dissolved away into the sky. That you bring, out of all the petty cares which surround you, a soul so sweet and sound and lofty, – this is a marvel and a delight to me; and I take a fresh draught of energy, of grace, and of satisfaction from it. It makes me think of that cool spring which is on the top of Chilhowee Mountain, and which, when one has toiled up the terrible hill, offers him new strength just at the fainting-point.

I have had a long and hard day, just like the afternoon on which we intruded into so many Washington domiciles. My work has finally been rewarded with just the place which suits me. It involves further help from you, but it so completely disposes of *me* that I have engaged the apartments. I found that by furnishing them I could secure many and material advantages. I get three rooms, and a sort of cuddy thrown in, for thirty-five dollars a month, *i. e.*, by the *real* month and not the factitious four-weeks-month of the ordinary boarding-house keepers: payable monthly. The building is a large white marble one, which contains a great many such *suites* of rooms, and is organized as a hotel, with all its freedom. In the basement is an excellent restaurant which is to send us our meals without extra charge. I enclose a bill of fare from which you can see how cheaply we can live. The great and inestimable advantage of this arrangement to me is: that its only *fixed* expense is the thirty-five a month, and I can then order from this bill of fare such food, and no other, as I am each day able to pay for in cash. I will thus have no leaden fears as to the board-bill weighing me down month after month, and will be able to live in such frugal manner as suits my purse.

I have gone over the furnishing-estimate with the landlady, and I find that I can put the rooms in good living order, carpets and all, for one hundred and fifty dollars. Now, instead of the thirty dollars a month which you were to send to me, I will ask you to advance this hundred and fifty to me, immediately. This will give me a local habitation, and a sense of home to which I have long been an utter stranger: and will make me very tranquil and contented. I can keep the rooms certainly for three years.

As soon as you receive this, send me a night-telegram, addressed

" Care of Mrs. S. B. Bird,
40 Mt. Vernon Place,
Baltimore,
Md. "

If the telegram says "yes", I will draw a sight draft on you
for $150, and get it cashed through a friend of mine who is a
banker here. I will then immediately furnish my rooms, and
get May here by the time our next week's board is out at
Chadd's Ford: for every day made in this way is money saved:
and moreover I do long to enter into these cosy rooms and
fall-to upon the poems that are now devouring *me*.[83]

Kiss Will for me, and God bless you, dear

Your

S. L.

To Bayard Taylor [84]

Baltimore, Md.

Oct. 8th 1877.

My dear Mr. Taylor:

I have been in the unsettled state of a
bear who goes poking about the logs and coverts in search of
a place to hibernate; and this nomadic condition has kept me
from answering your letter. I had thought of being in Washington during the winter. There was some prospect that
either a small consulate or some minor place in one of the
Departments would be given me. But, from what I can gather,
places of this sort are rarely obtained except by *personal* application and persistence. Of course I cannot come down to that,
and so have let the matter go. If anything should be offered
I will cheerfully take it, but I will do no urging or solicitation
of any sort.

I have engaged quarters here for the winter, and will bring
my family over, in about a week, from Chadd's Ford.

The editors of THE GALAXY write me that a poem of mine,
called "A Dream of the Age: To Richard Wagner," will appear in the November number.[85] As it is about time for that

---

[83] Lanier was now planning to take up his residence in Baltimore again after
an absence of eighteen months. His new quarters at the corner of Charles and
Lexington Sts. (see his letter of Oct. 19, below) were several blocks further
down town than his former lodgings in Centre St.

[84] Previously published, *Atlantic Monthly*, LXXXIV, 137 (July, 1899),
misdated Oct 6; reprinted, *Letters* (New York, 1899), pp. 204-205.

[85] Later included as No. VI of "Street Cries," in a modified version and with
a shortened title: "To Richard Wagner" (I, 102).

to be in print, – and as they are sometimes slow in remitting when I write, – will you take the trouble to call at Sheldons', (I think it is 8 Murray St.) and get the check and send it me? The poem is about seventy five or eighty lines, if I am not mistaken. I wouldn't bother you with this, but I really need the money. My address is "Care of Mrs. S. B. Bird, 40 Mt. Vernon Place, Baltimore, Md."

My "Bee" is in the Oct. Lippincott's.

Tell me what you are doing with Deucalion. Have you seen a poem by Swinburne of which the refrain is: "*Villon*, our sad mad bad glad brother's name"? Sad mad bad glad is not intended for a joke. It's a wild panegyric of Villon.[86]

Will you squelch the Atlantic Contributor who is unhappy about Goethe?

With cordial messages to Mrs. Taylor,

Your friend,

Sidney L.

To Robert S. Lanier

Baltimore, Md.
Oct. 14th 1877.

My dearest Father, Your letter is written with so much evident pain that I hasten to beg you not to take matters so much to heart on my account. Of course I need the money extremely — I never write you for it until the last resource is exhausted elsewhere: but if it cannot be had, it cannot, – and I do not wish you to worry over the inevitable. I do not doubt we will get through the squeeze somehow. I at least rejoice to know that your office-relations have all been readjusted and that matters promise to work more suitably in *that* quarter.

[86] The reference is to Swinburne's "A Ballad of François Villon."

In his reply, Oct. 13, 1877 (*Letters*, New York, 1899, pp. 202-204), Taylor reported that he attended to Lanier's mission about the Galaxy check and that he had at last finished his *Deukalion*. Then he added: "'Scribner's' are going to publish your poem on the Chestnut-trees, and have it illustrated by me! When I was last at Cedarcroft, I made the necessary sketch of the trees for them." ("Under the Cedarcroft Chestnut" appeared in the Jan., 1878, issue of *Scribner's*; the wood-cut, made from Taylor's drawing, was by Thomas Moran.)

I have secured some very cheap lodgings in this city, to which I am going to bring Mary as soon as I am [in] funds to do so.[87] It will be much easier for us to get along here than at the place where she now is. I had found it absolutely necessary to my peace of mind to settle finally upon some definite abiding-place for the winter: and as my chances of employment seem better here than in Washington, and as the lodgings – which I found by accident – seemed very cheap and possessed several other advantages for our way of life, I determined to take them. If I should be employed in Washington, I can run over here twice a week and thus be with my family at least as much as that until other arrangements could be made. I have been engaged for a week in getting these lodgings ready for occupation, and am quite tired out today.

And so I write no more, now. Keep up heart, my dear Father. I am quite full of hope and over-full of poetry. Perhaps this latter plethora will transfer itself to my now-empty purse, as soon as I can get into any such settled state of habitation with my family as will make me feel authorized to allow myself to write. I feel sure your industry and ability, under your new office-*régime*, will soon clear you from difficulties.

I would have sent you the Lanier books,[88] but have not yet received them. Having no place to put them, I asked Lippincott to keep my share in the store until further orders. I hope to get them here in a week.

A poem of mine called "the Bee" came out in the October LIPPINCOTT'S. I believe one of mine called "A Dream of the Age: To Richard Wagner", is to appear in the November GALAXY.

Love to Mama, and God bless you both.

Your son,

S. L.

---

[87] In a letter of Oct. 13, 1877, to his wife (here omitted) Lanier wrote: "I have been in a perfect maze of '*this* or *that*' all the week, with fitting up our rooms. . . . I am amazed beyond measure at the number of 'things' required to carry on the humblest existence." He added that he was moving into their new quarters immediately and wanted her and the boys to make the remove to Baltimore on Oct. 17; but it was a week later before they came.

[88] See note 54, above.

To John B. Tabb [89]

55 Lexington St.
Baltimore, Md.
Oct. 19th 1877.

My dear Friend:

Your last letter was forwarded to me from Chadd's Ford. I am in real sorrow about the *other* letter of which this informs me, and which has never reached me: for I fear it contained poems, or something of that nature, which you may possibly find it difficult to replace. Let me know how this is.

I rejoice to find that we will be so near together. My fate will fix me either in Baltimore or Washington for the ensuing winter, and, I hope, longer. It is now my expectation to bring my family here next Wednesday. I have found some rooms fronting on Charles St. (though the entrance is on Lexington, No. 55) in the large white marble building at the corner of Charles and Lexington. These I am trying to fit up in a sort of Arabian manner, *i. e.* in a manner which will admit easily of any move that may be necessitated by my health or business; and we are to have our meals sent·up from a restaurant below.

Here, then, if you should come to Baltimore at any time, you will find us: and I need not say how warm will be your welcome. Indeed, I would make my way out to you immediately; but for the next three or four days I will be very much absorbed in some perplexing matters which require my constant presence here. As soon as I can get my heart at rest about these, I shall certainly find you, in some way, if you don't previously find *me.* It would give me a real uplifting of the Spirit to grasp your hand again.

Perhaps you will care to see a poem of mine in the November GALAXY, headed " A Dream of the Age: To Richard Wagner." By the way, have you seen a volume of my poems, published last December by Lippincott?

[89] Previously published, Gordon Blair, *Father Tabb* (Richmond, Va., 1940), pp. 56-57. Tabb was now living at Ellicott City, near Baltimore (see note 70, above).

What have you done with the Scribner poem? Have you become a good pianist? And do you know the wonder and the glory of Beethoven from actually feeling his soul beating in the ends of your fingers, — for only those *do* know him who have played him ?

Answer me these interrogatories faithfully, my dear John, and hold me always

Your friend

S. L.

To Robert S. Lanier

Address:

55 Lexington St.
Baltimore, Md.

Oct. 21st 1877.

My dear Father:

        I write a line to ask that you will ship to me immediately, as freight (that is, *not* by Express) the yellow trunk which I left at your house last Spring. It has "Lanier" painted on it, and is the only one so marked. I think it remained in the passage up stairs. I will ask you to have it corded with a good rope, before sending. Please forward me the Bill of Lading when you ship.

This trunk has all my winter underclothing, and Mary's, in it, and the cold weather puts us in instant need of it.

I have found some quarters here in which we can live very economically, and have engaged them for the winter. My address in future is

55 Lexington St.
Baltimore, Md.

I am now occupying one of the rooms. I hope to get Mary and the children here on Wednesday next: but this depends on my success in getting some money meanwhile.

I was in Washington a few days ago, and did all that I was able to do in the way of forwarding my matters there. I saw Gen. Morgan, Senator from Alabama. He was extraordinarily kind, and volunteered to take charge of my affairs. I also had short interviews with Senator Lamar and Mr. Stephens. I failed to see the Representatives I wanted to meet: but wrote to them, the day after. These were Ligon, of Alabama, and Blount, of Georgia.[90]

I do not believe that anything will come of it, however. I find that every man of political prominence appears to have attained it by the help of others : and to these " others " he is bound hand and foot, in every matter connected with the distribution of office. As I have not helped any one to such prominence, I cannot expect to have consideration, under this system of *quid pro quo*. I am putting on foot many agencies to procure employment, here, – which I should infinitely prefer to anything in Washington. The Librarian of the Peabody Library is in need of an assistant, and would be glad to have me, as he has informed me: but just at present a decline in the Tennessee Bonds which constitute the Peabody Fund renders it impossible for the Trustees to appropriate any more money for that purpose. This is the place of all places in the world that I would rather have: and the probability is that a way, – of which I have not now time to write you – might be found to get it for me, in a very short time. I wish to go to the Library every day, and offer my services for a couple of hours, so as to familiarize myself with the routine of the business – which is a good deal more complicated than is generally supposed –, and thus to place myself in the direct road to the position I want. Of course, if anything offers at Washington, I will accept it, meanwhile: having my family, here, and visiting them occasionally. My friends are making inquiries among the lawyers, here, to see if a secretary's place can be found for me: and President Gilman is still trying to arrange some sort of place for me at the University. You will thus see that there is reason to hope I may find something to dispose of me permanently.

As for the Fernandina collectorship: there are two insuperable difficulties. One is that such places are given –and rightly

---

[90] Those here mentioned were J. T. Morgan (1824-1907), L. Q. C. Lamar (1825-1894), A. H. Stephens (1812-1883), Robert Fulwood Ligon (1823-1901), and James H. Blount (1837-1903).

– only to citizens of the places in which the vacancies occur: another is that it is simply impossible for me to make any further application for office than that now set on foot. My name has already been presented by my friends to the Treasury and State Departments, and I have in person asked Gen. Morgan to find me a clerkship of a Committee, besides requesting Ligon and Blount to co-operate with him in that endeavor. After being in Washington, and seeing the course of office-hunting there, I have deliberately determined that I will not engage in it, and I deeply regret even the requests that have been already made in my behalf. Nothing is more certain in my own mind than that *you* would feel exactly the same way after ten minutes in the Lobby among the poor ill-smelling mortals who are every day making it more and more a place where only rascality can find profit and where every honest man must sicken with shame and disgust.

You need not fear, as your letter indicates, that I will break down in health under any steady employment here. If I have managed to stand up at all under the unspeakable trials and labors of the last three or four months – which I have not spoken of to any one –, there is no doubt but I can go through with any work that may be given me.   I am perfectly clear in my own mind that a steady income of a hundred dollars a month, from any sort of labor of which I am capable, would make me a well man, comparatively.

I have been very busy in trying to get our quarters habitable by Wednesday.

When you have any money I should be glad to receive some. There is desperate need.

Love to Mama and Pringle.

Your son,

S. L.

To Robert S. Lanier

55 Lexington St.
Baltimore, Md.
Oct. 26th 1877.

My dear Father:

Yesterday morning Mr. Day popped in upon me: — a few moments afterward your letter with its most welcome enclosure arrived: and at eight o'clock last night May and the boys (from whom I have been separated for six weeks) joined me.[91] Such a happy reunion as we had! The fact is that the family had been bound in the Chadd's Ford harbor for some time by stress of financial weather: and this made our happiness all the more intense, as we sat in our cosy new quarters and gave ourselves up to the recital of our respective adventures.

I have not yet told you that about three weeks ago, after a very deliberate review of my experiences during the last four or five years, I came to the conclusion that the thing absolutely needful to my health – in truth, to my life – was to have some spot in which I might collect all my little belongings, and which might be in some sense, *mine*, as a home and permanent abiding-place, no matter how humble. I could not longer endure the idea of entering great cities, three or four times a year, with the dead load upon me of trying to find among the interminable boarding-houses some place which would be at least endurable to the many wants which people of our sort come to have. I therefore sat down and wrote Clifford, and got from him a hundred and fifty dollars: by the sale of some jewelry and a poem or two I raised a hundred more, and this I invested to the last cent in a lot of simple furniture and belongings, which I then placed in the rooms described to you in my last. Here, we are absolutely free to practice the economies which suit us; we have no servant: we have our meals in our own room, served from the restaurant. We are to have our gas-stove in a short time (when money is a little more

---

[91] In a letter to his wife, Oct. 23, 1877 (here omitted), Lanier gave his wife instructions for her trip to Baltimore and inclosed $70.00 with the following comment: " After incredible toil, suffering, patience, and a thousand stings and bitternesses and disappointments, I have managed to get a little money– an absurdly small sum– without parting irretreivably with any of thy dainty jewels."

plentiful), and we shall then get our own breakfast and supper in our own way, and have but one meal (dinner) from the restaurant each day. Although this is troublesome yet it is overwhelmingly preferable to any mode of life possible to us: for it gives us absolute freedom and absolute privacy, and he who has lived in boarding-houses will inevitably have learned to regard these as the two chief blessings of family life.

As for me, a sense of repose and of security have come with this arrangement which I have not known in a long time. If I can manage to maintain myself here, I shall be very happy, and it will go hard but I do some good work. I am in the near neighborhood of all the places I love: the Johns Hopkins University, the Peabody Library,[92] the Academy of Music, and a good gallery of paintings, – are but a short distance from me. Mary shares with me all these sentiments, and I do not know when I have seen her look as happy as she does this morning. I had made all my preparations without letting her know much of what was going on. For three weeks I have been scampering over Baltimore, diving into all the old odd shops and junkeries, and chaffering with Tom, Dick and Harry for carpets, chairs, stoves, tables, bedsteads, rugs, sheets, pillow-cases, and the thousand things that turn up unexpectedly as needs when one commences housekeeping. I finally got everything in habitable condition: my last pillow-case arrived only a couple of hours before May came last night: and although we are by no means complete, yet we can shift and contrive till the price of poetry rises.

It was in an emergency connected with this arrangement that I telegraphed you. If I find that I cannot get on without the other fifteen dollars until I sell a poem, I may draw for it to-morrow: likely I will, as I think I can't stave off the need longer than that.

There is no news from Washington. We have invitations to Katie Lanier's wedding. I will send you the Lanier book in a day or two, having now a place to put them.

Love to Mama, and God bless you,

Your son,

S. L.

[92] The Peabody Institute (facing illustration) is several blocks north of Lexington St. The present library building was not completed until the following year. (For The Johns Hopkins University, see X, 129.)

THE PEABODY INSTITUTE, BALTIMORE, 1874

Courtesy of the Peabody Institute Library

To Gibson Peacock [93]

55 Lexington St.
Baltimore, Md.
Nov. 3rd 1877.

My dear Mr. Gibson:

I have not had the courage to write you without enclosing the check for twenty five dollars which ought to have gone to you long ago. I still haven't a cent to send; and am writing only to answer your inquiries whose kindliness might otherwise go unacknowledged.

All sorts of things were promised to the friends who were good enough to intercede at Washington in my behalf: but nothing has come of it. In truth I should long ago have abandoned all ideas in that direction and resumed the thread of my magazine work, had it not been for illness which prevented me from writing much and thus kept me entertaining some little expectation. The hæmorrhage, however, which disabled me from work temporarily, has greatly relieved my lung, and I am now stronger than at any time in the last fifteen months. My whole soul is bursting with chaotic poems, and I hope to do some good work during the coming year.

I have found it quite essential to my happiness and health to have some quarters, however rude, which I could regard as permanent for the next four or five years,– instead of drifting about the world. We have therefore established ourselves in four rooms, arranged somewhat as a French Flat, in the heart of Baltimore. We have a gas-stove, on which my comrade magically produces the best coffee in the world, and this, with fresh eggs (boiled over the same handy little machine) bread, butter and milk, forms our breakfast. Our dinner is sent to us from a restaurant in the same building with our rooms, and is served in our own apartment without extra charge.

As for my plans for the future: I have set on foot another attempt to get a place in the Johns Hopkins University—: I also have a prospect of employment as an assistant in the Peabody Library here: and there is still a possibility of a com-

---

[93] Previously published, *Atlantic Monthly*, LXXIV, 187 (Aug., 1894); reprinted, *Letters* (New York, 1899), pp. 46-48.

mittee-clerkship in Washington. Meantime, however, I am just resuming work for the editors: my nearest commission is to write a Christmas poem for "*Every Saturday*",[94] an ambitious new weekly paper just started in Baltimore. The editor wishes to illustrate the poem liberally and use it as an advertisement by making some fuss over it. There! You have a tolerable abstract of my past, present and future.

Now, go thou and do likewise. Tell me what you and my dear Maria Peacock have been doing all this month, which has slipped by so like a dream. My wife — who is, by the way (this is a piece of news), simply the cream of all the angels— sends cordial greetings to you both, and so would the boys if they were not all asleep in their several beds.

Have you seen my Wagner poem in the November *Galaxy*? I have *not*: and as it was much involved, and as I didn't see any proof-sheet, and as finally the Galaxy's proof-reader is notoriously bad,– I suspect it is a pretty muddle of nonsense.

And so, God bless you both. Your friend,

Sidney L.

To Richard M. Johnston [95]

55 Lexington Street,
Baltimore, Md.,
November 6, 1877.

My Dear Col. Johnston,

Mrs. Lanier's illness on Saturday devolved a great many domestic duties upon me, and rendered it quite impossible for me to make the preparations necessary for

---

[94] "The Hard Times in Elfland" (I, 105), published in the Christmas Supplement of *Every Saturday*, Baltimore, Dec. 22, 1877. (No file discovered. Photostat in the Lanier Room, Johns Hopkins University, from a copy of this issue owned by Miss Carrie Speer, Americus, Ga.—see attached clipping from the Macon *Dainly Telegraph*, Dec. 25, 1933.)

The setting of this poem seems to be a faithful picture of the Lanier family gathered round the fireside of their Baltimore flat. (It is referred to in subsequent letters by Lanier: to Bayard Taylor, Jan. 6, 1878; to Charles Scribner, May 22, 1879.)

[95] Previously published, Mims, pp. 295-297, from which the present text is taken (MS not found). This is the earliest letter from Lanier to Johnston that has survived, though they had been friends since the winter of 1874.

my visit to you on Sunday. This caused me a great deal of regret; a malign fate seems to have pursued all my recent efforts in your direction.

I have attentively examined your "Dukesborough Tale." [96] I wish very much that I could read it over aloud in your presence, so that I might call your attention to many verbal lapses which I find and which, I am sure, will hinder its way with the magazine editors. I will try to see you in a day or two, and do this. Again, ascending from merely verbal criticism to considerations of general treatment, I find that the action of the story does not move quite fast enough during the *first* twenty-five pages, and the *last* ten, to suit the impatience of the modern magazine man.

Aside from these two points, – and they can both be easily remedied, – the story strikes me as exquisitely funny, and your reproduction of the modes of thought and of speech among the rural Georgians is really wonderful. The peculiar turns and odd angles, described by the minds of these people in the course of ratiocination (Good Heavens, what would Sammy Wiggins think of such a sentence as this!), are presented here with a delicacy of art that gives me a great deal of enjoyment. The whole picture of old-time Georgia is admirable, and I find myself regretting that its *full* merit can be appreciated only by that limited number who, from personal experience, can compare it with the original.

Purely with a view to conciliating the editor of the magazine, I strongly advise you to hasten the movement of the beginning and of the catastrophe: that is, from about p. 1 to p. 34, and from p. 57 to p. 67. The middle, i.e., from p. 34 to p. 57, should not be touched: it is good enough for me.

I would not dare to make these suggestions if I thought that you would regard them otherwise than as pure evidences of my interest in the success of the story.

Your friend,

Sidney L.

[96] "Mr. Neelus Peeler's Conditions," later collected in the third edition of Johnston's *Dukesborough Tales* (New York, 1883). Lanier is said to have negotiated its acceptance by R. W. Gilder, editor of *Scribner's* (where it was first published), and to have forwarded to Johnston the pay check—the first he had ever received for a story (see F. T. Long, "The Life of Richard Malcolm Johnston in Maryland, 1867-1898," *Maryland Historical Magazine*, XXXIV, 315-316, Dec., 1939).

To Mary Day Lanier

Pha. Nov. 8th 1877

Dear Heart, I pledged the flute and the silver for twenty five dollars, and herein enclosed is a P. O. order for that amount. I dislike making thee go so far as to the Post Office to collect this, but cannot now help myself. I send this in much haste, my negotiations here having kept me much beyond the time I expected. I slept at the Colonnade Hotel, Pha. last night. I go on directly to New York. Have seen Mrs. but not Mr. Peacock. They go to N. Y. tomorrow.

The enclosed sum is not as much as I expected to send thee. When the collector for the furniture instalments comes, just send him word that I am in New York and expect to be back certainly by Sunday. He will let it go over; they know me and are accommodating. Also, order thy breakfasts and suppers from the restaurant. In this way thou mayst possibly manage. If thou shouldst still be overpressed, go to Mrs. Bird, and tell her of my absence and expected-return, and get such overplus as thou shouldst need.

And God in Heaven have care of thee and my sweet young men, prays thy lover.

I pray thee do not on any account allow the old hard-faced lady to draw thee into any discussion at all. Pay what she demands, and leave the balance to me when I return.

To Mary Day Lanier

Westminster Hotel.
N. Y. Nov. 9th 1877

Dear Soul, I scrawl the hastiest of lines to say that there is no chance for me to return before Monday. I cannot see *anybody* until tomorrow afternoon. You had better forward my letters to the Westminster, as I may be absent longer even than Monday. I expect to see thy father tomorrow morning. He is in town, but I missed him today at the Astor House.

I think of thee with such solicitude as I cannot describe: it

seems as if thou wert so lonesome and unprotected in the great
house, there, and with the sinful old lady to trouble thee.

I am very well. My cold stays in my head, and gradually
decreases. I have not seen Mr. Taylor, or anybody, yet.

May thy house be the Heart of God, prays thy

husband.

To ROBERT S. LANIER

55 Lexington St.
Baltimore, Md.
Nov. 14th 1877.

My dearest Father:

Yours announcing the death of my dear
old Grandmother has reached us, and gives us many thoughts.[97]
I greatly wished to see her once more before she should leave
us, for it is now many years since I have been with her. Yet
it is impossible for anyone who loved her to wish a continuation of the fragmentary existence she was drawing out, and I
find a genuine pleasure in believing that she has rejoined the
partner with whom she lived so many bright and active years.
Surely there was never a simpler, finer, more loyal soul: and it
is good to believe that it has escaped finally from the tyrannous
decrepitudes of the worn-out body and has regained the glory
of its youth.

I have just returned from New York, where I have spent a
very busy week in renewing my connections with the Magazines, which had been discontinued so long in consequence of
my illness. Dr. Holland, (Ed. of SCRIBNER'S) was appreciative
enough to engage from me four papers on Southern life,[98] for
which I am to receive from three hundred and fifty to four
hundred dollars. Although he does not want the papers until
the last of next August, he very generously paid me a " re-
tainer " of two hundred dollars cash. This came just in time

[97] Sarah Vivian Fulwood Lanier had died Nov. 3, 1877.

[98] Neither this project nor the book on Georgia, mentioned in the following
paragraph, materialized. Lanier's long essay, " The New South " (V, 334),
published in *Scribner's*, Oct., 1880, may have been a substitute for the former
project.

to save me from I know not what extent of mortification and suffering: for, in order to get the bare necessaries of life, I had been compelled to borrow a great deal of money during the last four months, and this windfall enabled me to reduce my debt to at least manageable proportions.

Dr. Holland also introduced me to the "business-partner" of the house of Scribner, Welford & Armstrong. The latter carried me to his private room, and after some complimentary remarks asked my advice as to a very expensive book which was published some time ago by that firm. On examining the book, I found in it many charming wood-cuts of Georgia scenery, and I finally suggested to him that I should get up a work on Georgia similar to that on Florida which I wrote some years ago and which has been successful. The proposition seemed to strike him; and on Monday I had a second conference with him and another partner. They are to deliberate on it and write me their conclusion. I have much reason to believe that they will undertake it; and, if they do, I will secure employment thereby from next March until the end of the year. I should come South in April and devote the spring and summer to the accumulation of material, – travelling about various parts of Georgia, and seeing *you* among other good things. In the fall I should come back to my quarters here and write the book.

This is, at any rate, a pleasant prospect, and its origin was accompanied with circumstances which were gratifying, as showing that even during the inactive year of my illness my work has been growing silently into favor.

Meantime: I have a commission to write a Christmas poem for an ambitious weekly paper of Baltimore, which will bring me in some fifty to seventy five dollars when it is delivered. Not a line is yet written, however. It is to be in hand by the 1st December. Besides this I have a fair prospect of selling about a hundred and fifty dollars worth of matter to a couple of Magazines — the North American Review, and Lippincott's, but cannot look for the avails of these before six weeks from now.

My problem is therefore how to bridge the yawning chasm of the next three weeks. My two hundred was really spent before I received it, and is gone. If you can help me, it will be great help indeed.

We find our new mode of life to be very advantageous in many respects. We have no nurse. Mary gets our breakfast and supper with her own hands; and we have a dinner of three courses served to us in our own room daily for one dollar. Our entire expense for food is less than forty five dollars a month, upon a rigorous calculation which we have made.

Mr. Day is now with us, on his way home. He will probably remain a month, and *may* stay until Christmas.

He and Mary and the boys are at this writing dining out with an old friend, I staying at home because I am very tired with a cruel pressure of work.

Love to Mama and God bless you both.

Your son,

S. L.

I wish you would send this letter to Clifford, as it gives some account of my doings and plans: I really haven't strength to write him.

S. L.

To JOHN B. TABB [99]

55 Lexington St.
Baltimore, Md.
Nov. 22nd 1877.

My dear John:

A couple of weeks ago, I went to New York in order to renew my connection with the magazines, after the disruption thereof caused by my absence in Florida last Winter. After a few days in New York I returned here, and on the day your friend called was seized with a hæmorrhage quite suddenly. This was brought on by running about too much in New York, and has prostrated me very much until today, when I begin to feel like a man again.[100]

---

[99] Previously published, Gordon Blair, *Father Tabb* (Richmond, Va., 1940), pp. 57-58.

[100] In a letter to his father, Nov. 21, 1877 (here omitted), Lanier had written: "I have been in the prostration of a hæmorrhage for a week: yesterday being my first day out of my room."

The foregoing will explain to you, my dear, why your charming "Echoes" did not immediately return to your own bosom from mine, as well as why I have neither visited nor written you. I am under contract to furnish a Xmas poem by the 1st December, and this is going to keep me pinned down to work until that time, having been delayed by the visit and the illness aforementioned.

I do heartily rejoice with you in the favor with which your work seems to be regarded by the Magazine editors. I long to see you and talk with you about it all. I must tell you that ever since our parting I have retained a peculiarly tender remembrance of our comradeship at Point Lookout: upon analyzing the feeling I find that some of its strength arises from the circumstance that you are the only friend I ever had who was younger than myself. Most of my friendships have been with men who were old enough to be my father, and all with my seniors.

I'll hope to give you a hug, soon, *a la* Grizzly. Meantime, keep me well and truly posted of all your doings and writings. I should like to see your "Bridge". Does it run to the Other Shore ?

God bless you, says always

Your friend,

S. L.

To Sarah J. Farley

55 Lexington St.
Baltimore, Md.
Nov. 25th 1877.

My dearest Sarah:

Neither the haemorrhages; – nor the visits, through Philadelphia, to New York; – nor the pressure of the Magazines; – nor the frightful grind of poverty; – nor my lords and masters, those three boys; – nor the enormous demands of that gray-eyed Lady whom I serve; – nor all the powers of earth and hell combined: – shall longer prevent me from sending some sort of little love-letter which may convey to you how much you have been in my heart during all these æons

and eternities of time since I saw you.   If I could only run
over to you once a week and kiss your hand – even without
saying a word – it would be such a comfort!   A week is just
about as long as I can do without you.   One must have a
Sabbath every seven days, of some sort.   And you're always
such a lovely Sunday – like those that come in the early spring,
when all heaven seems to lie in the note of every song bird.

If I could stop making love to you long enough, I would
tell you that we are finally settled in Baltimore, that the Washington project (to my intense delight) is altogether abandoned, that we have four rooms in the very heart of town,
that my Comrade has a gas-stove on which she makes the most
delicious coffee and Avena (Oatmeal), and boils eggs which
are not as any other eggs that ever existed before, that this
aforesaid *menu* constitutes our breakfast, that our tea consists
of bread and milk, that we have a gorgeous dinner of three
courses brought up and served in our own rooms from a
restaurant which is in the same building with us, and that we
thus have secured the most perfect approach to family privacy
combined with freedom which our lot has ever brought us.
Although May has to work very hard – we have no nurse –,
yet she appears better and stronger in every way than for a long
time before.   The boys have all been victims of wretched colds:
and Harry is still quite ill, though up and about every day.
As for my good-for-nothing self I have had a couple of hæmorrhages which, though prostrating me much for a week or so
at a time, have left my general condition better than it has
been in a year.   I have resumed my old magazine life, and
have several pleasant commissions on hand.   Have you seen
a humorous poem of mine in APPLETON'S JOURNAL for December, called " A Puzzled Ghost in Florida "?   It was written at
the Brinton's.[101]

Here then you have all the details and particulars and so
forth and so on: and now straightway present my loyal service
to your Mother and ask her to send me word how she fares,
fully, as to one that loves her and would know all her environment.   While I am penning this sentence, I ask my little Sidney

---

[101] Caleb Brinton's farm at Chadd's Ford, where Lanier composed " A
Puzzled Ghost in Florida " (I, 99).

what message I shall send to Mrs. Farley for him? " Give her my love: and put down a kiss ", says he: and then adds, with earnest inquiry, " how *will* you send the kiss, Papa? " He now affixes a codicil: " write this down, Papa: that I hope to see her very soon." The other chickens are not by, but they would all send the same sort of freight.

Perhaps the summer will be a generous wave and will cast us up in the sweet hills about West Chester, where we may have sight of you again.

Write me, dear, all that you know to be wished for by your

faithful

S. L.

To Richard M. Johnston [102]

55 Lexington St.
Baltimore, Md.
Nov. 27th 1877

My dear Col. Johnston:

Your letter arrived while I was in New York, and only reached me after I came back.

Immediately on my return a severe hæmorrhage kept me *hors du combat* for several days, and I am just now beginning to get about again. In answer to your kind enquiries about Charley: the brave little fellow has been quite kept under by the failure of his long-continued boil to heal, and is still suffering so much inconvenience from it that we have been afraid to start him to school. I've just finished a long Christmas poem for " Every Saturday "; and have at this moment sent off a " *Song of the Chattahoochee* " to a Georgia editress.[103] The latter I particularly want to read to you.

---

[102] Previously published, *Maryland Historical Magazine*, XXXIV, 316 (Dec., 1939), misdated May 27. For Johnston's story, referred to in the last paragraph, see note 96, above.

[103] The Georgia periodical to which Lanier sent the " Song of the Chattahoochee " (I, 103), and in which it was first printed, has not been identified. In Lanier's letter of Nov. 30, 1877, following, he said it was " written for a little paper at West Point, Georgia "; but no such periodical has been found. (The Macon *Daily Telegraph and Messenger* for 1877-1878 has also been searched, in vain, for possible reprinting.) Both *Poems* (New York, 1884),

Pardon a hasty note.   Come in whenever you can, and let me see Mr. Neelus Peeler again before you send him off.   I am in a cruel press of work and write in a shameful hurry.

Your friend,

Sidney L.

To ROBERT S. LANIER

55 Lexington St.
Baltimore, Md.
Nov. 30th 1877.

My dearest Father:
                    I write immediately to prevent you from being further distressed on account of my illness.   Since the prostration has passed away, I feel all the better for the relief afforded by the hemorrhage.   This is always the case with me. I am now just as active and strong as at any time within the past year.   The hemorrhage was occasioned by my visit to New York, during which I overtaxed my strength.   It is now entirely over, and I am at hard work again.   I have just finished a long Christmas poem for a Baltimore paper, and another for a little paper at West Point, Georgia.   The latter was written at the request of Mrs. W. C. Lanier, wife of the banker at West Point, for a paper which is to be issued by a lady-friend of hers. It is called the " Song of the Chattahoochee ", and I have some suspicion that it is the best poem I ever wrote.   As soon as it appears I'll send you a copy.   I hope to forward you the Lanier books very soon.

I expect to change my plan of life very much for the better, in a week or so.   I find I can rent an elegant house for twenty five dollars a month, which is ten dollars a month less than we now pay for our four rooms.   The latter are in the midst of a business centre, and the noise and dust are great objections.

p. iii, and F. V. N. Painter, ed., *Poets of the South* (New York, 1903), p. 227, state that it was originally published in *Scott's Magazine*— the former giving the date as 1877, and the latter giving the place as Atlanta, Ga. But the only periodical bearing this title that has been discovered—*Scott's Monthly Magazine*—ceased to exist in 1869; and a search of its files fails to reveal Lanier's poem. The earliest verified printing is the posthumous one in the *Independent*, XXXV, 1601 (Dec. 20, 1883).

There are other disadvantages also which I cannot now detail. In order to make this change I have to anticipate some matters which will be coming in during the next six weeks, and have drawn up the enclosed draft which I would be glad for you to negotiate at some of the Macon banks.

I will be able to meet it promptly, and you need give yourself no concern about it.

Yours containing twenty five Dollars came duly. Mr. Day leaves us tomorrow, for the south. He will stop in Macon, and will be able to give you some account of us all here.

We have had very warm weather – almost like summer – until today when the thermometer has fallen to 29° at mid-day! It is now 26° (seven O'clock in the evening) and we'll have plently of ice in the morning. I have been walking about a good deal, and the clear crystalline air braces me up wonderfully.

Good night, and God bless you all.

Your son,

S. L.

To Gibson Peacock [104]

55 Lexington St.
Bo. Dec. 3rd 1877

My dear Mr. Gibson:

Your letter was heartily received by May and me, and the stamps brought acclamations from the three young men at the breakfast-table. We had been talking of you more than usual for several days: and May had been re-calling that wonderful Thanksgiving Day a year ago when the kindness of you and my dear Maria seemed to culminate in the mysterious Five-hundred-dollar-bill which came up on the breakfast-tray. What a couple you are, anyhow; you and that same Maria with the cape-jessamine-textured throat!

I indulged in a hemorrhage immediately after reaching home, which kept me out of the combat for ten days. I then plunged in and brought captive forth a long Christmas poem for *Every Saturday*, an ambitious young weekly of Baltimore.

---

[104] Previously published, *Atlantic Monthly*, LXXIV, 187-188 (Aug., 1894); reprinted, *Letters* (New York, 1899), pp. 48-49.

Have you seen my " Puzzled Ghost in Florida ", in *Appleton's* for December?

May and the boys have had wretched colds. May's still lingers, catarrhally, and gives her much trouble.

We had another key to the silver chest. It contained a second set of old family plate, which we now use daily and in which we take great comfort. There are no other papers concerning it.

I hope you had a pleasant visit in New York. Tell me of Miss Phelp's progress at the water-cure. I've just received a letter from Emma Stebbins. She is at the Cushmans', in Newport, and much improved in health. She has finished six chapters of her book on Miss Cushman, and may have it ready for the publisher by next fall.

Wife and I have been out to look at a lovely house today, with eight rooms and many charming appliances, which we find we can rent for less than we now pay for our four rooms. We think of taking it straightway, and will do so if a certain half-hundred of dollars for which we hope reaches us in time. God bless you both, is always the fervent prayer of your friend

Sidney L.

To John B. Tabb [105]

55 Lexington St.
Bo Dec. 6th 1877.

My dear Friend:

I also long *audire ac reddere voces* – as Horace hath it – with you, and have waited until the last moment to see if any happy chance might release me from work on your feast-day.[106] It seems not, however: I must go to Philadelphia

---

[105] Previously published, Gordon Blair, *Father Tabb* (Richmond, Va., 1940), p. 58.

[106] On Nov. 28, 1877, Tabb had paid a visit to Lanier, their first reunion since 1865, as he reported in a letter to his sister Hally Tabb: " I went to Balto this morning to see Mr Lanier & never have I been more cordially greeted. It did my heart good to see his face again, but it saddened me to find him so changed– I fear, poor fellow, he has not long to stay– His wife is a *lady*, so gentle and attractive that I quite lost my heart. She told me the children (three sweet little boys) had been quite excited about ' John Tabb's ' coming and wondered what manner of thing it could be that so pleased their father."

tomorrow afternoon, in order to be there on Saturday to transact some business. I am consoled a little for this disappointment by a charming prospect which opens itself to me — of
seeing you in my little home erelong and often. We have
found a delightfully situated house in Denmead St., just out of
Charles, and have taken it for a year. We expect to move
next week, and to be as happy as five mundane residents ever
become, – particularly when you shall render yourself with us.

I have just been reading, in St. Thomas a Kempis; " he doeth
much that loveth much." This gives me great comfort: for
when I lament, as I often must how little I *do* in a day, I will
think how much I love you in an hour, – and then the little
four walls of work will become as large as the heaven of
friendship – .

Faithfully yours,

S. L.

To Clifford A. Lanier

55 Lexington St.
Baltimore, Md.
Dec. 18th 1877.

My dear Clifford:

I had hoped to have some account of the
manner of Mr. Montgomery's death.[107] I was greatly pained
by the news, and wrote Auntie immediately. Was it not very
sudden?

I have come bump against the necessity of making a change
in our location. We find several objections here on the score
of health which are insuperable. We can get a charming house
for the same rent which we pay for our four rooms, and I have
taken one for a year. We hope to move in the course of the
next four or five days.

This move necessitates that I shall anticipate some revenues
which will be coming to me during the next forty days, and
I wish very much to get the enclosed draft arranged by you at

---

[107] Captain Richard M. Montgomery had married Lanier's Aunt Jane (widow
of Abram P. Watt) in Oct., 1876.

some of your Montgomery banks. You need give yourself no concern about prompt payment of the draft at maturity. My need of the money is absolute and immediate.

We are all in more or less discomfort from the weather which has been too warm for this part of the world. I believe I stand it better than any of the family. Mary is quite worn out with overwork and loss of sleep.

Secretary Sherman renews his assurance that the long-promised place shall soon be conferred on me; and I look for news from Gen. Dunn any day. Meantime, I am getting quite a half year's work for the magazines in progress.

I write hurriedly, amid a press of engagements which scarcely leave me time to eat.

God bless you all, fervently prays

Your

S. L.

TO JOHN B. TABB [108]

55 Lexinton St.
B⁰ Dec. 19th 1877.

My dear John, I have at length caught a flying half-hour, and have made a part of it serve for a critical examination of your "REPOSE."

I have two classes of remarks to offer, about it: the first class refers to matters of which I have *no* doubt; and the second to things which I *think* would heighten the effect.

1.

"To *drown* the ear" is a vigorous expression which does not precisely chime with the idea of "Lullaby". Would not "To soothe the ear", or some similar phrase, be better?

Again, "*My* brooding mind" would give the reader a clearer idea of what you are aiming at than "*the* brooding mind."

Again: "*Keen*" does not seem exactly the right adjective for that supreme "Intelligence" of which you are there speak-

---

[108] Previously published, Gordon Blair, *Father Tabb* (Richmond, Va., 1940), pp. 59-61.

ing. Would not something like " large Intelligence ", or " The All-Intelligence that spans &c ", be better ?

2

I am not sure that I precisely get the marrow of your thought in this quatrain:

> " And in this mystic *unison*
> Of Nature kind
> Each subtle *harmony* fulfils
> A *chord* designed."

Now, calling attention to the terms I have underscored, would it not be more precise to say:

> And in this mystic *harmony*
> Of Nature kind,
> Each subtle (*single tone*) fulfils
> A *chord* designed?

Again: would it not be better, in the last eight lines of the poem, to employ exclusively such adjectives as will serve to call the reader's attention to the main theme of the piece, *i.e.* Repose? For example, (purely as suggestion)

> — — — — — — —
>
> All speak one (*calm*) Original
> Whose power divine
> Hath wrought for them &c &c
> &c &c
> For all on gentle Ministrants
> Of (*peaceful*) Love,
> &c &c &c — — :

And upon this same principle would not some less active word than " *Outpourings* " be better: something equivalent to emanations, or the like subtle outgivings of placid Power?

Again: instead of having the rhythm that of four-feet lines alternating with two-feet lines, I am strongly impressed with the conviction that the poem would gain greatly in just that *large* and *tranquil* flow which suits its idea if you would attach each two-feet line to its preceding four-feet line and make the whole piece thus consist of rhymed couplets.

E. g. :

> I laid me down in solitude, but not alone:
> The Night was round me, and the stars above me shone.
> The Earth, my mother, pillowed me, and to her breast
> I nestled as a weary child that longs for rest.
> &c &c &c.

These long six-feet lines have a very peculiar *repose* in their placid movement: like the glassy surface of a stream which one knows is running but which seems in the twilight perfectly still. Your *ear* has guided you perfectly in the rhythm: it is only a re-arrangement of the component parts which is necessary.

"
_____
"

And now: do you think I would take the trouble of all these critical suggestions for a *poor* piece? The poem is very pretty, and very much like *you.* I fancy especially the lines from

> " But o'er the mystery of calm
>   The brooding mind,
>   &c &c

to

>   The depth sublime.

"
__ Mr. Eggleston's letter is very comfortable reading
"
indeed to me.[109] I suspect I am arrived at that stage of every career when one writes all the better if he has confidence in

---

[109] George Cary Eggleston had written a letter to Tabb, Dec., 1877, which had been forwarded to Lanier. In it he said: " I am delighted to get your note about Lanier. I have learned to know him in his work, which strongly reflects the spirit of the man, and I should greatly like to know him personally. . . .
" Yes, I wrote Lanier a hurried letter once, when I had learned by accident that he was ill, perhaps fatally so. . . . He wrote me a letter in reply which I shall keep, because, even more than his poetry, it reflects the rare spirit of the man who wrote it.
" Lanier has been badly entreated of the critics,– partly because his warmth and wealth of imagery and his intensity of expression offend the prevalent taste of the time for coldness and genteel reserve, and partly because the critics are asses sometimes, and are bewildered by anything which refuses to fit their conventional moulds. There is that in his work however which will make its way, spite of critical obtuseness, and in spite also, of the sometimes real redundancy of his rich imagery. . . . Lanier has undoubted genius, and if life is given to him he will do work which shall teach his critics new canons of criticism."

the sympathy of his auditory. You were a very good boy to send it. I hope soon to be in New York for several days, and will try to meet Mr. Eggleston.

I don't now see any possibility, my dear, for the 24th. It would be very delightful to me, to know your good friends, and to witness your solemnities: my heart would be quite warm, to both: but I am tied here during every moment of time, now, by matters which we will talk over some time.

And so: May you see, in your dream this night, the Ideal! that wondrous thing which many prattle of, but few know – is this day's closing prayer of

Yours faithfully

S. L.

To ROBERT S. LANIER

55 Lexington St.
Bo Dec. 19th 1877.

My dearest Father:

Is it entirely impossible to obtain the sixty day loan of a hundred and fifty? My need of it is so great and so immediately pressing that I write in haste to ask that you will get it for me, if there is any possible way. A month from now will probably see me entirely out of trouble: at any rate, I shall not have the least difficulty *then* in getting the amount named. But just now I have entirely employed all that is available, and this hundred and fifty is absolutely necessary.

I enclose a couple of letters which will interest you. The Col. James who writes from Texas is a Maryland gentleman who served with distinction in the Confederate army, and has, since the war, built up a great and flourishing college at Austin.[110] The other letter [111] is by the literary editor of the Evening Post, and is written to a friend of mine who is now beginning to acquire a fine reputation as a poet.

---

[110] Col. John G. James of the Texas Military Institute, Austin, Texas, had written Lanier on Dec. 6, 1877, asking his permission to include selections of Lanier's poetry in his forthcoming text-book, *The Southern Student's Hand-Book of Selections for Reading and Oratory* (New York, 1879).

[111] Eggleston to Tabb, Dec. 5, 1877, quoted in note 109, above.

The Peabody Concerts have commenced for the season,[112] and I am perfectly delighted to find that I am able to play through the daily rehearsals, of two hours each, without detriment. This seems simply marvellous, in view of my condition last winter. I find, too, that the terrible hoarseness which I was subject to, even during the summer, has quite disappeared, and the cold air now invigorates me, as of old. All this gives me great hope of doing a huge modicum of work during the coming year. I look forward to it with the greatest eagerness.

Please write me as soon as you receive this, if there is finally no possibility of getting the money. I am putting off many pressing matters from day to day, waiting for it.

God bless you all. I hope Mama is better. Please kiss her for me, and tell her that May is on her feet from seven in the morning until eleven at night, cooking, nursing, marketing, and a thousand other 'ings, and that she has thus been wholly unable to write any letters at all.

Your son,

S. L.

To Robert S. Lanier

33 Denmead St.[113]
Baltimore, Md.
Dec. 25th 1877.

My dearest Father:

How I wish I could inspire you with my own confidence in my future, financial and other ! Your letter indicates to me that you are allowing this to give you a thousand times more care than is necessary. If you compare my condition at present with what it was a year ago,– when I was entirely incapable of work, and separated by a thousand miles

---

[112] The first Peabody Concert of the season was given on Dec. 15, 1877. Seven others followed on Dec. 22, 1877; Jan. 5, 19, Feb. 2, 16, Mar. 2, 16, 1878 (see programs in the Charles D. Lanier Collection, Johns Hopkins University).

[113] Lanier's new residence on Denmead (now 20th) St. was on the outskirts of the Baltimore of that day (see J. C. French, " Sidney Lanier's Life in Baltimore," Baltimore *Sun*, Sept. 6, 1931, Literary Section, p. 16; and J. S. Short, " Sidney Lanier ' Familiar Citizen of the Town,' " *Maryland Historical Magazine*, XXXV, 121-146, June, 1940).

from my children – I think you must find cause for great rejoicing and hopeful augury.   My wife and I have just been
engaged in striking a balance of this sort between the present
and the past, and we agree in discovering many circumstances
in favor of the former.   We are now e[n]sconced in a comfortable house – we moved on Saturday – and are surrounded
by a hundred luxuries (to *us*) which have not hitherto seemed
possible.   The privacy, the sense of citizenship, the home feeling, are indescribably delightful; and I persuade myself continually that we have ceased, for a time at least, to " move
on ".   Our house is fifteen minutes ride from the centre of
business in town: and two lines of street cars run within a
couple of hundred yards of us.   We have a fine outlook across
an open space in front, plenty of play-ground all about for the
boys, and Druid Hill Park a five-minutes' walk from us.   The
dwelling is charmingly arranged, with nine rooms, and a stable
at the rear.   It fronts south, and the sun pours into all the
rooms of that side from morning till sunset.   I got carpets for
the parlor and dining-room from a dealer who receives his pay
in weekly instalments: we managed to fit up the sleeping-
rooms with the furniture we had already been using.   We are
altogether very comfortable, and our whole environment
pleasanter than ever since our wanderings began.

   As to the means of keeping this establishment in running
order, I hope to have something pleasant and certain to write
you erelong.   I don't think it worth while to feed you on
projects: but I beg you to give your mind ease about me.   If
the hundred and fifty cannot possibly be raised,— why, let it
go, dear Father, and do not pay it the compliment of worry.
I feel very indignant when I think that you have lived so long
in Macon, and have been so prompt in your business-rela-
tions,— and yet find such trouble in a matter of this sort.   But
my indignation is short-lived: for I reflect that it is worth more
than the subject of it.

   I send you a paper containing a Christmas poem, with an
illustration.   The latter was very pretty, in the original drawing, but was badly printed from the plate.   I believe the poem
is very well received.   Col. Richard M. Johnston called today
and gave vent to some very warm sentiments about it.

I suppose you have seen my poem, "Under the Cedarcroft Chestnut," in Scribner's for January. The drawing for the wood-cut was done by Bayard Taylor.

Your P. O. order arrived in time, and the boys had a superb lot of Christmas gifts. May and I arranged a big Austrian Pine in our new parlor last night as a Christmas tree, and Harry danced the wildest saraband about it this morning that ever was seen. Col. Johnston happened to come in while the gifts were still strewed about: he lifted up his hands and cried " This doesn't look as if Santa Claus was sick! " [114]

Mary and the boys join me in sending you a thousand Christmas greetings, which you are to share with our dear Mama. We rejoice to hear that this lady is better. How we should delight to have you both in *our* house ! Perhaps this summer may give us that pleasure. We have never yet heard whether Pringle retained his college-position.[115] Give him our love, also.

That God may bless you, dear Father, and bring you quickly out of all trouble, is the continual prayer of

Your son,

S. L.

[114] The allusion is to Lanier's Christmas poem mentioned above, "The Hard Times in Elfland."

[115] Pringle Morgan, Mrs. R. S. Lanier's son by a former marriage, had been suspended from Mercer College, Macon, because of a student prank.